Rocky Mountain Skiing

Revised Edition

Rocky Mountain Skiing

Revised Edition

Claire Walter

Fulcrum Publishing
Golden, Colorado

To Ral Sandberg
For all the summits and all the slopes below them.

Copyright © 1996 Claire Walter

Book design by Deborah Rich
Cover by Alyssa Pumphrey
Front cover photograph, U.S. Extreme Skiing Champion David Swanwick, copyright ©
1996 Tom Stillo Photographer
Back cover photographs: *top,* Silver Star Ski Resort copyright © 1996 Don Weixl;
bottom, snowboarder Gareth Van Dyk copyright © 1996 Tom Stillo Photographer

Library of Congress Cataloging-in-Publication Data

Walter, Claire.
    Rocky Mountain skiing / Claire Walter. — Rev. ed.
        p.   cm.
    Includes index.
    ISBN 1-55591-330-X (pbk.)
    1. Skiing—Rocky Mountains—Guidebooks. 2. Rocky Mountains—
Guidebooks.   3. Ski resorts—Rocky Mountains—Directories.
I. Title.
GV854.5.R62W35   1996
796.93'0978—dc20   96-33116
                                                                          CIP

Printed in the United States of America

0 9 8 7 6 5 4 3 2 1

Fulcrum Publishing
350 Indiana Street, Suite 350
Golden, Colorado 80401-5093
(800) 992-2908 • (303) 277-1623

Contents

Contents

Contents

Acknowledgments

The research for this book in a real sense began the first time I skied Colorado in 1971. I returned to the Rockies winter after winter, usually for an article and always with pleasure, until the lure was so potent that I moved west. I had been a *Skiing* magazine contributing editor for many years from a New York base when I told editor-in-chief Rick Kahl that I was thinking about moving to Colorado. His response was, "Can we keep you busy!" And *Skiing* has done just that. So thanks, Rick and his *Skiing* colleagues for giving me the opportunity to range throughout the Rockies in search of articles and article ideas. Visiting so many spurred this book into being.

In the past eight winters, I have skied my way between Canada and New Mexico. A list of individuals at ski resorts all over the Rocky Mountain West who helped me sort out the puzzle pieces would comprise another entire chapter, which is the last thing the patient folks at Fulcrum—Carmel Huestis, Alison Auch, Daniel Forrest-Bank, Sara Hanson, Jen Waters, Annie Reschak, Patty Maher, Deborah Rich, Alyssa Pumphrey, Bill Spahr, Pauline Brown and the rest—want to see from me. They've got enough to do without such a list. But thanks to you all, and enjoy the fruits of our efforts.

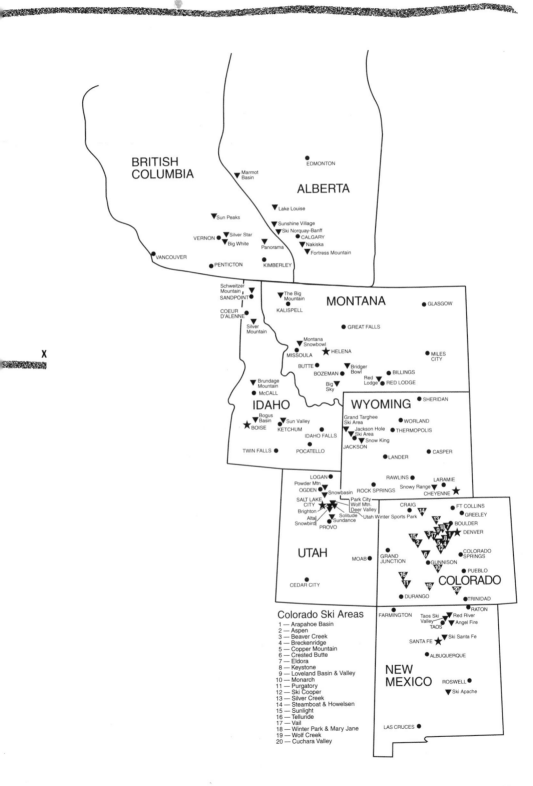

BRITISH COLUMBIA

ALBERTA

● EDMONTON

▼ Marmot Basin

▼ Lake Louise

▼ Sunshine Village
▼ Ski Norquay-Banff
● CALGARY

▼ Sun Peaks

VERNON ● ▼ Silver Star
▼ Big White
Panorama ▼

▼ Nakiska
● Fortress Mountain

● VANCOUVER

● PENTICTON

KIMBERLEY

Schweitzer Mountain ▼
SANDPOINT ●

▼ The Big Mountain
KALISPELL ●

MONTANA

● GLASGOW

COEUR D'ALENNE ●

Silver Mountain ▼

● GREAT FALLS

X

Montana Snowbowl ▼
MISSOULA ●

★ HELENA

● MILES CITY

BUTTE ●
BOZEMAN ●

▼ Bridger Bowl

Red Lodge ▼
● BILLINGS
● RED LODGE

Brundage Mountain ▼
● McCALL

Big Sky ▼

IDAHO

WYOMING

● SHERIDAN

Bogus Basin ●
★ BOISE

▼ Sun Valley
KETCHUM ●

Grand Targhee Ski Area ▼

● WORLAND

Jackson Hole Ski Area ▼
▼ Snow King
JACKSON ●

● THERMOPOLIS

IDAHO FALLS ●

TWIN FALLS ●
POCATELLO ●

● LANDER

● CASPER

LOGAN ●

Powder Mtn ●
OGDEN ●
▼ Snowbasin
SALT LAKE CITY ●
Park City ▼
Wolf Mtn. ▼
Deer Valley ▼
Brighton ●
Alta ●
Snowbird ●
Solitude ▼
Sundance ●
PROVO ●
Utah Winter Sports Park

RAWLINS ●
ROCK SPRINGS ●

● LARAMIE
Snowy Range ▼
★ CHEYENNE

CRAIG ●
14 ▼
13 ▼

● FT COLLINS
● GREELEY

15 ▼
2 ▼
3 ▼ 17 ▼
18 ▼ 1 ▼
5 ▼ 4 ▼
8 ▼
★ ● BOULDER
● DENVER

UTAH

MOAB ●

GRAND JUNCTION ●

6 ▼
9 ▼
GUNNISON ●
10 ▼

● COLORADO SPRINGS

● PUEBLO

CEDAR CITY ●

16 ▼
11 ▼

19 ▼
20 ▼

COLORADO

DURANGO ●

● TRINIDAD

● RATON

Colorado Ski Areas
1 — Arapahoe Basin
2 — Aspen
3 — Beaver Creek
4 — Breckenridge
5 — Copper Mountain
6 — Crested Butte
7 — Eldora
8 — Keystone
9 — Loveland Basin & Valley
10 — Monarch
11 — Purgatory
12 — Ski Cooper
13 — Silver Creek
14 — Steamboat & Howelsen
15 — Sunlight
16 — Telluride
17 — Vail
18 — Winter Park & Mary Jane
19 — Wolf Creek
20 — Cuchara Valley

FARMINGTON ●

Taos Ski Valley ▼
TAOS ●
▼ Red River
▼ Angel Fire

SANTA FE ★
▼ Ski Santa Fe

● ALBUQUERQUE

NEW MEXICO

● ROSWELL

▼ Ski Apache

LAS CRUCES ●

Introduction

Rising skyward in a chain that stretches from the desert of New Mexico to the tundra of Canada, the Rocky Mountains encompass dozens of ranges, comprising, in turn, thousands of peaks and valleys. Some are household names; others are unnamed, unexplored, virtually unknown. Separated from the nearest ocean by hundreds of miles of arid land, the Rockies are blanketed with deep feather-light snow each winter. Taken as a whole, the range is still the embodiment of wilderness. Yet etched onto a few dozen mountainsides are ski areas that turn that snow from a mantle of white, whose main function is to serve as a water source for the parched West, into the world's most compelling winter playground. What a by-product!

The Rocky Mountains of the geographer and the skier overlap but are not identical. The geographer views the whole of the chain but segments it pickily into ranges according to their geological history and climate, while the skier thinks of the Rockies as stretching from northern New Mexico into Canada. The U.S. resorts considered to be in the Rockies are in Colorado, Utah, New Mexico, Wyoming, Montana and Idaho. The spine of the Canadian Rockies form the border between Alberta and British Columbia, but some of the mountains of British Columbia's interior, while technically not part of the Rockies, offer similar skiing experiences. They are known throughout the skiing world for exceptional snow, eye-popping scenery and increasingly sophisticated resort living—in short, all the components of top-flight skiing.

After a lifetime in the Northeast, I moved to Colorado in 1988, and I still thrill to have the best skiing on Earth so close. Colorado ski areas tally close to one out of five skier visits nationwide each year, and I'm delighted to take credit

for a good number of them. Next door in Utah, 11 of the state's 14 ski areas—including the largest—lie within about an hour's drive of Salt Lake City International Airport, making this the densest, and most convenient, grouping of first-rate ski areas in the country. States to the north and south each have equally distinctive but less densely concentrated ski resorts, and the Canadian Rockies have a beauty, majesty and economy of their own. With the Canadian dollar being worth roughly one-third less than the U.S. dollar, it turns a ski trip to our northern neighbor into a bargain.

Conventional wisdom has it that it is impossible to be all things to all people, but in this guide I've tried to do just that—to create a more than passingly comprehensive guide to the great skiing and the ancillary options for lodging, dining, nonski activities and nightlife. I've included the big-name resorts that are shown regularly on *Lifestyles of the Rich and Famous* and smaller ones that are regional or even local in appeal but that merit consideration, especially by skiers looking for good snow and economy vacationing. I have come to savor the differences in scale and style and have tried to impart the flavor of each ski area and each resort town while writing a practical guidebook for those planning a western vacation.

This book was originally written primarily for Alpine skiers of all ability levels and budget constrictions. It has now come to encompass snowboarding, which is growing in popularity. When I write of "ski terrain," "ski area" or "the skiing," I am using the terms generically with no intention of excluding riders. The book also touches on joys of Nordic skiing, both on groomed trails and in the backcountry, near each Alpine area. Each chapter is meant to be a self-

Introduction

contained guide within a guide—an everything-you-always-wanted-to-know-about directory to each of the resorts that is covered. It is my hope that this was not too ambitious a project and that you will find it useful in planning your winter travels.

And now, a word about each section:

THE LAY OF THE LAND

An overall depiction of the layout of the resort and its ski area(s). Just a primer on how to get around.

GETTING THERE

Air, auto, Amtrak, plus transport tidbits between gateway and resort and transportation within the resort.

PROFILE

Designations of terrain (beginner/novice, intermediate and advanced—or green circle, blue square and black diamond) are meant to relate that ski area's runs to one another, not to compare them to another mountain, just as it says on a trailmap key. A black diamond at Silver Creek or Sunlight obviously is not the same as a black diamond at Jackson Hole, Taos or Snowbird. It is possible but tedious to paint an ultrarealistic picture of each skiing mountain with detailed descriptions of every run and every lift. So I've gone for the impressionistic approach, selecting the mountain sectors and runs that have touched me to create an accurate but less detailed portrait.

MOUNTAIN STATS

Self-evident—and straight from the ski areas. Some are specific, pinpointing lift capacity, el-

Perhaps the most famous shot in Colorado: the Maroon Bells, outside of Aspen. In winter, you can cross-country ski to this spot.

evation and so on to the exact number. Others round off. If you don't like the numbers, complain to the ski areas, not to me. It also includes on-mountain extras you ought to know about.

SKI SCHOOL PROGRAMS

Every ski school offers traditional class lessons (normally $1^1/_2$ to two hours and generally morning and afternoon) for all ability levels, plus private lessons throughout the day. The listing for each ski area is for other programs and special deals divided into "Introductory Programs" (never ever skied or snowboarded) and "Advanced and Specialty Programs" (intermediates and above). Although infant/toddler nurseries may not technically be part of a resort's ski school, for convenience I've listed such services along with kids' ski classes under "For Children" in the ski-school sections. "For Children" is broken down into "Nonskiing Children" (infant and toddler programs), "Skiing Children" (ski instruction, which may be combined with day care for the smallest children) and "Teens" (13 to 18 where such programs exist). Pay special attention to the reservations policies where they are stated. Where none are stated, walk-ins are welcome—to the best of my knowledge. If you have a question, call. Where no separate specific phone number is given, call the ski area's general number or the central reservations number. Instruction and other programs for racers and for disabled skiers are noted where available.

NORDIC SKIING

Rather than a definitive guide, this is an indication as to what kind of track skiing and backcountry options, including guided programs, are available at or near the Alpine resorts.

WHERE TO STAY

Like terrain evaluations, designations of luxury, mid-price and economy lodgings are compared to each other within one resort, not to those in another town. Luxury in Aspen, Deer Valley or Beaver Creek is a big notch higher (and pricier) than luxury elsewhere in the Rockies; economy in Pagosa Springs or Buena Vista is probably a cheap "mom-and-pop" motel with outside room doors—a kind of lodging that doesn't even exist in pricier ski resorts. Assume that all luxury and mid-price accommodations have private direct dial telephone and color TV, usually cable and frequently with one or more pay channels, such as HBO. Where I have unearthed an economy lodge or motel that does not offer these (or at least in common areas rather than rooms), I have specified that. I could also have written "covered parking" and/or "on-site parking" for the many, many properties that offer it, but in the interest of space, didn't. I've included enough lodging options in each resort and nearby town where skiers routinely and realistically stay to give you an idea of what is available. Every single property has not been included.

Summaries of services and facilities come from the latest resort accommodations directories, supplemented by calls to many of the properties themselves. Remember that most central reservations services can book an entire ski vacation, including air or Amtrak tickets, accommodations, car rental or other ground transportation, lift tickets, ski school, nursery, rental equipment and even special nonski activities.

DINING OUT

Assume the same parameters for dining. Expensive and elegant or informal and economical carry different connotations in different resorts. I purposely haven't wasted space on fast-food chain restaurants, because you know what they are like anyway.

xiii

NIGHTLIFE

A short overview of what to do after the lifts close down.

What you won't find here are lift ticket and other prices. Neither my editors nor I wanted this book to be outdated right after you buy it. We know that terrain expansions, lift replacements or additions, lodging construction and renovations and restaurant openings and closings represent ongoing changes in ski resorts and may not be totally accurate a year from this writing. Even lift prices, which in some cases are not announced until a few weeks before the ski season, would guarantee obsolescence within the first year of publication and hopelessness thereafter, and we didn't want that.

Claire Walter
Boulder, Colorado
August 1996

Rocky Mountain Skiing

Revised Edition

Colorado's
Big Five

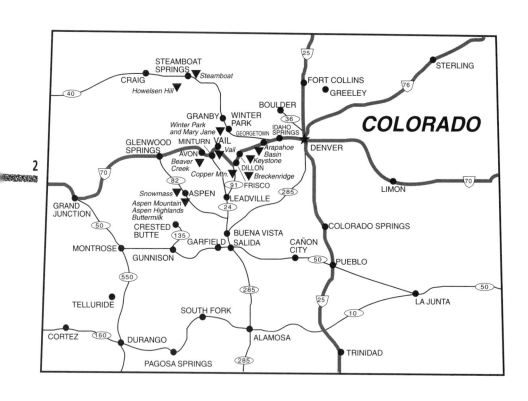

Colorado's Big Five

Vail photo by Jack Affleck

THE VAIL VALLEY

BACKDROP

Whenever anyone ranks U.S. ski resorts, Vail seems to come out on top. Little wonder, for it is a five-star resort town at the base of a superlative skiing mountain, a place that exudes unsurpassed quality, style and overall panache. Unlike any resort that preceded it, with the arguable exception of Sun Valley decades earlier, Vail was built for skiing. Its location on what was sheep meadow beside US Route 6 was not dictated by a town already in place, but rather by the promise of a huge beguiling mountain and deep cloud-light snow that falls upon it. Vail and its sister resort of Beaver Creek rack up roughly two million skier days a year—20 percent of Colorado's total, nearly as many as the entire state of Utah, and close to 4 percent of the annual total of the entire United States.

Vail's founding father, 10th Mountain Division veteran Pete Seibert, envisioned a quasi-Alpine village at the base of a massive ski area and made it happen. When it opened on December 15, 1962, with America's first gondola, three chairlifts and 10 miles of runs, Vail was already one of the country's largest ski areas, and by the end of the season, it had become one of the most successful. It remains so today, ranking as America's largest single-mountain ski area coupled with a world-class resort. Together, they form the heart of what has come to be called the Vail Valley.

In 1980, Vail Associates launched Beaver Creek, a second resort 10 miles to the west. This is a more intimate, more exclusive and less crowded resort than Vail, yet the two balance each other with precision. Vail Village and its tributaries offer all manner of lodging, dining and après-skiing, though perhaps a little thinly on the budget end, while Beaver Creek caters purely to the carriage trade with the greatest concentra-

tion of luxury lodging of any Colorado ski resort. Vail and Beaver Creek hosted the prestigious 1989 World Alpine Ski Championships and were awarded a reprise for 1999. The Vail Valley is now an annual stop on the World Cup circuit, and watching a race in person is a real thrill. In 1996, Vail Associates, which runs this ski colossus, installed a lift linking Beaver Creek with Arrowhead, a golf and ski resort in the Eagle River Valley. The connection gives Beaver Creek the greatest vertical of any Colorado ski area and creates the American semblance of an Alpine village-to-village ski experience.

The other focus at Beaver Creek is filling in the blank spaces on the resort map. One Beaver Creek, west of the Village Hall day lodge, finishes the mountainside development with a state-of-the-art pedestrian plaza, while Market Square is the new village focal point with an arts center, year-round skating rink, shops and restaurants. Both projects are scheduled for completion in 1997. Among the amenities will be moving sidewalks, a first at a North American ski resort. There is something intrinsically bizarre about sparing guests in a sports-oriented resort the burden of walking, but when you consider that Beaver Creek is seeking to solidify its reputation as a summer escape for people who perhaps are less fit than skiers, it makes some sense.

In the summer of 1996, Vail Associates announced an agreement to acquire Ralcorp's Keystone, Breckenridge and Arapahoe Basin and their real estate holdings, to create America's largest mountain resort company with roughly five million skier/snowboarder visits and about $300 million in annual revenues. The announced intention of this proposed merger was to create a stronger national and international marketing position. What it will ultimately mean for Vail-bound skiers is, at this printing, still unknown.

Even before the merger proposal, Vail had racked up so many firsts, mosts and bests that they almost defy enumerating. The overwhelming qualities Vail exudes all the time are harmony and class. The huge resort's myriad components fit together as neatly as a jigsaw puzzle, and you know that when Vail sets out to do anything, it's done right. No one ever accused Vail of being a low-key, low-profile bargain, but both the ski area and the resort set and meet such high standards that they provide surprising value for the top dollar you will pay to vacation there.

THE LAY OF THE LAND

As you drive down the west side of Vail Pass on I-70, you first reach East Vail, mostly private chalets and spacious townhouses beside a golf course, followed in short order by Golden Peak, Vail Village, Lionshead and Cascade Village. These interconnected resort bases are lined up between the highway and the ski mountain. Vail Village, the original Alpine-style resort, remains the leading entertainment and shopping center. Lionshead is mid-rise and modern, while Cascade Village is a growing development centered around a hotel and a small commercial area with private homes in the surrounding hills. Several subdivisions and a shopping center stretch along I-70's north side.

Continuing to the west, you then pass Dowd Junction, a former railroad switching station at I-70's intersection with US 24, leading south to Minturn, a popular option for funky dining and nightlife. The next town visible from the highway is Eagle-Vail, where many locals now live, and next comes Avon, which has grown rapidly with mostly economy lodging and services. It is also the gateway to luxurious Beaver Creek Resort. Just beyond is Arrowhead, the small golf and ski resort now interconnected with Beaver Creek. Edwards anchors the far western end of the Vail Valley with a growing number of economical restaurants, shops and lodgings—as well as Cordillera, a luxury resort high on the mountains above town.

Vail Village, Lionshead and Beaver Creek are true pedestrian villages, and the Vail Valley's ongoing success largely hinges on how well the car-free concept works. Therefore, Vail has developed one of the Rockies' best bus systems—now Colorado's second largest public transportation system after metro Denver. Free (and usually frequent) buses run on routes linking the Vail Transportation Center with the other centers from

Photo by Jack Affleck/Vail Assoc.

Inside the Vail Valley

early in the morning until late at night. Beaver Creek also has an on-demand Dial-A-Ride van service for guests, and large properties often have their own private shuttle vans, complimentary to guests as well. Low-cost bus services link Vail with Avon, Beaver Creek and Arrowhead.

GETTING THERE

Vail is 100 miles from Denver, a straight shot west on I-70. Major carriers serve Denver International Airport, from which rental cars and frequent van service are available. Among them are **Airport Shuttle of Colorado, (800) 222-2112, (970) 476-4467; Colorado Mountain Express, (800) 525-6363, (970) 949-4227** and **Vail Transportation, (800) 882-8872, (970) 476-8008.**

Vail/Eagle County Airport, 30 miles west of Vail, has become the gateway of choice for many Vail–Beaver Creek skiers, with nonstop flights from such major cities as Atlanta, Chicago, Dallas/Ft. Worth, Detroit, Los Angeles, Miami, New York (LaGuardia), Phoenix and San Francisco. There are also commuter connections between DIA and Colorado Springs Municipal Airport, and Vail/Eagle County. For information on direct flights and reservations, call **(800) 525-2257**.

Premier Passport is designed for the vacationer with two weeks of ski time and a desire to combine Aspen and Vail, both convenient from the airport at Eagle. It offers a lift pass to Aspen Highlands, Aspen Mountain, Beaver Creek, Snowmass, Buttermilk and Vail for a minimum of 10 out of 12 consecutive days, including one transfer between Vail and Aspen.

THE SKIING

Vail Mountain

Profile

Stretching 7 miles from the Mongolia surface lift to the Cascade Village chairlift, this is the giant of Rocky Mountain skiing in all measures except

Mountain Stats—
Vail Mountain

Resort elevation 8,120 feet
Top of highest lift 11,450 feet
Bottom of lowest lift 8,120 feet
Total vertical 3,330 feet
Longest run 4$^1/_2$ miles
Average annual snowfall 335 inches
Ski season mid-November (occasionally earlier, conditions permitting) to mid-April
Lifts one 12-passenger gondola, 10 high-speed quad chairlifts, 1 fixed-grip quad, 3 triples, 6 doubles, 6 surface lifts
Capacity 43,470 skiers per hour
Terrain 121 trails, 4,112 acres
Frontside 1,255 acres (32% novice and beginner, 36% intermediate, 32% advanced and expert)
Backside 2,617 acres (36% intermediate, 64% advanced and expert)
Snowmaking 347 acres
Night skiing limited beginner skiing, snowboarding and tubing at Eagle's Nest
Mountain dining Mid-Vail (including the CookShack) at Mid-Vail, Eagle's Nest (including the Wine Stube) at the top of the gondola, Two Elk Restaurant overlooking China Bowl, Dog Haus at the base of the Northwoods Express, Wildwood Smokehouse & Shelter atop Chair 3 and Wok 'n Roll at the base of the Orient Express, Buffalos next to PHQ and Buffalo's II, both at the top of Chairs 4, 5 and 11.
Snow reports (970) 476-4888

vertical drop—and it's no slouch in that department either, boasting a vertical of more than 3,300 feet. Vail is the nation's leader in uphill capacity, skiable acres and, most notably, acres of bowl skiing. The Back Bowls have enough aggregate acreage to rank ahead of such huge ski areas as Snowmass and Jackson Hole, and its 10 high-speed quad chairlifts are more than any place else in the world. Other than from the air, there is no place to see more than a fraction of Vail's grandeur. The skiing is so expansive and varied that it defies easy characterization. You can spend a week there and have a different skiing experience each day.

The easternmost section of Vail is Golden Peak, a hill that is small only in relation to the rest of the area, serving as headquarters for Vail's beginner lessons, race training, children's programs and snowboarding. A spectacular new base lodge debuted at Golden Peak in the winter of 1996–97, consolidating a ski school, lift ticket sales, retail and rental shops, a spacious bar and restaurant and other services under one roof. Also under that roof is a first even for the poshest Colorado resorts: condominium-type parking spaces selling for up to $40,000 each, which perhaps is a reasonable price for keeping those Range Rovers out of the weather.

Because it has been so since the resort's first day, the main entry into the ski terrain remains at the head of Bridge Street in Vail Village. Two generations of lifts have preceded the VistaBahn, a covered high-speed quad, as the main lift, which unloads at Mid-Vail. Numerous popular runs are arrayed in a semicircle above. Of the handful of trails cut through the dense woods below, primarily for returning to the village, Gitalong Road serpentines gently down the mountain and is the longest and easiest. Most of the skiing of this central part of the frontside is found on high. From Mid-Vail, there are two high-speed quad chairlifts: one angling off to the left to the Summit and one climbing straight up to Wildwood Shelter. More than a dozen wide relatively tame runs feed back to Mid-Vail and tend to attract crowds that like this congenial island in the sky. Sprinkled amid the blue squares and green circles are a handful of show-off diamonds. Mogul faces such as Skipper, Zot and Look Ma belie Mid-Vail's reputation as simply a playground for intermediates.

Vail's backbone is a long ridge whose high spots serve as the unloading areas for the upper frontside lifts and the chairlifts rising from the fabled Back Bowls. The Summit, at 11,480 feet, is Vail Mountain's highest point and the spot where three chairlifts from three different sectors (Chair 4 from Mid-Vail, Chair 11 from Northwoods and Chair 5 from the Back Bowls) converge. It's a busy spot rather than an imposing one. The "second summit" at Wildwood atop Chairs 3 and 7 is more impressive, graced with two lovely little lunch cabins that provide great smoked foods and an imposing view. Entry gates to the original Back Bowls are found at the tops of both Chairs 3 and 4.

By veering from Chair 4 down the face of the mountain rather than returning to Mid-Vail, you reach some of the legendary black-diamond trails. Riva Ridge, Riva Glade, Prima and Prima Cornice dominate this sector and drainage that separates the VistaBahn area and Northwoods. The Rivas eventually lead to the base, while the Primas spill into Northwoods. This was a secret spot until Chair 11 was turned into a high-speed quad. It is now a favorite with those who like steep, bumpy rock-ledge runs like First Step and North and South Rim. These steeps do gentle out into real cruising turf below. It is also possible to sneak in via the Northwoods slope, which gives the whole sector its name and is the only blue square.

If you follow a catwalk past Northwoods, you'll reach Chair 14 with a handful of short mountaintop novice runs. Beyond them, the easternmost frontside lift is the Highline chair, where Vail's iron-kneed young bloods pound themselves on Highline, Blue Ox and Roger's Run. This trio sports double diamonds, not because of sheer steepness, but because the bumps are allowed to build up until they are virtually unskiable. One of Vail's surprises is to happen upon one of them when it has just been groomed and to find that it isn't super steep after all. Chair 14 also serves as part of the access to the Far East and Vail's most recently developed, most expansive bowls.

But before leaving the frontside, you may explore Lionshead on the sprawling western end of the Vail massif. While everything from Mid-Vail east feels fragmented into tight groupings of trails, Lionshead offers mile after mile of ego-massaging cruising. Long fall-line runs and a rolling, stair-step mixture of flats and steeps characterize Born Free, Simba, Safari, Avanti and other trails in Vail's far west. With a new state-of-the-art, high-speed 12-passenger gondola and three fast quads, Lionshead accommodates hordes of skiers without getting crowded. Eagle's Nest is the top station of the gondola, and just below is a mild beginner area with two slow-moving lifts and a new snowboard park, all now lit for night skiing. When the lights are on, this is

Vail Mountain's new happening by night, but by day, it is still the purview of new skiers, and very small ones, who can practice on this high mild meadow and ride back down. This area now also boasts sledding and tubing hills, snowboard half-pipes and even a skating rink for day and night fun.

Most visitors, however, don't feel as if they've skied Vail until they've pointed their ski tips into the Back Bowls. Seven bowls—Sun Down, Sun Up, Tea Cup, China, Siberia, Inner Mongolia and Outer Mongolia—offer skiing of sensational scale that is unmatched anywhere else on this side of the Atlantic. Each bowl is many hundreds of acres of steadily pitched terrain scooped out of the backside of Vail Mountain. Sun Up and Sun Down, the two originals, are legitimate expert turf, while Inner and Outer Mongolia are far gentler, with blue-square pitches and a long runout to the Orient Express chair. China, Tea Cup and Siberia are mid-steep and megasized. Normally, a European-style piste is packed down the middle of each trough and the rest of the snow remains where nature put it (until skiers rearranged it). Their sheer dimensions mean that only a fraction of the bowls is ever groomed. There is no end to ways of skiing the bowls. You can cruise down the piste, simply enjoying the majestic scenery. You can ricochet from wall to wall, skiing your own personal roller coaster. You can traverse along a ridge and seek out the steepest wall to the bottom of the bowl. Perhaps you can even find some patches of untracked powder after the vast open areas have been skied out.

While the frontside runs are oriented toward the north to hold the snow, these south-facing bowls snare both the powder and the sunshine. Under optimal conditions, there is sublime skiing with soft snow and clement temperatures. Under the least favorable circumstances, the powder has been chopped up, frozen or melted to the consistency of oatmeal. In this most controlled skiing environment, the bowls are real naturals—the closest feeling to European skiing at an American resort. You have the option of playing in the bowls if they suit you or ignoring them if they don't. Few skiers other than timid novices stay away from the bowls. The Two Elk Restaurant, which seemed so monumental when it was

opened in the winter of 1991–92 atop China Bowl, was expanded by 50 percent the following summer, and three more lifts were added in the bowls. The High Noon triple chair and the West Wall platterpull make it easy for skiers to combine the original Back Bowls with the Far East—and fill some of those additional seats at Two Elk—while the Wapiti tow eliminates the skier's need to tuck and pole—and the snowboarders' need to dismount and walk—when returning to Two Elk or the frontside from the Orient Express.

You can think of Game Creek Bowl, which is tucked into the southwestern corner of Vail Mountain, as a bowl that happens to have some wide, tree-lined trails or as trail skiing that opens into a bowl at the bottom. It is also the site of the Game Creek Club, an exclusive private club that demonstrates that while you don't need to be rich to ski at Vail, you may need to be rich to afford the special facilities and services available to those who are willing to pay hefty membership fees.

When you are skiing the Back Bowls and look across the three more mouth-watering bowls that have the additional benefit of being north-facing, you are looking at Vail's proposed expansion area, probably for 1997–98. The easternmost is Commando Bowl, the middle one is Pete's Bowl and the western one is Super Bowl. Cumulatively, they comprise an additional 2,000 acres. Half is to be accessed by three more chairlifts, while another 1,000 acres or so are to be left undeveloped for a backcountry, off-piste type of skiing.

Beaver Creek

Profile

Beaver Creek is a gracious skiable mountain coupled with three exquisitely upscale little resort centers. The terrain starts from a compact base area and fans out into a sweeping arc above. The bottom of the original ski area is a gentle meadow, providing a generous beginner slope. The Centennial Express, a high-speed quad, is the main lift into the Beave's trail network, unloading two-thirds of the way up the mountain at Spruce Saddle. On this plateau sits one of the first attractive mountain lodges in Colorado. Because the mountaintop is crowned with novice runs and the Centennial quad is so fast, intermediate skiers often ski the bottom part of Beaver Creek, swooping down Latigo, Gold Dust and Fool's Gold—all delightful for their width and even pitch. Lower Centennial and Bear Trap beneath the main chair are trickier to reach and less trafficked. Dropping off the lower portion of Centennial are the black-diamond threesome Moonshine, Bootleg and Buckboard. Down to the skier's right, or east, of Spruce Saddle is Rose Bowl. Its one blue-square slope is an exhilarating cruiser wide as a football field, and its handful of black-diamond shots rival the Birds of Prey for steepness and bumps, but are a lot shorter.

Directly above Spruce Saddle are two more chairlifts leading to incredibly wide novice runs—a treat for new skiers. A trail called Red Tail angling off to the west (or left) of Spruce Saddle deposits skiers in the bottom of a small valley from which more chairlifts climb in three directions. Chair 9 serves a trio of super-steep trails—Goshawk, Peregrine and Golden Eagle, collectively known as the Birds of Prey—long, fall-line mogul runs that equal any in the state. Chair 11 leads to Larkspur Bowl, a swooping snowfield commodious enough for lots of lines through the powder. A long road continues along Larkspur Bowl's crest to McCoy Park, the ski-touring center—even more unusual at a summit than true novice turf. McCoy can also be reached via the Strawberry Park Express across the valley from the Centennial Express. A small web of intermediate runs return to the valley.

The third chair from Red Tail Camp climbs a peak between the Birds of Prey and Larkspur Bowl. Grouse Mountain offers 1,808 vertical feet of advanced and expert runs, continuing on the avian theme with names such as Screech Owl and Ptarmigan. They are both tough and delicate—a mixture of steep pitches of varying widths with some glades and occasional stands of trees. Nestled at the end of a signed-off trail between the Larkspur and Grouse Mountain runouts is Beano's Cabin, the Vail Valley's first on-slope membership club.

Debuting for the 1996–97 ski season is a bigger Beaver Creek, expanded by bringing Arrowhead into the fold. A single lift, climbing through

Mountain Stats—
Beaver Creek

Resort elevation 8,100 feet (Beaver Creek Resort)
Top of highest lift 11,440 feet
Bottom of lowest lift 7,400 feet (Arrowhead)
Total vertical 4,040 feet
Longest run 3$\frac{1}{2}$ miles
Average annual snowfall 330 inches
Ski season mid-November to mid-April
Lifts 5 high-speed quad chairlifts, 4 triples, 4 doubles, 1 surface lift
Capacity 20,640 skiers per hour
Terrain 85 trails, 1,529 acres (18% novice and beginner, 39% intermediate, 43% advanced and expert)
Snowmaking 457 acres
Mountain dining Spruce Saddle at the top of the Centennial Express, Red Tail Camp at the base of Chairs 9 and 11 and Taters at the top of the Strawberry Park Express
Snow reports (970) 476-4888

Bachelor Gulch, made it possible to link a small resort in the Eagle River Valley with the much larger, significantly higher one. Arrowhead was originally built as a luxury second-home and golf community on the lower "outside" slope of Beaver Creek, with a highly touted Jack Nicklaus–designed golf course and a small ski area that was originally another amenity, like a swimming pool or tennis courts, to the real estate development. Arrowhead's high-speed quad and handful of mostly intermediate runs on a 1,714-foot vertical serve as a new gateway to Beaver Creek. Piece o' Cake, the novice run, meanders down the mountain so gently that almost anyone can ski it. The black-diamond trails, which are more challenging than formidable, plus a handful of blue squares comprise Arrowhead.

When Beaver Creek Resort was designed as the Rockies' first gated community with limited vehicular access, the die was cast in the direction of exclusivity. Beano's Cabin, a private club open only to members during the day (though it hosts the general public for sleighride dinners in the evening). The idea of a private club—in the manner of St. Moritz or Gstaad—on an American mountain serves to solidify Beaver Creek's reputation as society playground. Beaver Creek deserves this reputation as a quiet oasis of elegance and luxury contrasted to the hustle of Vail. The addition of Bachlor Gulch to the Beaver Creek scene puts the final seal of poshness on to this very special resort.

SNOWBOARDING

Snowboarders range all over the vastness of Vail Mountain, trying to avoid only a few flat spots on green-circle roads and traverses. Golden Peak's berm and a half-pipe—each more than 300 feet long—are also powerful draws for young riders, and a halfpipe on the newly lighted novice area high on Lionshead, near Eagle's Nest, draws night riders. A variety of slides, jumps and other features draw snowboarders to the Jibline, off the Avanti Express lift. At Beaver Creek, Haywire, a gladed gully spiced with rollers, and Stickline, a steep tree-lined trail with table tops, jumps, log slides and other features designed by pro snowboarding star Brian Delaney, are two runs favored by snowboarders. A snowboarder's trail map, featuring both Vail and Beaver Creek, highlights top runs for riders and even specific snowboarding hot spots. The world's largest ski school incorporates a huge snowboard school. In addition, the Delaney Adult Snowboarding Camps and Boone Lennon's innovative Alpine snowboarding are taught in the Vail Valley. For details, see "Ski School Programs." Rental snowboards and boots are available at Golden Peak, Lionshead and Beaver Creek. Reservations are recommended.

SNOWCAT SKIING

Guided backcountry skiing on 3,000 acres in the Ptarmigan Pass area is suitable for intermediate through expert skiers. Groups are divided by ability, and tips on powder skiing are also offered. Fat skis are available for taming the powder and the crud. The full-day programs include transportation to the skiing area from designated resort pickup points to Vail Pass, guided snowcat skiing, optional fat skis and lunch. Reservations are required. **Vail SnoTours, P.O. Box 7, Vail, CO 81658; (970) 476-3239.**

SKI SCHOOL PROGRAMS

The Vail/Beaver Creek Ski School, with 1,500 instructors, offers a variety of services for skiers of all ages and abilities in all-day and half-day formats at the ski school meeting places at Golden Peak, Vail Village, Lionshead, Two Elk, Mid-Vail and Eagle's Nest at Vail and Spruce Saddle, Beaver Creek Village and Arrowhead at Beaver Creek. The Vail/Beaver Creek Ski School Teaching System encompasses nine levels of skill development. Each level builds on your accomplishments by blending skills you have mastered with new skills. Information on all the programs is available from the **Vail/Beaver Creek Ski School, (970) 476-3239.**

Introductory Program

Discover Skiing!: Full- and half-day beginner lessons or three-day programs, covering the basics of skiing. At Golden Peak, Lionshead and Beaver Creek.

Advanced and Specialty Programs

Breakthrough: Three-day lesson plan to help intermediate and advanced skiers leap up to their next skiing level. Parabolic skis available for this program.

SyberVision: Lesson enhancement, featuring videotapes of your skiing shown at on-mountain viewing centers for analysis.

Style Workshop: Ski groomed runs with grace. Afternoon class on finesse and techniques for effortless skiing by refining fundamental skills. At Mid-Vail and Eagle's Nest.

Mogul and Powder Workshops: Link controlled parallel turns over, around and through the moguls and in powder. Vail's "bumps and bowls class" to improve ability to see and ski down the fall line with precise turn mechanics. At Mid-Vail and Eagle's Nest.

Mountain Masters: Full day of coaching and hard skiing on various terrain and snow conditions.

Super Guides: Offered every Monday from Vail Village, orientation-type guided skiing on best groomed trails.

Vic Braden Ski Weeks: Energetic classes for all levels, from beginners to experienced skiers. Tailored to individual learning styles. Covers overcoming fear as well as refining technique. Personalized coaching based on Braden's training and research as a psychologist and sports coach.

Integrated Skiing Seminars: Led by certified Feldenkrais practitioner Margaret McIntyre. Classes include neuromuscular re-education to help coordination, balance and flexibility. Combination of carefully blended indoor and on-slope sessions.

Mountain Skills Workshop: More than just skiing. Tools for the backcountry skier as well as introduction to winter survival, animal track identification, avalanche awareness, nutrition and more.

Pepi's Wedel Weeks: High-energy, pre-Christmas and January ski weeks for intermediate and advanced skiers, packaged into full programs that include accommodations, lifts, instruction, gift packages and after-ski social activities.

Ultimate Back Bowl Workshop: Two-day workshop led by Chris Anthony and taught by top-level instructors for Level 8 and higher-level skiers. Two-day nonstop skiing on advanced terrain and challenging conditions. Complimentary use of shaped skis is optional.

Vail Moguls Camp: Pro mogul champs Scott Kauf and Patti Sherman-Kauf direct two-day mogul camp, including speed-control techniques, fine-tuning skiing skills and video analysis.

Women's Technique Weeks: Week-long program taught by women instructors with the input of a sports psychologist. Small groups of women. Relaxed and noncompetitive.

Rossignol Women's Workshops: Olympic gold medalist Diann Roffe-Steinrotter (who won her final World Cup race at Vail), Olympic silver medalist Christin Cooper, Olympic bronze medalist Cindy Nelson, overall World Cup champion Tamara McKinney and U.S. Ski Team alumna Kiki Cutter headline two-day sessions. Classes, lectures and opportunity to ski Rossignol demo equipment.

For Mothers Only: Three-day sessions (Monday through Wednesday); $2^{1}/_{2}$-hour midday lessons.

Snowboard Programs

Discover Boarding! for Adults: Covers basics of balance and control.

Freestyle: Full- and half-day classes on intermediate riding tricks, including twists, turns and acrobatics using half-pipe, jibline, snowboard parks, sliders and more.

Alpine: Full- and half-day classes concentrating on sweeping carved turns.

Three-Day Breakthrough: Premier program for intermediate and advanced snowboarders. Midday mountain tours include style and technique tips.

Delaney Adult Snowboarding Camps: Two- and three-day snowboard camps for adult beginners, intermediates and even experts. Directed by champs Brian and Kevin Delaney.

Quick Carve: Hybrid of snowboarding and Alpine skiing in terms of equipment and technique. Innovative technique developed by U.S. Men's Alpine coach and certified instructor Boone Lennon. Three-hour lesson leading to pure carved turns.

Special Programs

Vail Mountain Welcome Tour: Complimentary three-hour mountain tour for intermediate and advanced skiers. Introduction to terrain, led by a professional instructor. At Vail Village daily at 9:00 A.M.

Ski Tips: On-snow analysis by a professional instructor. Offered at 11:00 A.M. daily at Mid-Vail, Spruce Saddle and the top of the Arrowbahn.

Meet the Mountain: Become acquainted with the history, geology and wildlife of Vail and

The Children's Ski Centers at Vail and Beaver Creek offer ski adventures for preschoolers.

Photo by David Lokey

Beaver Creek mountains during a tour led by a knowledgeable guide. At Vail, complimentary Meet the Mountain Tours are 9:00 A.M. daily from Vail Village and from the Lionshead Information Kiosk. At Beaver Creek, they are at 1:00 P.M. on Sunday, Monday and Tuesday from Spruce Saddle.

For Families

Nonskiing Children

Small World Play School nurseries at Golden Peak and Beaver Creek accept children from 2 months to 6 years for all-day care from 8:00 A.M. to 4:30 P.M. There are three programs: infants (2 to 18 months), toddlers (18 to 30 months) and preschoolers ($2^1/_2$ to 6 years). Toddler and preschooler programs include lunch and snowplay. Complimentary parent pagers are available on request. Reservations required. **Children's Center** at **Golden Peak, (970) 479-2044**; at **Beaver Creek, (970) 845-5325.**

12 Skiing Children

Golden Peak, Lionshead and Beaver Creek Children's Ski Centers: Lessons, lunch and lift packages for ages 3 to 6. Centers are open from 8:30 A.M. to 5:00 P.M. mid-week and 5:30 P.M. on weekends. Mini Mice is an introductory exploratory program for children age 3, using snowplay with and without skis. Mogul Mice and Little Braves are geared for 4- to 6-year-old beginners. Both use the Magic Carpet. SuperStars are advanced beginners who ride the chairlifts with partners. Register by 9:45 A.M. Full-day lift-and-lesson packages are available for all levels.

Children ages 6 to 13 are divided into classes by age and ability. Discoverer for beginners, Mountain Explorer for intermediates and Black Diamond Club for experts. Lunch is supervised but not included in the cost. Children (ages 6 to 12) must be registered by 9:15 A.M.

Ske-Cology: An awareness of the mountain environment that offers ski-on treasure hunts, class races and other activities wrapped into all children's classes.

Discover Boarding! for Kids: First-time snowboarding lesson for first-graders and older.

Teens

Teen Guides: Full-day instruction offered during school holiday periods throughout the season for intermediate and advanced teens ages 13 to 18. Holiday Camps also offered. **Teen Activity Line, (970) 479-4090, (970) 476-3239.**

FOR RACERS

NASTAR: Run daily from 10:30 A.M. to 3:00 P.M. at Vail's Black Forest Race Arena off Chair 2 and from 11:00 A.M. to 3:30 P.M. on Beaver Creek's Bear Race Way. Pay-to-race self-time courses are at both of those locations.

HANDICAPPED SKIING

The Disabled Ski Program meets the needs of differently abled guests. Lessons are provided for a variety of challenges, including physical, emotional and learning disabilities. Adaptive rental equipment is available; reserve in advance. **(970) 479-3072.**

NORDIC SKIING

Nordic skiing instruction by the Vail/Beaver Creek Ski School and other programs are offered at the Golden Peak Cross-Country Center, Vail Nordic Center at the Vail Golf Course and Beaver Creek Cross-Country Center. Beaver Creek's is unique, with a high-mountain network of 32 kilometers of double-tracked trails plus skating lane, accessed from the Strawberry Park Express. Half- and full-day instruction, plus nature, backcountry, snowshoe, gourmet and overnight hut tours from intermediate-level skiers and up. Telemark and skating instruction also available, with both facilities offering cross-country lessons for children too. Arrowhead is the center for gourmet snowshoe tours. **(970) 845-5313, (970) 479-4391.**

Backcountry skiing, with or without a guide, abounds in the region. One of Colorado's most popular backcountry tours is the Shrine Pass Road, 12.2 miles from the Vail Pass summit to

Noteworthy

Vail and Beaver Creek have pioneered the development of truly innovative children's ski and after-ski programs. The resorts put out a Children's Adventure Map highlighting on-mountain theme areas at Vail and Beaver Creek and were among the first to designate slow-skiing zones for families and beginners. Vail also has set up a special toll-free number to dispense information on children's activities or to receive the **Vail Valley Fun Pak.** Call **(800) 4-SKI-KID.**

The children's ski school is exemplary. Vail took the concept of the terrain garden—normally simple cut-out figures and sculpted snow to help small children have fun while learning the basic skiing skills—and expanded it into Children's Mountain Adventure attractions that help youngsters with their skills and also teach them about the West. Thunder Cat Cave, the Indian Burial Ground and Gitchegumee Gulch are found on Lionshead. Fort Whippersnapper, Dragon's Breath Mine and a special kids' race course are at Golden Peak. Buckaroo Bowl for little beginners is at the bottom and the Indian Village, the Hibernating Bear Cave, the Indian Burial Grounds, the Aurora Mine and Tombstone Territory are higher up on Beaver Creek. Vail even produces a special children's trail map. To get a sense of how enchanting these theme environments are, watch an instructor lead a class to any of these areas or follow your own child through one. Vail also led in the development of Ske-Cology, a program now spreading across the country. This cooperative effort between ski areas and the U.S. Forest Service is designed to introduce children to the wondrous mountain environment, its plants, its animals and its fragility via special signage on designated trails.

In 1996–97, Vail launched what is the most complete, family-friendly evening diversion in the Rockies. The new Lionshead gondola now runs in the evening (you can ride it for free), and the Island in the Sky cafeteria in the Eagle's Nest lodge serves pizza, burgers and other casual favorites. But even better is the new mountaintop ice skating rink, night snowmobile tours and night lights on the Practice Park. Chair 15 now runs for night beginner skiing, and a new surface tow has been installed to access the new tubing hill and the new halfpipe. The facility is open seven nights a week. Also available in the evening is the long-running Kids' Night Out Goes Western, held selected Tuesdays and Thursdays at Vail and Beaver Creek. It features music, activities, "wagonwheel pizza" and a Wild West show. For details on the **Eagle's Nest Adventure Center,** call **(970) 476-9090.**

For details on all children's activities, phone the **Family Adventure Line, (970) 479-2048,** or check with the **Activities Desk at Vail, (970) 476-9090** or the **Beaver Creek Resort Concierge, (970) 845-9090.** Children's centers are open 8:00 A.M. to 4:30 P.M. Information (but not reservations) is available from the children's centers at **Golden Peak, (970) 479-4400; Lionshead, (970) 479-4450; Village Hall at Beaver Creek, (970) 845-5464.** Babysitting information is available from **Beaver Creek Resort Concierge, (970) 845-9090.**

Families traveling with infants and toddlers can rent cribs, playpens, rocking chairs, highchairs, booster seats and other furnishings delivered to guests' hotel or condominium in the Vail Valley from **Baby's Away, (800) 785-9030, (970) 926-5256.**

the town of Red Cliff. The route's highlights are exceptional scenery, including views of the Mount of the Holy Cross on clear days and a rollicking 2,400-foot downhill into town. Beginning ski-tourers can ski 2 miles from the parking area to the top of Shrine Pass and back down. Experienced skiers ready to do the whole route must leave one vehicle in Red Cliff.

Guided excursions, including hut tours using the 10th Mountain Division huts, can be arranged through the ski school. Vail is also the headquarters for **Paragon Guides,** which specializes in multiday backcountry excursions along the 10th Mountain Trail between the Vail and Aspen areas. **(970) 476-0553.**

WHERE TO STAY

Vail/Beaver Creek Reservations, (970)845-5745; Vail Valley Central Reservations, (800) 525-3875.

Noteworthy

Vail's Mountain Plus Ticket is designed to give vacationers flexibility with no penalty. Five-day or longer tickets can be used for Alpine skiing at Vail or Beaver Creek or selections from the Nordic menu, including cross-country trail fee and rental equipment or instruction, or Nordic or snowshoe tour **(970) 479-4213.**

---

14 Vail

Luxury Accommodations

Cascade Hotel & Club

Full-service 322-room resort hotel and conference center in Cascade Village. Chairlift just steps from the door and movie theater and excellent fitness center next adjacent. Large, sleek and newly renovated, with upscale services. Top health and fitness center adjacent. Popular lobby bar. Formerly the Westin Resort Vail, now under new management and focusing on an international clientele. AAA four-diamond rating. Daily housekeeping, 24-hour room service, bell staff, valet, valet parking, 24-hour front desk, concierge, private shuttle. Outdoor heated pool, two whirlpools, ski check, shops, restaurants, lounge, movie theater (adjacent), full athletic club (adjacent), ski lift with direct access to Lionshead, in-room refrigerators and bars. **1300 Westhaven Dr., Vail, CO 81657; (800) 420-2424, (970) 476-7111.**

Christiania Lodge

Vail classic, recently renewed, updated and upscaled. Vail's first owner-operated lodge, opened in 1963, now redone into six charmingly furnished suites. Excellent Vail Village location.

Newly renovated and refurnished with custom Bavarian-style interiors. Lodge rooms, suites and multibedroom condominiums. Exceptional convenience to the slopes. Daily housekeeping, complimentary breakfast, concierge. Lounge, outdoor heated pool, sauna, ski storage, some rooms with whirlpool tubs or steam showers. **356 E. Hanson Ranch Rd., Vail, CO 81657; (970) 476-5641.**

Game Creek Club Chalets

Exclusive private on-mountain chalets, the first opening in 1996–97 and plans for three more in subsequent seasons. Available to private groups, similar to Trapper's Cabin at Beaver Creek (see page 17). Book through Central Reservations.

Gasthof Gramshammer

Austrian-accented, 28-room lodge with five-star location, 18-karat charm and Vail pedigree. Rates are high and services can't match larger hotels, but legions of regulars don't mind at all. Daily housekeeping, buffet breakfast. Ski room, restaurant, bar, nightclub, ski shop. **231 E. Gore Creek Dr., Vail, CO 81657; (970) 476-5626.**

The Lodge at Vail

Vail's only Mobil four-star, AAA four-diamond hotel; also, member of prestigious Preferred Hotels and Resorts Worldwide group. One hundred well-furnished rooms and suites; 60 hotel rooms, the rest are two- and three-bedroom suites. Lovely public spaces, Austro-Swiss-inspired decor and matchless location in the heart of Vail Village and steps from the base of Vail Mountain. Rooms have humidifiers, refrigerators and marble bathrooms. Daily housekeeping, room service, 24-hour front desk, bell staff, valet, business services. Restaurants, lounge, heated outdoor heated pool, sauna, exercise facilities, whirlpool. **174 E. Gore Creek Dr., Vail, CO 81657; (800) 331-5634, (970) 476-5011.**

Marriott's Mountain Resort Vail

Somewhat urban ambiance, with 350 rooms in a high-rise tower. Recently renovated in fashionable mountain style. Excellent Lionshead location. Daily housekeeping, room service, 24-hour front desk, concierge, valet. Restaurants, lounge, indoor/outdoor heated pool, indoor and outdoor hot tubs, sauna, health and fitness facilities, guest laundry, in-room refrigerators, ski storage. **715**

W. Lionshead Cr., Vail, CO 81657; (970) 476-4444, (800) 228-9290 for Marriott reservations.

Sonnenalp Resort

Extraordinary resort property, with exquisite decor, outstanding service and international clientele. Tranquil oasis in heart of Vail Village. A lovely and perfect corner of the Alps manifested in the Rockies, from custom-made European furnishings down to the smallest custom touches. Complete overhaul and upgrade phased in over several years. Bavaria Haus has 88 lavish suites and demi-suites, each with fancy marble bathroom, gas-log fireplace, balcony, in-room safe and other extras; Swiss Haus and Austria Haus have simpler hotel rooms with views of Vail Village or Gore Creek. Resort offers special guided skiing, snowshoeing and other programs to guests. Daily housekeeping, bell staff, room service, 24-hour front desk, concierge. Restaurants, lounge, outdoor heated pool, hot tub, fitness facilities, two spas, business center. **20 Vail Rd., Vail, CO 81657; (800) 654-8312, (970) 476-5656.**

Vail Athletic Club Hotel & Spa

Small and sporty hotel with individually furnished rooms and suites and one of the best fitness centers in Vail Village, including a climbing wall. Spa packages available. Central Vail Village location. Daily housekeeping, 24-hour front desk, room service, valet, fitness classes, massage, beauty treatments. Restaurant, full fitness center, racquetball court, indoor pool, hot tub, sauna, Jacuzzi, indoor climbing wall, guest laundry, ski storage. **352 E. Meadow Dr., Vail, CO 81657; (800) 822-4754, (970) 476-0700.**

Mid-Priced Accommodations

Best Western VailGlo Lodge

Conveniently located lodge. Lionshead classic, offering functional and pleasant surroundings. Daily housekeeping, Continental breakfast. Pool, sauna, laundry. **701 W. Lionshead Cr., Vail, CO 81657; (970) 476-5506, (800) 528-1234** for Best Western reservations.

Black Bear Inn

Hand-hewn log B&B lodge, 1 1/2 miles west of Vail. Twelve cozy rooms, all with private baths and most with sitting bays. Congenial lobby with fireplace. Located on bus route. Ski and boot storage room. Daily housekeeping, full breakfast, afternoon snack, front desk and concierge. **2405 Elliott Rd., Vail, CO 81657; (970) 476-1304.**

Chateau Vail-Holiday Inn

One of the country's more congenial Holiday Inns. Vail standby with 120 rooms; also, some condominium units. Excellent and convenient location. Daily housekeeping, room service, 24-hour front desk. Hot tub, outdoor heated pool, restaurant, lounge, in-room refrigerators, ski storage. **13 Vail Rd., Vail, CO 81657; (800) 451-9840, (970) 476-5631, (800) HOL-IDAY** for Holiday Inn reservations.

Lion Square Lodge

Hotel rooms and multibedroom units, most with fireplaces, close to Lionshead gondola. Also known for conference facilities. Daily housekeeping, valet service, private shuttle, 24-hour front desk. Heated outdoor pool, hot tubs, saunas, restaurant, guest laundry. **660 W. Lionshead Pl., Vail, CO 81657; (800) 525-5788, (970) 476-2281.**

15

L'Ostello

Contemporary, casually elegant 52-room hotel with distinctive decor and continental ambiance. Dramatically different for Vail generally and Lionshead in particular. Recent total renovation. Daily housekeeping, room service, 24-hour front desk, continental breakfast, private shuttle. Restaurant, lounge, outdoor heated pool, hot tub, workout facility, individual home entertainment centers, in-room refrigerators. **705 W. Lionshead Cr., Vail, CO 81657; (800) 283-8245, (970) 476-2050.**

Tivoli Lodge

Informal, well-priced lodge between Vail Village and Golden Peak, and an easy walk to both. Alpine style, friendly atmosphere and good value. Daily housekeeping, breakfast, complimentary coffee, tea and hot chocolate all day. Outdoor heated pool, whirlpool, sauna, ski storage. **386 E. Hanson Ranch Rd., Vail, CO 81657; (970) 476-5615.**

Vail Village Inn

Hotel rooms in main inn and multiroom condo units in Village Inn Plaza Condominiums. Condos feature fireplaces, kitchens. All in prime central location. Daily housekeeping, 24-hour front desk, concierge, full breakfast for inn guests. Restaurants, lounge, outdoor heated pool, sauna and hot tub (in condo building for condo guests only), ski storage. **100 E. Meadow Dr., Vail, CO 81657; (800) 445-4014, (970) 476-5622.**

Economy Accommodations

Apollo Park Lodge
Lodge in the heart of Vail Village. Simple kitchen units. Popular with families. Daily housekeeping. Heated outdoor pool. **442 S. Frontage Rd. East, Vail, CO 81657; (800) 872-8281, (970) 476-5881.**

Roost Lodge
West Vail bargain with friendly family atmosphere. Daily housekeeping, Continental breakfast, shuttle. Heated pool, hot tub. **1783 Fall Line Dr., Vail, CO 81657; (800) 873-3065, (970) 476-5451.**

16

Condominiums and Homes
Condominium management and rental firms in the Vail Valley include
Bighorn Rentals, (970) 476-5532
Cascade Village Properties, (800) 228-3000, (970) 476-6106
Destination Resorts, (800) 322-VAIL
East Vail Rentals, (970) 476-6636
Vail Management Co., (970) 476-4262
Vail Resort Rentals & Realty, (800) 456-VAIL
Skier's Homestay arranges economical accommodations in private homes on bus routes, **(970) 476-2571.**

Antlers at Vail
Casual studio to three-bedroom units. Very convenient to Lionshead gondola. Condos with fully equipped kitchens at moderate hotel-room rates, all with balconies. Hotel-style front desk, daily housekeeping. Outdoor heated pool, hot tub, guest laundry. **680 W. Lionshead Pl., Vail, CO 81657; (800) 843-8245, (970) 476-2471.**

Evergreen Lodge
One- to three-bedroom condominiums in large room lodge between Vail Village and Lionshead. Hotel facilities and services. Daily housekeeping, 24-hour front desk, concierge. Restaurant, out-door heated pool, hot tub, sauna, hot tub, ski storage. **250 S. Frontage Rd. West, Vail, CO 81657; (800) 284-8245, (970) 476-7810.**

The Lodge at Lionshead
Well-equipped studio to three-bedroom units, all with full kitchens, most with fireplaces and some with Gore Creek views. Daily housekeeping, hotel-style front desk. Outdoor heated pool, sauna, guest laundry. **380 Lionshead Cr., Vail, CO 81658; (800) 962-4399, (970) 476-2700.**

Manor Vail Lodge
Sprawling complex at the base of Golden Peak. Top pick since Vail's earliest days. Units of various sizes—all with kitchens, most with fireplaces, balconies or patios. Major renovation underway. Daily housekeeping, 24-hour front desk. Restaurant, lounge, outdoor heated pool, sauna, Jacuzzi. **595 E. Vail Valley Dr., Vail, CO 81657; (800) 950-VAIL, (970) 476-5651.**

Marriott's Streamside at Vail
Timeshare resort just west of Vail with especially well priced studio to two-bedroom units, all with full kitchens. Luxury property out of Vail's hustle, but accessible to the action. Excellent for families. Clubhouse with nightly movies. Twenty-four-hour front desk, complimentary shuttle. Indoor/outdoor pool, hot tubs, Jacuzzi, racquetball courts, game room. **2254 S. Frontage Rd. West, Vail, CO 81657; (970) 476-8667, (800) 228-9290** for Marriott reservations.

Montaneros in Vail
One- to four-bedroom units, some with lofts. Individually decorated luxury condos, most with fireplaces and balconies, in popular family complex close to Lionshead gondola. Plain exterior but spacious units with high ceilings and views. Daily housekeeping, 24-hour front desk. Outdoor heated pool, hot tub, sauna, Jacuzzi, ski storage, restaurant, guest laundry. **641 W. Lionshead Mall, Vail, CO 86157; (800) 444-VAIL, (970) 476-2491.**

Mountain Haus
Large, sleekly furnished units in top location next to the Covered Bridge. Excellent TV/VCR systems, fireplaces and other luxury extras. Daily housekeeping, 24-hour front desk, concierge. Fitness

center, outdoor heated pool, saunas, whirlpools. **292 E. Meadow Dr., Vail, CO 81657; (800) 237-0922, (970) 476-2434.**

Sandstone Creek Club

Comfortable, reasonably priced mountainview units sleeping up to 10 people. Located across the highway from town. Daily housekeeping, private shuttle. Heated indoor/outdoor pool, hot tubs, sauna, exercise room, racquetball court, game room, billiard room, laundry, lounge. **1020 Vail View Dr., Vail, CO 81657; (800) 421-1098, (970) 476-4405.**

Simba Run

Sixty handsomely appointed one- and two-bedroom units with fireplaces. Contemporary architecture and furnishings. Located $1^1/_2$ miles west of Vail Village, with private shuttle or town bus options. Daily housekeeping, private shuttle, 24-hour front desk. Indoor pool, exercise facility, hot tub, steamroom. **1100 Fall Line Dr., Vail, CO 81657; (800) 321-1489, (970) 476-0344.**

Vail International

Thirty-five one- to three-bedroom condos between Vail Village and Lionshead. Fine location, yet some of Vail's most affordable prices. Short walk to lifts. All units with fireplaces, kitchens, balconies and outside corridors. Daily housekeeping, hotel-style front desk. Outdoor heated pool, hot tub, saunas, guest laundry, ski storage. **303 E. Lionshead Cr., Vail, CO 81657; (970) 476-5200.**

Vail Racquet Club

Spacious one- to three-bedroom condominiums and three-bedroom townhomes, located in East Vail on bus route. Complimentary use of one of the resort's top athletic clubs. Daily housekeeping, hotel-style front desk, concierge. Restaurant, lounge, full health and racquet club, sauna, Jacuzzi, ski storage. **4690 Vail Racquet Club Dr., Vail, CO 81657; (970) 476-4840.**

Beaver Creek

Luxury Accommodations

Hyatt Regency Beaver Creek

One of the top hotels in ski country. Impeccable 300-room hotel, beautifully furnished with spa-cious bathrooms. Elegantly rustic style, top-of-the-line services and abundant facilities. Ski-in/ski-out. Special singles, single parents and ski-and-spa packages. Lobby is popular evening gathering spot. Camp Hyatt, supervised day and evening children's activities. Twice-daily housekeeping, concierge, valet parking, ski valet, room service, fitness classes, massage. Indoor/outdoor heated pool, six hot tubs, children's locker rooms, fitness center, restaurants, lounge, shops, salon. **P.O. Box 1595, Avon, CO 81620; (970) 949-1234, (800) 233-1234** for Hyatt reservations.

The Pines Lodge

Exquisite 60-room lodge with excellent mountain views, featuring the opulence and level of service associated with fine hotels' concierge floors. Each room has refrigerator, humidifier, hair dryer and TV with VCR (with a video library, as well as a paperback best-seller library on site). Near Chair 12 and cross-resort ride from the main base area. Housekeeping three times daily, hot water bottle in bed, 24-hour front desk, overnight laundry service, ski valet, full American breakfast, après-ski refreshments, afternoon tea. Restaurant, lounge, heated outdoor pool, whirlpool, saunas, fitness equipment, business service center, library. **P.O. Box 36, Avon, CO 81620; (800) 859-8342, (970) 845-7900.**

Trapper's Cabin

Not a lodge in a conventional sense but a secluded four-bedroom cabin high on the mountain that may be rented by groups of up to 10. The ultimate in relaxation and privacy (no television or telephone). Typically, guests ski to Trapper's in the late afternoon and ski out the morning of departure. Rate is high, but includes cocktails, gourmet dinner, breakfast the next morning and a two-person staff to prepare, serve and clean up—and priceless privacy. Services include luggage transfer, private chef, personal cabin keeper. Outdoor hot tub. **P.O. Box 915, Avon, CO 81620;** for reservations or emergency contact, **(800) 859-8242, (970) 845-5787, (970) 845-9700.**

Condominiums

Beaver Creek Lodge

Seventy immaculate suites, from one-bedroom kitchenette suites to luxurious five-bedroom suites, all with fireplaces. Daily housekeeping, 24-hour front desk, continental breakfast. Indoor/outdoor heated pool, spa, sauna, steamroom, workout facilities, restaurants, lounges, salon. **P.O. Box 2578, Avon, CO 81620; (800) 732-6777, (970) 845-9800.**

The Charter at Beaver Creek

This large 155-unit complex combines European style and American spaciousness into one exceptional condo lodge. Also combines condominium convenience with hotel services. Units of one to five bedrooms. Daily housekeeping, 24-hour front desk, concierge, Continental breakfast, private shuttle. Restaurants, lounge, indoor pool, indoor and outdoor hot tubs, health club, sauna, ski storage. **P.O. Box 5310, Avon, CO 81620; (800) 525-6660, (970) 949-6660.**

Park Plaza

Spacious and well-appointed condos in the heart of Beaver Creek. Master suites have oversize whirlpool tubs. Elegant atmosphere. Fine service and unbeatable location. Daily housekeeping, complimentary Continental breakfast, hotel-type front desk. Indoor pool, sauna, Jacuzzi, ski storage, restaurant. **P.O. Box 358, Avon, CO 81620; (970) 845-7700.**

Poste Montane

Beaver Creek classic, located in the center of Beaver Creek Village. Lodge rooms and suites in property with European flavor and friendly American service. Guests have access to athletic club and heated outdoor pool. Hotel-style front desk, concierge, daily housekeeping, continental breakfast included. Sauna, Jacuzzi, ski storage. **P.O. Box 5480, Avon, CO 81620; (800) 497-9238, (970) 845-7500.**

SaddleRidge at Beaver Creek

Built as a private corporate conference center. Now an ultraluxury resort. Antique- and memorabilia-filled "clubhouse" with dining and recreational facilities and 12 exquisite two- and three-bedroom "mountain villas," furnished as lavishly as the public spaces. Multiline telephones, fireplaces, balconies, deluxe kitchens and bathrooms with steam showers and whirlpool tubs. Easy ski-in, but a short walk or van shuttle to the slopes. Meals served in a clublike dining area. Daily housekeeping, massage, concierge.

18

Indoor/outdoor heated pool, fitness facilities, hot tub, restaurant, lounge. **P.O. Box 915, Avon, CO 81620; (800) 859-8242, (970) 845-8165.**

St. James Place

Sizeable timeshare complex, well-located in Beaver Creek Village. Luxury one- to three-bedroom units, each with gas fireplace, stereo, VCR and humidifier. Twenty-four-hour front desk, concierge, daily housekeeping. Indoor pool, indoor and outdoor hot tubs, fitness facilities, sauna, steamroom, ski lockers. **P.O. Box 1512, Avon, CO 81620; (970) 845-9300.**

Avon

Mid-Priced Accommodations

Christie Lodge

Moderately priced kitchenette units. Fireplaces, balconies. Daily housekeeping, 24-hour front desk. Indoor/outdoor heated pool, hot tubs, saunas, athletic club, restaurant, lounge, guest laundry. **0047 E. Beaver Creek Blvd., Avon, CO 81620; (800) 551-4326, (970) 949-7700.**

Comfort Inn

Functional economy motel. Many amenities for the money. Daily housekeeping, complimentary Continental breakfast, 24-hour front desk. Heated pool, hot tub. **P.O. Box 5510, Avon, CO 81620; (800) 423-4374, (970) 949-5511, (800) 424-6423** for Comfort Inn reservations.

Condominiums

The Seasons at Avon

Several spacious condominium units from studios to three bedrooms, within walking distance of the Arrowhead lift. **P.O. Box 1256, Avon, CO 81620; (800) 859-8242, (970) 845-5787.**

Minturn

Mid-Priced Accommodations

Eagle River Inn

This 1894 downtown landmark, redone in a chic Southwestern style, operates as a 12-bedroom B&B inn. Daily housekeeping, continental breakfast, afternoon wine-and-cheese hour. Hot tub overlooking Eagle River. **P.O. Box 100, Minturn,**

CO 81654; (800) 344-1750, (970) 827-5761.

Edwards

Luxury Accommodations

The Lodge at Cordillera

Luxurious 28-room country inn on 3,000 mountaintop acres in growing resort community. Noted for Restaurant Picasso and outstanding spa and now noteworthy golf course. Many lodge rooms with private fireplaces, some with lofts. Daily housekeeping, van service, massage and beauty treatments. Indoor pool, hot tub, fitness center, cross-country center, restaurant, lounge. **P.O. Box 1110, Edwards, CO 81632; (800) 548-2721, (970) 926-2200.**

Economy Accommodations

Lazy Ranch

Historic farmhouse, originally built in 1904, now charming Victorian-style B&B inn. Family-owned and run; set on 60 acres. Just four charming rooms, each with distinctive theme. An oasis of western tradition in a valley rapidly being over-developed. Daily housekeeping, full breakfast. **0057 Lake Creek Rd., Edwards, CO 81632; (970) 926-3876.**

DINING OUT

Vail

Alfredo's

Sumptuous restaurant in the Cascade Hotel & Club specializing in northern Italian and new American cuisine. Non-smoking restaurant. "Taste of Alfredo's" is a prix fixe dinner that changes monthly. Dinner only in 1996–97. Renovation and extended hours planned in 1997. Children's menu. **Cascade Hotel, 1300 Westhaven Dr., Cascade Village (970) 476-7014.**

Alpenrose

Charming tea room serving breakfast and lunch by day and intimate, romantic restaurant by night. Formal Swiss and Continental cuisine, in-

Vail's aprés-ski scene starts early—and is especially beguiling on a warm spring afternoon.

cluding excellent game and unbelievable pastry, plus a fine wine list. Seductive ambiance. Reservations recommended. **100 E. Meadow Dr., Vail; (970) 476-3194.**

Ambrosia

Gourmet continental cuisine in an elegant, romantic restaurant. A Vail classic, specializing in veal, lamb, duck and seafood. Gorgeous pastries. **17 E. Meadow Dr., Vail; (970) 476-1964.**

Los Amigos

Longtime favorite Mexican restaurant for lunch, après-ski and dinner. Various "flavors" of nachos, plus other zesty appetizers. Chile rellenos, fajitas and enchiladas are faves. Moderate prices. Children's menu. Located next to the VistaBahn. **318 Hanson Ranch Rd., Vail; (970) 476-5847.**

Antlers Room

Cozy Austrian look and rich Austrian fare served at dinner; lunches are a tad lighter. Terrific desserts. Reservations recommended. **Gasthof Gramshammer, 231 E. Gore Creek Dr., Vail; (970) 476-5626.**

Bart & Yeti's

Casual, good-humored spot known for great burgers and sandwiches, plus chili, ribs and chicken-fried steak. Nightly pasta special. Moderate prices. Beers on tap and wine by the glass or bottle. Children's menu. Takeout available. Reservations not accepted. **551 E. Lionshead Cr., Lionshead, Vail; (970) 476-2754.**

Blu's

Casual setting for eclectic American cuisine, featuring both light and hearty dishes from all sorts of culinary traditions. Menu features Roasted Farmhouse Duck, Breast of Southwest Chicken, Kick Ass California Chicken Relleno, Pistacchio Schnitzel, Calamari Caesar Salad and other creations. Also, unusual breakfast selections. Extensive wine list. Reservations not accepted. **193 E. Gore Creek Dr., Vail; (970) 476-3113.**

Bully Ranch

English pub in the Sonnenalp's Bavaria Haus serves fancy feasts, as well as traditional fish-and-chips, burgers and concoctions from the salad bar. Casual, big-screen TV. Reservations accepted. **Sonnenalp Resort, 20 Vail Rd., Vail; (970) 476-5656.**

Cafe Colorado

Southwestern-style mesquite cooking. Unusual renditions of shrimp, steak and seafood in pleasant streamside location. Also salad bar, light meals and sandwiches, plus daily breakfast buffet. Early-bird specials. Reservations accepted. **Evergreen Lodge, 250 S. Frontage Rd. West, Vail; (970) 476-7810.**

Clancy's Windy City Irish Pub

Chicago-style pizza, pasta, burgers and beer in big-city pub setting. Reservations accepted. **1300 Westhaven Dr., Cascade Village; (970) 476-3886.**

Cucina Rustica

Italian country cuisine coupled with Vail style. Popular skier's buffet breakfast. Fine for dinner and also good choice for breakfast or lunch. **The Lodge at Vail, Vail; (970) 476-5011.**

Fondue Stube

The place to go for this Swiss specialty. Also, seafood fondue. **Holiday Inn–Chateau Vail, 13 Vail Rd., Vail; (970) 476-5631.**

Game Creek Club

Exclusive luncheon club ($24,500 initiation fee, $1,200 annual dues plus food and beverage tab) now available to anyone who can afford the price of dinner—OK, a pricey dinner. Ride the Lionshead gondola and take a snowcat-drawn sleigh to new club in Game Creek Bowl. Excellent six-course dinner, with limited menu but choices for several courses, similar to the successful Beano's Cabin dinners at Beaver Creek (see page 22). Full bar and good wine list. Reservations required. On the mountain; **(970) 479-4275.**

Hong Kong Cafe

American cafe food at lunch and Chinese dishes at dinner. Also, light appetizers after skiing. Reservations not accepted. **227 Wall Street, Vail; (970) 476-1818.**

Imperial Fez

Moroccan cuisine, including meat, seafood and strict vegetarian offerings. Couscous a predictably delicious specialty. Lavish decor and dramatic presentation. Multicourse dinner menus, with two prix fixe options. Entertainment and dancing. Children under 6 may share adult's entrée. Reservations recommended. **Vail Run, 1000 Lions Ridge, West Vail; (970) 476-1948.**

Jackalope Cafe & Cantina

Fun-filled Tex-Mex atmosphere and food. Breakfast, lunch and dinner. Good appetizer selection. Stuffed jalapeño camarones, fajitas, burritos and enchiladas are favorites. Also, nightly dinner specials and gringo options available. Shuffleboard, pool, late bar service. **West Vail Mall, Vail; (970) 476-4314.**

K. B. Ranch Co.

Good steaks and seafood plus a huge salad bar at this informal Lionshead eatery. Reservations recommended. **Lion Square Lodge, 660 Lionshead Pl., Vail; (970) 476-1937.**

Lancelot

A favorite for more than 20 years. Longtime purveyor of such traditional favorites as prime rib, seafood and chicken. Updated menu also features pasta and vegetarians specials. Friendly restaurant in the center of the village. Caesar is the house salad. Hearty soups to hearty desserts. No smoking in the dining room; cigarettes only in the bar. Children's menu. Reservations recommended. **201 Gore Creek Dr., Vail; (970) 476-5828.**

The Left Bank

Elegant and romantic restaurant overlooking Gore Creek, known for outstanding French cuisine, desserts and continental service. Fine wine list. One of Vail's long-standing best restaurants. Reservations recommended. **Sitzmark Lodge, 183 Gore Creek Dr., Vail; (970) 476-3696.**

Lord Gore
Spacious restaurant serving continental cuisine. Prime location at the base of Golden Peak. Prime meats too, all expertly prepared and well served. Chateaubriand and Colorado lamb are specialties. Vail institution known for dramatic tableside cooking, plus children's menu. Reservations recommended. **Manor Vail, Vail; (970) 476-4959, (970) 476-5000, Ext 303.**

L'Ostello Italian Bistro
Purveyor of nouvelle Italian pastas, vegetables, seafood and other light fare. **L'Ostello Lodge, 705 W. Lionshead Cr., Vail; (970) 476-2050.**

Ludwig's
Continental fare with light nouvelle flair at this charming restaurant. Serves buffet breakfast, brunch and dinner. Dinner reservations recommended. **Sonnenalp Resort, Bavaria Haus, 20 Vail Rd., Vail; (970) 476-5656.**

Michael's American Bistro
Trendy purveyor of modern American dishes made with excellent, imaginatively combined ingredients. Outstanding appetizers and desserts—and everything between. Mixed Seafood Grill and Mixed Shellfish Grill typify new twist on old standbys. Meats, seafood, poultry and many meatless options. Wood-burning pizza oven too. Extensive wine list. Downstairs Mediterranean bistro offers light lunches, beverages from cappucino to cognac and good tapas bar. Sometimes, live entertainment too. Restaurant reservations recommended. **Vail Gateway Mall, 12 S. Frontage Rd., Vail; (970) 476-5353.**

Montauk Seafood Grill
Good fare from the sea in good-looking eatery. Emphasis is on seafood, but steaks, chops and pasta also available. **549 Lionshead Cr., Lionshead, Vail; (970) 476-2610.**

The Ore House
Vail veterans make pilgrimage to this venerable steakhouse "under the clock tower." Steaks, prime rib, chops and ribs are long-standing favorites. Poultry, seafood and vegetarian specialties reflect contemporary tastes. Moderate prices. Takeout available. **232 Bridge St., Vail; (970) 476-5100.**

Red Lion
Big, busy restaurant that has been around almost since Vail's beginnings. Hickory-smoked barbecue, big burgers, soups and salads. Continuous service from 11:00 A.M. Good for après-ski as well as moderately priced lunch or dinner. Takeout available. **304 Bridge St., Vail; (970) 476-7676.**

Salad Garden
Inexpensive and healthful cuisine in center-Vail location. All-you-can-eat buffet at breakfast, lunch and dinner. Sixty-item salad bar, including pasta offerings. Pizza also available, to eat in or take out. Low prices, no-tipping policy and children under 12 half-price (under 3, free). Desserts too. **Mountain Haus, 292 E. Meadow Dr., Vail; (970) 476-8862.**

Seasons at the Green
Sleighride dinner to American down-home meal. Wrangler Steve Jones's big Belgian draft horses ferry sleigh to pleasant restaurant at golf course/Nordic center, which in the evening is secluded and off-the-beaten-Vail-path. Three-course dinner, prepared country style and served family style. Adult and children's rates. Reservations required. **Vail Golf Club, East Vail; (970) 476-8057** for reservations.

Siamese Orchid at Vail
Thai specialties including curries and stir fries, in a stylish setting. **Vail Gateway Mall, 12 S. Frontage Rd., Vail; (970) 476-9417.**

Stuberl Restaurant
Charming restaurant offering four- to six-course prix fixe menu in one nightly setting. Reservations required. **Austria Haus, Sonnenalp Resort, 20 Vail Rd., Vail; (970) 476-5656.**

Sweet Basil
Modern cuisine, fine service and a good selection of wine in a pleasant cafe-style environment. Lunch and dinner. **193 Gore Creek Dr., Vail; (970) 476-0125.**

Terra Bistro
Innovative dishes served in sprightly, high-ceiling room. Air of contemporary elegance—and smoke-free too. Interesting melding of European, Oriental and American flavors, including Fennel

and Leek Soup with Tapenade and Red Pepper Puree or Sweet Potato-Poblano Ravioli with Gorgonzola Vinaigrette for starters, or Five Spiced Salmon Box with Sweet Soy, Grilled Rice Lake, Eggplant Salsa and Steamed Spinach as an entrée. Many seafood and vegetarian choices. Reservations recommended. **Vail Athletic Club, 352 E. Meadow Dr., Vail; (970) 476-6836.**

La Tour
Classic Vail restaurant serving classic French cuisine. A Vail tradition since the mid-1960s. Extensive menu, focusing on long-standing favorites plus newer versions of *la cuisine de France.* Sautéed Breast of Quail in Foie Gras Truffle Sauce, Moules Marinière and other specialties practically spring from the pages of a Peter Mayle description of French food. Imported and California wines. Dinner nightly (except Monday). Reservations recommended. **Vail Center Building, 122 E. Meadow Dr., Vail; (970) 476-4403.**

22 The Tyrolean
Wild game and other award-winning continental and American specialties in an atmosphere of Alpine elegance. Daily specials. Dinner only. Children's menu. Reservations recommended. **400 E. Meadow Dr., Vail; (970) 476-2204.**

Up the Creek
Stylish eatery with good food at moderate prices. Salads, pastas and seafood are specialties at

Beaver Creek has developed into an elegant, self-contained resort village.

Photo by Jack Affleck/Vail Assoc.

lunch and dinner. On Gore Creek, downstairs from the Children's Fountain. Reservations suggested. **223 Gore Creek Dr., Vail; (970) 476-8141.**

Vendetta's
Heart-of-Vail location. Traditional northern Italian cuisine at lunch and dinner, plus excellent après-ski scene. Seafood and veal are specialties in atmospheric downstairs dining room. Upstairs pizza bar for casual eating at lunch, after-ski, dinner and late into the evening, plus pizza delivery anywhere in Vail Village and Lionshead. Dinner reservations suggested. **291 Bridge St., Vail; (970) 476-5070.**

The Wildflower
Elegant restaurant with well-prepared, well-served modern American fare at dinner. **Lodge at Vail, Vail; (970) 476-5011.**

Beaver Creek

Beano's Cabin
Slopeside private lunch club high on the mountain open for six-course sleighride dinners, featuring steak, lamb, chicken or fish and nightly entertainment. Other specialties: pizza from wood-fired oven, soup of the day and fine desserts. Full bar and extensive wine list. Children's menu. Two seatings. Reservations required. On the mountain; **(970) 949-9090** for reservations.

Coyote Cafe
Mexican foods, salads, sandwiches and even Spaghettios in a casual fun setting. **Beaver Creek Village; (970) 949-5001.**

Crooked Hearth
Breakfast, lunch and dinner specialties in this casual hotel restaurant. A touch of wine-cellar ambiance. Pan pizzas, fondue and interesting salads are the dinner. More than 100 beers plus wine by the glass and special schnapps. **Hyatt Regency Beaver Creek, Beaver Creek; (970) 949-1234.**

Golden Eagle Inn
Substantial lunches and creative American cuisine at dinner in this pleasant restaurant in the center of Beaver Creek Village. Specializes in ranch-raised game, carefully prepared and presented. Excellent vegetarian entrées, salads and

pastas too. Reservations accepted. **Village Hall, Beaver Creek; (970) 949-1940.**

Grouse Mountain Grill
Breakfast and dinners in spacious dining room with mountain views. Dinners on the creative and contemporary side. Steak, seafood, pasta and game, imaginatively prepared and beautifully presented. Caters to appetites from light (Grilled Ahi Tuna on Vegetable Ribbons with Mango Sauce) to hearty (Double-Cut Pork Chop with Tomato-Apple Chutney and Pickled Fig, with Roasted Garlic Cream Potatoes on the side). Excellent wine list. Children's menu. Dinner reservations recommended. **The Pines, Beaver Creek; (970) 949-6000.**

Legends
Bills itself as "Rancho Deluxe," for Southwestern overlay to its interesting menu. Crab & Jalapeño Won Tons with Red Pepper Jelly as appetizer or Crispy Half Duck with Tequilla-Raspberry Sauce typify cross-cultural mix. Fine seafood, steaks, poultry and pasta. Smaller meals also offered for lighter appetites—and at lower prices. Good wine list. Reservations recommended. **Poste Montane Lodge, Beaver Creek; (970) 949-5540.**

Mirabelle
Delightful, renovated homestead turned into an elegant restaurant specializing in finely tuned Provençale cuisine and a wine list to match. Delightful ambiance and excellent service. Reservations recommended. **55 Village Rd., near Beaver Creek entrance; (970) 949-7728.**

Patina Ristorante
Formal setting for innovative and classic Italian dishes. Top any meal with Tiramasu for a sybaritic treat. Elegance and style prevail in spacious, high-ceiling hotel dining room overlooking the slopes. **Hyatt Regency Beaver Creek; (970) 949-1234.**

traMonti
Elegant atmosphere and classic Italian cuisine. Large menu, with special emphasis on extensive choice of antipasti to outstanding entrées and rich desserts. Excellent pasta and risotto selection available in appetizer or entrée portions. **The Charter, Beaver Creek; (970) 949-5552.**

Avon

The Brass Parrot
Good old down-home cookin', including chicken-fried steak, fried chicken and other traditional American favorites. **Avon Market Center, Avon; (970) 949-7770.**

Cassidy's Hole in the Wall Saloon
Longtime favorite for eating and meeting offering moderately priced American and Southwestern fare, daily at lunch and dinner. Large selection of moderately priced steaks and barbecue specialties. Also, lots of appetizer choices, generous sandwiches with fries or country slaw and salads. Children's menu. **Benchmark Shopping Center, 82 E. Beaver Creek Blvd., Avon; (970) 949-9449.**

Chicago Pizza Factory
All sorts of pies. Eat in, take out or have delivered. **Avon Market Center, Avon; (970) 949-4210.**

China Garden
Mandarin and Szechuan dishes. Takeout available. **Avon Center Building, Avon; (970) 949-4986.**

Mosato's
Nippon in Avon. Japanese cuisine and sushi bar. **Avon Market Center, Avon; (970) 949-0330.**

Minturn

Booco's Station
Casual restaurant specializing in barbecued ribs, down-home country fare, steak and Mexican dishes. Great selection of appetizers, including fabled Killer Nachos and Pig-Out Combo Plate. Live jazz. Reservations accepted. **455 Main St., Minturn; (970) 827-4224.**

Chili Willy's
Casual Tex-Mex spot known for good margaritas and lively atmosphere. Fajitas, Rellenos de Camarones, several chicken dishes and Texas-style barbecued ribs are specialties. Mix-and-match combination plates from Tex-Mex classics. Sopapilla Basket a great dessert, but it's okay, because Chili Willy's uses only canola oil for frying. Reservations accepted. **101 Main St., Minturn; (970) 827-5887.**

Colorado's Big Five

Minturn Country Club
Fun, funk and fabulous steaks and salad bar. Grill your own meat over charcoal. **Main St., Minturn; (970) 827-4114.**

Pasta Palace
Lots of hearty fare at non–Vail Valley budget prices. Light on decor; heavy on value. Antipasti, salads and soups as starters. Choice of pasta entrées, in *piccolo* or *grande* portions for various appetites. Select pasta (linguine, fettucini, penne regati, fusilli or spaghetti) and top with choice of over a dozen sauces. Also, catch of the day, chicken, veal and pizza. Non-smoking dining room. Children's menu. Reservations accepted. **410 Main St., Minturn; (970) 827-9204.**

The Saloon
Minturn standby known for lots of noise, lots of food and lots of fun. Good appetizers, terrific entrées and assorted combination plates. Also the place to go for quail, served by the piece as an appetizer or several on the plate as a main course. **146 N. Main St., Minturn; (970) 827-5854.**

Edwards

Champions Tavern
Local hangout for burgers, chicken, salads and prime rib. Casual pool table and dart board atmosphere. Breakfast, lunch and dinner. Three miles west of Avon. **Edwards Business Center. US 6, Edwards; (970) 426-2444.**

Fiesta's
New Tex-Mex spot with optional all-American dishes. **57 Edwards Access Rd., Edwards; (970) 926-3048.**

Four Eagle Ranch
Sleighride dinner to rustic barn, for casual barbecue fare served buffet style. Friendly country atmosphere. Reservations required. Located west of Edwards. **Drawer 70, Wolcott, CO 81655; (970) 926-3371.**

June Creek Grill
Outstanding contemporary dinners served nightly (except Sunday and Monday). Award-winning chef. Lovely atmosphere. Reservations requested. **Sonnenalp Golf Club, 1265 Berry Creek Rd., Singletree, Edwards; (970) 926-3528.**

Markos Pizza & Pasta
Very inexpensive lunches (but very far from the slopes) and moderately priced Italian dinners. Pizza and pasta. Beer and wine. Eat-in or carry-out. Also, delivery within a limited area. **Edwards Plaza, Edwards; (970) 926-7003.**

Restaurant Picasso
One of Colorado's top restaurants, in terms of cuisine, views and price. Contemporary and imaginative French cuisine, including two multicourse, prix fixe menus, the "Discovery Menu" and spa menu. Excellent wine cellar. Top-flight service. Reservations suggested. **The Lodge at Cordillera, Edwards; (970) 926-2200, Ext. 176.**

Timber Hearth Grille
Antique horsedrawn sleighride to lovely restaurant in Cordillera's golf clubhouse for dinner. Innovative creations in the finest Cordillera tradition, all with Southwestern flair. Fireside cocktails and appetizers. Live entertainment some nights. Reservations required. **The Lodge at Cordillera, Edwards; (970) 926-5588.**

Nightlife

The Vail Valley offers abundant opportunities for everyone to unwind from the skiing day. Vail is Aspen's main rival as the shopping mecca of the Rockies. Excellent, elegant and interesting shops, galleries and boutiques vie with eating and dining places as after-skiing diversions. In pedestrian-oriented Vail Village, Lionshead and growing Beaver Creek Village, terraces are popular when it's warm. In the village, traditional after-ski action centers around such watering holes as the Red Lion, the Hong Kong Cafe, Pepi's Bar and Vendetta's, which offers a well-priced pizza and draft beer special. The King's Club in the Sonnenalp Resort serves high tea and cocktails, and features live piano or harp, all in a serene fireside setting. Fitzwilliam's in the Lodge at Vail, at the bottom of Golden Peak, is a longtime favorite and offers happy-hour specials.

Lionshead, Bart and Yeti's, Garfinkel's and Trail's End—the latter right in the gondola building—fill up fast, and Garfinkel's has become the most rockin' spot in Vail for a few years. In Cascade Village, Clancy's and the lobby lounge the Cascade Hotel & Club are the places to be. At Beaver Creek, after-ski activity centers around the lobby bar and the Crooked Hearth, both in the Hyatt, at Players Pub, the resort's happy-hour headquarters in the Beaver Creek Lodge, and at the Coyote Cafe, a ski and sports bar. In East Vail, Anthony's is the only place to be—because it's the only place with après-ski.

There's lots of live, loud entertainment, yet quietly civilized piano players can be found in several boîtes as well. Pianist Peter Varvra has been entertaining for years at what was the Westin and is now the Cascade Hotel & Club. The Hyatt and the Pines Lodge at Beaver Creek and the King's Club in the Sonnenalp and Mickey's in the Lodge at Vail in Vail Village are among the others with fine piano playing for après-ski and sometimes later. Many places offer live entertainment some or most evenings, but none stress it more than **Louie's,** below the Hong King Cafe, which specializes in live jazz in a non-smoking environment; reservations recommended for all shows, **(970) 479-9008.**

Vail's best family after-ski offerings are unrivaled. The new Lionshead gondola now runs in the evenings and access a new high-mountain evening activities center with beginner night skiing, snowboarding, tubing, ice skating, snowmobile tours and casual dining. In addition to a teen hangout in the Lionshead Auxiliary Building, at the base of the parking structure, three evening programs are aimed at younger children. The Vail Ski School's matchless demo team puts on a sizzling show called Hot Winter Nights every Wednesday at Golden Peak. Admission is free. There are also two evenings of dinner and live entertainment heavy on audience participation, **Family Night Out** (children of all ages and their parents) and **Kids' Night Out Goes Western** (ages 5 to 12, no parents). For reservations call **(970) 476-9898.** Families, including older children and teens, flock to Fun and Games, which features popular diversions in an alcohol-free environment. Everything from Cracky Crab for toddlers to old-fashioned boardwalk games to high-tech hit video games is on tap in this amusement center, well located at Crossroads in Vail Village.

For adults, late-night action blankets the Valley. Vail has a reputation for high style and prices, but there's an abundance of stylistic and even budgetary options. On the casual end, there's the foot-stomping glee of a Tex-Mex evening in Minturn, a round of drinks and a game of pool at Clancy's or the Jackalope. Cassidy's Hole in the Wall in Avon has recently been gentrified and is a mingling spot for budget-minded yuppies. The Club at the head of Bridge Street gets a young, dance-crazy crowd, while the designer-jeans-and-diamonds gang dances at Sheika's well into morning, and hungry late-nighters stop in at Vendetta's, which serves until 2:00 A.M.

For more information, contact **Vail Assn., P.O. Box 7, Vail, CO 81658; (970) 476-5601; Vail Tourism & Convention Bureau, 100 E. Meadow Dr., Vail, CO 81657; (970) 476-1000.**

ASPEN AND SNOWMASS

BACKDROP

Aspen is the larger-than-life grande dame of Colorado skiing. It is the name both of an effusively glamorous, celebrity-studded, determinedly picturesque town and of one of America's classic ski areas. Aspen is the resort skiers love to hate—or just plain love. To purists, the town of Aspen is the only place to sleep and party and Aspen Mountain is the only place to ski. In reality, the name Aspen now loosely encompasses four ski areas, two resorts and a sphere of influence all the way to Glenwood Springs.

Aspen's Victorian core, sparkling with expensive restaurants, nightspots, shops and galleries, remains the heart of a now-sprawling, eclectic town with residences ranging from mobile homes on a mine dump that is an EPA superfund site to multimillion-dollar hillside mansions. With 90 percent of its lodging ski-in/ski-out, built-from-scratch Snowmass is a less imposing resort that puts a human face on the supernatural excess of its more prestigious neighbor.

THE LAY OF THE LAND

Colorado Hwy 82 leads from Glenwood Springs southeastward over Independence Pass, except in winter when the pass is closed and the road dead-ends on the eastern fringes of Aspen. Officials are constantly promising (or threatening) to continue widening the entire stretch of this narrow and treacherous two-laner and/or supplement it with a rail link from Glenwood Springs. Until (or unless) that is completed, it remains a scenic but weather-vulnerable and congested 42-mile byway, which has developed city-style morning and evening rush-hour snarls. Before you

26

reach Aspen from Glenwood, you come to a turn-off to Snowmass Village, a slopeside resort built in tandem with the largest of the four ski mountains. Continuing toward town, in short succession, you pass the airport, Buttermilk, the access road to Aspen Highlands and finally the northwestern quadrant of Aspen itself. Laid out in a grid, with the commercial center pushed right up against Aspen Mountain's steep slopes.

GETTING THERE

During the ski season, commuter flights from Denver operate year-round to Sardy Field, the local airport between Aspen and Snowmass, and ski season service non-stops has recently existed from various gateways, more during some winters than others. Amtrak has daily east- and west-bound trains to Glenwood Springs (42 miles). It is also possible to fly to Denver International Airport (220 miles), Grand Junction's Walker Field (130 miles) or Vail/Eagle County Airport (70 miles). Rental cars are available, and **Colorado Mountain Express, (800) 525-6363, (970) 949-4227,** and **Airport Shuttle of Colorado, (800) 222-2112, (970) 949-5032,** provide van service to Aspen and Snowmass. The winter drive from Denver to the Aspen area is west on I-70 and from Grand Junction east on I-70 to Glenwood Springs and then southeast on Route 82. Premier Passport is a lift pass good at the four Aspen Skiing Co. mountains (Aspen Mountain, Aspen Highlands, Snowmass and Buttermilk) and two Vail Associates mountains (Vail and Beaver Creek) for a minimum of 10 out of 12 consecutive days; it includes one transfer between Aspen and Vail (in either direction).

A car is usually more trouble than it's worth in the Aspen area. The Roaring Fork Transit Agency (RFTA, pronounced "raft-ah") runs free public buses around the town of Aspen, to Highlands and Buttermilk, and between Aspen and Snowmass, free for skiing and for a nominal charge in the evening. For information, call the **Rubey Park Transportation Center in Aspen (970) 925-8484** or the **Snowmass Village**

Photo by Paul Hilts, Aspen Skiing Company

Transportation Center, (970) 923-2543. The Galena Street Shuttle also offers free service in downtown Aspen. The Village Shuttle does the same in Snowmass, and low-cost Dial-A-Ride service operates between 12:45 A.M. and 7:00 A.M. when the Village Shuttle is shuttered for the night.

THE SKIING

Aspen Mountain

Profile

Aspen Mountain undeniably reigns as the flagship of the Aspen Skiing Co.'s four ski areas, bestowing bragging rights on all who ski it well. There is no beginner terrain and nothing for shaky novices either. The lightest hue on a trail sign is blue, and black diamonds abound. It takes at least solid intermediate skill to ski anywhere on the mountain—and more than that to navigate the routes to the bottom.

The ski terrain appears, on the trail map, to be arranged in a Y-shaped layout. The Silver Queen gondola forms the stem of the Y and continues all the way to the top, while upper-mountain chairlifts are embraced in the Y's arms. Intertwined runs on the lower slopes of the mountain, west of the gondola base, are effectively an appendix to this main network. A topographical map shows that the Y actually rolls over three steep ridges—from west to east, Ruthie's, Bell and Gentleman's. Trails and glades are found on all three ridgetops, the slopes down their sides and the gullies between them.

Of the two access points into the ski terrain, the main one, just steps from downtown, is at the Little Nell hill, the launching pad for the six-passenger Silver Queen gondola that speeds skiers 3,267 vertical feet in just 13 minutes. An alternate route consisting of three chairlifts (Little Nell, Bell Mountain and Chair 3) now could only be considered if the gondola were not operating or if the lines for it were exceptionally long. The second access is via Chair 1-A and Ruthie's chair, a pair of slow-moving relics on the west side of the ski area that take five minutes longer to climb

Colorado's Big Five

500 feet less than the other three lifts. Skiers staying on the northwestern edge of town, those managing to park there or simply unwilling to stand in the morning gondola line use these chairs.

The summit of Aspen Mountain is where nearly everyone skis because the upper runs are by far the most interesting and have the best snow. With the advent of the gondola, some savvy skiers discovered that it is often faster to ski all the way to the bottom than endure the lift mazes on top. Still, for most people, the usually harrowing, always crowded and often icy mountain egress via Spar Gulch and Little Nell, the lowest, shadowiest slope, is best done just once a day.

The ski area is laid out in the old mode, with short, demanding trails and whatever connectors are needed to link them. Bell must be considered the ski area's center. The deep, steep-walled drainage separating Bell and Ruthie's is Spar Gulch; that between Bell and Gent's is Copper Bowl. The runs funneling into Spar Gulch are the most popular. Lift 3, the mountain's only high-speed quad, parallels the Spar drainage's east side to the summit. This chair offers the most direct access to ample intermediate runs, as well as to Bell's glades and steeps. Still, some diehard lovers of Bell's bumps and trees are willing to endure a long runout and a ride up the old Bell Mountain chair.

Lift 6, a short double on the west side of Spar, leads to Ruthie's ridge. Experts shoot back into Spar via the tight east-facing tree and bump runs collectively called the Mine Dumps, a name you'll find on no trail map but on locals' lips, while middling skiers head for the blue-square terrain on Ruthie's face on the area's western edge. This upper lobe is where you'll find Roch Run, the first cut trail on the mountain, and mogul fields like Zaugg, Short Snort and Last Dollar. The somewhat confusing and little trafficked web of trails at the bottom of Ruthie's gets less sun and is altogether less appealing than the upper mountain. Though these trails sport the same array of blue squares and black diamonds you'll find on high, they seem to be the private territory of local youngsters.

Gentleman's Ridge, the newest terrain, thrusts almost defiantly eastward, challenging

skiers to discover its steep fall-away trails. Gent's upside is its exposure, making it a good bet for morning sun. Its steepest drops build awesome bumps but lose the light early in the afternoon. The downside is the pokey fixed-grip quad that takes as long to climb 1,100 feet as the gondola does to climb the entire mountain. Without the cachet, sentimental attraction or the mountain restaurants of the older domain, Gent's doesn't get much attention—or crowds either.

Aspen Mountain's three eating places are all on the Bell-Ruthie's side. Sundeck near the summit has the best panoramas. Bonnie's, on a promontory overlooking Tourtelotte Park near Lift 6, is viewed as the most fashionable. La Baita, site of the venerable Ruthie's, is the newest mountain restaurant.

Aspen Mountain is the ultimate grown-ups' ski area. You will find few children, no snowboarders and not even many skiers who effect the shredder look. Even though wannabe experts have increased since the gondola was installed, the mountain still attracts a high level of skier—both in skill and in style, proving that it's possible to look great and ski well. These folks continue to ski there because they like to be in the rarefied company of their peers who also look extra good and ski extra well.

Snowmass

Profile

You don't compare Snowmass to Aspen Mountain; you contrast them, for they are 12 miles and light years apart. While Aspen Mountain's runs are wedged into a mountain that almost folds in on itself, Snowmass's long, smooth trails are laid generously across a broad massif. Aspen Mountain's 625 skiable acres on one complex are difficult to envision, while Snowmass's 2,575 acres sprawled across four interconnecting peaks are easily depicted. As a result, Aspen Mountain feels like staccato bursts of snowy steeps, while Snowmass skis as smoothly as a sibilant symphony. Aspen Mountain physically dominates the old town of Aspen, yet the new resort of Snowmass Village nestles comfortably against the ski terrain of its namesake area. While Aspen Mountain tends to intimidate and demand a measure of caution, Snowmass's ultra-wide runs inspire skiers to shift into a higher gear and soar as never before. Their development nearly a quarter of a century ago literally changed the face of American skiing.

Snowmass's terrain is fan-shaped. Assay Hill and the traditional day skiers' parking lot are at the point, Snowmass Village above slightly to the right and above that the Big Burn and Sam's Knob sectors. Campground trails are off to the right, like a ribbon attached to the fan's edge. The Funnel chair angles sharply to the left from Assay Hill, passing the bottoms of the Alpine Springs and Naked Lady lifts and leading to Elk Camp, whose summit is the fan's upper left-hand point. The Two Creek lift rises up from Snowmass's newest base like a second ribbon. From the top of Elk Camp to the top of the Big Burn, the area boundary arcs along a long ridge with skiing on various mountain faces, but essentially you might think of Snowmass as north and northeast-facing.

Other than a handful of beginner lifts at the very bottom, Snowmass's lower chairs are de-

signed to move skiers up and out, and up is where you want to be. Most skiers walk to the edge of Fanny Hill, slide to the Burlingame triple chair and don't come down again until afternoon. From Burlingame, it's a straight shot via the Sam's Knob chair to a peaklet on which perches a congenial restaurant. Down the hill to the right is Campground with more than 2,400 vertical feet of long, never crowded, rarely groomed steeps. Because Snowmass is considered primarily an intermediate haven, expert skiers will often have runs like Bear Claw or Wildcat or Zugspitze all to themselves.

A handful of relatively short intermediate runs on the front side of Sam's Knob lengthen when you continue down to Burlingame, while those on the backside lead to the Big Burn high-speed quad chairlift to 11,835 feet, Snowmass's highest lift-served spot. Up to a quarter of a mile wide and $1\frac{1}{2}$-miles long, "the Burn" inspires novices to ski like intermediates, intermediates to ski like experts and experts to enjoy the rare thrill of supercharged skiing down what feels like limitless terrain. The Burn is so expansive that it never seems crowded, but because growing trees

Mountain Stats—
Buttermilk

Resort elevation 7,945 feet
Top of highest lift 9,900 feet
Bottom of lowest lift 7,870 feet
Total vertical 2,030 feet
Longest run 3 miles
Average annual snowfall 200 inches
Ski season early December to early April
Lifts 1 high-speed quad chairlift, 5 doubles, 1 platterpull
Capacity 7,500 skiers per hour
Terrain 45 trails, 410 acres (35% beginner and novice, 39% intermediate, 26% advanced and expert)
Snowmaking 108 acres (27%)
Mountain dining Cafe West at the bottom of Lift 3, the Cliffhouse at the summit
Snow reports (970) 925-1221 or **(888) ASPENSNOW (277-3676)**

have begun to poke even through deep snow, some of the Burn now skis like an open glade.

Sheer Bliss, which could be the appropriate name for nearly anything at Snowmass, is a long lift serving a web of steepish runs on the south side of the Big Burn. The upper portion of Green Cabin, a particularly beautiful and tranquil blue trail, flows along the bottom of the drainage separating the Big Burn/Sheer Bliss area from High Alpine on the next peak. The most direct access to High Alpine is via two chairs, Wood Run chair from the base and then either Alpine Springs or Naked Lady. A handful of intermediate runs are served by these chairs, but essentially, they are transit lifts to the steep mogul terrain atop High Alpine's rounded summit. A broader valley separates High Alpine from Elk Camp, the southernmost sector. By riding either the Two Creeks quad or the Funnel chair to the Elk Camp quad, skiers reach the scenic top of half-a-dozen long, medium-wide and steadily pitched trails that epitomize Snowmass skiing—in their own way as much as the Big Burn. These are the kind of cruising trails through stunning scenery that most skiers love, but many skiers will also want to take some time to visit the new wildlife and nature center at the top.

Two Creeks debuted in 1995–96, with a new base area, including a lovely log day lodge and a high-speed quad chairlift linking into the Elk Camp sector. More opulent second-home sites are sprinkled around the aspen forest and ancient meadows of the lower mountain, and the languid cruising runs leading down to them enable real estate people to market ski-in/ski-out access for this new development. Well above the real-estate frenzy and building boom, Snowmass offers expert skiers and snowboarders two breathtaking high-mountain bowls. A control gate at the top of the Big Burn plus a hike or free snowcat ride an additional 400 vertical feet to The Cirque. A deceptively easy glide from High Alpine's southernmost run leads to the cliffs of the Hanging Valley Wall. Both bowls have chutes, headwalls and super-steep faces and are as extreme as Snowmass gets, and challenging black-diamond terrain by the standards of any ski area in the Rockies.

Buttermilk

Profile

Snowmass has such impressive statistics and such a glorious reputation that people expect a great deal of it, but Buttermilk, as the smallest mountain operated by the ski company is currently called, always comes as a surprise because people don't anticipate much. Located just west of town, it has better than a 2,000-foot vertical and 410 skiable acres, which would make it a worthy Eastern destination area. In Aspen, it's the beguiling bunny hill. After a dump, powder-loving locals descend on the snow-holding trees of the Tiehack sector, but normally, visitors pass by as they shuttle between Aspen and Snowmass, without a clue as to how good the skiing can be.

The terrain wraps around three sides of Buttermilk and adjacent Tiehack. The three points of access are the main Buttermilk base, which is visible from Route 82; Tiehack, around the corner to the left and Buttermilk West, around the right side. Tiehack and West have small day skiers' lots that are useful and chairlifts that are relics. Their lack of speed cuts down on the number of runs that can be wedged into a day, which is why the addition of a high-speed quad on Buttermilk's frontside replacing another relic was so welcome. One thing you don't want at Buttermilk is frustration from too few runs, because the area is such unexpected fun. Skiers and snowboarders have their choice of Tiehack's trees and steeps, lower Buttermilk's exemplary terrain for beginners and small fry and Buttermilk West's long, gentle trails laced through the woods.

In addition to these widely publicized and well-known features, it holds a wild card—Buttermilk's secret bowl. When you first board the Summit Express or the Savio chair, which is the upper one of the frontside lifts, you'll see nothing extraordinary until the chair passes over a knoll and dips slightly, unfolding the view of a broad bowl below. The trail map is not very elucidating, for what looks like a bowl is drawn as a wide spot on the trail, where Friedl's, Savio and Buckskin spill into No Problem. Still, for many skiers, if it looks like a bowl and skis like a bowl, it is a bowl—and it may just rank as one of the few ski surprises in the Aspen area.

Aspen Highlands

Profile

Located on Maroon Creek Road, which climbs up a deep valley between Aspen Mountain and Buttermilk's Tiehack side, Aspen Highlands, once an independently owned ski area and the rebel on the Aspen firmament, is now the new star in the Aspen Skiing Co. galaxy. Highlands's unprepossessing base lodge and handful of beginner lifts are at the narrow frontside of a steep-flanked mountain. The ski area boasts dozens of runs on a huge vertical.

Once the Aspen Skiing Co. took Highlands over, it replaced four of the longest, slowest, most tedious lifts in Colorado with two high-speed quads that more than cut the base-to-summit ride time in half, 20 minutes on two chairs instead of nearly 45 on four lifts. The Exhibition chair climbs from the base to the Merry-Go-Round area and the Loge Peak chairlift rises to

Mountain Stats—
Aspen Highlands

Resort elevation 7,945 feet
Top of highest lift 11,675 feet
Bottom of lowest lift 8,040 feet
Total vertical 3,635 feet
Longest run $3^1/_2$ miles
Average annual snowfall 300 inches
Ski season Thanksgiving to mid-April
Lifts 2 high-speed quad chairlifts, 5 doubles, 1 platterpulls
Capacity 8,645 skiers per hour
Terrain 81 trails, 619 acres (20% beginner and novice, 33% intermediate, 47% advanced and expert)
Snowmaking 115 acres
Mountain dining Merry-Go-Round at the top of Exhibition
Snow reports (970) 925-1221 or **(888) ASPENSNOW (277-3676)**

the summit, providing extraordinary views and accessing Highlands's most thrilling steeps. On one side of the razorback ridge that is Loge's, you'll find the fabulous tree skiing of Olympic Glades; on the other, seven double-black freefalls etched into an area nicknamed Steeplechase. Many skiers and snowboarders prefer to stay in this high-mountain paradise, so the old Cloud Nine and Olympic chairs remain as backups to the Exhibition quad. All the green-circle slopes and trails are below Merry-Go-Round.

Highlands is a complex ski area and with the installation of the high-speed quads, you can now get the full flavor of the terrain and its stunning variety. Its trail map resembles a virtual warren of trails. You can follow what crowd there is, follow an Ambassador on a free mountain tour or explore on your own and let your ski tips or the nose of your board lead the way, but Highlands has a way of dishing up surprises. You might come up a passle of tree-lined sluices dropping off an easy catwalk and not realize that they're even skiable. You can ski long, wide boulevards groomed as carefully as your eccentric aunt's poodle. You can find an unexpected bump run or seek out the chance to show off on Ricardo's, right above the Merry-Go-Round Restaurant. You can revel in the exhilaration of bombing down the Golden Horn, a near-secret off-side run that is steep and smooth and oodles of fun. And if you're an Aspen veteran who never previously bothered with the Highlands, you can wonder how you could possibly have ignored so much great terrain.

SNOWBOARDING

Aspen Mountain is Colorado's only remaining skis-only ski area, except for selected post-season weekends in high snow years when the other three areas have closed and snowboarders are also permitted. Elsewhere, snowboard facilities abound. There's a huge snowboard park on Buttermilk's Spruce Run and another between Slider and Funnel at Snowmass. Good snowboarders love the Tiehack trees, Highlands radical steeps and the vast Cirque atop Snowmass as well as the long peek-a-boo trails of Campground below. And those who either want to learn snowboarding or improve can sign up with the Delaney Adult Snowboard Camps, which developed at Buttermilk. Also at Buttermilk is the annual mid-December Boarding Festival, with free lessons for all levels of rider, on-snow events and other activities.

SNOWCAT SKIING

Guided tours of up to 10 skiers have exclusive access to 1,500 powdery acres off the backside of Aspen Mountain in deluxe heated snowcats. Groups average 9,000 vertical feet a day. The ski school runs this program for intermediate and advanced skiers For reservations, call **(970) 925-1220, Ext. 3549.** Registration is at the Ski School Desk in the gondola base building.

Free Snowmass Cirque Tours are available, conditions permitting, for experts every 15 minutes from the Up 4 Pizza Restaurant on the Big Burn. Sign-up begins first thing in the morning and is first-come, first-served.

SKI SCHOOL PROGRAMS

In 1995–96, the concept of adult ski instruction underwent a wholesale revolution at Aspen and Snowmass. In place of traditional class lessons with their sometimes unwieldy sizes, the newly renamed Ski Schools of Aspen replaced semi-private-style half- and full-day programs for intermediate and advanced skiers. Groups maxed out at three skiers, so that three students and one ski pro, renamed from the traditional "ski instructor" position to a more prestigious one drawn from the golf and tennis worlds, could ride a high-speed quad together. Information and reservations, **(800) 525-6200, (970) 923-1227.**

Introductory Programs

Learn-to-Ski and Learn-to-Board: Group lessons for Levels 1 to 4. Introductory lessons for skiers and snowboarders at all mountains but Aspen Mountain.

First Time on Skis or Snowboard: Economical three-day program, including lift ticket, rental equipment and guarantee that beginners will be able to ski or snowboard from the top of Buttermilk Mountain or the Two Creeks quad or they'll get an extra day's lesson free.

Delaney Snowboard Camp: Two-day clinics using the champion Delaney brothers' innovative teaching method, available for adult beginners, **(970) 920-7528.**

John Clendednin's Ski Doctors: Combination of skiing or snowboarding introduction indoors on a simulator with on-slope experience. Five-hour lesson starts at the Aspen Club and continues on one of the four mountains.

Advanced and Specialty Programs

Free Advice from the Pros: Ski for the camera and get free tips from the pros, daily at Snowmass and daily except Saturday and Buttermilk.

Mountain Masters: Intensive four-day workshop, Monday through Thursday, for intermediate and advanced skiers. Five hours a day for Levels 5 to 10 at Aspen Mountain and Snowmass. Part of the Ski Schools of Aspen Breakthrough series. Reservations strongly suggested.

Women's Ski Seminars: Four-day workshop, Monday through Thursday, taught by women, for women, with confidence-building as well as ski instruction. Levels 3 to 10 at Buttermilk and Snowmass. Part of the Ski Schools of Aspen Breakthrough series. Developed in 1981–82, one of the longest-running such programs. Reservations strongly suggested.

SCX Semi-Private: Specialty classes for Levels 5 to 10, utilizing the Elan SCX super sidecut ski.

Delaney Snowboard Camp: Continuation of Delaney approach for intermediate and advanced adult snowboarders; two-day weekend clinics. Available at Buttermilk and Aspen Highlands. One session for women only. For information and reservations, **(970) 920-7528.**

Kim Reichhelm's Women's Ski Adventures: Four-day program of small groups and intensive workshops. Package includes four nights' lodging, breakfast and dinner, lift tickets, video taping and evening activities. Offered a couple of times during the season. For information and reservations, **(800) 992-7700.**

Break Out of the Intermediate Rut: Five-day total saturation clinic developed by Lito Tejada-Flores. Package includes lessons and lift tickets, video analysis, daily indoor session and wrap-up party. Reservations and information, **(800) 626-6200.** Lodging package also available with the **Inn at Aspen, (800) 952-1515.**

Quick Carve: New system of Alpine snowboarding, an innovative hybrid of skiing and snowboarding developed by coach Boone Lennon.

The Magic of Skiing: Five-day program based on the mind-body relationship and conflict resolution applied to skiing. Offered several times a season for all levels. Part of the Ski Schools of Aspen Breakthrough series. For information, call **Aiki Works, (970) 925-7099.**

Fit Over Fifty: Al Myers, Aspen native, 79 years old in 1995–96 and author of *Success Over Sixty,* developed five-day inspirational program including skiing, fitness and lifestyle planning. Available several times during the season at Buttermilk Mountain. Part of the Ski Schools of Aspen Breakthrough series.

Photo by John Bing/Buttermilk Mountain

Aspen Academy: Four-day skiing and snowboarding led by PSIA Demo Team members. Includes teaching skills and potential recruitment by Ski Schools of Aspen.

Special Programs

Ski Ambassadors: Volunteers on hand all four mountains to give complimentary meeting-the-mountain tours and to staff information kiosks throughout the day. Tours are available to intermediate skiers and better and start at Guest Services daily at 10:00 A.M. and 1:30 P.M. Locations are the top of Lift 7 at Aspen Mountain, top of the Exhibition lift at Highlands, top of the Summit Express at Buttermilk and both the top of the Coney Glade lift and the bottom of the Elk Camp lift at Snowmass.

Fresh Track Nature Tours: Offered once (Aspen Highlands), twice (Aspen Mountain and Buttermilk) or three times a week (Snowmass), led by naturalists from the Aspen Center for Environmental Studies for intermediates and better, **33** aged 8 and older. Tours are free, but you need a lift ticket.

First Run on Ajax: Sign up at the Aspen Mountain ticket office for a drawing Sunday, Tuesday and Thursday for first tracks for three winners and one guest each for 8:15 A.M. "first tracks" down the empty Ajax the following morning, escorted by a ski pro.

Performance Centers: Unique on-mountain centers devised by skiing's biomechanics guru Harald Harb, who believes that better skiing be-

Snowboarding is a big hit at Buttermilk Mountain, Aspen Highlands and Snowmass Ski Area, where wide, evenly groomed slopes provide plenty of fun for both beginning and advanced riders.

gins with proper body alignment. Centers build custom-designed footbeds, adjust boot cuffs and adjust foot and ankle balance. Located at the tops of Aspen Mountain and Buttermilk and under the Coney Glade lift at Snowmass.

Freestyle Friday: Weekly show put on by about 20 top-bump skiers and big-air competitors weekly from January through mid-April. Great view from the Merry-Go-Round Deck. A 25-year tradition at Highlands.

Multi-Day Lift Ticket Option: Unused regular multiday lift ticket redeemable for cross-country ski rental and/or lesson, snowshoe rental and/or tour, indoor tennis court time or athletic club privileges, all at the Snowmass Lodge and Club.

For Families

Nonskiing Children

Aspen and Snowmass are the only major resorts in Colorado that have no true baby nurseries. The Aspen Skiing Co.'s children's centers do not take infants, and at this writing, neither does any other licensed day care in the Aspen-Snowmass area. Families with children 18 months and younger can call **Super Sitters, (970) 923-6080,** to arrange for child care. The picture brightens for families with toddlers and preschoolers when the Snow Cubs Play School kicks in. This fine facility in the Timbermill Building at Snowmass Village Mall has a full-day play program for ages 18 months to 4 years with indoor and outdoor activities and lunch, including naps for the younger group and skiing for the older group. Children use a special contoured beginner area on Fanny Hill and a Magic Carpet conveyor lift. Reservations, **(970) 923-0563.**

Skiing Children

Preschool ski programs are offered at all mountains except Aspen Mountain for half-day or full-day, including hot lunch and snack. Reservations required for all preschool programs, Big Burn Bears (ages 4 to kindergarten) at **Snowmass, (970) 923-0570;** Powder Pandas (ages 3 to 6) at **Buttermilk, (970) 925-0563** and Snow Puppies (ages $3^1/_2$ to 6) at **Highlands, (970) 544-3025.**

Kids' Lessons: At Snowmass and Buttermilk for children ages 7 to 12. Half-day for first-time skiers; full-day for others. Five-day package with videotaping, picnics and other activities. Children need to bring money for lunch, which is supervised.

Noteworthy

The Aspen Skiing Co. issues a children's trail map, highlighting areas of interest and child-oriented routes such as the Green Dino Outdoor Adventure at Highlands (the Green Dino is an "environmental dinosaur"), No Problem Territory at Buttermilk and the abundance of Surprises in Snowmass. In addition to slow-skiing zones on all four mountains, the Panda House at Buttermilk is a separate facility for preschoolers, with its own gentle ski hill and surface lift. Seven- to 12-year-olds love Fort Frog, a children's learning and video center. Aspen also offers a couple of special services for families. The Max the Moose Express, escorted by instructors from the Panda Ski School, transports children from Aspen hotels and lodges to Buttermilk in the morning and back to the Silver Queen gondola in the afternoon. The Greeno Deeno Express is a four-mountain shuttle for children and their parents or instructors. Free Kids' Fairs are held at the Bumps Base Lodge at Buttermilk every Wednesday afternoon staring Christmas Week. Children can pick up a Kid's Passport to Fun at any ski school desk or ticket office and register for the Birthday Club, which results in a birthday card, messages and greetings from new friends at Snowmass and Aspen. Nighthawks is an evening program for ages 3 to 12, staffed by ski school personnel, with dinner and activities. It's available by the hour; reduced rates for additional children in the same family.

The local franchise of **Baby's Away** rents cribs, high chairs, strollers, packs, toys, humidifiers and other child and baby needs. They deliver to condos all over the Aspen-Snowmass area and will have the equipment set up when you arrive. For information and reservations, call **(800) 948-9030, (970) 920-1699.**

Teens

The ski school offers a ski week of classes for skiers and snowboarders ages 13 to 19 roving around all three mountains with up to five hours of high-energy action, daily, lunch, plus fun races, barbecue and supervised social events. In the evening, the **Aspen Youth Center** draws local and visiting youngsters from 5th to 12th grade. Free admission includes dances, basketball and movie nights, games and videos. An on-site "diner" serves inexpensive food.

FOR RACERS

Spider Sabich Race Arena: Excellent recreational racing facility off the Burlingame lift at Snowmass. Location of area's recreational race clinics and special events.

NASTAR: Courses at Cabin Trail at Snowmass Ski Area, Savio on Buttermilk, Exhibition at Aspen Highlands and Silver Dip Swing on Aspen Mountain. Available daily somewhere at Aspen. Race course hours vary.

Cooper/Tache Race Program: Directed by the husband-and-wife team of 1984 Olympic silver medalist Christin Cooper and pro racer Mark Tache. Weekday course that may be booked by the day, week or season. Recommended for intermediates and above looking to hone their racing skills. Held at Tiehack Racing Center and at the base of the Little Nell chair on Aspen Mountain.

Speed Course: Only lift-serviced course for speed skiing and snowboarding in the United States. Skiers and riders reach speeds of 35 to 65 miles per hour in timing trap. Three-hour sessions, once a week from 9:30 A.M. to 12:30 P.M. Certificate given at end of run. Located on Slot, off Sam's Knob.

Rolling Stone Ski Challenge: Fun race and après-ski party every Tuesday at Highlands. Registrants can win free gear and grand prize at the end of the season. Entry fee and goodie bag to all participants, **(970) 544-3018.**

HANDICAPPED SKIING

Challenge Aspen provides discounted lift tickets, complimentary lift ticket for volunteer ski buddy, instruction (two-hour to six-hour lessons by appointment) and adaptive equipment for individuals with various disabilities. For information and reservations, call **Challenge Aspen, (970) 923-0578.** For blind and visually impaired skiers, **BOLD** operates on a similar formula structure; call **(970) 923-3811.**

NORDIC SKIING

With nearly 80 kilometers of free groomed trails, cross-country skiing in the Aspen-Snowmass area is so extensive that it is sometimes referred to as "the fifth mountain." The **Aspen/Snowmass Nordic Council** maintains, but does not patrol or in any other way service, these touring trails, said to be the largest system of free maintained tracks in North America, **(970) 925-1940.** Easy golf-course skiing, rentals and instruction are offered on 4 kilometers at the Aspen Cross-Country Center off Route 82, **(970) 925-2145,** between Aspen and Buttermilk and 30 kilometers at the **Snowmass Club Cross-Country Center, (970) 923-3148.** Any day of a multiday ticket may be redeemed for ski or snowshoe rental and/or lesson at the Snowmass Club Cross-Country Center.

Aspen's best-known Nordic facility is at Ashcroft, a mining ghost town 12 miles up Castle Creek, where the Ashcroft Ski Touring Unlimited maintains 30 kilometers of excellent groomed trails and operates gourmet lunch and dinner tours. The **Pine Creek Cookhouse,** 2 kilometers from the Ashcroft trailhead, is known for its excellent ski-to lunches and dinners. For information, call **(970) 925-1971.** Ashcroft is the gateway to the spectacular Maroon Bells–Snowmass Wilderness and Alfred A. Braun Hut System. Aspen is also the headquarters and one end of the Tenth Mountain Trail Assn., linking it with Vail to the northeast. This 230-mile route system includes 13 huts and lodges en route for overnights and is America's premier high-Alpine hut system. The six-hut Alfred A. Braun Hut System between Aspen and Crested Butte to the south is similar but smaller. **Tenth Mountain Trail Assn.** handles reservations for both; **(970) 925-5775.** Strong backcountry skiers with excellent winter wilderness skills can handle these routes themselves, but for anyone else, a guide is strongly recommended for backcountry adventures.

WHERE TO STAY

Aspen

Aspen Central Reservations, (800) 262-7736, (970) 925-9000.

Luxury Accommodations

Hotel Jerome

Century-old, exquisitely restored landmark. Not only a local but also a national treasure, combining an authentic Victorian atmosphere with modern luxury. Ninety-three spacious rooms (including 50 suites) furnished with fine antiques and faithful reproductions. All rooms with marble bathrooms, remote-control TVs, refrigerators and mini-bars; suites with large Jacuzzi tubs and separate stall showers. Twice-daily housekeeping, room service, valet parking, concierge, valet/laundry service, courtesy transfers to airport, ski lifts and other local destinations. Three restaurants, bar, heated swimming pool, sundeck, Jacuzzi, fitness room. Business services, doorperson, bell staff, concierge, room service, 24-hour front desk. **330 E. Main St., Aspen, CO 81611; (800) 331-7213, (970) 920-1000.**

Hotel Lenado

Elegant boutique hotel with distinctive lobby and 19 lovely rooms. Daily housekeeping. Rooftop hot tub, library, lounge. **200 S. Aspen St., Aspen, CO 81611; (800) 321-3457, (970) 925-6246.**

The Little Nell

Elegant and highly honored hotel. Base of the Silver Queen gondola. Contemporary city sophistication combined with resort casualness. Ninety-two rooms (including eight suites and five executive suits) with sybaritic marble bathroom with deep tub set in a mirrored alcove, separate stall shower and two vanities; mini-bar and refrigerator; remote-control color TV with VCR, two phones and a gas-log fireplace. Hotel and restaurant honored with AAA Five Diamonds and Mobil Five Stars; in 1996 only one of 14 North American properties with the highest honors in both rankings. Also member of prestigious Relais & Chateaux group. Twice-daily housekeeping, concierge, 24-hour front desk, room service, bell staff, ski valet, overnight ski tuning, valet/laundry

services, valet parking, massage, business services, guest privileges at the Snowmass Club & Lodge's fitness and tennis center. Restaurant, lounge, outdoor pool, hot tub, sauna, fitness center, courtesy airport transfers, shops. **675 E. Durant Ave., Aspen, CO 81611; (800) 525-6200, (970) 920-4600.**

Ritz-Carlton Aspen

Elegant, opulent "mountain-style" hotel one block from the Silver Queen gondola. Large and lavish, with 257 rooms (including 33 suites) with marble bathrooms and three phones. Ritz Carlton Club level keyed off and offering even higher level of service than Ritz Carlton "regular." Twice-daily housekeeping, 24-hour front desk, concierge, room service, bell staff, valet parking, business services, sports concierge, dry cleaning and laundry, massage. Four restaurants, two lounges, outdoor pool, two hot tubs, fitness center, steamroom, saunas, beauty salon, shops. **315 Dean St., Aspen, CO 81611; (970) 241-3300, (800) 241-3333** for Ritz-Carlton reservations.

Sardy House

Historic Victorian mansion, now an elegant 14-room, six-suite inn. Rooms feature feather comforters, whirlpool tubs, robes. Known equally for lace-curtain charm and fine food. Four Stars from Mobil. Twice-daily housekeeping, concierge, valet, full breakfast. Restaurant, pool, hot tub, sauna, restaurant. **128 E. Main St., Aspen, CO 81611; (800) 321-3457 (970) 920-2525.**

Mid-Priced Accommodations

Aspen Club Lodge

Fine modern property with scale and facilities far more than a normal "lodge." Ninety guest rooms and suites. Southwestern style. Units offer TV with VCR, CD players. Non-smoking rooms available. Guest privileges at the Aspen Club fitness center. The nearby Aspen Club Condominiums under the same management. Upscale and high end of mid-price range. Restaurant, lounge, pool, hot tub, sauna. Daily housekeeping, room service, concierge, ski concierge, courtesy airport transfers, complimentary daily newspaper, 24-hour front desk, full breakfast buffet. **709 E. Durant St., Aspen, CO 81611; (800) 882-2582, (970) 925-6760.**

Aspen Meadows

Design dream. Winterized landmark complex designed by Bauhaus architect Herbert Bayer for the Aspen Institute. Secluded and spacious West End location. Ninety-eight pristinely furnished rooms (including 58 suites). Features include living/study area, wet bar, mini-refrigerator, coffee maker and TV with VCR. Restaurant, library lounge, fitness center, heated pool, Jacuzzi. Daily housekeeping, bell staff, 24-hour front desk, complimentary shuttle service, massage and facials. **845 Meadows Rd., Aspen, CO 81611; (800) 452-4240, (970) 925-4240.**

Fireside Lodge

Congenial ski-lodge atmosphere with Aspen views and recently redecorated rooms and public spaces. Continental breakfast, daily housekeeping. Fireplace lounge, pool, hot tub, breakfast loft. **130 W. Cooper Ave., Aspen, CO 81611; (970) 925-6000.**

Independence Square Hotel

Centrally located on the Mall, downtown and one block from the mountain. Twenty-eight mini-suites with kitchenettes decorated in country French style. Daily housekeeping, continental breakfast buffet, après-ski refreshments, airport shuttle. Rooftop hot tub, sundeck, library, ski lockers. **404 S. Galena St., Aspen, CO 81611; (800) 633-0336, (970) 920-2010.**

Hotel Aspen

Centrally located and moderately priced. Room features include refrigerator, wet bar and in-room coffee maker. Jacuzzi tub and balcony rooms also available. Heated outdoor pool, Jacuzzi. Daily housekeeping, breakfast, after-ski refreshments. **110 W. Main St., Aspen, CO 81611; (800) 527-7369, (970) 925-3441.**

Inn at Aspen

Sprawling 114-unit hotel with studios, including five one-bedroom apartments. Base of Buttermilk. Fitness center, indoor/outdoor pool, hot tub, sauna, restaurant, lounge, video game room. Daily housekeeping, room service, courtesy airport and town van service, massage and personal trainer available. **38750 Hwy 82, Aspen, CO 81611, (800) 952-1515, (970) 925-1500.**

Photo by Carl Yarbrough/Aspen Skiing Company

Aspen Mountain, with tight gladed trails and daring bump runs, is an expert skier's dream come true. It has been luring skiers since 1946–47.

Molly Gibson Lodge

Intimate yet elegant little inn. Fifty rooms and suites, some with large Jacuzzi tubs, wood-burning fireplaces and kitchens, others simpler and less expensive. Three blocks from town. Daily housekeeping, courtesy airport van, continental breakfast, après-ski bar. Two pools, two hot tubs, lounge. **101 W. Main St., Aspen, CO 81611; (800) 356-6559, (970) 925-3434.**

Economy Accommodations

Heatherbed Mountain Lodge

Pleasant informal inn at Highlands base. Small economy rooms and commodious studios with kitchenettes, all recently redone. Lobby fireplace and deck overlooking Maroon Creek. Four-poster beds, quilts, down comforters. Housekeeping, full breakfast, after-ski chili. Pool, hot tub, sauna. **Maroon Creek Rd., Aspen, CO 81612; (800) 356-6782, (970) 925-7077.**

Colorado's Big Five

Little Red Ski Haus

The last of Aspen's shared-bath bargain lodges (some rooms with private facilities). Champagne location on a near-beer budget. Popular with young skiers. Daily housekeeping. **118 E. Cooper Ave., Aspen, CO 81611; (970) 925-3333.**

St. Moritz Lodge

European-style lodge, five blocks from downtown. Standard rooms, dorms and one- to four-bedroom apartment units. Affordable ski lodge in residential neighborhood. Friendly and casual. Pool, whirlpool, sauna. **334 W. Hyman Ave., Aspen, CO 81611; (800) 817-2069, (970) 925-3220.**

Ullr Lodge

Casual lodge in Aspen's West End has 23 units. Non-smoking hotel rooms and one- and two-bedroom kitchen units. Family-owned and traditional. Quiet hours after 10:00 P.M. AAA and Mobil recommendations. Daily housekeeping, après-ski hour, full breakfast for room guests, afternoon tea. Indoor/outdoor pool, hot tubs, guest laundry. **520 W. Main St., Aspen, CO 81611; (970) 925-7696.**

Condominiums and Homes

Aspen Alps

Individually decorated luxury two-, three- and four-bedroom units, each with fireplace and balcony, adjacent to gondola. Good location and good hotel-type service. Daily housekeeping, courtesy airport transfers. Pool, hot tub, sauna. **700 E. Ute Ave., Aspen, CO 81611; (800) 228-7820, (970) 925-7822.**

Aspen Square

Large complex with 102 luxury studio to two-bedroom units. Fireplace units, each with full kitchen and outside deck Across from gondola. Moderate prices for top location and hotel-type services and free underground parking (the latter not to be taken for granted in the center of Aspen). Daily housekeeping. Outdoor heated pool, outdoor hot tub, saunas, new fitness center. **617 E. Cooper Ave., Aspen, CO 81611; (800) 862-7736, (970) 925-1000.**

Chalet Lisl

Modest, and modestly priced, studio and one-bedroom units. Hot tub, game room, ski tuning bench, game room, library. **100 E. Hyman Ave., Aspen, CO 81611; (970) 925-3520.**

The Gant

Large resort-style property with 120 luxurious one- to four-bedroom condos. Each with fireplace and balcony. Located at the base of Aspen Mountain and three blocks from town. Two heated pools, three hot tubs, two saunas. Guest privileges at nearby health clubs at nominal fee. Daily housekeeping (including dishwashing), complimentary morning newspaper, full-service front desk, concierge, complimentary airport and town van service, grocery delivery, ski valet. **610 West End St., Aspen, CO 81611; (800) 345-1471.**

Lift One Condominiums

Moderately priced one- to three-bedroom condos. Twenty-seven units. Base of Aspen Mountain. Daily housekeeping. Heated pool, hot tub, saunas, living room with fireplace, guest laundry. **131 E. Durant St., Aspen, CO 81611; (800) 543-8001, (970) 925-1670.**

The Prospector

Luxurious, centrally located timeshares with rentals available. One-bedroom units have wet bar, private balcony, hot tub and sauna. Daily housekeeping, courtesy airport transfers, Continental breakfast. **301 E. Hyman Ave., Aspen, CO 81611; (800) 522-4525, (970) 920-2030.**

Management companies running many condo units and private homes include
Aspen Central Properties, (970) 925-7301
Aspen Classic Properties, (970) 925-5759
Aspen Club Property Management, (800) 882-2582, (970) 920-2000
Aspen Resort Accommodations, (970) 925-4772
Coates, Reid & Waldron, (970) 925-1400, (800) 22-ASPEN
Condominium Rental Management, (800) 321-7025, (970) 925-2260
Rocky Mountain Residential Sales and Management, (970) 925-2526

Snowmass

Snowmass Central Reservations, (800) 598-2005, (970) 923-2000; fax (970) 923-5466.

Luxury Accommodations

The Silvertree

Slopeside hotel with 262 rooms and suites (most with private patio or balcony) and expansive public spaces, all in a pleasing, contemporary style. In-room refrigerators, coffee makers, hair dryers and Nintendo available on TV. Convenient to the slopes, the Snowmass Mall and the Snowmass Conference Center. Daily housekeeping, 24-hour front desk, bell staff, room service, concierge, massage available. Restaurants, piano bar, two heated pools, hot tubs, fitness center, steamroom, sauna, ski and rental shop. **P.O. Box 5009, Snowmass Village, CO 81615; (800) 525-9402, (970) 923-3520.**

Snowmass Lodge & Club

Newly redone 76-room country club-style resort hotel, plus 60 one- to three-bedroom villa units on 567 acres. Boasts lavish spa, year-round racquet sports courts and fine restaurant. Site of Snowmass's cross-country center. Complete hotel services, daily housekeeping, 24-hour front desk, bell staff, slopeside ski concierge at the Timbermill for lodge guests (includes overnight ski storage), courtesy shuttle to Aspen. Health and fitness spa, pools, hot tubs, steamrooms, indoor tennis, squash, racquetball, ski rentals, Nordic center, children's nursery, restaurant, lounge. **P.O. Drawer G-2, Snowmass Village, CO 81615; (800) 525-0710, (970) 923-5600.**

Mid-Priced Accommodations

Wildwood Lodge

Hospitable mid-size hotel with convenient location and good value. Newly remodeled guest rooms and suites with mini-refrigerators and coffee makers. Daily housekeeping, 24-hour front desk, courtesy airport transfers, coffee, complimentary continental breakfast. Outdoor heated pool, hot tub, sauna, guest laundry, restaurant, lounge. **P.O. Box 5037, Snowmass Village, CO 81615; (800) 525-9402, (970) 923-3520.**

Mountain Chalet

Largely remodeled and well-maintained, this Snowmass standard retains its popularity. Daily housekeeping, courtesy airport transfers, complimentary breakfast. Fitness center, pool, hot tub, sauna, restaurant, lounge. **P.O. Box 5066,** Snowmass Village, CO 81615; (970) 923-3900.

Pokolodi Lodge

Small, well-situated lodge provides in-room refrigerators and coffee makers. Daily housekeeping, 24-hour front desk, courtesy airport transfers, pool. **P.O. Box 5640, Snowmass Village, CO 81615; (800) 666-4556, (970) 923-4310.**

Stonebridge Inn

Well-located contemporary lodge with 95 recently refurnished rooms, featuring in-room refrigerators and coffee. Daily housekeeping, 24-hour front desk, courtesy airport transfers, complimentary continental breakfast. Restaurant, lounge, Outdoor heated pool, hot tub, sauna, ski storage. **P.O. Box 5008, Snowmass Village, CO 81615; (800) 922-7242, (970) 923-2420.**

Condominiums and Homes

Chamonix

Upscale two- and three-bedroom ski-in/ski-out condos, each with good kitchen, whirlpool bathtub, steam shower and washer and dryer. Daily housekeeping, 24-hour front desk, grocery shopping and delivery service, courtesy airport transfers and village transport. Pool, hot tub, sauna, ski rentals. **P.O. Box 6077, Snowmass Village, CO 81615; (800) 365-0410, (970) 923-3232.**

The Crestwood

Slopeside condo hotel with 120 individually decorated studio to three-bedroom apartments. Each with fireplace, full kitchen and bathroom for each bedroom, balcony with gas barbecue and washer/dryer. Daily housekeeping, hotel-type front desk, courtesy airport transfers, grocery and liquor shopping. Pool, two whirlpools, sauna, exercise room. **P.O. Box 5460, 400 Wood Rd., Snowmass Village, CO 81615; (800) 356-5949, (970) 923-2450.**

The Laurelwood

Modestly priced studio units. Two levels up from Snowmass Mall; close to slopes and Snowmass Mall. All with kitchens, balconies and fireplaces; some with upgraded furnishings. Front desk, housekeeping daily except Sunday. Pool, hot tub. **P.O. Box 5600, Snowmass Village, CO 81615; (800) 356-7893, (970) 923-3110.**

Management companies running many condo units and private homes include
Alpine Property Management, (800) 543-0839, (970) 923-5860
Aspen Snowmass Care, (970) 923-4488
Coates, Reid & Waldron, (800) 222-7989, (970) 923-4750
Destination Resorts, (970) 923-2420
Snowmass Lodging Co., (800) 365-0410, (970) 923-3232
Snowmass Home Rentals (Paraelee and Company), (800) 999-0816, (970) 923-3636
Village Property Management, (800) 525-9402, (970) 923-4350.

DINING OUT

Aspen

Ajax Tavern
California wine country trendy restaurant at base of gondola. Owners of heralded Tra Vigne and Mustards Grill in Napa transplanted concept and style to the Rockies. Lunch, after-ski and dinner. Stylish look. Strong Mediterranean influences on taste. Dinner reservations recommended. **865 E. Durant Ave., Aspen; (970) 920-9333.**

Bentley's
Soups, salads, seafood, steaks, ribs and an outstanding selection of beers in this Victorian-style eating and entertainment establishment. Full bar, featuring beers from around the world. Lunch and dinner. **Wheeler Opera House, 328 E. Hyman Ave., Aspen; (970) 920-2240.**

Boogie's Diner
The '50s and '60s return to Aspen at this funky eatery. Rock and roll. Daily Blue Plate Special, a Catch of the Day, meat loaf, turkey, fountain treats and other family-friendly fare. **534 E. Cooper Ave., Aspen; (970) 925-6610.**

Cache Chache
Attractive restaurant. Could be called "Cachet Cachet," for it is a long-standing favorite with Aspen's chic set. Cuisine described as "innovative southern French," a clever melding of Provençale and northern Italian. Seafood Riso with Saffron Prawns, Calamari and Mussels or Tian of Lamb Tataloille, Candied Garlic, Spinach and Potato Crowns. Great pastries, high prices but fashionable crowd and a scene that remains one of Aspen's best. Surprisingly, children's menu too. Reservations recommended. **Mill Street Plaza, 205 S. Mill St., Aspen; (970) 925-3835.**

The Cantina
Merry Mexican restaurant known for well-priced, well-portioned Tex-Mex and Southwestern dishes and generous margaritas at lunch and dinner. Tacos, burritos and enchiladas predictable menu items, generally served in poultry, meat and veggie versions. Daily specials. Small children's selection. **411 E. Main, Aspen; (970) 925-3663.**

Century Room
Fine dining in the refined atmosphere of the Hotel Jerome's top dining room. Comfortable and elegant setting for excellent and romantic dinners. Extensive menu with traditional and contemporary meats, poultry, game, seafood and meatless offerings. Excellent desserts. Reservations recommended. **Hotel Jerome, 330 E. Main St., Aspen; (970) 920-1000.**

Chanin's Grill
Succulent steaks and superb fresh seafood, with lobster featured. Clubby, slightly western atmosphere, naturally an upscale version, but prices on the moderate side. Early bird prix fixe special attracts budget-watchers. Excellent salads and even a vegetable platter with grilled tofu for health-watchers. Reservations recommended. **205 S. Mill St., Aspen; (970) 920-2334.**

The Crystal Palace
Opulent decor, celebrity diners and a good cabaret spoofing the famous and infamous are the drawing cards in this popular theater/restaurant. Prime rib a perennial favorite, in adult or child's portion. Aspen at its smartest—in every sense of the word. One and occasionally two seatings nightly. Reservations required. **300 E. Hyman Ave., Aspen; (970) 925-1455.**

Eastern Winds
Large selection of dishes from several Chinese provinces including Szechuan, Hunan and Mongolian, plus some with Polynesian touches—

especially in the exotic drink area. Moderate prices. Lunch specials, all-you-can-eat menu and takeout available, and free delivery in Aspen. **520 E. Cooper Ave., Aspen; (970) 925-5160.**

The Grill
Ribs, chicken, fish, steak and anything else the chef can think of to throw on the grill served in this casual spot. **307 S. Mill, Aspen; (970) 920-3700.**

Guido's
A corner of the Alps transported to the Rockies. Large menu suffused with rich European specialties and a Continental atmosphere keep Aspenites returning to this longtime favorite. Great desserts. Reservations recommended. **403 S. Galena, Aspen; (970) 925-7222.**

Giuseppi Wong
There's the Italian menu and the Chinese menu— and the humorously self-style "confusion" menu in the middle. Try Thai Chicken Pizza, Pine Cone Fish, Marco Polo Risotto or Palermo Pad Thai for new taste sensations. Interesting and delicious. Reservations recommended. **517 E. Hopkins Ave., Aspen; (970) 544-0222.**

Jacob's Corner
High on Victorian ambiance and liveliness. Informal side of the Hotel Jerome's dining options, serving great breakfasts and lunches in a wonderful Gilded Age setting. Breakfasts include heart-healthy offerings. Lunch is light and luscious. **330 E. Main St., Aspen; (970) 920-1000.**

Little Annie's Eating House
Long-time Aspen favorite. Filling, casual fare such as BBQ ribs and chicken, burgers, killer potato pancakes and great pastas in a relaxed and very popular restaurant. Lunch, dinner or late supper, and good for drinks too. Children's menu. **517 E. Hyman Ave., Aspen; (970) 925-1098.**

Main Street Bakery
A little funky. Excellent for freshly baked breakfast pastries. Hearty soups, salads and pastries for lunch. Small dinner menu, with grilled meats, poultry and seafood, vegetarian dishes and nightly specials. Beer and wine. Casual and moderately priced. **201 E. Main St., Aspen; (970) 925-6446.**

Mezzaluna
West Coast chic transplanted to the heart of the Rockies equals a fashionable watering hole. Busy and crowded. Modern adaptations of Italian specialties only a bit of the lure. **600 E. Cooper, Aspen; (970) 925-5882.**

Milan's
Classic and creative northern Italian and other continental specialties, plus seafood and game. Pastas available in full or half portions. Reservations suggested. **304 E. Hopkins, Aspen; (970) 925-6328.**

Mirabella
The accent is Mediterranean, with dishes from France, Italy, Greece, Spain, Lebanon and other Middle Eastern countries. Interesting and memorable. Reservations suggested. **216 S. Monarch, Aspen; (970) 920-5555.**

Mother Lode
Longtime Aspen favorite with pasta, seafood and extensive vegetarian menu, plus excellent wine list. **925 E. Hyman, Aspen; (970) 925-7700.**

New York Pizza
Pizza by the slice or whole, with 20 toppings. Both New York–style and deep-dish pizza as well as pasta, subs, salads and other family favorites. Super-casual upstairs pizza place. Food served from late morning until the wee hours. Takeout and free delivery in Aspen too. Beer and wine. **409 E. Hyman, Aspen; (970) 920-3088.**

Pine Creek Cookhouse
One of the Aspen area's distinctive treats. Historic mining-camp cookhouse, now a unique restaurant. Gourmet lunch, dinner and lavish Sunday brunch at this fabled restaurant at the Ashcroft Touring Center. Take a sleighride or ski in (using a miner's lamp after dark) to be rewarded with expansive views of the Elk Mountains (except after dark—unless the moon is full). Reservations required. **11399 Castle Creek Rd., Ashcroft; (970) 925-1044.**

Piñons
Very high in the pantheon of ethereal Aspen eateries. Attractive purveyor of innovative American cuisine with a Colorado touch. "Eclectic" toned-down Southwestern decor. Creative food in wild combinations of influences that work for diners

41

with fat wallets and a penchant for places exhibiting finely tuned good taste. Game, meat and seafood. Exceptional desserts. Highly rated award-winning restaurant. Reservations required. **105 S. Mill, Aspen; (970) 920-2021.**

Poppie's Bistro Cafe

Good service, fine contemporary cuisine and excellent baked goods (both breads and desserts) are the hallmarks of this innovative eating place. Setting is a charming and cozy Victorian home. Reservations recommended. **834 W. Hallam, Aspen; (970) 925-2333.**

Pour La France!

Moderately priced cafe, one of a small chain, known for good soups, salads, sandwiches and pastries. Good bet for breakfast. Turns into a bistro in the evening with fine Gallic and adapted dishes in a pleasant setting. Full bar, Takeout available. **413 E. Main St., Aspen; (970) 920-1151.**

Renaissance

42 A jewel of a modern French restaurant, with exceptional and imaginative food, immaculate service and a refined ambiance. The nightly prix fixe menu dégustation is one of Aspen's civilized treats with a multicourse feast and wines paired to each course an option. Modern French cuisine with international and interesting touches. Lighter options in the R Bar, upstairs bistro. Award-winning cuisine, practically from opening day. Reservations strongly recommended. **304 E. Hopkins, Aspen; (970) 925-2402.**

The Restaurant at the Little Nell

"American Alpine Cuisine" purveyor is elegant, expensive and exquisite. Main dining room of the Little Nell Hotel. Classy, subdued atmosphere on the formal side with fine linens, china and flatware. Serves three meals a day—and does them all well. Dinner reservations strongly recommended. **675 E. Durant, Aspen; (970) 920-6330.**

Sardy House

Restaurant of a lovely Victorian inn. Fine breakfast, dinner and Sunday brunch in a gorgeous dining room. Food tends toward stylish specialties that may be grilled, sautéed, roasted or seared. Dinner reservations recommended. **128 E. Main, Aspen; (970) 920-2525.**

Silver City Grill

Downstairs eatery purveying such casual food as burgers (beef, chicken or turkey), sandwiches (including cheese steak for homesick Philadelphians), ribs and seafood for lunch and dinner. Family favorite, and tops with locals too. Lunch and dinner. Takeout and fast delivery service. **308 S. Hunter, Aspen; (970) 925-6658.**

Skier's Chalet Steak House

True family restaurant. Perfect for skiers with big appetites and tight budgets. Moderately priced restaurant at the base of Lift 1-A serving steaks, pork chops, chicken and seafood for more than 45 years. Home-baked bread and salad tossed at the table. Beer and wine. **710 S. Aspen St., Aspen; (970) 925-3381.**

Smuggler Land Office

Mining era memorabilia and atmosphere overlaid with modern flair and style. Oysters, crab cakes, shrimp and other seafood, plus some Cajun and Creole specialties. Premium wines by the glass. Salad and pasta bars. Lively, multilevel spot also has popular bar and hot entertainment. **415 E. Hopkins, Aspen; (970) 925-8624.**

The Steak Pit

Established in 1960 and recently moved to a new in-town location. Traditional rather than trendy. Aged steak, prime rib (generous "house cut" or gargantuan "waiter's cut"), lobster, crab and fish accessorized with baked potato, fries or rice. Selections from the fine salad bar and a large wine list. Dinners nightly. Specialty coffees and good desserts. **Hopkins & Monarch, Aspen; (970) 925-3459.**

Syzygy

Eclectic menu tracing French, Southwestern, Italian and Oriental roots in this trendy restaurant, where one goes to see and be seen as well as dine. Casually classy ambiance—at a price. Extensive wine list. Award-winning restaurant. Reservations requested. **520 E. Hyman, Aspen; (970) 925-3700.**

Takah Sushi

Coastal-quality sushi, plus tempura and whole-fish specialties in one of the most highly regarded and top-ranked Japanese restaurants in the West. Excellent sushi bar. Also, specialties from other Pacific Rim countries. Tempura Fried Ice Cream and Jane's Addiction are unique desserts. Reservations requested. **420 E. Hyman, Aspen; (970) 925-8588.**

T-Lazy-7 Ranch
Fun and funky evening. Sleighride to big barn for all-you-can-eat western dinner featuring grill-your-own rib-eye steak. Cash bar. Country-and-western band with dancing. Wednesday and Thursday nights. Reservations required. **Maroon Creek Rd., Aspen; (970) 925-7254.**

Ute City Bar & Grill
New restaurant in old building. Now specializing in modern bistro fare with interesting international touches. Colorado aged beef, game and pastas with a variety of sauces. Excellent vegetarian choices too. Full-service bar, tapas bar and microbrews. **Galena & Hyman, Aspen; (970) 920-4699.**

The Wienerstube Restaurant
Austrian dishes and pastries (breakfast and beyond). Attractive restaurant exuding Austrian gemütlichkeit despite its spacious size and its location in a modest modern building. Reservations suggested for dinner. **633 E. Hyman, Aspen; (970) 925-3357.**

Snowmass

La Bohème & La Brasserie
Ever-changing French menu, with touches from other cuisines, in a lovely restaurant in an upper gallery of the Snowmass Mall. Restaurant serves full dinners in leisurely continental fashion, plus earlybird three-course prix fixe. Adjacent Brasserie also features lighter, more casual menu at lunch and dinner—salads, grill items and vegetarian elections. Reservations suggested. **315 Gateway Building, Snowmass Village Mall, Snowmass Village; (970) 923-6804.**

The Brothers Grille
California kitchen and cuisine in a sprightly, contemporary slopeside restaurant. Hotel restaurant serving breakfast, lunch and dinner. Choice of starters and drinks, pizza, pasta, sandwiches and heftier entrées—or a combination, such as a Blackened Prime Rib Sandwich. Full bar.

Silvertree Hotel, 100 Fall Ln., Snowmass Village; (970) 923-3520.

Burlingame Cabin Dinner Rides
Comfortable 32-passenger snowcat-pulled sleigh to cozy log cabin. Western decor and western dinner. One seating. Bluegrass duo entertains. Good food, with wine beer and other beverages included. Children aged 7 to 12 half-price. Reservations required. Tours available. Departure from **Ticket Pavilion, Snowmass Mall, Snowmass Village; (970) 923-0575.**

Butch's Lobster Bar
A corner of New England in the Rockies. Huge appetizer menu, mainly shellfish—raw and otherwise. Moderately priced entrées include more seafood, meats, poultry and pasta. Specialty is lobster, available steamed, grilled or stuffed and then baked. Daily fish menu. Children's menu. Desserts change nightly. Full bar. Reservations recommended. **Timberline Condos, Snowmass Village; (970) 923-4004.**

Cowboys
Saddle up at this western-theme restaurant and bar for lunch, after-ski nibbles or dinner. Pasta, game, seafood and beef, including the restaurant's rendition of London Broil. Children's menu. Dinner reservations suggested. **Silvertree Hotel, Snowmass Village; (970) 923-5349.**

Krabloonik
Hear the huskies howling as you cozy into a rustic log building to dine on some of the finest game in the West in a distinctive atmosphere. Fallow deer, elk, pheasant and combination game entrées lead the list. Excellent fish selection too. Lunch, dinner and Sunday brunch. Reachable on cross-country skis or by vehicle. Reservations accepted for lunch and strongly suggested for dinner. **4250 Divide Rd., Snowmass Village; (970) 923-3953.**

Mayfair Deli & Pizza
Bistro style and pizzeria prices. Several varieties of pies, mostly California-style, plus hot and cold sandwiches, quiche, soup, salads and light fare. Freshly baked bread and pastries. Full bar. Take-out or delivery available. **Gateway Building, Snowmass Village Mall; (970) 923-5938.**

Colorado's Big Five

Sage
Fine wining and dining with a European flair in an excellent hotel restaurant at the Snowmass Lodge. Breakfast, lunch and really fine dinner. "High country bistro" styling. Moderate prices, especially given the spaciousness, ambiance and creative cuisine. Trendy as well as traditional dishes. Also, "health and fitness menu" and children's menu. Dinner reservations strongly recommended. **Snowmass Club, Snowmass Village; (970) 923-0923.**

Sno' Beach
The spot for filling breakfasts. Also, good choice for lunch (subs, sandwiches, burritos) or dinner (full entrées or pizza and pasta bar). Full bar service. Also, cappuccino bar. Casual upstairs location. Children's menu. **Snowmass Village Mall, Snowmass Village; (970) 923-2597.**

Snowmass Stables Dinner Rides
Two nightly departures to rustic log cabin. Hearty country-style meal. Live country music. Reservations required. **Brush Creek Stables, Snowmass; (970) 923-3075.**

The Stew Pot
A longtime Snowmass favorite with moderately priced soups, stews, sandwiches, salads and ice cream. Children's menu. Wine and beer available. **Snowmass Village Mall; (970) 923-2263.**

The Tower
Snowmass institution for light eating, heavy dining and entertainment. Burger, soup and chili lunches. Colorado beef, seafood and pasta dinners. Soups, salads and vegetarian specials for lighter appetites. Earlybird dinner specials. But best known for bartender/musicians who entertain après-skiers of all ages. Children's menu. **Snowmass Village Mall, Snowmass Village; (970) 923-4650.**

Wildcat Cafe
Economical meals in off-the-beaten-track location in a shopping complex that includes the resort's biggest supermarket. Breakfast, lunch, light snacks and early dinner. Casual coffee-shop atmosphere, with good bloody Marys and microbrews. Children's menu. **Snowmass Center, 0065 Kearns Rd., Snowmass Village; (970) 923-5990.**

NIGHTLIFE

Aspen has a reputation as a swinging, action-filled, celebrity-studded resort, and indeed, there are all sorts of options for music and merriment —and for spending money. Shopping (window or otherwise) and people-watching are time-honored after-ski activities, but as more wealthy and famous people have settled on Aspen as their chosen ski resort, the most glittering social events are increasingly private—as the growing number of Aspen caterers (and even security services) demonstrates. For some visitors, wandering around after dark while browsing the toniest, highest priced shops between Palm Beach and Palm Springs and hoping to spot celebrities—perhaps with a refreshment stop at the antique red popcorn wagon, which serves popcorn, crepes and sandwiches almost till dawn's early light—is still enough evening entertainment.

But of course, participant après-ski remains lively, from the obligatory beer at the Ajax Tavern at the base of mountain where the fabled Little Nell Deck and Shlomo's used to be and extending to the wee hours. The J-Bar in the Jerome remains meeting-and-greeting central through the evening. The Little Nell is the place for a drink—often with high-flying jazz Tuesdays through Saturdays—or for the civilized ritual of high tea. The bar at the Ritz-Carlton has a cocktail hour with mellow live music. The Red Onion has been an Aspen tradition practically since skiing began

44

Snowmass Mountain's well-groomed and varied terrain provides great opportunities for group and family skiing.

there. Syzygy has live music, and the Flying Dog Brew Pub, the first brewery in Aspen in this century, is a revived tradition for great microbrews and meals to match. O'Leary's is a place to go for pizza, but mainly to drink and mingle. Eastern Winds has happy hour with an Oriental-Polynesian tilt. The Aspen Club Lodge, Cantina, Mezzaluna and the Tippler are also lively and fun. Where people go changes with the season—although at peak periods, every place is crowded. The Smuggler Land Office has an especially good happy hour with terrific wines by the glass. The Caribou Club is desirable but private, so copping an invite must be considered a coup. The Crystal Palace's wait staff puts on a devastating revue. Chanin's bar serves well into the night. The Wheeler Opera House is the site of cultural events, comedy shows, pop music and name entertainers. Piñons gets the celebrities and the trendies who follow them. Packaged entertainment has, alas, hit Aspen too. In addition to the Hard Rock Cafe (and its predictable T-shirts), Planet Hollywood has landed with occasional live entertainment.

Aspen and Snowmass do have more down-home options as well. Maxfield's in the Grand Aspen Hotel has a sports bar ambiance, complete with big-screen television, pool, darts and lots of locals. For Aspen's version of "down home," try the Shooters Saloon, with a country-and-western tilt, or the T-Lazy-7 Ranch beyond

Aspen Highlands for a western-style evening with barbecue dinner and toe-tapping, two-stepping music.

At Snowmass, you can step out of your skis and begin après-skiing at the Timbermill, where the Snowmass Mall meets the slopes. The Tower, very nearby, is a perennially popular magic and comedy bar with bartenders who are musicians and crack jokes too. Cowboys in the nearby Silvertree Hotel offers country-and-western music and dancing. You'll find live jazz piano at La Bohème. Zoom's Saloon is Snowmass's best sports bar for light food, big-screen TV, darts, pool and other games. What passes for the counterculture in greater Aspen tends to gather at the Woody Creek Tavern, on the distant outskirts of town. **The Ultimate Taxi** is an ancient Checker cab equipped with a knock-out sound system, mirror ball, fog machine and all the trimmings of a disco on wheels. **(970) 925-0361.** Aspen's new Community Youth Center attracts youngsters ages 11 to 20.

45

For more information, contact **Aspen Skiing Co., P.O. Box 1248, Aspen, CO 81612, (800) 525-6200, (970) 925-1220; Aspen Chamber Resort Assn., 425 Rio Grande Pl., Aspen, CO 81611, (800) 262-7736, (970) 925-1940 and Snowmass Resort Assn., P.O. Box 5566, Snowmass Village, CO 81615, (800) 598-2004, (970) 923-2000.**

STEAMBOAT

BACKDROP

By grace of size, location, snow conditions and what can only be called force of personality, Steamboat is firmly entrenched in the pantheon of Colorado's top five ski resorts. It is less opulent and attracts fewer celebrities and tycoons than Vail and Aspen, but Steamboat's antichic, aw-shucks atmosphere has its own potent appeal. The heart of Steamboat is the ski area that spreads across five peaks, but its soul is still the old ranching center of Steamboat Springs. Western wear and western crafts still draw more shoppers than fancy imports. And the town's annual Winter Carnival, which began in 1912, is one of the best such events in the West. Like other aspects to Steamboat Springs, the inclusion of tourists has planed down the carnival's rough edges but it does remain rooted in the real American West.

No ski resort in the state has a more finely honed reputation for bottomless powder and open-hearted western atmosphere than Steamboat. It comes by both honorably. Though Steamboat, like every other resort in the West, has had occasional lean snow years, it is usually blessed with constant and steady dumps. In January 1996, 259 $3/4$ inches of snow fell on the summit of Steamboat, a single-month record, and a good part of the season total, a memorable 441$1/2$ inches. The resort was virtually buried of the kind of snow Steamboaters call "champagne powder," and it seemed that every day was a powder day. More than any other in Colorado, Steamboat commands its regional scene. It is the only ski resort in the northern part of the state, and the ski area itself is on a massive, multipeaked mountain that creates a constant presence over the broad Yampa River Valley.

THE LAY OF THE LAND

Steamboat Springs is located just west of Rabbit Ears Pass on US 40, northern Colorado's major east-west highway. The Mountain Village at the base of the Steamboat Ski Area has most of the lodging, some of the restaurants and shops and all of the significant ski facilities. It consists of The Gondola Square and Ski Time Square, which are the two main plazas, and The Village Center and Torian Plum Plaza, plus surrounding lodgings. The ski resort is 2 miles east of town, and frequent shuttle buses link the two.

GETTING THERE

Steamboat's direct-to-resort flight program is the oldest and largest in the Rockies, with major airline service to Yampa Valley Regional Airport, most recently from Chicago, Dallas–Ft. Worth, Houston, Los Angeles, Minneapolis–St. Paul and Newark. Commuter flights are available from Denver. This jetport is 22 miles west of town. Steamboat Springs's own small airport is 5 miles from town, but at this writing had no commercial service, though it was expected to resume for the 1996–97 ski season. Rental cars are available at both airports. Some properties provide complimentary van service from the local STOLport.

Scheduled ground transportation between Yampa Valley Regional, Denver International Airport and the resort are offered by **Alpine Taxi & Limo, (800) 343-7433, (970) 879-2800; Colorado Mountain Express, (800) 882-7736,** and **Steamboat Express, (800) 545-6050, (970) 879-3400.**

Steamboat is 157 miles northwest of Denver and 172 miles from Denver International Airport. Driving options include I-70 through the Eisenhower Tunnel to the Silverthorne exit, north on Colorado 9 and then west on US 40, or west on I-70 to US 40 over Berthoud Pass. The drive takes between three and four hours, depending on traffic and road conditions. You won't need a car at Steamboat. Free Steamboat Springs Transit buses (also called town, city or SST buses) connect the town and mountain resort. For scheduling or other information, call **(970) 879-5585.**

PROFILE

Steamboat is a big ski area, looming over the broad Yampa River Valley and coming across as muscular rather than refined. Because of the open topography and the rounded, wooded mountains, it gives the appearance of being a gentle giant. Steamboat does have steep runs and challenging terrain, but the topography itself is not intimidating. It's just when you stand at the top of a fall-away mogul run that your heart skips a beat. You don't get that sensation simply by looking up at the mountain. In fact, you don't even get a real sense of the ski area's scale until you are in the middle of it.

The Steamboat resort is a modern development built around two anchors. Gondola Square is at the bottom of North America's first eight-passenger gondola, and Ski Time Square is at the base of the Christie II and III chairlifts. Since these are the only lifts up the mountain, the resort center is truly a hub. Skiers unload at Thunderhead, a rounded crest that is the linchpin of Steamboat skiing. Atop Thunderhead is a multilevel lodge with cafeteria, sit-down restaurant and barbecue. In other contexts, a mountain of Thunderhead's scale—a gondola and eight lifts on a 2,200-foot vertical—would be a ski area in its own right. Four little lifts at the base rise slowly up a perfect slope for beginners and small children. Three others serve a lush web of novice and intermediate trails, and yet another is beside the Bashor race area. Yet, for all the statistics and steepness, Thunderhead remains the hors d'oeuvre to multicourse skiing gluttony you can indulge in at Steamboat. Most of the terrain is tucked behind three far higher peaks—Mt. Werner, Storm Peak and Sunshine Peak— sprawling along one gigantic massif. It's a complicated mountain parcel, with well-defined drainages between the peaks and ridges that comprise it. You must ski down behind Thunderhead to reach any of those three peaks that form the main part of the ski terrain. Creek drainages, which appear as tilted valleys that snag the snow, separate the peaks of the Steamboat massif.

If you head down to the left, you come to Burgess Creek, with lifts rising out of it to Storm Peak, the lower slopes of Mt. Werner and back up to Thunderhead. Werner is the westernmost point of the Steamboat massif and, at 10,568 feet, it's the highest as well. The Bar UE and Storm Peak lifts climb to the Storm Peak summit. Experts tackle the ridge from there and ski the Chutes, Ridge and Cowtrack just below the ski area boundary, while intermediates angle to Mt. Werner's Big Meadow. Steamboat's most recent expansion in 1996–97 was for another triple chairlift and an additional 179 acres of mostly intermediate terrain to Morningside Park on the backside of Storm Peak. Buddy's Run is a generous intermediate run between Storm and Werner. Storm Peak's east side is composed of broad slopes and open glades, an enticing introduction to powder places. This is the kind of skiing that makes the spirits soar—a capacious, steadily canted white trough that provides dream skiing, especially under a mantle of fresh snow. From the Four Points chairlift, bumpers ski Storm Peak's lower slopes and such steeps as Tornado, Cyclone, Twister and Hurricane. These trail names sound like roller coasters, and they do have a bit of that excitement.

By skiing down to the right from Thunderhead, you come to Priest Creek on the eastern side of the ski area. The Sundown Express climbs to the top of Sunshine Peak, while Elkhead is the return lift to Thunderhead. It is also possible to ski between the two almost equally high summits—on Traverse from Sunshine to Storm and Highline the other way. These are the twin giants of Steamboat skiing—two high vertexes on a long ridge sloping eastward from Mt. Werner offering unexcelled terrain for intermediate and expert skiers. Even more than Storm, Sunshine Peak offers the quintessential Steamboat skiing.

To the left of the parallel chairs' unloading areas, Closet and Shadows are the names given to a forest of firs and aspens so perfectly spaced that they seem to have been placed there by the god of glade skiing. The terrain is steep but steady, expansive yet enfolding—altogether some of the best tree skiing in Colorado. Sunshine also offers trail skiing—Three O'Clock and Twilight for skiers of the steep and Two O'Clock and One O'Clock for those who like their runs a bit tamer. However, since there's such good tree skiing between the cut runs, the woods are a hard-to-resist temptation. You can also ski off to the right of the chairs to Tomahawk, which follows Sunshine's eastern shoulder in a broad, gentle arc. A series of intermediate shots are alternatives from Tomahawk to Quickdraw and Flintlock below. A small sub-peak nestles against Sunshine's lower flanks with a trail or two for each ability level, including Rolex, the only brand-name run on the mountain. This section of the mountain boasts the attractive Rendezvous Saddle lodge, with its cafeteria, Ragnar's restaurant and broad deck for days when it's not snowing.

Howelsen Hill, a small local hill, which has produced 26 Olympic ski racers and jumpers, is the reason Steamboat Springs has named itself Ski Town USA. It has just five trails (all intermediate and advanced), two lifts and 440 vertical feet, but it is also steep (37.5-degree grade), making it ideal for slalom training and landing ski jumpers, which is what local youngsters do. Visitors come to night ski, to watch the thrilling action at the international-caliber ski-jumping complex, to ride the half-pipe, to skate at the

48

bottom of the hill or simply to make a pilgrimage to the mighty midget that has produced so many great champions, **(970) 879-2170, (970) 879-8499.**

SNOWBOARDING

Steamboat is high on riders, and by 1996–97, there should be four-and-a-half terrain parks on the mountain. Number one is the Sunshine Lift Line Terrain Park on the southside liftline (and visible from the chair) is 400 yards of action, featuring table tops, rollers, a snake, a wu-tang launcher, fun box and other jumps. It was designed by local riders and has been fine-tuned. Dude Ranch features a terrific half-pipe, and two additional parks are slated for Big Meadow served by the Bar U-E chair and Giggle Gulch served by the Christie lifts. The half-a-terrain garden is Kids' Park on Spike, a down-sized version of the popular Sunshine Lift Line Park scaled just for kids. Steamboat's chutes, trees and brassy steeps are also treasured by riders—as is that fabled powder.

SNOWCAT SKIING

Steamboat Powder Cats offers full-day guided powder adventures at Buffalo Pass along the Continental Divide. The heated cats hold groups of 12 to 14. Powdercats roam over 15 square miles of the Routt National Forest. Groups commonly make ten 1,000-vertical runs per day. You should be a strong, athletic skier of at least intermediate ability to participate, but the program does include free powder lessons, continental breakfast during orientation at Steamboat and lunch served in Powdercats' high-country cabin. Fat skis are recommended. **Steamboat Powder Cats, P.O. Box 1468, Steamboat Springs, CO 80477; (800) 288-0543, (970) 879-5188.**

SKI SCHOOL PROGRAMS

All levels of ski and snowboarding classes and privates available. For information on all programs except those with a separate number, call the **Steamboat Ski & Snowboard School, (970) 879-6111, Ext. 531.**

Introductory Program

Learn to Ski Weekends: Two-hour class lesson, beginner lift ticket and rentals during selected early-season weekends.

Advanced and Specialty Programs

Sunrise Workshop: Sessions from 8:45 to 10:00 A.M., with instructor-guides who lead groups to first-on-the-mountain terrain and give pointers useful in the conditions encountered. For parallel skiers and above. Available Monday through Friday during key holiday periods.

Style Clinic: Three-hour lesson to help parallel skiers and above develop rhythm and flow.

Bumps Clinic: Three-hour class for advanced adults and teens who want to learn mogul technique.

Super Side-Cuts Clinic: Learn the secrets of "instant carving" using these new skis. For intermediate skiers and above.

Steamboat's chutes, trees, steeps and deep powder are ideal for both riders and skiers.

Photo by Larry Pierce/Steamboat Ski Corporation

Colorado's Big Five

Telemark Workshop: Five-hour session, offered once a month.

Women's Ski Seminars: Top female instructors lead mid-week programs, offered in one- and three-day versions.

Adult Ski Week: Traditional ski weeks for all ability levels, starting Monday and ending Friday. Same instructor all week. Includes five two-hour lessons, on-mountain barbecue, NASTAR race, video analysis and souvenir pin.

Snowboarding: Three-hour morning lesson for all levels.

Telemark: Using cross-country skis (preferably metal-edged) on Alpine slopes.

Billy Kidd Center for Performance Skiing: Olympic medalist and World Champion **Billy Kidd** and his coaching staff lead intensive two- and three-day programs for intermediates and better in four areas: racing, bumps, challenge (i.e., extremes, trees, racing, etc.) and snowboarding. Small classes (limited to six or fewer participants). Available for teens and adults. **(970) 879-6111, Ext. 543.**

Special Programs

Every day that the former Olympic medalist and World Champion Billy Kidd is in town, he meets intermediate skiers and better at the Thunderhead Lodge at 1:00 P.M. for a run down Heavenly Daze. When he's not around (or even when he is), you can get the lowdown on skiing or snowboarding with mountain hosts, who offer information, directions and complimentary mountain tours Sunday and Monday mornings at 10:30 from the upper terminal of the Silver Bullet gondola. It is also possible to ski or ride with a U.S. Forest Service ranger Thursdays, Fridays and Saturdays (check information center for times) and learn about the forest and mountain habitat and indigenous flora and fauna.

For Families

The Kids' Vacation Center organizes skiing and off-slope activities for tots to teens, including some evening supervision. Reservations are required for all programs, **(970) 879-6111, Ext. 469.**

Nonskiing Children

Kiddie Corral: Nursery and day care for ages 6 months and to nonskiing 6 year olds. Direct-from-the-slopes access available for nursing mothers. Divided into Infant, Toddler and Preschool groups. Outstanding facility. Lunches included for children 2 and older; parents need to provide lunch (but need not be present) for under 2. Reservations required, **(970) 879-6111, Ext. 469.**

Skiing Children

Buckaroos: For ages 2 through kindergarten. Includes all-day care and supervision plus a one-hour private lesson to introduce little ones to skiing. Only regular ski school program in the Rockies with ski lessons for children under three.

Sundance Kids: Beginner lesson program for age ages 3½ to kindergarten. Children use kids' learning area with two Magic Carpet conveyor lifts and two Mighty–Mite surface tows. More advanced skiers use more difficult terrain. Half-, full- and multiday options. Full and multidays include lunch. Equipment additional.

Mavericks: Similar format to Sundance Kids, but with smaller class sizes and a little less ski time. Ages 3½ to 4 who are willing to ski.

Rough Riders: Junior ski school with instruction in all-day programs, including lunch, for first graders to age 15.

Teens

Steamboat Teens: Fast-moving classes for intermediates and advanced skiers ages 13 to 18. Offered during holiday periods. Full-day and multiday programs, including lunch.

Billy Kidd Center for Performance Skiing: Series of two-, three- and six-day programs for adults and teens who are intermediate to advanced skiers feature small classes, extensive video, evening technical sessions and Billy Kidd's active presence. Reservations required, **(970) 879-6111, Ext. 543.**

Senior Skiers: Sunday through Thursday, the Over-the-Hill Gang meets at 9:00 A.M. for a day of skiing—reduced 20 percent for ages 65 to 69 and free for ages 70 and over.

Noteworthy

Steamboat etched its way into the consciousness of America's skiing families with the introduction of Kids Ski Free in 1982, enabling children 12 and under to ski free, stay free and occasionally rent free when parents buy a five-day or longer lift ticket and stay in a participating property. Starting in 1996–97, there are no longer holiday blackout periods to this offer. A similar deal, but with reduced rather than free skiing, is now available for teens ages 13 to 15, plus discounted equipment rental. Steamboat also offers a free season pass to children 12 and under with the purchase of a parent's or guardian's adult season pass, and older students through high school get a discounted pass.

The mountain has designated three slow-skiing family zones and several slow-skiing and snowboarding areas. Rough Rider Basin is terrific, a kids-only area with a Wild West theme, including teepees, a log cabin playhouse, Fort Rough Rider and separate surface lifts. Adults are only permitted when accompanied by a child.

Kids Adventure Club at Night offers evening care for ages $2^1/_2$ to 12 in indoor "camp" environment, nightly except Sunday and Monday. Includes pizza, snacks, games, movies and rest time. Discount for additional children in the same family. Program runs from 6:00 to 10:30 P.M. Once a week, ages 8 to 12 go to climbing gym or hot springs pool. Available by the evening or by the hour. Night Owls is new evening program for teens, ages 13 to 18, including supervised trip to town, climbing gym, movie or other activities. Available Wednesday, Thursday and Friday nights from mid-December to late March. Reservations required by 4:30 P.M. for either program, **(970) 879-6111, Ext. 469.**

The local franchise of **Baby's Away** rents cribs, playpens, high chairs and other baby needs; **(800) 978-9030, (970) 879-2354.**

51

FOR RACERS

NASTAR: Daily at the Bashor Race Area from 10:30 A.M. to 12:30 P.M.
NASTAR Race Clinics: Two-hour classes including coaching, video analysis and two-run NASTAR race. Available Tuesdays, Thursdays and Saturdays for adults and children.
Billy Kidd Center for Performance Skiing: Small specialized classes for recreational racers a key component of the center. See "Advanced and Specialty Programs" on p. 49.

HANDICAPPED SKIING

The **Steamboat Ski School** has instructors qualified to teach physically and developmentally disabled skiers. **(970) 879-6111, Ext. 531.**

NORDIC SKIING

The **Steamboat Ski Touring Center** below the ski area base has 30 kilometers of groomed and set trails across the Steamboat Golf Course and into surrounding hills and meadows along Fish Creek. Instruction for all levels and full- and half-day guided backcountry tours are offered, **(970) 879-8180.** A shorter track at the base of Howelsen Hill, close to town, is also lighted for night skiing, **(970) 879-2043. Vista Verde Guest Ranch,** 25 miles north of Steamboat Springs, grooms an additional 30 kilometers, with double tracks and skating lanes, and also provides access to the backcountry. Guests ski free, but the cross-country facilities are also open to the general public; **(800) 526-RIDE, (970) 879-3858.**

Rabbit Ears Pass, just east of the resort, is a popular close-by spot for skiing miles of marked but not maintained Forest Service roads. They range in length from 1.7 to 7 miles and in challenge from moderate to difficult. Some are multi-use routes shared with snowmobilers, and parking is ample. Information is available from the **U.S. Forest Service Ranger Station** at **57 Tenth St. in Steamboat Springs, (970) 879-1870.** Other popular backcountry areas nearby both for ski and snowmobile tours include **Buffalo Pass, (970) 879-1870; Pearl Lake State**

Park, (970) 879-3922; Stagecoach State Recreation Area, (970) 736-2436, and Steamboat Lake State Park, (970) 879-3922.

WHERE TO STAY

Steamboat Central Reservation Services, (800) 922-2722, (970) 879-0740, fax (970) 879-4757.

Luxury Accommodations

Sheraton Steamboat Resort and Conference Center

Full-service, high-rise hotel with 267 rooms (each with two double beds) and three suites. Ski-in/ski-out location with similar convenience to shops and restaurants of Ski Time Square and Gondola Square. Many rooms with private balconies. Children 17 and younger stay free in parents' room. Daily housekeeping, 24-hour front desk, room service, valet/laundry, door staff, concierge, complimentary shuttle from STOLport, massage, complimentary daily newspaper. Restaurants, lounges, heated outdoor pool, hot tubs, saunas, steamrooms, ski storage and rental. **P.O. Box 774808, 2200 Village Inn Court, Steamboat Springs, CO 80477; (800) 848-8878** out of state, **(800) 848-8877** in Colorado, **(970) 879-2220; (800) 325-3535** for Sheraton reservations.

Mid-Priced Accommodations

Best Western Ptarmigan Inn

Comfortable 78-room slopeside lodge with traditional Alpine architecture, contemporary decor and modern amenities. Some units with mini-refrigerators. Daily housekeeping, room service, complimentary après-ski hors d'oeuvres. Restaurant, lounge, outdoor heated pool, hot tub, sauna, ski storage, ski rental. **P.O. Box 773240, Steamboat Springs, CO 80477; (800) 538-7519, (970) 879-1730, (800) 528-1234** for Best Western reservations.

Harbor Hotel

The 62-room hotel is the most charming part of a downtown complex that also includes a 23-room motel and 24 one- and two-bedroom condominiums. Well-furnished with English antique-style furniture and Victorian wallpaper coverings. Some non-smoking rooms. The adjacent motel has modern decor, and the condos make up the only such property downtown. Daily housekeeping, 24-hour front desk, complimentary Continental breakfast, Wednesday night après-ski wine and cheese party, guest services desk. Spa, hot tubs, steamroom, guest laundry, lounge. **P.O. Box 774109, Steamboat Springs, CO 80477; (800) 543-8888, (970) 879-1522.**

Holiday Inn

Eighty-two rooms, two suites and many services. Mini-microwaves, small refrigerators and hair dryers in rooms are among the extras in some rooms. Located 1 mile south of the ski area. Daily housekeeping, 24-hour front desk, 24-hour room service, complimentary shuttle. Whirlpool, game room, fireplace lounge, 24-hour restaurant, ski shop, hair dryers in rooms. **P.O. Box 5007, 3190 S. Lincoln Ave., Steamboat Springs, CO 80477; (800) 654-3944, (970) 879-2250, (800) HOL-IDAY** for Holiday Inn reservations.

The Inn at Steamboat Bed & Breakfast

Seven exquisite, antique-filled rooms created within the shell of a burned-out church. Music conservatory, outdoor hot tub. Also, adjacent two-bedroom Southwestern-style house available for rent. Non-smoking property. Lavish, full breakfast daily, complimentary après-ski wine, daily housekeeping. **442 Pine St., Steamboat Springs, CO 80477; (970) 879-5724.**

Overlook Lodge

Well-priced, 117-room hotel between mountain and town with many on-site amenities. Sixteen loft suites with kitchenettes. Decorated with a western motif. Daily housekeeping, room service, complimentary shuttle, complimentary buffet breakfast. Indoor pool, hot tub, saunas, game room, lounge, restaurant. **P.O. Box 770388, Steamboat Springs, CO 80477; (800) 752-5666, (970) 879-2900.**

Sky Valley Lodge

Twenty-four-room in two beam and moss-rock lodges on a secluded lane, 2 miles up Rabbit Ears Pass. Tranquility, pleasingly rustic charm and sweeping views of the Yampa River Valley. Daily housekeeping, breakfast buffet, complimentary shuttle to mountain, complimentary ski storage at Ptarmigan Inn. Outdoor hot tub, restaurant. **P.O. Box 773132, Steamboat Springs, CO 80477; (800) 538-7519, (970) 879-7749.**

Economy Accommodations

The Alpiner

Bavarian-style inn in downtown Steamboat Springs. Thirty-two recently remodeled rooms, some adjoining. Family atmosphere. Daily housekeeping, complimentary morning and afternoon shuttle to mountain. Use of complimentary ski storage at Ptarmigan Inn, complimentary coffee. In-room coffee. **P.O. Box 770054, Steamboat Springs, CO 80477; (800) 538-7519, (970) 879-1430.**

Nite's Rest Motel

Family-style budget units (some with kitchens, all with in-room coffee) within walking distance of downtown entertainment. Daily housekeeping, Jacuzzi. **P.O. Box 770068, Steamboat Springs, CO 80477; (800) 828-1780, (970) 879-1212.**

Condominiums

The Atriums at Eagle Ridge

Very large (up to 4,000 square feet) luxury condominiums. Upscale appointments such as Jacuzzis, steam showers, several fireplaces and gourmet kitchens—even a lap pool in one unit. Daily housekeeping, concierge, complimentary shuttle. Heated pool, hot tub. **P.O. Box 5184, Steamboat Springs, CO 80477; (800) 545-9292, (970) 879-0720.**

Bear Claw

Opulent ski-in/ski-out property overlooking the lower slopes. Each of the 67 individually decorated condos features balcony, full kitchen, VCR and private ski locker. Daily housekeeping, concierge, complimentary shuttle. Pool, hot tub, sauna, lounge, game room, guest laundry. **2420**

A skier carves a telemark turn on one of Steamboat's hard-to-beat powder days.

Ski Trail Ln., Steamboat Springs, CO 80487; (800) 232-7252, (970) 879-6100.

Kutuk

Imaginatively decorated, well-appointed luxury condos in a rustic Southwestern style. Two- to four-bedroom units are convenient to the slopes and contemporary in style. Daily housekeeping, complimentary shuttle, complimentary welcome bottle of wine, complimentary morning coffee and doughnuts. Outdoor hot tubs, complimentary guest laundry. **P.O. Box 2995, Steamboat Springs, CO 80477; (800) 525-5502, (970) 879-6605.**

La Casa Townhomes

Twenty-four stylish condos with high ceilings, wet bar with ice maker, fireplace, well-appointed kitchen with large pantry and washer and dryer. Huge units (two-bedroom, three-bath to four-bedroom, five-bath) with luxurious decor, designed for entertaining. Adjacent to the slopes. Daily housekeeping, complimentary shuttle, complimentary welcome bottle of wine. Outdoor hot tubs, complimentary guest laundry. **P.O. Box 2995, Steamboat Springs, CO 80477; (800) 525-5502, (970) 879-6036.**

The Meadows at Eagle Ridge

Deluxe two- to four-bedroom condos with Jacuzzis, steam showers and fireplaces in master bedrooms of some units. Well-appointed kitchens, exquisite decor and washer and dryer are in each unit. Daily housekeeping, concierge, complimentary shuttle. Heated pool and hot tub. **P.O. Box 5184, Steamboat Springs, CO 80477; (800) 545-9292, (970) 879-0720.**

Norwegian Log Condominiums
Eleven large, individually decorated condominiums each with fireplace, balcony, whirlpool tub, washer and dryer and well-appointed kitchens. Charming and distinctive ambiance, plus ski-in/ski-out location. Daily housekeeping, concierge. **P.O. Box 5184, Steamboat Springs, CO 80477; (800) 545-9292, (970) 879-0720.**

The Phoenix
Fifty-seven two- to four-bedroom units with full kitchens, moss-rock fireplaces, balconies and walk-to-lifts convenience, at moderate prices. Daily housekeeping, private complimentary shuttle. Washer and dryer in each unit, heated outdoor pool, two hot tubs, rec room, party kitchen. **P.O. Box 881120, Steamboat Springs, CO 80488; (800) 525-7654, (970) 879-7654.**

Ramada Vacation Suites at Steamboat Springs
Timeshare resort with one- and two-bedroom suites with kitchens. Lobby fireplace, coffee bar, spa, sauna. **1485 Pine Grove Rd., P.O. Box 774306, Steamboat Springs, CO 80477; (970) 879-1211.**

The Ranch at Steamboat
Luxury leader among Steamboat condos, with 88 one- to four-bedroom townhouses on 36 private acres overlooking the Yampa River Valley, yet because it is not slopeside, it is a good value. Each finely designed and decorated unit has a well-equipped kitchen, slope-facing balcony, electric barbecue and washer and dryer. Services equal those of a fine hotel. Daily housekeeping, 24-hour front desk, concierge, complimentary on-call shuttle. Outdoor heated pool, three hot tubs, two saunas, recreation room with 40-inch TV and VCR. **One Ranch Rd., Steamboat Springs, CO 80487; (800) 525-2002, (970) 879-3000.**

The Rockies
Eighty well-priced fireplace units from loft studios to three bedrooms, with mountain views and doorstep cross-country skiing. Daily housekeeping, complimentary shuttle to lifts, outdoor heated pool, two hot tubs, guest laundry. **P.O. Box 881120, Steamboat Springs, CO 80488; (800) 525-7654, (970) 879-7654.**

Shadow Run
Economical condos with such desirable extras as full kitchens and washer and dryer in each of the 81 units, ranging from one bedroom to two bedrooms plus loft. Daily towel service. Indoor and outdoor hot tubs, sauna. **P.O. Box 774288, Steamboat Springs, CO 80477; (800) 525-2622, (970) 879-3700.**

Ski Time Square
Unbeatable resort-center location, just steps from the lifts, for 50 moderately priced units from studios to two bedrooms plus loft. Daily towel service. Indoor and outdoor hot tubs, sauna, guest laundry, ski lockers. **P.O. Box 774288, Steamboat Springs, CO 80477; (800) 525-2622, (970) 879-3700.**

Ski Trail
Twenty-five moderately priced one- to three-bedroom units with fireplaces and ski-in/ski-out convenience. Full kitchens and fireplaces in each. Daily housekeeping. Use of pool and hot tub, guest laundry. **P.O. Box 881120, Steamboat Springs, CO 80488; (800) 525-7654, (970) 879-7654.**

Thunderhead Lodge & Condominiums
Sixty-nine spacious condos plus 56 lodge and hotel rooms. Efficiencies through two-bedroom loft units with full kitchens and gas fireplaces. Modern furnishings. Well-situated at the base of the slopes. Luxury ski-in/ski-out property with hotel-type services. Daily housekeeping, 24-hour front desk, bell staff, guest services desk, complimentary evening shuttle, welcome bottle of wine (most units), complimentary morning coffee. Heated outdoor pool, three indoor hot tubs, two restaurants, lounge, guest laundry, ski storage. **P.O. Box 2995, Steamboat Springs, CO 80477; (800) 525-5502, (970) 879-9000.**

Torian Plum
Exceptional luxury condos in attractive mid-rise building directly at the base of the mountain. Ski-in/ski-out and fine views, tops for facilities and

services. Units feature gas-log fireplaces, gourmet kitchens and whirlpool tubs in master bath. Daily housekeeping, bell staff, concierge, complimentary shuttle. Heated outdoor pool, two hot tubs, sauna. **1855 Ski Time Sq., Steamboat Springs, CO 80487; (800) 228-2458, (970) 879-8811.**

Trappeur's Crossing
Excellent services and a top "clubhouse" with recreational facilities. Each of the 25 two- to four-bedroom condos, two blocks from the lifts, has a full kitchen, private balcony and gas-log fireplace. Daily housekeeping, complimentary ski shuttle, concierge. Heated indoor/outdoor pool, two hot tubs, sauna. **1855 Ski Time Sq., Steamboat Springs, CO 80487; (800) 228-2458, (970) 879-8811.**

The Village at Steamboat
Situated at the Steamboat resort access road, this complex features 22 bright spacious studios and one-bedroom units (some with lofts) and an excellent clubhouse for sports and recreation. Daily housekeeping, complimentary shuttle, complimentary morning coffee and doughnuts. Indoor and outdoor pools, hot tubs, sauna, steamroom, racquetball courts, guest laundry, party kitchen. **P.O. Box 775168, Steamboat Springs, CO 80477; (800) 525-5502, (970) 879-2931.**

Management companies and rental agencies for condominiums, town houses and private homes include
Big Country Management, (800) 872-0763
Colorado Resort Services, (800) 525-7654
Mountain Castles, (800) 525-4537 (970) 879-1311
Mountain Resorts, (800) 525-2622, (970) 879-3700
Special Places of Steamboat, (800) 848-1960, (970) 879-5417
Ski Town Management, (800) SKI-TOWN, (970) 879-9300
Steamboat Home Management, (800) 523-9384
Steamboat Premier Properties, (800) 228-2458, (970) 879-8811
Steamboat Resorts, (800) 525-5502, (970) 879-8000.

You can have your condo stocked with groceries and alcoholic beverages; for information, call **The Grocery Company of Steamboat Springs, (970) 879-8333.** You can mail your order to them at **P.O. Box 2669, Steamboat Springs, CO 80477,** or fax it to **(970) 879-4186.**

DINING OUT

The Branding Iron
Lots of Italian pasta dishes, but top sirloin is considered the house specialty. Sandwiches and kids' menu too. Also happy hour drink specials and entertainment in the lounge. **Overlook Lodge, 1000 Highpoint Dr., Steamboat Springs; (970) 879-2900.**

Buddha's Burritos
Whimsical concept of "edible enlightenment." Small downtown place for huge burritos. Homemade, using top ingredients. **Fifth St. and Yampa, Steamboat Springs; (970) 870-1661.**

Buffalo Wild Wings & Weck
Light-hearted and fun. Nicknamed BW-3. Buffalo-style wings, Weck-Burgers, Beef-on-Weck and other wackily named specialties. Full bar and full menu until closing. **729 Lincoln Ave., Steamboat Springs; (970) 879-2431.**

The Butcher Shop
Friendly, family-owned restaurant, founded in 1971. Fine aged beef in a matchless variety of cuts and methods of preparation. Also, fresh seafood and Rocky Mountain trout. Salad bar too. Distinctive wine list. Kids' menu. **Ski Time Sq., Mountain Village; (970) 879-2484.**

Cantina
Mexican specialties, thick-crust pizza and Tex-Mex salads. Daily specials. Children's specials, plus menu proclaiming, "Prizes awarded to well-behaved children." Moderately priced lunch and dinner. Also good happy hour. **818 Lincoln Ave., Steamboat Springs; (970) 879-0826.**

Cipriani's
Fine northern Italian cuisine in a restrained, intimate and elegant atmosphere. Specialties include Osso Buco Milanese, Duckling Stuffed with Garlic and Rosemary and Pasta with Langostinas

and Roasted Peppers. Excellent selection of fine Italian wines. Reservations required. **Thunderhead Lodge, Ski Time Sq., Mountain Village; (970) 879-8824.**

The Coral Grill
Best known for ultrafresh fish and shellfish (including oysters and Maine lobster), but Colorado beef and lamb also available. Excellent salads. Menu changes seasonally. Daily specials served. Excellent wine list. Fine bar menu. Reservations recommended. **Sundance Plaza, Anglers Dr., off US 40, Steamboat Springs; (970) 879-6858.**

Cugino's
Moderately priced pizza, antipasti, pasta, Philly hoagies, sandwiches and other casual Italian dishes. Delivery service. **826 Oak St., Steamboat Springs; (970) 879-5805.**

Dos Amigos
Terrific for tacos, and seafood enchiladas are tops. Ditto for maragritas. New York steak and prime rib too. Small children's menu. Half-price appetizers until 6:00 P.M. and bar menu till midnight. Locals' favorite hangout. Popular Tex-Mex spot for drinking and dining on reasonably priced and hearty portions. Limited reservations accepted. **Ski Time Sq., Mountain Village; (970) 879-4270.**

El Rancho
Mexican-American tradition since the mid-'50s, long before Steamboat Springs became a ski resort. Affordable fajitas, steaks, salads and sandwiches. All-you-can-eat chicken-fried steak dinners some nights. Well-known by locals and savvy, early-dining (until 9:00 P.M.) visitors. Also hearty breakfast and lunch choices. Full bar, featuring good margaritas, bloody Marys (make your own on weekends) and five imported beers on tap. **425 Lincoln Ave., Steamboat Springs; (970) 879-9988.**

Harwig's Grill
Finger foods plus international grilled specialties. More than 40 wines by the glass. Resort's largest selection of single-malt scotch. Lavish dessert tray. Informal atmosphere. **911 Lincoln Ave., Steamboat Springs; (970) 879-1980.**

Hazie's
The sit-down restaurant at the Thunderhead Lodge does prix fixe dinners Tuesday through Saturday evenings a week, combining Continental cuisine, romantic atmosphere and a great view of the valley. Live piano music. Price includes the gondola rides. Reservations recommended. On the mountain; **(970) 879-6111, Ext. 469.**

Heavenly Daze Brewery Grill
The house that microbrews built also offers terrific pub fare at lunch and dinner. Soup, salad, sandwiches, half-pound burgers, steaks and pasta. Children's menu. Entertainment aplenty. **Ski Time Sq., Mountain Village; (970) 879-8080.**

Johnny B. Good's Diner
Fifties-style diner featuring family-pleasing atmosphere, plus old-time rock 'n roll nostalgia for the first baby boomer wave. Hand-patted burgers, fountain drinks and other blasts from the past. Breakfast until 2:00 P.M. then sandwiches and dinners. **738 Lincoln Ave., Steamboat Springs; (970) 870-8400.**

L'Apogée
Elegant and atmospheric restaurant specializing in contemporary French cuisine. Creative salads, classic soufflés made with nontraditional ingredients, splendidly prepared game and other appetizers, entrées and desserts. Three Stars from Mobil. Menu changes weekly. Daily specials too. Huge, award-winning wine list. Reservations required. **911 Lincoln Ave., Steamboat Springs; (970) 879-1919.**

Mattie Silks
Candlelight ambiance and fine steaks, seafood, pasta and Continental cuisine in longtime Steamboat classic. Decadent desserts. Western-Victorian atmosphere that fits with overall Steamboat style. Outstanding wine list. Alternative to rather pricey dining room is Mattie's Cat House Cafe, located in the bar and serving appetizers, light entrées, sandwiches and espresso. More than 50 imported beers and large selection of wines by the glass. Reservations recommended. **Ski Time Sq., Mountain Village; (970) 879-2441.**

Mazzola's

Popular restaurant recently relocated to in-town location. Huge selection of affordably priced pizza in two sizes, pasta and other family favorites with an Italian accent, both northern and southern varieties. Pizza is award-winner. All-you-can-eat salad bar. Kids' portions. Most excessively delicious dessert is hot fudge calzone. Takeout and delivery available. Breakfast served until 11:00 A.M., lunch/dinner menu until 10:00 P.M. and pizza till midnight. Full bar. Reservations recommended. **917 Lincoln Ave., Steamboat Springs; (970) 879-2405.**

La Montaña

Creative versions of Southwestern and Mexican food. Low-ceiling casual charm, like a corner of Santa Fe. Award-winning chefs. Specialties include Red Chili Pasta, Stuffed Shrimp with Jalapeño Hollandaise and five varieties of fajitas. Also known for fabulous frozen margaritas and Mexican beers. Greenhouse dining. Mesquite grilling. Children's menu. Takeout too. Reservations suggested. **Après Ski Way and Village Dr., Mountain Village; (970) 879-5800.**

Old Town Pub & Restaurant

Friendly downtown spot for everyone—families, partiers, old and new friends. Large portions of filling fare: soups, sandwiches, salads, terrific burgers for light appetites and Baby Back Ribs, prime rib, pasta and seafood for those who really want to dig in. Full bar. Lots of entertainment and congeniality. Lunch, dinner and Sunday brunch. **Sixth & Lincoln, Steamboat Springs; (970) 879-2101.**

Old West Steakhouse

Rugged cuts of Colorado beef, well-prepared seafood and hometown Western atmosphere. Something for everyone—happy-hour munchers, hungry diners, light-eating kids and adults grazing on late-night nibbles. Reservations recommended. **1105 Lincoln Ave., Steamboat Springs; (970) 879-1441.**

Panda Garden

Large selection of Szechuan and Mandarin dishes. General Tsao's Chicken, Treasures of the Sea, Romeo and Juliet, Volcano Shrimp and Peking Duck are house specialties. Congenial lounge. Happy hour hors d'oeuvres, including

Steamboat's fabled "champagne powder" packs into the glades, providing tree skiers with ample first-tracks opportunities.

Photo by Cynthia Hunter/Steamboat Ski and Resort Corp.

57

half-price Szechuan appetizers on weekdays. Takeout and free delivery available. Reservations suggested for parties of four or more. Located near City Market. **Central Park Plaza, off US 40, Steamboat Springs; (970) 879-2622.**

Ragnar's

On-mountain restaurant known for fine table-service lunches also serves snowcat-drawn sleighride to dinner Thursday, Friday and Saturday evenings (more during holiday weeks). Fine Scandinavian and Continental specialties at this memorabilia-filled restaurant at Rendezvous Saddle. Dinner price includes gondola and sleigh rides and entertainment. Reservations recommended for lunch, required for dinner. **(970) 879-6111, Ext. 469.**

Roccioso's

Informal Italian cafe with such classic light fare as crostini, calamari and mussels. Also, excellent Goat Cheese-Filled Pumpkin Ravioli, Spaghetti Salsiccia and Herbed Chicken Over Linguine. More casual both in ambiance and in menu selection than Cipriani's, upstairs. Italian wines by the glass or bottle. Reservations not accepted. **Thunderhead Inn, Ski Time Sq., Mountain Village; (970) 879-8824.**

Steamboat Smokehouse

Hickory pit-smoked meats (brisket is tops), turkey, ham, sausage and ribs come in a sandwich, on a dinner plate or by the pound. Condo dwellers can buy a whole smoked ham, turkey or brisket. Moderate prices. Bar service. TV for "sports fans." Eat in or take out. Children's menu. **912 Lincoln Ave., Steamboat Springs; (970) 879-5570.**

Steamboat Yacht Club

Contemporary decor and fine seafood, steaks and prime rib, all well-prepared in a sophisticated riverfront setting. Daily specials. Greenhouse dining with view of Howelsen Hill, especially fun on Wednesday nights when there's ski jumping (restaurant provides house binoculars). Appetizers and light entrées in the lounge. Fireplace lounge. Reservations recommended. **811 Yampa Ave., Steamboat Springs; (970) 879-4774.**

58 Tugboat Grill and Pub

Lively spot for drinking, mixing, mingling and, oh yes, dining on soups, salads, Mexican selections and sandwiches. Western atmosphere, heavy with local seasonings. Breakfast plus same menu at lunch and dinner. Top après-ski spot with live entertainment. Children's menu. **Ski Time Sq., Mountain Village; (970) 879-7070.**

Western Barbecue Buffet

All-you-can-eat barbecue, featuring prime rib, chicken, ribs and trout. Also salad bar, vegetable du jour, potatoes and dessert for all. Cash bar. Live country-and-western entertainment and dancing. Price reduction for children under 12 and free for 5 and under. Price includes gondola ride to Thunderhead Lodge. On the mountain; **(970) 879-6111, Ext. 469.**

Windwalker Sleighride Dinner

Horsedrawn sleigh to cozy log cabin. Known for Ribeye Steak with all the trimmings, including Cowboy Beans. Barbecued chicken or vegetarian lasagna by advance request. Country-and-western dancing, live entertainment and casual fun. BYO wine or beer. Reservations required. Office located at **Gondola Square; (800) 748-1642, (970) 879-8065.**

Winona's

Reasonably priced downtown restaurant serving three meals a day. Breakfast from homemade muffins, bagels and other basked treats to excellent Eggs Benedict, omelettes, waffles and other morning fuel. Create-your-own-sandwich lunches. Reasonably priced dinners, popular with families, include soups, salads, pasta, burgers, interesting entrées and great desserts. Non-smoking restaurant with many vegetarian items. Children's menu. **617 Lincoln Ave., Steamboat Springs; (970) 879-2483.**

NIGHTLIFE

With a few miles separating the slopes and downtown Steamboat Springs, it is natural that the early evening action centers around the base of the mountain. Buddy's Run at the Sheraton, Dos Amigos, Heavenly Daze Brewery, The Inferno, the Tugboat Grill and Pub, The Time Out Sports Bar and the Motherlode are the busiest places right after the lifts close. The Inferno puts on a dynamite happy hour and features the shot wheel, with shot prices as low as 35 cents. After 9:00 P.M., the action switches from pub-style dinner to music, live or courtesy of a DJ. The Tugboat starts early and keeps going with live entertainment and dancing. Time Out has both a huge TV screen (12 by 15 feet!), several merely large ones and large picture windows overlooking the ski slopes. Dos Amigos's appeal is a combination of congeniality, great margaritas and half-price appetizers till 6:00. The resort's first microbrewery, Heavenly Daze, has three floors of fun. You wonder, with happy hour every evening, live entertainment, a game room and a hot nightclub, how they manage to get any brewing done, but they do—and the results have been award-winners at the Great American Beer Festival. The Conservatory at the Thunderhead Lodge does an après-ski grill offering.

Off-mountain and other downtown spots vie for some of the early business with happy hours, munchie menus and appetizer specials. The Old Town Pub & Restaurant has become a popular downtown spot with great drinks (especially their hot concoctions), four large-screen televisions showing ski movies and rollicking congeniality. The Steamboat Yacht Club starts with happy hour and ends with mellow late-evening socializing in the fireside lounge. Steamboat also is the rare ski town with two movie theaters (one in town, one in the Mountain Village), and you might also catch a Steamboat Community Players performance.

Late-crawlers' main choices are the Clock Tower, the Inferno and the Tugboat Saloon, all in the Mountain Village, and at the Old Town Pub and the Steamboat Smokehouse, both downtown. The Cantina offers free happy-hour appetizers, big-screen TV, video games and dart boards. BW-3 has many different beers and a large dance floor. Hotel lounges also offering entertainment include the Greenhouse at the Holiday Inn, Branding at the Overlook Lodge and the Conservatory at the Thunderhead Lodge. You can make a whole evening of BBQ dinner, country and western entertainment, dancing and gondola transport at the western BBQ in the Thunderhead Lodge, Tuesday through Saturday. Children

are welcome. The Steamboat Springs Restaurant and Retail Liquor Assn. sponsors a free Tipsy Taxi service for those who shouldn't be driving after partying; ask the waiter or bartender.

Sports don't stop when the sun sets. Families often head to the Howelsen Hill skating rink or lighted ski runs, or to the Steamboat Springs Health & Recreation Assn., whose three natural hot mineral pools, lap pools, waterslide and snack bar are open well into the evening. The Kids' Vacation Center has a Kids Adventure Club at Night offering evening child care for $2^1/_2$- to 12-year-olds. Tuesday through Saturday and Night Owls for teens (see "For Families," p. 50).

For more information, contact **Steamboat Ski & Resort Corp., 2305 Mt. Werner Cr., Steamboat Springs, CO 80487; (970) 879-6111; Steamboat Springs Chamber of Commerce Resort Assn., P.O. Box 774408, Steamboat Springs, CO 80477; (970) 879-0880.**

SUMMIT COUNTY

BACKDROP

There is no single style of resort that typifies Summit County and no specific type of person who chooses to ski there. More than any other group of ski areas in the country, Summit County exhibits an eclectic balance between locals (who are from Denver and other Front Range cities) and foreigners (who might hail from London, Los Angeles or Lubbock), between day trippers and ski weekers, between hard-working beginners, hard-core experts and hard-playing après-skiers. This absence of an overall, definable identity both of the skiers and the places they ski ensures limitless permutations to skiing and après-skiing in a compact geographical area, where you never know with whom you'll be rubbing elbows in a lift line or at a bar.

Summit County offers skiing at four areas totaling nine peaks and one high Alpine cirque during a season that wraps around the calendar from October, when Keystone cranks up, until June or later, when A-Basin shuts down. That twosome, plus the Breckenridge ski area, are owned by the same corporation and skiable on one lift ticket. Among them, this trio logs more than 2.5 million skier/snowboarder visits every season, and Copper Mountain, which is operated by a separate corporation, usually weighs in with another million, meaning that Summit County has more slope use than the entire state of Utah. Legions are day-skiers from Denver, but vacationers can choose among five remarkably different places to stay, dine, shop and party. Three (Breckenridge, Copper and Keystone) are true resorts, snaring the publicity and building reputations, but two (Dillon and Frisco) are sporty little boomtowns with rapidly expanding lodging, dining and other off-slope options—and locals to share them with.

In mid-1996, as this edition was in preparation, Vail Associates, which owns Vail and Beaver Creek, announced an agreement to purchase Keystone, Arapahoe Basin and Breckenridge from Ralcorp. The merger had not been finalized by the time the book went to press, and even once approved, was not expected to impact operations or programs for the 1996–97 season—at least not significantly. However, the picture could change radically in the future, so with this chapter especially, be aware that what you read here was in place in the summer of 1996.

THE LAY OF THE LAND

Keystone and Copper Mountain are modern built-for-skiing resorts, while Breckenridge is a historic mining town with a huge, three-peak ski area. Dillon and Frisco are bedroom communities without skiing, while Arapahoe Basin is a ski area without a place to stay. I-70 tunnels under the Continental Divide at Loveland Pass, spilling skiers into the county. US Route 6 snakes over Loveland Pass. Just west of this spectacular pass is Arapahoe Basin, an American classic which dates from the immediate post–World War II era and is the country's premier high-Alpine ski area. The road drops into a valley at Keystone Resort's doorstep. You can also reach Keystone from I-70's Dillon-Silverthorne exit, the first off-ramp west of the tunnel.

As the first of the real class acts in the Rockies, Keystone was designed with concern for the total vacation experience. Built from scratch with no skimping and expanded with no letdown of standards, it is known for first-rate facilities and services, an exceptionally long ski season (thanks in part to outstanding snowmaking), excellent family facilities, Colorado's largest mountain conference center and more on- and off-slope features than you can shake a ski pole at. Many of the resort's own lodgings are a short ride from the lifts, but the developing River Run village at the base of the Skyway gondola is changing the complexion of the resort. Designed by much-lauded, Canada-based IntraWest, this slopeside pedestrian village is harmonious and user-friendly, combining the charm of a traditional European village with the infrastructure of a modern American resort. The lakeside Keystone Lodge, the cornerstone of Keystone Village a short shuttle ride from the slopes, has earned AAA's coveted Five Diamond honors almost every year since 1977, and hundreds of condominiums are scattered about the resort with discretion and taste.

Next to the west is the Frisco exit, also used for Breckenridge, 9 miles to the south. Beyond, right along the highway, Copper Mountain butts against the eastern side of Vail Pass.

Each resort in the county has its own shuttle system, and Summit Stage serving the three resorts with each other and with Dillon, Frisco and Silverthorne for lodging, shopping dining and entertainment access. The KAB Express links the Keystone, Arapahoe Basin and Breckenridge ski areas. All these bus systems are free, and most run well into the evening. A car can be useful but isn't really necessary.

GETTING THERE

Keystone is 75 miles west of Denver and 90 miles from Denver International Airport via I-70. You can exit at Loveland Pass and take US 6, the scenic but hairpin-turn pass road past Arapahoe Basin, to the Keystone Resort or continue through the Eisenhower Tunnel to the Dillon exit, then backtrack 6 miles on US 6 to the resort. Breckenridge is 85 miles from Denver and an even hundred from DIA, also via I-70 to the Frisco exit, then south on Route 9 for 9 miles. Copper Mountain is directly off I-70, 75 miles west of Denver and 90 miles from DIA. Transportation between the airport and Keystone, Breckenridge and Copper Mountain is provided by **Airport Shuttle of Colorado, (800) 334-7433, (800) 222-2112, (970) 668-7433** and by **Resort Express, (800) 334-7433.**

Photo by Bob Winsett/Breckenridge

Inside Summit County

THE SKIING

Keystone

Profile

The mountain on which the Keystone ski area developed rises from the base like a densely wooded wall. The few trails emerging from the trees are runouts from the upper mountain, where the topography is both more textured and gentler. This deceptively modest view of the area doesn't begin to hint at the size or the quality of the skiing. Most of Keystone Mountain's terrain spreads out high, out of sight, and behind the main mountain is North Peak and behind that is The Outback. The skiing on this chain of ski mountains is surprising in terms of its dimensions and delightful in terms of its sheer quality.

At the base of the original lifts up the frontside of Keystone Mountain is a cluster of buildings around a day lodge called the Mountain House. It includes ski rental shops, a ski school and a children's center and is the original base area. Skiers head directly to more than half a dozen lifts at the bottom, ranging from the slow lifts on the Checkerboard Square beginner slope to a high-speed quad, the Peru Express. It and the older Packsaddle double chair veer off to the right along either side of Packsaddle Bowl, a graceful slope nudged into Keystone's western shoulder offering excellent mountaintop novice and snowboarding terrain. The handful of steep trails to the bottom, Keystone's original black diamonds, are no longer often skied. The Peru Express is the quickest route to the mild ego skiing on Schoolmarm, Last Chance, Ballhooter and other dark greens and light blues, and to nearby Gold Rush Alley, a kids-only terrain garden with a mining theme.

The Argentine double chair angles left from the base to the core of Keystone's exquisite intermediate terrain and the three upper-mountain chairlifts that serve them, the Montezuma Express quad and two doubles, all named after old mining sites. These three lifts unload at various points along the summit ridge, from which you

Mountain Stats— Keystone

Resort elevation 9,300 feet
Top of highest lift 11,640 feet
Top of hike-to terrain 11,980 feet
Bottom of lowest lift 9,300 feet
Total vertical 2,340 feet
Longest run 3 miles
Average annual snowfall 230 inches
Ski season late October to late April
Lifts two 6-passenger gondolas, 3 high-speed quad chairlifts, 1 fixed-grip quad chair, 3 triples, 6 doubles, 5 surface lifts
Capacity 26,251 skiers per hour
Terrain 95 trails, 1,104 acres (8% beginner and novice, 55% intermediate, 37% advanced and expert)
Snowmaking 850 acres
Night skiing until 9:00 P.M.; every lift ticket—multiday, single-day or afternoon is valid for night skiing too
Mountain dining Summit House on Keystone Mountain; The Outpost (including the Alpenglow Stube and Der Fondue Chessel at night) on North Peak
Snow reports (970) 496-4111, (303) 733-0191 metro Denver

can reach Flying Dutchman, Frenchman, Wild Irishman and Paymaster. Such meandering, impeccably groomed runs are the reason behind Keystone's long-standing reputation as a novice and intermediate skiers' mountain. Keystone was a Colorado snowmaking pioneer, and its snowmaking system just keeps getting better. The area also has been a leader in grooming and snow farming.

The six-passenger Skyway gondola rises from a second base area called the Village at River Run at the eastern end of the resort, unloading at the highest point of the main mountain. Nearby are the top stations of the Montezuma, Ida Belle and Saints John lifts. Most mid-level skiers explore the runs off these upper chairs, only occasionally continuing all the way to the base. Additional novice and intermediate trails cascade down the eastern sector of Keystone's front face, with the option of the Erikson triple or the gondola for a really long run. With the gondola making night skiing feasible and comfortable, thirteen frontside runs are lighted to create America's largest single-mountain night-skiing operation. At twilight, Keystone's snowcats groom the illuminated runs, and since any ticket—multiday, full-day, half-day or night—is good until the 9:00 P.M. (closing time), there's generally a can't-quit-when-the-snow's-so-good crowd skiing under the lights.

The runs Diamond Back, Ambush, Powder Cap and Bullet on North Peak are the area's premier bump bastions, while the Glades, Geronimo and Cat Dancer are not only super steep but also have double fall lines to make them trickier. While experts in the two previous decades tended to youth, as expressed in invulnerable ligaments and an eagerness to keep battling the North Peak bumps, The Outback is black-diamond terrain for the nineties. It tallies 12 high intermediate runs and advanced terrain that are geared more to elegant, technique-testing skiing, as well as penetrable, skiable woods that meet a parallel contemporary demand for ungroomed adventure terrain. The Outback nearly equals North Peak in vertical, exceeds it in number of trails and tops it in summit elevation. Its modern-mode trails are etched through the woods, following the contours of the land and islanded with stands of trees to provide both visual appeal and skiing interest. Near the top, the trees thin out to a wide glade called the Black Forest, and then they fade completely at The Outback's summit, just above timberline. The Outback Bowls, a couple of hundred acres of tree-free bowls, are accessible by a short walk up from the top of the chairlift. They funnel into deep drainages on either side of the Outback.

Keystone was one of Colorado's remaining holdouts in permitting snowboarding. That *was*, but not longer is the case. When the area decided to allow it for the 1996–97 ski season, they did so with their customary whole-hog commitment. A spectacular $2.5 million snowboarding park was built in Packsaddle Bowl, high on the mountain with night skiing, a half-pipe and all manner of cool terrain features.

Mountain Stats—
Arapahoe Basin

Base elevation 10,800 feet
Top of highest lift 12,450 feet
Top of hike-to terrain 13,050 feet
Bottom of lowest lift 10,800 feet
Total vertical 1,670 feet
Longest run 1½ miles
Average annual snowfall 360 inches
Ski season early December (or whenever there is enough snow) at least until June, often later
Lifts 1 triple chairlift, 4 double chairs
Capacity 6,566 skiers per hour
Terrain 61 trails, 490 acres (10% beginner and novice, 50% intermediate, 40% advanced and expert)
Mountain dining Exhibition Warming Hut with outdoor barbecue, Midway Beach, barbecue and outdoor dining during "nice" days only
Snow reports (970) 468-4111, (303) 733-0191 (metro Denver).

Arapahoe Basin
Profile

Arapahoe Basin is America's highest lift-served ski area, topping out at a literally breathtaking 12,450 feet above sea level—and 600 feet higher if you care to hike. It snares more than 350 inches of snow a year, and at these altitudes, melt-off is late. The ski season runs regularly into June, often into July (sometimes August). This pristine playground where the ski terrain flirts with the timberline looks like a wild corner of the Alps, with vistas of craggy, tree-free peaks etched in high relief against the azure sky. Statistically, A-Basin with five chairlifts serving 27 runs on a 1,670-foot vertical is not among Colorado's giants. But in terms of steep terrain and panoramic splendor, it has few peers and no betters. Ninety percent of the terrain is rated for strong intermediates and experts, but a soft surface of beguiling spring corn invites all who are comfortable on their skis or boards to cruise the rooftop of the Rockies on their own terms.

The main building is unapologetically a base lodge—nothing more, nothing fancier. It looks, feels and is functional. Nearby are a little beginner double chair and a long triple, leading to two additional chairlifts for those who stick to the vast expanse on the upper sections of the cirque. Tucked out of sight is Palivacinni, a lift that serves several runs. Its fabled namesake from below looks like a free fall with white pimples stuck upon it. What looks so perpendicular is actually just very steep, but because it is so bumped up, Palivacinni has been a mogul skiing mecca for decades.

With few trees on A-Basin's expansive sweep of snow, you can follow the marked and named routes or pick your own. True variety comes from the way nature folded the massif upon itself, creating broad fields, minibowls, long chutes, little bumps and bigger humps—and the way everyone chooses to ski it. Hardcore ski-it-as-it-lies sorts traverse from the top of the Lenawee lift to a high face called the East Wall, which provides a backcountry sense of altitude, isolation and on-going challenge.

A rustic warming hut at the top of the Exhibition chair is a mecca in its own right. In winter, even the hardy need to warm up on occasion, but in spring, it offers one of the best outdoor barbecues in the Rockies. In fact, A-Basin—more than anyplace else—demands good weather, good visibility and good snow, either knee-deep powder or forgiving spring corn to be really enjoyable. But when those conditions are met, you won't find better skiing in Colorado.

Ski School Programs

For information call **(800) 255-3715, (970) 468-4170.**

Introductory Programs
Learn to Ski: Beginner lift ticket and two-and-a-half-hour lesson; optional rental equipment. For first-time Level 1 skier.
Novice Skier: Same as above, for Levels 2 and 3.
Snowboarding: Two-hour introductory lesson.

Advanced and Specialty Programs
Skier's Package: $2^1/_2$-hour mid-level lesson and all-mountain lift ticket for Levels 4, 5 and 6; rental equipment optional.
Ski Workshops: $2^1/_2$-hour mid-level lesson and all-mountain lift ticket for Levels 7 and 8; rental equipment optional.
Personalized Performance Skiing Workshops: Three days of coaching, viedo analysis and lift tickets. Maximum four people per group. Available selected weeks for Levels 5 to 8.
Ladies' Day: Four-hour lesson, with or without included lift ticket, every Thursday and Saturday for Levels 4 to 8.
Mahre Training Centers: See "For Racers," below.

For Families
Information and reservations for child care and junior ski school are available by calling **(800) 255-3715.**

Nonskiing Children
The Keystone Children's Center: Day care for infants from 2 months, toddlers and nonskiing preschoolers (includes snowplay for children 3 and older). Available during the day and until 9:00 P.M. during night skiing. Reservations required.

Skiing Children
Mini-Minors: Offered at Keystone and A-Basin. Lift/lunch/rental/lessons package for children ages 3 and 4. Full-day program with maximum of eight children per class.
Minor's Camp: Full-day lift/lunch/lesson/rental programs for children ages 5 to 12.

Teens
Teen Program: Full-day lift/lunch/lesson/rental programs for youngsters ages 11 to 16; available selected holiday and school-vacation weeks.

For Racers

Mahre Training Centers: Two formats, three and five days respectively, of lift tickets and coaching, including a half-day with either Phil or Steve Mahre, both Olympic medalists. Offered several times during the winter and spring. Uses racing principles but designed to enhance skiing skills as well as racing prowess. Exclusive to Keystone and A-Basin.

Ski Challenge Race Course: Coin-operated race course, Packsaddle Race Arena.
NASTAR: Packsaddle Race Arena.

Nordic Skiing

The Keystone Cross-Country Center offers cross-country skiing, skating and telemark instruction and 20 miles of prepared trails both in the Snake River Valley and high in the mountains with access via gondola, plus guided excursions into the Montezuma Valley and Arapaho National Forest. Family classes and moonlight tours are exceptionally popular. Ski and snowshoe rentals are available. Two-day workshops, designed especially for women by former U.S. Ski Team Olympian Jana Hlavaty, with women instructors, **(800) 255-3715.**

Easy (and easily accessible) backcountry skiing abounds in and near Montezuma. From the Peru Creek trailhead, you can ski a quite gentle and scenic route into a vast basin with remnants of old mines. The route up from Montezuma toward Sts. John and beyond is steeper, but both are suitable for ski and snowshoe touring.

Where to Stay

Keystone Resort

The address for all Keystone properties is **P.O. Box 38, Keystone, CO 80435. Keystone Reservations, (800) 468-5004.**

Luxury Accommodations

Chateaux d'Mont

Slopeside lodge with just 15 suites and extra personalized services, such as fresh flowers, champagne and a tin of candies as a welcome; a grocery package in each unit and fire in each fireplace lighted by the concierge. Full concierge service, twice-daily housekeeping, nightly turndown service, complimentary continental breakfast, après-ski cocktails. Remote control cable TV with three complimentary pay channels, robes and hair dryers in each unit, full kitchens, ski lockers.

Keystone Lodge

Understated luxury in award-winning, contemporary 152-room hotel with the best facilities and services in Summit County. Charming lakeside location. All rooms with lake and mountain views. Most convenient access to conference center. Daily housekeeping, turndown service, valet parking, ski check, room service, 24-hour front desk, concierge. Restaurants, lounge, fitness facility, swimming pool.

Mid-Priced Accommodations

The Inn at Keystone

Tasteful contemporary lodge. Walking distance (150 yards) to Keystone lifts and close to resort. Restaurant serves huge and moderately priced buffet breakfast. Daily housekeeping, 24-hour front desk. Three outdoor hot tubs, restaurant.

Ski Tip Lodge

Historic stage stop that was turned into county's first ski inn by A-Basin and Keystone founders Max and Edna Dercum. Now a charming country

Noteworthy

Keystone offers a variety of packages with free lodging for children sharing their parents' accommodations. Children's lift rates extend to age 14. Children's movies for ages 3 and up are shown every Friday evening at the Keystone Lodge. MonteZuma's, the new teen center in Keystone Village, offers video games, pool, table tennis, foozball, big-screen TV and snacks.

Baby's Away rents cribs, high chairs, humidifiers, strollers, packs, toys and other child and baby needs and delivers to condos all over Summit County. For information or reservations, call **(800) 979-9030, (970) 668-1571.**

inn, known for authentic early Colorado charm and fine food. Feels like a New England country inn with overtones of western history. Formerly isolated and rustic setting; now being enveloped by new development, but still an oasis of traditional atmosphere. Fourteen quaint and rustic rooms. Restaurant, fireplace lounge. Daily housekeeping, buffet breakfast.

Condominiums

Some 800 well-appointed condominium units from studios to four-bedroom townhomes dot the resort, all with access to swimming pools, saunas and/or hot tubs and a centralized check-in and telephone system. "Mountain View Premium

Colorado's Big Five

Condominiums" receive daily "deluxe" housekeeping, including linen change, general straightening, towel and trash service. Others receive daily "regular" housekeeping, including bed makeup with "deluxe" service every third day. River Bank Lodge is the first signature accommodation at the developing Village at River Run. With unsurpassed access to the gondola, on-site concierge, outdoor hot tub and moderately sized but extremely well-furnished one- and two-bedroom suites with kitchens, gas fireplace and stereo TV. Among the oldest units, Argentine, Decatur, Edgewater, Lakeside, Lenawee, Montezuma and Willows are closest to Keystone Lake; Argentine and Edgewater are most convenient to the Lodge, shops and restaurants. Homestead, Lodgepole and Pines are clustered north of the central village in one grouping, and Flying Dutchman, Soda Spring and Wild Irishman are in another. Children 12 and younger stay free in their parents' lodge room or condominium unit.

Dillon and Silverthorne

Summit County Central Reservations, (800) 356-6365, (970) 468-6222.

Mid-Priced Accommodations

Hampton Inn

Recently upgraded 160-room motel off I-70. Good value and predictable atmosphere. In-room irons and ironing boards, hair dryers and coffee makers. Daily housekeeping, 24-hour front desk, complimentary continental breakfast. Restaurant, heated indoor pool, hot tub, ski shop, guest laundry. **P.O. Box 368, Silverthorne, CO 80498; (800) 321-3509, (970) 468-6200.**

Lake Dillon Lodge

Large motel with 127 modern rooms and suites. Centrally located just off I-70, close to skiing and Silverthorne Factory Outlets. Family-friendly. Twenty-four-hour front desk, daily housekeeping. Indoor pool, Jacuzzi, game room, restaurant, lounge. **P.O. Box 552, Dillon, CO 80443; (800) 727-0607, (970) 668-5094, (800) 528-1234** for Best Western reservations, **(303) 825-7423** Denver direct.

Economy Accommodations

Alpen Hütte

Bargain rooms in friendly lodge. Free ski shuttle. **P.O. Box 919, 410 Rainbow, Silverthorne, CO 80498; (970) 468-6336.**

Super 8 Motel

Just off I-70. Summit County affiliate of well-known budget chain. Daily housekeeping. **808 Little Beaver Trail, Dillon, CO 80435; (800) 843-1991, (970) 468-8888, (800) 800-8000** for Super 8 reservations.

Condominiums

Coeur du Lac Lakefront Condos

Well-appointed one- to three-bedroom condos with lake view, kitchen, fireplace. Pool, hot tub, sauna, game room. **P.O. Box 2664, Dillon, CO 80435; (970) 696-6962.**

Eggers Condos

Comfortable one- to three-bedroom units. Complete clubhouse. **P.O. Box 1406, Dillon, CO 80435; (970) 468-2261.**

Lake Dillon Condotel

Thirty one- and two-bedroom lakeview units, individually furnished and most recently updated. First condos on the lake; the only thing between the property and the lake is a 1-acre lawn and the bike path. Midweek cleaning on six-day or longer stay. Game room, guest laundry, large indoor hot tub. **401 W. Lodgepole, Dillon, CO 80435; (800) 323-7792, (970) 468-2409.**

Spinnaker at Lake Dillon

Twenty-eight timeshares with rentals often available. Good value for well-equipped luxury units. Washer and dryer and fireplace in each. Daily housekeeping available for extra charge. Indoor pool, hot tub, sauna. **P.O. 2519, Dillon, CO 80435; (970) 468-8001.**

Yacht Club Condominiums

Forty-seven individually decorated units of one to three bedrooms. Economical and ideal for families. Great views of Lake Dillon and Ten Mile Range. Cleaning on arrival and departure. Hot tub, sauna, guest laundry. **410 Tenderfoot Rd., Dillon, CO 80435; (800) 999-2123, (970) 468-2703.**

Management companies for Dillon area condominiums include
Columbine Management, (800) 289-7666, (970) 468-0611
Gold Mine Management, (970) 468-9123
Hansen Management, (800) 635-3434, (970) 468-1465
High Country Travel & Tours, (800) 367-1654 out of state, (800) 999-0823 in Colorado, (970) 468-1020
Mountain Condominium Management Co., (800) 525-3682, (970) 468-0566
Mountain View Properties, (800) 451-5948, (970) 468-2601
Omni Business Management, (800) 727-2397, (970) 468-5846

Dining Out

Keystone Resort
Reservations for all resort restaurants are available from the **Keystone Activities Desk, (800) 354-4FUN, (970) 468-2316.**

Alpenglow Stube
Classy mountaintop restaurant serving gourmet lunch and ultragourmet six-course dinners of new western regional cuisine. Fireside dining, romantic and elegant. Specialties include game and other regional ingredients, all prepared innovatively and served elegantly. Open kitchen where chefs welcome conversation with guests. Outstanding wine list. Dinner price includes gondola rides. Dinner reservations required. **The Outpost atop North Peak.**

Bighorn Southwestern Grille
Trendy Southwestern-style dining with large, comfortable booths and interesting Southwestern cuisine. Popular with families. **Keystone Lodge.**

Der Fondue Chessel
Swiss-style fondue and raclette at the top of North Peak, plus live entertainment. Filling and fun. Children's menu. Price includes gondola rides. **The Outpost.**

Edgewater Cafe
Casual atmosphere, light fare and fine view of the skaters on Keystone Lake. Good family spot for breakfast, lunch or dinner. **Keystone Lodge.**

Arapahoe Basin and Keystone's Outback Bowls represent the oldest and newest challenges for skiers and riders in eastern Summit County.

The Garden Room & Steakhouse
Airy and attractive restaurant with continental and American specialties, many prepared tableside. Keystone's place for fine cuts of beef and fresh seafood. Reservations suggested. **Keystone Lodge.**

Gassy's
Barbecue for the hungry, salads for the health-conscious or both as a compromise. Casual lunch and dinner spot at the base of Keystone Mountain. **Mountain House.**

Ida Belle's Bar & Grille
Casual lakeside spot for lunch, after-ski munchies and Mexican-style dinners. Elwood's Hot Sauce is the seasoning of choice. Half-pound burgers and big sandwiches, plus Tex-Mex favorites. Draft beer and draft root beer served in mason jars, and down-home nibbles to match. Children's menu. **Keystone Village.**

Keystone Ranch
Exquisite log ranch house serving extravagant six-course dinners in spacious and relaxed setting. Colorado cuisine—local ingredients imaginatively prepared and presented. Excellent wine list. Classy lounge. Lavish desserts, served in the parlor before a roaring wood fire. Reservations required. **Keystone Golf Course.**

Razzberry's
Pleasant, modern restaurant with mountain views. Bistro-style cuisine. Excellent salad bar. Also serves buffet breakfast. **The Inn at Keystone.**

Colorado's Big Five

Ski Tip Lodge
Cozy beamed dining room with outstanding four-course dinners in the American mode. Quaint, romantic, perennial favorite. Fine wines. Excellent from appetizers to desserts. Reservations required. Montezuma Rd.

Nonnino's
Fun-filled dining experience for families. Popular pastas and other traditional favorites. Keystone Village.

Dillon and Silverthorne

Alice's Restaurant
Lovely restaurant serving classic meats, seafood and poultry. Reservations accepted. **119 LaBonte, Dillon; (970) 468-9808.**

Antonia's
Off-the-highway location, near shopping center. Gourmet pizza and other Italian specialties. Casual atmosphere. Good selection of American wines. Reservations suggested. **817 US Hwy 6, Dillon; (970) 468-5055.**

Arapahoe Cafe
Historic log cabin restaurant near Lake Dillon. Serves hearty, home-style meals, including breakfast, and lighter fare too. Good prices. Seafood (notably trout), steaks and roast duckling dinner. Daily specials. Takeout available. The Bar

Diners sample fine Colorado cuisine at Keystone Resort's Alpenglow Stube, the highest gourmet restaurant in North America.

Photo by Ken Redding/Keystone

Down Under for entertainment. **626 Lake Dillon Dr., Dillon; (970) 468-0873.**

Old Dillon Inn
A Summit County classic. Lively, laid-back nightspot with filling Mexican food, great drinks, entertainment by the decibel and dancing. Ultracasual. Reservations not accepted. **311 Blue River Pkwy, Silverthorne; (970) 468-2791.**

Pug Ryan's Steakhouse
Steaks, prime rib and seafood. Two "bars": the oyster bar and "bar"becued ribs are specials. Clever and fun. Children's menu. Reservations accepted. **101 Dillon Place, Dillon; (970) 468-2145.**

Ristorante Al Lago
Family-owned restaurant specializing in fine northern Italian cuisine near Lake Dillon. Atmosphere is slightly casual and nice. Veal, chicken and seafood specialties, all served with soup, salad, pasta and fresh bread. Known for wildlife on the hoof outside the windows. Reservations suggested. **240 Lake Dillon Dr., Dillon; (970) 468-6111.**

Silverheels
Southwestern specialties, smokehouse meats, tabletop cooking and Spanish-style tapas with a stateside twist. Candlelit hacienda atmosphere. Reservations suggested. **Wildernest, 81 Buffalo Dr., Silverthorne; (970) 468-2926.**

Snake River Saloon
Après-ski is the draw, but steaks and other simply prepared dinners are good too. Entertainment mecca well into the night. **23074 US Hwy 6, Dillon; (970) 468-2788.**

Sunshine Cafe
Moderately priced and healthy breakfast, lunch and dinner. Convenient to factory outlets and a good alternative to the fast-food restaurants that dominate the area. Casual, cute and award-winning as well. **Summit Place Shopping Center, Silverthorne; (970) 468-6663.**

Nightlife

Because Keystone has skiing under the lights seven nights a week, the ski and après-ski elements meld into each other. The base lodges get the early crowds. Gassy's and the Last Lift Bar in the Mountain House at the main base of Keystone Mountain are tried-and-true favorites. Gassy's is somewhat mellow, while Last Lift has loud live entertainment. Keysters at the River Run base has a full bar and munchie menu, live entertainment, dancing and even sing-along karaoke. In Keystone Village, Ida Belle's is lively and fun with shuffleboard, sports TV and a jukebox to fill the spaces. If you're skiing A-Basin, you might do your first après-skiing at Sixth Alley. The piano at the Tenderfoot Lounge in the Keystone Lodge is mellow and melodious. Warren Miller's latest ski movie is shown every Saturday evening at the Lodge. Youngsters hang out at MonteZuma's, Keystone's top teen spot.

Just off campus, the Snake River Saloon gets a loud, young crowd that loves to dance to nearly nonstop rock and roll. Bandito's Cantina across the street has family-style après-ski (balloons for the kids, beer for the grown-ups) and a "snow bar menu" from 4:00 P.M. on. The Bar Down Under in the Arapahoe Cafe does a good happy hour, while the Old Dillon Inn stomps with live country-and-western music and potent margaritas late into the night and is one of the Rockies' perennial hot spots. Keystone also is the closest resort to the sprawling factory outlet complex at Silverthorne. Free buses go there, and many of the stores are open late.

For more information, contact **Keystone Resort, P.O. Box 38, Keystone, CO 80435; (800) 486-0188.**

Breckenridge

Profile

Breckenridge is the big kahuna of Summit County skiing. Not only is it the biggest ski area and biggest town, but it also has the longest history, and, if that weren't enough, it is geographically in the middle between Keystone and Copper. Breckenridge's three interconnected mountains and adjacent off-piste peak provide an awesome variety of ski experience skiable on a fully interchangeable lift ticket shared with Keystone and Araphaoe Basin, and the town is fun that won't quit.

Main Street, the town's prime artery, is a strip of fancied-up Victoriana offering the best après-ski in Summit County, and the town's old part comprises the largest nationally registered historic district in Colorado. Christmas decorations garland the lampposts throughout the winter, giving the street an air of nonstop winter festiveness, and the shops are pleasant and, contrasted with other major resort towns, affordable. Breck's nightspots crank up early and keep going till long after the rest of the county has buttoned down. And the restaurants come in diverse cuisines, styles and prices.

Much of the life in Breckenridge is beyond Main Street, but you'd never know it from the evening parade. Promenading skiers, peripatetic shoppers, cranked-up revelers and diners make Main Street a must-do for anyone visiting Summit County. The ski area and the town between them host a provocative array of special events, from the annual Ullr Fest celebrating the Norse god of winter to World Cup ski competitions in which the exploits of contemporary gods clad in Lycra inspire celebrations of their own. Modern accommodations surround the lively and historic core, and the skiing is excellent as well.

The names of the mountains of the Ten Mile Range—Peak 7, Peak 8, Peak 9 and Peak 10—that comprise the Breckenridge Ski Area may not stir the imagination, but their scope, scale and collective variety will make your heartbeat quicken. Any one of these mountains by itself would be worthwhile skiing. Together, they add up to a compelling giant, and taken in concert with its Summit County neighbors, they are hard to surpass for variety and quality.

The original Breckenridge, Peak 8 on the northern end of the present lift-served area, displays the kind of balance of terrain difficulty that was necessary when this was the ski area in its entirety. You can still ski it for days without getting bored. The Colorado Express rockets skiers to a broad plateau on which the Vista House day lodge is located. Advanced skiers traverse northward along the Columbine run and drop down into such black and blue back trails as High Anxiety, Boreas or Rounders, while intermediates go south to a selection of graceful middle-steep boulevards. Novices don't ride the quad at all but stick to the easy greens at the bottom.

Peak 8 also is the gateway to some of Breckenridge's most demanding skiing. This high-altitude terrain elevates Breck into a top draw for good skiers—all kinds of good skiers and snowboarders too. The southern flank of Peak 8's main section—the upper portion of the bottom of Peak 8, if you will—is an ultrasteep quartet of bump battlefields. The most notable is Mach 1, on which high-level mogul competitions are regularly held, while Southern Cross, Tiger, Goodbye Girl and the woods between them offer some ungroomed gnarl for powder pigs. For skiers aiming higher, the Columbine Traverse off the quad flirts with the timberline and leads to a T-bar accessing most of Breckenridge's double-black diamond bowls. North Bowl to the right of the T-bar wears dark blue and black and is your best bet if you're a first-timer in the high and the steep. A track along the ridge to the left lets you drop into the curved white walls of Contest and Horseshoe wherever you choose. These precipitous tandem bowls provide a thrilling ride. The Back Bowl on the other side of the ridge is also a steep arc but one that is dotted with trees. Skiers strong of legs and lungs can trek 30 to 45 minutes to Imperial Bowl, topping out at a hair under 13,000 feet. This 60-acre double-black cirque, the highest in-bounds skiing in America, boasts 1,000 vertical feet of what feels very much akin to ultrasteep backcountry skiing. Peak 8 is also the gateway to Peak 7—not lift-served but within the ski area's confines of ungroomed but controlled off-piste terrain. Peak 7 is steep—and

Summit County knows steep. The most vertical pitches approach 36 degrees, comparable to LuLu and Mach 1 on Peak 8 and Palivacinni at A-Basin.

Peak 9 has developed into the heart of the ski area. The Quicksilver, one of Peak 9's two detachable quads and the first such lift in North America, takes off from the outskirts of town. It isn't high-speed by more recent standards, but the legions of novices who ski gingerly down the languorous green-circle runs on the lower mountain don't mind the lack of a really swift ascent. By contrast, the Mercury SuperChair is the newest and longest of Breck's quartet of four-seaters, climbing from the slopeside Beaver Run Resort to the Peak 9 summit in less than 10 minutes. Once there, you will find a web of pleasing, tree-lined intermediate runs on the frontside and another gaggle of awesome double-diamond glades collectively known as the North Face. Devil's Crotch, Hades and Mine Shaft are names meant to rightly convey the impression of someplace high, steep and deep plus trees.

Peak 10 provides Breckenridge's final claim as an expert's haven—and for skiers treasuring powder-holding steeps, putting Peak 10 at the end is saving the best for last. The Falcon SuperChair follows the ridgecrest, with black runs dropping off on both sides. Most of Peak 10's north flank is devoted to The Burn, a precipitous glade, wide enough for safety yet steep enough for challenge. On the south, a half-dozen chutelike trails cut through the woods, luring the mogul skiers and holding the powder in inverse proportion. Cimarron is sufficiently pitched to have hosted World Cup giant slalom and slalom races.

Breckenridge's main peaks are interlinked by lifts, roads and crossover slopes that meld into one eclectic ski area that could easily be three distinctive ones. It is feasible to ski all three in a day, but the best strategy for a multiday stay seems to be to explore one chunk at a time, according to your ability.

Getting There

As an alternate to Denver International Airport, Breckenridge is 125 miles west/northwest of Colorado Springs Airport. Transportation is available from **Airport Shuttle of Colorado, (800)**

Mountain Stats— Breckenridge

Resort elevation 9,600 feet
Top of highest lift 12,231 feet
Top of hike-to terrain 12,988 feet
Bottom of lowest lift 9,600 feet
Total vertical 3,398 feet
Longest run $3\frac{1}{2}$ miles
Average annual snowfall 255 inches
Ski season early November to late April
Lifts 4 high-speed quad chairlifts, 1 fixed-grip quad, 1 triple, 8 doubles, 4 surface lifts
Capacity 24,830 skiers per hour
Terrain 135 trails, 2,023 acres (20% beginner, 31% intermediate, 49% advanced and expert)
Snowmaking 731 acres
Mountain dining Vista Haus (including Piz Otto's) at the top of Peak 8, Falcon's Aerie at the top of Peak 9
Snow reports (970) 453-6118

222-2112, (970) 668-5466. The free Town Trolley links downtown and Peak 9, running every 20 minutes between 9:00 A.M. and midnight. Free shuttle buses are less picturesque than the trolley, but the route system is more extensive and include both base areas as well as Four O'Clock and French Street condo locations.

Snowboarding

Breckenridge has been hospitable to alternative sports too, and, as an early snowboard center, it has a fine halfpipe, and shredders have also compiled their own inventory of favorite spots.

Ski School Programs

Daily class and private lessons meet at the Peak 8, Peak 9 Village and Mercury lift base areas.

Introductory Program
Beginner Lesson: First-time skiers do not need a lift ticket while in class with an instructor.

Advanced and Specialty Programs
The European Experience: Multiday guided skiing with an instructor for two to eight skiers or riders.
Catch the Wave: Adult snowboarding clinics.

Colorado's Big Five

Women's Skiing Seminars: A series of three-day-long weekends taught by women, for women.

Special Program

Guided mountain tours are free, according to demand but by appointment only. Contact the Skier Services Activities Desk.

For Families
Nonskiing Children

Breckenridge has two children's centers, one each at Peak 8 and Peak 9 (see below). Both centers are open from 8:30 A.M. to 4:30 P.M. Infant Care (ages 2 months to 1 year) and Toddler Care (ages 1 and 2) are available only at Peak 8. Older toddlers are in a snowplay program. Reservations required, **(800) 789-7699, (970)453-5000.**

Skiing Children

Ski School for Children: Half- and full-day programs for ages 3 and older available at Peak 8 and Peak 9 Children's Centers. Full-day programs include lunch. Morning lessons only for 3-year-olds; morning and afternoon for 4- and 5-year-olds. Preschoolers ski free, but rental equipment is additional. Children ages 6 to 12 also need beginner or all-mountain lift ticket. Snowboarding instruction available.

Teens

Ski-School for Teens: Separate classes for 13- to 17-year-olds formed when possible. Half- and full-day options. Lift tickets and rentals additional.
Teen High Adventure Camp: High-energy ski and snowboard programs for ages 13 to 18 during holiday and popular vacation periods.

For Racers

NASTAR: Daily from 11:00 A.M. to 3:30 P.M. on Country Boy (Peak 9) and Freeway (Peak 8).
Self-time Race Courses: Country Boy (Peak 9) and Freeway (Peak 8).

Handicapped Skiing

A ski program for those with physical or developmental disabilities is offered in cooperation with the **Breckenridge Outdoor Education Center, (970) 453-6422.** Breckenridge is a regular early-December venue for the Disabled Ski Challenge.
Ski for Light: One of the Rockies' most extensive learn-to-ski programs for the blind.

Nordic Skiing

The Breckenridge and Frisco Nordic Centers are under the same management and share an interchangeable trail pass. The **Breckenridge Nordic Center** has more than 23 kilometers of groomed track set in the valleys below Peaks 7 and 8. Rentals, lessons and snowshoeing are available, **(970) 453-6855.** The **Frisco Nordic Center's** 35 kilometers of trails are groomed daily for classical skiing and skating, with much of the system also offering great views of Lake Dillon. It also offers rentals, lessons and snowshoeing, and it has a particularly congenial log day lodge, **(970) 668-0868.** Both centers offer a lesson guarantee and free afternoon beginner lessons. **Whateley Ranch,** 2 miles north of town, has an additional 15 kilometers of trails, **(970) 453-2600.** Miles of marked backcountry trails are found primarily south of Breckenridge.

Noteworthy

Family travel is a lot easier if you have all the equipment you need for your child but don't have to transport it from home. **Baby's Away,** which now has franchises all over the major resorts of the Rockies, is headquartered in Summit County. It rents cribs, high chairs, humidifiers, strollers, packs, toys and other child and baby needs and delivers to condos all over the county. For information or reservations, call **(800) 979-9030, (970) 668-1571.**

Rapid Rentals has similar gear, as well as VCRs, video games such as Sega Genesis and Game Gear and Super Nintendo, hair dryers, irons, blenders and typewriters. For information or reservations, call **(970) 453-9100.**

Where to Stay

During January and the first week in February, Breckenridge's Ski Free/Stay Free package provides a fifth free night to guests who book in advance four nights of lodging and three days of skiing for the price of four. **Breckenridge Resort**

Chamber Central Reservations, (800) 221-1091, (970) 453-2918.

Luxury Accommodations
Allaire Timbers Bed & Breakfast
Luxurious mountain inn with 10 rooms, each with private deck plus two suites, all with river rock fireplace, private bath and hot tub. Cozy yet luxurious log lodge. On ridge overlooking town and ski slopes. One-third mile from downtown. Daily housekeeping, full breakfast. Great room with fireplace, reading loft, sun room, outdoor hot tub. **P.O. Box 4653, Breckenridge, CO 80424; (800) 624-4904, (970) 453-7530.**

Breckenridge Hilton Resort
Full-service hotel across the street from Peak 9 slopes. Extensively remodeled before the 1994–95 ski season. All 208 commodious units have refrigerator, wet bar and coffeemaker. Extremely popular with British skiers. Children stay free in their parents' room. Daily housekeeping, 24-hour front desk, room service, valet parking. Restaurant, lounge, swimming pool, hot tubs, saunas, exercise room, ski rental shop. **550 Village Rd., P.O. Box 8059, Breckenridge, CO 80424; (800) 321-8444. (970) 453-4500, (800) HILTONS** for Hilton Hotels reservations.

The Lodge at Breckenridge
Splendidly located spa resort on Boreas Pass. Lodge has 45 individually decorated rooms and suites, fine (and healthful) dining and full health and beauty spa. Set on 32 acres. Great views from indoors and huge decks. Daily housekeeping, concierge, private in-town shuttle, aerobics classes, massage and beauty treatments. Restaurant, full health spa and racquetball center, full-size indoor pool, two indoor hot tubs, two outdoor hot tubs, saunas, racquetball. **112 Edwards Dr., Breckenridge, CO 80424; (800) 736-1607, (970) 453-9300.**

Mid-Priced Accommodations
Breckenridge Mountain Lodge
Informal in-town lodge. Rooms have one or two double beds or one king. Daily housekeeping. Restaurant, lounge, hot tubs, outdoor pool, ski rental shop. **600 S. Ridge St., Breckenridge, CO 80424; (800) 525-2224, (970) 453-2333.**

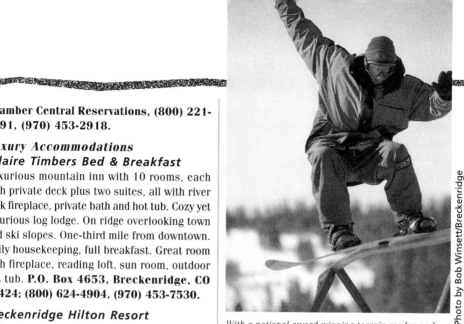

With a national award-winning terrain garden and World Cup-level half-pipe, Breckenridge offers some of the best snowboarding in the Colorado Rockies.

Fireside Inn
Breckenridge's first B&B—New England-style. Nine rooms with private bath and TV, plus economy dorm for 20 budget skiers. Fireplace parlor. Daily housekeeping, breakfast. Hot tub. **114 N. French St., P.O. Box 2252, Breckenridge, CO 80424; (970) 453-6456.**

Ridge Street Inn
Charming and cozy 1890 Victorian B&B. Six rooms with private baths. Fireplace parlor, library. Daily housekeeping, full breakfast, afternoon tea. Limited guest use of kitchen facilities. **212 N. Ridge St., P.O. Box 2854, Breckenridge, CO 80424; (800) 452-4680, (970) 453-4680.**

The Wellington Inn
Stylish new luxury B&B with fabulous in-town location. Combines Victorian atmosphere and modern amenities. Just four rooms—and an excellent restaurant. All rooms with private baths. Daily housekeeping, full breakfast, after-ski refreshments. Fireplace in lounge area, hot tub. **200 N. Main St., Breckenridge, CO 80424; (800) 655-7557, (970) 453-9464.**

Williams House
This historic home is now a beautifully furnished, antique-filled B&B with just six rooms, plus two in a cottage. All rooms with private

Photo by Bob Winsett/Breckenridge

73

baths. Great location. High end of "mid-priced." Full breakfast, après-ski refreshments, daily housekeeping. Hot tub. **303 N. Main St., Breckenridge, CO 80424; (800) 795-2975, (970) 453-2975.**

Economy Accommodations
Breckenridge Park Meadows Lodge
Traditional ski lodge with 32 moderately priced kitchenette units. Ski-in from Four O'Clock Run. Cozy and comfortable. Daily housekeeping. Hot tub, game room, guest laundry, common area with fireplace. **110 Sawmill Rd., Breckenridge, CO 80424; (800) 344-7669, (970) 453-2414.**

Breckenridge Wayside Inn
Thirty-eight rooms and three condo units. Tranquil surroundings across from golf course. Great views. Informal and friendly. Daily housekeeping, continental breakfast, after-ski refreshments. Outdoor hot tub, large stone fireplace in lobby. **165 Tiger Rd., P.O. Box 2666, Breckenridge, CO 80424; (800) 927-7669, (970) 453-5540.**

Evans House Bed & Breakfast
Tradition at a modest price. Centrally located 1886 Victorian, now small and simple inn with four rooms with private or shared baths, and a casual common room. Hospitable and friendly; children welcome. Full breakfast. **P.O. Box 387, Breckenridge, CO 80424; (970) 453-5509.**

The Swiss Inn B&B
Immaculate economy B&B. Five private rooms and dorm-style accommodations for eight additional. Friendly inn. Daily housekeeping, full breakfast. Two sitting rooms (one with TV, one quiet), hot tub. **P.O. Box 556, Breckenridge, CO 80424; (970) 453-6489.**

Tiger Run Resort
Large RV resort with paved sites and full hookups for winterized rigs. Also 20 rustic cabins accommodating up to six. On-site recreation. Hot tub, convenience store, guest laundry. **85 Tiger Rd., Breckenridge, CO 80424; (800) 895-9594, (970) 453-9690.**

Condominiums
Beaver Run Resort
Technically a condominium, but functionally a huge, full-service resort with 520 rooms and ho-

tel-style services. Options range from hotel rooms and spa studios to four-bedroom suites with gourmet kitchen and fireplace. Peak 9 ski-in/ski-out. Daily housekeeping, 24-hour front desk, concierge, bell staff. Lounge, restaurants, deli, liquor store, ski rental shop, two pools, seven hot tubs, saunas, exercise room, 18-hole indoor minigolf, video arcade, guest laundry. **620 Village Rd., Breckenridge, CO 80424; (800) 525-2253, (970) 453-6000.**

Claimjumper Condominiums
Ten spacious three-bedroom, four-bathroom luxury townhouses sleeping up to 16. All have washer/dryer, VCR, stereo, microwave and individual sauna. Slightly outlying location, across from new rec center. Walking distance to shuttle. Housekeeping schedule varies. Indoor/outdoor pool, indoor and outdoor hot tubs, laundry. **P.O. Box 3789, Breckenridge, CO 80424; (800) 343-8942, (970) 453-5830.**

Marriott Mountain Valley Lodge
New 85-unit timeshare. Luxurious units, some with fireplaces or whirlpool tubs. Well-priced packages for guests willing to attend a 90-minute sales pitch; regular rentals. Peak 9 ski-in/ski-out location. Pool. **P.O. Box 1157, Breckenridge, CO 80424; (800) 754-8886, (800) 754-8911** for sales-oriented packages.

River Mountain Lodge
Sizable complex across the street from Four O'Clock Run. Walk to town. Has 110 units, from studios to two bedrooms, with full kitchen, terrace and washer/dryer. Daily housekeeping, continental breakfast. Health club, weight room, pool, steamroom, sauna, indoor and outdoor hot tubs, lounge, ski rental shop. **100 S. Park Ave., Breckenridge, CO 80424; (800) 325-2342; (970) 453-0533.**

Village at Breckenridge
Four mid-rise towers with 347 rooms, from hotel rooms to studios and larger one- to three-bedroom apartments and "chateaux" in the others. Much recent renovation. Ski-in/ski-out complex, slopeside, at base of Peak 9; walking distance to town. Thirteen buildings in all, including shops and restaurants on site. Ski packages, family packages and other attractive deals. Daily house-

keeping, 24-hour front desk. Health club, two indoor/outdoor heated pools, 12 hot tubs, ice skating, restaurants, lounges. **535 S. Park Ave., Breckenridge, CO 80424; (800) 845-2624, (970) 453-2000.**

Wedgewood Lodge
Fifty-three studio to three-bedroom slopeside units in Victorian-style townhome complex. Ski-in from Four O'Clock Run. Limited housekeeping, front desk, fresh flowers in each condominium. Indoor/outdoor spa sauna, access to pool. **535 Four O'Clock Rd., Breckenridge, CO 80424; (800) 521-2458, (970) 453-1800.**

Woods Manor Condominiums
Twenty-four luxury one- and two-bedroom units in a secluded setting south of town with mountain views. Quality decor and furnishings. Extras include whirlpool tubs, washer and dryer and stone fireplace in each unit. Daily housekeeping available for extra charge, clubhouse with hot tub, steamroom and sauna. **P.O. Box 3239, Breckenridge, CO 80424; (970) 453-4000.**

An extremely large portion of Breckenridge's accommodations are condo style, and most are spacious and well equipped. Many are slopeside, with a dense concentration near the Four O'Clock Run and the new Snowflake lift between Peaks 8 and 9. Others flank Main Street or are on the outskirts of town. Many management companies package accommodations, airfare and even lift tickets. Among the companies managing several condominium complexes and private homes are

Alpine Meadows, (800) 866-1228, (970) 453-1226
Alpine Valley Realty, (800) 331-9561, (970) 453-1762
AMR Lodging (Affordable Mountain Rentals), (800) 334-9162, (970) 453-0833
Boreas Pass Realty, (800) 525-3687, (970) 453-6131
Asset Management Co., (970) 453-6480
Breckenridge Accommodations, (800) 872-8789, (970) 453-9140
Breckenridge Central Lodging Co., (800) 858-5885, (970) 453-2160

Breckenridge Vacation Rentals, (970) 453-2136
Collection of Fine Properties, (970) 453-0533
Executive Resorts Rental, (800) 424-8400, (970) 453-4422
East-West Resorts, (800) 525-2258, (970) 453-2222
Four Seasons Lodging, (800) 848-3434, (970) 453-1403
Gold Point Lodging (timeshare), (800) 231-3780, (970) 453-1910
Peak Property Management, (800) 458-7998, (970) 453-1724
Ski Country Resorts & Sports, (800) 633-8388, (970) 453-4474
Summit Mountain Rentals, (800) 383-7382
Tonti Management, (800) 521-2458, (970) 453-1800
White Cloud Lodging Co. (rents private homes), **(800) 345-0593, (970) 453-1018**
Year-In & Year-Out Management, (800) 446-4172, (970) 453-0721

Frisco

Mid-Priced Accommodations
Best Western Lake Dillon Lodge
Has 127 large rooms. Good value. Located just off I-70. Summit Stage main transfer center right outside door. Daily housekeeping, 24-hour front desk, room service, bell staff. Indoor pool, hot tub, game room, restaurant, lounge, ski rental shop. **1202 N. Summit Blvd., Frisco, CO 80443; (800) 727-0607, (970) 668-5094, (800) 528-1234** for Best Western reservations.

Galena Street Inn
Fifteen-room B&B in the center of Frisco—one the Tower Room with commanding views and a romantic atmosphere. Some combinable into family suites. All rooms with private bath and well appointed. Four have fireplaces and three have private porches. Classic comfort and simple style, with Neo–Mission-style furnishings and natural-fiber bed linens and down comforters. Daily housekeeping, full breakfast, afternoon tea. Hot tub, sauna, ski room. **First Ave. and Galena, Frisco, CO 80443; (800) 248-9138, (970) 668-3224.**

Colorado's Big Five

Twilight Inn

Twelve-room B&B with country decor. Some private baths. Daily housekeeping, breakfast. Hot tub, steamroom, two living rooms. **308 Main St., Frisco, CO 80443; (970) 668-5009.**

Economy Accommodations
Frisco Inn

Former stagecoach stop and railroad depot. Now rustic eight-room, shared-bath lodge with 10-room private-bath motel annex. Daily housekeeping. **P.O. Box 1325, Frisco, CO 80443; (970) 668-3389.**

Sky-Vue Motel

Budget rooms (some kitchenette units), two blocks from Main St. Quiet and economical. Daily housekeeping, courtesy coffee. Indoor pool, hot tub. **305 Second Ave., Frisco, CO 80443; (970) 668-3311.**

Snowshoe Motel

Budget motel near the center of town. Kitchenette available. Daily housekeeping. **521 Main St., Frisco, CO 80443; (970) 668-3444.**

Woods Inn

Western-style, art-filled B & B with seven bath-sharing rooms. Daily housekeeping, breakfast, hot tub, two sitting rooms, reading room. **P.O. Box 1302, Frisco, CO 80443; (970) 668-3389.**

If you like your skiing on the wild side, Breckenridge fits the bill with steeps like these on 108 acres of extreme terrain that includes pitches approaching 50 degrees.

Condominiums
Cross Creek

Spacious modern condominium complex in quiet location on the outskirts of Frisco. Two- and three-bedroom units, some bilevel, with full kitchens, whirlpool tubs, fireplaces, satellite TV, washer and dryers and decks overlooking Ten Mile Creek. Club house with indoor/outdoor pool, spas, sauna, game room with fireplace. **P.O. Box 1966, 223 W. Creekside Dr., Frisco, CO 80443; (970) 668-5175.**

Dining Out

Breckenridge

Adams Street Grill

Attractive and spacious California-style restaurant with Southwestern overlay (a.k.a. contemporary American cuisine). In short, trendy look, trendy fare, yet moderate prices. Lunch, après-ski and dinner. Dinner reservations suggested. **10 W. Adams Ave., Breckenridge; (970) 453-4700.**

Blue Moose

Top natural-food restaurant in the county. Casual. Great breakfasts and vegetarian offerings at lunch and dinner, plus natural steaks. Good value. Full bar. Takeout available. **540 S. Main St., Breckenridge; (970) 453-4859.**

Breckenridge BBQ

A taste of country Texas in the mountains of Colorado. Frolicsome atmosphere and hearty meals at lunch and dinner. **301 Main St., Breckenridge; (970) 453-7313.**

Briar Rose Restaurant

Downtown charmer. Old-time ambiance. Serves classic favorites, including prime rib, veal, seafood, steak and especially game. Extensive wine list. Reservations accepted. **109 E. Lincoln Ave., Breckenridge; (970) 453-9948.**

Cafe Three Eleven

Healthy gourmet food, but singularly sinful desserts to balance things off. Breakfast, lunch and après-ski. Casual non-smoking restaurant in the **Main Street Mall, 311 S. Main St., Breckenridge; (970) 453-7657.**

Photo by Bob Winsett/Breckenridge

Downstairs at Eric's

Big, brassy spot for young crowd, families and anyone else with a yen for well-priced burgers, pizzas, munchies and more. Light fare at lunch and dinner, but mostly live entertainment. **111 S. Main St., Breckenridge; (970) 453-1401.**

Fatty's Pizzeria

Popular for pizza, with choice of white or whole wheat dough. Also homestyle Italian dishes, soups, sandwiches, burgers and salad bar. Moderate prices, easygoing atmosphere. Sports shown on big-screen TV. Takeout available. **106 S. Ridge St., Breckenridge; (970) 453-9802.**

Gold Pan Restaurant & Bar

Filling Mexican fare in old Breckenridge saloon, still going strong day and night. Big breakfasts served till noon. Pizza prevails in the evening. Funky fun. **103-5 N. Main St., Breckenridge; (970) 453-5499.**

Hearthstone

Popular restaurant for roast beef, seafood, chicken and pasta dinners. Casual atmosphere in shell of elegant century-old home. Non-smoking policy. Early-bird specials. **130 S. Ridge St., Breckenridge; (970) 453-1148.**

Horseshoe II

Big, busy restaurant. American food and boistrous American ambiance. Children's menu and easygoing atmosphere, popular with families. Moderate prices. Serves breakfast, lunch and dinner. **115 S. Main St., Breckenridge; (970) 453-7463.**

Mi Casa

Cheery cantina, popular with families and budget-watchers. Also good seafood. Dining room is non-smoking. Lunch and dinner, plus excellent happy hour, cocktails, takeout. **600 S. Park Ave., Breckenridge; (970) 453-2071.**

Nordic Sleigh Rides

Sleighride to old mining camp for generous steak dinner. Scott Joplin–style ragtime entertainment. Departure from Breckenridge Nordic Center, accessible by town shuttle. Reservations required. **P.O. Box 64, Breckenridge; (970) 453-2005.**

Pasta Jay's

Popular Boulder eatery's second branch in ski country. Rich, flavorful and unsubtle dishes at lunch and dinner. Non-smoking dining area. **326 S. Main St., Breckenridge; (970) 453-5800.**

Pierre's Restaurant

Fine dining, derived from nouvelle French and nouvelle American influences but now decidedly individualistic. Fresh ingredients and individually prepared dishes equals fine dining in fine surroundings. Excellent wine list. Reservations recommended. **137 S. Main St., Breckenridge; (970) 453-0989.**

Poirrier's Cajun Cafe

Fine renditions of Cajun and Creole cuisine transported to the mountains. Moderately priced lunch and dinner. Award-winning chef. **224 S. Main St., Breckenridge; (970) 453-1877.**

Rasta Pasta

Combine Italian-based pasta with distinctive Jamaica seasonings for a unique taste. Atmosphere also unique. Lunch, dinner and bar service. Non-smoking dining room. Reservations accepted. **411 S. Main St., Breckenridge; (970) 453-7467.**

Spencer's Steaks & Spirits

Hotel restaurant serving breakfast, lunch and dinner. American–style food, including hearty seafood, steaks and a humongous salad bar. Dinner reservations suggested. **Beaver Run Resort, Breckenridge; (970) 453-7975.**

St. Bernard Inn

Considered one of the top restaurants in Summit County. Antique-filled, atmospheric charmer in a restored Victorian building. Northern Italian cuisine, fine meats, excellent desserts and first-rate wine list. Early-bird specials. Reservations suggested. **103 S. Main St., Breckenridge; (970) 453-2572.**

Tillie's Restaurant & Saloon

Popular spot for a drink and the best burgers in Breck. Lunch and dinner. Takeout available. **215 S. Ridge Rd., Breckenridge; (970) 453-0669.**

Colorado's Big Five

Top of the World
Rustic elegance, mountain views and healthy cuisine wrapped into one classy package. Healthful renditions of American and Continental cuisine for breakfast, lunch, dinner and Sunday champagne brunch. Medium to high prices. Nonsmoking restaurant. Reservations suggested. **Lodge at Breckenridge, 112 Edwards Dr., Breckenridge; (970) 453-4500.**

Village Pub
Breakfast, lunch and dinner at the base of Peak 9. Burgers, appetizers and a children's menu for light appetites. Steaks, ribs, chicken, seafood and specialty burritos for hungry adults. Happy hour and live entertainment. **Bell Tower Mall, Breckenridge; (970) 453-0369.**

The Wellington Inn
Lace tablecloths, candlelight and antique decor make this a romantic Victorian treasure. Yet, casual atmosphere and moderately priced Rocky Mountain regional and German dishes, including popular Beef Wellington, Trout Almondine and Wienerschnitzel. Dinner and Sunday champagne brunch. No smoking in dining room. Reservations accepted. **200 N. Main St., Breckenridge; (970) 453-9464.**

Frisco

Barkley's Margaritagrille
Slogan is "More than Just Mexican," which adds signature prime rib, chicken, seafood and vegetarian meals to the menu. Good burgers. Children's menu. Microbrews in addition to margaritas. Happy hour. Fun atmosphere with big-screen TV, pool and live entertainment some nights. **620 Main St., Frisco; (970) 668-3694.**

Blue Spruce Inn
Charming log cabin inn. Fine prime ribs, seafood, lamb and veal combines continental and Rocky Mountain taste and style. Excellent wine list. Reservations suggested. **20 W. Main St., Frisco; (970) 668-5900.**

Charity's
A little pseudo-Victorian and a lot of variety and good spirits. American grill entrées featured, including char-broiled steaks, seafood and burgers. Also, good pasta. Cocktail lounge open late. Full bar. **307 Main St., Frisco; (970) 668-3644.**

Golden Annie's
Casual dinners featuring fajitas, steak, seafood and smoked barbecue specials over mesquite coals. Daily specials. Full bar and cocktail lounge. **603 Main St., Frisco; (970) 668-0345.**

Two Below Zero Dinner Sleigh & Wagon Rides
Atmospheric dinner rides in two 14-passenger mule-drawn sleighs. Two departures from Frisco Nordic Center nightly except Sunday. Freshly prepared dinner served in cozy heated tent camp in the woods. Start with vegetables and dip. Shrimp as an appetizer, grilled sirloin and chicken breast combo, baked potato, French bread and peach cobbler for dessert. Hot beverages included; BYO wine or beer. Reservations required. Discount for children 11 and under. **P.O. Box 845, Frisco, CO 80443; (800) 571-MULE, (970) 453-1520.**

Nightlife

Breckenridge has more après-ski activity than the rest of Summit County combined—and that's saying a lot. The Bergenhof at the base of Peak 8, Tiffany's at Beaver Run and the Maggie, the Village Pub and Jake T. Pounder's at the bottom of Peak 9 snag a big chunk of the immediate after-skiing crowd. Josh's also has a good D.J. and great scene. The Maggie spices its après-ski with karaoke sing-alongs, and Pounder's has live entertainment and, being legally owned by a mutt

Although a free trolley and bus system exist, visitors to Breckenridge can also choose to experience the charm of the Victorian town by old-fashioned means.

Photo by Bob Winsett/Breckenridge

named Jake who was adopted from a pound, serves its snacks in dog dishes. In town, happy hour prevails at the Adams Street Gill, Breck's Pub and Eatery, Briar Rose, Downstairs at Eric's, Hearthstone, Horseshoe II, Mi Casa, Pasta Jay's, Salt Creek Saloon and the Village Pub. Some keep corking until 2:00 A.M.—though the crowd thins considerably when it's snowing and the next day presents the prospect of a powder morning.

The Gold Pan maintains its historic swinging-door saloon ambiance with pool tables—but is updated with a CD jukebox. It claims to be the longest continuously operating bar between St. Louis and San Francisco. The Breckenridge Brewery & Pub is a microbrewery with five kinds of outstanding beer and ale on tap at all times, pool tables and a perpetual air of après-ski min-gling. The Alligator Lounge specializes in live blues and jazz, and also has specials on well drinks and pints some nights. There's live entertainment at the Breckenridge Cattle Company, the Briar Rose and most notably Downstairs at Eric's. Breck's Lounge has dancing and live entertainment, while Tiffany's in Beaver Run is a nightclub with a D.J. and dancing. If, for some reason, Breckenridge doesn't offer enough diversion, **Aces & Eights** offers casino shuttles to Central City with door-to-door service from anywhere in Summit County; **(970) HOT-7777.**

For more information, contact **Breckenridge Ski Corp., P.O. Box 1058, Breckenridge, CO 80424; (970) 453-5000; Breckenridge Resort Chamber, P.O. Box 1909, Breckenridge, CO 80424; (970) 453-2918.**

Copper Mountain

Profile

Copper Mountain is an especially well-configured ski area coupled with a self-contained resort at its base. Its beauty is its simplicity—fine skiing, fine resort facilities and a sense of logistical manageability that makes it ideal for families and others seeking a relaxed, uncomplicated ski vacation. It has neither the effusive services and woodsy elegance of Keystone nor the long history and contemporary brassiness of Breckenridge, but it receives (and deserves) authentic devotion from loyal skiers, both those who commute for a day from the Front Range and those who cross the ocean to vacation there.

Its family appeal is unsurpassed. As one of the first ski resorts in the country to make a major commitment to children, Copper's Belly Button Baby and Belly Button Bakery (the latter where one of the most popular activities is cookie baking) is a day-care prelude to an exceptional children's ski school. Adults fare just as well. The Copper Mountain Ski School Satisfaction Guarantee provides an additional lesson at no charge or a refund to any skier dissatisfied with a class. Copper seldom has had to pay out on this guarantee.

Accommodations are primarily condominiums (though Copper is also the site of the only Club Med ski village in North America), and the buildings—while appearing a bit scattered on the

80

Copper Bowl, with 900 acres of challenging terrain, represented the largest expansion in Colorado for the 1995–96 season. It upped Copper's skiable acreage to nearly 2,500.

snowy valley floor because they were also sited for summer around a golf course—are attractive if unspectacular mid-rises. The appearance is one of no-nonsense sporty comfort, which is most suitable for a year-round resort heavier on athletics and outdoors than on passive pleasures and indoor activities. The entire resort has been honored with AAA's four diamonds for facilities, services and amenities. Nevertheless, Copper is a casual place where the living is easy, the skiing is great and the hot action is only a commute away.

The skiing is found on two major mountains—Copper Peak on the left (or east) and the steeper Union Peak on the right (or west). The lower portions of both are textured into ridges and drainages, while the tops are scoopy bowls and white-coned peaks poking above the timberline.

Although the lifts rise from four distinct bases, the resort hub mandates where the prime ones are located. Two high-speed quad chairlifts bracket the newer Copper Commons and the older, clocktower-topped Center Building, which between them hold the main cafeteria, ticket sales, children's and adult ski schools, checkrooms and other ski-area service facilities. The American Flyer angles westward, climbing lower Union Peak to a knob just before the mountain steepens seriously. Nearby is a small snack hut and below are some of the finest, least crowded intermediate runs in Colorado, served by the Timberline Express, a mid-mountain chair. Because this lift and the beguiling blues it serves are suspended between service facilities, skiers get and stay on a roll, tending to make fewer pit stops, food stops and rest stops than they might if tempting skier services were visible. The result, especially with this high-speed lift that replaced two older doubles, is a lot of skiing.

Nestled into one of Copper's farthest corners, still lower and farther west, is Union Creek with a separate base lodge, ski school desk and Chairs K and L exclusively for a fabulous novice area. This is a place for new skiers to practice in sequestered comfort and safety from down-rushing experts. Of the interlacing green-circle runs in this Copper corner, none is more wider, steadier or more confidence-building than Roundabout. Advanced skiers and snowboarders

Photo by Ben Blankenburg/Copper Mountain Resort

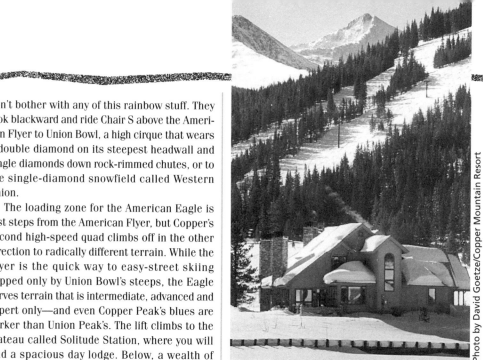

Photo by David Goetze/Copper Mountain Resort

don't bother with any of this rainbow stuff. They look blackward and ride Chair S above the American Flyer to Union Bowl, a high cirque that wears a double diamond on its steepest headwall and single diamonds down rock-rimmed chutes, or to the single-diamond snowfield called Western Union.

The loading zone for the American Eagle is just steps from the American Flyer, but Copper's second high-speed quad climbs off in the other direction to radically different terrain. While the Flyer is the quick way to easy-street skiing capped only by Union Bowl's steeps, the Eagle serves terrain that is intermediate, advanced and expert only—and even Copper Peak's blues are darker than Union Peak's. The lift climbs to the plateau called Solitude Station, where you will find a spacious day lodge. Below, a wealth of long, luscious blue-square runs lead back to the base, while Chair E continues upward. Mogul maniacs use it to yo-yo a quartet of bump runs, but most skiers continue to Copper's best bowl skiing. At the top, Chair R climbs up a long gentle scoop between Copper Peak and Union Peak, serving novice long runs that give relatively new skiers the sense of top-of-the-mountain skiing.

A catwalk skirts the top of the mogul runs to Storm King, a swift little Poma lift that dumps skiers just below Copper Peak's 12,360-foot summit, Copper's open-air room with a view with nonstop vistas of the Ten Mile Range and the mountains beyond. The curving slope off the western side is Hallelujah Bowl, a hootin', hollerin' pitch that spills skiers into Enchanted Forest's glades or Bariloche's ungroomed steeps. Both ultimately feed into Coppertone, a long, easy-skiing cruiser at the bottom of the drainage between the lower parts of Copper and Union Peaks. To the east is Spaulding Bowl, sheerly hollowed out of the mountain. Skiing Spaulding and riding Storm King is a popular circuit for lovers of the steep.

True-blue bump skiers don't dawdle in the bowls. They are likely to take a hard left from Chair E into the perpendicular headwall known as Resolution Bowl, which deceptively gentles into a plateau before steepening again into a fearsome quartet of mogul runs. Cross Cut, Highline, Sawtooth and Cabin Chute are black

The Woods at Copper Creek are just steps away from the ski slopes at Copper Mountain, a resort known for its compact, convenient layout.

pitches with triple-black bumps, and skiing them well takes legs of steel and nerves to match. The entire lower eastern side of Copper Peak has equally awesome bump runs reached by skiing down from the top of E, which is how vacationers do it, or from Chairs A and B/B1, which is how day-skiing bumpers do it—from the parking lot directly to the steeps. These trails sport names like Triple Treat, Too Much, Formidable, Ore Deal and Treble Cliff. These are names that invite respect, and the trails they label demand it as well.

The resort's complexion changed in 1995–96 with the addition of a chairlift in Copper Bowl, 900 acres of high-alpine challenge—the largest terrain expansion in Colorado that season. You can plunge into Copper Bowl from the top of the R lift, Union Peak's S Lift or the Copper Peak summit from the Storm King Poma. Catch your breath, drink in the views of this vast bowl with Tucker Mountain straight ahead and Jacque Peak off to the right, and dive in. The main entry point is from the R Lift, down a knee-knocking route called Six Shooter. You might prefer the heady snowfields of Union Peak, or you might traverse all the way to the Fremont chutes, where you might discover some powder no one yet found. For advanced and expert skiers and snowboarders, it doesn't get any better than Copper Mountain's newly exposed, and very seductive, backside.

Yet despite Copper's bowls, bumps and beginner haven, it has its place in the realm of the regular recreational skier and snowboarder. Intermediate terrain like Andy's Encore, Collage and their like is unsurpassed. The segmented layout means that every level of skier has the sense of a ski area designed just for his or her level, and vacationing doesn't get much easier than having a comfortable condo to nestle into at the base of such an engaging mountain for all types of skiers.

The Lay of the Land

Copper mountain is right off I-70, making it one of the Rockies most accessible resorts. Copper Road leads directly to the Mountain Plaza building, with central check-in for most condominium properties. Condos are located in the Village Cen-

Noteworthy

During portions of the 1995–96 ski season, Copper Mountain threw open the door for novice skiers with totally free use of lifts K and L in January and late in the season. The resort expected about 3,000 people, but 51,000 took advantage of its generosity, at times overwhelming the parking lots and day lodge. Due to its astonishing success but the pressure it put on facilities and on paying customers, the program has been scaled down.

ter, surrounding the main base area with the day lodge and children's center; the East Village around the golf course and Lift B and the West Village between the main base and the Union Creek beginner area and Nordic Center. Free buses operate from 8:00 A.M. to 11:00 P.M., connecting lodging centers and also service the outlying day skiers' parking lots.

Snowboarding

Copper Mountain was one of the first resorts to welcome snowboarders, and the payback for

their congeniality was that it became the area of choice for a small cadre of bad dudes who showed up in the early 1990s. But the lousiest of the louses who gave the whole sport a black eye have taken their attitudes elsewhere, and Copper is again as congenial a place to ride as it is to ski, with snowboard instruction plugged into the ski school curriculum, easy-riding novice slopes and formidable steeps and natural terrain features.

Ski School Programs

Ski School desks are situated at The Center, Union Creek and Solitude Station. For all information or reservations for special workshops call

Noteworthy

Children's rates extend to age 14, and even better deals are offered for multiday ticketing.

(800) 458-8386, Ext. 7827; (970) 968-2318, Ext. 6326.

Introductory Program
Class Lesson and Beginner Lift Ticket: Moneysaver for novice skiers and snowboarders. Early-season versions are also available.

Advanced and Specialty Programs
Advanced Skiing Seminars: Small groups (maximum six skiers) ski all kinds of snow conditions on Copper's toughest terrain, learning how to handle bumps, powder, crud and steeps. Two-day workshops with videotaping and after-ski party.
Women's Skiing Seminar: Two- and three-day clinics for women, taught by women. Focus on getting off a plateau, overcoming fear and setting goals.
Telemark Clinics and Telemark Race Clinics: Half-day, one-day or two-day workshops with instruction, video and tuning and waxing tips.

For Families

Nonskiing Children
Belly Button Babies and Belly Button Bakery, located in Mountain Plaza, offer day-care for chil-

dren ages 2 months and older. Outdoor play and skiing (including equipment) are available for children ages 3 and older. Reservations required. **(800) 458-8386.**

Skiing Children

Copper Mountain's Children's Ski School, head-quartered in the remodeled Center where the rental shop is also located, offers full-day supervision, lunch and instruction, divided into Junior Ranch (ages 4 to 6) and Senior Ranch (ages 7 to 12). Beginners start on a handle tow in the fenced-off Kids Arena next to the Center. Reservations are not taken, but registration begins at 8:00 A.M. Copper Choppers, Shred with the Choppers, Scooters and Super Scooters are consecutive-weekend programs for children within commuting distance, including bus transportation from Denver, Boulder and other Front Range locations. For information call **(800) 458-8386.**

For Racers

Fast Camps: Intensive two-day camp with practice and timed runs in gates, coaching and video analysis. Introductory Fast Camps also offered.
NASTAR: Daily at 1:00 P.M. on the Loverly Trail.
NASTAR Workshop: Daily two-hour class beginning at 10:30 A.M. at the bottom of G Lift.
Self-Timer: Coin-operated race course on the Loverly Trail.
Snowboard Racing Series: Season-long shred meets.
Telemark Race Clinic: Two-day clinic include instruction, lift tickets, video analysis, equipment and waxing lectures and evening socials.

Nordic Skiing

Copper Mountain's 25 kilometers of machine-set tracks and skating lanes wind from Union Creek through the valleys of the Arapaho National Forest. Eat, Ski and Be Merry! is a popular tour and culinary treat wrapped into one fun-filled day in mid-February, and instruction in cross-country and telemark skiing, wildlife tours, overnight hut trips, gourmet hut trips and other backcountry excursions are also offered throughout the winter. **Copper Mountain Cross-Country Center, (970) 968-2882, Ext. 6342.**

Photo by Ben Blankenburg/Copper Mountain Resort

Mountain Stats— Copper Mountain

Resort elevation 9,712 feet
Top of highest lift 12,313 feet
Bottom of lowest lift 9,600 feet
Total vertical 2,601 feet
Longest run 2.8 miles
Average annual snowfall 280 inches
Ski season Mid-November to early May
Lifts 3 high-speed quad chairlifts, 6 triples, 8 doubles, 4 surface lifts
Capacity 29,190 skiers per hour
Terrain 116 trails; 2,433 acres (23% beginner and novice, 36% intermediate, 41% advanced and expert)
Snowmaking 270 acres
Mountain dining Solitude Station atop the American Eagle with full lunch menu, Flyers atop the American Flyer and I Lift for sandwiches and snacks
Snow reports (970) 968-2100

Where to Stay

83

Mid-Priced Accommodations

Club Med

Excellent value. All-inclusive packages for lodging, meals, lifts, instruction and entertainment.

Two two-hour ski or snowboard lessons daily (plus special December racing clinics) for all ages and abilities from Club Med's own instructors. Petit Club (for children ages 3 and older), Mini Club (ages 4 to 7) and Kids Club (ages 8 to 11) skiing and entertainment for youngsters; nightly music and dancing for adults. All rooms with twin beds and private bath. Housekeeping service, meals included, après-ski entertainment and refreshment, morning and afternoon stretch and fitness classes. Restaurant, ski rental shop, outdoor hot tub, sauna, piano bar, large-screen TV, guest laundry. **50 Beeler Pl., Copper Mountain, CO 80443; (970) 968-2161. For reservations only, call (800) CLUB-MED.**

Condominiums

Copper Mountain Reservations, (800) 458-8386. Other than Club Med, accommodations are condo-style, ranging from lock-off hotel rooms to four-bedroom luxury townhomes. Half a dozen management companies actually run the lodgings, but the sense of one resort with across-the-board standards prevails. During selected weeks throughout the ski season, there is a Kids Stay Free/Ski Free policy. All overnight guests at the resort enjoy complimentary access to the

excellent Copper Mountain Racquet & Athletic Club. Village Square units are located close to the lifts and well-priced activities. Mid-price units are found in Foxpine, The Lodge, Mountain Plaza and Telemark Lodge. The most deluxe are the Woods at Copper Creek and Legends at Copper Creek on the eastern end of the resort. Built for accessibility to the golf course, they are comparatively secluded and tranquil in winter. Facilities vary, but some complexes have their own hot tubs, saunas and other recreational facilities.

Dining Out

The Clubhouse

Buffet breakfast and lunch. Sandwiches, salads, burgers and barbecue on the sundeck. Drinks from the full-service bar. Golf clubhouse in summer sets the atmospheric tone. **Base of B Lift, Copper Mountain; (970) 968-2318, Ext. 6514.**

Creekside Pizza & Deli

Best—or is it only?—pizza at Copper Mountain. **Snowbridge Square, Copper Mountain; (970) 968-2033.**

Farley's Prime Chop House

Burgers, steaks, Mexican dishes and a lot of après-skiing locals. Pool table. **104 Wheeler, Copper Mountain; (970) 968-2577.**

Imperial Palace

Mandarin and Szechuan specialties. Bargain buffet lunch. Pleasant setting. Takeout available. Reservations accepted. **Village Square, Copper Mountain; (970) 968-6688.**

O'Shea's Copper Bar

Casual place for breakfast, lunch, après-ski or dinner. Great nachos. Also gourmet sandwiches, burgers and salads. Reasonable prices. Nightly entertainment. **Base of American Eagle, Copper Mountain; (970) 968-0882.**

Pesce Fresco

Sprightly modern decor and contemporary cuisine, with breakfast, lunch and dinner service. Sandwiches, salads, burgers and pasta lead the lunch list. Seafood and homemade pasta specialties tops for dinner. Full bar, comprehensive wine list and after-ski entertainment on weekends too. Dinner reservations recommended. **Mountain**

84

Photo by Ben Blankenburg/Copper Mountain Resort

Plaza Building, Copper Mountain; (970) 968-2318, Ext. 6505.

Rackets

Spacious, slightly Southwestern restaurant. Fresh and healthful cuisine, mainly fresh fish and pasta. First-rate salad bar. **Copper Mountain Racquet & Athletic Club, Copper Mountain; (970) 968-2882, Ext. 6386.**

The Steak Out

Copper's place for beef. Après-ski spot too. **0760 Copper Rd., Copper Mountain; (970) 968-2023.**

Nightlife

Après-ski at Copper starts early with a fun-filled, family-friendly show at the Copper Commons day lodge, and it remains low-key. The B Lift Pub, O'Shea's and Farley's are more traditional watering holes. Pesce Fresca is a stylish bar in the center of the resort. All four feature live entertainment some nights; Farley's and B Lift have good pool tables, and O'Shea's is the place for dancing. Locals hang out at The Steak Out. The Pub downstairs in Copper Commons features a clublike atmosphere and English ale. Kokomos upstairs is louder and livelier. Club Med has it all—with dinner and entertainment for its own guests, and, in a very un–Club Med–like fashion, welcomes outsiders as well. Breckenridge's considerable evening action is a free Summit Stage ride away, and **Casino Coach Tours, (800) 297-8444, (970) 668-LUCK,** operates gaming tours to Central City and Blackhawk.

For more information, contact **Copper Mountain Resort, P.O. Box 3001, Copper Mountain, CO 80443; (970) 968-2882.**

WINTER PARK

BACKDROP

Winter Park is a big-time ski area coupled with a resort town in the making. Local as the flavor is, Winter Park is a real destination resort with terrain, lifts, snow conditions, on-mountain facilities and proximity to a major airport that equals or exceeds the top ski spots in the Rockies at prices that are hard to beat. Nevertheless, hobbled by extremely limited ski-in/ski-out lodging and a town center still working hard to forge an identity, Winter Park lacks the feeling of full-fledged resorthood. As a day-trip and weekend area for Colorado skiers for more than half a century, there's a huge on-hill capacity and a low-key town with lodging for thousands of guests near the ski area—often tucked appealingly into the woods—and the quickly improving town. A true base village is in the works, to be developed by Hines, the firm that is also working on a base development at Aspen Highlands.

There are some other unique elements that distinguish Winter Park from its peers. While it operates, as do most western American ski areas, on U.S. Forest Service land, the city of Denver owns the ski area's assets, which are run by a not-for-profit corporation. The railroad passes right by the resort. Amtrak stops in Fraser, just to the north, and the weekend Ski Train is a decades-old Denver tradition that drops skiers off steps from the lifts (vacationers can enjoy it in a package that includes the train ride and a night at Denver's historic Oxford Hotel; **[800] 228-5838, [303] 628-5400).** Located at the West Portal of the Moffat Tunnel, Winter Park has preserved the railroad link by giving many of its trails and facilities railroad names. It is one of just two Colorado ski areas where Nordic skiing (jumping as well as cross-country) is as valued as Alpine. The Children's Center is spacious, self-contained and tops for children ages 2 months to 12 years, and Discovery Park is a sensational 30-acre learning center for beginning snowboarders and skiers. In addition, the very best facilities and programs for the disabled in the country—perhaps the world—are found at the National Sports Center for the Disabled in the Balcony House.

Despite steady stream growth and improvements, Winter Park has not lost sight of the budget-conscious skier and snowboarder. Innovative multitier ticketing and the Powder Express Pass, a frequent-skier program combining direct-to-lifts discounted mountain access, keeps Winter Park high on the leader among fussy Front Range skiers. With three interconnected mountains, a fleet of lifts, including seven high-speed quads and an hourly capacity of nearly 30,000, and major plans for a base village and still more terrain, the ski area has long been in Colorado's big leagues, but the town is catching up. The result is champagne skiing on a near-beer budget with some specialty elements unmatched elsewhere in ski country.

THE LAY OF THE LAND

After descending from Berthoud Pass, you first reach the access road to the Mary Jane sector and then the main Winter Park base area, which is eventually supposed to be developed as a base village. Old Town Winter Park is nearby. Finally, the highway serves as the main street of the town of Winter Park, which is small but quite spread out. Fraser, 2 miles to the north, has additional lodging, eating places and stores.

GETTING THERE

Winter Park is 67 miles from Denver and 82 miles from Denver International Airport, via I-70 west to US 40 west over Berthoud Pass. Airport shuttle services are provided by **Home James, (800) 451-4844, (970) 726-5060.** The resort can also be reached by daily Amtrak service to

Fraser with taxi or van transport to all properties. On weekends and holidays from mid-December to early April, the **Ski Train** departs from Denver's Union Station at 7:00 A.M. and returns from Winter Park's base at 4:00 P.M., offering a breathtaking two-hour ride through deep canyons and 29 tunnels, culminating in the 6.21-mile Moffat Tunnel under the Continental Divide, **(970) 296-4754.** The **Lift, (970) 726-4163,** is a wide-ranging free bus service, connecting most of the lodges with the ski area and town.

PROFILE

Winter Park is the name of a town and the overall name for a massive ski area, which has three lift-served mountains forming a triangle. The Winter Park and Mary Jane sectors are along the highway, behind which are Vasquez Ridge and Parsenn Bowl. Three chairlifts rise from the original Winter Park base, two just for lower runs, and the high-speed Zephyr Express quad climbing to the Sunspot summit at 10,700 feet. This first-cut trail system consists of a handful of relatively narrow, rather steep runs. The best known of these old-style classics are Hughes, Little Pierre and Ambush, now often used for racing with excellent visibility for spectator events.

Winter Park's summit is crowned with the elegant Lodge at Sunspot, and its charms for average recreational skiers are in the much wider, substantially easier topside trails cascading below on all sides and ample lifts to them all. Tucked into a broad basin is Snoasis, arguably the most cleverly named mid-mountain lodge in skidom. Above are such wide boulevards as Cranmer and Allan Phipps, and several chairlifts to take skiers back up. An indication of the popularity of this beguiling part of the main mountain is the number of lifts; an indication of how well they work is that the runs never feel crowded. Nearby Discovery Park, one of the best ideas to come along for new skiers and snowboarders, is a wonderful 30-acre sheltered mini-area at midmountain for beginners. Accessible by chairlift from the base and served by its own slow-moving, using-friendly triple chair, it features four slopes and trails ideally configured for new skiers, snowboarders, disabled skiers and small children.

The Prospector Express angles from Snoasis to a subsidiary peak with growing significance—as skiers slowly discover the Winter Park that lies "beyond" the immediately obvious. A handful of runs return to Snoasis and another handful lead to the long, gentle trails along the tame valley of the main mountain's rear flank. Named after Alice in Wonderland characters—Tweedle Dee, Cheshire Cat, Jabberwocky and the like—these trails are as endearing for novices and intermediates to ski as their names would suggest. Beyond is Vasquez Ridge, whose high-speed quad seems unnecessary for the half dozen existing runs balanced for all ability levels and for the relatively few skiers who presently venture there, but the Vasquez is slated as a gateway for future expansion.

88   Interlinked with Winter Park/Vasquez—but firm with its own identity—is Mary Jane, an adjacent mountain that has less vertical than the Winter Park side but, in all other measures, is the mightier. It has terrain that is overwhelmingly for high intermediates and experts (just 6 percent is designated "beginner"), gets more

The legendary bumps and steeps of Mary Jane provide some of the best mogul skiing in North America. Mary Jane, Winter Park and Vasquez Ridge are fully interconnected.

snow each season, has a more intense rugged mountain feeling and has gained a reputation with experts for long, steep runs. In fact, many locals ski only the Jane and say they are going there rather than to Winter Park, and it does provide a sense of being a totally separate ski area that just happens to be connected with another, easier one. Mary Jane's base lodge is tucked at the end of an access road. The nearby Galloping Goose chair serves a mild beginner slope, but all others—including the high-speed Summit Express quad—access fairly steep, steeper and steepest terrain. There are narrow bumped-up slots through the woods, short bumped-up headwalls, long bumped-up ridge and gully runs—in fact, there's very little that's not a bumped-up something.

Phantom Bridge, Needles Eye and Rifle Sight Notch are among the frontside bruisers. Hole-in-the-Wall, Awe-Chute, Baldy Chute and Jeff Chute, accessible through a control gate off a run called Derailer, which separates Mary Jane's front and back sectors, are rock-rimmed couloirs of such narrowness and pitch that you wonder why Winter Park management doesn't give them an extra diamond or two. These perilous chutes, as well as longer, wider mogul runs such as Trestle, Runaway, Long Haul and Brakeman, comprise the steeper portion of Mary Jane's backside, which also tames into a gentler part of the mountain with easier runs and glades. The Sunnyside chairlift divides the backside with all but one of the blue squares on one side of the lift and all but one of the blacks (and that one a blue-black, not a true black) on the other.

Behind and above Mary Jane is Parsenn Bowl, the ski area's thrust above the treeline. Accessed from the top of Mary Jane, the Parsenn offers more than 1,000 feet of vertical from wide open playgrounds to nifty tree skiing below. Intermediates can handle the quarter of the terrain that is groomed, and experts find a special level of challenge to the three-quarters that is not. Breathtaking panoramic views and a wild backcountry flair further characterize Parsenn Bowl.

Photo by Byron Hetzler/Winter Park Resort

Connector trails and lifts link the area's four mountains with each other. Access from Winter Park's Sunspot to Mary Jane is via a steep bump run called Outhouse. To get from the Vasquez to Mary Jane, you must ride the High Lonesome high-speed quad. To return from Lunch Rock atop Mary Jane to the Vasquez, you ski the greens of Switchyard or Lonesome Whistle. The links from Winter Park to the Vasquez are via an easy run called Hookup. Corona Way arcs around the entire base of the Mary Jane, and The Corridor feeds skiers from Mary Jane's base to Winter Park's. Parsenn Bowl skiers return to the base via Mary Jane.

SNOWBOARDING

Three terrain parks make Winter Park and Mary Jane super for snowboarders. Jumps, slides and similar features are on Mad Tea Party and Lower Cranmer (the latter is known

Noteworthy

Winter Park starts adult beginners on a rolling people mover called a Magic Carpet at Sorenson Park at the base of the slopes. From there, they move on to Discovery Park, an outstanding learn-to-ski zone encompassing thirty acres of gentle terrain, a slow-moving triple chairlift, several skill-building stations and even restroom facilities. The Skier Improvement Center has embraced the super sidecut ski and offers special lessons using this latest technology.

Winter Park is one of just three areas in the country (and the only within the Rockies) to host the inaugural and second year of Women's National Ski & Snowboard Week, with classes at all levels for and by women, including visiting ski champions, as well as workshops, seminars and social activities.

Mountain Stats— Winter Park

Resort elevation 9,000 feet
Top of highest lift 12,060 feet
Bottom of lowest lift 9,000 feet
Total vertical 3,060 feet
Longest run 5.1 miles
Average annual snowfall 350 inches
Ski season mid-November through late April
Lifts 7 high-speed quad chairlifts, 5 triples, 8 doubles
Capacity 34,023 skiers per hour
Terrain 121 trails, 1,414 acres (19% beginner and novice, 38% intermediate, 43% advanced and expert)
Snowmaking 280 acres (25 trails)
Mountain dining The Lodge of Sunspot at the Winter Park summit with the Provisioner marketplace-style cafeteria and table-service dining room; Snoasis with cafeteria, Mama Mia's Pizza Parlour and Oasis bar; Lunch Rock Cafe at the top of Mary Jane; Sundance Cafe on Vasquez Ridge at the top of the Pioneer Express
Snow reports (303) 572-SNOW (Denver number)

89

as Knuckle Dragon) on the Winter Park side, while Stone Grove is Mary Jane's magnet for snowboarders who like to ride in the woods. This steep and gnarly glade is just off the trail called Sleeper and most directly accessible from the Challenger chairlift.

SKI SCHOOL PROGRAMS

The ski school is now called the **Skier/Rider Improvement Center,** with locations at the Balcony House, Mary Jane Center and The Lodge at Sunspot, **(970) 726-1551.**

Colorado's Big Five

Introductory Programs

Discover Skiing and First Time Class Lessons: First day free with purchase of all-day adult lift ticket; second and third days discounted throughout the month of January. Available for skiers and snowboarders.

Learn for Free: Free beginner lessons with all-day lifts during January.

Advanced and Specialty Programs

Basic Turns, Intro to Parallel, Parallel Breakthrough and Perfect Parallel: Intermediate classes from Level 2.

Intro to Bumps, Carve Clinics and Mogul Masters: Specialty classes on advanced skiing techniques.

Performance Lab: One-on-one analysis of skiing from top instructions who assess all aspects of

Snowboarders are welcome to enjoy all of Winter Park Resort's 121 trails—from the gentle beginner terrain in Discovery Park to the bumps of Mary Jane.

90

your skiing, including stance, skills and equipment. Mechanical adjustments of equipment include canting and footbeds. Video sessions before and as followups to class. Three-hour diagnostic workshop and equipment evaluation. Reservations required.

First Tracks: One-hour, two-person lesson starting half an hour before the lifts open to the public. Perfection on a powder day.

Last Tracks: One-hour, two-person lesson starting at 3:00 P.M.

Snowboard Workshops: Three-hour clinics for Levels to 7. Also, women-only snowboard clinics.

Special Program

Free Mountain Tours are offered daily, departing from the top of the Zephyr Express lift at 10:30 A.M. Even nonskiers can enjoy the mountains via by taking a tour in heated, enclosed snowcat. Reservations at the Guest Services Desk.

For Families

The **Children's Center** is located adjacent to the West Portal Station day lodge at the Winter Park base. Rental equipment is available in the shop right in the Children's Center. Reservations are required for day care but not accepted for skiing programs. Rental equipment is optional with all skiing programs. Hours are 8:00 A.M. to 4:00 P.M. **(970) 726-5514, Ext. 337.**

Nonskiing Children

Day Care: Nonski care, lunch and supervision for children ages 2 months to 5 years. Half- and full-day options (lunch included in full-day).

Skiing Children

Ute Tribe: Ages 3 to 6: Full-day program orienting children to skiing. Small beginners start on fenced-off Mt. Maury beside the Children's Center. Includes lunch.

Cheyenne Tribe: Ages 5 to 6; program similar to Utes.

Navajo Tribe: Instruction, all-day supervision, lunch, lift ticket and progress card for children in first to third grade.

Arapahoe Tribe: Fourth-graders through age 12, including lift ticket, lunch, instruction and video.

Photo by Byron Hetzler/Winter Park Resort

Kid's Snowboard Lesson: One-day class for fourth grade through age 12.

Arapaho Tribe: Instruction, all-day supervision, lunch, lift ticket and progress card for children in fourth grade to age 12.

Ski with Winter Park Willie: The skiing moose mascot interacts and skis with children; the Guest Services Desk has Willie's schedule or call **(970) 726-5514, Ext. 1727.**

Teens

Teen Program: Special groups for teens ages 13 to 16, intermediate to advanced skiers and snowboarders form during Christmas vacation and month of March.

FOR RACERS

NASTAR: Daily, starting at 10:30 A.M. on Cranmer, above Snoasis.

Dual Coin-Op: Coin-operated pay-to-race course on Lower Cranmer.

Racer Tune Up: $1\frac{1}{2}$-hour classes for levels 4 to 7, focusing on racing technique. Offered Tuesday, Thursday and Sunday.

Winter Park Competition Center: In addition to organizing the recreational programs above, the center provides ongoing coaching and training for youngsters ages 6 through high school age at all levels of Alpine racing, freestyle skiing and ski jumping.

HANDICAPPED SKIING

Winter Park has the largest and finest ski program for the disabled in the world. The National Sports Center for the Disabled, established in 1970 and headquartered in the Balcony House day lodge, provides low-cost lessons by trained volunteer and professional instructors and special adaptive equipment for individuals with all sorts of disabilities. The Winter Park Disabled Ski Team is an offshoot that trains serious competitors in various racing disciplines. The barrier-free West Portal Station day lodge accommodates wheelchairs.

In addition to great downhill skiing at Winter Park Resort, the Fraser valley is also home to outstanding cross-country skiing, found in the groomed trails at Devil's Thumb Ranch and Snow Mountain Ranch as well as extensive terrain in the backcountry of Arapaho National Forest.

NORDIC SKIING

Devil's Thumb Ranch, (970) 726-8231, in nearby Fraser offers 105 kilometers of cross-country trails for all ability levels, plus lessons, ski rentals and snowshoeing. The YMCA's noteworthy **Snow Mountain Ranch, (970) 887-4628,** has 100 kilometers of groomed trails (3 kilometers lit for night skiing and some particularly suited for skating). The trails of Snow Mountain Ranch and Devil's Thumb are adjacent, just requiring crossing US 40. The Experimental Ranger Station in the **Arapaho National Forest, (970) 887-3331,** has marked but not groomed trails, which are free. From the Jim Creek trailhead, right across the highway from Winter Park, you can take a wonderful backcountry excursion to a gorgeous and isolated mountain-ringed basin.

WHERE TO STAY

Winter Park Central Reservations, (800) 729-5813, (970) 726-5587.

Luxury Accommodations

C Lazy U Guest Ranch

Exceptional, highly honored dude and guest ranch with fine winter program. Rustic and secluded. Mobil Five Stars; AAA Five Diamonds.

91

Colorado's Big Five

Lovely log main lodge with open-beam ceilings, fireplaces and Indian art. One- to three-bedroom fireplace units decorated with warmth and charm. Wonderful views and 40 kilometers of groomed cross-country trails (equipment free). Twenty-five miles from Winter Park. A bit of formality at dinner. Daily housekeeping, fresh fruit delivered to room each day, complimentary shuttle to transportation and ski area. Sauna, hot tub, racquetball, game room, TV room, children's indoor play area, cross-country ski trails, ski shop, dining room, bar, lounge, sledding and tubing hill, ice skating, horseback riding. **P.O. Box 378-B, Granby, CO 80446; (970) 887-3344.**

Grand Victorian

New 10-room neo-Victorian set among the pines. Seven bedrooms and three suites with fireplaces and private Jacuzzis. All bathrooms and luxuriously appointed. Entire lodge is secluded, romantic and sumptuous. Extra-long beds. Non-smoking inn. Daily housekeeping, full breakfast, after-ski fondue and complimentary spirits. **P.O. Box 0145, 78542 Fraser Valley, Winter Park, CO 80482; (800) 204-1170, (970) 726-5881.**

Iron Horse Resort

Winter Park's most deluxe property. Condo-hotel with 130 contemporary units from lodge rooms to two-bedroom, three-bath suites. Full-service property with many amenities. Intermediate and better skiers can ski in and out. Daily housekeeping, 24-hour front desk, complimentary local shuttle, bell staff. Indoor/outdoor pool, hot tubs, athletic club, racquetball, restaurant, lounge, ski shop. **P.O. Box 1286, Winter Park, CO 80482; (800) 621-8190, (970) 726-8851.**

Vintage Hotel

Sleek newly refurnished five-story hotel with 121 modern rooms and suites, many with kitchenettes and fireplaces. Excellent facilities for a reasonable price. Daily housekeeping, 24-hour front desk, movie rentals. Hot tubs, sauna, game room, ski storage, restaurant, lounge, courtesy van. **P.O. Box 11369, Winter Park, CO 80482; (800) 472-7017, (970) 726-8801.**

Mid-Priced Accommodations

Alpen Rose

Outside looks Rockies rustic; inside a corner of Austria. European-style B&B with five bedrooms, all with private baths (one with jetted tub). Down puffs, handmade quilts and Austrian furnishings. Surrounded by aspen and pine trees, yet offering a view of the Continental Divide. Charming and reasonably priced. Non-smoking. Daily housekeeping, full breakfast, afternoon refreshments. Outdoor hot tub, sitting room with fireplace. **P.O. Box 769, Winter Park, CO 80482; (970) 726-5039.**

Arapahoe Ski Lodge

Old-fashioned ski lodge in the heart of Winter Park. Family owned and operated. Fourteen rooms with two double or twin beds and private baths. Cozy and functional. Packages include Modified American Plan (breakfast and dinner) and ski packages. Continental breakfast always included. Lounge, recreation room with fireplace, heated indoor pool, hot tub. **P.O. Box 44, Winter Park, CO 80482; (800) SKI-0094, (970) 726-8222.**

Byers Peak Bed & Breakfast

Six-room Alpine-style B&B in Fraser, within walking distance of shops and restaurants (Winter Park's downtown amenities are 2 miles away) and shuttle ride to the slopes. Simple and classical European-style furnishings. All rooms with king- or queen-size beds, private bath and phone. No smoking and no children under 10. Ski storage, restaurant adjacent. **5 County Rd. 72, Fraser, CO 80442; (970) 726-8256.**

Gasthäus Eichler

Simply furnished but extremely comfortable chalet-style inn atop one of Winter Park's best restaurants. Fifteen rooms with down comforters, whirlpool bathtubs, hair dryers and phones. Meal plan includes daily breakfast and dinner in lodge's outstanding German-American restaurant. Daily housekeeping, complimentary van service at peak times. Restaurant, lounge, ski shop. **78786 Hwy 40, Winter Park, CO 80482; (970) 726-5133.**

Raintree Inn

Fifty-eight-room mountain-view hotel. Well-appointed and contemporary. Non-smoking rooms available. Daily housekeeping, 24-hour front desk, continental breakfast included, movie rentals. Indoor pool, two hot tubs, two saunas, ski shop, restaurant, lounge. **P.O. Box 299, Winter Park, CO 80482; (800) 726-3340, (970) 726-4211, (303) 642-0550** (Denver direct).

Super 8 Motel

New 60-room motel in the center of Winter Park. All rooms with queen beds, and some rooms are non-smoking. Children 12 and under stay free in parents' room. Daily housekeeping, 24-hour front desk, free local phone calls, complimentary continental breakfast. **P.O. Box 35, Winter Park, CO 80482; (970) 726-8088. (800) 800-8000** for Super 8 reservations.

Woodspur Lodge

Great views from spectacular setting against the Arapaho National Forest. Spacious common area. Four miles from ski area. Daily housekeeping, all-you-can-eat meals. Sauna, hot tub, game room, bar. **P.O. Box 249, Winter Park, CO 80482; (970) 726-8417.**

Economy Accommodations

Beaver Village Lodge

Friendly 55-room lodge with motel-type rooms (no TV). Daily housekeeping, 24-hour front desk. Indoor pool, two hot tubs, restaurant, lounge. **P.O. Box 21, Winter Park, CO 80482; (800) 666-0281, (970) 726-5741.**

Candlelight Mountain Inn

A true anomaly: a B&B inn that courts families. Comfortable rooms with private or shared baths. Kitchenette available. Located between Winter Park and SilverCreek and close to Snow Mountain Ranch. Quiet location, well off the highway.

Photo by Byron Hetzler/Winter Park Resort

The award-winning Lodge at Sunspot at the top of Winter Park mountain offers two dining options: The Provisioner, a food marketplace, and the Dining Room, for fine lunches or special dinners.

Family rates. Non-smoking inn. Full breakfast. Outdoor hot tub, game and toy rooms. **P.O. Box 600, Winter Park, CO 80482; (800) KIM-4-TIM, (970) 887-2877.**

Englemann Pines

Melding of antique and contemporary styles into one cozy entity. Rooms named after Swiss ski villages. One room has private fireplace and Jacuzzi, while others share baths. TV room with fireplace. B&B plan, and guests have kitchen privileges. Daily housekeeping, breakfast. **P.O. Box 1305, Winter Park, CO 80482; (970) 726-4632.**

Olympia Motor Lodge

AAA-rated comfortable motel in the center of town with 15 units, some with kitchenettes. Queen-size beds. **P.O. Box 204, Winter Park, CO 80482; (800) 548-1992, (970) 726-8843.**

Snow Mountain Ranch

Run by the YMCA of the Rockies. Huge retreat on 4,950 acres. Affordable accommodations and exceptionally family- and group-appropriate in the new 79-room Indian Peaks Lodge (rooms sleep up to six and have private bathrooms and balconies), four older 47-room lodges (rooms sleep up to four or five people) and 45 two- to seven-bedroom cabins and RV spaces. Ideal for cross-country skiers; 14 miles from Winter Park Ski Area. Daily housekeeping, 24-hour front desk, morning and afternoon ski shuttle, day care. Olympic-size indoor pool, whirlpool, indoor roller rink, Nordic center with instruction and equipment rental, volleyball and basketball courts, gym, restaurant, ski rental shop, horseback riding. **P.O. Box 169, Winter Park, CO 80482; (970) 887-2152.**

Sundowner Motel

Central location on US Hwy 40 in downtown Winter Park. Spacious and functional rooms with enough comfort features to merit Three Diamonds from AAA. Easy walk to town. Daily housekeeping, courtesy coffee. Outdoor hot tub, TV with HBO. **P.O. Box 221, Winter Park, CO 80482; (970) 726-9451.**

Viking Ski Lodge

Mostly economy to mid-range guest rooms, plus deluxe suite and mini-suite. Two miles from ski area and walking distance to downtown restaurants and shops. Daily housekeeping, continental breakfast, complimentary coffee. Game room, whirlpool, sauna, ski shop, fireplace lobby. **78956 US Hwy 40 & Vasquez Rd., Winter Park, CO 80482; (970) 726-8885.**

Condominiums and Homes

Beaver Village Condominiums

Twenty buildings with 10 to 20 condominiums in each, all with full kitchen and fireplace. Linen exchange at front desk, 24-hour front desk. Recreation center with indoor pool and three hot tubs, guest laundry, complimentary transportation to and from Amtrak station. Located on the edge of town, $1^{1}/_{2}$ miles from the ski area. **P.O. Box 349, Winter Park, CO 80482; (800) 824-8438, (970) 726-8813.**

Bed & Breakfasts of Winter Park

Offers personal home-stay-type experiences in distinctive and personal lodgings along The Lift's routes. Prices and facilities vary but may include fireplaces, hot tub, complimentary refreshments, use of kitchen and other details. Prices also vary

from very reasonable to upper end. **P.O. Box 3434, Winter Park, CO 80482; (970) 726-5360, (970) 726-5039.**

Braidwood Condominiums

Small property with 12 especially well-appointed units, each with full kitchen, microwave, balcony and whirlpool bathtub. Private, yet just a block off US Hwy 40 near town. Linen and towel change on request. Use of Hi Country Haus facilities. **P.O. Box 3095, Winter Park, CO 80482; (970) 726-9421.**

Silverado II Resort & Conference Center

Fine facilities with an attractive price tag. Self-contained resort with 72 one- and two-bedroom suites, individually decorated. Housekeeping every second day; manager on duty 24 hours a day. Ski area shuttle, indoor pool, two hot tubs, two saunas, restaurant, lounge. **490 Kings Crossing Rd., Winter Park, CO 80482; (800) 777-1700, (800) 654-7157, (970) 726-5753.**

Snowblaze Athletic Club & Condominiums

Functional and attractive one- to three-bedroom condos a block from downtown and $1^{1}/_{2}$ miles from ski area. Private sauna, kitchen and fireplace in each multibedroom unit. Also, hotel-style studios. Fine athletic club with weight room, indoor pool, saunas, hot tubs, racquetball. Daily housekeeping, complimentary ski shuttle. **P.O. Box 66, Winter Park, CO 80482; (970) 726-5701.**

Hundreds of condominium units are scattered around Winter Park and beyond to Fraser. Among the management companies are

Alpine Peaks, (970) 726-8822
Condominium Management Co., (800) 228-1025, (970) 726-9421
Continental Property Management Co., (800) 824-8449, (970) 726-5585
Destinations West, (970) 726-8881
Summit at Winter Park, (800) 443-2781, (970) 726-8834
Wirsing & Co., (800) 626-6562

DINING OUT

Byers Peak Restaurant
Historic stage stop, now good restaurant. Popular favorites from many cuisines, including nachos, fettuccine, Veal Parmigiana, Wiener Schnitzel, Breast of Chicken Hawaiian Style. Also, many cuts of steak. Salad bar. Children's menu. **US Hwy 40, Fraser; (970) 726-8256.**

Carvers Bakery & Cafe
Quaint and informal restaurant located in old log structure, tucked in behind far newer Cooper Creek Square of downtown Winter Park. Home-baked pastries and excellent breads. Espresso bar. Breakfast, lunch and dinner, from light to hearty. Equally appealing to those seeking low-fat dishes as those desiring decadent desserts. Generous salads, good sandwiches, interesting entrées. Beer and wine. Takeout available. **93 Cooper Creek Way, Winter Park, (970) 726-8202.**

Crooked Creek Saloon
Locals' favorite spot for inexpensive Mexican, stir-fries, bar food, steaks, burgers and salads. Calendar of Specials means a different entrée every day of the month. Small kids' menu. Cocktails and entertainment too. **US Hwy 40, Fraser; (970) 726-9250.**

Dashing Through the Snow
Three-mile sleighride to rustic backcountry cowboy cabin. Excellent food. Entrée choices are baron of beef and chicken Marco Polo, with all the trimmings. BYO wine or beer. Entertainment. Old-fashioned, fun atmosphere. Also, three bonfire rides each day. Reservations required by noon on day of ride. **(970) 726-5376.**

Deno's Mountain Bistro
Longtime downtown Winter Park favorite. Large menu with something for everyone, from continental cuisine to favorite American steaks and sandwiches, seafood and bistro specials, to pasta and munchies. Combinations for the indecisive. Pizza and calzone (eat in or take out) also popular. Nightly pasta, beef and poultry specials. Award-winning wine selection and 75 beers. Lunch, dinner, and late-night dining. Reservations accepted. **78911 US Hwy 40, Winter Park; (970) 726-5332.**

Dinner at the Barn
Horsedrawn sleighride through the woods to historic homestead barn for gourmet dinner and live country entertainment. Dinner features Boneless Stuffed Chicken Breasts with Sage Dressing, well garnished. Vegetarian option. Dessert and hot cider, coffee, tea or chocolate included. BYO wine or beer. Local transportation included. Advanced reservations required. **(970) 726-4923.**

Fontenot's Cajun Cafe
Casual Cajun place north of town, best for piquant Louisiana seafood. Best known for Cajun and Creole specialties, but also interesting pasta dishes and daily specials. Affordable wines by the glass or bottle. Non-smoking restaurant. Family-friendly. Reservations accepted. Takeout available. **Park Plaza Shopping Center, US Hwy 40, Winter Park; (970) 726-4021.**

Gasthäus Eichler
Atmospheric and elegant award winner in the Gasthäus Eichler. Specializes in classic Austrian and German cuisine, including veal, roasted duck and other game and Chateaubriand for two. Some entrées available in children's and seniors' portions. Exquisite desserts. Fireside cocktail lounge. Reservations recommended. **78786 US Hwy 40, north of downtown Winter Park; (970) 726-5133.**

Hernando's Pizza Pub
Unique pizzas, generously portioned Italian sandwiches, pasta—all at moderate prices. Full bar. North of town. **78199 US Hwy 40, Winter Park; (970) 726-5409.**

The Last Waltz
Specializes in Tex-Mex, some sandwiches, popular soup-and-salad combos at lunch. Similar dishes plus appetizers and popular homestyle entrées at dinner. Very modest prices. North of town. Consistently ranked as locals' favorite by Winter Park's weekly newspaper. Cocktails. **Kings Crossing Shopping Center, 78336 US Hwy 40, Winter Park; (970) 726-4877.**

Photo by Byron Hetzler/Winter Park Resort

At Winter Park, kids five and under ski free. The resort boasts plenty of groomed trails, a variety of fun nonski activities for the family and lots of affordable lodging in the area.

96

The Lodge at Sunspot

Gorgeous mountaintop lodge serving memorable dinners as well as traditional lunches. Gondola cabins attach to Zephyr Express chairlift for fast, comfortable ride to the mountaintop—nicknamed the "Sunsport Starride." Elegant four-course dinners served Thursday, Friday and Saturday evenings. Specialties include fresh fish, buffalo prime rib, filet mignon and specialty chicken dishes. Appetizer, soup, salad and choice of entrée included in dinner; outstanding desserts à la carte. Pricey but worthwhile. Also, fireplace lounge adjacent to dining room. Reservations recommended. **Winter Park Ski Area; (970) 726-5514.**

Rails Restaurant

Contemporary continental and American specialties in a sleek restaurant. Unusual adaptations include blackened ribeye and filet mignon stuffed with crabmeat and blue cheese. Light fare at the bar. Homestyle breakfast. **Iron Horse Resort, Winter Park; (970) 726-8851.**

Ranch House at Devil's Thumb

Elegant gourmet meals in a gentrified rustic setting, a 1937 homestead with splendid views.

Warm and cozy atmosphere and fine views. Breakfast, lunch and dinner. Dinner reservations accepted. Also, dinner sleighrides with stop for hot cider or hot chocolate over a campfire and gourmet dinners at the restaurant. Live music. Children's rates. **Devil's Thumb Ranch, Fraser; (970) 726-5632, 726-5633.**

The Slope

Dining for all tastes and budgets. Expectations is a fine dining room in a setting that is surprisingly intimate for a place with a reputation for rowdy action. Pizza, burgers, munchies and more served in the Mary Jane Club. **Old Town Winter Park; (970) 726-5727.**

La Taqueria

Good Mexican food, reasonably priced and generously portioned. Best green chili in the valley. Burritos featured. Quesadilla Grande for big appetites. Salsa bar. Children's menu. Combination plates available. Children's menu. Great margaritas, premium beers and varietal wines. **Cinema Plaza, Winter Park; (970) 726-0280.**

Winston's

Hotel restaurant in The Vintage serving breakfast and dinner. Warm atmosphere. Mostly American cuisine, with steak and seafood featured, but with influences from other culinary traditions, including ever-popular pasta creations. Relaxed restaurant. Gorgeous 19th-century bar. Dinner reservations accepted (door-to-door van service available). **The Vintage, Winter Park; (970) 726-8801.**

NIGHTLIFE

Après-ski gets an early start at the Derailer Bar in West Portal Station (live music most nights) and the Sports Bar and Club Car at the Mary Jane Center (live music on weekends). Several spots rollick into the night. The Slope in Old Town Winter Park, not far from the ski area, boasts hot bands, a D.J., a big dance floor, light food, cold drinks and an arcade. Deno's is popular with après-skiers who like to watch sports on 10 (count 'em, 10) big-screen TVs. Quieter spots include The Shed, The Ranch House Saloon and the Divide Grill. The Hideaway is a perennial favorite for après-ski, late-night celebrations, dinner or some combination. It's worth the drive to Fraser to mingle at the Crooked Creek Saloon (dance floor, live music some nights, pool every night). Live music is also featured occasionally (generally weekends and on some other nights) at Adolph's, Byers Peak, Deno's, the Last Waltz and the Old Town Cookhouse. And, of course, as every Colorado resort must now have a good brew pub, you'll find good microbrews and American-style pub fare at the new Winter Park Pub.

Families and the perpetually energetic like Fraser's tubing hill, with two lighted sliding slopes, tows and inner tubes for rent or Snow Mountain Ranch between Winter Park and Granby for night cross-country skiing, swimming, basketball or volleyball. Both are extremely reasonably priced. A little costlier but no less fun are Sno-Scoot rentals from Mountain Madness; these snappy little vehicles can be driven around two tracks by youngsters not yet old enough to operate snowmobiles. You can lose (or spend) more at the low-stakes casinos of Central City and Blackhawk, approximately a one-hour ride. If you don't want to negotiate Berthoud Pass at night or hassle with parking, **Home James** runs charter vans, **(970) 726-5060.**

For more information, contact **Winter Park Resort, P.O. Box 36, Winter Park, CO 80482, (970) 726-5514; Winter Park/Fraser Valley Chamber of Commerce, P.O. Box 3236, Winter Park, CO 80482; (970) 726-4118.**

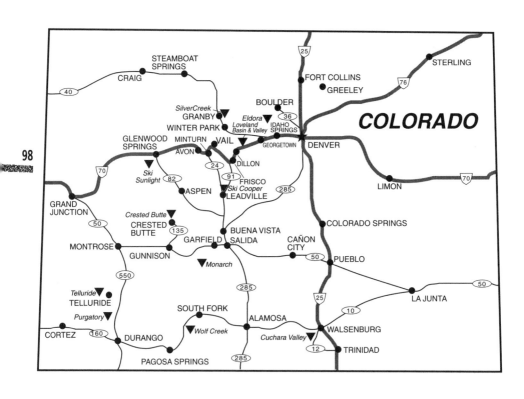

STEAMBOAT SPRINGS
STERLING
CRAIG
FORT COLLINS
GREELEY
40
76
BOULDER
SilverCreek
GRANBY
Eldora
Loveland Basin & Valley
36
COLORADO
WINTER PARK
IDAHO SPRINGS
GLENWOOD SPRINGS
MINTURN
VAIL
AVON
Georgetown
DENVER
70
Ski Sunlight
82
DILLON
24
91
FRISCO
70
ASPEN
Ski Cooper
LEADVILLE
285
LIMON
GRAND JUNCTION
Crested Butte
COLORADO SPRINGS
50
CRESTED BUTTE
135
BUENA VISTA
CAÑON CITY
MONTROSE
GARFIELD
SALIDA
GUNNISON
Monarch
50
PUEBLO
550
285
50
Telluride
25
LA JUNTA
TELLURIDE
SOUTH FORK
ALAMOSA
10
Purgatory
285
CORTEZ
160
Wolf Creek
Cuchara Valley
WALSENBURG
DURANGO
12
TRINIDAD
PAGOSA SPRINGS
285

Colorado Classics

Photo by Claire Walter

99

SILVER CREEK

THE LAY OF THE LAND

Silver Creek is set on a broad west-facing hillside in a portion of the Colorado Rockies that is both gentler and still more rural than most of the state's resort areas. Home construction is mushrooming on the open hillsides that flank the access road, but deer and elk still do roam the property, and it is anyone's guess when density and traffic will chase them elsewhere. The ski area is at the high point of the access road and consists of two small peaks with lifts rising from a common base area.

BACKDROP

Silver Creek is the winsome midget of Colorado ski resorts. Small, self-contained, it occupies a special niche in a state dominated by giants. It is best for budget-watching families who want congenial skiing, good instruction, sufficient diversion for nonski hours and a place where children can enjoy a measure of independence in a safe and comforting environment. The resort, an ambitious four-season development in Middle Park (one of the several wide valleys within the Colorado Rockies) now owned by a Brazilian family, has grappled for recognition against larger, better appointed competitors. In large measure, it has succeeded, carving a place for itself as a learn-to-ski center. New skiers and snowboarders find comfort in what in the large context of Rocky Mountain skiing is overwhelmingly undemanding terrain, and they are nurtured by a fine ski and snowboarding school that essentially does little but teach beginners and its guaranteed learn-to-ski (or ride) program. For the many people who first tackled snowy slopes there, Silver Creek will always shine as the place where they first stepped into ski or snowboard bindings.

Still, Silver Creek has real limitations. Restaurants and other services are, at this writing, exceptionally limited, but the resort has tried to offer value packages, create a family-oriented environment, offer complimentary shuttle service to Granby and host special events to compensate. These events, from skiing with Santa Claus on Christmas Eve to Girl Scout Cookie Sample Day—and most especially SilverBear Ski Weeks—are kid-pleasers that keep families coming back and recommending Silver Creek to friends who want to learn how to ski.

GETTING THERE

Silver Creek is 78 miles from Denver and 93 miles from Denver International Airport via I-70 and US 40. **Home James** offers van service from Denver International Airport. Reservations are recommended, **(800) 451-4844, (970) 726-5060.** The **Amtrak** train via the California Zephyr between Chicago and San Francisco stops daily in Granby, 2 miles away, **(800) USA-RAIL.**

A complimentary ski shuttle runs during the day between lodgings and the base area; a less frequent courtesy shuttle operates to Granby in the evening. Silver Creek is also 15 miles north of Winter Park, enabling vacationers to ski a bigger mountain for a day or two and tap into the dining and nightlife of a larger resort area.

PROFILE

The skiing cascades, mainly with gentleness, down East and West Mountains, two adjacent hills with common base facilities and the separate Milestone beginner knoll in between and the teeniest beginner slope, served by a slow moving carpet called the Bear Bahn, off to one side right next to the Sterling Base Lodge. Milestone has two ultragentle slopes and a slow double chair

staffed by lift operators as reassuring as Mr. Rogers. Silver Creek's One-Day Guaranteed Start to Ski program assures that you will be able to ride the Milestone lift and ski down in just one day.

East Mountain is the lower and gentler of the two peaklets that comprise the bulk of Silver Creek. Served by a triple chair, it offers confidence-building novice and intermediate runs of considerable length. Buckhorn, a $1^1/_4$-mile ribbon of snow-covered reassurance is arguably the area's single most popular run. That run conquered, newly minted novices can easily work their way to East Mountain's slightly steeper runs—Easy Money down the fall line and the slightly winding Drifter and Gettles.

West Mountain, served by another triple, is a bit higher and more challenging. Dragon Lady and Speculator would merit blue squares at most ski areas but are blue-black at Silver Creek, while Head Hunter and Sleuth are steeper still and occasionally sprout mogul fields. Widowmaker is permitted to bigger build bumps. Jackpot, a blue square even by Silver Creek standards, is the newest trail on West Mountain—a response to guests' request for an easy route down the more challenging side of the area.

SNOWBOARDING

Silver Creek puts snowboarding right on a par with skiing—another smart move for a resort that caters to families. Rental boards are equipped with easy-to-operate K2 Clicker bindings. This easy-cruising area, with many wide runs, continues to appeal as riders get better. There is also an earth-bermed halfpipe in Lone Pine Bowl on the lower port of West Mountain.

SKI SCHOOL PROGRAMS

Introductory Programs

One-Day Guaranteed Start to Ski: Ski Milestone after one or two days or money refunded. One-day package is for lifts, lessons and rental equipment for new skiers ages 13 and older.

Inside Silver Creek

Over the Hill Gang International Learn to Ski Program: Designed for mature beginner (age 50 and over) and taught by instructors of that age. Package includes lift ticket, $3^3/_4$-hour lesson and rental equipment. Available Wednesdays and Saturdays.

Women Only: Beginner program to encourage women to learn by eliminating pressure to compete with men. Women instructors. One- and two-day options.

For Families

Nonskiing Children

Silver Creek Nursery & Child Care: Nursery for children ages 6 months to 7 years. Hourly, half-day and full-day (including lunch). Discounts for additional children in family. Reservations recommended, **(800) 448-9458.**

Skiing Children

Cinnamon Bears: For children ages 3 to 5, lift ticket, lessons, rental equipment, supervision and lunch on full-day program; all but lunch on half-day.

SilverBears: Lift ticket, lessons, rental equipment and lunch on full-day program; all but lunch on half-day. Divided into SilverBear Cubs (ages 6 and 7) and SilverBears (ages 8 to 12).

Kids' Snowboarding: Daily for ages 6 to 12. Full-day program including equipment, lesson, beginner lift ticket and lunch.

FOR RACERS

NASTAR: Offered Saturday and Sunday on East Mountain course.

NORDIC SKIING

Silver Creek's exceptionally scenic 25-mile Nordic trail system adjoins the Alpine area, and a trail pass includes two lift rides since its access is from the top of the Milestone chairlift. It contains a variety of loops and cut-offs and has groomed trails varying from very easy to rather difficult. Instruction and rental equipment are also available. Through a cooperative effort with Snow Mountain Ranch/YMCA of the Rockies, skiers can use 140 kilometers of Nordic routes on two adjacent areas. Some of the trails are lightly groomed, while others are trackset. Shadow Mountain Ranch marks but does not groom cross-country trails on its 1,000-acre spread. For

---

Mountain Stats—
Silver Creek

Resort elevation 8,202 feet
Top of highest lift 9,202 feet
Bottom of lowest lift 8,202 feet
Total vertical 1,000 feet
Longest run 1 1/2 miles
Average annual snowfall 180 inches
Ski season Thanksgiving day to mid-April
Lifts 2 triple chairlifts, 1 double, 1 platterpull, 1 moving carpet for beginners
Capacity 5,400 skiers per hour
Terrain 251 acres, 33 trails (30% beginner and novice, 50% intermediate, 20% advanced and expert)
Snowmaking 50% of terrain
Night skiing on 1 slope, for children only
Snow reports (800) 618-snow, (970) 448-9458

---

more information on other regional ski-touring options, see "Winter Park" chapter in this book.

WHERE TO STAY

In addition to lodging at Silver Creek Resort, skiers stay in Granby, down in the valley. Shuttle service to the slopes makes this a viable, hassle-free option. **Silver Creek Ski Resort, (800) SKI-SILV, (800) 618-SNOW, (970) 887-3384.**

Luxury Accommodations

C Lazy U Ranch

See Winter Park, "Where to Stay" listing; ranch also runs free shuttle to Silver Creek.

Mid-Priced Accommodations

The Inn at Silver Creek

Large 342-room resort hotel 2 miles from the lifts. Accommodations in hotel rooms, studios, larger suites, some with kitchens and/or fireplaces. On shuttle route. Children 12 and younger stay free in parents' room. Housekeeping, 24-hour front desk, complimentary shuttle to Silver Creek. and Winter Park. Heated pool, hot tub, weight and exercise rooms, sauna, tanning salons, two racquetball courts, restaurants, lounges, game room, guest laundry, shops. **P.O. Box 4222, Granby, CO 80446; (800) 926-4386, (970) 887-2131.**

Economy Accommodations

Blue Spruce Motel
Fourteen-unit motel. Some kitchenette units. Four miles from resort; walking distance to local restaurants. No in-room phones. Daily housekeeping. **P.O. Box 285, Granby, CO 80446; (970) 887-3300.**

El Monte Motor Inn
Three buildings with three kinds of rooms, 52 in all. Cozy lodge rooms with handmade furniture, plus family studios and larger "deluxe" rooms. Economy to mid-price range. Pets permitted. Daily housekeeping, restaurant, lounge, hot tub. **P.O. Box 105, Granby, CO 80446; (800) 282-3348, (970) 887-3348.**

Little Tree Inn
Well-appointed 48-room motel; some kitchenette units. Three miles from ski area. Children 12 and under stay free in parents' room. Daily housekeeping, hot tub, guest laundry. **P.O. Box 800, Granby, CO 80446; (800) 446-1663, (970) 887-2551.**

Shadow Mountain Ranch
Seven rustic cabins with kitchenettes, plus two-room fireplace lodge where hot beverages are always available. Now operating on a B&B plan. Fifteen minutes to Silver Creek. Groomed but not trackset cross-country trails on site. **P.O. Box 963, Granby, CO 80446; (970) 887-9524.**

Snow Mountain Ranch/YMCA of the Rockies
See Winter Park, "Where to Stay" listing; ranch also runs free shuttle to Silver Creek.

Condominiums

Lakeview Condominiums
Sixteen two- and three-bedroom condos with fireplaces and great views. Guests can use recreational facilities at Inn at Silver Creek. Location is at the resort, on the shuttle route. Limited housekeeping, pool, hot tub. **P.O. Box 4031, Silver Creek, CO 80446; (970) 887-2461, (970) 465-0069.**

Mountainside at Silver Creek
Resort's most convenient ski-in/ski-out condominiums with 120 one- to three-bedroom units, many with gas fireplaces, lofts and private hot tubs. Children ages 17 and younger stay free with parents. Located on shuttle route. Housekeeping. **P.O. Box 4104, Silver Creek, CO 80446; (800) 223-7677, (970) 887-2571.**

Soda Springs Ranch
Luxury condo complex with 120 one-, two- and three-bedroom condominiums, some with kitchen, whirlpool and/or washer and dryer. Restaurant gets raves for charm and food. In scenic countryside, 11 miles from Silver Creek. Housekeeping. Health club, restaurant. **9921 US Hwy 34, #20, Grand Lake, CO 80447; (970) 627-8125.**

Noteworthy

The ski terrain is extremely compact and funnels into one main base area, making it ideal for youngsters to go off on their own when not in a class or with their parents. Three ski parks located off East Mountain's Buckhorn Trail provide a fun learning environment for youngsters 14 and younger, and parents may enter only with their children. There's now also kids only night skiing.

Silver Creek's Family Skiing Passport is a special bargain lift ticket for a family of four (including two children ages 6 to 12; children ages 5 and younger ski free anytime). SilverBear Ski Weeks are family ski weeks in January, featuring free skiing for children to age 12 when accompanying at least one skiing adult on two- to five-day lift ticket, plus teddy bear or other stuffed animal. Special events include Smokey Bear visit, magic show, lollipop ski race, teddy bear parade, Ben & Jerry's ice cream party, Red Baron pizza party and movie night. Reservations are required, **(800) 448-9458.**

The Summit at Silver Creek
Well-appointed complex with 72 one- to three-bedroom units, many with fireplaces, lofts and/or private whirlpool tubs. Ski in from East Mountain but shuttle to base of lifts. Housekeeping, indoor

pool, outdoor hot tub. **P.O. Box 650, Granby, CO 80446; (800) 827-9226, (970) 887-2561.**

DINING OUT

Bertie's
Antique-filled old-timey family restaurant. Cozy and comfortable. Breakfast all day long. Lots of homemade country food—soups, chili, chicken fries, tortillas, pies. Granby's oldest restaurant under same management. **52 Fourth St., Granby; (970) 887-3632.**

Caroline's Cuisine
Highly praised restaurant serving French and other Continental specialties. Cozy lounge. Good wine list. Piano and live jazz on weekends. Reservations accepted. **9921 US Hwy 34, Granby; (970) 627-9404.**

The Deli
104 Casual stop for sandwiches, soups, salads, sweets. **Inn at Silver Creek, Silver Creek; (970) 887-2131.**

El Monte Motor Inn Ranch Kitchen
Western-style family restaurant. Big breakfasts, served all day long. Also lunch and dinner. Made-from-scratch baked goods. Entrées include pork chops, steaks, trout, seafood, chicken and all kinds of Mexican specialties. Full bar. **519 W. Agate Ave., Granby; (970) 887-3348.**

The Longbranch
Family-run western-style restaurant with huge menu selection from various cuisines. Internationally trained owner-chef. Number-one specialties are German dishes. Also pasta, Mexican food and American favorites such as steaks, sandwiches, seafood. Children's menu. Moderate prices. Reservations accepted. Also small two-room B&B. **185 E. Agate Ave., Granby; (970) 887-2209.**

Mel's Diner
Old-fashioned, family-run cafe. No relation to the TV show—there's really a Mel who owns the place. Huge burgers and great burritos, plus dinner entrées such as pork chops, roast beef, ham, chicken, steaks. Homemade pies and soups.

Photo courtesy Silver Creek Resort

Kids receive the red carpet treatment at Silver Creek.

Daily specials. Very reasonable prices. **551 E. Agate Ave., Granby; (970) 887-3364.**

NIGHTLIFE

Entertainment is largely of the make-your-own-fun variety. The only place currently to go for entertainment is the Black Bear Tavern at the Inn at Silver Creek. This is a mellow, intimate bar with a fireplace and easy-listening music.

The resort's latest diversion is snowbiking, which is especially appealing to those who find skiing, let alone snowboarding, to be intimidating—or just want an evening change of pace. The bicyclelike device has regular handlebars but runners instead of wheels, and riders also wear mini-skis on their feet. It is safe, stable and lots of fun. Snowbiking is available nightly from 5:00 to 9:00 P.M.

The Silver Spur is Granby's liveliest nightspot with music and dancing, and some people like to spend an evening in the board-sidewalk-town of Grand Lake, the western gateway to Rocky Mountain National Park and a noteworthy snowmobile center.

For more information, contact **Silver Creek Resort, P.O. Box 1110, Silver Creek, CO 80446; (800) 448-9458, (970) 887-3384, (303) 629-1020** (Denver).

ELDORA MOUNTAIN RESORT

BACKDROP

This midsize Front Range ski area has an ambitious name—and one that's a bit misleading. By Colorado's lofty standards, its statistics are more "hill" than "mountain"—though portions of its most challenging terrain has a high-mountain flavor and the high peaks of the Continental Divide are visible from the backside—and there is no "resort" component to the ski area as it is understood in terms of accommodations, dining and other such amenities. Nevertheless, Eldora offers quality skiing at a very modest price little more than an hour from Denver and just over half an hour from the sporty and lively college town of Boulder, which has all of those services in abundance. Boulder is the home of the University of Colorado, and Eldora is where its elite NCAA ski teams train and intramural recreational squads race. Because Boulder is at an elevation of roughly 5,500 feet, skiing at Eldora, some 4,000 feet higher, and staying in town is a fine compromise for folks who find it uncomfortable to spend 24 hours a day at the altitude of most of Colorado's ski areas. Denver is a doable commute (especially for a business traveler squeezing in a little Colorado skiing), but makes less sense than staying, dining and partying in Boulder.

Eldora remains a modest, mostly local ski area popular with Front Range families and thrifty, energetic students. In fact, in 1995–96, when Aspen made headlines by raising its top, peak-season one-day lift ticket price to $52, Eldora made news by actually lowering its ticket price by $2. Reachable by low-cost public bus directly from downtown Boulder, Eldora is especially suitable for older children, pre-driver's li-

Inside Eldora Mountain Resort

cense teens and skiers wishing to spend some time on the slopes during a business trip to Boulder. The area's proximity to Colorado's big population centers has always made it popular with families, and its new children's center and children's programs are as good and comprehensive (especially on weekends and school vacations) as a small area can be expected to provide. The entire base area has been upgraded and made more efficient. Improved and expanded snowmaking is really the difference between marginal skiing and rather good skiing, especially at Eldora, where the nearby Continental Divide creates such unpredictable weather that snow might fall generously or not at all. Lean years or not, it is worth noting that the 24-hour world snowfall record—76 inches—was set at Silver Lake below nearby Albion Peak.

¹⁰⁶ THE LAY OF THE LAND

The nearest town is Nederland, and the nearest city is Boulder, 21 miles away. To skiers spoiled by big-resort, major-highway accessibility, the route to Eldora seems to be all access road—first a relatively generous two-lane state highway, then a far narrower two-lane mountain road to the base area. A free area shuttle connects the base lodge, Little Hawk beginner area and the touring center, but the closest accommodations and dining are several miles away.

GETTING THERE

Eldora Mountain Resort is 21 miles from Boulder, via Route 119 (Boulder Canyon), then south to County Rd. 130 to County Rd. 140. From Denver, take I-25 north to US 36 west, then proceed as above. The ski area is also reachable via **RTD** bus direct from the downtown Boulder bus station (14th and Walnut Streets), **(303) 442-0100.**

PROFILE

As you pull into the Eldora parking lot, you will see three lifts on a small hill to the left, two parallel chairlifts—a triple and a double—straight ahead that rise far higher and a rambling base complex on the right. The left-hand lifts serve a variety of short runs, from the beginner smoothie called Little Hawk to the bumped-up expert shot of Upper Chute or the slalom steepness of the Corkscrew racing trail. If you don't mind a lot of Midwest-style yo-yoing, you can manage a good amount of vertical in a few hours. Challenge and Cannonball, Eldora's twin main chairlifts, serve some dozen main-mountain blue-square and black-diamond trails. These old-style classics etched through the woods for interest give the frontside a more complex feel than the modest vertical would suggest. Psychopath, Challenge and Liftline grow impressive moguls before being cut back to cruising smoothness. Windmill is a good start to black diamonds, because the blue on top steepens to blackness over the lower portion. Jolly Jug, Powderhorn and Sunset are legitimately intermediate, while Jolly Jug Glades, which isn't at all treacherous, is a blue-square glade run that is lots of fun.

The remaining glades comprise much of the Corona Bowl area on the mountain's backside. This terrain, which is served by the country's only natural gas-powered chairlift, was closed for several years, but sophisticated snowmaking, grooming and aggressive revegetation have made Corona's four wide, steep and handsome trails and the double-diamond glades beside them skiable through the season. This part of the mountain is truly steep, with the kind of interesting terrain variations and pitch that you won't usually find at a local area. When the trail named Corona beside the lift named Corona in the mountain sector called Corona Bowl is groomed, it is a beguiling cruising run, but bumps, steeps and awesome trees are what you'll mostly find on the backside of Eldora. As a bonus, views of the Continental Divide from The Lookout at the summit are worth the price of a lift ticket.

SNOWBOARDING

Eldora was one of the first areas in Colorado to welcome snowboarders with special facilities and programs, and it now not only courts riders but is making an unusual effort to integrate skiing and snowboarding. The area's new Alpine terrain park, called the Bone Yard, is open both to snowboarders and skiers and is more about attitude than separation. Snowboarders easily take to the park's log slides, table tops, spines, quarter-pipes and jumps, but hot and adventuresome skiers are invited to try them too. The park is located on the Dream and Scream trail.

SKI SCHOOL PROGRAMS

Introductory Program

Beginner's Special: Bargain lift-lesson-rental package for beginning skiers and snowboarders; same program without lifts for beginner cross-country skiers.

Advanced and Specialty Programs

Advanced Workshops: Intensive $1^1/_2$-hour workshops at advanced skill levels.
Women's Wednesdays: Six consecutive Wednesdays of Alpine or cross-country skiing and socializing.
Mom's Monday: See below, under "Skiing Children."
Carving Clinic: Fine-tuning snowboarding technique and talk.
Telemark Clinic: Three-hour clinics offered in conjunction with Front Range outdoor shops.

For Families

Nonskiing Children
The Eldorable Nursery: New 2,000-square-foot nursery with full- and half-day care for children ages 3 months to 6 years. Reservations recommended.

Skiing Children
Little Mac: Monday afternoon club, consisting of half-day lift ticket, lesson and rental equipment for children ages 4 to 6. Offered in conjunction

Mountain Stats—
Eldora Mountain Resort

Top of the highest lift 10,600 feet
Bottom of lowest lift 9,200 feet
Total vertical 1,400 feet
Longest run 2 miles
Average annual snowfall 120 inches
Ski season mid-November to mid-April
Lifts 1 triple chairlift, 5 doubles, 3 surface lifts
Capacity 7,500 skiers per hour
Terrain 43 runs on 386 acres (20% beginner and novice, 55% intermediate, 25% advanced and expert)
Snowmaking 370 acres
Mountain dining at the top of Corona Bowl
Snow reports (303) 440-8700

with Mom's Monday, a five-week series of women-only downhill or telemark classes, lifts and rentals.
Mountain Explorers: All-day lift tickets, two classes, rental skis or snowboard and lunch offered daily for ages 4 to 12.
Mini-Trekkers: Six- and 12-week version lesson and supervision program for children ages 4 to 6.
Ski Trek: Same basic format as Mini-Trekkers, but for school-age children and teens, ages 7 to 18, including an introduction to racing. Also, Nordic version for ages 5 to 12.
Saturday Shredders: Snowboarding classes for children ages 10 to 18.

FOR RACERS

Citizen Racing Workshops: Coaching and training drills for recreational and Masters racers.

NORDIC SKIING

The Eldora Nordic Center is the closest track system to Boulder and Denver. Headquartered in a sprightly log building, it offers cross-country ski instruction, a ski and rental shop and light lunch service. Forty kilometers of marked groomed trails in a scenic network. Half are trackset; half are left trackless for skaters. The ski school offers a full range of instruction for adults, children, skaters, classic racers and telemarkers, and the Nordic Center takes overnight reservations in the Tennessee Mountain Cabin on the eastern extreme of Eldora's trail system. There are also vast backcountry options in the nearby Roosevelt National Forest and the Indian Peaks Wilderness. Information is available from the **U.S. Forest Service, Boulder Ranger District Office, (303) 444-6600.**

WHERE TO STAY

Nederland and Mountain Area

Luxury Accommodations

Gold Lake Mountain Resort
Secluded mountain resort, with seventeen charming and cozy cottage accommodations, most with fireplaces. Rustic yet stylish and romantic—and still, families are welcome. Daily housekeeping. Restaurant, lounge, health club, hot tub, ice skating. **3371 Gold Lake Rd., Ward, CO 80481; (800) 450-3544, (303) 459-3544.**

Mid-Priced Accommodations

Goldminer Hotel
Homey B&B in historic mining town of Eldora. Five-room inn. Two rooms in log lodge, built in 1897, plus three cozy cabins with kitchens. Full breakfast, lounge with TV, hot tub. **601 Klondyke Ave., Eldora, CO 80466; (800) 422-4629, (303) 258-7770.**

Lodge at Nederland
Rustic log lodge in the center of Nederland, a short drive (or RTD bus ride) to the mountain and within walking distance of restaurants and entertainment. Daily housekeeping. Hot tub. Rooms have coffee makers, refrigerators and hair dryers. Suites also have fireplaces. **55 Lakeview Dr., Nederland, CO 80466; (800) 279-9463, (303) 258-9463.**

Peaceful Valley Lodge
Informal and comfortable family-owned resort combining Western and Tyrolean styles. Fifty-five lodge rooms plus 11 cabins, some with hot tubs, varying degrees of size and opulence, all with private baths and some with fireplaces or balconies. All meals served on-site; meal plans. Evening entertainment. Daily housekeeping, 24-hour front desk, meal service. Cross-country track, ski rentals, two dining rooms, indoor pool, hot tubs, lounge. **Star Route, Box 2811, Lyons, CO 80540; (303) 747-2881.**

Economy Accommodations

Nederhaus Motel
Closest motel accommodation to Eldora. Pleasantly furnished, unpretentious motel, plus family cabin for up to six and several suites. On Boulder RTD bus route. Ski packages available. Cafe open for breakfast and lunch. Daily housekeeping, 24-hour front desk, free shuttle to Eldora and Central City. **686 Hwy 119 South, Nederland, CO 80466; (800) 422-4629, (303) 258-3585.**

Sundance Lodge
Rustic 12-room lodge. Recently remodeled, simple rooms. Restaurant adjacent. **23942 Hwy 119, Nederland, CO 80466; (303) 258-3797.**

Boulder

Information (but not reservations) on further Boulder area lodging is available from the **Chamber of Commerce, (303) 442-1044.**

Luxury Accommodations

Boulder Victoria Historic Bed & Breakfast
Exquisitely restored and elegantly furnished B&B. Prime downtown setting, close to Boulder's best shops and restaurants, as well as to RTD station and Eldora bus. Rooms with steam showers and private balconies. Daily housekeeping, breakfast (in dining room or in bed), afternoon tea. **1305 Pine St., Boulder, CO 80302; (303) 938-1300.**

Hotel Boulderado
Landmark turn-of-the-century hotel in downtown Boulder with 160 traditionally and beautifully furnished guest rooms, many in a new wing. Regular stop for airport limousine and close to Boulder Bus Terminal. Soaring, leaded-glass-domed lobby with mezzanine bar (live entertainment) and congenial ambiance. Daily housekeeping, room service, 24-hour front desk, one-day laundry and valet service, bell service, hourly airport shuttle (fee service). Three restaurants, oyster bar, three lounges. **2115 Thirteenth St., Boulder, CO 80302; (800) 433-4344, (303) 442-4344.**

Magpie Inn
Exquisite B&B in a historic Mapleton Hill mansion. Five romantic fireplace rooms. Grace and charm, plus convenience to downtown Boulder. Daily housekeeping, full breakfast, afternoon refreshments. **1001 Spruce St., Boulder, CO 80302; (303) 449-6528.**

Regal Harvest House
Full-service hotel with urban and resort amenities. Recently refurbished in lodgelike style with 270 rooms and suites, many with mountain views. Children 17 and younger stay free in parents' room. Adjacent to Boulder Creek Path, a paved jogging, cycling and rollerblading route. Daily housekeeping, 24-hour front desk, room service, hourly airport shuttle (fee service). Restaurant, fireplace lobby, lounge, five indoor and 10 outdoor tennis courts, outdoor volleyball and basketball courts, two whirlpools, fitness facilities. **1345 28th St., Boulder, CO 80302; (800) 222-8888, (303) 443-3850.**

Mid-Priced Accommodations

Alps Boulder Canyon Inn
New country inn west of town along Boulder Canyon, en route to Eldora. Twelve antique-filled rooms with private baths and fireplaces; some with private balconies and oversize tubs. English country decor. Daily housekeeping, full breakfast, afternoon tea. **38619 Boulder Canyon, Boulder, CO 80302; (303) 444-5445.**

Best Western Golden Buff Lodge
Well-serviced, 112-room motor inn, distinguished by restaurant serving healthful, natural cuisine three meals a day. Daily housekeeping, 24-hour front desk. Health club, hot tub, sauna, in-room refrigerators. **1725 28th St., Boulder, CO 80302; (800) 999-BUFF, (303) 442-7450; (800) 528-1234** for Best Western reservations.

Boulder Mountain Lodge
Family-owned lodge in quiet country location, yet close to Boulder, en route to Eldora. Suites with full kitchens. Video games available. Family-friendly. Daily housekeeping, hot tubs, TV lounge. **91 Four Mile Canyon Dr., Boulder, CO 80302; (800) 458-0882, (303) 444-0882.**

Briar Rose
Atmospheric B&B inn, with something of an English country house ambiance. Nine charming rooms in main house and cottage furnished with period antiques; all with private baths. Non-smoking inn. Guests receive local health-club pass. Close to Boulder Creek Path. Daily housekeeping, full breakfast, afternoon and evening tea. **2151 Arapahoe Ave., Boulder, CO 80302; (303) 442-3007.**

Broker Inn
Full-service hotel close to university. Rooms have Victorian touches, brass beds and recliners. Broker Restaurant, known for all-you-can-eat shrimp bowl for starters. Club with D.J., dancing and top singles' action. Daily housekeeping, 24-hour front desk, room service, bell staff, hourly airport shuttle (fee service). **30th and Baseline Rd., Boulder, CO 80303; (800) 358-5407, (303) 444-3330.**

Economy Accommodations

Above Boulder Lodge
Rustic and comfortable country lodge. Casual family atmosphere and economy rates. Kennel, babysitting available, extensive video library, accepts collect calls for reservations. Lounge with big-screen TV, hot tub. **Sugarloaf Mountain, Boulder, CO 80306; (303) 258-7777.**

Foot of the Mountain Motel
Simple economy motel, close to city and Boulder Canyon. Family-owned. In-room refrigerators. Daily housekeeping, complimentary coffee. **200 Arapahoe Ave., Boulder, CO 80302; (303) 442-5688.**

DINING OUT

Nederland

Aki Sundance
Small, rustic restaurant. Great views. Outstanding breakfasts, including unique versions of eggs Benedict and other standards. A little of everything but mostly American food at lunch and dinner with steaks and vegetarian dishes featured. South of Eldora turnoff on Peak to Peak Hwy. **23942 Hwy 119, Nederland; (303) 258-3797.**

Assay Office
Quirky saloon featuring steaks, chicken and Mexican food. Casual and fun, with live entertainment several nights a week. **35 E. First St., Nederland; (303) 258-7001.**

Marvin's Garden
Casual, moderately priced western-style restaurant specializing in steaks, seafood and poultry. Friendly and pleasant. Also ample breakfasts. Model airplanes adorn the walls. Sizable early-bird special menu. Children's menu. Weekend reservations recommended. **110 Jefferson, Nederland; (303) 258-7398.**

Neopolitan's Italian Restaurant
Small restaurant with big following. Locals call it "Neo's." Large variety of dishes, from sandwiches and pizza to veal entrées. Pasta specialties. Takeout available. Beer and wine. Reservations accepted. **Wolftongue Square, 885 First St., Nederland; (303) 258-7313.**

Pioneer Inn
Rustic, casual and lively favorite with locals. Western look inside and out. Breakfast until noon, then lunch and dinner. Sizable charcoal-grilled burgers, generous sandwiches, Mexican entrées, steaks and barbecued chicken. Full bar and good munchie menu. Live entertainment four nights a week. **15 First St., Nederland; (303) 258-7733.**

The Place Upstairs
Pleasant and cozy, with dining area rambling through several small, interconnected rooms. Good variety of dishes, from classic to moderately innovative. Vegetarian specials. Sunday brunch. Outstanding desserts. Complimentary glass of wine with Eldora lift ticket. Reservations accepted (suggested on weekends). **Wolftongue Square, 885 First St; (303) 258-7822.**

Terragawa
Small casual eatery serving good, homemade fare in Formica-table casual atmosphere. Breakfast dishes and both Oriental and Tex-Mex plates at lunch and dinner. Reasonably priced combo plates from both culinary traditions. Located on "backside" of Village Shopping Center. **20 Lakeview Dr., Nederland; (303) 258-0455.**

Whistler's Cafe
Good breakfasts, including "mountain muffin" and veggie omelettes. Salads, soups, sandwiches and kids' menu at lunch. Low prices. **121 Jefferson St., Nederland; (303) 258-7871.**

NIGHTLIFE

Eldora's own Alpenhorn Bar predictably gets most of the immediate après-ski. Later, it's all in Nederland, a funky little mountain town, or down in Boulder. In Nederland, live entertainment is available four nights a week at the Pioneer Inn and three nights at the Assay Office, which also has darts, cribbage, checkers and chess. Several of the local restaurants have lounges or bars, but the draw is more conviviality and friendliness than organized entertainment. Boulder has ample restaurants and nightlife, from several brew pubs to a dinner theater. Eldora and Nederland are little more than half an hour from the mining towns turned gambling meccas of Central City and Blackhawk.

For more information, call or write **Eldora Mountain Resort, P.O. Box 1697, Nederland, CO 80466-1697, (303) 440-8700; Boulder Chamber of Commerce, 2440 Pearl St., Boulder, CO 80302, (303) 442-1044.**

LOVELAND VALLEY AND BASIN

BACKDROP

This high-alpine ski area under the brow of the Continental Divide is Colorado's most open secret. Locals arrive in droves early in the season when other ski areas aren't yet open and return even more enthusiastically when party season gears up in mid-March. Those in the know keep skiing until almost every other area in the state is closed, and, even after Loveland itself shuts its lifts, backcountry types climb a thousand or so feet above the top lifts to ski the highest snowfields until they melt into patches so small that it's no longer worth the effort. The area's skier traffic tends to take an odd dip in mid-winter when all of the state's areas are corking and those as high as Loveland can get cold and windy, meaning that the lines are minimal and the prices remain reasonable. Nevertheless, out-of-state skiers regularly bypass it on I-70, glancing up at the tree-lined lower trails, upper snowfields and the odd transfer lift that links Loveland Valley and Loveland Basin but not stopping to sample Loveland's convenience, economy and splendid scenery.

With no on-site lodging or other glitter to mar Loveland's purity, it remains quaint, reminding everyone how skiing used to be—inexpensive, casual, fun. Other than lucky Denverites who drive little more than commuting distance, skiers must sleep somewhere, and the choices are Georgetown and Idaho Springs, two former mining towns to the east, and Dillon, Silverthorne and other Summit County communities just on the west side of the tunnel. People combining business or conventioneering in Denver with a day or so off to ski sometimes stay in the city, and several metro motels even offer ski packages.

The ski area's improbably romantic name is derived from the high mountain pass just up the road, which in turn was named for William A. H. Loveland, a 19th-century tycoon who opened the pass to commerce with his Bakerville and Leadville Wagon Road and was also president of the Colorado Central Railroad. Today, the ski area utilizes the love connection, in a whimsical Denver advertising campaign featuring testimonials from skiers as to why they love Loveland. February 14 is a big day at the ski area, which annually hosts a complimentary mass wedding for couples who'd like to get hitched on the hill.

THE LAY OF THE LAND

Loveland is defined as much by what it doesn't have as by what it does. It is a ski area pure and simple, with none of the trappings that characterize the lavish full-service neighboring resorts. In fact, the most convenient accommodations and dining are in Georgetown, a quaint and historic mining town 12 miles and a long way downhill to the east. Loveland has no high-speed lifts, no fancy restaurants, no slopeside lodging. But this white-clad arc does have one of the state's longest ski seasons (normally mid-October to early May), second-highest snowfall (an average of 375 inches annually) and matchless proximity to Denver (56 miles, just before the entrance to the Eisenhower Tunnel and therefore before any harrowing passes). As you drive up the interstate, the first part coming into view to the left is Loveland Valley, with two chairlifts, an ultra-mild beginner slope and three steepish, never-crowded trails. Both a horizontal double chair which runs weekends and a free shuttle link which runs daily link this satellite to the main base, 200 feet and about a third of a mile higher, where all the main lifts and lion's share of the terrain are found.

GETTING THERE

Loveland is 56 miles west of Denver and 78 miles from Denver International Airport. It is located on the east side of Loveland Pass and the Eisenhower Tunnel, immediately adjacent to I-70.

PROFILE

Loveland is a mid-size ski area that skis big. With a base elevation of 10,600 feet, most of the skiable acreage consists of broad bowls and open snowfields, and the altitude means that the snow starts to fall early, piles deep, keeps falling well into spring and lasts long. When you are above the treeline, with lifts crossing those seamless sheets of snow and high peaks forming a grandiose panorama, you feel that you are in the Alps. Only the sound of the siren signaling that an overheight vehicle has tried to enter the tunnel or a glimpse of the silvery double ribbon of I-70 far below brings you back to Colorado.

Loveland Valley is both an exemplary off-the-beaten track learning area and a nice out-of-the-way spot for skiers who like to yo-yo a handful of steeper runs. As long as Chair 3, which serves Loveland Valley's vertical max, was an ancient, slow-moving double, there were no lines and minimal skier traffic. But with the upgrade of this lift to a quad, the Valley's complexion is changing, especially as skiers and snowboarders discover how congenial tree-rimmed trails can be on a snowy blustery day.

Still, the overwhelming majority of Loveland skiers stick to the expansive Basin, and Chair 4 upgrade or not, they will probably continue to do so. Chair 1, a triple, climbs from the south side of the main base area nearly a thousand feet to Rock House, a picnic cabin perched above a half dozen steep chutes and another half-dozen wide intermediate runs cut through the trees, which are extremely popular with bumpers, jumpers and snowboarders.

Loveland Basin's primary draw spreads across the entrancing white cirque of uncommon width above Chair 2, a slow-moving chairway to heaven if ever there was one. This lift provides the main access to the area's incomparable above-timberline snowfields. As you languish on the ride, imagine what Loveland was like three decades ago, when a tractor tow and half a dozen rope tows served as uphill transport in that very sector and fifteen minutes on a chairlift would have seemed like sheer luxury.

When you unload at the 12,280-foot level, stop to take in the scenery that is as spectacular as any view in the Rockies. To the south is another lift, Chair 6, and the slightly gladed bowl whose runs have such gambling names as North and South Blackjack, Dealer's Choice, Royal Flush and Deuces Wild, which turned out to be rather prophetic in light of the gambling now legalized at nearby Central City and Blackhawk. These are relatively mild runs, which means there are no losers in the Chair 6 game.

On either side of the highest lift-served spot at Loveland are Bennett's and Ptarmigan, which must be considered the heart of the area. It's there that one of the best spring party places is found—the E-Tow Cabin, where the aroma of barbecue mingles with the fresh mountain air, where snow volleyball is played fervently and where the essence of an old-time good time prevails. Well, maybe not totally old time, for the sound to spike by is reggae.

Chair 4, the double visible just above the east portal to the Eisenhower Tunnel, long served Loveland's inbounds periphery—a generous, mainly south-facing trough rippled with chutes and ridges above and dotted with trees below for great glade skiing. That terrain still skis nicely, and the magical isolation, so far above the tunnel, is typical of the Loveland sense of space, dimension and super snow. Zip Basin provides a backcountry feeling to skiers who choose not to hike. Named after the Zipfelberger Ski Club, Denver's top ski group more than half a century ago, Zip Basin is a fitting tribute to a ski-it-as-it-lies approach to the sport. Snowcats pack a few European-style pistes onto Zip's expansive 150 acres, but essentially the snow falls, blows, melts, freezes and gets tracked naturally. When there's powder, Zip is as close to heaven as its altitude would suggest. When the weather has done a nasty deed, dicey conditions turn Zip's dark blue terrain into menacing black.

Noteworthy

The area stocks quality rental skiwear and accessories, and of course ski and snowboard gear, for business travelers or others who can escape from nearby Denver for a day on the slopes. With Loveland's Snow Guarantee, anyone dissatisfied with ski conditions gets a full refund if ticket is turned in by 10:00 A.M. Also, lifts open at 8:30 A.M. on weekends and holidays, half-an-hour before the regular midweek start.

SNOWBOARDING

With so much terrain at and above the treeline, Loveland Basin is particularly appealing to snowboarders. Natural features shine, and the area supplements it with a snowboard park called Shredland. Its features are an 80-foot sidewinder quarter-pipe, Evil Knievel–inspired 30-foot gap jump, table top and pyramid-shaped "fun box" for tricks limited only by the rider's skill, strength and imagination.

SKI SCHOOL PROGRAMS

Loveland Ski School, (303) 569-3203.

Introductory Program

Never-Ever Package: Full- or half-day lesson, rental equipment and beginner lift ticket.

Advanced and Specialty Programs

Ladies' Day: All-day clinic for intermediate and advanced skiers, including bumps, racing, powder and backcountry technique. Held every Wednesday through March. Reservations accepted.
Advanced Lesson Package: Lift ticket and half-day lesson for adults, Level 4 to 9.

Special Program

Skier Services representatives lead complimentary meet-the-mountain tours daily at 10:30 A.M. for intermediate and advanced skiers.

For Families

Nonskiing Children

The nursery at Loveland Basin provides day care for children ages 1 or older for indoor and often outdoor play. Special low rates for second child in family. Lunch option available. Reservations recommended, **(800) 736-3SKI.**

Skiing Children

Club Kid: Ski school for children (ages 3 to 12), including all-day lessons and supervision, equipment rental, goody bag and SKIwee or MINIrider progress card, is headquartered at Loveland Valley and offers a sheltered beginner learning area with Mitey-Mite lift. Children must check in no later than 30 minutes before the lesson, which starts at 10:00 A.M.
3 Day Progressive Kids' Package: Three-day lift, lesson, rental and lunch package for children ages 3 to 12, based on SKIwee foundation.
Parent-Tot Program: One-hour lesson for parents and children, focusing on how to ski together safely and have fun. Parents learn what to expect from their skiing 2- to 4-year-old.

114

FOR RACERS

Loveland Basin Racing Club: Not-for-profit organization for serious junior and adult racers. LBRC, P.O. Box 1542, Evergreen, CO 80439; (303) 989-7575, (303) 571-5580.

WHERE TO STAY

In addition to the lodgings in nearby Georgetown and Idaho Springs, east of Loveland, some skiers stay in Summit County, through the Eisenhower Tunnel and down in the next major valley. Driving distance is about the same. All can be booked through **Loveland Central Reservations, (800) 225-LOVE.**

Georgetown and Silver Plume

Mid-Priced Accommodations

The Hardy House
Quaint B&B with five bedrooms (two joined into a suite with TV and VCR), all charmingly furnished with private bath. The rather luxurious suite price drops to economy when shared by three or four. Limited kitchen privileges. Daily housekeeping, full breakfast. Hot tub. **605 Brownell, Georgetown, CO 80444; (303) 569-3388.**

Kip on the Creek
Quiet charm. Just three guest rooms in B&B on banks of Clear Creek. Country atmosphere and decor. No children under 15. Daily housekeeping, full breakfast. **1205 Rose St., P.O. Box 754, Georgetown, CO 80444; (800) 821-6545, (303) 821-2923.**

Economy Accommodations

Brewery Inn
Closest lodging to Loveland ski areas. Hundred-year-old Victorian house, furnished in antiques. Three guests rooms with one shared bath; first-

floor suite with fireplace and private bath. Daily housekeeping, continental breakfast. **P.O. Box 473, Silver Plume, CO 80476; (800) 500-0209, (303) 569-2284.**

Georgetown Motor Inn
Functional, well-priced motel. Dining adjacent. Walking distance to town and 12 miles from ski area. Lift tickets can be purchased on-site. Daily housekeeping, Continental breakfast. Hot tub. **P.O. Box 277, Georgetown, CO 80444; (303) 569-3201.**

Super 8 Motel
Recently renovated 54-room property with Old West motif. Right off highway. Daily housekeeping, 24-hour front desk, complimentary breakfast toast bar. Hot tub, ski lockers. **1600 Argentine St., P.O. Box 308, Georgetown, CO 80444; (303) 569-3211, (800) 800-8000** for Super 8 reservations.

Private Homes

Guest Houses
Referrals to historic and individually decorated private homes and cozy cabins accommodating from two to 12 for a minimum of two-night stays. All with central heating, full kitchens, fireplaces or wood stoves, linens and such extras as sauna, oversize tub or exceptional views. **Georgetown/ Buehler Resort Service, P.O. Box 247, Georgetown, CO 80444; (303) 569-2665.**

Idaho Springs

Mid-Priced Accommodations

Argo Motor Inn
Comfortable, price-worthy motel. All rooms with queen-size beds; some creekside and/or with fireplace. Pets allowed. Dining nearby. Ski packages available. Daily housekeeping, courtesy coffee. Greenhouse spa and exercise facility, coin laundry. **P.O. Box 837, Idaho Springs, CO 80452; (303) 567-4473.**

Indian Springs Lodge
Mineral-springs resort with 30-room lodge and 20-room inn. Springs known by the Indians as "Healing Waters of the Great Spirit." Weekend entertainment and dancing in lounge. Daily

housekeeping. Massage available, mineral pool, cave baths, private hot tubs, "Club Mud," restaurant, lounge. **302 Soda Creek Rd., Idaho Springs, CO 80452; (303) 623-0250.**

Economy Accommodations

Blair Motel
Remodeled motel with good-size rooms and family suites. Dining nearby. Daily housekeeping. **345 Colorado Blvd., Idaho Springs, CO 80452; (303) 567-4661.**

H&H Motor Lodge
Budget-watchers' motel. Some units with kitchenettes. Daily housekeeping. Hot tub, guest laundry. **2445 Colorado Blvd., Idaho Springs, CO 80452; (303) 567-2838.**

Peoriana Motel
Thirty-one rooms and family suites, some with kitchenettes. Three restaurants adjacent. Daily housekeeping. Hot tub. **2901 Colorado Blvd., Idaho Springs, CO 80452; (303) 567-2021.**

Rest Haven Motel
Clean, comfortable, value motel with some kitchenette units. Restaurants within walking distance. Daily housekeeping. **2631 Colorado Blvd., Idaho Springs, CO 80452; (303) 567-2242.**

DINING OUT

Georgetown

The Happy Cooker
Nifty restaurant with fine breakfasts and lunches in Victorian house. Homemade breads and quiches are tops. Artwork displayed on walls. **412 Sixth St., Georgetown; (303) 569-3166.**

The Ram
Well-regarded, long-established restaurant in historic brick bank building. Stylish and atmospheric. Lunches are casual, with burgers, sandwiches and Tex-Mex. Dinners are fancier. Wednesday all-you-can-eat pasta night. Full bar. **606 Sixth St., Georgetown; (303) 569-3263.**

Colorado Classics

The Renaissance
Georgetown's culinary champion. Lovely atmosphere as a bonus. Fine northern Italian cuisine, with exquisitely sauced veal, chicken, beef, seafood and game. Huge portions. Home-baked breads. Extensive quality wine list. Dinner nightly except Monday and Tuesday; lunches on weekends only. Reservations recommended. **1025 Rose St., Georgetown; (303) 569-3336.**

Silver Queen
Popular downtown restaurant. Saloon-style, both in atmosphere and in menu. Filled with historic photos and memorabilia. **500 Sixth St., Georgetown; (303) 569-2961.**

Idaho Springs

Beau Jo's Pizza
A Colorado classic for great atmosphere, pitchers of beer and mix-and-match pizzas (crusts, sauces, toppings to order). Salad bar. Big and brassy. Decorated with patrons' napkin artwork. **1517 Miner St., Idaho Springs; (303) 567-4276.**

Buffalo Company
Fun and funky western restaurant. Breakfast, lunch, dinner and après-ski action well into the night. Best known for buffalo burgers, but the variety starts with breakfast burritos and extends to wee-hours munchies. Nightly dinner specials. **1617 Miner St., Idaho Springs; (303) 567-2729.**

Tommy Knocker Brew Pub
Restaurant is Victorian style; adjacent brew pub is contemporary and "industrial," with tanks and other brewery paraphernalia as decorative (as well as functional) elements. Trendy, yet casual. Pub-style and deli-style food and microbrews. Lunch and dinner. **1401 Miner St., Idaho Springs; (303) 567-2688.**

NIGHTLIFE

Après-ski opening salvos are fired at the Rathskeller, a pleasant and busy lounge in the Loveland Basin lodge. In Georgetown, the Silver Queen is the liveliest. In Idaho Springs, the places to be are BeauJo's, the Buffalo Company and Tommy Knockers. Although they are open late, drawing locals, these spots (especially those in Idaho Springs) are busiest on weekends when skiers returning to Denver stop for something to eat and drink but wind down earlier than nightspots in ski resort towns.

For more information, contact **Loveland Ski Areas, P.O. Box 899, Georgetown, CO 80444; (303) 571-5580** in Denver, fax **(303) 569-2288; Clear Creek County Tourism Board, P.O. Box 100, Idaho Springs, CO 80452; (800) 88-BLAST, (303) 567-4660,** fax **(303) 567-4605.**

SKI COOPER

Photo courtesy Ski Cooper

BACKDROP

The heroic exploits of the Tenth Mountain Division in Italy during World War II are the stuff of which legends are made. Ski Cooper, a small ski area located at Tennessee Pass where the high-altitude training center of Camp Hale was located, is the keeper of the flame. Set in a high range of the Rockies, Cooper is just a half-hour drive from Copper Mountain (via Route 91) or Vail and Beaver Creek (via Route 24), yet it can provide a day of low-key contrast to the big-mountain, full-resort skiing experience of its neighbors. Coupled with accommodations in the old mining town of Leadville, Ski Cooper makes for an awesomely affordable ski weekend or vacation. Without pretending that Cooper's terrain, lifts or amenities even come close to approaching the larger resorts', it is worth noting that the full-day lift ticket is half the price or less of its more glamorous neighbors—and the unique ambience of Leadville is not only inexpensive but priceless as well.

Leadville, at 10,152 feet (nearly twice Denver's elevation), is America's highest city. It is also awash with mining history and legend. Various metals have been mined in and around Leadville, the greatest boomtown of the 1870s. The town boasts several small museums and displays open for limited winter hours. Catch any you can between ski runs for a fascinating look at Colorado's past. In very few places can you combine skiing with so much unvarnished atmosphere.

THE LAY OF THE LAND

Ski Cooper is a ski area, pure and simple. It is located at a high pass, 10 miles north of Leadville via Route 24, a scenic mountain highway. The ski area is set back against the Continental Divide, enhancing the feeling of old-fashioned and isolated informality. This sparsely

Mountain Stats— Ski Cooper

Resort elevation (Leadville) 10,152 feet
Top of highest lift 11,700 feet
Bottom of lowest lift 10,500 feet
Total vertical 1,200 feet
Longest run 1.4 miles
Average annual snowfall 260 inches
Ski season Thanksgiving through the end of March or early April
Lifts 1 triple chairlift, 1 double, 2 surface lifts
Capacity 3,300 skiers per hour
Terrain inbounds, 26 runs on 365 acres (30% beginner and novice, 40% intermediate, 30% advanced and expert); Chicago Ridge Snowcat terrain, 1,600 acres (all high intermediate, advanced and expert)
Snow reports (719) 486-2277

populated region of soaring peaks is too high for agriculture, so the sense of near-wilderness is palpable in this spectacular part of a scenically endowed state.

GETTING THERE

Ski Cooper is 110 miles from Denver via I-70 and Route 91, with a backtrack from the northwest via Route 24 just on the outskirts of Leadville.

PROFILE

Ski Cooper's terrain is draped over two sides of a broad, rather gentle mountain providing a friendly and beguiling playground for beginner and intermediate skiers. The runs are exceptionally wide, and most are consistently pitched and visually appealing too. The double chair climbs from the base area to a canted summit ridge, where it meets the triple rising from the backside. All but two of the trails on the front face are marked with green circles or blue squares, while the backside runs include a handful of black diamonds as well.

You can create a lovely rhythm to your skiing day by working your way across first one side of the mountain then the other, or perhaps by skiing all the greens, then the blues and finally the blacks—or the reverse. With just two major lifts terminating very close to each other, this rare kind of mix-and-match skiing is easy. In addition to uncommonly wide and constant trails, there is a fair amount of tree skiing, particularly on the backside. With a low lift capacity and relatively little traffic, especially during the week, Cooper's stashes last and last.

The platterpull-served beginner slope at the base is as tame and gentle as a slightly canted tabletop. Even the shakiest beginner or tiniest preschooler quickly can ski such a mellow run. With the seamless snow of a high-altitude ski area and sufficient separation from the main frontside runs, the slope is a confidence-builder too. For skiers recently graduated from beginner to novice status, Cooper is just the ticket. Sitzmark and Mayfield on the front and Tenderfoot and Eagle on the back continue the ego-boosting of the beginner slope. All are bracketed by lovely intermediate runs—some fringed or dotted with trees here and there for an open-glade sense. The majority of the blacks are short, steep drops off the end of the mountaintop ridge where the lifts unload. However, these short shots are but a teaser for Cooper's ace in the hole—snowcat skiing the ungroomed chutes, glades, snowfields, bowls and drainages of Chicago Ridge (see below).

SNOWBOARDING

Just as Ski Cooper is a congenial, low-cost place to ski, it is a congenial, low-cost place to snowboard with beginner packages, lessons, rental equipment and suitable terrain and specialty clinics. Snowboards and snowcats are a great mix, and riders love cat service on Chicago Ridge, which is fantastic for snowboarding too. Ski Cooper also builds a snowboard terrain park as soon as snow accumulations permit.

SNOWCAT SKIING

Ski Cooper operates **Chicago Ridge Snowcat Tours** on terrain that is physically separate from the lift-service ski area. It is nothing less than spectacular with runs up to 3,000 feet long and 1,200 vertical feet—and fantastic scenery to match. Two snowcats take up to 18 skiers and snowboarders a day plus guides into 1,800 acres that top off above the timberline at a spine-tingling 12,600 feet above sea level. The experience in the powdery playground, nearly five times the inbounds lift-served area, is one of the best in the Rockies. Full-day skiing or snowboarding, including lunch, and a half-day version operate daily except Tuesday from mid-December until early April. Reservations required. **(719) 486-2277.**

Photo courtesy Ski Cooper

Chicago Ridge Snowcat Tours are practically like having a private mountain, with 1,800 acres of terrain.

SKI SCHOOL PROGRAMS

Introductory Programs

Never-Ever Package: Bargain-rate, two-hour morning or afternoon lesson, beginner lift ticket and rental equipment.

Snowboard Lesson Package: Two-hour snowboard lesson, rentals and all-mountain lift ticket, for beginners and better.

Advanced and Specialty Programs

Women's in Powder Clinic: Two-day intro to backcountry skiing, including a day on Chicago Ridge; includes fat skis, three meals, lift tickets and instruction. Offered on a weekend in late February.

Snowboarding Clinics: Two-day snowboarding clinics, including one for women only, including two days of lessons, board rental, lifts and three meals.

Women on Boards: One-day snowboard clinic.

For Families

Nonskiing Children

Nursery: Full- and half-day care with optional lunch for children ages 2 to 6. Nursery care can be combined with private lesson and rental

equipment for small beginning skiers. Reservations required. **(719) 486-2277.**

Skiing Children

Learn-to-Ski: Children's beginner package including two-hour morning or afternoon lesson, rental equipment and beginner lift ticket.

Snowboard Lesson: Lift, lesson and rental packages available for ages 8 and older.

Panda Patrol: Full day of supervision, skiing, lessons and lunch rental for children ages 4 to 10, with rental option. Child's package with private $1\frac{1}{2}$-hour lesson available. Reservations required.

FOR RACERS

NASTAR and race clinics available.

NORDIC SKIING

The Piney Creek Nordic Center, adjacent to Ski Cooper, prepares 25 kilometers of tracks and skating lanes and offers rentals and instruction in diagonal, skating and telemarking. Snowshoe rentals are also offered. The system's foundation are trails used by the 10th Mountain Division troops. Three short trails near the Nordic Center, including a loop that passes a roadside memorial

119

Colorado Classics

Photo courtesy Ski Cooper

Ski Cooper's gentle lift-served terrain is a winter playground for kids.

to America's crack ski and mountain tops, are for novices, and the rest are for intermediate and advanced skiers; (719) 486-2117. The Nordic Center also runs dinner tours to the nearby Tennessee Pass Cookhouse; see "Dining Out," below.

Most of the Leadville area's remaining ski touring is south of town, with miles of marked

Noteworthy

Children 5 and under ski free when accompanying an adult.

and mapped routes, mainly along unplowed roads, accessible from trailheads at the Leadville National Fish Hatchery, Colorado Mountain College and Twin Lakes. The Twin Lakes Nordic Inn, along Route 82 south of Leadville, is a century-old stage stop on the Independence Pass route, with access to limitless backcountry skiing in the San Isabel National Forest as well as up the unplowed pass road. The inn puts out a useful brochure outlining the recommended touring routes. Rental equipment is available, but most guests are good skiers who bring their own, **(719) 486-1830. Sawatch Naturalist & Guides** are knowledge locals experienced in the backcountry who offer ski and snowshoe guiding, **(719) 486-1856.** Several of the 10th Mountain Division system huts are accessible from the Leadville area; see Aspen chapter, page 35.). **The San Isabel National Forest Leadville**

Ranger District Office in Leadville also has backcountry information, **(719) 486-0749.**

WHERE TO STAY

Leadville–Twin Lakes Lodging, (800) 933-3901, (719) 486-3900.

Note that guests staying at most of the properties below can buy discounted lift tickets at Ski Cooper.

Mid-Priced Accommodations

The Apple Blossom Inn

Historic 1879 banker's home with five charming guest rooms furnished with wonderful antiques. Daily housekeeping, full breakfast, complimentary morning paper, complimentary rec center passes. Guest laundry, kitchenette available. **120 W. Fourth St., Leadville, CO 80461; (719) 486-2141.**

Delaware Hotel

Charming Victorian-style rooms and suites in historic hotel located in the historic heart of downtown. Some small but all well-furnished and atmospheric. All with private baths. Daily housekeeping, continental breakfast. Hot tub, restaurant. **700 Harrison Ave., Leadville, CO 80461; (800) 748-2004, (719) 486-1418.**

Grand West Village Resort

Private one-, two- and three-bedroom lodges with full kitchens, laundry, Jacuzzi tubs, gas fireplaces, TVs with VCRs and ski-equipment storage on 154 forested acres overlooking the Arkansas River Valley. Located between Leadville and Ski Cooper. **P.O. Box 967, Leadville, CO 80461; (800) 691 3999, (719) 465-0702.**

Leadville Country Inn

Ten romantic rooms in 1893 Victorian. Quiet location, yet close to downtown. Antique furnishings (including antique copper soaking tub). Daily housekeeping, full gourmet breakfast. Hot tub, guest laundry. **127 E. Eighth St., Leadville, CO 80461; (800) 748-2354, (719) 486-2354.**

Pan Ark Lodge

Forty-eight comfortable suites with moss-rock fireplaces, kitchens and mountain views. Pets allowed. Nine miles south of town with great mountain views including Mt. Elbert, Colorado's highest peak. AAA-rated motel. Daily housekeeping, guest laundry. **5827 Hwy 24 South, Leadville, CO 80461; (800) 443-1063, (719) 486-1063.**

Peri & Ed's Mountain Hideaway
Family-friendly B&B in 1875 boardinghouse. Home-like, with five guest rooms, parlor and cozy kitchen/dining room. One block from main street. Daily housekeeping, full breakfast. **201 W. Eighth St., Leadville, CO 80461; (719) 486-0716.**

Twin Lakes Nordic Inn
Fascinating lodge and restaurant in secluded setting south of Leadville. Built in 1879 as a stagecoach stop and once a brothel; now full of rustic charm and tradition in tiny National Historic District. All rooms individually decorated and have imported feather beds. Some private, some shared baths. A significant drive through Leadville to Ski Cooper, but worthwhile for history and ambiance. Excellent restaurant, lounge and ski-touring options. Daily housekeeping. Restaurant, lounge, outdoor hot tub, video room/library. **6435 Hwy 82, Twin Lakes, CO 81251; (800) 626-7812, (719) 486-1830.**

Wood Haven Manor
Exquisite 1899 "bankers' row" Victorian home now a lovely B&B. Four distinctively furnished rooms. Parlors and formal dining room for congenial socializing. Luxury and intense charm at a moderate price. Daily housekeeping, full breakfast. **807 Spruce St., Leadville, CO 80461; (800) 748-2570, (719) 486-1484.**

Economy Accommodations

Club Lead
Family-style B&B inn with deliberate bunkhouse atmosphere. Various accommodations, from bargain dorms to rooms with queen-size beds. Daily housekeeping, courtesy shuttle, full breakfast. Game room, hot tub. **500 E. Seventh St., Leadville, CO 80461; (719) 486-2202.**

Lazy JB Motel
Budget motel close to town. Twelve newly done rooms. Pets permitted. Daily housekeeping.

1515 Poplar St., Leadville, CO 80461; (719) 486-3155.

Mountain Peaks Motel
Simple motel north of downtown. Ground-level units. Knotty-pine decor. Daily housekeeping. **1 Harrison Ave., Leadville, CO 80461; (719) 486-3178.**

Timberline Motel
Located downtown, within walking distance of restaurants and bars. AAA motel. Daily housekeeping. **216 Harrison Ave., Leadville, CO 80461; (719) 486-1876.**

Private Homes

Alpine Realty
Manages and rents private homes in and around Leadville. Amenities, facilities and housekeeping policies vary. **P.O. Box 321, Leadville, CO 80461; (800) 571-2782, (719) 486-1866.**

DINING OUT

Callaway's Restaurant
Breakfast and lunch, plus fine dining in Delaware Hotel. Leadville's fanciest restaurant, serving northern Italian and French cuisine. Charming and gracious. Children's menu. Nightly specials. Excellent desserts. Reservations suggested. **700 Harrison Ave., Leadville; (719) 486-1418.**

La Cantina
One of the most popular of Leadville's well-priced, spotlessly clean Mexican restaurants. Carefully prepared, lavishly portioned meals. Good-size, friendly restaurant. Moderate prices. Mexican beer. Children's menu. **1942 Hwy 24, Leadville; (719) 486-9927.**

Golden Burro Cafe & Lounge
Family-style restaurant founded in 1938. Home-style breakfast, lunch, dinner and Sunday brunch. Homemade soups, pies and other baked goods. Large portions at moderate prices. Children's and seniors' menu. Booths, tables and counter service, plus takeout. **710 Harrison Ave., Leadville; (719) 486-2679.**

Colorado Classics

Grill Bar & Cafe
Popular place for margaritas, beer and well-prepared Mexican specialties. Moderate prices. Takeout available. **715 E. Elm St., Leadville; (719) 486-9930.**

Leadville Prospector
Great mountain setting 3 miles north of Leadville. Fine dining. Soup and bean kettles, beef, seafood, pasta and baby back ribs. Nightly dinners except Monday and Sunday brunch. Reservations recommended. **2798 Hwy 91, Leadville; (800) 844-2828, (719) 486-3955.**

Matilda's Cafe
Budget Mexican for the lunch bunch and early diners. Casual. Kids' menu. Takeout available. **323 E. Fourth St., Leadville; (719) 486-1071.**

Pastime Saloon
Oro City Chinese bar is centerpiece of this venerable (and recently restored) saloon, founded in 1878. Big burgers (including buffalo meat), ribs and wings. Kitchen open Wednesday through Sunday, Full bar; drink specials. **120 W. Second St., Leadville; (719) 486-9986.**

The Prospector
Dinners start with homemade soup and beans, salad bar and freshly baked breads. Fine seafood, aged steaks and daily specials follow. Log building in lovely mountain setting north of town. Children's menu. Reservations are recommended. **Hwy 91, 3 1/2 miles north of Leadville; (719) 486-2117.**

Tennessee Pass Cookhouse
Guided skiing or snowshoeing on groomed trails to backcountry cookhouse for four-course, prix fixe dinner. Fee includes equipment and headlamps. Wild game, lamb, trout and pasta are centerpieces for gourmet, healthful meal. Reservations required. Also, sleigh and snowmobile rides at lunch. **Piney Creek Nordic Center, Ski Cooper, Leadville; (719) 486-1750.**

Twin Lakes Nordic Inn
Breakfast, lunch and dinner in charming fireside dining of 1879 stagecoach stop, now an inn. Excellent German and American cuisine. Children's menu. Imported German wine and beer. **6435 Hwy 82, Twin Lakes; (719) 486-1830.**

Wild Bill's Hamburgers & Ice Cream
Charbroiled burgers and other casual food, including chili and soups. Children's menu. Very reasonable prices. Takeout and free delivery available. **200 Harrison Ave., Leadville; (719) 486-0533.**

NIGHTLIFE

Immediate après-ski might start with a quick wine or beer at the base lodge but soon moves to town. The brassiest local bars, which maintain (and perhaps embellish) the old mining boomtown flavor, are the Silver Dollar Saloon and the Pastime Saloon. The Silver Dollar claims to be "Leadville's oldest bar where Silver Kings once met," while the Pastime boasts of being "the oldest original saloon on [old] State Street." Both date from 1878–79 and are funky, fantastic and fun today. The Pastime, with a rowdy and illustrious history in the days when Leadville's ladies of the night headquartered there, now inexplicably specializes in delicious tropical drinks, while the Silver Dollar nurtures the atmosphere of an Irish bar. The Scarlett Inn Tavern has a dance floor (live music on weekends), pool table and other games. The Grill Bar has good margaritas, but it, the Golden Burro and the Golden Rose bars cater mostly to diners. The Silver King downtown and The Prospector and Twin Lakes Nordic Inn, both outside of town, all have cozy lounges, conducive to conversation.

For more information, contact **Ski Cooper, P.O. Box 896, Leadville, CO 80461; (719) 486-3684; fax (719) 486-3685; Greater Leadville Area Chamber of Commerce, 809 Harrison Ave., P.O. Box 861, Leadville, CO 80461; (800) 933-3901, (719) 486-3900.**

SUNLIGHT MOUNTAIN RESORT

Photo by Gary Hubbell

BACKDROP

Glenwood Springs, with its mammoth outdoor spring-fed pool complex steaming in sight of highway and railroad alike, is one of Colorado's distinctive towns. It has attracted warm-weather visitors for a century. Sunlight, the local ski area, is a congenial, uncrowded ski hill where the ambiance is strictly low-key, a marked contrast to the international glamour embodied in Aspen and Snowmass, the nearest ski-country neighbors. With Aspen's prices somewhere in the stratosphere and many everyday goods no longer available in town at all, Glenwood Springs has experienced a spillover boom with resort workers shopping and even living there. High on the list of appeals for winter visitors is economy. In addition to an abundance of well-priced in-town accommodations, ranging from the historic and luxurious to the most basic of bargain motels, Sunlight had held its single-day lift ticket price from 1991–92 through 1996–97.

The bottom line is that you can stay in Glenwood Springs, ski a few days at Sunlight where the snow is good, the atmosphere is friendly and the lift and lesson prices low—and cap the vacation with a few days skiing Aspen, Snowmass, Vail or Beaver Creek. Scheduled bus service to Aspen and Snowmass eases the commute on Route 82 or I-70—all at moderate prices. Though the fine print changes from season to season, there are normally inclusive packages for lodging in Glenwood Springs and skiing at Sunlight plus Aspen, Snowmass, Vail or Beaver Creek in some combination (and soaking in the famous Hot Springs Pool, the world's largest spring-fed outdoor hot pool). In fact, with or without combining Sunlight and the other resort

Colorado Classics

areas, economical Ski, Swim and Stay packages prevail for lodgings in Glenwood Springs; the town is also a daily Amtrak stop, making it a top choice for skiers who prefer not to fly or drive.

THE LAY OF THE LAND

Glenwood Springs, located in a scenic, temperate valley carved by the Colorado River, is a town of hit-and-miss development in an area of incredible scenic beauty. The downtown has been upgraded over the years into a lively and attractive place. While some Glenwood Springs lodging is outlying, much of it is within walking distance of the Hot Springs Pool and downtown shops and restaurants. The ski area is located in a scenic and still rural area 10 miles southwest of town—and more than 2,000 feet higher. Sunlight Mountain has limited on-site lodging, but there is a free ski shuttle from town to the mountain, **(970) 945-7491.** As you approach the ski area, the first of Sunlight's runs to come into view from the road is the dauntingly steep Defiance glade. It would be enough to make tentative skiers make a U-turn for the hot pool, but there's no place to turn around until the ski-area parking lot. That's where the comfort element kicks in, because the simple base area is surrounded by runs of all pitches and widths, and there's even an ultra-gentle beginner area on one side of the lot.

124

GETTING THERE

Glenwood Springs is 157 miles west of Denver and 89 miles east of Grand Junction (and their airports). The drive from Denver International Airport, via I-70 through scenic Glenwood Canyon, takes about three hours and from Grand Junction's Walker Field, about 1 1/2 hours. Aspen's Sardy Field is 40 miles to the southeast, via Route 82, and Vail/Eagle County Airport is a comparable distance to the east via I-70. **Airport Shuttle of Colorado** has bus service between Glenwood Springs and both Aspen and Vail; **(800) 222-2112,** as well as DIA. **Amtrak's California Zephyr** between Chicago and San Fran-

cisco stops daily in Glenwood Springs, **(800) USA-RAIL. Greyhound/Trailways** also has daily bus service, **(970) 945-8501.**

Mountain Stats—
Sunlight Mountain Resort

Resort elevation 5,746 feet (Glenwood Springs)
Top of highest lift 9,895 feet
Bottom of lowest lift 7,885 feet
Total vertical 2,010 feet
Longest run 2 1/2 miles
Average annual snowfall 260 inches
Ski season Thanksgiving through early April
Lifts 1 triple chairlift, 2 doubles, 1 surface lift
Capacity 4,600 skiers per hour
Terrain 445 acres, 55 trails (20% beginner and novice, 55% intermediate, 25% advanced and expert)
Snowmaking limited
Snow reports (970) 945-7491

PROFILE

Sunshine Meadow and its tame, secluded surface lift—across the parking lot from the main base—is Sunlight's convenient teaching hill, but the skiing that counts is three dozen trails arranged in an appealing semicircle above the day lodge. Although there are just three chairlifts, they are so functionally placed that they permit easy and convenient access to the whole network, and all runs eventually funnel back to the base too. The Tercero chairlift ferries skiers a quarter of the way up the mountain. Novices can ride it all day to ski Sunlight's bottom-of-the-hill, green-circle slopes, which are football field-wide, gentle yet interesting. Tercero also accesses the Enchanted Forest, a natural aspen glade that became such a favorite children's playground that area management eventually named and signed it and most recently added a terrain garden with miniature gates, bumps and swales to make this midway area both more fun and more productive for children's ski classes.

Better skiers use the Tercero triple only as a prelude to Primo, the mile-long chair to the surprising summit of Compass Mountain, Sunlight's official name. It is a near-10,000-foot peak with knock-your-ski-socks-off views of Mt. Sopris and an endless panorama of other, less distinctive mountains. Novices can enjoy the vista and ski the 2¹/₂ mild miles of the scenic Ute Trail skirting the area's western boundary, where they often meet the aerobically aggressive climbing Ute on cross-country skis. The complicated web of trails embraced by Ute is most suitable for intermediates. Locals know the lay of the land quite well, but visiting skiers can confuse, surprise and delight themselves with the unexpected variety of routes that can be made by skiing Ute to Sundance, Ute Cutoff, Segundo Road or Blue Catwalk, from which the choices multiply to Joslin, Peace Pipe or Dawson. Or they can shock themselves by dropping from blue runs into the black turf of Crystal, Showdown, Holiday Hill or Segundo. So many skiers prefer these western runs that Segundo angles off to serve just this sector.

Skiing the eastern runs, which are set farther apart but are generally more challenging than the western ones, requires riding Primo. The eastern sector has its own rim run—a combination of Grizzly and The Parks, following the curving gentle descent of the ridge, fringed with trees and wonderful for relaxed skiing. A plunge into the Upper Glade or Zephyr, marked with a black diamond or two, serves as a wake-up call for even the most enervated skier. Farther down, a straight run from Grizzly instead of a left turn means a bone-rattling descent of Defiance, the steep, partially gladed slope seen from the highway on arrival. Advanced skiers thrive on having successfully defied Defiance; intermediates feel proud for having done it, and errant novices shouldn't be there in the first place.

Defiance is but a warm-up for Sunlight Extreme on the far end of East Ridge or Sundown Glades notched into the lower portion of the ridge, which rank among Colorado's steepest inbounds skiing. Access is via control gate, and the runs, which nip and tuck among the trees, are never groomed. Patrol nicknames have become

Sunlight is home to boarders and skiers alike. The area offers well-priced beginner packages that include a lesson, lift ticket and rental.

codified, with such shots as Rapid Transit, The Heathen, Tod's Ride and The Slot now on the trail map. The map doesn't begin to communicate the pit-of-the-stomach knot that develops when you first look down at these shots, and neither do statistics, but it's enlightening to compare these rigorous double blacks with their overall 37-degree pitch (and a maximum drop off a ledge that reaches 52 degrees) with the average U.S. black diamond pitch to 27 to 33 degrees. The extreme vertical is a relatively modest 750 feet, but the steepness and the ungroomed naturalness of the snow conditions makes it feel like a thousand or more.

SNOWBOARDING

With the exception of a few flats on the long traverses from the summit, Sunlight's prevailing fall-line trail design and compelling East Ride steeps make for wonderful riding. There's a fine snowboard park just east of the base lodge, with quarter turns, camel bumps, rail slides and other obstacles. Lessons, rentals, races and specialized clinics are available too.

SKI SCHOOL PROGRAMS

Introductory Programs

Note that many programs are available for ages 7 through adult. Check-in required one-half hour before lesson times.

Beginners Package: Lifts, single- or double-session lesson and ski or snowboard equipment rental for first-timers.

Adult Learn to Snowboard Workshop: Beginner workshops on specific Saturdays during the season.

Adult Learn to Telemark Workshop: Beginner workshops on specific Saturdays during the season.

Advanced and Specialty Programs

Alpine Classics: For intermediate and advanced adult skiers on Sunday and Friday afternoons.

Women's Workshops: Latest in women's skiing techniques for women skiing easy blue to black runs. Focuses on mental as well as physical aspects of skiing. Available Saturdays.

Mountain Masters: Two-hour technique and confidence-building workshop. Available Saturdays.

Sunlight is a mid-sized mountain with big-league views. Mt. Sopris, one of Colorado's landmark peaks, is visible from Sunlight's summit.

For Families

Nonskiing Children

Cricket Corner: Day care (half or full day, including lunch) for children ages 6 months to 6 years. Reservations are accepted, but not required.

Skiing Children

Super Tots: One-hour private lesson available for children ages 3 and older. Full ski school program with supervision, lesson and rental equipment for children ages four and five. Lunch is included in full-day program. Reservations available.

Youth Packages: Beginner package with lift, equipment and single- or double-session lesson.

NORDIC SKIING

Sunlight's cross-country center offers 27 kilometers of tracks, two warming huts, rental equipment and track, skating, telemark and snowshoeing instruction. The trails are especially wide, with 10 kilometers of trackset on the sides and groomed a skating lane in the middle. Use is free. The Back Country Cabin is stocked with self-service hot drinks and snacks and is available for a rustic overnight stay; the Ski Shelter also has drinks and a wood stove. While fitness fanatics can ski up Ute trail's $2^1/2$ miles and more than 2,000 vertical feet, less ambitious skiers can purchase a single-ride ticket and ski down the mountain. The annual 10-kilometer Coal Dust Classic, established in 1967, is one of Colorado's oldest cross-country citizen races. Of the abundant backcountry tours, one of the most unusual is Avalanche Creek, winter feeding grounds for bighorn sheep, off Hwy 133 about an hour's drive from Glenwood Springs. The **White River National Forest Office** in Glenwood Springs has information and maps on backcountry skiing; **(970) 945-2521.**

WHERE TO STAY

Glenwood Springs Central Reservations, (800) 221-0098.

Photo by Sunlight Ski Photography

Luxury Accommodations

Cleveholm Manor

Monumentally built, exquisitely furnished B&B inn also known as Redstone Castle. Palatial yet secluded with extraordinary views and matchless ambiance. Sixteen exceptionally furnished rooms. A commute to skiing (but worth it). Dinners divine too. Daily housekeeping, breakfast. Restaurant, lounge. **0058 Redstone Blvd., Redstone, CO 81623; (970) 963-3463.**

Mid-Priced Accommodations

First Choice Inn of Glenwood Springs

One of the largest motels in town, with 123 modern rooms. Children stay free in parents' room. Daily housekeeping, 24-hour front desk, room service. Restaurant, lounge, game room, guest laundry. **51359 Hwy 6 & 24, Glenwood Springs, CO 81601; (800) 332-2233, (970) 945-8551.**

Hot Springs Lodge

Has 107 rooms, standard and deluxe categories. Deluxe with in-room mini-refrigerator, remote-control TV and patio or balcony; some with king-size beds. Poolside lodge, with exceptional convenience to all hot-springs facilities. Discounts to pool facilities and massage. Adjacent athletic club. Ski/swim packages. Daily housekeeping, shuttle to train station and other transportation, 24-hour front desk. Poolside restaurant, lounge, athletic club, outdoor hot tub (not connected to Hot Springs Pool), guest laundry, game room in-room coffee and safe. **415 East Sixth St., Glenwood Springs, CO 81601; (800) 537-SWIM** in Colorado only, **(970) 945-6571.**

Hotel Colorado

Landmark 128-room hotel, opened in 1893, adjacent to Hot Springs Pool. Historic Italian building with Victorian antique furnishings. Rooms range from large and luxurious to compact and cute, and room rates range from moderate to high (for Glenwood Springs, but still a lot of history for a little money). Daily housekeeping, 24-hour front desk, bell staff, room service. Restaurants, lounge, full health club, hot tub, sauna. **526 Pine St., Glenwood Springs, CO 81601; (800) 544-3998, (970) 945-6511.**

Hotel Denver

Historic hotel across from Amtrak station and easy walking distance to Hot Springs Pool and downtown. Three-story atrium. Sixty rooms and suites in Art Deco style with in-room coffee. Some non-smoking rooms. Pets permitted. Children stay free with parents. Ski and ski/swim packages. Daily housekeeping, 24-hour front desk, room service, complimentary morning newspaper. Restaurant, lounge, fitness facilities. **402 Seventh St., Glenwood Springs, CO 81601; (800) 826-8820, (970) 945-6565.**

Ramada Inn of Glenwood Springs

Large and lively hotel two blocks from Hot Springs Pool and three blocks from downtown. Full-service hotel with 125 well-appointed rooms and some suites each with kitchen, in-room steam bath and fireplace. Children ages 18 and younger stay free in parents' room. Pets permitted. Discounted health club privileges. Ski/swim packages. Daily housekeeping, 24-hour front desk, room service, train shuttle, bell staff. Restaurant, lounge, indoor pool, hot tub. **124 W. Sixth St., Glenwood Springs, CO 81601; (800) 332-1472, (970) 945-2500, (800) 228-2828** for Ramada Inn reservations.

Economy Accommodations

Adducci's Inn

Pleasant B&B accommodating just 12. Walking distance to Hot Springs Pool. Children welcome; babysitting can be arranged. Full breakfast, complimentary wine. Restaurant, lounge, hot tub. **1023 Grand Ave., Glenwood Springs, CO 81601; (970) 945-9341.**

Cedar Lodge Motel

Forty-eight-room-motel outside town on Route 82. Well-equipped and recently remodeled. AAA motel. Skier discounts. Some kitchenette units; one honeymoon suite. Ski/swim packages. Daily housekeeping, Continental breakfast. Indoor hot tub, sauna, guest laundry. **2102 Grand Ave., Glenwood Springs, CO 81601; (800) 341-3761, (970) 945-6579.**

Colonial Inn Motel

Ultra-clean 16-room motel. Traditionally furnished, with king- and queen-size beds. AAA motel. Walking distance to restaurants and indoor shopping mall. Daily housekeeping, train shuttle, in-room coffee. **5871 Hwy 6 & 24, Glenwood Springs, CO 81601; (800) 841-0255, (970) 945-6279.**

Glenwood Motor Inn

Forty-five-room motel two blocks from Hot Springs Pool. Some rooms with refrigerators and microwaves. AAA-rated. Daily housekeeping, train shuttle. Restaurant (breakfast and lunch), hot tub, sauna. **141 W. Sixth St., Glenwood Springs, CO 81601; (800) 543-5906, (970) 945-5438.**

Glenwood Springs Hostel

Main street hostel for young skiers—and anyone on a budget. Downtown Victorian with later additions. Glenwood and Aspen buses stop at the door. Dorm-style accommodations and private rooms. Loans from lost-and-found from skiers who have forgotten something. Kitchen privileges. **1021 Grand Ave., Glenwood Springs, CO 81601; (800) 9-HOSTEL, (970) 945-8545.**

Hideout Cabins

Modern housekeeping cabins of various sizes, some with fireplaces. Secluded wooded setting on road to Sunlight. Guest laundry. **1293 County Rd. 117, Glenwood Springs, CO 81601; (800) 987-0779, (970) 945-5621.**

Knotty Pine Lodge

Four motel rooms and 17 cabins sleeping up to eight guests. Some fireplace and kitchen units. Pets accepted. Rustic style. Slightly outlying; short drive to Hot Springs Pool. Restaurant across the street. Daily housekeeping, guest laundry, game room. **2706 Grand Ave., Glenwood Springs, CO 81601; (800) 726-5940, (970) 945-6446.**

Red Mountain Inn

Motel rooms and family units with kitchenettes and fireplaces. Located 1^1/2 miles west of town. Restaurant nearby. Pets accepted. Daily housekeeping. Hot tub, heated pool, guest laundry. **51637 Hwy 6 & 24, Glenwood Springs, CO 81601; (800) 748-2565, (970) 945-6353.**

Sunlight Bavarian Inn

Casual ski inn at base of ski area. Twenty-one cedar-paneled rooms of various configurations, each accommodating from two to six. Non-smoking rooms available. Half of the rooms have views right up at the ski slopes. Walking distance to lifts. Midweek ski packages. Daily housekeeping. Restaurant, lounge, outdoor hot tub, lighted skating rink, game room. **10252 County Rd. 117, Glenwood Springs, CO 81601; (800) 733-4757, (970) 945-5225.**

Condominiums

Brettelberg Condominiums

Only ski-in/ski-out lodging at Sunlight Mountain Resort. Simple, economical and quiet family units in Alpine-inspired buildings with porches, fireplaces, kitchens. Units range from studios sleep two to one-bedroom condos sleeping up to six. Walk to base lodge, with cafeteria serving breakfast and lunch, plus après-ski lounge. Satellite dish and in-room movies. Ski/swim packages. Daily housekeeping. Guest laundry, game room. **11101 County Rd. 117, Glenwood Springs, CO 81601; (800) 634-0481, (970) 945-7421.**

DINING OUT

Adducci's

Centrally located Continental restaurant. European specialties with an Italian accent. Very nice meals and entertainment. **1023 Grand Ave., Glenwood Springs; (970) 945-9341, (970) 928-8520.**

Bayou Cajun Restaurant

Fun-filled place with Louisiana food and down-home atmosphere. Casual and fun. Dinner only. **52103 Hwy 6 & 24, Glenwood Springs; (970) 945-1047.**

Buffalo Valley Inn

Friendly and congenial. Recently expanded. Legitimate western decor and atmosphere, but now cross-culturally owned by Swiss proprietor of Sopris Restaurant. Lots of cowboy and Indian memorabilia. Specialties are barbecued meats, chicken slow-smoked over applewood, plus buffalo, pasta, steaks and prime rib. Salad bar. Monday and Tuesday all-you-can-eat steamed shrimp special, Wednesday and Thursday prime rib. Lunch and dinner, and Sunday brunch. Full bar and entertainment. **3637 Hwy 82, Glenwood Springs; (970) 945-5297.**

China Town Restaurant
Mandarin and Szechuan, plus Japanese dishes served in the Fuji Room. Friendly non-smoking, no-MSG restaurant. Full bar. Lunch and dinner; daily specials. Takeout available. **2830 Glen Ave., Glenwood Springs; (970) 945-0307.**

Daily Bread
Good downtown stop of breakfast, featuring delicious home-baked breads and pastries. **729 Grand Ave., Glenwood Springs; (970) 945-6253.**

The Devereux Room
Hotel Colorado's fine-dining room. Baronial setting. Good service. Breakfast, lunch and Continental cuisine and American favorites at dinner. Nightly specials, including prime rib and Rocky Mountain trout. Champagne Sunday brunch. Moderately priced but extensive wine list. **526 Pine St., Glenwood Springs; (970) 945-6511.**

Doc Holliday's Saloon
Mexican food, steaks, sandwiches and burgers in popular saloon. Antique bar and old-time photos. Lunch and dinner. Reservations accepted. **724 Grand Ave., Glenwood Springs; (970) 945-9050.**

Dos Hombres
Mexican mecca for families looking for reasonably priced meals. Shrimp fajitas are house specialty; so are generous margaritas for family members of drinking age. Open daily for lunch and dinner. **51783 Hwy 6 & 24, Glenwood Springs; (970) 928-0490.**

Fireside Inn
Affordable dining with hearty portions. Smoked baby back ribs a specialty. Prime rib, steaks, seafood, chicken and German dishes too. Big salad bar. Large children's menu. Buffet for midweek lunch and Sunday brunch. Reservations ac-

Boarders can show off their skills (and crashes) on rail slides and other natural obstacles in Sunlight's snowboard terrain garden.

cepted. **51701 Hwy 6 & 24, Glenwood Springs; (970) 945-6613.**

Florindo's
Congenial and pleasant non-smoking restaurant serving northern and southern Italian dishes. Lotsa pasta. Milk-fed veal and seafood too. Daily specials. Large wine list; cocktails. Fine homemade desserts. Weekday lunch; dinner nightly except Sunday. Reservations accepted and recommended for parties of six or more. Takeout available. **721 Grand Ave., Glenwood Springs; (970) 925-1245.**

Kettle Restaurant
Super-casual family restaurant open 24 hours. Daily breakfast buffet. Soup tureen and 40-item salad bar at lunch. Children's and seniors' menu. **510 Laurel St., Glenwood Springs; (970) 945-9766.**

Marshall Dillon's
Glenwood's favorite steakhouse. Steak, ribs, pasta and seafood at dinner nightly. Hungry locals come for all-you-can-eat buffets: Mexican on Mondays, Italian on Wednesdays and Chinese on Fridays. Discount to First Choice Inn guests. **51359 US Hwy 6 & 24, Glenwood Springs; (970) 945-0605.**

Nineteenth Street Diner
Retro American tradition. Breakfast all day long plus lunch and dinner at appropriate hours. Extremely affordable homemade food. Full bar. **1908 Grand Ave., Glenwood Springs; (970) 945-9133.**

129

Rick's

Fine dining in lovely white-tablecloth restaurant. Classic foundation with progressive and contemporary interpretation. French sautés and seafood are specialties, all done with light, healthful approach. Cocktails and outstanding extensive wine list. No smoking. Dinner nightly except Sunday. Reservations recommended. **6824 Hwy 82, Glenwood Springs; (970) 945-4771.**

Sopris Restaurant

Well-known Swiss owner/chef presides. Fine dining on European and American specialties at surprisingly moderate prices. Veal, steak, seafood and vegetarian plate featured. Comfortable and exceptionally attractive. Good service at surprisingly moderate prices. Cocktails and wine list. Children's menu. Five miles south of town. Reservations suggested. **7215 Hwy 82, Glenwood Springs; (970) 925-7771.**

130

NIGHTLIFE

Ski Sunlight's Last Turn bar in the recently expanded base lodge gets the first après-ski wave, which spills onto the sunny adjacent deck in spring. In and around town, good nightspots include the Bayou Cajun, Doc Holliday's Saloon, The Loft, The Rivers and the Springs Restaurant & Bar. The new Glenwood Canyon Brewing Co. in the Hotel Denver is a popular spot for an elbow-bending evening. The Palm Court Bar & Grill and the Bamboo Bar in the Hotel Colorado between them serve light meals and also have a CD jukebox, pool table and electronic darts. There's a pool and a view of the hot springs pool from the Club Car of the Hotel Denver. The 1,000 Silver Dollar Bar at the Buffalo Valley Inn is worth a visit, even if just for the attraction. The Nineteenth Street Diner has a full bar and a big-screen TV, a 1990s adornment to a 1950s kind of place. You can dance to country-and-western music at Celebrations in the Ramada Tuesday through Saturday, and you can hear live jazz at the Sopris on Tuesday nights. Still, Glenwood Springs cannot be considered as one of Colorado's hot spots at night, with many places' last call at 10:00 P.M. most nights.

No one, young or old, seems to ski at Sunlight without visiting the Hot Springs Pool, an understandable Glenwood Springs institution. The pool—actually a huge complex of hot spring-fed pools of various sizes and temperatures, water slides, dressing rooms and swimsuit and towel rentals—is open daily (except the second Wednesday of each month) until 10:00 P.M.

For more information, contact **Sunlight Mountain Resort, 10901 County Rd. 117, Glenwood Springs, CO 81601; (800) 445-7931, (970) 945-7491; Glenwood Springs Chamber Resort Assn., 1102 Grand Ave., Glenwood Springs, CO 81601; (970) 945-6589.**

MONARCH

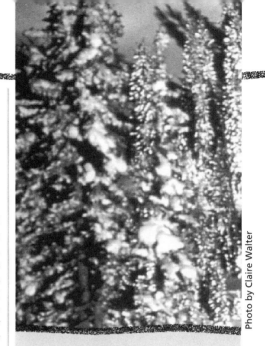

Photo by Claire Walter

BACKDROP

In the realm of powder skiing, Monarch is indeed royalty. This high-altitude ski area sweeps as grandly across the Continental Divide as a queen, wearing a mantle of new snow as regally as if it were an ermine cape. Monarch is situated just east of the Divide in Colorado's south-central mountains. The powder dropped from the so-called "Monarch Cloud" gets tracked by early birds, but it generally still hasn't been trashed by the time the next dump hits. Monarch's fabled "powder policy" endears the area with new snow-aholics. After a night's snowfall, terrain is opened as early as the Patrol declares it safe—no waiting until 9:00 o'clock. That kind of attitude has endeared Monarch to several generations of powderhounds.

The ski area is characterized by a mature forest of well-spaced pine and fir that draw powder pigs like a magnet attracts iron filings. Every few yards along any of the 54 cut trails, tracks angle into and out of the trees, telling of yet another skier or snowboarder who ventured into the deep. The secret of the area's linger-longer cover is that nearly everything within its boundaries is skiable—not just the trails and bowls you'll find on the map but also the uncharted powder shots through the trees.

Despite this noble abundance of powder, Monarch's low prices, functional facilities and unpretentious friendliness keep it essentially a spot for day skiers and weekenders and no-frills vacationers who drive in from Oklahoma, Kansas and even northern Texas. The fanciest lodgings and restaurants around are low-priced and low-key, making it a natural destination for budget-watchers. The area is trying to appeal to a wider spectrum of destination guests by quietly upgrading the nearby Monarch Lodge and laying plans for an eventual expansion. For years, improvements were stymied because the area was controlled by the Seattle-based Seventh Elect Church of God in Israel, whose entire membership consisted of three elderly eccentrics. Sprung from the bizarre setup in 1991 when it was purchased by a Japanese-backed investment company, which tabled a long-wished-for lift expansion into the Great Divide area, which offers some of Colorado's best snowcat skiing, when the powers that be decided that remaining a mid-size, economical area with big snow was the best strategy for the future.

In the summer of 1996, Monarch changed hands and direction again. A new Los Angeles–based investment group purchased the area, renamed it Monarch Ski and Snowboard Area and began talking about upping lift capacity, improving the base area and marketing more aggressively to out-of-state skiers. Those who like Monarch just as it is—a snow-laden bowl not overwhelmed with infrastructure—had better get their turns in quickly, for some of the old plans and some new ones that will change the nature of the place may be instituted in the next few years. Then again, if history is a teacher, perhaps they won't. In either case, no matter who "owns" it, the ultimate control of Monarch lies in the clouds—those clouds that are so generous winter after winter after winter.

THE LAY OF THE LAND

Like such other venerable ski areas high on mountain passes as Arapahoe Basin, Loveland, Ski Cooper and Wolf Creek, Monarch is simply a ski area. The nearest beds are in the Monarch Lodge, 3 miles from the lifts, and the nearest true towns are neighboring Poncha Springs and Salida 12 miles to the east and Buena Vista beyond. A free shuttle bus connects lodge and mountain, but skiers are on their own for all other transport.

GETTING THERE

The Monarch Lodge and Monarch ski area are on US 50 on the east side of Monarch Pass, Colorado's second most-traveled east/west road (after I-70), and although the snowfalls can be

prodigious, it is excellently maintained. Coming from the east, you miss the final steeps of the pass. Two major-city airports have the best air service: Denver is 166 miles via US 285 and US 50, and Colorado Springs is 120 miles via Colorado Route 115 and US 50. The closest airport with scheduled flights is Gunnison, 47 miles to the west via US 50 (and over the pass). A rental car is necessary from any of these airports.

PROFILE

Monarch's terrain is enfolded by a grandly sweeping ridge that is shaped into an open-sided bowl. The ridge spikes into two gentle peaks and a sub-peak pokes up from the middle. It's shaped a bit like a mountainous amphitheater with an upside-down ice-cream cone in the center. Three deep, gently pitched runs follow three drainages enfolded in the cirque, conveying upon this modest ski area distinctive sectors and a big-mountain feel. Yet a simple, rustic base lodge and a preponderance of family skiers and snowboarders give the place an endearing feeling of rusticity and permanence. Follow-the-sun skiing (when it's not snowing) gives skiers at bargain-priced Monarch a priceless benefit not available at ski areas where all the runs face north. A great percentage of Monarch's terrain is suitable for beginners and novices. Tumbelina, the beginner chair near the base lodge, serves some excellent novice terrain, the children's area is great for little ones and the 54 cut runs are fairly apportioned for all ability levels. But the tree skiing between these runs adds an ample measure of challenge, making Monarch surprisingly good for advanced and expert skiers—the kind who would normally eschew a ski area with just four double chairlifts and a ho-hum vertical of just over 1,000 feet.

The Breezeway chair angles northward from the base area accessing half a dozen intermediate and advanced trails, plus little cutoffs through the woods and legitimate glades. Team up with a local if you want to discover such secret spots as Surprise 1, 2 and 3, a trio of snow-holding chutes between Little Mo and Slow Mo. You can find B's Bash on the trail map, but you'll need help in finding B's Trees, a hidden glade beside it.

By contrast, The Meadows, near the area's eastern boundary, is less concealed. This splendidly textured stand of widely spaced trees usually retains untracked snow and is especially treasured by telemark skiers.

A brief ridge-top walk from the top of Breezeway leads to the Outback, a wide semi-steep snowfield that is no less than sublime when plastered with a deep mantle of fresh snow. Early birds with good skills take regular fall-line turns that create picture-perfect tracks. To preserve as much of the powder for as long as possible, the patrol sets several vertical fences with control gates down the Outback, so that traversing skiers don't track out the snow without really skiing it. The Outback narrows suddenly, funneling into a wide runout at the bottom of a drainage, feeding into a run called Snowburn. This in turn leads to the base of the Panorama chair, which reaches Monarch's highest elevation. Hundreds of peaks from the Elk Range near Aspen to Pikes Peak looming over Colorado Springs are visible, and if there were one spot in Rocky Mountain that merited a European-style view restaurant, this would surely be it.

The Panorama chair accesses steep terrain that for most regulars is the best of Monarch. Sheer-Rock-O, the aptly named liftline run, is steep and narrow and most attractive to young hotshots who like to show off for lift riders. Two green-circle trails follow the ridgeline in both directions, literally following the Continental Divide. From the Great Divide to the right, you can drop into High Anxiety, Frazzle, Zipper and Dire Straits, a demanding black-diamond quartet. Between them, there's tree skiing galore, the most harrowing parcel being the small jumpable cliffs nicknamed Horseshoe and tucked between Zipper and Dire Straits. If the blacks are too scary and the unmarked tree turf unthinkable, you can continue to the end of Great Divide and ski Ticaboo or Snowburn back to the bottom of Panorama.

Skywalker is the easy trail off the left side of the Panorama. Novices can drink in the scenery (even stopping at a mountaintop picnic table if they choose) and then follow the trail to equally mild Sleepy Hollow all the way to the base. Sleepy Hollow is a wide meander down still another drainage. Children especially are drawn

Mountain Stats— Monarch

Resort elevation 9,543 feet (Monarch Lodge)
Top of highest lift 11,950 feet
Bottom of lowest lift 10,790 feet
Total vertical 1,160 feet
Longest run 2 miles
Average annual snowfall 350 inches
Ski season mid-November to early April
Lifts 4 double chairlifts
Capacity 4,500 skiers per hour
Terrain inbounds, 54 trails, 637 acres (21% beginner and novice, 37% intermediate, 42% advanced and expert); Great Divide Snowcat terrain, 900 acres (all high-intermediate to expert)
Snow reports (800) 228-7943, (719) 539-3573

into Pinball, a steep little trough that appears on no map but is known by local youngsters for its jumpy bumps and banks on which to turn. Insider skiing starts early at Monarch. The lower section is called the Glade, a mild tree run near the bottom, and it is fun as well.

Better skiers ride the Panorama lift and shoot down Mirage, a black run that mirrors the foursome on the other side of the chair, or Turbo and Short-n-Sweet, nearby intermediate runs and more trees between them as well. Advanced skiers also have the option of climbing a small knoll above a switchback on Skywalker and skiing yet another broad powder-caked snowfield called Curecanti Bowl. The climb, not onerous but nevertheless longer than the one required to reach the Outback, separates those willing to work to get to the powder from those willing to work only to ski the Outback. With a maximum vertical of 500 feet, Curecanti spills into Sidewinder and finally to Lower Tango, yet another green down the bottom of yet another drainage.

The Garfield chair climbs up the mid-area inverted cone between the Sleepy Hollow and Lower Tango drainages. The "back" of this subpeak lies up against the main cirque, and a ridge at the top points back toward the base area. The runs from this ridge tend toward the steep-drop, double-fall line variety—terrain to get your knees cranking and your heart pumping. Again, the trees beckon too. The Garfield chair also accesses Romp, which skirts the high side of the

133

Lower Tango drainage, giving novices and intermediates half a dozen easier runs. At the far end of the inbounds terrain, just across from the Breezeway chair, is Gunbarrel, Monarch's original trail, and nearby is an unmarked, arrow-straight, phone booth–narrow cut that follows an old rope-tow line.

SNOWBOARDING

At Monarch, snowboarding enjoys regal status, with snowboard instruction for all ages and all abilities to terrain that begs for riders. Monarch's terrain—both lift- and snowcat-served—includes the kinds of steady fall-line slopes, great trees and challenging trails that snowboarders love. The sensational Meadows Snowboard Park between the Great Divide and Ticaboo trails features rail slides, quarter-pipe, spine, big air jumps and smooth transitions. There is also a half-pipe.

134

SNOWCAT SKIING

Monarch boasts of having Colorado's steepest snowcat terrain. The Great Divide is a 900-acre playground for advanced and expert skiers and snowboarders. Two guides accompany each group of up to eight on runs of 1,000 to 1,400 feet. The terrain ranges from true-blue intermediate to what the patrol describes as black, double-black and triple-black, encompassing glades, meadows, cliffs, chutes and still more trees and all packed with fluffy snow that lingers and lingers. Backcountry skiers named some of the best spots even before the cat service started. Smith & Jones, named after two popular goggle manufacturers, are expert chutes. Colombia and Mexico are free-fall slopes of 40 degrees and more. OOTS, which is short for "orgasms on the spot," is a fabulous, near-vertical tree run. Single runs, half-day and full-day excursions are offered at a price that is among the most reasonable in the Rockies.

SKI SCHOOL PROGRAMS

Monarch Ski and Snowboard School, (800) 228-7943, (719) 539-3573.

Introductory Program

Never-Ever Package: All-lifts ticket, ski or snowboard rental equipment rental and two-hour lesson.

Advanced and Specialty Programs

Lift & Lesson Package: Lift ticket, ski rentals and two-hour lesson at novice/intermediate and above levels.
Snowboard Clinic: $1^1/2$-hour lesson for all levels.
Women's Workshops: Morning coffee, two-hour lesson at all levels, lunch and videotaping, taught by women for women.
Advanced Skier Workshops: Weekend package of four hours of instruction, videotaping and Saturday wine and cheese party. Designed for adults who want to improve their technique. One-day option also offered.

For Families

Nonskiing Children
Children's Center: Nursery and day care for children ages 2 months to 6 years. Hourly, all-day and half-day options. Reservations recommended.

Skiing Children
Team Ski: Instruction options for ages 3 to 6 offered in conjunction with day care in the Children's Center. Options include morning or afternoon lessons; afternoon for ages 5 and 6 only. Packages available.
Kidski: All-day lift, lesson and lunch program for children ages 7 to 12. Classes for all levels. Rental equipment optional.

FOR RACERS

Race Clinics: Available through Ski and Snowboard School.
NASTAR: Thursdays, Fridays and weekends. Register at Guest Services Desk in main base lodge.

NORDIC SKIING

Monarch has a 3-kilometer beginner cross-country loop, but the most popular route is up the Old Monarch Pass Road. The options for this tour are to ski out from and back to the ski area, or to use the car-shuttle technique—ski one way over the pass and ride the other way. The longest downhill, a hoot-and-holler 7 miler, is one of Colorado's most fun ski tours. Equipment rental and instruction in such Nordic skills as cross-country skiing, skating, telemarking and backcountry skiing, as well as guided ski or snowshoe tours into the backcountry is available from **Monarch Mountain Guides, (800) 228-0675, (719) 539-4506.** The San Isabel National Forest puts out an informative brochure on Monarch, including a self-guided nature ski trail trek, which is available at the ski area. The Sawatch Range abounds with backcountry tours, including popular ones to the ghost town of St. Elmo and around Cottonwood Pass west of Buena Vista. **The U.S. Forest Service** can be reached at **(970) 533-3591.**

WHERE TO STAY

All accommodations are economy to mid-price. There is no central reservations number; contact individual properties, or check with the **Chaffee County Lodging Association,** which operates a referral service for properties in Salida, Buena Vista and Poncha Springs, **(719) 539-8822.** Availability is updated hourly for last-minute skiing plans when there's big powder.

Monarch/Garfield

Monarch Lodge
One-hundred-room lodge, including 31 kitchenette units. Recently redecorated and moderately priced. Functional and unpretentious, but many facilities for après-ski activities. Lodge has best deals on lift/lodging packages. Closest to ski area (3 miles). Daily housekeeping, 24-hour front desk, complimentary ski shuttle, massage therapist. Indoor pool, outdoor hot tub, sauna, fitness center, racquetball, game room, restaurant, lounge. **#1 Powder Pl., Monarch, CO 81227; (800) 332-3668, (719) 539-2581.**

Mountain Cabin Rentals
Three miles east of ski area, close to Monarch Lodge. Great setup for large families and groups. Four rustic cabins sleeping from 6 to 20 people (the latter was a schoolhouse built in 1880s). All have full kitchens, completely stocked. Tranquil (no phones). No housekeeping service, but linens are supplied. **General Delivery, P.O. Box B, Monarch, CO 81227; (719) 539-4057.**

Buena Vista

(Forty-five minutes via US 285 and US 50). For information (but not reservations), contact **Buena Vista Area Chamber of Commerce, P.O. Box 2021, 343 South Hwy 24, Buena Vista, CO 81211; (719) 395-6612.**

The Adobe Inn
Five distinctively furnished rooms in a hacienda-style B&B inn. Each room with private bath and interesting furnishings, including antiques and imports. Non-smoking property. Daily housekeeping, full breakfast. Restaurant, solarium, hot tub, library. **303 Hwy 24 North, Buena Vista, CO 81211; (719) 395-6340.**

Cottonwood Hot Springs Inn & Spa
Twelve-room country inn plus three housekeeping cabins in secluded setting. Original lodge founded in 1878. Claims to have Colorado's "purest" hot spring. Some privacy-fenced spas sunk into redwood decks cantilevered over Cottonwood Creek. Vegetarian and traditional meals served family-style. Tranquil, with no in-room phones or television. TV with VCR in main lodge only. Children 12 and younger half-price. Dining room, hot tubs, exercise and weight room. **10999 Hwy 306, Buena Vista, CO 81211; (719) 395-6434.**

Great Western Sumac Lodge
Inexpensive AAA-approved lodge. Thirty rooms, some nonsmoking. Children 12 and younger stay free. Pets welcome. Daily housekeeping, complimentary coffee, free local calls. **428 Hwy 24 South, Buena Vista, CO 81211; (719) 395-8111.**

Colorado Classics

Thunder Lodge
Eight family-size cabins nestled in the trees along Cottonwood Creek. Western and Native American decor. Complete kitchens. Views of Collegiate Peaks. **207 Brookdale, Buena Vista, CO 81211; (719) 395-2245.**

Vista Court Cabins & Lodge
Five new lodge rooms and eight log cabins on 2$\frac{1}{2}$ mountain-view acres. Restaurant, outdoor hot tub. **1004 W. Main, Buena Vista, CO 81211; (719) 395-6557.**

Poncha Springs

(About 25 minutes via US 50.) For information (but not reservations), contact **Poncha Springs Town Hall, P.O. Box 74, Poncha Springs, CO 81242; (719) 539-6882,** or the Heart of the Rockies Chamber of Commerce (see below).

Poncha Lodge
Fourteen-room budget motel right on the highway, 12 miles from ski area. Rooms with one, two and three beds; most rooms with stall showers, two with tub and shower. **P.O. Box 298, Poncha Springs, CO 81242; (719) 539-6085.**

Rocky Mountain Lodge
Simple motel 5 miles from Salida and 13 miles from Monarch. Restaurant across the street. Rustic and casual. One- and two-bedded rooms. Ten units; some efficiencies. Daily housekeeping. **446 E. US 50, P.O. Box 172, Poncha Springs, CO 81242; (719) 539-6008.**

The Yellow House at Maysville
Roadside landmark, now sprightly three-room B&B inn between highway and river. Country feeling. Art gallery and gift shop on site. Located 5 miles west of Poncha Springs. Two outdoor hot tubs overlooking the river (also available for rental by the hour). Daily housekeeping, full country breakfast. **16665 W. US 50. Poncha Springs, CO 81242; (800) 294-7531, (719) 539-7531.**

Salida

(About 30 minutes via US 50.) For information (but not reservations), contact **Heart of the Rockies Chamber of Commerce, 406 US Hwy 50, Salida, CO 81201; (719) 539-2068.**

Best Western Colorado Lodge
Thirty-five rooms, including 10 mini-suites with whirlpool baths, king- or queen-size bed and refrigerator. Next door to Mineral Hot Springs. New indoor swimming pool complex. Daily housekeeping, complimentary coffee, complimentary HBO. Indoor pool, hot tub, two Jacuzzis, two guest laundries. **352 W. Rainbow Blvd., US 50 West, Salida, CO 81201; (719) 539-2514; (800) 528-1234** for Best Western reservations.

Friendship Inn of Salida
Simple motel with extras at budget rates. King- and queen-size waterbeds. Discount Hot Springs Pool and Monarch lift tickets to guests. AAA motel. Express drive-in check-in, daily housekeeping, free local calls, Continental breakfast. Heated swimming pool, indoor hot tub, game room. **7545 US 50 West, Salida, CO 81201; (719) 539-6656, (800) 453-4511** for Friendship Inn reservations.

Heart of the Rockies Campground
Budget overnights for RVers in park that's gone year-round. Pull-through sites. Outdoor heated pool, showers, arcade. **16105 US 50, Salida, CO 81201; (800) 496-2245, (719) 539-4051.**

Holiday Inn Express
New economy motor inn, affiliated with national chain. Six rooms with private jetted tubs; family suites. Daily housekeeping, Continental breakfast. Heated indoor pool, spa. **7400 US 50 West, Salida, CO 81201; (719) 539-8500, (800) HOL-IDAY** for Holiday Inn reservations.

Log Cabin Court
Cabins with kitchenettes on the banks of the Arkansas River. A local landmark for more than 50 years. Housekeeping. **Hwy 291, 536 E. First St., Salida, CO 81201; (719) 539-4793.**

Redwood Lodge
Twenty-eight individually decorated units from comfortable hotel-type rooms to luxurious mini-suites with private hot tubs. Some non-smoking rooms. AAA Four Diamond property with landscaped grounds. Great views of Sangre de Cristo and Sawatch Ranges. Daily housekeeping, two outdoor hot tubs, sundeck. **7310 Hwy 50, Salida, CO 81202; (800) 234-1077, (719) 539-2528.**

River Run Inn

Historic Victorian homes on the Arkansas River, now fine B&B with five rooms and dorm. Children welcome. Daily housekeeping. Breakfast. **8495 County Rd. 160, Salida, CO 81201; (800) 385-6925, (719) 539-3818.**

Western Holiday Motel

Rambling in-town motel within walking distance of restaurants and Hot Springs Pool. Newly remodeled rooms with individual heat controls. Daily housekeeping. Outdoor heated pool, indoor hot tub, in-room coffee. **545 W. Rainbow Blvd., US 50, Salida, CO 81201; (719) 539-2553.**

DINING OUT

Monarch

Syncline Restaurant

Breakfast, lunch and dinner served in pleasant remodeled dining room of the Monarch Lodge. Varied menu with standard to slightly exotic dishes. Moderate prices. **Monarch Lodge, Monarch; (719) 539-2581.**

Buena Vista

Buffalo Bar & Grill

Quality beef in general and prime rib in particular are main specialties. Also chicken, chops, smoked ribs and seafood. Soups and sauces homemade daily. Dinner nightly. **710 US 24 North, Buena Vista; (719) 539-9931.**

El Duran y Miguel

Casual Mexican place with large portions, budget prices and relaxed, vibrant atmosphere. The green chili is renowned. **301 E. Main St., Buena Vista; (719) 395-2120.**

Poncha Springs

Grimo's

Popular Italian dishes, especially veal, pasta and seafood. Family-owned restaurant known for mid-price range and good food. Casual pool-table atmosphere of bar spills over to restaurant. **146 S. Main St., Poncha Springs; (719) 539-2903.**

Salida

Country Bounty Restaurant

Breakfast, lunch and dinner. Known for full menu selection and homemade pies and cobblers. Family-friendly, smoke-free and very hospitable. Gift shop. **413 W. Rainbow Blvd., Salida; (719) 539-3546.**

First Street Cafe

Downtown cafe in historic brick building with old-fashioned atmosphere, old-time prices but new-style fare. Mexican platters, vegetarian specials and traditional steak, chicken and shrimp. Breakfast, lunch and dinner (early only, as closing is at 7:00 P.M. on weekdays). Daily specials, soup and salad bar and great desserts. Wine and beer, including microbrews. **137 First St., Salida; (719) 539-4759.**

Il Vicino

Oak-fired pizza oven, fresh microbrewed beers and contemporary Italian ambiance equal Chaffee County hot spot. Salads sandwiches and pastas served at lunch and dinner. **136 E. Second St., Salida; (719) 539-5219.**

Windmill Restaurant

False-front western-style building beckons tourists, as does promise of gift shop. Lots of antiques and memorabilia. Large restaurant has friendly service and good food. Steak, seafood and Mexican food at modest prices. Soup and salad bar; dessert tray. Children's menu. Lounge with full bar service. **720 US 50 East, Salida; (719) 539-3594.**

NIGHTLIFE

The Sidewinder Saloon in Monarch's base lodge has a full bar and limited food service. Afterwards, the best bet is Taylor's in the Monarch Lodge. There is some nightlife in all the nearby Arkansas River Valley towns, but it tends to end early and concentrates on weekends.

For more information, contact **Monarch Ski & Snowboard Area, #1 Powder Pl., Monarch, CO 81227; (800) 228-7943, (719) 539-2581,** or the local and regional information sources (see Buena Vista, Poncha Springs and Salida "Where to Stay," above).

CRESTED BUTTE

BACKDROP

Crested Butte has every tangible element people look for in the Rockies: a broad spectrum of terrain, ample snow and sunshine, base-of-the-lifts resort convenience coupled with the charm of a nifty old town nearby and adequate restaurants, nightspots and non-ski activities to fill a week. Yet the scale of the total resort is comparatively modest, and such intangibles as down-home friendliness and an absence of pretensions draw skiers who are put off by glitz and glamour. The result is an unintimidating, people-pleasing destination with a lot going for it.

Crested Butte is the name of a picturesque village in the heart of Colorado, where western-cut clothing, cowboy hats and pickup trucks are part of life. When Crested Butte began promoting itself as "the real West," no one criticized the resort for inaccuracy. This old mining town, whose center is now a National Historic District, wallows in Victorian charm. The ski area and base village spread under the commanding presence of Mt. Crested Butte, which dominates the scenery much as the Matterhorn dominates Zermatt. The ski terrain wraps halfway around the sloping apron of land that surrounds this exceptionally photogenic peak. At the base of the main lifts is Mt. Crested Butte, a little complex that includes a sleek hotel, a preponderance of condominiums and just enough shops and eateries to combat cabin fever.

Since it's too far from the Front Range to appeal to day-trippers, the ski area of Crested Butte has made extra efforts to devise good deals for vacationers, especially those who travel in off-peak times, and to offer excellent air access from key cities and special attention to beginners, clubs, families and other groups. In 1991–92 Crested Butte, already a leader in free early-sea-son ski instruction as well as good deals for families, introduced totally free, no-strings-attached skiing between Thanksgiving and mid-December, snaring record crowds. The program has been tweaked since then. It is now generally available from just after Thanksgiving to mid-December and again in spring—and it remains one of the best deals in skidom.

THE LAY OF THE LAND

As you drive the 28 miles northward from Gunnison, you'll get a sense that the Western Slope is brash and unforgiving, consisting of rugged, rolling high prairie set against a mountain backdrop. There's an open feeling to the land, where working ranches outnumber dude ranches and a true rural flavor prevails. It's a sudden transition from sparsely populated ranchland to new subdivisions and then to the pretty town that has become such an attractive vacationville. Three miles north of town—up a road that is steeper than it looks—are its namesakes, the ski mountain and the resort at its base.

The resort development is at the northern end of a relatively small stairstep-shaped parcel of land, almost entirely surrounded by the Gunnison National Forest, with loosely drawn plans for another (more glamorous) development over the hill from the present Mt. Crested Butte, where many private homes have already been built. Since the traffic won't bear that expansion yet, the present balance between small authentic town and small resort remains.

GETTING THERE

Gunnison (28 miles) is served with nonstop flights from Chicago, Dallas–Fort Worth, Atlanta and Houston and commuter service from Denver International Airport. **Alpine Express** provides transfers via shuttle vans and/or buses; **(800) 822-4844, (970) 641-5074.** It's easy to be in Crested Butte without a car, since free buses run until midnight—about every 15 minutes between

the town and the mountain and about every 20 serving the resort condo areas.

Crested Butte is 230 miles (about four and one half hours) from Denver. The most direct route is US 285 south to US 50, west over Monarch Pass to Gunnison and north on Route 135 to Crested Butte. From Colorado Springs (198 miles, four hours), follow US 24 west to US Route 50 and continue as from Denver. If the weather is dicey, your car is ill-equipped for heavy snows and/or you're simply uncomfortable on high pass roads, an alternative is Route 114, looping south around Monarch Pass. From Denver or Colorado Springs, take US 285 southward at Saguache, then Route 114, which rejoins Route 50 just east of Gunnison and substitutes North Pass (10,149 feet) for Monarch Pass (11,312 feet), although it is about 50 miles longer.

PROFILE

Until (or unless) a new resort center is constructed, the main port of entry to Crested Butte's ski terrain remains the informal and decidedly unprepossessing base village of Mt. Crested Butte. It is no place of beauty, but it is functional and exceptionally convenient—just steps from a high-speed quad, a triple chair and the nursery area. As you are looking uphill, most of the ski terrain is up to the left and out of sight. A few hundred feet down to the right the Peachtree chair accesses gentle novice terrain, and beyond, one of the last T-bars in captivity serves the racing hill. The Silver Queen quad lift directly accesses a handful of steep runs that, by turns, are groomed for super-cruising or allowed to bump up. Good skiers switch to the Twister chair on the upper portion of this sector to ski such steep shorts as Crystal, Twister, Jokerville and Upper Keystone. International, which is often the downhill course for the U.S. Alpine Ski Championships, is the area's longest black-diamond trail. Better skiers veer off to the ungroomed double blacks farther to the right—Peel, Forest and Hot Rocks.

Hospitality to new skiers is a Crested Butte signature, and from the base the Keystone lift

Inside Crested Butte

Mountain Stats—
Crested Butte

Resort elevation 9,375 feet
Top of highest lift 11,875 feet
Bottom of lowest lift 9,100 feet
Total vertical 2,775 feet
Longest run 2.6 miles
Average annual snowfall 300 inches
Ski season Thanksgiving to mid-April
Lifts 2 high-speed quads, 3 triples, 4 doubles, 4 surface lifts
Capacity 15,960 skiers per hour
Terrain 85 trails, 1,160 acres (13% beginner and novice, 30% intermediate, 57% advanced and expert)
Snowmaking 238 acres
Mountain dining Paradise Warming House at the bottom of the Paradise lift (including Bubba's full-service restaurant), Twister Warming House at the bottom of the Twister lift
Ski reports (970) 349-2323
Note The new Ticket Plus enables guests on a five-day or longer ticket to exchange a day of skiing for another activity, including cross-country skiing, snowmobiling or a balloon ride

angles to the left where novices find more than half a dozen easy trails. Some are clear-cut, barrier-free paths of comfortable width and pitch, while others are gently and prettily gladed. It would take a new skier half an hour or better to make a round-trip. The Keystone triple chair is also the most convenient for Crested Butte's ample intermediate terrain. Close to its top station is the unloading ramp of the Teocalli chair, which angles upward from the left. This is one of three lifts that serve the mostly intermediate runs "around the corner" from the front side. Teocalli and Paradise, the area's second high-speed quad, angle off slightly from one another, each climbing along one side of a broad, wooded U-shaped valley into which a web of blue-square runs have been cut. Some, like Meander, are mild baby blues; others, like Upper Ruby Chief, are headwalls that turn dark blue when they bump up or are wind-scoured to almost ice. Lower than the Teocalli/Paradise area and around another "corner" is the East River double chair, which serves Double Top Glades and Resurrection, two steepish trails, plus a few blue-square trails.

To the casual skier, the small hill off to the side from the Keystone chair is the ski area's most puzzling development. The Painter Boy triple chair climbs just 525 feet to the top of this mild knob with three wide, easy slopes. Rising 680 vertical feet from nowhere on the other side are the Gold Link triple and three easy blue runs. The mystery is solved when you discover that this is the area projected for Crested Butte's hoped-for second resort center.

There is no mystery to the North Face. When it opened for lift-served skiing in 1987, this ultra-steep gladed area hanging above East River catapulted Crested Butte from a mostly intermediate ski area to a mecca for extreme skiers. Previously only accessible by a 20-minute (or longer) walk—a serious workout at 11,400 feet above sea level—the North Face, now accessed by a short surface lift, comprises some 400 acres of terrain so extreme that double black diamond designation does not quite seem to suffice. From somewhere above East River to somewhere above Paradise Bowl is the North Face, which was etched into the face by some primeval force and includes breathtaking bowls, harrowing headwalls and sheer chutes. The running gag is that the ski patrol never has to do any rescue work on the North Face; they simply wait at the bottom with body bags.

It is the greatest concentration of lift-served, never-groomed high-expert terrain in Colorado—and one of the best such caches in the skiing world. When you stand at the end of one of the two entrances to the North Face, with the platterpull behind you and your tips poised over a precipice, you are committing yourself to a run that will draw from you all manner of emotions, simultaneously or consecutively—awe and fear, excitement and ecstasy, reverence or reverie. But this isn't a dream. It's the reality of skiing Spellbound Bowl, Phoenix Bowl, Slot, Staircase, Cesspool, Last Steep or dozens of other spots whose names don't appear on the trail map. Reality only returns when you slide into Upper Treasury or Black Eagle, the contrast mellowing those respectable blue squares into what suddenly appear to be manicured flats.

The success of this lift-served extreme terrain prompted the area to put a T-bar to access

Teocalli Bowl, above the Paradise Headwall, upping the double-black turf by 130 acres to a total of 550 and, more importantly, boosting Crested Butte's vertical over the magic 3,000-foot mark. Skiing's strong, gutsy few are separated from its

Ski Free

Since 1991–92, Crested Butte has offered free lift tickets to early-season skiers. Currently, they are available from after Thanksgiving to before Christmas and again at the end of the season. Sleep in your car if you wish. No minimum stays or overnights at a specific property are required—in other words, no strings attached.

weaker, meeker many just by the access to this newest sector. It's a bit of a climb to the High Lift, and anybody who can't handle it has no business on The Headwall or in Teocalli Bowl to the left of the T-bar or Monument, Forest, Peel and Hot Rocks, the chutes and bowls to the right. If you are feeling really strong, heft your skis on your shoulder, and climb another 700 feet (a steep 700 feet at that) to the pinnacle of Crested Butte itself—12,162 feet above sea level and 3,000 feet above the resort. Drink in the view, catch your breath and ski down the creamy snowfield on the peak's northern side. When it tames out, you're back to choosing which black or double-black you wish to ski. If you accomplish it, it's an achievement to be proud of, and you know you'll have earned a massage or a long soak in the hot tub.

Crested Butte is a great place with misleading names. Not only is there built-in confusion when sorting out the old town of Crested Butte, the pinnacle of Crested Butte and the ski area of Crested Butte, plus the resort of Mt. Crested Butte, but many of the trail names are nondescript. The North Face ultra-expert sector isn't a face but a complex snowscape of bowls, ridges, cliffs and walls. There are gentle runs with such steep-sounding names as Roller Coaster and Lower Twister. Only the bottom portion of the Keystone run is served by the Keystone lift. Upper

Keystone is served by the Silver Queen quad chair. But confused nomenclature in no way diminishes great skiing.

SNOWBOARDING

Crested Butte traditionally has welcomed non-traditional winter-sports practitioners. Telemarking got its start on the slopes of Crested Butte. Management also saw the need for some real extreme terrain at a ski area whose initial development was intended to be mild. So it is not surprising that the Butte also embraced the 'board. In addition to a snowpark, the mountain's long gentle trails are well suited to learning (and the ski school offers entry-level as well as advanced classes), and its radical steeps are heaven for top riders. In fact, they were the site of the first-ever U.S. Extreme Snowboarding Championships.

141

SKI SCHOOL PROGRAMS

The ski school desk is in the Gothic Building at the base of the lifts; **(970) 349-2251.**

Introductory Programs

First Timer: All-day Level 1 group lesson, two hours in the morning and two in the afternoon, for new skiers and snowboarders. First Timers

Glades, open slopes, traditional trails and true extreme terrain await skiers, snowboarders and telemarkers.

Photo by Tom Stillo/Crested Butte

booking a minimum three-hour private lesson get 10 percent off; lift ticket included.

Blast Off: One all-day beginner lesson and three-day lift ticket.

QuickStart: Skiers who cannot ski the beginner runs off the Keystone chair by the end of a full-day program with four hours of lessons can get a full refund or return until they are able to do so.

Free Never-Ever Lessons: Inaugurated in 1989, free beginner class lessons for those seven years and older (including adults!) during Ski Free. New skiers progress from station to station, where an instructor works on one skill at a time until the students are ready to board the chairlifts. Class size varies from almost-private to mob-scene, but students progress at their own pace—and the price is right.

Intro to Snowboarding: Four-hour lesson with optional limited lift ticket and rentals.

Advanced and Specialty Programs

Workshops: Specialized two-hour workshops in Turning Fundamentals (Levels 2 to 5), Senior Skiers (Lessons 2 to 9), Bumps, Powder or Parallel (Levels 5 to 9) Ski the Extreme (Level 9), Parabolic Workshop (Levels 6 to 9, including free parabolic ski rentals on Tuesdays, Thursdays and Saturdays), North Face Workshop (Levels 6 to 9) and Groomed Ski Workshop (Levels 2 to 9). Snowboarding Workshops in Carving, Gates, Moguls, Powder, Steeps, Freestyle and Jibbing.

Telemark Lessons: Two-hour morning lessons, including rentals, offered daily.

Kim Reichhelm's Women's Ski Adventures: Traveling women's clinics at Crested Butte more often than at any other resort. Five-day program including coaching, lift tickets, lodging, airport transfers, welcome and awards dinners, product demos and much more. **Women's Ski Adventures, (800) 992-7700** out of Connecticut, **(203) 454-2135** in state.

Extreme Team Advanced Ski Clinics: The Egan and DesLauriers brothers' multiday workshops for experts held at Crested Butte a couple of times each winter.

Adult Snowboarding Workshops: Two-hour workshops with a maximum of four participants focusing on carving, gates, moguls, powder, steeps, freestyle and jibbing. Packages including lift tickets and rentals also available.

Ski Mountaineering and Other Specialty Programs: Avalanche courses, winter mountaineering skills and tours, French-style Centre du Ski Fantastique and other unique programs. **Adventures to the Edge, (800) 349-5219, (970) 349-5219.**

Special Program

Meet the Mountain Tours: Free orientation daily from the quad. Special steep-and-deep tours of the extreme areas are also offered to advanced skiers only.

For Families

Nonskiing Children

Buttetopia Children's Center in the Whetstone Building is headquarters for Buttetopia Toddler Program and Day Care, as well as the children's ski school Mites, Miners and Buttebusters programs, which can be booked by the full or half-day. **(970) 349-2259.**

Nursery: Infant care for newborn to 6 months. Ratio is one caregiver for two infants. Available by the hour. Reservations recommended.

Toddler Program: Day care, lunch and supervised age-appropriate activities, lunch, snacks for children ages 6 months to potty trained. Reservations recommended.

Day Care: Day care, supervision and age-appropriate activities for toilet-trained preschool non-skiers to age 7. Reservations not required.

Annie's Kiddie Center: Independent child care center for non-skiers, aged 1 to 10. Licensed day care for ages 1 to 3. Indoor and outdoor activities, specifics depending on age and weather. Also, supervised evening campfire cookouts. Open daily from 8:30 A.M. to 9:00 P.M. Drop-ins welcome. **621 Gothic Rd., Mt. Crested Butte, CO 81225; (970) 349-9262.**

Skiing Children

Mites: Introduction to skiing for potty-trained 2- and 3-year-olds. Age- and skill-appropriate skiing and off-snow activities. Includes lift ticket, lunch and equipment rental.

Miners: For skiers ages 4 to 7 of all ability levels from Level 1 to Level 9 (occasionally, there are truly high-level little skiers). Includes lift ticket, lunch and equipment rental.

Buttebusters: Group lessons, supervision and lunch for all ability levels for ages 8 to 12. Includes lift tickets and lessons; rental equipment additional.

Tag-Along Lessons: Parents may participate in lessons of children to age 12. One- to three-hour lessons, enabling parents to be actively involved in their child's or children's instruction.

Kid's Snowboarding Workshop: One-on-one instruction for youngsters ages 7 to 12. All ability levels.

Teens

Teen Program: Full-day and half-day classes for all ability levels, from first-timers to black-diamond-level experts. For ages 13 to 17.

FOR RACERS

NASTAR: Offered Wednesdays. Sign up at the information desk in the Gothic Building.
Coin-Operated Course: Open daily on Smith Hill. Racing clinics/instruction available.

HANDICAPPED SKIING

The Physically Challenged Program is supported by proceeds from lift tickets, with a slopeside office in the Gothic Building. Advance reservations are required, **(970) 349-2296.**

NORDIC SKIING

The Crested Butte Nordic Center, operated by the CB Nordic Council and headquartered at Big Mine Park right at the edge of the downtown area, grooms 20 to 30 kilometers of trails daily for class skiing and skating. Twenty kilometers are available directly from the Nordic Center, the longest an easy 9-kilometer loop called The Bench, while the remainder is reached from the trailhead at the bottom of the Kebler Pass Road. Track skiing, lessons at all levels and organized half-day and all-day tours (minimum of three

people) operate out of the **Nordic Center, (970) 349-1707.** Crested Butte was the birthplace of modern American telemark skiing, and lessons at the Alpine area can be booked at the **Gothic Building Ski School Desk, (970) 349-2282.**

Adventures to the Edge offers an assortment of winter mountaineering programs, including winter peak climbs and ski-downs, backcountry hut tours and ski and snowshoe tours of various sorts. The company is run by Jean Pavillard, a French mountain and ski guide (and former Crested Butte Ski School director who returned to his roots), and offer programs that are quite unique in the Rockies, **(800) 349-5219.** You can put all your Alpine skills to the test by skiing hut to hut. The Alfred A. Braun Hut System's southern end is near Crested Butte (the northern is near Aspen). For information and reservations, contact the **Tenth Mountain Trail Assn., (970) 925-5775.**

WHERE TO STAY

Crested Butte Central Reservations, P.O. Box A, Mt. Crested Butte, CO 81225; (800) 544-8448, fax (970) 349-2307.

Luxury Accommodations

Crested Butte Club

Seven luxury suites, with gas fireplaces and antique furnishings in the Victorian style. In historic downtown Crested Butte. Full athletic club (aerobics, lap pool, weight room, racquetball, steam baths, hot tubs, massage). Also, Nordic Center nearby. Daily housekeeping, full breakfast buffet, complimentary after-ski refreshments. Full health and fitness facility, sun deck, piano bar, lounge. **P.O. Drawer 309, 512 Second St., Crested Butte, CO 81224; (970) 349-6655.**

Grande Butte Hotel

Sleek hotel at the base of the lifts with 261 spacious rooms and suites, each with a wet bar, in-room coffee maker, whirlpool bathtub, private balcony and cable TV with in-room movies. Daily housekeeping, room service, 24-hour front desk, bell staff, concierge, valet, attended ski check. Two restaurants, two lounges, indoor swimming

Photo by Tom Stillo/Crested Butte

Free riders heading for the hill exude Crested Butte's youthful exuberance.

pool, fitness room, sauna, hot tub, game room. **P.O. Drawer A, 500 Gothic Rd., Mt. Crested Butte, CO 81224; (800) 544-8448, (970) 349-7561.**

Mid-Priced Accommodations

The Claim Jumper
In-town B&B inn. Outside, a contemporary log cabin; inside, a Victorian charmer filled with museum-quality memorabilia. Six humorous theme rooms, including the Sports Fan Attic, Ethyl's Room and Prospector's Gulch. All rooms with private baths. Non-smoking inn, Daily housekeeping, gourmet breakfast. Redwood hot tub, sauna, game room, sun room. **P.O. Box 118, 704 Whiterock, Crested Butte, CO 81224; (970) 349-6471.**

Manor Lodge
Unprepossessing 58-room lodge a short walk from the lifts. Some rooms with fireplaces. Four suites. Optional meal plan at Casey's Restaurant & Bar. Complimentary continental breakfast, daily housekeeping. Restaurant, lounge, hot tub, sauna, guest laundry. **P.O. Box 729, Crested Butte, CO 81224; (800) 826-3210, (970) 349-5308.**

Mountainlair
Designed for families and groups. Has 125 over-sized rooms with two king or queen beds, refrig-erator, in-room coffee, cable TV with first-run movie channel. Hotel located 200 yards from Silver Queen Lift at base of mountain. Ample parking. Daily housekeeping. Two outdoor hot tubs, coin laundry. **600 Emmons Rd., Mt. Crested Butte, CO 81224; (800) 544-8448, (970) 349-8000.**

Nordic Inn
Family-owned 25-room lodge near the lifts. Norwegian touch at this all-American resort. Friendly atmosphere and weekly wine-and-cheese parties. Twenty-four rooms, each with two double beds, and two suites. Daily housekeeping, Continental breakfast. Outdoor hot tub, sun deck. **P.O. Box 939, Crested Butte, CO 81224; (970) 349-5542.**

Economy Accommodations

Cristiana Guesthaus
Affordable B&B lodge. Twenty-one rooms with one queen-size or two double beds. All have private baths. Television lobby. Comfortable and relaxing non-smoking inn. Daily housekeeping, Continental breakfast buffet, complimentary hot beverages available all day. Deck, hot tub, sauna, ski storage. **P.O. Box 427, 621 Maroon, Crested Butte, CO 81224; (970) 349-5326.**

Elizabeth Anne Bed & Breakfast
Charming Victorian, now an economical four-room B&B. Largest room accommodates up to six. All rooms with private baths. No smoking. Children welcome. Full breakfast. Hot tub. **P.O. Box 105, 703 Maroon, Crested Butte, CO 81224; (970) 349-0147.**

Elk Mountain Lodge
Historic miners' hotel, built in 1919. Completely and beautifully renovated. Nineteen quaint rooms with queen-size beds and private baths. Moderate priced option in downtown Crested Butte. Daily housekeeping, full breakfast. Lobby bar, indoor hot tub. **P.O. Box 148, 129 Gothic Ave., Crested Butte, CO 81224; (800) 374-6521, (970) 349-7533.**

Purple Mountain Lodge
Comfortable in-town classic ski lodge in a historic building, built in 1927. Five rooms accommodating one to three guests each. Three with

private baths, two share. Lobby with massive stone fireplace. Non-smoking inn. Daily housekeeping, full breakfast. Sun room, hot tub. **P.O. Box 897, 714 Gothic Ave., Crested Butte, CO 81224; (970) 349-5888.**

Condominiums

Crested Mountain Village

This catch-all name embodies lodge rooms and one-, two- and three-bedroom condos in half a dozen Mt. Crested Butte properties (many ski-in/ski-out). Common areas vary, but all units (except lodge rooms) have full kitchen, fireplace and balcony, and many have washer and dryer. Daily housekeeping. Swimming pool, hot tubs, saunas. **P.O. Box 99, Mt. Crested Butte, CO 81224; (800) 544-8448, (970) 349-7555.**

The Gateway

Deluxe ski-in/ski-out units. One-bedroom, one-bath to three-bedroom, three-bath condos. Each unit with fireplace, private balcony, TV with HBO and washer and dryer, full kitchen. Daily housekeeping. Hot tub, sauna. **P.O. Box 5004, 701 Gothic Rd., Mt. Crested Butte, CO 81225; (800) 821-3718.**

Paradise Condominiums

Walking distance of the T-bar and the free resort shuttle. Standard two-bedroom, two-bath to four-bedroom plus loft, four-bathroom units, each with fireplace, full kitchen, washer and dryer, private balcony. Daily housekeeping. Three hot tubs, sauna. **P.O. Box 2A, Mt. Crested Butte, CO 81224; (800) 544-8448, (970) 349-2800.**

The Plaza

Twenty-nine two-bedroom, two-bathroom units and 15 three-bedroom, three-bathroom units with full kitchens, fireplace, washer and dryer, private balcony and color TV with HBO. Hotel-type services. Short walk to the lifts. Daily housekeeping. Restaurant, lounge, indoor and outdoor hot tubs, steam bath, sauna, ski rental and repair, convenience/liquor store. **P.O. Box A, 11 Snowmass Rd., Mt. Crested Butte, CO 81225; (800) 433-5684, (970) 349-2900.**

Snowcrest Condominiums

Located across the pedestrian bridge from the lifts. Two- and three-bedroom, two-bath units

with freestanding fireplace and balcony. Full kitchens, some with ice maker and microwave. Spacious and functionally furnished. Daily towel and trash service. Outdoor hot tub, coin laundry. **P.O. Box 1330, Crested Butte, CO 81224; (800) 451-5699, (970) 349-2400.**

Gunnison

The college town of Gunnison, down valley, also offers accommodations, including real budget motels and a handful of nice B&Bs that are more economical than those in Crested Butte. Alpine Express (the same folks who run the airport shuttle) operate low-priced ski shuttles with four downvalley stops (two along US 50, one at Ohio Creek and one in Almont) and two at Crested Butte, one at the four-way stop at the eastern end of town and one at the resort. For information on Gunnison lodgings, contact the **Gunnison Country Chamber of Commerce, P.O. Box 36, Gunnison, CO 81230; (800) 323-2453, (970) 641-1501.**

DINING OUT

The Artichoke

Base-of-the-lifts convenience. Popular for midday breaks, lunch and après-ski. Dinner specialty is steaks and prime rib, but the best bets are burgers, salads and other casual daytime fare. **Treasury Building, 10 Crested Butte Wy., Mt. Crested Butte; (970) 349-6688.**

Bacchanale

Italian specialties, from linguine with popular sauces to various classic veal and poultry selections. "Eat pasta, ski fasta" is the restaurant's slogan. Sandwiches for lighter appetites. Open for dinner only. Children's portions available. Reservations requested. **208 Elk Ave., Crested Butte; (970) 349-5257.**

The Bakery Cafe

Fresh-from-the-oven breads and pastries in a casual downtown cafe. Crested Butte institution. Also serves overstuffed sandwiches, quiches and soups. Salad bar. Large selection of vegetarian and low-fat items. Hearth-baked pizza (and pizza and pitcher deals) from 4:00 to 9:00 P.M. Beer, wine, espresso, cappuccino and latte available. Bakery Kids' Meal featured. **302 Elk Ave., Crested Butte; (970) 349-7280.**

The Bistro

Downtown cafe dispensing breakfast, lunch, dinner and Sunday brunch. Everything from stuffed croissants and eggs Benedict to barbecue ribs and chicken. Large selection of vegetarian items at all meals. Extensive wine list and lots of microbrews to choose from too. Great desserts. Children's menu. Espresso and cappuccino. **229 Elk Ave., Crested Butte; (970) 6107.**

Le Bosquet

Charming purveyor of French specialties (plus a bit of pasta) in a romantic setting. Sophisticated and interesting dinner menu, including Scallop and Salmon Mousseline in White Zinfandel Sauce, Rack of Venison with Wild Mushroom and Pheasant Raviolis, Braised Lamb Shack with French Lentils and many more. Chateaubriand for Two carved at tableside. In addition, lunch and twilight dinner specials. Fine desserts. Reservations suggested. **201 Elk Ave., Crested Butte; (970) 349-5808.**

Donita's Cantina

Filling Tex-Mex fare at moderate prices. Enchiladas, tacos, burritos, tostadas, fajitas and quesadillas with various fillings and in various combinations. Friendly and lively. Good drinks and great salsa. Reservations not accepted. **330 Elk Ave., Crested Butte; (970) 349-6674.**

Giovanni's Grande Cafe

Casually elegant hotel restaurant with fine northern Italian fare. Decor smacks of city sophistication, the menu is very Italian and yet the combination fits right in to the Rocky Mountains. Daily specials. Reservations requested. **Grande Butte Hotel, Mt. Crested Butte; (970) 349-4066, (970) 349-4999.**

The Gourmet Noodle

Fresh pasta and a variety of sauces, all delicious and interesting. Entrée prices cover a wide range, from inexpensive to pricey. In addition to pastas, Chicken Picatta, ravioli, lasagne, veal and game. Full bar, but best known for good wine selection. Open for dinner only. Children's por-

tions available. Reservations requested. **411 Third St., Crested Butte; (9780) 349-7401.**

Karolina's Kitchen

Well-priced home-cookin' in casual setting. Lunch and dinner. Build-your-own deli sandwiches, breakfast favorites, burgers and sandwiches, appetizers, chili and house specialties such as barbecued chicken and grilled flank steak. Rotating specials: Monday, Mexican; Tuesday, meatloaf with mashed potatoes and gravy; Wednesday, pasta; Thursday, chicken-fried steak; Friday, roast beef with gravy—all appropriately accompanied. Full bar. **127 Elk Ave., Crested Butte; (970) 349-6756.**

Lazy F Bar

Crested Butte's only horsedrawn sleighride dinner. Two rides, at 5:00 and 7:00 P.M., on Tuesday, Thursday, Friday and Saturday evenings. Five-course meal, including entrée choice of steak or Cornish hen. BYO wine and beer. Reservations required before noon on day of dinner, **(970) 349-5793.**

MacMahon's

Small and cozy, with stained-glass lamps, neon lights and other objects. Moderately priced downtown eatery. Specializes in steak, pasta, Mexican and grilled items from hot dogs to tuna steaks. Children's portions. Singles table. Lunch, excellent happy hour and dinner. Dinner reservations accepted. **229 Elk Ave., Crested Butte; (970) 349-6107.**

Paradise Sleighride Dinner

Snowcat-drawn sleigh departs Tuesdays, Thursday and Saturday evenings at 5:30 P.M. for evening of merriment in Bubba's at the Paradise Warming Hut. Entrée choice of prime rib, New York steak, Rocky Mountain trout and chef's nightly special. Hors d'oeuvre buffet, salad, dessert and wine included. Cash bar for stronger stuff. Sleigh departs from Rafters' deck, Mt. Crested Butte. Reservations required. **(970) 349-2211, (970) 347-2213.**

Roaring Elk Restaurant

Casual hotel restaurant serving three meals a day. Breakfast buffet and light lunches with selection of soups, salads, sandwiches and other offerings. Dinners feature such all-American classics as Chicken Fried Steak, Fried Chicken, rainbow trout and various cuts of steak. Friday evening, New England-style fish and chips. Sunday evening, prime rib and salad bar. Lounge adjacent for full bar service. **Grande Butte Hotel, Mt. Crested Butte; (970) 349-4042.**

The Slogar Bar & Restaurant

Slogar's expands the meaning of the expression, "down-home cooking." Humongous portions of skillet-fried chicken and steak, accompanied by gut-busting heaps of mashed potatoes, creamed corn and baking powder biscuits with honey butter. Served family-style in a nifty downtown landmark. Children's portions and take-out available. Reservations recommended. So is a loose belt. **517 Second St., Crested Butte; (970) 349-5765.**

Penelope's

Cheerful greenhouse restaurant serving nightly dinners and Sunday brunch. Examples of sophisticated dinner menu offerings: Rabbit Pâté on the appetizer list, Herb Crusted Salmon as an entrée and Crème Brûlée as dessert. Brunch starts early—at 8:30 with breakfast favorites. Lunch items available after 11:00 A.M. **120 Elk Ave., Crested Butte; (970) 349-5178.**

Soupçon

Enchanting place coupling delicious and sophisticated meals, mostly French, with a charming lace-curtain setting. One of downtown Crested Butte's oldest buildings, originally a miner's cabin. Two nightly seatings, at 6:00 and 8:15 P.M. Non-smoking restaurant. Reservations requested. In the alley off Second St. behind Kochevar's, **127 Elk Ave., Crested Butte; (970) 349-5448.**

Swiss Chalet Bierstube & Restaurant

Day starts with great breakfast buffet, including homemade müsli and pastries, plus eggs, omelettes, French toast and more. Dinner is Austro-Swiss (plus a little Italian): Gorgonzola Gnocchi, Bratwurst Platter, Wiener schnitzel, Aprikosen Quail and other dishes. Daily appetizer, entrée and dessert specials. Non-smoking restaurant. Children's menu. Fine happy hour too. Dinner reservations accepted. **621 Gothic Rd., Mt. Crested Butte; (970) 349-5917.**

Twister Warming House Fondue Party

Real fun evening, every Wednesday and Sunday beginning at 4:30. Ride Keystone lift for three-course cheese fondue at the Twister Warming House at mid-mountain. Ends with torchlight procession and everyone skiing down an easy run. Children's rate, one-third reduction. Reservations required. Contact the Information Desk in the Gothic Cafeteria, **(970) 349-2211, (970) 349-2213.**

NIGHTLIFE

"Casual" and "fun" are the words that most often come to mind when describing Crested Butte evenings. Because there are so many ski groups, the action varies with the degree of rowdiness or piety that binds the participants of any given ski week. Students from Western Colorado State College in Gunnison guarantee that a certain amount of early-evening merriment always prevails, but it's up to the guests to keep it going.

Rafters in the Gothic Building starts shaking early with an après-ski "sneak peek" at the band plus canned music and happy-hour drink specials. Sandwiches, fajitas and other filling fare are available, but the real action starts on Fridays and Saturdays at 9:00 P.M., when the band returns for good. Pool, video games, foosball and laser karaoke are also popular in some circles. Also at Mt. Crested Butte, The Artichoke's long happy hour (3:00 to 6:00 P.M.), low prices and good munchies (of course including artichoke dip) make it a winner. Casey's shows free ski movies during its busy happy hour, which also features daily drink specials, a good bar menu, some of the Butte's best pizza and often live entertainment. The Swiss Chalet Bierstube & Restaurant has a terrific happy hour every afternoon. Features a good bar menu and Paulaner Oktoberfest on tap, and a live bluegrass band on Sunday evenings. The Wood Creek Tavern features video games, big-screen TV, Foozball, electronic darts and satisfying bar food.

The top downtown action is at Kochevar's and the Wooden Nickel, which bill themselves respectively as "the area's oldest active saloon" and

Colorado Classics

"Crested Butte's oldest bar." The distinction is a subtle, and irrelevant, difference for both are rowdy and fun. Kochevar's, dating back to 1896, is the site of one of Butch Cassidy's scrapes with the law. There's pool, shuffleboard and darts, and home-style food is available from Karolina's Kitchen next door. The Nickel serves killer drinks, shrimp, sandwiches and BBQ and general merriment, especially during its two happy hours, one from 3:30 to 6:00 P.M. and the other from 10:30 P.M. to midnight. The Powderhouse has a short (one-hour) but potent happy hour, with the availability of 42 tequilas, 21 beers and the promise of "unlimited margarita possibilities."

The Idle Spur is a new brew pub with good beer, live music and food. Talk of the Town is bargain après-ski, with early- and late-evening happy hours and 75¢ draft and $1 schnapps specials. Such cheap eats as hot dogs, chili, pizza and snacks fortify the body, while shuffleboard, pool, darts, video games, Foozball, bowling and video games challenge the coordination—if not the intellect. MacMahon's entices après-skiers with a wide selection of beer on tap, wines and great frozen drinks, plus four big-screen TVs, Foozball, video games and darts. The Idle Spur Steakhouse and Microbrewery has a swell happy hour with nine handcrafted beers, offers live music and also grills up great steaks and more.

A couple of places fill the restrained end of the nightlife spectrum. The Princess pours excellent wines and champagnes (including private reserve) by the bottle or glass, serves exquisite desserts, dispenses after-dinner drinks and features an espresso and coffee bar. The town's oldest bar is installed at the Crested Butte Club, where a piano player holds delightful court.

For more information, contact **Crested Butte Mountain Resort, P.O. Box A, Mt. Crested Butte, CO 81225; (970) 349-2211; Chamber of Commerce, P.O. Box 1288, Crested Butte, CO 81224; (800) 545-4505, (970) 349-6438.**

Crested Butte at sunset.

Photo by Tom Stillo/Crested Butte

TELLURIDE

Photo by T.R. Youngstrom/Telluride Ski & Golf Co.

BACKDROP

Telluride is following in Aspen's tracks from mining boomtown to booming tinseltown. In the seventies, Telluride was still a used-up mining town with what can be described as a "developing" ski area, much as Aspen had been in the fifties. In the eighties, the mountain's reputation for prodigious powder, blue skies and steep, uncrowded slopes began luring skiers from all over the country. In the nineties, a new boom is hitting Telluride with the force of a typhoon. Again like Aspen, instead of prospectors going for the gleam, an incoming wave—initially the most selective skiers in the land and, more recently, celebrities of all stripes—has discovered this corner of southwestern Colorado. Telluride is situated at the head of a remote valley where the waters of the San Miguel River tumble from dramatic mountains that have been compared, favorably, to the Alps. Again like Aspen, Telluride is a town, a mountain, a state of mind.

Today, there are two Tellurides. The original one is western Americana. This old Telluride is untrammeled Victorian has been overlaid with a fashionable luster with interesting shops, galleries, excellent restaurants and B&Bs behind the fancy fretwork and colorful facades. Though the town has gussied up its historic buildings and polished its act, it retains much of its funky charm. Telluride has become one of America's finest and most fashionable ski areas, yet the back streets have still not been paved.

New Telluride, more properly called Mountain Village, is an upscale development in the heart of one of the world's best ski areas. It bears more similarities to Beaver Creek than to anyplace else in the Rockies. Mountain Village, which incorporated in 1995 as a separate town, is a burgeoning second-home community where the streets are not only paved but smoothly so. It conveys the kind of contemporary status that famous faces confirm. Geraldo Rivera, Daryl

Colorado Classics

Hannah, Sting, James Taylor, Dustin Hoffman and Clint Eastwood have skied (or, in Sting's case, snowboarded) on Telluride's slopes or hung around town. Actress Susan St. James, designer Ralph Lauren, television's Oprah Winfrey, and filmmaker Oliver Stone even have houses at or near Telluride; so does the Clorox bleach heiress. Donald Trump and Marla Maples sought refuge at Telluride while Ivana cavorted in Aspen. Tom Cruise and Nicole Kidman were married at Telluride, and Christie Brinkley and real-estate developer Richard Taubman embarked on their short-lived marriage in a mountaintop ceremony. Sylvester Stallone got into a tussle with a lift operator who didn't show him sufficient respect. Rocky's antics won him no friends in town, and the Brinkley-Taubman union dissolved in a matter of months. Despite the occasional paparazzi assault that accompanies such visitors, Telluride's unsurpassed skiing and ardor for the sport exhibited by legions of locals maintain its persona as a true ski town.

150

THE LAY OF THE LAND

Telluride is physically at the end of the road, at the termination of Route 145, which twists for an hour from the nearest major highway to the outskirts of town. The term for topography like this is "box canyon," and old Telluride is surrounded by 13,000- and 14,000-foot peaks of awesome beauty. The isolation means that the ski area never gets crowded and that the historic town was left alone for decades. Old Telluride is etched with a traditional grid of streets lined with Victorian buildings. Colorado Avenue, a wide boulevard, is the main street. A few paved and more unpaved streets flank and intersect the boulevard. Where the sidewalks end, the ski area begins. The famous Front Face looms over the town like a high white wall on which ski tracks have been laid.

Tucked into a scoopy mid-mountain plateau behind the Front Face is Telluride Mountain Village, the glossy new resort development in the heart of the ski terrain. A terrific new option to the tedious roundabout by car or free San Miguel Transit Co. shuttle between the old and new re-

sort components, is a new 2½-mile, up-and-down gondola that operates during the day for skiing and at night for après-skiing.

GETTING THERE

Flying in is the best bet—when the weather is good. However, even though the Telluride Regional Airport has recently been expanded, it is still weather-vulnerable and flights are often diverted to Montrose, 65 miles away. When that happens, complimentary transportation between Montrose and Telluride is offered. It is also possible to fly into Grand Junction Airport, 127 miles to the northwest. Durango Regional Airport is 125 miles to the southeast. Rental cars are available at all four airports. Among the companies operating airport shuttles are **Skip's Taxi, (970) 728-6667; Telluride Transit, (970) 728-6000,** and **Mountain Limo, (970) 728-9606.** Denver International Airport is 335 miles from Telluride. The 7- to 8-hour drive (via US Hwy 285 or I-70 to Colorado 141, and then to US 50, to US 550 to Ridgway, then Route 62 and finally Route 145) is not an option most visitors seriously consider.

PROFILE

Even if you haven't been to Telluride in years, you'll recognized the traditional entrance to the ski area is via two chairlifts on the edge of town, Coonskin and Oak Street. The Oak Street lift rises so sharply over fearsome Front Face—3,165 vertical feet of relentless challenge—that it feels like a cross between an elevator and a chairlift. Once known as much for intimidating moguls as for radical pitch, these have been somewhat recut and are now periodically groomed by winch cat to accommodate aging baby boomers who still love the steeps but can do without so many bumps. Still, groomed or not, ski the near-vertical likes of The Plunge, Spiral Stairs or Kant-Mak-Em, and you're good. Ski them well, and you're great. Ski them well all day, and you're a superstar. What will strike you as brand new and old at the same time is the town station for the new gondola. Sleek modern cars emerge from and disappearing into what looks like an old mining building—in fact, a new creation designed to resemble something weathered and historic. The long-planned gondola is the express service into Gorrono Basin in the heart of Telluride's terrain and to Mountain Village. The Coonskin lift rises beside a small base facility and provides the best connection to ski area from the west end of town.

If the Front Face is too much, or your skiing isn't quite enough, Gorrono Basin is the place to ski. This is a powdery playground etched with 21 immaculately groomed, confidence-building intermediate runs. Glide down Tomboy, Hermit, See Forever or Butterfly, and you'd never know that you are on one of the toughest skiing mountains in the Rockies. The Meadows at the bottom of the Gorrono lifts is a 100-acre beginner slope of uncommon width and gentle pitch, and beside it, Telluride Mountain Village is a visionary dream of slopeside splendor. This is also the site of a truly unique, multi-purpose lift called a Chondola. This hybrid lift uses detachable-chair technology and has both chairlift seats and gondola cars hanging from the cable. It serves as a conventional ski lift for the Meadows and also as transportation from housing and Big Billie's, the newest of Telluride's ski-to eating places.

Sharing a base area with the Chondola bottom across the village from the Gorrono lifts is the Sunshine Express. It rises to the gentle Sunshine Peak summit with fabulous views and modest skiing. Nicknamed "the lift to nowhere," this high-speed quad—astonishingly, at 2 miles, the world's longest—currently leads to just a handful of ego-pleasing novice and intermediate trails. It

Mountain Stats— Telluride

Resort elevation 8,725 feet (Telluride); 9,500 feet (Mountain Village)
Top of highest lift 11,890 feet
Top of hike-to terrain 12,247 feet
Bottom of lowest lift 8,725 feet
Total vertical 3,165 feet
Total hike-to vertical 3,522 feet
Longest run 2.85 miles
Average annual snowfall 300 inches
Ski season Thanksgiving to mid-April
Lifts 1 gondola, 2 high-speed quad chairlifts (1 Chondola), 2 triples, 5 doubles, 1 platterpull
Capacity 11,716 skiers per hour
Terrain 64 trails, 1,056 acres (24% beginner, 51% intermediate, 25% advanced and expert)
Snowmaking 155 acres
Mountain dining Gorrono Ranch mid-mountain in Gorrono Basin with cafeteria service, patio and bar; Gorrono Saloon, next door for beverages, soup and chili; Giuseppi's, on top of Lift 9, with Italian specialties and indoor and outdoor seating with spectacular panoramic views.
Snow reports (970) 728-3614

151

provides access to private homes and is the gateway to the future when Prospector, Palmyra and San Joaquin Bowls are developed. A major hurdle was overcome with the signing of a complex multi-party letter of agreement for the future development of nearly a thousand additional acres of sparkling high-alpine terrain.

Although it has a reputation for real challenge, you can ski Telluride all week without encountering a single black diamond. In fact, three-quarters of the terrain is for beginning and intermediate skiers, and Telluride has so much "easiest" and "more difficult" terrain that the area has seen fit also to divide green runs into single and double circles and blue ones into single and double squares. The remainder of Telluride's runs, splayed in a white arc high above Gorrono Basin, are largely for experts. There is a long ridge connecting the Plunge summit at the top of the Oak Street lift with a currently undeveloped peak called Gold Hill. Its 12,247-foot summit has long been an out-of-bounds favorite of powder pigs willing to hike from the top of Chair 6. In recent years, Gold Hill's 400 acres of tree-free steeps and expert glades are inbounds—meaning they are patrolled, not groomed—but you have to earn your turns by hiking up to ski there, which is not a trivial effort at this altitude.

Chair 6 also shoots skiers up the ridge's precipitous wall, where the steeps of Silverglade, Electra and Apex await the strong. Not as long as the Front Face, but occasionally narrower and in places more constricted by boulders, this powdery sector reinforces Telluride's reputation as a true skier's mountain. The Rockies have numerous ski areas that exceed Telluride's acreage and trail census, but this is a mountain with medium statistics, big views and a grand reputation as one of the best places in the West to ski, with its powdery steeps and monster bumps responsible for its far-ranging preeminence.

SNOWBOARDING

Telluride's new Ride Park, designed by a local snowboarder of some repute, is located just below Gorrono Ranch. The 800-foot-long, 80-foot wide park boasts table tops, gap jumps, a 12-foot quarter-pipe and other features. East Drain and West Drain are two natural half-pipes, and much of the mountain is congenial for riders. Telluride is the rare ski area that provides snowboarders with a special Meet the Mountain Tour, available for free, three times a week. The resort also hosts the annual Nike ACG Surf the Rockies Snowboard Derby in April, and has other events on its calendar and a snowboarding gear in its rental program and snowboarding lessons for all levels available in its ski school.

SKI SCHOOL PROGRAMS

Adult ski school information, **(970) 728-7514.** Ski school desks are located at the Coonskin base area and Mountain Village.

Introductory Program
Beginner Package: Beginner lesson, lift ticket and rental equipment; multiday discounts.

Advanced and Specialty Programs
Specialty Clinics: Midday and afternoon ski clinics on Alpine, Nordic, bumps, telemarking and racing. Snowboard clinics are available for bumps, racing and freestyle. All are offered from 10:50 A.M. to 1:00 P.M. and 1:20 to 4:00 P.M., they are long enough for intense and productive instruction. In addition, Powder Morning Clinics are scheduled from 8:40 to 10:45 A.M.
Women's Week: Three- or five-day programs for and by women, plus evening activities.
Mini-Ski Week: Three-day series of morning clinics with the same instructor.

Special Programs
Meet the Mountain: Free tours meet daily at the top of the Lifts 3 and 7; a snowboarders' version meets Sunday, Monday and Friday. Snowshoe Tours along the ridge between Mountain Village and the valley floor meet Monday, Wednesday and Friday at 1:00 P.M. at the base of Lift 3.

For Families
Advance reservations are strongly recommended for children's ski programs, **(970) 728-7545.**

Nonskiing Children
Village Nursery: Nursery care for infants and toddlers ages 2 months to 3 years. Toddler program includes lunch. Reservations, **Skier Services, (970) 728-4424, (800) 544-0507.**

Skiing Children
Utes: One-on-one introduction to skiing for 3-year-olds, available in conjunction with Village Nursery. Rental equipment available.

Miners: Group lessons for 4- to 6-year-olds Packages include lunch; free lifts to age 5.

Explorers: Full-day ski instruction at all levels and lunch for elementary schoolers ages 6 to 12, lift tickets additional.

Teens
Teen Club: Skiing and socializing for teens ages 13 to 18, available during holiday and high-sea-

son weeks. Focuses on bumps, racing, freestyle all-terrain skiing for wide-track, parallel to advanced skiers. **(970) 728-7514.**

FOR RACERS

NASTAR: Daily on the NASTAR Hill. Two-hour NASTAR Pacesetter Clinics coached by the race course pacesetter available daily at 10:50 A.M. Hot Combo package of three two-hour clinics available.

Franz Klammer Slalom: Daily from 10:00 A.M. to 3:00 P.M. on the Franz Klammer timed-run course.

Telluride Race Week: Three- and five-day programs during selected weeks from December to March with a PSIA-certified race instructor.

Masters Club: Two-hour non-holiday race clinics in club format for Town Series participants.

HANDICAPPED SKIING

The **Telluride Adaptive Ski Program** is experienced in teaching people with most physical disabilities. Disabled skiers ski free, with half-price lift tickets for guides and buddies. There is a charge for half- or full-day instruction. Equipment and ski buddy/guide service are available. For information and reservations, call **(970) 728-4424.**

NORDIC SKIING

Thirty kilometers of groomed cross-country trails lace through the area, including 10 to 14 kilometers in Prospect Basin and Magic Meadows at the top of Sunshine Peak. The Telluride Nordic Center in Town Park offers rentals instruction in classic skiing and skating. Trail grooming and development is undertaken by the **Telluride Nordic Association, (970) 728-6911.**

The San Juan Mountains offer some of the best backcountry touring in the Rockies, and the

Photo by Grafton M. Smith/Telluride Ski & Golf Co.

San Juan Hut System route traverses some 70 kilometers of the most scenic segments between Telluride and Ouray and offers accommodations in five small, rustic huts, each sleeping 12, about 7 miles apart. Guides are available. For information and reservations contact **San Juan Hut System, P.O. Box 1663, Telluride, CO 81435; (970) 728-6935.**

153

HELI-SKIING

Guided Alpine adventures and Nordic heli-skiing in the backcountry are offered by **Telluride HeliTrax, P.O. Box 1560, Telluride, CO 81435; (970) 728-4904.**

WHERE TO STAY

Telluride Central Reservations, (800) 525-3455.

Luxury Accommodations

Hotel Columbia

New boutique hotel at the base of Oak Street chairlift and new gondola. Nineteen well appointed rooms with fireplaces and private balconies, plus two penthouse suites with kitchens. Bathrooms have 6-foot-long claw-foot tubs and steam showers. Decor is elegantly casual, with over-stuffed chairs and sofas and a luxurious country look. Concierge, room service from Cosmopolitan Restaurant. Restaurant, lounge, ski lockers (also boot dryers), in-room coffee and mini-bar, library and adjacent deck, exercise room, roof-top hot tub, business center. **300 W. San Juan Ave., P.O. Box 800, Telluride, CO 81435; (800) 201-9505, (970) 728-0660.**

The Ice House
Modern 42-room lodge in renovated four-story elevator building with central atrium. All units have handmade Southwestern furniture, refrigerators and private balconies. Restaurant adjacent. Daily housekeeping, Continental breakfast, après-ski refreshments, room service by La Marmotte. Steamroom, hot tubs, two guest lounges with television, library. **P.O. Box 2909, Telluride, CO 81435; (800) 544-3436, (970) 728-6300.**

New Sheridan Hotel
Historic landmark and now one of the best small hotels in the Rockies. New Sheridan is new again, thanks to stem-to-stern remodel. Thirty-two exquisite and opulent rooms and suites, combining Victorian grace and style with modern conveniences and unbeatable downtown location. Mid- to upper price range. Beautifully and romantically furnished. Non-smoking hotel. Packages. Twenty-four-hour front desk, complimentary Continental breakfast and afternoon tea, daily housekeeping. Restaurant, lounge, ski room, rooftop hot tub. **231 W. Colorado Ave., Telluride, CO 81435; (800) 200-1891, (970) 728-4351.**

The Peaks at Telluride
Outstanding Telluride Mountain Village location, with doorstep skiing. Spectacular and splashy hotel, with 181 deluxe rooms and opulent suites. All have refrigerators, VCRs and bathrooms with dual marble vanities and hair dryers. Huge (42,000 square feet) spa, exceptionally well-appointed and staffed. Spa programs are available. Ski and ski/spa packages. Twice-daily housekeeping, 24-hour front desk, laundry and valet services, concierge, room service, library, video rentals, business services, guest services staff, ski concierge, bell staff, full spa services (fitness assessment, cardiovascular fitness center, massage, beauty treatments). Indoor and outdoor heated pools, water slide, three whirlpool tubs, three saunas and steamrooms, day-care center, ski shop, ski locker room, restaurants, lounges, boutiques. Complimentary airport and town

shuttle. **P.O. Box 2702, Telluride, CO 81435; (800) 789-2220, (970) 728-6800.**

Pennington's Mountain Village Inn
Luxurious country inn at Mountain Village gateway, 1 1/2 miles from lifts. Lovely and romantic country French decor. Expansive views. Doorstep cross-country skiing and bus to lifts. Posh rooms with stocked in-room refrigerators, private decks and sybaritic bathrooms. Daily housekeeping, full breakfast, room service (breakfast), après-ski happy hour (including champagne, brandy, hot beverages and hors d'oeuvres). Library lounge, indoor hot tub, steamroom, game room, ski lockers, guest laundry, use of kitchen. **P.O. Box 2428, Telluride, CO 81435; (800) 543-1437, (970) 728-5337.**

The San Sophia
Elegant and intimate inn. Newly built in the Victorian style with overlays of western and Southwestern elements. Sixteen posh rooms (not all large, but all lovely) with oversized tubs for two, stall showers and brass beds (queen, two doubles or king) topped with handmade quilts. Top rooms have TV with built-in VCR and the best views. Steps from the Oak Street lift. Daily housekeeping, concierge, buffet breakfast, après-ski refreshments. Outdoor hot tub, library, ski room, observatory in turret. **3300 W. Pacific St., Telluride, CO 80435; (800) 537-4781, (970) 728-3001.**

Mid-Priced Accommodations

Alpine Inn Bed & Breakfast
Restored 1907 house on edge of downtown historic district. Nine individually decorated rooms. Daily housekeeping, full breakfast. Glassed-in solarium, indoor hot tub. **P.O. Box 2398, Telluride, CO 81435; (970) 728-6282.**

Bear Creek Bed & Breakfast
Eight charming rooms with queen beds. Adjacent to Town Park; walking distance to lifts. Daily housekeeping, full breakfast, après-ski refreshments. Sauna, steamroom, rooftop deck. **P.O. Box 1797, Telluride, CO 81435; (970) 728-6681.**

Johnstone Inn
Warm and romantic B&B in town with eight rooms, each with private bath of white marble and brass. Recently restored and furnished in

period pieces and down comforters. Non-smoking inn. Daily housekeeping, full breakfast, après-ski refreshments. Hot tub, complimentary laundry room. **P.O. Box 546, Telluride, CO 81435; (800) 752-1901, (970) 728-3316.**

Manitou Hotel Bed & Breakfast

Attractive B&B overlooking San Miguel River. Convenient location at base of Oak Street lift and new gondola. All rooms have private bath, refrigerator and either two queen-size beds or one queen and one sofa bed. Decor is country style. Daily housekeeping, Continental breakfast buffet, après-ski refreshments. Fireplace parlor, outdoor hot tub. **P.O. Box 756, Telluride, CO 81435; (800) 233-9292, (970) 728-3803.**

Skyline Guest Ranch

Delightful, family-owned guest ranch; heartfelt hospitality. Classic ski-lodge ambiance. Cabins with kitchenettes plus small, cozy rooms in main lodge. Sheepskin mattress covers, down comforters and other feel-good frills. Wonderful photographs on the walls. Good and hearty food; meal plans. Cross-country skiing on-site, with free equipment for guests. Daily housekeeping, full breakfast, après-ski refreshments, complimentary van. Outdoor hot tub, library, cross-country skiing. **P.O. Box 67, Hwy 145 South, Telluride, CO 81435; (970) 728-3757.**

Tomboy Inn of Telluride

Well-located, well-priced lodge rooms, studios and one-bedroom units. Full kitchens and balconies. Daily housekeeping, hot tub, steamroom, game room, sun deck. **P.O. Box 2038, Telluride, CO 81435; (800) 446-3192, (970) 728-6621.**

Economy Accommodations

Victorian Inn

Victorian in name only. Motel built in 1976. Comfortable with sizable rooms. Central location between main drag and lifts. Daily housekeeping, Continental breakfast, outdoor hot tub, sauna. **P.O. Box 217, Telluride, CO 81435; (800) 537-2614, (970) 728-6601.**

Condominiums

Telluride Resort Accommodations is now the major condominium rental and management company in town, **(800) 536-7754, (970) 726-6621.** Other management companies include **Alpine Rentals, (800) 376-9769, (970) 728-3388**
Premier Mountain Resorts, (800) 750-8750, (970) 728-4077
Telluride Lodge Rentals, (800) 662-8748, (970) 728-6621
These companies handle rentals in the following complexes and elsewhere in town and Mountain Village.

Aspen Ridge Townhomes

Ski-in/ski-out Mountain Village complex. Luxurious and spacious three-bedroom, three-bath units, each with great room, washer and dryer, private garage, steam shower and gas fireplace.

Bridal Veil

Classy one- and two-bedroom townhomes with full kitchens, washers, dryers and distinctive furnishings.

Cimarron Lodge

155

Comfortable 52-unit complex at base of Coonskin lift, close to ski school and some shops and quick walk to town. One to three bedrooms, plus such amenities as microwave ovens, whirlpool bathtubs and washers and dryers. Also, 12-unit inn with hotel rooms and efficiencies. Daily housekeeping, indoor hot tub, sauna, guest laundry, restaurant, lounge.

Etta Place

Base-of-mountain convenience and great views. One- to three-bedroom units with great views. Penthouses are especially sybaritic, with private hot tub and upscale furnishings. Outdoor pool, hot tub.

Kayenta Legend House

Luxurious Mountain Village condos with ski-in/ski-out convenience. Two- and three-bedroom units with whirlpool tubs, fireplaces, balconies. Cathedral ceilings and large windows maximize views.

LuLu City

Spacious, decorator-furnished one- to three-bedroom condos close to lifts. Eight of 53 units have private tiled steamrooms and 6-foot hot tubs. Outdoor pool, hot tub.

Colorado Classics

Manitou Riverhouses
Ten quiet and well-furnished studio to two-bedroom units with mountain and river views. Complex designed for maximum seclusion and privacy. Close to lifts and main street. Outdoor hot tub.

Riverside Condominiums
Luxurious one- to three-bedroom units with great views. Dramatic 30-unit building. Full kitchen and washer and dryer are standard. Ski lockers, outdoor hot tub.

Viking Suites Hotel
Conveniently located property, 500 feet from Coonskin lift. Hotel front desk and some hotel services. Bedroom with queen beds, living area with bunks, sofa bed, kitchenette, dining area. Good value. Outdoor pool, hot tub.

DINING OUT

Baked in Telluride
Light meals, pizza, snacks, fresh baked goods. Opens at 5:30 A.M. for real earlybirds. Great for breakfast; lunch and dinner also served. Brew pub added in 1991, serving lasagna, nachos and other pub fare to accompany freshly brewed, crafted beers. Local hangout. Free in-town delivery. **127 S. Fir, Telluride; (970) 728-4775.**

Border House Salsa Cafe
Bright little eating place. Mexi-breakfasts, maxi-lunch, munchie après-ski and multi-option dinners in this informal restaurant. Mix-and-match dishes at moderate prices. Margaritas, sangria and Mexican beer head the beverage list. Key Lime Pie is the leadoff dessert. **200 S. Davis, Telluride; (970) 728-5114.**

Campagna
Italian country cuisine in historic house. Tuscany comes to Telluride. Small and simply decorated restaurant. Menu changes nightly, with dishes ranging from exotic to traditional Italian fare. Fine wine list. Reservations recommended. **435 W. Pacific; (970) 728-6190.**

Cosmopolitan
Modest-size restaurant with big ideas which famed chef Chad Scothan brought to Telluride.

Columbia's hotel restaurant serves breakfast, lunch and dinner. Highly imaginative cuisine, expertly prepared and beautifully presented. Contemporary flair. Grilled specialties, seafood and fine desserts. Menu changes frequently. Dinner reservations recommended. Excellent wine list. **300 W. San Juan Ave., Telluride; (970) 728-1292.**

Deep Creek Sleigh Rides
Nightly dinner sleigh ride, featuring rib eye steak dinner, vegetable, dessert and beverage. Chicken, trout or vegetarian plate also available on request. Reservations required. **(970) 728-3565.**

Evangeline's
Small, charming restaurant specializing in New Orleans cuisine, from creative appetizers to rich desserts. Menu changes nightly and includes à la carte and prix fixe selections. Lunch indoors or on large patio. Reservations recommended. **646 Mountain Village Blvd., Telluride Mountain Village; (970) 728-9717.**

Excelsior Cafe
Very atmospheric cafe serving regional Italian cuisine with a stylish flair. Excellent appetizers, grilled entrées, vegetarian dishes, salads and desserts. Delicious thin-crust pizza. California and Italian wines featured. Reservations accepted. **200 W. Colorado, Telluride; (970) 728-4250.** Delivery available, **(970) 728-5509.**

Fat Alley BBQ
Pork ribs, beef ribs, chicken and all sorts of southern-style side dishes. Even vegetarian platters. Moderate prices. Super-casual eating area in authentic Victorian. Order at the counter; food is brought to your table—or packed up to go. **112 S. Oak St., Telluride; (970) 728-3985.**

Floradora Saloon
Brassy and fun restaurant, serving steaks, burgers, sandwiches, salads and mountain-town atmosphere. Sports memorabilia. Longtime Telluride favorite—under same ownership "forever." Soup and salad bar. Children's menu. Reservations not accepted. **103 W. Colorado Ave., Telluride; (970) 728-3888.**

Honga's Lotus Petal

Wide variety of healthy natural foods, creatively served. Eggrolls from various culinary traditions, lemon grass flavors from Southeast Asia, Chinese chicken, sushi from Japan and gado gado from Indonesia reflect pan-Asian traditions. Small restaurant with additional greenhouse dining. Eat in, takeout and delivery. Children's portions available. **137 E. Colorado Ave., Telluride; (970) 728-5134.**

Legends of the Peaks

Excellent restaurant in the Peaks, offering cuisine in the modern mode. Decor is beam-ceiling rustic, but stylish and elegant. Traditional American fare with Southwestern influences inspire "Colorado ranchlands" fare. Peaks Performance Cuisine features low-fat, low-calorie, energy-boosting dishes. Fine wine list, fine decor, fine service. Also, children's menu. Serves breakfast, lunch and dinner. Lunch is lighter and faster, with soups, salads, sandwiches and express luncheon buffet. Dinner reservations recommended. **The Peaks at Telluride, Mountain Village; (970) 728-6800.**

La Marmotte

French couple runs excellent French restaurant serving authentic French cuisine. Fittingly, charming country French ambiance. Good wine list and exemplary desserts. Reservations recommended. **150 W. San Juan, Telluride; (970) 728-6232.**

The Powder House

Downstairs restaurant specializing in popular American dishes, plus game, poultry, pasta and seafood. Nightly specials include crab legs and prime rib. Reservations accepted. **226 W. Colorado Ave., Telluride; (970) 728-3622.**

New Sheridan Restaurant

Slick, contemporary new dining mecca in the restored New Sheridan Hotel. Fine dining in a fine new restaurant. Exotic and interesting menu, including game, seafood and other house specialties. Good wine list. Reservations recommended. **231 W. Colorado Ave., Telluride; (970) 728-9100.**

Skyline Ranch

Public welcome for dinner in charming dining room of classic ski lodge and guest ranch. Ample

Noteworthy

Ski Telluride Half Price is a unique program for budget-watchers who are willing to commute up to an hour to the slopes in return for bargain off-season lodging in outlying communities and half-price lift tickets. The town of Ouray, just over the hill by proverbial crow flight but 50 miles by road and better than an hour's drive away in winter, started it by tapping in to Telluride's overflow with economical packages that include lodging, half-price lift tickets all season long, plus use of the town's famous thermal spring pools. **Ouray** is a popular summer destination nicknamed "The Switzerland of America" and has ample lodgings of many types and price ranges, all offering low-season rates in winter, **(800) 228-1876, (970) 325-4323.** With the success of this program, it developed into the regional promotion, spreading to **Ridgway, (800) 754-3131; Montrose, (800) 348-3495;** and **Cortez, Dolores and Mancos, (800) 253-1616.** Ouray is the most charming. Ridgway has the easiest commute, 37 miles on well-traveled secondary roads. Montrose feels more like a small city than a country town. And the last three are the most convenient for combining with Mesa Verde National Park. A car is mandatory for all.

157

portions of Continental and American specialties, notably game, beautifully done. Menu changes nightly with four entrées, splendid desserts. Eight miles from town. **Turkey Creek Mesa, Hwy 145 South; (970) 728-3757.**

Sofio's Mexican Cafe

Popular spot for hearty portions of good food. Small breakfast menu of big breakfast specialties. Equally ample dinners. Tostadas, burritos, tacos, four kinds of fajitas, the proverbial whole enchilada. Also, meat, seafood and veggie entrées. Good margaritas and selection of Mexican beers. Moderate prices. Reservations accepted. **110 E. Colorado, Telluride; (970) 728-4882.**

Station One

Located in the restored train depot at the base of the mountain, now a restaurant and brew pub. Traditional elegant entrées such as Beef Wellington and lobster in the more formal dining.

Also, casual dining room with full fondue menu. Lunch and dinner. **300 W. Townsend Ave., Telluride; (970) 728-3773.**

Swede-Finn Hall

Historic social hall, now good spot for light meals, full dinner or just a drink and entertainment. Bar menu includes appetizers, sandwiches and light fare and is available from mid-afternoon to later evening. Dinner menu features steak, chicken, game, poultry and pasta. Bar and dining area upstairs; billiards below. Microbrews, good wine list and terrific mixed drinks. Reservations accepted. **417 W. Pacific St., Telluride; (970) 728-2085.**

The Tavern at the Village

Village restaurant which showcases the old Brunswick Bar that once graced the Sheridan. Light lunches, mostly soups, salads, pizza, pasta and sandwiches. More formal dinner menu with varied dishes, including interesting contemporary creations such as Seafood Wellington, Pepper Seared Ahi with Cabernet Rice and Grilled Lamb Salad. **Blue Mesa Lodge, 117 Lost Creek Ln., Telluride Mountain Village; (970) 728-0741.**

T-Ride Country Club

Informal upstairs eatery "where everyone's a member." Family favorite for moderate prices and easy-going atmosphere. Pub food, burgers, sandwiches, pasta and entrées strong in the steak department. Salad bar. Lunch, after-ski nibbles and dinner. Children's menu. **333 W. Colorado Ave., Telluride; (970) 728-6344.**

NIGHTLIFE

Telluride made its reputation attracting active young skiers, so it isn't surprising that active young après-skiers also prevail after dark. As Telluride Mountain Village develops and as people get used to the gondola hop between the old and new communities, more after-ski and nightspots will gain popularity, but so far, most of the action still centers in and around downtown Telluride. Leimgruber's Bierstube, an expanded cabin known for good beer and German food, and the Border House, a new Tex-Mex place, get early crowds.

Later, the action moves to Colorado Avenue, the main street downtown. The Fly Me to the Moon Saloon has entertainment, pool table, drinks. Three billiards tables, which is a fancier way of saying pool, are in the basement of Swede-Finn Hall. The Last Dollar Saloon, a long-standing favorite, is an old western bar with a huge selection of beers, pool, darts and stone fireplace. There's always a game on at the Floradora and at the T-Ride Country Club. You can also find entertainment and lively crowds at the Roma Bar, O'Bannon's Irish Pub and the New Sheridan Bar, an authentic and recently gentrified turn-of-the-century classic for drinks and socializing.

Good microbrews are available at two brew pubs, Station One (formerly the San Juan Brewing Co.) in the spectacularly restored railroad depot and at Baked in Telluride. Eddie's has twelve beers on tap, an interesting wine list and espresso—something for everyone. A dinner sleighride with entertainment, a movie at the local cinema or something special at the historic Sheridan Opera House (now run by the Sheridan Arts Foundation) provides a change of pace. The Teen Youth Center's Voodoo Lounge is where kids gather. The House is a congenial in-town meeting place with cards, backgammon, games, chess and pool to break the ice.

For more information, contact **Telluride Ski & Golf, Inc., 562 Mountain Village Blvd., P.O. Box 11155, Telluride, CO 81435; (970) 728-6200; Telluride Chamber Resort Assn., P.O. Box 653, Telluride, CO 81435; (970) 728-3041.**

PURGATORY

BACKDROP

Durango is on the route between the Indian-Hispanic culture of the Four Corners to the west and the Alpine atmosphere of the San Juan Range to the north. The town is also the jumping-off point for Mesa Verde National Park, just 37 miles to the west, renowned for its spectacular Anasazi ruins and overwhelmed with summer tourists, which translates into accommodations for more than 6,000 guests, which further translates into excellent off-season lodging prices and bargain ski packages at rates too low to seem real.

Once southwest Colorado's main rail hub, downtown Durango now sparkles with assiduously preserved frontier flavor (stop for a drink or dinner at the Strater Hotel, where Louis L'Amour wrote many of his works), garnished with the necessities of modern-day tourism—chain motels, all manner of restaurants and shops ranging from souvenir sellers to designer factory outlets.

Thirty minutes away is Purgatory, Colorado's most southwesterly major ski area—and heaven on earth for skiers seeking lots of snow, sunshine and friendly fun. Such a high proportion of these skiers have traditionally come up from the Sunbelt rather than in from the coasts or down from the Midwest that the twangy drawl of Texas or New Mexico starts to sound like the indigenous speech pattern.

Purgatory hasn't yet joined the big leagues—and most loyal patrons hope it never will—but the area finally got its first big-league accoutrement with the addition of the first high-speed quad chair in 1995–96. In fact, the Hermosa Park chair isn't not just another high-speed lift but is purportedly the fastest super-quad in the Southwest. It unsnarled one of the major bottlenecks on the mountain, for it replaced a real slow-moving double in the heart of the terrain.

Purgatory provides really good skiing, but the resort knows that the entire beguiling southwest-

ern corner of Colorado has a lot going for it. Therefore, Purgatory sells a Total Ticket for stays of four days or longer. Any day can be devoted to Alpine skiing, cross-country skiing, a trip to the

Mountain Stats— Purgatory

Resort elevation 8,900 feet
Top of highest lift 10,822 feet
Bottom of lowest lift 8,793 feet
Total vertical 2,029 feet
Durange elevation 6,512 feet
Longest run 2 miles
Average annual snowfall 250 inches
Ski season Thanksgiving to early April
Lifts 1 high-speed quad chairlift, 4 triples, 4 doubles
Capacity 13,600 skiers per hour
Terrain 75 trails, 745 acres (23% beginner and novice, 51% intermediate, 26% advanced and expert)
Snowmaking 250 acres
Mountain dining Powderhouse Restaurant near top of the Engineer Chair; Cafe de los Piños and Dante's Restaurant near top of the Grizzly Peak chair
Snow reports (970) 247-9000, (505) 984-8738

GETTING THERE

The Durango–La Plata County Airport, 16 miles southeast of town, has flights from Denver, Dallas–Fort Worth, Phoenix, Houston and Albuquerque. Rental cars are available and are recommended if you want to move easily between resort and town, but some lodging properties offer complimentary airport transfers and/or ski shuttle transportation. Though Purgatory-Durango is 350 arduous miles from Denver, it is a far easier 210-mile, four-hour drive from Albuquerque via US 44 and US 550.

PROFILE

Looking at the two frontside chairlifts from Purgatory's small village is a lot like gazing at an iceberg from a ship's deck: There's a lot more out of view. Those lifts climb the end of a long, east-facing ridge. The ridge curves around, stretching to the west, where five additional chairs and most of the 75 runs are found. These snow-holding runs, facing primarily north, are arranged roughly in order of difficulty. Most of the easy ones are near the village, most of the tough mogully steeps are at the back, and lots of intermediate turf is in the middle—all powdered with more than 250 inches of snow during an average year.

In some parts of the country, Purgatory's iceberg-tip frontside alone would constitute a decent ski area. Below the village is the Columbine Station beginner area with two lifts (free for children under 6), while the Needles triple chairlift and the Spud double climb 1,485 vertical feet from the village. This frontside group of a dozen-odd intermediate and expert trails are the most consistently pitched at a ski area known for its stair-step skiing, and they are sheer delight in the morning when the sun warms them even as the rest of the ski area is still in snow-firming shadow. Blue squares decorate steady fall lines, while black diamonds grace runs of more variety. Of those, Styx is steep, narrow and bump-ridden down the entire vertical, while Lower Hades and Pandemonium are shorter but equally mogully.

Sky Ute Casino or Mesa Verde National Park, a snowmobile ride, a sybaritic experience at the Trimble Hot Springs, a sleighride dinner or even a ride on the fabled Durango & Silverton Narrow Gauge Railroad.

THE LAY OF THE LAND

Durango is an attractive, lively town closer to the Four Corners (where Colorado, Utah, New Mexico and Arizona touch) than to a major city in any of those states. The Purgatory ski resort is a 27-mile straight shot up US 550—a spectacular drive along the Animas Valley. The resort is a compact, modern slopeside village at the base of the lifts with the Village Center Building, functioning as a day lodge for the ski area and general activities center. Some of the larger Durango properties operate free ski shuttles. There may also be limited city-run bus service; for current information, call **(970) 259-LIFT.** A free shuttle does operate around the resort itself, linking parking lots, the Columbine Station beginner area, touring center and base village.

Upper Catharsis is as narrow as a tunnel and sports two diamonds before widening and taming to merit just a single diamond near the bottom.

If the scale embodied in just the front of the mountain is your frame of reference, the rest of the ski area comes across as a beautiful bonus. You can reach these remaining lifts and runs from the tops of Needles and Spud or more directly by taking the Twilight double, which angles deep into the trail system from the village. The runs off Twilight are mostly easy-street greens—the tamest of which is so flat a serpentine that it is called Walk-A-Lot, which must be a triumph of honesty in ski-trail nomenclature. As it stretches westward, the main mountain is textured with smaller vertical ridges and drainages between them. Many of the runs alternate steeps and flats, creating interest and variety on a less-than-commanding vertical and also making it easier for improving skiers to get the feel of the next-highest level of terrain. The three longest of the four additional chairlifts, which run roughly parallel to each other, climb up from a broad flat valley and access three distinct mountain sectors.

Lifts 2 and 3 serve most intermediate runs. You can ski a wonderful group of blue squares—some straight fall-line shooters, others graceful arcs—from Engineer, an upper-mountain double chair. You can move over one more sector to the west, where the Hermosa Park Express, Purgatory's first high-speed quad, which is nearly twice as long, accesses additional mid-level terrain. Purgatory's intermediate terrain, noteworthy because of both its quantity and its quality, is concentrated at these two lifts. Between them is a handful of easier runs, while the blacks like Wapiti and double blacks like Bull Run begin to appear on the map, west of the Grizzly Peak chair.

The end of Purgatory's daisy-chain terrain is the sector known as The Legends, served by the Legends triple chair unloading at more than 10,800 feet. Although it is the high point of a long ridge rather than a dramatic peak in its own right, it is one of the most spectacular ski area summits in Colorado because of the view. La Plata, Mission Ridge, East Needles, Eolus, Sunlight, Windom and West Needles—all Fourteeners or nearly so—are arrayed in exceptional splendor. If you are a black-diamond addict, take a moment to savor the panorama. Even if you are an intermediate skier, as long as you can manage the blue run called The Legends and board the lift at a loading ramp part-way up to avoid any black diamonds, do make the effort just for the scenery; there is an easy way back.

If you are an expert, The Legends (the mountain sector, not the intermediate trail of the same name) is where you'll spend your time. Legends offers narrow powder shots through the trees, long bump runs (some with double fall lines to escalate the challenge) and tight glades. Before The Legends was developed, Purgatory was a wonderful destination for the 90-plus percent of the skiing population that actually prefers novice and intermediate terrain; with the addition of The Legends, the area leapt into the realm of offering legitimate challenge for those who can legitimately handle it.

SNOWBOARDING

Purgatory's Snowboard Park off the Engineer chairlift varies with snowfall, season and changing input from local riders who help build it. Typically, it features quarter-pipes, a terrain garden,

Photo by Larry Pierce/Purgatory Resort

Getting air at Purgatory, Colorado's southwesternmost major ski area.

logs, rails, slides, barrels and assorted jumps. Demon, a green-circle run that serves as the main egress off the mountain, is a generous natural half-pipe, and savvy riders run it in midday when it's not too crowded. The frontside is popu-

Noteworthy

Children in ski school get free lift tickets.

lar with snowboarders too, both because of the abundance of black-diamond steeps and because it offers direct-to-lift return without any bothersome traverses. Like their skiing counterparts, advanced and expert snowboarders do like The Legends because of the unadulterated steeps and absence of slow-moving beginners. However, the tradeoff is a tedious traverse along the mountaintop BD&M Expressway, a run so tame that it deteriorates into true flats along a few stretches.

162

SKI SCHOOL PROGRAMS

The ski school desk is on level 2 of the Village Center. If you need equipment, reserve through the **Rental Hotline, (800) 699-6423.**

Introductory Program

First Things First: Economical half-day beginner or snowboarding lesson.

Advanced and Specialty Programs

Women's and Mens' Performance Weekend Workshops: Two-day women's or mens'program with instruction, lunch, video and social program for intermediate and advanced skiers.

For Families

Reservations required for **Cub Care, Polar Bears and Grizzly Bears, (970) 385-2144.**

Nonskiing Children

Cub Care: Day care for non-skiers age 2 months to 3 years. Full-day with lunch or half-day with snack.

Skiing Children

Children's ski classes use the SKIwee progression. Participants receive a scorecard noting their daily progress.

Polar Bears: Introduction to skiing for 3- and 4-year-olds. Emphasis on skiing, with limited indoor activities. Full-day with lunch and half-day options. Use of beginner skis included.

Grizzly Bears: For children ages 4 to 5, using Alpine skis and boots. Full-day with lunch and half-day options. Rentals available, but not included in cost.

Kodiak Clan: Classes for 6- to 12-year-olds, with groups divided by age and ability. Full-day with lunch for all ability levels. Half-day beginner lessons in the afternoon and intermediate and advanced groups in the morning. Rentals available, but not included in cost.

Outer Limits: Supervised skiing experience for youngsters aged 6 to 12 who ski the mountain— and like to ski hard. Work on NASTAR racing, bumps, parallel turns and other advanced skills. Afternoons only. Rentals available, but not included in cost.

Shred Bears: Snowboarding lessons, lift and lunch for children who weigh 35 pounds or more. Full-day with lunch for all ability levels. Half-day beginner lessons in the afternoon and intermediate and advanced groups in the morning. Rentals available, but not included in cost.

FOR RACERS

NASTAR: Daily from 10:00 A.M. to 3:00 P.M. at the Pitchfork Race Arena below the Powderhouse Restaurant near Lift 2.
NASTAR Race Clinic: Daily at 12:30 P.M.

HANDICAPPED SKIING

The Durango/Purgatory Adaptive Sports Assn. is a not-for-profit group providing sports opportunities for the physically or developmentally disabled. Reservations required, **(970) 259-0374.**

NORDIC SKIING

The Purgatory Touring Center is just north of the ski resort entrance on US 550. It has 16 kilometers of tracks groomed for classic cross-country and skating. The routes wind through the Cascade Creek Valley. The touring center offers instruction and equipment rental. The Tamarron Hilton Resort has its own 8-kilometer groomed track. For an unsurpassed backcountry experience, Mesa Verde National Park, though a longish ride, offers an unusual setting for ski touring. Endless backcountry touring options in the San Juan Mountains are possible. Guides are available through **Southwest Adventures, (970) 259-0370.**

WHERE TO STAY

Purgatory Central Reservations, (800) 979-9742, (800) 525-0892; Durango Central Reservations, (800) 525-8855.

Luxury Accommodations

Strater Hotel
Historic and opulent landmark built in 1887, furnished in authentic turn-of-the-century style. Family-owned and full of history. Claims to have

Noteworthy
Animas City Adventure Park between the Hermosa Park Express and the Engineer lift is a wonderful children's terrain garden, featuring a ski-through obstacle course, replicas of historic storefronts and signs teaching youngsters about western history and the mountain environment.

the world's largest collection of Victorian walnut furniture. Best of the 93 rooms truly deluxe; standard ones smaller but charming. Central location in the heart of downtown Durango. Diamond Circle Theatre (live productions at Christmas and in summer) on-site. Ski packages. Daily housekeeping, turndown on request, 24-hour front desk, bell staff, room service, complimentary valet parking. Hot tub, restaurants, lounge. **699 Main Ave., Durango, CO 81302; (800) 247-4431, (970) 247-4431.**

Tamarron Hilton Resort
Award-winning 750-acre golf resort where winter is off-season. Accommodations in 100 spacious rooms in main lodge (plus 270 two- and three-bedroom condominiums, some open in winter peak times or on demand). Casual elegance and fine service, facilities and dining. Spectacular setting and views to match. On-site cross-country skiing, après-ski and other entertainment and recreation. Ski packages. Daily housekeeping, 24-hour front desk, bell staff, activities desk, room service, laundry, complimentary shuttle, full breakfast included. Indoor/outdoor pool, hot tub, workout room, cross-country skiing, ski shop, two dining rooms, deli, lounge, game room, ski shop and other retail outlets. **P.O. Box 3131, Durango, CO 81302; (800) 678-1000, (970) 259-2000, (800) 221-2424** for Hilton reservations.

Mid-Priced Accommodations

Best Western Lodge at Purgatory
One- and two-bedroom suites with kitchens. Short walk to ski area. Daily housekeeping, 24-hour front desk. Indoor pool, hot tub, restaurant, lounge, ski shop. **49617 US Hwy 550 North, Durango, CO 81301; (800) 637-7727, (970) 247-9669, (800) 528-1234** for Best Western reservations.

Colorado Classics

Best Western Rio Grande Inn & Suites

Has 138 rooms, including some deluxe rooms with whirlpool baths and some suites. Ski packages. Daily housekeeping, 24-hour front desk, complimentary airport transportation, complimentary continental breakfast, après-ski cocktail hour. Indoor pool, hot tub, sauna. **400 E. Second Ave., Durango, CO 81301; (800) 245-4466, (970) 385-4980, (800) 528-1234** for Best Western reservations.

Comfort Inn

Functional motel overlooking Animas River. Rooms have two queen- or one king-sized bed. Ski packages. Daily housekeeping, complimentary 24-hour coffee, complimentary continental breakfast, 24-hour front desk. Hot tubs, solarium. **2930 N. Main Ave., Durango, CO 81301; (800) 525-0892, (970) 259-5373.**

Country Sunshine

Lovely six-room inn, 15 minutes south of the Purgatory ski area. Four rooms with private baths; two share. One two-room suite accommodating four and featuring moss-rock fireplace. Eclectic furnishings, from early American to country. Refreshment bar always available. Guests may use kitchen and laundry facilities. Non-smoking B&B. Breakfast bar, daily housekeeping. **35130 US 550 N., Durango, CO 81301; (800) 383-2853, (970) 247-2853.**

Days Inn Durango

Large, well-equipped motor inn $3^1/_2$ miles north of town. Rooms have two double beds or one king bed and in-room safes. Pets permitted. Ski packages. Daily housekeeping, 24-hour front desk, complimentary continental breakfast, complimentary in-town and ski shuttles, massage available. Indoor Olympic-size pool, fitness room, two saunas, two large hot tubs, restaurant. **1700 Animas View Dr., Durango, CO 81301; (800) 329-7466, (970) 259-1430, (800) DAYS-INN** for Days Inn reservations.

General Palmer Hotel

Downtown landmark, built in 1898, with exquisitely restored Victorian lobby and quaint, individually decorated rooms. A teddy bear waits on each bed. Four Diamonds from AAA. Continental breakfast served in sunny solarium. Ski packages. Daily housekeeping, 24-hour front desk, bell staff. Hot tub, restaurants, lounge. **567 Main Ave., Durango, CO 81301; (800) 523-3358, (970) 247-4747.**

Jarvis Suite Hotel

Landmark building renovated into 22 suite-style kitchen units from studios to two bedrooms. Renovated in 1995. Within walking distance of all downtown attractions. Some non-smoking rooms. Extras from playing cards to hair dryers available at front desk. Ski packages. Daily housekeeping. Hot tub, guest laundry. **125 W. 10th St., Durango, CO 81301; (800) 824-1024, (970) 259-6190.**

The Leland House

Ten charming rooms including six three-room suites with full kitchen facilities. All with private baths. Furnished with antiques and period pieces, accented with photos and memorabilia. Daily housekeeping, turndown on request, full gourmet breakfast. **721 E. Second Ave., Durango, CO 81301; (800) 664-1920, (970) 385-1920.**

Red Lion Inn

The best of the new in-town hotels, with 159 well-appointed rooms with king or queen beds, in-room coffee, irons and ironing boards. Spacious lobby and full services. AAA's Four Diamonds. On Animas River, within easy walking distance of downtown. Pets permitted. Ski packages. Daily housekeeping, 24-hour front desk, room service, bell staff, seasonal concierge, complimentary airport shuttle. Indoor pool, weight room, sauna, hot tub, dining room, lounge, hair salon. **501 Camino del Rio, Durango, CO 81301; (800) 547-8010, (970) 259-6580.**

River House

Sprawling ranch house at the edge of Durango. Seven rooms, all with private baths and each individually decorated. Charming bed and breakfast overlooking Animas River. Living room with fireplace, wet bar, pool table and big-screen TV. Full healthy breakfast in plant-filled atrium. Daily housekeeping, full breakfast, sports massage available. Outdoor hot tub. **495 Animas View**

Dr., Durango, CO 81301; (800) 254-4775, (970) 247-4775.

Rochester Hotel

Historic (built in 1891–92) and operated continuously as a hotel for more than a century. Now redone as delightful inn with 15 large rooms, all with private baths, decorated on the motif of old western movies filmed in and around Durango. Stay in Butch Cassidy and the Sundance Kid, a king bedded, garden view room; Across the Wide Missouri, a deluxe room with its own kitchenette; Naked Spur with two queen-sized beds or a dozen other rooms named after a dozen different films. Daily housekeeping, Continental breakfast. **726 E. Second Ave., Durango, CO 81301; (800) 664-1920.**

Vagabond Inn

Charming in-town B&B. Bridal suite with four-poster bed and private Jacuzzi. Economy motel rooms also available. Daily housekeeping, breakfast. Hot tub, guest laundry. **2180 Main Ave., Durango, CO 81301; (970) 259-5901.**

Economy Accommodations

Spanish Trails Inn & Suites

Seventy-six well-priced units of different designs. Every room or suite has microwave and mini-refrigerator or kitchen. Located across from grocery store. Daily housekeeping, 24-hour front desk. Guest laundry. **3131 Main Ave., Durango, CO 81301; (970) 247-4173.**

Sunset Motel

Bargain packages. Family units. Member of National 9 Inn group. Daily housekeeping, morning coffee. Hot tub, sauna. **2855 Main Ave., Durango, CO 81301; (800) 524-5999, (970) 247-2653.**

Condominiums

Note that all Purgatory Village condominiums (i.e., those with Sheol St. addresses plus Purgatory Village Hotel) are at the base of the mountain, offer airport transport and have daily housekeeping.

Angelhaus

Modern style and affordable prices. Comfortable one- to three-bedroom fireplace units 150 yards from the base area. Fully equipped with dish-

washer and microwave. Some non-smoking units. Daily housekeeping. Guest laundry, indoor hot tub. **455 Sheol St., Durango, CO 81301; (800) 356-1397, (970) 247-8090.**

Brimstone Condominiums

Ski-in/ski-out units sleeping up to 10. Wood-burning fireplaces and full kitchens, outdoor hot tub. **400 Sheol St., Durango, CO 81301; (800)-323-SKI-2, (970) 259-1066.**

Cascade Village

Large modern resort condo complex a mile from the ski area. Spacious, beautifully furnished units from studios to three-bedroom apartments with fireplaces, stereos, whirlpool tubs and balconies. Benchmark Building is activity center. Linen and trash service daily, full midweek cleaning on five- to seven-night stays, complimentary scheduled ski-area shuttle, airport shuttle on request. Indoor pool, indoor and outdoor hot tubs, steamroom, sauna, exercise room, game room, ski shop, restaurant, lounge, general store. **50827 US Hwy 550 North, Durango, CO 81301; (800) 525-0896, (970) 259-3500.**

Purgatory Townhouse

Studio to two-bedroom units with views of slopes or West Needles, plus fireplaces, private decks and patios. Indoor hot tub. **337 Sheol St., Durango, CO 81301; (800) 223-ISKI, (970) 247-0026.**

Purgatory Village Hotel

Condo-style suites with hotel services. Heart of resort village with lifts right outside the door. Sleekly and attractively furnished. Bell staff, 24-hour front desk, complimentary airport transfers. Outdoor/indoor pool, hot tub, restaurant, guest laundry. **P.O. Box 2082, Durango, CO 81301; (800) TRY-PURG, (970) 247-9000.**

Silver Pick Resort

Deluxe contemporary hotel rooms and one- and two-bedroom units with full kitchens. Some with fireplaces. Located 1 mile south of the ski resort, a short ride from the lifts. Satellite TV. Some non-smoking units. Daily housekeeping, mid-stay full clean, complimentary shuttle. Hot tub, game room, restaurant, lounge, ski shop. **48475 US Hwy 550, Durango, CO 81301; (800) 221-7425, (970) 259-6600.**

DINING OUT

Amici's Italian Grill
Family owned and operated. Veal, seafood, pasta, steaks and New York–style pizza. Full bar. Lunch and dinner. **948 Main Ave., Durango; (970) 247-4144.**

Ariano's
Somewhat casual atmosphere but fine food. A tad pricey, but worth it. Northern Italian specialties include fresh pasta, milk-fed veal, chef's specials. Many Italian wines. Espresso and cappuccino. Reservations not accepted. **150 E. Sixth St., Durango; (970) 247-8146.**

Cafe Cascade
Spacious and stylish restaurant masquerading as a cafe. Fresh fish, game, aged beef and Southwestern specialties. Expensive but good. Reservations accepted. **Cascade Village, 50827 US Hwy 550 North, Purgatory; (970) 385-1870.**

Carver's Bakery and Brew Pub
Bakery and cafe in front (great breakfast, plus lunch and dinner too) and one of Colorado's earliest brew pubs in the rear. Casual and still as popular with locals as with visitors. Moderate prices. Takeout available. **1022 Main Ave., Durango; (970) 259-2545.**

Edgewater Dining Room
River-view dining room serving regional American cuisine. Salmon is a specialty. Also, prime rib, Rocky Mountain trout, rack of lamb and other classics. Salad bar. Breakfast, lunch and dinner. Reservations accepted. **Red Lion Inn, 501 Camino del Rio, Durango; (970) 259-6580.**

Farquahrts
Pizza is the specialty, but Italian and Mexican dishes are also served. Takeout and free delivery offered. Hang out all evening. **725 Main Ave., Durango; (970) 247-5442.**

Father Murphy's Pub & Gardens
Irish pub serving homemade soups, salads, sandwiches and light entrées. Low-cholesterol local longhorn beef, but fish 'n chips for those who care not. Nightly specials. **636 Main Ave., Durango; (970) 259-0333.**

Francisco's
Mostly Mexican fare for diners with big appetites and small budgets. Also beef, chicken and seafood. Children's menu. **619 Main Ave., Durango; (970) 247-4098.**

Gazpacho
Stylish new restaurant specializing in "northern New Mexican" cuisine. Many dishes have Tex-Mex names, but the preparation is distinctive. Children's menu. Takeout available. Reservations accepted. **431 E. Second Ave., Durango; (970) 259-9494.**

Henry's at the Strater
Three meals a day served in atmospheric hotel dining room. Certified Black Angus beef featured. Dinner reservations required during holiday periods, accepted at other times. **699 Main Ave., Durango; (970) 247-4431.**

Kachina Kitchen
Mexican and Native American fare, and combinations, like the "Navajo Taco," all prepared from scratch. Extremely casual seating area, and takeout also available. **Durango Mall, 800 S. Camino del Rio, Durango; (970) 247-3536.**

Lady Falconburgh's Barley Exchange
Durango's largest selection of beers: 150 domestics, microbrews and imports, 20 on tap. Serving from lunch to late dinner. Casual beer garden atmosphere. New favorite with locals. **640 Main Ave., Durango; (970) 385-6776.**

Main Street Grill
Small and intimate. Serving continental cuisine, pasta and the ubiquitous Mexican items. Moderate prices. Casual atmosphere. **1017 Main Ave., Durango; (970) 385-6776.**

Mama's Boy
Italian favorites, such as pizza, pastas and calzone. Dinner specials. Casual. **3600 Main Ave., Durango; (970) 247-0060.**

The Ore House
Casual, laid-back ambiance. Durango's top steak house, with seafood, salad bar and children's menu. **147 Sixth St., Durango; (970) 247-5707.**

Palace Grill

Romantic restaurant. Adapted Victorian decor. Award-winning purveyor of fine continental specialties, aged beef, poultry, seafood and good desserts. Nightly specials. Sizable wine list. High end of price scale. **3 Depot Pl., Durango; (970) 247-2018.**

Purgatory Creek

The sitdown restaurant in the Purgatory resort center. Breakfast, lunch and dinner. Emphasis is on Mexican food. Full bar. **Purgatory Resort; (970) 385-2108.**

Randy's

High-backed booths and low-key look. Slow-cooked prime rib, steaks, seafood, pasta and poultry. Children's menu. Reservations suggested. **152 E. Sixth St., Durango; (970) 247-9083.**

Red Snapper

Fine seafood, home-baked breads, a 40-item salad bar and killer desserts (notably Death by Chocolate, which is just that). Oyster bar. Mellow atmosphere. Children's menu and saltwater aquariums to divert youngsters while they wait. Reservations accepted (suggested for large parties). **144 E. Ninth St., Durango; (970) 259-3417.**

San Juan Cafe

Breakfast, lunch and dinner in attractive resort hotel restaurant. Pasta, steaks, seafood and poultry featured at dinner, also, excellent salads. At dinner, the cafe goes atmospheric with linens and fresh flowers on the tables. Full bar. Dinner reservations accepted. **Tamarron Hilton Resort, 40292 US Hwy 550 North, between Purgatory and Durango; (970) 259-2000.**

The Sow's Ear

Grilled meats, poultry and seafood are the specialties in this busy restaurant at the Purgatory access road. Reservations accepted. **49617 US Hwy 550 North, Durango; (970) 247-3527.**

NIGHTLIFE

Farquahrts at the mountain has the resort's loudest après-ski just after the lifts close, and its downtown sibling sees the action later. Live rock and roll is the Farquahrts' trademark at both locations. The Olde Schoolhouse Cafe, 2 miles south of the ski resort, is a favorite after-ski hangout, with good casual food and drink and free pool. Downtown boosters want you to keep going. They invite visitors to "tango in Durango" with some 60 places to eat and drink, 13 art galleries, three movie houses and a registered National Historic District with quaint shops (and more than its share of regular nonquaint souvenir shops and factory outlets too). Customers mount the stage and sing along at A. J.'s Grill and Sports Bar, which also has big-screen TV, pool tables and a jukebox. Sweeney's Grubsteak has a good bar with Animas Valley views. Durango may have the only brew pub located in the rear of a bakery. It's Carver's, a local hangout and lots of casual fun. Lady Falconburgh's Barley Exchange is a newer entry on the beer scene, with 150 domestic and imported beers, 20 on tap, and a vibrant atmosphere popular with locals.

Hotel lounges are popular. The San Juan Lounge at Tamarron, 8 miles south of Purgatory, has a relaxed atmosphere and nightly entertainment, and the Flume Lounge in Cascade Village just north of the ski resort is suitable for a relaxing fireside evening. There's a similar feeling in the Red Lion's Edgewater Lounge, which is also restrained and gets kudos for complimentary hors d'oeuvres during happy hour. Fort Lewis College is the site of special sports, cultural and entertainment options.

For more information, contact **Purgatory Ski Resort, 1 Skier Pl., Durango, CO 81302; (970) 247-9000; Durango Area Chamber Resort Assn., (800) 979-9742, P.O. Box 2587, Durango, CO 81302; (800) 525-8855, (970) 247-0312.**

WOLF CREEK

BACKDROP

Wolf Creek is an anomaly of Colorado skiing. With 465 inches of snow in a normal year, it is the state's snowfall leader by so much—an average of more than 6 feet a year over runner-up Loveland and 10 feet or more over most other mountains—that the other ski areas would rather pretend that it didn't exist within the state's borders. That's all right with Wolf Creek, which is so far south that it is closer to Albuquerque than to Denver, meaning that both its generous snow clouds and most of its skiers come from the south. Not only is its personality split between a Colorado address and a New Mexico tilt, but it even copes with schizoid area codes. Wolf Creek sits virtually astride Colorado's southernmost pass, and to phone the lodgings west, you dial 970; to call those to the east, it's area code 719.

There's nothing ambivalent about the skiing though. Wolf Creek's colossal snow cover and low-key ambiance have drawn skiers for more than half a century, and the area remains much as it has been for decades—simply extraordinary powder on a darned good mountain. Sure, they groom the place—even with a winch cat on some of the super-steeps—but it's the great snow and the rugged, old-time skiing-as-it-lays aspect that make Wolf Creek worthwhile for anyone seeking an alternative to manicured, pampering, costlier places to ski.

THE LAY OF THE LAND

The Wolf Creek ski area is located immediately adjacent to US 160, just west of the summit of Wolf Creek Pass. Pagosa Springs is 23 miles to the west, and South Fork is over the pass and 18 miles to the east. These towns are where accommodations and dining—mostly low-priced and ultra-casual—are found. The drive from the west is a few miles longer but easier. Shuttles, which are not free, connect the towns with the ski area; **Pagosa Springs Shuttle, (800) 523-7704, (970) 731-4123** and **South Fork Shuttle, (800) 874-0416, (719) 873-5547.**

GETTING THERE

Wolf Creek is 237 miles from Albuquerque and 246 miles from Denver. The closest airport with commercial service is Durango–La Plata County Airport, 57 miles west of Pagosa Springs. Rental cars are available. **Stevens Field** in Pagosa Springs is open to private planes, **(970) 731-2127.**

PROFILE

Wolf Creek is so high that the forest near its 10,350-foot base is thin enough to invite tree skiing, and, at the summit, treeless bowls, snowfields and cornices offer phenomenal see-forever, ski-where-you-wish skiing. Very gentle beginner and low-intermediate runs are available for new skiers, but, in reality, Wolf Creek primarily comes across as an intermediate and advanced skiers' paradise. Not only do blues and blacks prevail on the trail map, but some skill and confidence are needed to navigate the trees and the powder and the variably textured terrain that make the area so special.

Three day lodges are close to one another at the base. The Prospector Lodge is small and simple, with limited cafeteria offerings. Wolf Creek Lodge is larger and more fully equipped. It serves hot and cold meals and has a bar and a big outdoor deck called The Outside for burgers on those days when there's actually sun. Base Camp is the newest of all with snack service and a large indoor area and for thrifty brown-baggers who bring their own lunch. The Sport Center houses

rental and retail shops and the ticket office.

A small beginner area is just outside the Wolf Creek Lodge, while most of the area's easier trails are off the Bonanza and Dickey chairs that angle toward the west from below the Prospector Lodge. Skiing the lacework of comfortable trails provides novice and intermediate skiers with essentially a separate area. Kelly Boyce Trail, a gentle meander along Wolf Creek's western perimeter, is like most of the trails—wide and blanketed with soft, well-groomed snow. Only Gun Barrel, the liftline run under Dickey, merits a black. The top section is short and very moguly and throws a quick jolt of reality into the overconfident novices who seem compelled to try it. There is mercy, however, since the lower part isn't fearsome, but it's steeper than anything else on this part of the mountain.

The Treasure triple chair, just east of the Wolf Creek Lodge, is the area's main lift, while the Boyce lift is a zippy surface lift that parallels Treasure and can be used for overflow on peak days. Alberta Face, a totally inbounds mogul pitch of exceptional width, is Wolf Creek's show-off run for bumpers for it is visible from the top of the Treasure chair. Treasure and Boyce unload on a broad mountaintop, below which are Wolf Creek's more demanding trails. Treasure also accesses the bowls and woods and cornices in both directions. This high terrain doesn't add significantly to the total vertical, but it escalates the experience, and at such an altitude, the short hike to the control gates is demanding. Exhibition and Bonanza Bowl to the west of the lift are steep, broad, powder playgrounds that end with a funnel into Treasure and Windjammer, parallel cruising runs back to the base. As expansive as they feel, they pale in contrast to what stretches to the east of the chair.

Prospector, Glory Hole and Boundary Bowl (which is no longer the boundary) are wide cirques, graceful and alternately somewhat steep and very steep. Alberta Peak, Montezuma and Step Bowl—even steeper than the other three—comprise 100 acres of extreme terrain and requiring a hike in and a hike out as well. These high bowls have it all when it comes to scenery, but the most excellent adventure available at Wolf Creek remains skiing the Water Fall. You

Inside Wolf Creek

start down the wide, steep precincts of Montezuma Bowl and follow Navajo Trail along the eastern perimeter until you reach one of seven control gates into the Water Fall Area, an ungroomed parcel of tight trees, open glades, neat drainages, little headwalls, jumps and surprising powder shots. You ski down to a shuttle pickup area for a snowcat tow back up to the base. It is out-of-bounds-style wilderness skiing with no need to hike—nor any extra charge for the snowcat.

SKI SCHOOL PROGRAMS

Introductory Program

Beginner's Package: Four hours of ski or snowboarding instruction and beginner lift ticket at an economical price.

Advanced and Specialty Programs

Three-Day Super Special: Three-day ticket and three two-hour lessons for all ski and snowboarding ability levels. Days are consecutive.

Ladies' Day Workshops: One-day sessions throughout the season; some with emphasis on racing, fashion show or other special theme.

For Families

Nonskiing Children
The ski area does not provide day care but can provide a list of private facilities in Pagosa Springs and South Fork.

Skiing Children
Wolf Pups: Full- and half-day lesson program for children ages 5 to 8. Lifts included when riding with an instructor or parents; lunch included on full-day program. Magic Carpet, moving conveyor lift, designed especially for Wolf Pups.

Hot Shot Adventurers: Full- and half-day program for skiers ages 9 to 12. Emphasis is on skill improvement and mountain exploration.

FOR RACERS

Wolf Creek Fun Series: Five-race series, periodically from December to March.

Special races: Martin Luther King's Birthday, Presidents' Day, Mardi Gras, St. Patrick's Day; also Rusty Cup Town Challenge and annual Antique Ski Race.

NORDIC SKIING

The **Alpen Haus Ski Center** at the Fairfield Pagosa Resort has 10 to 15 kilometers of marked ski trails and cross-country rentals; **(970) 731-4141, Ext. 2020.** Backcountry skiing abounds, though in many cases, skiers share trails with snowmobilers. While in other parts of Colorado, this kind of situation would be a recipe for conflict, there is cooperation in the high country around Wolf Creek Pass. The Powder Busters Snowmobile Club of South Fork maintains 165 miles of dual-use trails and issues a trail map and brochure for all; write to **Powder Busters, P.O. Box 454, South Fork, CO 81154.**

WHERE TO STAY

Pagosa Springs

For information (but not reservations), contact **Pagosa Springs Chamber of Commerce, P.O. Box 787, Pagosa Springs, CO 81147; (800) 252-2204, (970) 264-2360.**

Mid-Priced Accommodations

Best Western Oak Ridge Motor Inn
Eighty-room motel on the fringes of downtown, across from hot springs. Offers packages and discount lift tickets. Children under 12 stay free in parents' room. Pets allowed. Daily housekeeping, 24-hour front desk, complimentary coffee. Indoor pool, sauna, Jacuzzi, hot tub, game room, restaurant, lounge, guest laundry. **P.O. Box 1799, Pagosa Springs, CO 81147; (970) 264-4173; (800) 528-1234** for Best Western reservations.

Echo Manor Inn
Fourteen-room bed and breakfast. Restful with television and phones only in common areas.

Daily housekeeping, full country breakfast. Hot tub, gift shop, TV/game room. **P.O. Box 3366, Hwy 84, Pagosa Springs, CO 81147; (970) 264-5646.**

Pagosa Lodge
Comfortable 100-room resort hotel. Some suites. Value packages. Daily housekeeping. Restaurant, lounge, indoor pool, sauna, enormous hot tub, game room. **P.O. Box 2050, Pagosa Springs, CO 81147; (800) 523-7704, (970) 731-4141.**

The Spring Inn
Newly remodeled motel units. Located on banks of San Juan River. Use of mineral hot springs complimentary to guests. Daily housekeeping, massage therapy. Mineral springs, weight room, video rentals. **P.O. Box 1799, Pagosa Springs, CO 81147; (800) 225-0934, (970) 264-4168.**

Economy Accommodations

Davidson's Country Inn
B&B lodge. Access to swimming pool and hot tub at another location. Phone and fireplace in common area. Use of kitchen permitted. Eighteen miles from ski area. Daily housekeeping, full breakfast included. Game room. **P.O. Box 87, Pagosa Springs, CO 81147; (970) 264-5863.**

First Inn
AAA-rated motel with 33 rooms. Lift and lodging packages. Restaurants nearby. Daily housekeeping, complimentary coffee. Hot tub, guest laundry. **P.O. Box 952, Pagosa Springs, CO 81147; (970) 264-4161.**

High Country Lodge
Twenty-five rooms plus four cabins sleeping up to eight; some non-smoking. Children 12 and younger stay free. Ski packages. Housekeeping. Hot tubs, restaurant, tubing hill with rope tow, guest laundry **P.O. Box 485, Pagosa Springs, CO 81147; (970) 264-4181.**

Condominiums

Fairfield Pagosa
Resort with 100 units in timeshare complex. Fully equipped with kitchens, fireplaces, Jacuzzi tubs and more. Various sizes, accommodating up to eight people. Outdoor pool, hot tub, sauna, Danish cold plunge, ski shop, cross-country ski-

---

Mountain Stats— Wolf Creek

Top of highest lift 11,775 feet
Bottom of lowest lift 10,350
Total vertical 1,425 feet
Longest run 2 miles
Average annual snowfall 465 inches
Ski season early November to early April
Lifts 2 triple chairlifts, 2 doubles, 1 platterpull, 1 rolling conveyor for beginners
Capacity 6,000 skiers per hour
Terrain 50 trails, 800 acres (20% beginner and novice, 45% intermediate, 35% advanced and expert)
Snow reports (800) SKI-WOLF, (505) 984-8738

---

ing. **P.O. Box 4040, Pagosa Springs, CO 81147; (970) 731-4123, Ext. 2089.**

Pagosa Central Management is a rental and management agency for condominiums and homes over a wide area. All units have kitchens, fireplaces and television; some have hot tubs, phones and/or cable TV. **P.O. Box 900, Pagosa Springs, CO 81147; (800) 945-0182, (970) 731-2215.**

Sunetha Accommodations handles more than 150 reasonably priced condos, most with full kitchens, some luxurious. Packages, discount lift tickets available. **P.O. Box 2366, Pagosa Springs, CO 81147; (800) 365-3149, (970) 731-4344.**

South Fork

For information (but not reservations), contact **South Fork Chamber of Commerce, P.O. Box 577, South Fork, CO 81154; (800) 571-0881, (719) 873-5512.**

Mid-Priced Accommodations

Riverbend Resort
One of the closest lodgings to ski area—14 miles. Property bordered on two sides by national forest. Popular with groups. Ten fireplace cabins (largest sleeps up to 12) with kitchens. Pets al-

lowed. Hot tub, recreation room, guest laundry. **P.O. Box 129, South Fork, CO 81154; (719) 873-5344.**

Wolf Creek Ski Lodge

AAA-rated 49-unit motel at the eastern end of Wolf Creek Pass surrounded by 155 miles of groomed cross-country and snowmobile trails. Small pets allowed. Ski packages, discount lift tickets, seniors' discounts. Four outdoor hot tubs, ski lockers, restaurant, lounge, billiards room. Complimentary shuttle service to ski area. **P.O. Box 283, South Fork, CO 81154; (800) 874-0416, (719) 873-5547.**

Economy Accommodations

The Inn Motel

Sixteen motel rooms, six two-room units and three cabins with kitchens and fireplaces. Pets allowed. Housekeeping, Continental breakfast. Hot tub, guest laundry. **P.O. Box 474, South Fork, CO 81154; (800) 233-9723, (719) 873-5514.**

172

Spruce Ski Lodge

B&B format. Motel plus old-style ski lodge with two budget dorms sleeping five to 10 each, with TV and phone in common area. Also, housekeeping units with kitchen, fireplace and TV. Ski packages. Pets allowed. Home-style cooking. Housekeeping, full breakfast. Hot tub. **P.O. Box 181, South Fork, CO 81154; (800) 228-5605, (719) 873-5605.**

Wolf Creek is a ski area, pure and simple, with day-use facilities at the base.

Photo by Keoki Flagg/courtesy Wolf Creek Ski Area

Wolf Creek Ranch

Eight large motel rooms with kitchenettes and six fireplace cabins with full kitchens. At 10 miles, closest accommodation to ski area. Hot tub, ice skating, snowmobiling. **P.O. Box 242, South Fork, CO 81154; (800) 522-9653, (719) 873-5371.**

Condominiums

Rocky Mountain Associates manages and takes reservations for cabins and condos on the east side of Wolf Creek Pass; **P.O. Box 526, South Fork, CO 81154; (719) 873-5688.**

DINING OUT

Pagosa Springs

Moose River Pub

Southwestern and Mexican dishes, plus steaks, burgers and seafood. Casual. Lunch and dinner. **Park Ave. & N. Pagosa, Fairfield Village; (970) 731-5451.**

Ole Miner's Steakhouse

Pleasant atmosphere. Steak and shellfish, teriyaki and other types of preparation. Salad bar. Children's menu. **Hwy 160, 3 1/2 miles east of town; (970) 264-4268.**

Pagosa Hunan Restaurant

Chinese dishes served from lunch through dinner. All-you-can-eat Sunday buffet. Budget-watcher's prices. **River Center, E. Hwy 160, Pagosa Springs; (970) 264-5022.**

Riverside Restaurant

Casual downtown spot for inexpensive char-broiled burgers, sandwiches, broasted chicken. Breakfast till 11:00 A.M. **439 San Juan St., Pagosa Springs; (970) 264-2175.**

The Rose

Cute, casual downtown cafe. Breakfast and lunch. Salads, burgers, soups, home-baked pies. Reasonable prices. **408 Pagosa St., Pagosa Springs; (970) 264-2055.**

South Fork

Brown's Country Store
Open daily except Monday for breakfast, lunch and dinner. Also, Sunday buffet (brisket is the specialty) and Friday night pizza buffet. **W. Hwy 160, South Fork; (719) 873-5582.**

Hungry Logger
Family restaurant. Large soup and salad bar. Homemade pies, cinnamon rolls and bread. Charbroiled steaks. **W. Hwy 149, South Fork; (719) 873-5504.**

Mother Lode Restaurant
Texas-style ribs and barbecue. Motto: "Pig in or pig out." Open daily except Monday for lunch and dinner. Friday night all-you-can-eat catfish. Reservations suggested. **W. Hwy 160, South Fork; (719) 873-0245.**

Rock A Way Inn
Family restaurant with full bar. Country atmosphere specializing in charbroiled steaks and seafood. Open daily except Tuesday for breakfast, lunch and dinner. Reservations required for dinner. **W. Hwy 160, South Fork; (719) 873-5581.**

NIGHTLIFE

The Glory Hole at the ski area offers immediate après-ski. Neither nearby town is known for abundant nightlife but the best bets are the Best Western Oak Street Inn in downtown Pagosa Springs and Fairfield Pagosa on the western outskirts, each with a lounge and music. In South Fork, Quakies Lounge and Croakers offer live music and other entertainment.

For more information, contact **Wolf Creek, P.O. Box 2800, Pagosa Springs, CO 81147, (970) 264-5629; Pagosa Springs Chamber of Commerce, P.O. Box 787, Pagosa Springs, CO 81147, (800) 252-2204, (970) 264-2360 or South Fork Chamber of Commerce, P.O. Box 577, South Fork, CO 81154, (800) 571-0881, (719) 873-5512.**

CUCHARA VALLEY

BACKDROP

Cuchara Valley is out of the Colorado skiing mainstream. Farther south than Wolf Creek and farther east than Eldora, it's not the closest skiing to Denver and Colorado Springs, the metro areas which between them account for roughly three-quarters of the state's population. However, it is a short, easy drive from Pueblo, Walsenburg and Trinidad. Cuchara also appeals to Oklahomans, Texans and Kansans who are comforted by a ski resort that can be reached without negotiating any treacherous mountain passes. While other areas are closer daytrips for Colorado Springs's skiers, vacationers flying into the Springs's increasingly popular airport find it exceptionally convenient.

Economy is another reason to ski there. Cuchara's prices are among Colorado's lowest. Going along with the low prices is a laid-back, low-key spirit. You won't feel out of place without a great wardrobe. The weather is generally so benign that whatever you already own is more than modish enough for this jeans-over-longjohns resort. Cuchara also carries some conversational weight. If you like to be the first on your block to ski someplace different, Cuchara is a good bet. The resort closed before the 1989–90 season, reopened for the winter of 1993–94, closed again, and finally got its act together under new management in 1995–96.

THE LAY OF THE LAND

Cuchara sits in a high valley, surrounded by spectacular scenery. The towering Sangre de Cristo Mountains just to the north and west are one of the Rockies' most breathtaking ranges, and even in the context of this splendid landscape, the Spanish Peaks are distinctive. Indians called this pair of steep-sided summits Huajatolla, which means "breasts of the world." The Spanish Peaks also conjure up the romantic old West. They have spawned myths of mysterious spirits, legends of hidden Indian gold and tales of prospectors who tried to find it. Soaring up to 7,000 feet and visible across the prairie for a hundred miles, they served as landmarks for traders and settlers on the Santa Fe Trail. These pioneers passed them by to follow their own dreams farther west. The Spanish Peak are in-your-face visible from much of Cuchara's terrain.

Cuchara Village, a small, quirky western-style hamlet on Colorado 12, offers further accommodations, dining, entertainment and atmosphere. It features a funky general store, post office, restaurant, saloon and some accommodations.

GETTING THERE

From the I-25 exit at Walsenburg, take US 160 west to Colorado 12. This is a 32-mile green-circle drive through a scenic canyon but with no mountain passes. Cuchara is $3^{1}/_{2}$ hours (186 miles) from Denver and $2^{1}/_{2}$ hours (114 miles) from Colorado Springs, which also boasts the closest significant airport. Cuchara has plans to offer packages including air, lodging, lift tickets and bus transportation from Colorado Springs as early as the 1996–97 ski season, so check with the resort's reservation service to determine whether that has been instituted.

PROFILE

From the highway, Cuchara appears to be an insignificant little ski area just to the right of the Spanish Peaks, but what you see from the approach is just a trio of the easternmost trails. The base area isn't all that inspiring either. Even when you look over the beginners—sliding, standing, supine or in some other on-snow pose—your view is of a lot of rather flat terrain. But from the modest base, you can see three

174

chairlifts, and the map shows a fourth somewhere off to the left, as well as a modest number of named trails. Chair 3, the one to the summit, holds the most promise for interesting terrain and decent vertical, while Chair 5 is out of sight and therefore remains an unknown.

But Cuchara is the odd area where the trail map is a basic handbook rather than a baedeker. It orients you but doesn't lead you step by step, which depending on your outlook, can be disquieting or rather exciting. The skiing unfolds with unexpected complexity. In addition to a baker's dozen major trails named runs, a bunch of nameless little cutovers cascade from the top like a mass of tangled spaghetti. The big runs are straightforward routes down the fall line with deviations only out of respect for the mountain's contours. The small ones scramble the stew, with a net result that Chairs 3 and 5 access a satisfying range of green, blue and black routes in all sorts of combinations.

The wild card is Gallina Gulch, a slight misnomer for a run that is less a gulch than a meandering green-circle road that touches or crosses everything on Cuchara's eastern flank. This creates confusion and opportunities for collisions but also multiplies the skiing possibilities. Since the area—how to put it kindly?—has thus far not overspent on trail signs, you are presented with mysterious options every few hundred feet. Stay on the road or rattle your bones in the bumps straight ahead? You never know where you are till you've been there, and if you want to repeat or avoid a certain combination, doing so presents another sort of challenge. In fairness, Cuchara has pulled off a coup simply by rising twice from the near-dead, and during the longest hiatus, it was shut tight as a Space Shuttle airlock, and a single employee kept the resort from falling apart.

A short walk up from Chair 3 takes you to The Burn, a 45-acre, funnel-shaped clearing that is lightly gladed, a lot of fun to ski, and offers a spectacular view of the Spanish Peaks. But the trail map again has the power to deceive. What appears on paper to be a perimeter trail called Burn Out actually slices through the trees. It often gets rutted like a bobsled track and the best line is twisty as the race course at Monte Carlo.

Photo by Claire Walter

Inside Cuchara Valley

You can ski it flat out or with linked checks and wedges, and you might find yourself ricocheting through hard-packed hairpins, where you'll probably be dusted by snowboarders or a typical 12-year-old on 150s. The Burn may not be a true black-diamond bowl, but Burn Out certainly is a black-diamond run-out.

SNOWBOARDING

Half-pipe and snowboard park off Lift 5 are geared for snowboarders, but they range all over the mountain, getting air off the many road crossings and snaking through The Burn's trees.

SKI SCHOOL PROGRAMS

Introductory Program

Learn to Ski Packages: Lift, lesson and rental packages, based on the Perfect Turn, franchised progression of instruction at all levels.

Advanced and Specialty Programs

Perfect Turn: Franchised progression of instruction, which includes video self-analysis, goal-setting and a guarantee which enables a skier who does not reach the set goal to repeat the class free.
Mogul, Powder and Racing Clinics: Offered on demand, usually weekends and holidays.

For Families

Nonskiing Children

OK Corral: Supervised day dare for children ages 2 months to 3 years. Half- and full-day with lunch. Children taken to snowplay area, based on children's ages and weather.

Skiing Children

Sundance Kids: Ski classes for children ages 4 to 12 years, following the Perfect Turn principle. Packages including lifts, instruction, lunch and equipment rentals available.

NORDIC SKIING

A wealth of hiking trails are skiable in winter. The $2^1/_2$-mile Bonnett Trail starts directly at Cuchara Valley and connects with the 12-mile Indian Creek, one of the region's longest and finest. It is also possible to make a loop out of Bonnett, a small portion of Indian Creek and the Dodgetown Trail, which terminates downvalley from Cuchara. Old summer routes over Cordova Pass and along La Veta Pass narrow-gauge railroad line are interesting ski touring routes too.

WHERE TO STAY

Cuchara

Cuchara Valley information and reservations, **(800) 227-4436** out of state, **(719) 742-3163** in Colorado.

Mid-Priced Accommodations

Cuchara Cabin Rentals

Seven stocked cabins, located between one-quarter mile and $3^1/_2$ miles from Cuchara. All differently furnished and equipped. Some non-smoking. Largest accommodate 11. Company also handles condo rentals. **P.O. Box 677, La Veta, CO 81055; (719) 742-5490.**

Echo Canyon Ranch

Not "luxury" in the five-star sense, but pricey for Cuchara Valley. Low-season rates in winter. Hospitable ranch atmosphere. Great views. Accommodates 40 in mountain lodge and cabins. No phones or TVs in rooms. Large-screen TV and VCR in lobby. Fifteen minutes from slopes. Cross-country on property. Shuttle to slopes, breakfast and dinner served. Daily housekeeping. Outdoor hot tub, game room, video games. **P.O. Box 328,**

La Veta, CO 81055; (800) 341-6603, (719) 742-5524.

Economy Accommodations

Cuchara Inn
Rustic 44-room lodge-style room hotel in the boardwalk village of Cuchara. Many rooms are quite large. Some with fireplace, kitchen, and/or views of Yellow Pine Ranch. Daily housekeeping. **29 East Ave., Cuchara, CO 81055; (719) 742-3685.**

Yellow Pine Ranch
Historic ranch, taking guests since 1927. Walking distance of Cuchara Village. Accommodations in nine cabins, each sleeping two to maximum of eight. Full kitchens. Open Christmas vacation. **15880 State Hwy 12, Cuchara, CO 81055; (719) 742-3528.**

Condominiums

The most convenient lodgings are the 125 condominiums at Cuchara Valley. One- to three-bedroom units with kitchens and fireplaces are within walking distance of the lifts. Aspen Leaf Village are slopeside units, each with two bedrooms, one bath, and a kitchenette. The larger Sunwatcher units each have two bedrooms, two-and-a-half baths, loft with sleep sofa and full kitchen. Sun Mountain units are the largest, with three bedrooms, two or three baths, full kitchen, and washer and dryer. Property managers who rent Cuchara Valley lodgings include **All Seasons Property Management, (800) 453-2241; American West Builders, (800) 287-3879; Cuchara Cabin Rentals, (719) 742-5490,** and **Security Properties, 800-CUCHARA.**

La Veta

This small town 15 miles from Cuchara Valley Resort offers additional lodging options and small-town charm. Information is available from the **La Veta/Cuchara Chamber of Commerce,** (719) 742-3676.

Mid-Priced Accommodations

La Veta Inn
Historic hotel, recently restored and reopened. All rooms individually decorated with period and

---

Mountain Stats—
Cuchara Valley

Resort elevation 9,248 feet
Top of highest lift 10,810 feet
Bottom of lowest lift 9,284 feet
Total vertical 1,526 feet (1,562 feet from the top of The Burn)
Longest run 2^1/2 miles
Average annual snowfall 230 inches
Ski season mid-December to early April
Lifts 1 triple chairlift, 3 doubles
Capacity 5,000 skiers per hour
Terrain 24 trails, 300 acres (40% beginner and novice, 40% intermediate, 20% advanced and expert)
Snowmaking 75%
Night skiing offered on selected weekend nights off Lift 4
Snow reports (719) 742-3163

---

antique furniture, done in Santa Fe country colors. Currently seven rooms and three suites, two with full kitchens. One family suite has a kids' room with two bunkbeds and own television. Atmosphere is at once both family-oriented and romantic. Fireplace lobby, restaurant, bar. Daily housekeeping. **103 W. Ryus Ave., La Veta, CO 81055; (719) 742-3700.**

The 1899 House
Vintage home, now a delightful B&B inn. Furnished with antiques. Five bedrooms, all with private lavatory or bath, plus private cottage with kitchenette and fireplace. Non-smoking inn. Full breakfast, daily housekeeping. **314 S. Main St., La Veta, CO 81055; (719) 742-3576.**

Hunter House B&B
Stucco home, built in 1906, furnished with antiques and filled with owner's interesting collections. Large-screen TV with surround sound; VCR with choice of movies. Three rooms with shared bath, a charmer with footed tub and French shower. Non-smoking inn. Well-behaved children welcome. Fireplace den, patio with outdoor fireplace for mild weather. Large choice of from-scratch breakfast offerings (including homemade biscuits, farm-fresh eggs, specialty meats, homemade preserves), specialty coffees and teas in

178

Moderate prices, modest lifts and a mid-size mountain characterize the Cuchara experience.

the morning and after skiing, daily housekeeping. **115 W. Grand Ave., P.O. Box 427, La Veta, CO 81055; (719) 742-5577.**

Economy Accommodations

Circle the Wagons
Twelve simple motel rooms and 15 winterized RV spaces with full hookups including cable TV (bathhouse open in winter for showers and laundry). One-and-a-half blocks from downtown. Daily housekeeping. **124 N. Main, La Veta, CO 81955; (719) 742-3233.**

La Veta Motel
Nine units, from one-room efficiency cabin to two-bedroom suite with kitchenette. Located one block from main street, right on Cucharas River. Senior citizens' discounts; special weekly rates. Guest laundry, satellite TV. Daily housekeeping. **404 S. Oak St., La Veta, CO 81955; (719) 742-5303.**

DINING OUT

Baker Creek Restaurant
Base of lifts location. Lower base building, open for lunch and dinner. Mostly Mexican, pasta and local special-cut steaks. Cathedral ceiling with exposed beams and great views of slopes. Southwestern decor, including designer tables inlaid with copper. **Resort Base, (719) 742-3163, Ext. 236.**

Positively Main Street
Adobe-style building, part of the Zocolo Plaza complex. Art gallery, musical recital hall and natural food (but not necessary vegetarian or health-food) dispensary under one roof. Red Lion Tea Room for tea, cheese and other gourmet specialties. Breakfast, lunch and dinner. **222 Main St., La Veta; (719) 742-5505.**

La Veta Inn Restaurant
Fine new hotel restaurant. American specialties, but on the gourmet side. Santa Fe colors. Specials added to breakfast and dinner menu on Sundays. Great breakfasts from fruit plate to biscuits and gravy. Serves breakfast, lunch and dinner. Reservations recommended for dinner. **103 W. Ryus Ave., La Veta; (719) 742-3700.**

Milagro Cafe
Stylish Southwestern restaurant in attractive adobe building. Art on walls for sale. Serves popular Mexican dishes such as tacos, burritos and enchiladas, including versions with a creative, contemporary touch. Also nightly specials, which might include Chicken Carbonata with Flour Tortilla for the adventurous and ribeye steak for traditionalists. Dinner Friday through Monday evenings. Reservations accepted. **103 E. Francisco, La Veta; (719) 742-0288.**

Silver Spoon Restaurant
Beautiful. Located on Cucharas River, which makes an S right through the property. Fine dining on a combination of French, German and Italian specialties, all in innovative renditions. All dishes prepared to order, including many meat and seafood sautés finished with unique sauces. Situated between village and ski resort. Open

daily for lunch and dinner. Reservations requested. **16894 Hwy 12, Cuchara, (719) 742-3764.**

Timbers Restaurant
One of the more upscale restaurants in rural Huerfano County, with steaks, seafood, Italian and Mexican specialties. Pleasantly atmospheric. **Cuchara Village; (719) 742-3838.**

NIGHTLIFE

The day lodge serves beer and wine, and the elegant Baker Creek lodge at the base of the mountain sees evening action. It starts with after-ski and running through the dinner and sometimes highlighted with music and dancing. The bar has a slight western theme, with copper-topped tables and large fireplace. The ultra-funky Boardwalk Saloon in Cuchara Village is a virtual grandma's attic of memorabilia and an atmosphere that is both cozy and lively, with liquid refreshment and occasional karaoke entertainment. In town, the La Veta Sports Pub & Grub is younger, livelier and louder, while the lounge at the new La Veta is more stylish and subdued. Zocolo Plaza is developing into an interesting place for evening diversion.

For more information, contact **Cuchara Ski Valley, Resort Box 3, 946 Panadero Ave., Cuchara, CO 81055, (800) 227-4436, (719) 742-3163; Huerfano County Chamber of Commerce, 400 Main St., Walsenburg, CO 81089, (719) 738-1065, (719) 742-3163. Walsenburg-Huerfano Visitors' Center, 400 Main St., Walsenburg, CO 81089, (719) 738-1065.**

Photo by Claire Walter

Convenient condominiums are located at Cuchara Ski Valley. Other lodging options from RV spaces to quaint B&B inns are found nearby.

Utah

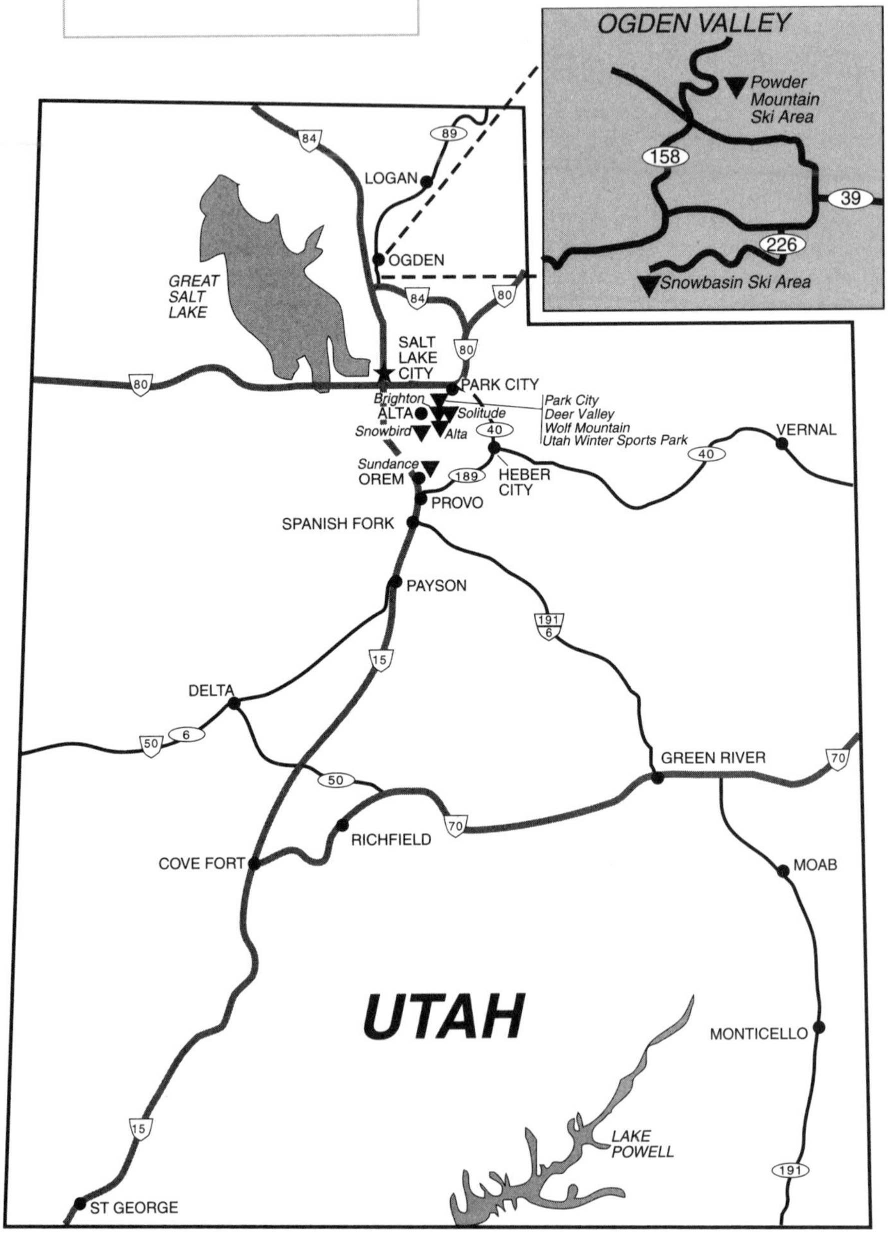

180

OGDEN VALLEY

▼ Powder Mountain Ski Area

158

39

226

▼ Snowbasin Ski Area

GREAT SALT LAKE

84

89

LOGAN

OGDEN

84

80

SALT LAKE CITY

80

PARK CITY

Brighton

ALTA

Snowbird

Alta

Solitude

Park City
Deer Valley
Wolf Mountain
Utah Winter Sports Park

40

VERNAL

40

Sundance

OREM

189

HEBER CITY

PROVO

SPANISH FORK

PAYSON

191
6

15

DELTA

50   6

50

GREEN RIVER

70

RICHFIELD

70

COVE FORT

MOAB

UTAH

MONTICELLO

15

LAKE POWELL

191

ST GEORGE

Utah

Photo by Lori Adamski-Peek/Park City Ski Area

181

THE PARK CITY AREAS

BACKDROP

Of the snow-holding valleys etched into the Wasatch Mountains east of Salt Lake City, Parley's Canyon has by far the most facilities. With three major ski areas, a historic mining town, the sparkling ski jumping and bobsled venue for the 2002 Olympics and ongoing development from one end of the valley to the other, it dwarfs everything else in the state. Park City, a picturesque former mining center and by far Utah's largest ski town (and most would argue its only ski town), is home base for the U.S. Ski Team. It is one of the most complete resorts in America boasting all manner of winter sports, a vibrant art scene and a wide range of lodgings. It started out as a long, skinny town with a true main street now alive with restaurants, shops, nightspots and skiers to patronize them all in a manner that is more reminiscent of Colorado than of other Utah resorts. Main Street is flanked with steep side streets that are a crazy quilt of old miner's cottages, newer in-fill homes, an old school here, a church there, a shrinking handful of empty lots between and new sprawling new development on all sides.

The namesake Park City Ski Area is Utah's leader in terms of vertical drop, number of lifts, lift capacity and skiable acreage. Because of Utah's biggest snowmaking system, Park City has also become respected as the reliable host of one of the top events in skiing. America's Opening is sometimes a season-launching World Cup event and sometimes a pro race in late November. In 1996–97, Park City replaced a high-speed quad chairlift with a high-speed six-seater, the first in the Rockies. The area is truly all things to all skiers, and its calendar is filled with special events from its opening through the rollicking Snowshine Festival as the ski season winds down.

Bracketing Park City like snow-covered bookends are Wolf Mountain and Deer Valley. The trio is rather like a retail district that has Neiman-Marcus on one side, K-Mart on the other and Macy's in the middle. Wolf Mountain is a low-key favorite with day skiers from Salt Lake, just as it was when it was called ParkWest, and the closest it gets to being crowded is a busy Saturday when they all show up. It is inexpensive, unpretentious, friendly and simple—an old-style ski area in the truest, finest sense of the phrase.

Deer Valley, by contrast, is the most unabashedly upscale ski resort in Utah, perhaps all of North America. The original developers and the investors who have followed had a vision of elegant perfection in skiing, lodging and guest services, and the Deer Valley of today is true to the vision. This exquisite aerie boasts deluxe accommodations, super-groomed slopes and trails, arguably the best on-mountain dining in the country and ski valets and other services that bring the standards of top hotels onto the slopes. Stein Eriksen, the ageless 1952 Olympic champion, has a lodge here bearing his name and is Deer Valley's director of skiing. Custom-built mountain homes, grand in proportions and splendid in style dot the mountains, and celebrities like Robert Urich, Johnny Carson and Charles Gibson who have mountain homes there embue Deer Valley with additional cachet.

THE LAY OF THE LAND

Park City—the town and the ski area—is located in a wide spot in Parley's Canyon on the far end of the Wasatch, taken from the perspective of a Salt Lake City skier. This canyon—actually more a wide valley than a Cottonwood-style canyon—is the giant of Utah skiing. The Utah Winter Sports Park, built for the 2002 Olympics, is closest to the canyon mouth. The town of Park City and its three ski areas are father up the road—first Wolf Mountain, then the town of Park City and the Park City ski area and finally Deer Valley.

Visitors headquarter in three main locales. Those who put a premium on après-ski tend to stay in town, where the selection of eating places and nightspots ranks as the best in the West. Families usually prefer living at the mountain base, loosely called the Resort Center, which is within walking distance of the children's ski school, skating rink and main ski lifts. And those who prefer luxury and tranquility, and can afford to do so, stay at Deer Valley. Free shuttle buses link downtown Park City, the Resort Center and Deer Valley, so picking one won't deny you access, day or night, to the other.

GETTING THERE

Salt Lake City International Airport is one of the least weather-vulnerable gateway airports in ski country, with more than 500 flights a day. Rental cars are available. The 27-mile drive takes about 40 minutes via Interstate 80 and Utah 224. Scheduled van service is provided by **All Resort Express (800) 457-9457; Lewis Bros. Stages, (800) 826-5844, (801) 649-2256, (801) 359-8347** and **Park City Transportation Services, (800) 637-3803, (801) 649-8567.** Salt Lake City is also a daily **AMTRAK** stop, **(800) USA-RAIL.** A car is superfluous at the resort. Free buses connecting town, outlying lodging and all three ski areas operate from 7:45 A.M. to 12:30 A.M. Also, a free trolley shuttles back and forth along Main Street.

THE SKIING

Park City

Profile

As a mountain, the Park City ski area is not dramatic to look at, but the skiing goes on forever. It rises above the town like a rumpled comforter with only a fraction of what's available visible from the base. Even on the mountain, there's no vantage point from which to see the entire area. Some skiers find the section they like best and stay there run after run—efficiency skiing at its best. Others prefer to wander helter-skelter, thrilled at finding new terrain and awed by its magnitude and variety. The only thing the layout

Photo by Lori Adamski-Peek/Park City Ski Area

183

doesn't let you do is ski from the very top to the very bottom in one continuous run.

The main entrance into this vast paradise is from the Resort Center. Your first choice at the start of a skiing day is to gondola or not to gondola. If you opt for the former on a peak day, you might have to wait half an hour or more for the leisurely 23-minute ride, for Park City's four-passenger, two-stage gondola—as old as the area itself—travels at a stately pace, and a fast modern replacement for it has long been predicted. The speedier alternatives to gondola-ing are to ride the Ski Team and Prospector chairs or even the Pay Day, Crescent and Pioneer chairs to the same place. The rides take roughly the same time—but the cumulative lift-line time on the chairs is usually shorter. Skiers overnighting near Main Street have the option of taking the Town Lift, putting the skiing nearer to the doorsteps of more people and unclogging the Resort Center on busy mornings. The gondola and the Silverlode, Thaynes and Motherlode chairlifts unload at the Summit House, one of Park City's mountain restaurants, a place so busy that it feels like a high-altitude Times Square. Skiers head in to or out from coffee or lunch or simply a pit stop, ski over to the bump runs on Thaynes or pass through en route to Jupiter Bowl.

If you look down from the air, Park City resembles a large Y formed by two main ridges that merge at mid-mountain to form a broader ridge that angles back, back and still farther back—first gently and then very steeply to the summit. The Town lift rises up one fork of the Y, the Ski Team chair climbs over another and the first stage of the gondola essentially sails over the drainage between them. The heavily forested

Freshly groomed slopes on a sunny morning.

main mountain has acres and acres of aspens, giving even the lower portions an airy, open feeling. The Pay Day quad ferries skiers from the gondola base to the same ridge, and a handful of runs drop off it back into that drainage. The most famous frontside run, Pay Day, is a beguiling blue used for World Cup openers and for night skiing as well. Across the way, half a dozen never-crowded, slalom-steep trails slash down the frontside off the Ski Team chair, while four really easy ones are found off the nearby First Time and Three Kings chairs. All of this combines into a lower mountain that looks and feels like a midsized, bowl-shaped ski area unto itself. But skiers, by and large, pass through and over this sector and ski on high.

The lion's share of Park City's runs—most of the blues and a load of black bumpers—cascade off the Ski Team Ridge and the main ridge forming the undulating north wall of a huge, deep drainage called Thaynes Canyon. From Thaynes, the modern Resort Center is out of sight and out of mind, but history is palpable as you ski past old mining buildings and hoists that pepper the landscape. Skiers can return via a choice of four chairlifts—in order from the "front" of the ski area, the King Consolidated and Silverlode high-speed lifts, the Mortherlode triple and the Thaynes double. Most skiers pack into the triangle formed by the second stage of the gondola, King Con and Silverlode. The runs off King Con are the easiest, and the terrain becomes progressively steeper toward the "back" runs served by the Thaynes lift, but with the gee-whiz factor and line-gobbling haul, the Silverlode six-place lift is Park City's newest triumph.

Like Baby Bear's porridge, most of the 10 busy, blue-square runs in this sector are "just right," a mile or so long on verticals of around 1,000 feet. The Hoist, Double Jack and Thaynes off the Thaynes chair are mean mogul runs—a fair bit longer, a lot steeper and always demanding of skill and alertness. The Hoist's midsection has an awesome drop-off where first-timers least expect it, while Thaynes (the trail, not the lift or the canyon run) has a steady fall line to mitigate the challenge—a bit. The Thaynes side is mostly the preserve of better skiers, yet novices love Claimjumper, the single most popular run at Park

Photo by Lori Adamski-Peek/Park City Ski Area

City, a generous slope that start from the Summit House, follows the main ridge (the one that is the stem of the Y) and curves down a small drainage right to the maze for the Prospector lift.

The other side of the main ridge is as little trafficked as the lower mountain. With a lift of its own, the Pioneer triple, such lovely green-circle runs as Webster and Bonanza, one diamond-wearing bowl and some of the best mountain dining this side of Deer Valley, this sector is a bit like Park City's hidden treasure. The steep little cirque called Blueslip Bowl is especially attractive, for it is tacked onto the back of the main ridge and is never crowded.

The far end of the main ridge serves as the access to Jupiter Bowl, a steep cirque segmented into four side-by-side bowls that vaulted Park City into Utah's major leagues. To ski Jupiter Access, a connector trail, is to drop into a wilder, more challenging world. The Jupiter chair rises quickly above dense woods to scrubby trees that tough it out near the timberline. There you'll find rocks and chutes, steep faces and tricky fall lines. When you disembark at 10,000 feet, the panorama is dramatically Alpine. Jupiter Bowl arcs off to the left, a double-diamond sea of white spiked with dark, tenacious evergreens. More trees and a slope pitched still more alarmingly characterize Silver Cliff, 6 Bells and Indicator, routes located toward the center of the bowl. West Face, on the far side, has fewer trees and is slightly less steep than the others. Powderhounds hike beyond Jupiter Peak and ski East Face into Puma Bowl or on to McConkey's. From these latter two, you must ski all the way down to the Pioneer chair and take two lifts to retrace your tracks. Off to the right of the Jupiter double is Scott's Bowl, which is ridged and rilled and channeled into challenges of various stripes.

Still, for every powder pig in the bowls or bumper on Thaynes, there are hundreds of skiers of every ilk working their way gingerly down the greens, confidently cruising the blues and tackling the blacks with varying degrees of skill. They return to Park City for its scale, its variety, its grooming and even its on-mountain restaurants.

Snowboarding

When the 2002 Olympics were awarded to Salt Lake City, Park City was tabbed to host the

---

Mountain Stats—
Park City

Resort elevation 6,900 feet
Top of highest lift 10,000 feet
Bottom of lowest lift 6,900 feet
Total vertical 3,100 feet
Longest run 3 1/2 miles
Average annual snowfall 350 inches
Ski season mid-November to late April
Lifts one 4-passenger gondola, 1 high-speed six-passenger chairlift, 1 high-speed quad, 1 fixed-grip quad, 6 triples, 4 doubles
Capacity 23,000 skiers per hour
Terrain 89 trails, 2,200 acres (16% beginner and novice, 45% intermediate, 39% advanced and expert)
Snowmaking 420 acres
Night skiing on Pay Day, 4:00 to 9:00 P.M., nightly from Christmas through March
Mountain dining Snow Hut at the bottom of the Prospector chair, Summit House at the top of the gondola, Mid-Mountain Restaurant near the lower portion of the Pioneer chair
Snow reports (801) 647-5335

185

---

snowboarding events, which was ironic, since the area prohibited snowboarding. This is changing in 1996–97, and riders will finally join skiers on Park City's slopes. There are no initial plans to build a half-pipe, snowboard park or any other special terrain features, but rentals and lessons for adults and youngsters are available.

Ski School Programs

Beginner to low intermediate classes meet at bottom of the Pay Day chair; intermediate to advanced classes meet at the summit area and Silverlode chair. Reservations recommended, **(800) 227-2SKI, (801) 649-8111.**

Introductory Programs
Beginner Lessons: Half-day (2 hours) or all-day (4 hours) group lessons, featuring Elan parabolic skis. Also, 3- and 5-day learn-to-ski programs. Snowboard version also offered.

Advanced and Specialty Programs
PCSA Women's Ski Challenge: Three- or four-day program of skiing with women of all ability

levels and taught by women and directed by former member of U.S. Ski Team Kristi Terzian. Philosophy is based on lots and lots of skiing. Includes welcome reception, lifts, Continental breakfast, stretching sessions, personal video to take home, seminars and social activities. Low-intermediate to advanced ability.

Mountain Experience Class: Four-hour class for high-intermediate and advanced skiers. Instructor-guides for learning plus discovering Park City's terrain.

For Families
Park City Ski School, (800) 227-2SKI.

Nonskiing Children
The Park City ski area has no infant/toddler nursery; for a list of off-mountain day care, see "Child Care" section on page 190.

Skiing Children
Kinderschule: Little children's ski school (ages 3 to 6), with full program of skiing, crafts, snacks, quiet time and supervision. Private lessons are recommended for all beginners and for 3-year-olds. Registration between 8:30 A.M. and 9:45 A.M. for morning or full day; pickup must be by 4:30 P.M. Prepaid reservations are required during peak holiday periods and suggested throughout the season, **(800) 227-2SKI, (801) 649-8111.**

Mountain Adventure: For 3- to 6-year-old wedge christie and better skiers. Includes other Kinderschule activities and lift pass.

Youth School: Adult prices and class schedules for children ages 7 to 13. Youngsters are grouped by age and ability. In addition to two-hour morning and afternoon lessons, the ski school offers an optional all-day package with supervised lunch for children ages seven to twelve. Three- and five-day packages available.

For Racers

NASTAR: Wednesday, Thursday, Friday and Saturday on Lost Prospector Trail.
Race Clinic: Training in racing technique for all ages and ability levels. Includes timed runs.
Coin-Operated Racing: Dual-format course on Clementine.
Eagle Race Arena: Site of Alpine technical

events for the 2002 Winter Olympics. Now available for group, league and night racing and race training.

Handicapped Skiing

Disabled Ski Lessons: Specialized one-on-one lessons for individuals with physical and/or mental disabilities. For information on skiing and other sports programs contact the **National Ability Center, (801) 649-3991.**

Deer Valley

Profile

Deer Valley shares with its neighbors a post office and multimountain skiing that is mostly hidden from sight of the base but otherwise, it is in a different league—not because of the terrain as much as what area management has done with it. It is the Mt. Meticulous of the Rockies, the Rolls Royce of ski mountains, the Maxim's of mountain dining, the Stanford Court of ski resorts. This final simile is deliberate, since the owner of the superluxe San Francisco hotel was one of the developers of the exquisite Utah ski complex. Deer Valley offers perfectly fine skiing escalated to the extraordinary ranks thanks to the most lavish services in skidom, starting with the valet who unloads your skis from the car, continuing through all food and hospitality elements and extending to the lift attendants who brush the snow off the thickly padded chairlift seats for you. Such outrageous pampering and elegant facilities have literally changed the face of American skiing, discreetly challenging every other upscale area to keep up or shut up.

Deer Valley's peaks are rounder and friendlier than the sharp ridges and deep valleys that comprise the terrain of Park City and Wolf Mountain, and all but the most demanding of the runs are manicured. The main base area for day skiers (meaning anyone coming up from Park City or farther afield) is Snow Park. As soon as you drive up, helpful green-jacketed ski valets will zip your skis off your car, the first of the extra services that characterize Deer Valley. The elegant Snow Park base lodge was recently expanded to the tune of $10 million. Right outside the door are a beginner area and a pair of parallel chairlifts, one a high-speed quad to ferry skiers to the top of Bald Eagle. There you'll find the mid-area resort center called Silver Lake Village. The higher mountains and more challenging skiing lie beyond.

At 9,400 feet, Bald Mountain is Deer Valley's highest point, and below it is the best terrain—both in terms of quantity and quality. Lifts rise from four spots around Bald Mountain's generous apron, meeting on the humpy summit. The Wasatch chair, Bald Mountain's main lift, has been upgraded to a quad, and all of its more than two dozen trails are marked blue and black. Most of them start out following the fall line like plumb lines, just curving gracefully near the bottom to lead back to the nearest chairlift. The runs tend toward broad boulevards, carefully groomed to keep them skiable and encourage the nonstop cruising that its well-heeled, mid-life clientele prefers.

Still, mindful and responsive to criticism that its skiing was too controlled and too clean to be interesting, Deer Valley now lets some of the blacks mogul up and remain rougher, less predictable, more demanding. In fact, there is a double-black area called Mayflower Bowl on Deer Valley's eastern fringe—as far from Snow Park and Silver Lake as you can get in that direction and still be inbounds. This bowl and the nearby expert trails off the Mayflower chair snare the morning sun and challenge stronger skiers before they're too weary. Because Deer Valley essentially remains such a true-blue cruising mountain, the trees don't get tracked quickly. The deep grove between the Sultan liftline and Ruins of Pompeii and the unsigned triangular stand of aspens between Tycoon and Reward are regarded as the best glades on the mountain.

When the first lift was installed on Flagstaff Mountain, its 800 vertical feet made it feel like a capricious afterthought, and it tended not to get crowded. But with the addition of the Northside Express, Deer Valley's first high-speed quad, on the far side of Flagstaff, it became evident that the short original lift was just good planning. Flagstaff's runs are quintessentially Deer Valley—long, loping boulevards designed for fast, smooth skiing. They are also the gateway to Empire Canyon, accessible via pay-per-ride snowcat skiing starting in January '96 and slated for lift-

Mountain Stats— Deer Valley

Resort elevation 8,200 feet (Silver Lake Village)
Top of highest lift 9,400 feet
Bottom of lowest lift 7,200 feet
Total vertical 2,200 feet
Longest run 2 miles
Average annual snowfall 250 inches
Ski season early December to early April
Lifts 3 high-speed quad chairlifts, 8 triples, 2 doubles
Capacity 23,800 skiers per hour
Terrain 67 trails, 3 bowls, 1,100 acres (15% beginner and novice, 50% intermediate, 35% advanced and expert), plus snowcat-accessed bowl skiing
Snowmaking 290 acres
Mountain dining Silver Lake Lodge at Silver Lake Village, between the Viking and Sterling lifts
Snow reports (801) 649-2000

served skiing. This vast parcel lays to rest any remaining notions that Deer Valley is too easy, too tame, too groomed, too flat, too predictable. The canyon is so broad—it's a valley, really—that the mountainsides enfolding it don't look steep from a distance. It's not until you're on the top de-

The luxurious lobby of the Stein Eriksen Lodge combines European charm and western American spaciousness.

Photo courtesy Deer Valley Resort

ciding where to ski, or in the middle of a heart-pounding run, that you realize how challenging Deer Valley's back bowls really are. Daly Bowl is a magnet for strong skiers. The easiest of its nine chutes is a hefty black diamond; the hardest might be triple blacks, especially in the context of Deer Valley. Eventually, four to five chairs are planned for this fantastic part of the mountain. On the other side of the ridge from Daly Bowl is Park City's McConkey's Bowl, presenting the tantalizing possibility of area-to-area skiing, a joint lift ticket or other future cooperation.

Noteworthy

Limited Ticket Sales: To keep the lines down and the runs uncrowded, Deer Valley limits lift ticket sales at peak periods. At times, there may be room only for holders of season passes, Christmas passes (a special eight-day holiday pass) and limited day tickets or vouchers. Ticket reservations are suggested for peak times; **Central Reservations, (800) 424-DEER, (801) 649-1000.**

At most ski areas, mountain restaurants merely merit a mention. At Deer Valley, they deserve the rapturous praise that has been heaped upon them. Describing the self-service buffets at Snow Lake and Silver Lake Lodges as cafeterias would do them a disservice, for the food and ambiance set new standards for ski areas. Nevertheless, prices are on a par with other good ski areas, but with ingredients and preparation that you would normally find in a first-rate restaurant. This is totally in character for a resort where quality is the watchword and "you get what you pay for" the philosophy of guests who want the best.

Ski School Programs

The ski school desk is located on the Plaza Level of the Snow Park Lodge. Reservations for all levels of skier from beginner up recommended for ski school, especially at peak times. **Central Reservations** can book them, **(800) 424-DEER.**

Advanced and Specialty Programs

Black Diamond Workshop: Five-hour clinic for advanced skiers to improve skills in various terrain and snow conditions.

Specialty Workshops: Parallel Breakthrough, Mountain Extreme, Style Workshop, Super Sidecut Clinic and Ladies Only, afternoon clinics for experienced skiers 18 and older who want to fine-tune a specific aspect of their skiing.

Women's Winter Escape: Three days of specialized clinics for women, by women. Available a couple of times a season.

For Families

The Snow Park Lodge expansion of 1995 included the addition of an excellent and expanded child-care facility.

Nonskiing children

Deer Valley Child Care Center: Infant care is for wee ones, 2 to 24 months, and day care provides indoor supervision and activities for nonskiers ages 2 to 12. Full- and half-day programs; lunch with full day. Hours are from 8:30 A.M. to 4:30 P.M. Reservations required. You can also call **Rent a Nanny** and book child care by the hour, day or vacation, **(801) 597-3652.**

Skiing Children

Bambi Special: One-hour private lesson within framework of Child Care Center program for children ages 3 to 5. Reservations required.

Reindeer Club: Group lessons for children ages 4 1/2 through kindergarten, operating out of the Child Care Center. Full-day lessons, play and lunch. Beginners start on Snow Safari, the little children's jungle-theme terrain garden. Bambi Slalom is a special race where each child receives an achievement medal and a special treat. Reservations required.

Adventure Club: Group lessons for first-graders through age 12; morning and afternoon classes and lunch.

Teens

Teen Equipe: Workshop for teens ages 13 to 18

Noteworthy

Kids Karnival Night is a fun social program from 6:00 to 9:00 P.M. for children ages 5 to 12. Games, activities, entertainment, dinner and snacks included. Offered select evenings Christmas through New Year and other peak times.

to ski together in a challenging environment. Coaching is on "dynamics of advanced skiing."

For Racers

Stein Eriksen Medalist Challenge: Two runs on a giant slalom course and a chance to compete against 1952 Olympic gold medalist Stein Eriksen's pace-set time and perhaps win a medal; daily on Race Course above Silver Lake Lodge. Available Fridays from 10:00 A.M. to 3:00 P.M.

Medalist Challenge: Two giant slalom runs and a chance to win a medal, competing against the time posted by Deer Valley pacesetters. Course times vary.

Self-Timed Dual Course: Tuesday, Thursday, Saturday and Sunday from 10:00 A.M. to noon on the Race Hill.

Handicapped Skiing

Skiing and year-round recreation for disabled children and adults, **(801) 649-3991.**

Wolf Mountain

Profile

Wolf Mountain, formerly ParkWest, has long struggled for recognition. It offers lower single-day lift tickets to keep locals coming, participates in the multi-area voucher book to attract visitors and for years was the only local area to permit snowboarding, drawing riders with two half-pipes and fabulous off-trail terrain. Yet, with all that, it remains so little trafficked that, except on Saturdays when Salt Lakers flock in, there aren't any real mazes feeding the seven lifts, including two quads with high-speed upgrade capabilities—the mountain's first new lifts in ages.

Like Park City, the mountain doesn't look like much from below—just a few lifts, a handful of base buildings and a broad beginner slope on which remarkably few people seem to be skiing. What you see is just the tiniest hint of what you get, because the real terrain is all out of sight. For many skiers who are fussier about snow and terrain than about status or frills, Wolf Mountain is outta sight as well. Also like Park City, this area is built on heavily wooded ridges, with easier skiing along the tops and in the valleys and the challenging pitches and great tree skiing

down the flanks. However, where Park City's ridges form a Y shape, Wolf Mountain's are roughly parallel but staggered, creating a ski area that pushes deep back from a base but is very narrow from boundary to boundary. Beginners ski the tapering end of the front ridge. Two long double chairs—Tomahawk up the first (Lookout Mountain) and Ironhorse up the second (Ironhorse Peak)—are all that's required. Intermediates tend to ski the predictably smooth blues on the ridge crests and valley floors, while advanced skiers have a real field day. Bearclaw, Badlands and Grizzly are narrow and slash relentlessly down the drop-away fall line. Massacre and Geronimo Ridge build Wolf Mountain's baddest bumps, while Bronco Bowl, which is more wall than bowl, offers genuinely extreme skiing. Rock 'n Roll, Porcupine and Three Tower off the south side of Ironhorse are phenomenal powder chutes—the peer of any in the Wasatch. The new Saddle Peak Ridge quad increases Wolf Mountain's vertical and adds some 300 acres of intermediate-level bowl and glade terrain.

Snowboarding

For years, first as ParkWest, then as Wolf Mountain, this was the only game in town for snowboarders. Even with riders now welcome at Park City, Wolf's reputation, casual friendliness, knockout terrain features, low prices and layout that is now well known and admired in the snowboarding community will keep it on the top of the heap. The mountain has five half-pipes and a snowboard park, lit for night riding, with rails, log slides, hits and table tops, as well as new Pipe Dragon to keep the half-pipes in top condition. The snowboard component of the ski school has a reputation as one of the best around.

Ski School Programs

Introductory Programs
Learn to Ski/Snowboard Package: Three-day introductory special to skiing or snowboarding.

Special Programs
Hidden Peaks: Two-hour complimentary meet-the-mountain tour for skiers and snowboarders. Meets daily at 10:00 A.M. at the ticket office.

For Families
Kids Central: Play-care, skiing, supervised lunches and snacks and rental equipment in one place. Special program for children ages 3 and younger, including one-on-one lessons; full-day plus activities for children ages 4 to 9.

190

Utah Winter Sports Park

Profile
Words like "unique" and "singular" are overused, but it's safe to say that the Utah Winter Sports Park is unique in the United States (Calgary's Olympic Park is similar). Nicknamed "Park City's fourth ski area," it was built for the 2002 Winter Olympics, and it is a singular sensation. You can watch athletes training on the bobsled and luge run. Ski jumps of all sizes and ramps for the aerial specialty of freestyle skiing are available to spectators—and even participants. The sports park features two-hour recreational ski-jumping instruction program. Using your regular Alpine gear (but no poles, please), you'll get a chance to soar off a tiny jump, a bigger one, a still bigger one—just like Eddie "the Eagle" Edwards. There's one slo-o-o-ow double chairlift that accesses the top of the big 90-meter jumping hill and a little day lodge. Actually, it's an evening lodge

too, for ski jumping has become a popular evening diversion in the Wasatch. For information, **Utah Winter Sports Park at Bear Hollow, P.O. Box 682-382, Park City, UT 84068; (801) 649-5447.**

Snowcat Skiing
The joy of backcountry snowcat-served skiing is available a short distance from Park City at Thousand Acre Ranch. An all-day package includes roundtrip transportation from the resort to the ranch, a full day of guided cat skiing (typically seven to eight runs), use of wide powder skis and lunch. **Park City Powdercats, P.O. Box 2340, Park City, UT 84060; (800) 635-4719, (801) 649-6583.**

For Families
Because two of the three ski areas in the valley, including the largest one, do not offer infant and toddler day care, independent day care is more important than in most ski towns. **Creative Beginnings** accepts children ages 4 weeks to 2 years and non-skiers to age 12 from 7:00 A.M. to 6:00 P.M. weekdays and 8:00 A.M. to 5:00 P.M. weekends (evening care with reservations), **(801) 645-7315.** The other option for infants is for a babysitter to come to your hotel or condo. You can find someone through **Guardian Angel, (801) 640-1229, Rent A Nanny, (801) 597-3652** and **Nanny 'N Me, (801) 483-9455.**

If you are traveling with an infant or toddler and need to rent a crib, playpen, highchair or other supplies, contact the local franchise of **Baby's Away, (800) 379-9030, (801) 645-8823.**

Nordic Skiing
The most convenient trail system is at the **White Pine Touring Center** on the Park City Golf Course. It offers 18 kilometers of tracks over both flat and rolling terrain, none too demanding, plus instruction and rental equipment, **(801) 649-8710** (year-round), **(801) 649-8701** (November 15 to end of season). In 2002, Mountain Dell Park near the mouth of Parley's Canyon will host the Olympic cross-country races. Right now, it's one of Park City's best-kept skiing secrets, with some 18 to 20 miles of tracks and skating lanes groomed on a county golf course. The ski season kicks in around mid-December and usually lasts until early

April. With a relatively low elevation, it's a good place for visitors to acclimate to Utah's altitude, and with a sledding hill, great when youngsters are too heavy to tote around in a carrier but too young to ski a lot. At this writing, there was still no infrastructure to speak of, and the grooming is a voluntary, cooperative effort between a local Nordic club and area ski shops. Until someone figures on a way to exploit Mountain Dell's commercial value, the skiing is free. For information, call **Wasatch Touring, (801) 359-9361.**

Jeremey Ranch, 8 miles from Park City, just off I-80, has 65 kilometers of trails from flat beginner to challenging hills. Instruction and a full-service ski shop are on the premises, **(801) 649-2700. The Homestead**, a wonderful country resort, 20 minutes by car from Park City, has 19 kilometers of cross-country tracks, lessons and rentals, **(800) 327-7220, (801) 654-1102.**

Off-Piste Skiing

If you are a strong, confident skier, consider signing up for the **Interconnect,** a thrilling guided ski tour that is a sampler of the best Utah has to offer. It combines use of some lifts and trails with off-piste skiing between the ski areas, all in a guided group of 6 to 14 skiers. Skiing five areas in three valleys or four areas in two without hiking or helicoptering is the only such European-style experience available in the United States. On the four-area itinerary (Tuesday, Thursday, Saturday), you'll start at Snowbird and ski to Alta, Brighton and Solitude. On the five-area version (Monday, Wednesday, Friday, Sunday), you'll start from Park City's Jupiter Bowl and ski into Big Cottonwood Canyon. There you use the runs and lifts of Solitude and Brighton, and then continue to Alta. It is also possible that the five-area tour will someday become six with the eventual addition of Deer Valley's Daly Bowl as the start. Both renditions include a private lunch and van

transfer back to the origin point. Reservations required, **(801) 534-1907.**

WHERE TO STAY

Park City

Note that many Park City properties participate in the Toucan promotion, two nights of lodging for the price of one, early (before Christmas) and late (after April 1) in the season, and Park City and Deer Valley match reduced lift ticket prices to this time period. **Park City Reservations, (800) 227-2SKI; Park City Chamber Resort Assn., (800) 453-1360.**

Luxury Accommodations

The Gables

Cozy and well-appointed one-bedroom suites at the base of the ski area. Each unit with jetted tub, fireplace and full kitchen—and fine views. Daily housekeeping, concierge services. Ski locker room, outdoor hot tub, sauna. **P.O. Box 905, 1335 Lowell Ave., Park City, UT 84060; (800) 443-1045, (801) 647-3160.**

Olympia Park Hotel

Well-appointed property with 206 large hotel rooms and 75 condominiums, located 1½ miles from the lifts in Prospector Square. Children 12 and younger stay free in parents' room. Ski Easy Packages include fanny pack on arrival, skiers' buffet breakfast, pack lunch to take skiing and complimentary après-ski beverages. Daily housekeeping, 24-hour front desk, bell staff, concierge, room service. Two restaurants, private club, atrium pool, sauna, hot tub, exercise room, game room, gift shop, ski rental shop. **P.O. Box 4439, 1895 Sidewinder Dr., Park City, UT 84060; (800) SKI-EASY, (801) 355-0910.**

Silver King Hotel & Silver Cliff Village
Spacious, deluxe condominiums, from studios to three-bedroom spa suites, with hotel services. Each unit has full kitchen with microwave, washer/dryer and wood-burning fireplace. Located at ski area base, 100 yards to lifts. Daily housekeeping, 24-hour front desk, valet laundry. Indoor/outdoor pool, hot tub, sauna. **P.O. Box 2818, Park City, UT 84060; (800) 331-8652, (801) 649-5500.**

Washington School Inn
Distinctive B&B in Park City's first schoolhouse (1889), listed on the National Register of Historic Places. Recipient of AAA Four Diamond honors; member of Great Inns of North America. Gracious and exquisitely furnished with antiques and Park City historical memorabilia. One block from Main Street and Town Lift. Daily housekeeping, breakfast, après-ski refreshments. Hot tub, fireplace lounge. **P.O. Box 546, Park City, UT 84060; (800) 824-1672, (801) 649-3800.**

Mid-Priced Accommodations

Blue Church Lodge & Townhouses
Elegantly furnished bed and breakfast in historic church building in "uptown" Park City, close to Main Street and Town Lift. On National and Utah Registers of Historic Places. Lodge has seven units of various sizes. Across the street, under same management, spacious two-bedroom condos (some with loft) with fireplace and spa. Midweek housekeeping (daily for extra fee), Continental breakfast. Indoor and outdoor hot tubs, game room, guest laundry, ski lockers. **P.O. Box 1720, 424 Park Ave., Park City, UT 84060; (800) 626-5467, (801) 649-8009.**

Chamonix Lodge
Traditional ski lodge with 24 functional rooms, all with private bath, queen-size bed, TV with VCR, in-room coffee maker (restocked daily), mini-refrigerator and most with balconies. Various room styles, sizes and rates. Short walk to gondola. Daily housekeeping. Sauna, indoor hot tub, free guest laundry. **P.O. Box 3327, 1450 Empire Ave., Park City, UT 84060; (801) 649-8443.**

Imperial Hotel
Historic 11-room hotel at the top of Main Street. Delightful landmark—downhill to dinner and nightlife, uphill returning. Daily housekeeping, Continental breakfast and après-ski refreshments included. Hot tub, sauna. **P.O. Box 2203, Park City, UT 84060; (800) 669-8824, (801) 649-1904.**

Old Miners' Lodge
Delightful hillside B&B, built in 1893, within short walk of Town Lift. Antique-filled rooms have private bath, down comforters and pillows. Relaxing library with fireplace. Phone in living room. Fine services and unsurpassed atmosphere. Like being a guest in a gracious home. Nonsmoking establishment. Daily housekeeping, nightly turndown service and towel replacement, full breakfast included, complimentary après-ski refreshments. Outdoor hot tub, ski lockers. **P.O. Box 2639, Park City, UT 84060; (800) 648-8068, (801) 645-8068.**

The Inn at Prospector Square
Large, full-service condo-hotel with 100 hotel rooms and 140 spacious condos to three bedrooms, with kitchenettes. Two miles from lifts. Children 12 and younger stay free in parents' room. Top athletic club used by U.S. Ski Team also has Park City's largest pool. Daily housekeeping, 24-hour front desk, free luggage storage (and complimentary changing rooms) on arrival and departure days, complimentary shuttle to ski area and downtown, massage. Full athletic club, indoor pool, hot tub, sauna, tanning room, steamroom, racquetball, exercise and weight room, restaurant. **P.O. Box 1698, 2200**

Sidewinder Dr., Park City, UT 84060; (800) 453-3812, (801) 649-7100.

Park Station Condominium Hotel

Hotel services for well-appointed one- to three-bedroom condominium units with wood-burning fireplaces. Next to Town Lift and easy walk to Main Street. Limited number of non-smoking rooms available. Daily housekeeping, 24-hour front desk, valet service, VCR and movie rentals. Indoor and outdoor hot tubs, sauna, guest laundry. **P.O. Box 1360, Park City, UT 84060; (800) 367-1056, (801) 649-7717.**

Radisson Inn Park City

Large, contemporary hotel with attractive decor and all services. All rooms equipped with robes, hairdryers, mini-bars and in-room movies. Children 17 and younger stay free in parents' room and those 12 and under eat free. Daily housekeeping, concierge, 24-hour front desk, room service, complimentary buffet breakfast. Indoor/outdoor pool, hot tub, sauna, ski rentals, gift shop, restaurant, private club, liquor store. **2121 Park Ave., P.O. Box 1778, Park City, UT 84060; (800) 345-5076, (801) 649-5000, (800) 333-3333** for Radisson reservations.

Shadow Ridge Resort Hotel & Conference Center

Large, tastefully decorated condo-hotel, two minutes' walk from lifts. Lock-off hotel room to two-bedroom suites with full kitchens, fireplaces and private balconies. Special deals for returning guests. Daily housekeeping, 24-hour front desk, bell staff, concierge services, massage available. Indoor/outdoor pool, indoor hot tub, sauna, fitness equipment, guest laundry, ski lockers. **P.O. Box 1820, Park City, UT 84060; (800) 451-3031, (801) 649-4300.**

Snowed Inn

Ten-room neo-Victorian inn designed in impeccable style and beautifully furnished with antiques. Very romantic and charming. Excellent restaurant. One mile from Wolf Mountain, 2 miles from Park City. Daily housekeeping, Continental breakfast. Outdoor hot tub, restaurant. **3770 N. Hwy 224, Park City, UT 84060; (800) 545-SNOW, (801) 649-5713.**

The Yarrow Resort Hotel

Well-equipped and long popular Park City hotel. Located just outside town and $1/2$ mile from the lifts. Children 12 and younger stay free in parents' room. Shopping center directly behind hotel; short ride to downtown and lifts. Daily housekeeping, 24-hour front desk, room service, guest service desk. Outdoor swimming pool, outdoor hot tub, sauna, restaurant, cocktail lounge, liquor store, shops, ski rentals and repair, barber/beauty shop. **P.O. Box 1840, 1800 Park Ave., Park City, UT 84060; (800) 927-7694, (801) 649-7000.**

Economy Accommodations

Acorn Chalet Lodging

Economical units located 80 yards from ski center. Hotel rooms and one- and two-bedroom units with kitchenette and gas fireplace. Management says its rates are "flexible during low season." Phone in hall. Access to hot tub, pool and sauna. Packages available. Housekeeping available at extra charge. Ski lockers. **1314 Empire Ave., Park City, UT 84103; (800) 443-3131, (801) 649-9313.**

Chateau Après Lodge

Long-running hit with Park City bargain seekers. Traditional ski lodge. Thirty-two rooms with private baths, plus dorm, with total accommodations for 52. TV in lobby and private rooms. Casual, youthful atmosphere. Only 150 yards from lifts. Daily housekeeping, Continental breakfast included, restaurant. **P.O. Box 578, 1299 Norfolk Ave., Park City, UT 84060; (801) 649-9372.**

Star Hotel

Ten-room Main Street lodge, established in 1931, now a simple, friendly, family-style ski lodge. A true bargain too. Cooked-to-order breakfast and dinner included. **P.O. Box 777, Park City, UT 84060; (801) 649-8333.**

Condominiums

Chamonix Groupe & Chalets

Modestly priced units to two bedrooms, plus private home and chalets in complex. Full kitchens with microwaves; gas or wood fireplaces. Walking distance to lifts. Housekeeping every three to four days. Hot tub, sauna, ski lockers. **2065 Lucky John Dr., Park City, UT 84060; (801) 649-2618.**

The Lodge at the Resort Center
Large, modern, ski-in/ski-out complex with studio to four-bedroom condos with full kitchens and fireplaces. Heart of lift-base resort complex; easy walk to shops, restaurants, skating rink. Daily housekeeping, on-site check-in, 24-hour management, concierge services, valet parking, massage. Indoor/outdoor pool, hot tubs, sauna, fitness equipment, ski lockers, guest laundry. **P.O. Box 3449, Park City, UT 84060; (800) 824-5331, (801) 649-0800.**

Marriott's Summit Watch
New timeshare, part of Marriott Vacation Club. Luxurious studios to two-bedroom units, located at the foot of Main Street, close to the heart of downtown. All units with full kitchen and commodious jetted tub in master suite. Some with laundry facilities and some smoke-free. Daily housekeeping, concierge. Restaurant, fitness facility, pool, hot tub. **642 Main St., Park City 84060; (800) 223-0933, (801) 647-4100.**

Mine Camp Inn
Cozy one- to three-bedroom condos, each with kitchenette and gas fireplace. Located off Main Street, equidistant to Park City and Deer Valley lifts. On-site check-in, sauna, indoor hot tub. **P.O. Box 3151, Park City, UT 84060;. (800) 543-7113, (801) 649-2577.**

PowderWood Resort
Well-appointed, award-winning complex with one- and two-bedroom condos, 6 miles from ski area. All with quality furnishings, gas fireplaces and full kitchens. Previous AAA Four Diamonds winner. Daily or midweek housekeeping (price differential), free ski shuttle, wine-and-cheese social, ski movie showings (including popcorn). Recreation center, pool, outdoor hot tub with gazebo, weight room, steamroom, hydrotherapy pool, game room, sledding hills, guest laundry, on-site cross-country skiing. **6975 N. 2200 West, Park City, UT 84060; (800) 223-7829, (801) 649-2032.**

Snowflower Condominiums
Located 100 feet from Park City's Three Kings chairlift. Condos of all sizes from studios to five bedrooms. Each has individual hot tub and wood-burning fireplace. Midweek housekeeping (additional at extra charge), 24-hour front desk. Two outdoor hot tubs, ski lockers, guest laundry. **P.O. Box 957, Park City, UT 84060; (800) 852-3101, (801) 649-6400.**

Condominium management and reservations companies with properties in various complexes (but often central check-in locations for those without a front desk) include

Acclaimed Lodging, (800) 552-9696, (801) 649-3736
Accommodations Unlimited, (800) 778-8581, (801) 649-1128
Blooming Enterprises, (800) 635-4719, (801) 649-6583
Budget Lodging, (800) 522-SNOW, (801) 649-2526
Central Reservations of Park City, (800) 243-2032, (801) 649-6654
Condominium Rentals of Park City/Intermountain Lodging, (800) 221-0933, (801) 649-2687
David Holland's Resort Lodging, (800) SKI-2002, (801) 649-1801
Identity Properties, (800) 245-6417, (801) 649-5100
Jupiter Property Management, (800) 453-5789, (801) 649-5900
Park City Reservations, (800) 453-5789, (801) 649-9598
R&R Recreation & Resort Properties, (800) 348-6759, (801) 649-6225
Resort Property Management, (800) 243-3932, (801) 649-6606
Resortside Properties, (800) 255-6163

Deer Valley

Deer Valley Central Reservations, (800) 424-DEER.

Luxury Accomodations
Goldener Hirsch Inn
Exquisite slopeside hotel, modeled after fabled

small hotel in Salzburg, Austria. Twenty deluxe minisuites, some with fireplaces and private deck. Hand-painted Austrian pine furniture. Distinctive style and flawless taste. Outstanding and attractive restaurant. Daily housekeeping, complimentary Continental breakfast, room service, concierge, valet. Indoor/outdoor hot tubs, sauna, restaurant, fireside lounge and bar, gift shop, ski storage facilities. **P.O. Box 859, Park City, UT 84060; (800) 252-3373, (801) 649-7770.**

Stein Eriksen Lodge

Stylish, luxury lodge with 113 recently renovated rooms and suites and memorable public spaces, all done in a distinctive Norwegian-inspired contemporary design. Outstanding high-touch personal services. Associated with the lodge are luxurious condominiums with up to four bedrooms with designer furnishings, wood-burning fireplace, washer and dryer, full kitchen, jetted bathtub and lodge services (including housekeeping). Awarded Four Stars by Mobil. Twice-daily housekeeping, 24-hour front desk, room service, concierge, room service, complimentary shuttle within Park City. Outdoor pool, hot tub, sauna, fitness center with massage available, restaurants, lounge, liquor store, ski rental and repair, shops. **P.O. Box 3177, Park City, UT 84060; (800) 453-1302, (801) 649-3700.**

Condominiums and Homes

Deer Valley Lodging

Luxury condos and superluxe private homes throughout Deer Valley. Many units also have lofts for additional space. Facilities vary but often include private hot tub, sauna, pool and/or fireplace. Services include daily housekeeping and often hotel-style valet and bell services as well. **P.O. Box 3000, Park City, UT 84060; (800) 453-3833, (801) 649-4040.**

Salt Lake City

This city offers accommodations in all price ranges for 10,000 visitors. Many lodgings feature ski packages. For information call the **Salt Lake Convention & Visitors Bureau, (801) 521-2822.** Transportation between Salt Lake and the Park City ski areas is via rental car or **Lewis Bros. Stages.**

Other Locations

Best Western Landmark Inn

Located off I-80, short ride to Park City—and even closer to Utah Winter Sports Park. Large rooms, most with refrigerators. Lots of amenities. Children 12 and younger stay free in parents' room. Daily housekeeping, 24-hour front desk, free shuttle service to resort. Indoor pool, hot tub, exercise area, restaurant, guest laundry, big-screen TV in lobby. **6560 N. Landmark Dr., Park City UT 84060; (800) 548-8824, (801) 649-7300, (800) 528-1234** for Best Western reservations.

The Homestead

Top-ranked resort, 20 minutes from Park City, specializing in total winter vacation. Charming country inn on large property. Offers well-priced packages with lodging, breakfast and dinner daily, five days' Alpine skiing, on-property snowmobiling and cross-country skiing, dinner sleighride and rental car. B&B lodge rooms for adults and apartment-style suites for families and groups. Four Diamonds from AAA. Daily housekeeping, 24-hour front desk, bell staff, scheduled shuttle to Park City. Children's rates too. Restaurants, lounge, liquor store, pool, hot tub, sauna, cross-country center, snowmobiles. **P.O. Box 99, Midway, UT 84032; (800) 327-7220, (801) 649-2060.**

195

DINING OUT

Park City

Adolph's

Fine Continental dining in clubhouse of Park City Golf Course/Nordic Center. Veal Adolph (with shallot-mushroom cream sauce) is the house specialty. Other dishes include classics such as Chateaubriand for Two, Utah Golden Trout Meuniere and Venison Steak, Hunter Style. Daily specials, one a seafood dish. Also serves fondue and excellent desserts, some flamed. Two seatings. Piano bar. Reservations required. **Park City Municipal Golf Course, Park City; (801) 649-7177.**

Baja Cantina

Jumping Mexican place at base of lifts. Combination plates, plus burritos, enchiladas, chili and other specialties—all served in generous portions. Menu tags lower-fat entrées for the health-conscious. Fish tacos a real treat. Non-smoking restaurant. Children's menu. Open for after-ski, lunch, dinner and Sunday brunch. **Resort Center; (801) 649-BAJA.**

Bangkok Thai on Main

Moderate prices and interesting dishes, available in choice of spiciness level from a green circle for mild to don't-you-dare symbol for extra-spicy. Lovely atmosphere and carefully prepared dishes. Lots of choices for vegetarians. Non-smoking restaurant. Takeout available. Cocktails, beer and wine. **255 Main St., Park City; (801) 649-THAI.**

196

Bistro 7000

Spacious, modern slopeside restaurant with a few dishes for each of several popular cuisines—some Mexican, some pasta, some grilled goodies and lots of hearty American. Good spot for lunch, après-ski or dinner. Full and petite steaks and ribs, plus seafood and good salads served with warm bread. Non-smoking restaurant. Children's menu. **Resort Center; (801) 649-7062.**

Burgie's

No better place for a burger. Big beefy half-pounder, Little Burgies from the kids' menu and every size between. Also, abundant choice of seasonings. Alternative burgers include turkey, buffalo, lamb and veggie. Sandwiches too. Casual backyard barbecue atmosphere. Lunch and dinner. Cocktails, beer and wine. No smoking. Takeout available. **570 Main St., Park City; (801) 649-0011.**

Cafe Terigo

Informal and attractive cafe. Midsize menu with lots of sprightly grilled specialties plus good pastas and outstanding salads. Innovative contemporary cooking. Fine desserts. Lunch and dinner. No smoking. **424 Main St., Park City; (801) 645-9555.**

Cisero's Ristorante & Bar

Moderately priced pasta and sandwiches at lunch. Italian accent permeates the full dinner menu, featuring pizza, pasta, grilled meats, seafood and veal. "Soon-to-be-famous house dressing." Pleasing atmosphere, at once casual and nice. Entertainment. Also Sunday brunch. **306 Main St., Park City; (801) 649-5044.**

The Eating Establishment

Boisterous and fun—and smoke-free too. Inexpensive and casual. Breakfast served all day. Burgers and sandwiches at lunch. Ditto at dinner, plus pasta, seafood and chalkboard specials. Also, big for barbecues: beef brisket, baby back ribs and mesquite chicken. Rich desserts. **317 Main St., Park City; (801) 649-8284.**

Eating Establishment Express

Big breakfast at the base of the Park City lifts. Also, sandwiches, salads and fried fare (fish and chips, seafood basket, buffalo wings, chicken fingers) for lunch and dinner. Takeout available. **Resort Center** (behind ticket office); **(801) 649-7289.**

1800 Park Avenue Cafe & Pub

Lots of food for little money. A menu of special menus, including breakfast specials until 11:30 A.M. weekdays, sunset steak dinners from 4:00 to 6:00 P.M. nightly, bargain lunches, Sunday brunch, an all-you-can-eat prime rib buffet Friday and Saturday evenings and free shrimp in the pub part. **The Yarrow, 1800 Park Ave., Park City; (801) 649-7000.**

Grub Steak Restaurant

Long-running hit steak house, known for big portions, including trip to the salad bar or Caesar salad tossed at the table, plus starch and fresh vegetables. Also chicken, ribs and seafood, similarly accompanied. Mix-and-match combination dinners. Children's menu. Good desserts. Closed Sunday. Reservations suggested. **Prospector Square Hotel, 2210 Sidewinder Dr., Park City; (801) 649-8060.**

Irish Camel

Funky spot that bills itself as "Irish Pub & Mexican Grub." Selection of nachos to start—or to stick with. Lunch and dinner. Popular Tex-Mex dishes, à la carte or on combo platters, with choice of red or green sauce. Seafood specials. Salads and pizza too. Takeout available. **434 Main St., Park City; (801) 649-6645.**

Main Street Deli

Breakfast bagels (served all day), eggs and other specials, plus sandwiches, salads and baked goods at lunch. Several fresh-ground coffees. Carrot cake is house specialty. Also serves sandwiches of all sorts from lunch menu for supper (until 9:10). Children's menu. No smoking. Cocktails. Takeout. **525 Main St., Park City; (801) 649-1100.**

Mileti's

Long-popular Italian restaurant—with a few ethnic aberrations such as gravlax, Texas barbecue shrimp and mesquite-grilled Atlantic salmon. But essentially known for fine, filling appetizers, homemade pastas and a variety of hearty Italian entrées. Early-bird specials. Daily dessert specials. No smoking. Cocktails and wine. Dinner only. Reservations suggested. **412 Main St., Park City; (801) 649-8211.**

Morning Ray

Want a good hearty breakfast? Let Morning Ray shine on you anytime after 7:00 a.m. Omelettes, pancakes, huevos rancheros and homemade granola. Fresh-baked pastries and specialty coffees. Sandwiches and salads at lunch. Various soft drinks and beer. **268 Main St., Park City; (801) 649-5686.**

Radigan's

Hotel restaurant serving breakfast, lunch and dinner. At dinner, steaks, seafood and prime rib are featured. English-style mixed grill. Also pasta selection. Nightly specials including wild game. Salad bar. No smoking. Children's menu. Dinner reservations recommended. **Radisson Hotel, 2121 Park Ave., Park City; (801) 649-5000, Ext. 150.**

Red Banjo

Family-owned pizza parlor. Park City institution since 1962. Three sizes; all sorts of toppings. Also broasted chicken, spaghetti, salads. Takeout and delivery available. **322 Main St., Park City; (801) 649-9901.**

Snowed Inn

Full-course prix fixe dinners in opulent, romantic dining room. Two seatings. Also, sleighride dinner to cabin for Dutch-oven dinner, featuring soup, chili, warm bread, camp potatoes, prime rib or mesquite-grilled chicken, dessert and hot beverages. Includes entertainment. One trip per evening. Reservations required for both. **3370 N. Hwy 224, Park City; (801) 649-5713.**

Szechwan Chinese Restaurant

Big menu. Lots of variety. Popular Szechuan and other regional specialties, plus interesting offerings like Three Kinds of Mushrooms, Chinese Chicken Salad and Mongolian Beef. Lunch specials. Takeout available. Delivery after 5:00 P.M. **438 Main St., Park City; (801) 649-0957.**

The Taco Maker

Fast, inexpensive Mexican food. Tacos plus nachos, fajitas, burritos, enchiladas and salads. Kids' dinner. Also, good snack stop for shakes, smoothies, candy, nuts, sundaes and other treats. Drive-through and takeout available. **Prospector Square, 1640 Bonanza Dr., Park City; (801) 649-9850.**

Texas Red's

Humorous chili-parlor atmosphere. Chili and other Tex-Mex fare. Dinners include satisfying pit barbecue ribs, chicken, and steak and such down-home southern favorites as chicken fried steak, catfish and hushpuppies. Luckenbach Special Combo is a gut-buster with ribs, beef and sausage on a mound of sauerkraut. Lunch specials. Children's menu. **440 Main St., Park City; (801) 649-REDS, (801) 649-9997.**

Training in racing technique for all ages and ability levels includes timed runs.

Photo by Lori Adamski-Peek/Park City Ski Area

Zoom Roadhouse Grill

Sundance is infiltrating Park City, not just with the Sundance Film Festival, but now with this casual pub and restaurant. Features "refreshed" versions of classic American dishes from neighborhood restaurants across America, the kind that are disappearing under the tidal wave of cookie-cutter chains. Moderately priced sandwiches, entrées, appetizers and desserts. Large restaurant, set in historic Union Pacific Railway Depot. Wide choice of popular and hand-crafted liquors, wines from small vineyards and microbeers. Lunch and dinner. Reservations accepted. **660 Main St., Park City; (801) 649-9108.**

Deer Valley

The Mariposa

Fine dining at Silver Lake Lodge. Lovely cafe serving a blend of classic and contemporary cuisine. Small menu of innovative uses of classic ingredients and concepts: Crisp Pheasant Dumplings with Bok Choy and Chinese Sausage Sauté, Roasted Chicken Breast Filled with Spinach, Green Leeks and Shiitake Mushrooms, Filet of Beef Wrapped in Maple Peppered Bacon and the like. Weekly specials. All done especially well. Gracious service. No smoking. Reservations suggested. **Silver Lake Lodge, Deer Valley; (801) 645-6724.**

The Forest Room

Intimate 40-seat restaurant added during Eriksen Lodge's 1991 renovation. Specializes in regional mountain cuisine, including wild game, grilled or spit-roasted, garnished creatively and served elegantly. No smoking. Reservations suggested. **Stein Eriksen Lodge, Deer Valley; (801) 649-3700, Ext. 83.**

Glitretind Restaurant

Lodge dining room serves breakfast, skier's buffet lunch and Sunday brunch. Also famous for fine dining on international specialties. Meticulous preparation and service. Stylish and expensive. Daily specials. Homemade desserts. Reservations suggested. **Stein Eriksen Lodge, Deer Valley; (801) 649-3700, Ext. 83.**

Goldener Hirsch

Hotel restaurant serves very European buffet breakfast, plus lovely lunch and elegant dining. Excellent selection of finely prepared meat, poultry and trout with an Austrian accent. Moderately priced European Ski Buffet at dinner features wild game chili, soup, smoked trout and salmon, special entrée, salads, fruit and outstanding and unusual desserts. No smoking. Reservations recommended. **Goldener Hirsch Inn, Deer Valley; (801) 649-7770.**

High Country Snowmobile Dinner Ride

Drive a powerful sled with handwarmers across the meadows and over the powder for lunch or dinner in the backcountry. Ride and meal are about three hours. Lunch is a deli-style sandwich, snack and beverage, served outdoors. Dinner is prepared and served at Deer Valley's Silver Lake Lodge and includes choice of steak, chicken or salmon, plus salad, baked beans, rolls, soft drink and dessert. Second passengers pay half-price. Reservations required. Free shuttle from anywhere in Park City, **(801) 645-7533, (801) 222-0882.**

McHenry's Grill

A little bit of several cuisines (Southwestern, Italian, all-American). Deer Valley's most casual dining. Grill pizzas are good as starters or lighter fare. No-cholesterol chocolate cake is a satisfying special dessert. Children's menu. Lunch and dinner. Reservations not accepted at lunch; are at dinner. **Silver Lake Lodge, Deer Valley; (801) 545-6623.**

Seafood Buffet at the Snow Park Restaurant

Seafood Buffet features large selection from natural buffet, hot appetizers, hot entrées and desserts—all at one price (lower for children). Exceptional and ample offerings of fresh fare from the sea such as live Maine lobster, steamed or broiled to order. Also, prime rib or side of grilled salmon from the adjacent Carvery. Menu changes nightly. Excellent desserts. Reservations recommended. **Snow Park Lodge, Deer Valley; (801) 645-6632.**

Silver Lake Restaurant

Widely acclaimed as best lunch at an American mountain restaurant. Wide selections including salads, grilled specialties and hot entrées, all beautifully displayed. Continental breakfast too, featuring outstanding baked goods. **Silver Lake Lodge, Deer Valley; (801) 649-1000.**

Heber City

The Homestead

Spacious dining room of country inn 20 minutes from Park City—worth a journey. Lovely ambiance and nicely prepared and served dinners. Traditional to trendy dishes. Breakfast, lunch, dinner and Sunday brunch. Children's menu. Reservations recommended. **700 Homestead Dr., Midway; (801) 649-2060, (801) 654-1102.**

NIGHTLIFE

Despite Utah's complex (though now substantially eased) liquor laws, Park City has always managed a vibrant après-ski scene. The action starts at the gondola base, notably at Steeps, which has music in the late afternoon, the Baja Cantina, which has terrific margaritas and Ziggy's for pizza and beer, moving later in the evening to Main Street, where you'll find about a dozen bars and clubs. The Cozy is a hit with the music-and-madness crowd. Other popular spots are Cisero's and The Club, which draw college-age partiers. Adolph's with its piano bar and Mileti's are quieter, while The Alamo is a classic pool and dart board bar. The Wasatch Brew Pub is Utah's first. It's got a good sports bar and gets most popular with every kickoff, slam dunk and even ski race. The really mellow set, more inclined to elegant après-ski, prefers the civility of tea in the soaring lobby of the Stein Eriksen Lodge and 221 Baker St. or a quieter drink in the lounges of any of the Deer Valley lodges.

The Homestead offers an excellent dinner sleighride with five-course dinner (including their spectacular specialty, chateaubriand flambé); a couple of other companies also mount dinner rides via sleigh and even snowmobile. Another popular nighttime diversion is skiing itself on Pay Day, Utah's longest illuminated run, from 4:00 P.M. to 9:00 P.M. **Park City Performances** puts on musicals, comedies and dramatic plays; call **(801) 649-9371** for the season's schedule and ticket information. If Park City and environs can't supply enough action, there's also **Casino Caravans' Gambler's Tour,** with a scheduled bus to Wendover, Nevada. Departure is at 5:00 P.M. and return is at approximately 2:00 A.M., **(800) 876-LUCK, (801) 649-DICE.**

199

For more information, contact **Park City Ski Area, P.O. Box 39, Park City, UT 84060, (801) 649-8111; Deer Valley Resort, P.O. Box 1525, Park City, UT 84060, (800) 424-DEER, (801) 649-1000; Wolf Mountain Ski Area, 4000 Wolf Mountain Dr., Park City, UT 84060, (801) 649-5400, fax (801) 649-7374; Park City Chamber of Commerce/ Convention & Visitors Bureau, P.O. Box 1630, Park City, UT 84060, (800) 453-1360, (801) 649-6100.**

LITTLE COTTONWOOD CANYON

BACKDROP

The Mormons have the mouth of Little Cottonwood Canyon (their famous genealogical vaults are there), and skiers have the rest. Little Cottonwood, the jewel of the Wasatch, is the site of the legendary Alta and Snowbird, two of the country's most celebrated meccas for lovers of the steep and deep. This dramatic rock-rimmed valley snares some 500 inches of cloud-light powder every winter. While both areas have ample options for beginning and intermediate skiers, their reputations rest on their vast expert terrain. Though both resorts will always remain small, both by management choice and geography of the tight valley floor, the skiing is truly big league. Both ski areas offer 2,000 or more acres of terrain—a lot of it truly high end—with relatively modest uphill capacities. If every space on every lift at either of those ski areas is filled, it's still just over 20,000 skiers an hour—which doesn't begin to create a crowd, especially on the tough stuff.

Alta, at the canyon's end, is a classic resort with a handful of quaint, unpretentious lodges scattered about the base of an enormous snow-kissed ski area. It debuted in 1938 with America's second chairlift (after Sun Valley). The spirit behind Alta was Alf Engen, a skimeister in the old mode who directed the Alta Ski School for 40 years. The resort looks much as it did 30 years ago, with eight chairlifts and five classic ski lodges that combine tradition, atmosphere and charm—and its lift tickets are so inexpensive that they seem like fugitive prices from a previous decade. Although the view from the base is an intimidating headwall, all but the most super experts ski gentler pitches out of sight.

Snowbird is similar to Alta in resort size but offers a stark contrast in style, scale and lift prices. It was conceived and designed in the modern mode, founded and funded by Dick Bass, with an oil fortune and a reputation as an adventurer (he was the oldest man to climb Mt. Everest and the first to reach the highest peaks on all the continents). When Snowbird opened in 1971, its cachet was instant, and it still occupies the pinnacle of powder prestige. Snowbird has a 125-passenger tram, eight chairlifts, four well-appointed mid-rise lodges arranged around a pedestrian plaza and lift ticket prices that are in the ballpark with other major Utah resorts. With 3,240 vertical feet of fall-line skiing, this behemoth offers great powder and challenging glades, chutes and headwalls. In addition to ranking as a top experts' paradise, Snowbird caters to sometime skiers, young skiers and even non-skiers via free tours led by mountain hosts, one of Utah's best kids-ski-free deals and one of the finest health and beauty spas in the West.

THE LAY OF THE LAND

Snowbird is 7 miles up Little Cottonwood Canyon and Alta is a mile beyond that, a pristine pocket of white just 25 miles from a city with a population topping a million. There is extremely limited skiing between the two. Both are self-contained, walk-about resorts (Snowbird by design, Alta by necessity). Alta's free shuttle links lift base areas and parking lots, and Snowbird's free shuttle operates throughout the resort. Hourly transportation between the two resorts is via Utah Transit Authority public bus, which also transports skiers into the canyon from Salt Lake City accommodations (see below).

GETTING THERE

For information on Salt Lake City Airport, which is less than 30 miles from the Little Cottonwood

Photo courtesy Alta Ski Resort

resorts, see the "Park City" chapter in this book. Airport shuttle services are offered by **Canyon Transportation, (800) 255-1841. UTA, (801) BUS-INFO,** operates buses from various points in the Salt Lake Valley into Little Cottonwood Canyon and hourly shuttle service between the two resorts. By car, Snowbird and Alta are about a 45-minute drive (more if snowslides shut the lower canyon or heavy traffic slows it down). The directions sound complicated: I-80 East to Route 215 South, to exit 6 at 6200 South to Wasatch Blvd. and then to Utah 210, but really, a car is neither necessary nor even desirable at Alta or Snowbird. If you insist on driving, tune your radio to the Travelers' Information Station at AM 530 to monitor road conditions and canyon closure; the transmission range is 2 to 3 miles from the canyon mouth.

THE SKIING

Alta

Profile

Alta is all about mystique, a unique aura formed by history, tradition, legendary skiers working through legendary powder, distinctive lodging, location and rough-hewn challenge that no one wants to see tamed. Alta also remains a skier's mountain, where snowboarding is as foreign a concept as snowmaking. Alta sells the conventional all-lifts ticket, but also full- and half-day beginner tickets, a 10-ride pass and even a single-ride ticket. (The ski area does nothing but sell the tickets, run the lifts and maintain mountain safety; private independent businesses handle food services, lodging, equipment rental and all that other stuff.) The lifts start loading at 9:15 A.M., or as soon as avalanche control work has been completed, and they run until 4:30 P.M., which is up to an hour later than most Rocky Mountain ski areas. But then, the patrol, area management and Alta regulars understand that a long ski day is required to adequately honor the snow—for it most likely will fall again that very night.

Alta's mythical frontside steeps are arguably the single most intimidating sight in American skiing. You see them as soon as you round the

Inside Little Cottonwood Canyon

bend—perpendicular chutes from the sky, a free-fall rampart on which people are miraculously skiing. This skiing is fly-on-the-wall, roped-in climber on a cliff, special effects designed to startle movie audiences stuff—except that these are real skiers working down a real slope often covered with downy snow. The most immediately visible sectors of Alta's terrain are among its most challenging. If you look at the right side of

Mountain Stats—
Alta

Resort elevation 8,550 feet
Top of highest lift 10,650 feet
Bottom of lowest lift 8,550 feet
Total vertical 2,100 feet
Longest run 3 1/2 miles
Average annual snowfall 500 inches
Ski season mid-November through third week in April
Lifts 2 triple chairlifts, 6 doubles, 4 transfer tows
Capacity 10,550 skiers per hour
Terrain 39 trails, 2,200 acres (25% beginner and novice, 40% intermediate, 35% advanced and expert)
Mountain dining Watson Cafe at the base of the Germania lift, Alpenglow at the base of the Sugarloaf and Cecret lifts
Snow reports (801) 572-3939

the trail map, Alta is mostly black with just a couple of ribbons of blue down the area's westernmost drainage. This spare and spartan area has only the conventional three trail signs, but two and perhaps even three black diamonds would not be out of place on Alf's High Rustler, Stone Crusher or Lone Pine. This high-impact first view, the reality of terrain once you're on it and the skiers who have mastered it give birth to Alta's reputation, its mystique.

The mystique is buried in powder, which seems to make it grow. A few other ski areas equal its 500 inches on an average year, but none exceeds it. Deep-snow skiers—pure classic stylists who glide through the snow like angelfish in an aquarium and wannabe extremists who bash and jump in the modern mode—queue up for the Collins and Wildcat lifts after each snowfall, which can mean day after day of inspiring new snow. If they had their druthers, they'd be on the heels of the patrol, which opens one sector after another as soon as each is declared to be or made safe. These lifts begin close to each other and veer off, serving different runs of essentially the same challenge. Wildcat is also the name of a massive and sheer face, stretching west from the Wildcat lift, on which some super-steep snowfields and chutes have been etched. When the snow is stable and the patrol concurs, it is possible to ski the snow-packed elevators called the Baldy Chutes off the top of Mt. Baldy. Wildcat and adjacent Westward Ho by themselves equal the high-expert terrain of most mountains in the West. Start at the top of Nina Curve, Schuss Folly and Collins Face on the east side of the Collins

202

Very big mountains totally dominate the very small resort of Alta.

chair and you feel a fall will land you right on top of the patrol headquarters' roof.

Collins and Wildcat also serve as access lifts to the Germania chair to the summit of this massif, home of Alta's fabled Rustlers. In what passes for a major improvement at immutable Alta, this lift was upgraded from a double to a triple in 1991–92. If you're a chicken—albeit, probably an exceedingly sensible chicken—you can ski Mambo, Ballroom and Main Street and still ride Germania with the fearless ones. If you're brave, you can plunge right into Sun Spot and a vertical parcel mysteriously named Race Course to West Rustler, a grand snowfield fringed with trees. There's even a route over a saddle that Alta marks with a blue square, but it would still be a diamond in most jewel boxes. When the patrol gives its OK signal, you can angle across the High Traverse to the legends among legends. You can pull on your rip cord and attempt Stone Crusher, whose name may have its origins in Alta's past as a mining camp but whose double entendre is not lost on today's skiers. Or you can keep going until you get to Alf's High Rustler, reverently named after Alf Engen, who invented modern powder skiing. The bottom of this run is the one that looks like a theatrical backdrop above the Alta Lodge. At the top, it's just as steep but a fraction of the width.

Photo courtesy Alta Ski Resort

Alta does have a gentler side, a high, snow-filled cirque called Albion Basin and the wide-open drainage below it called Sunnyside and as long and gentle a run as any novice could wish. The back of Germania/Rustler ridge actually forms one wall of Albion. It's called the Greeley area, and parts of it—Glory Hole, Yellow Tail, East Greeley and Greeley Bowl—are wide and steep and wonderful. The best of them catch the morning sun, if it's not still snowing, and offer 1,300 vertical feet of seamless powder skiing. If you have the skill and the stamina, hike, pole, skate or pray your way to the far end of a ridge that forks off from the High Traverse and drops into Eddie's High Nowhere or Gunsight, which boast an additional 500 feet and dump skiers in the bottom of Albion Basin. Devil's Elbow and Roller Coaster, below the Sugarloaf chair that brings skiers back up to the High Traverse, are relatively easy runs back there. Cecret Saddle, up the other side, is yet another high, wide snowfield of respectable pitch.

Albion Basin also offers terrific tree skiing. The Cecret chairlift, midway on the slopes of Albion Basin, accesses the gentlest slopes and most beguiling glades. The Supreme chair, which rises to Alta's highest point, offers more—yes, still more—steeps. Tree runs such as White Squaw, Piney Glade and So Long hold the powder from storm to storm, and Sidewinder snakes its way down the drainage between Spiney Ridge and Piney Glade. Sunset, at the area's far western boundary, might just be the best late-afternoon black diamond in the Rockies.

Ski School Programs

Introductory Programs
Beginner through intermediate groups (Levels 1 to 5) meet at the Albion base; most advanced classes (Levels 6 to 9) meet at the bottom of the Germania lift. Class and private lessons are 2 hours long, though half-day (3-hour) and full-day (6-hour) privates are available. The **Alf Engen Ski School, (801) 742-2600,** offers traditional quality Alpine ski instruction for all levels from rank beginners to true experts, with telemark lessons by appointment.

Advanced and Specialty Programs
Afternoon Workshops: 2½-hour afternoon workshop for four highest level classes: Skill Builders for Level 6 and Bumps, Bumps, Bumps; Skill Builders; Conditions Du Jour and Diamond Challenge for Level 7 and above.

Silver Meisters: Senior ski experience for strong skiers, Levels 6 to 9, scaled back only to a relaxed pace. Groups split into two levels. Three-hour classes meet at 9:30 A.M. at the Albion lift. Available on Fridays and Sundays. Reservations encouraged.

For Families
Nonskiing Children
Alta Children's Center: Infant care (for children ages 3 months and older) and day care (for nonskiers 12 years or younger). Located on the top level of the Albion Ticket Building. Hours are 8:30 A.M. to 5:00 P.M. Lunches with special dietary needs served on request. Half- and full-day options. Reservations encouraged; **(801) 742-3042.**

Skiing Children
Children's Private Lessons: For children 3 and younger.

All-Day Adventures: Four hours of skiing lessons with lunch. Levels 1 and 2 include beginner tow, Levels 3 and 4 include beginner lifts and all-lifts ticket included for Levels 5 to 9. For ages 4 to 12. Drop-off as early as Children's Center opens and pickup until it closes; supervision before and after skiing.

Mini Adventure: Half-day version with two hours of class lessons, lunch and half-day child care.

Mountain Explorers: Five-hour lesson including lift and lunch for children ages 7 to teens who are good skiers and in good physical condition; Levels 6 to 9. Friday afternoon race and late-afternoon ice cream party.

203

Noteworthy
Children are invited to participate in the Ske-Cology program, a cooperative effort between the Alta ski area and the U.S. Forest Service to introduce children to the wondrous mountain environment, its plants, its animals and its fragility.

For Racers

"A" Race: Alta's signature recreational racing program. Friday and Saturday challenge race (bring a friend). Goal is Alta A, based in age-group format, compared with pacesetter's time. Register at any ticket office or at the top of the race course at the top of the Sunnyside lift. One or two timed runs at the Sunnyside Race Arena. Awards follow (everyone gets a pin).

Snowbird

Profile

If Alta is an old classic, Snowbird ranks as a modern one, with the same high standards of skiing terrain, snow conditions, convenient lodging and its own version of the Little Cottonwood mystique. But Snowbird is run differently. Not only is there a contrast in architectural style, but there's a contrast in operational philosophy too. Like Alta Ski Lifts, Snowbird Ski & Summer Resort is a company that handles mountain operations, but it also built and operates the lodgings, runs the central reservations office, the ski school, the restaurants, a tennis club down the valley and even its own underground water reservoir.

Snowbird looks big, is big and skis tough. In all measures that count, it is one of the behemoths of Rocky Mountain skiing. It has 3,240 continuous vertical feet of skiing, meaning you can ski it top to bottom in one nonstop run, with no intermediary lifts from the bottom of a higher peak to the top of a lower one—one of the very few mountains where this is possible on a vertical exceeding 3,000 feet. Snowbird is a functional, no-nonsense ski area dominating a functional, no-nonsense ski village. Except that the snow is 500 inches of Wasatch powder and there are trees galore, Snowbird is reminiscent of the dramatic new French ski resorts that put demanding skiing at the doorsteps of extremely particular skiers. Unlike neighboring Alta, however, Snowbird designates "Most Difficult" terrain with a single black diamond and "Experts Only" with double black.

The most direct way to the core of the steeps that are Snowbird's mark of greatness is via the

Mountain Stats—
Snowbird

Resort elevation 8,100 feet
Top of highest lift 11,000 feet
Bottom of lowest lift 7,760 feet
Total vertical 3,240 feet
Longest run $3^1/_2$ miles
Average annual snowfall 500 inches
Ski season mid-November to early May (conditions permitting)
Lifts one 125-passenger tram, 8 double chairlifts
Capacity 10,100 skiers per hour
Terrain 66 trails, 2,000-plus acres (25% beginner and novice, 30% intermediate, 45% advanced and expert)
Snowmaking 25 acres
Night skiing on Chickadee
Mountain dining Mid-Gad Restaurant at the top of the Mid-Gad Lift
Snow reports (801) 742-2222, Ext. 4285

tram, whose huge red and blue cabins have virtually become a symbol for the ski area. So popular is this lift, which hoists 125 skiers up 2,900 vertical feet in just $7^1/_2$ minutes, that many people gladly pay more a day to ride it instead of sticking just to the chairlifts. The tram unloads atop Hidden Peak, at 11,000 feet the highest lift-served summit in the Wasatch. All around are craggy summits and fanning out below is some of the most awe-inspiring ski terrain in America.

The eastern side of Hidden Peak stretches out into a ridge that separates Snowbird from Alta. A vast, super-steep cirque enfolds this sector like half of an embrace. The steep half, a generous bowl known as High Baldy, curves around a vast trough known as Peruvian Gulch, a ski-anywhere cirque of impressive dimension. Cirque Traverse follows the ridgeline under the tram cable. Drop down the Peruvian side and you'll have a choice of virtually vertical, double-diamond walls that run out into the single-diamond domain of Primrose Path and Silver Fox, whose lower portions are two stars in Snowbird's galaxy of magnificent bump runs. Chip's Run and Chip's Bypass are a blue-square twosome down the low part of Peruvian Bowl. The runs on this side of the area kind of scramble up about midway down. The steeps merge briefly before fanning out again into a quartet of marked headwall runs, while Chip's arcs way off to the side, a blue-square traverse called Rothman Way materializes out of the steeps and another blue called Who Dunnit curves way out from the bottom of the trail system like the handle of a coffee cup.

The west side of Hidden Peak falls away as a broad-beamed snowfield called Regulator Johnson. Above it is Little Cloud, Snowbird's highest snow pocket and site of its best spring skiing. The Little Cloud chair permits yo-yo skiing on this sector—sublime when there's powder or spring corn or well-formed moguls or just gorgeous afternoon sun. These runs spill into the Gad Valley, a huge funnel-shaped drainage that starts with a medley of headwalls, glades, intermediate serpentine runs and mogul pitches and both narrows and flattens midway down into a group of wide trails and super-slopes for novice and intermediate skiers. From some of the upper-mountain steeps, experts can ski blacks almost all the way to the base; from others they must endure blue and even green runouts. Enter into this huge drainage via the Gad Chutes on high or the a black-diamond trio (Barry Barry Steeps, Wilbere Bowl and Wilbere Chute below), and you're on some truly stunning steeps. You'll eventually end at the Mid-Gad Restaurant and the tamer runs below. You can either return to the base or head over to the Mid-Gad chair, which angles off sharply from mid-mountain.

At other ski areas, it seems logical to describe the novice and intermediate terrain first and work up to the exciting stuff. In Little Cottonwood Canyon, the easy terrain comes naturally as an afterthought, though Snowbird's green circles, while modest in number, are very appealing—and skiing on a mountain with such a reputation does seem to motivate beginners to graduate from the greens. Chickadee, right by the lodging base, is a lovely little beginner run with a small, slow chairlift. Snowbird's newest lift, called Baby Thunder, serves seven outstanding novice and intermediate trails tucked into a remote corner of the lower mountain. Big Emma, served by the Mid-Gad chair—wide as a football field—is a splendid, confidence-building novices' playground. There is at least one solid intermediate route off each chair, so that you can experience the flavor of Snowbird

Photo courtesy Alta Ski Resort

"Little Cottonwood Canyon" and "powder" are synonymous in American ski lingo.

even if you aren't ready for its blacks, but Bananas, Bassackwards, Madam Annie's and Wilbere Ridge comprise a good network of mid-range runs, all on the western side of the mountain. They tend to snake around, interlacing with the blacks and providing access to the trees, so that you don't need to commit an entire summit-to-base run to click up a notch to advanced terrain.

Snowboarding

With a huge, unremitting vertical, Snowbird is for snowboards—ideal terrain, with the kinds of off-trail steeps, chutes and trees, as well as an abundance of roads to jump in order to get air that riders love.

Ski School Programs

The **Snowbird Ski School** has desks at Snowbird Center and in the Cliff Lodge, or call **(801) 742-2222, Ext. 5170.**

Introductory Programs

First Timers: Half-day lesson, rental equipment and use of the Chickadee chairlift.
Beginning Snowboarding: All-day session, with half-day option.
Adult Super Class: Half- and full-day classes, Levels 1 to 5 (10 being the highest at the Snowbird Ski School) meet at the Chickadee chair. Chickadee ticket free for ski school participants.

Advanced and Specialty Programs

Adult Super Class: Half- and full-day classes, Levels 6 to 9 meets at Ski School Lane meeting area and combines skiing and coaching.

Style Workshop: 2½-hour afternoon workshop on moguls and other advanced skills, Levels 5 and 6.

Bumps & Diamonds Workshop: 2½-hour afternoon workshop on moguls and other advanced skills, Levels 7 through 9.

Mountain Experience: More an adventure than a lesson. Full day of off-piste skiing, with tips on skiing the powder, the steeps, the crud, whatever materializes. Group skis the most challenging terrain, seeking out powder and other diverse snow conditions Optional rental of wide skis for powder and crud. Level 9 only. Meet at Snowbird Center Plaza Deck.

Snowboarding Workshop: 2½-hour morning or full-day workshop for all levels of snowboard-ing for adults and older children.

Silver Wings: Special classes for skiers Level 7 to 9 classes who are 50 years and older. Available Wednesday and Thursday, led by Junior and Maxine Bounous. Also, one five-day seniors' seminar per season (usually mid-February).

Junior's Seniors: Complimentary morning program every Tuesday from 10:00 A.M. to noon for skiers 62 and over, with casual skiing, strategies for skiing in flat, light, funny snow and other conditions and congeniality among one's peer seniors. Low-cost afternoon session from 1:15 to 4:00 P.M. Meets at the Ski School Lane meeting area.

Alta regulars are among the best powder skiers in the land.

Women's Seminars: For women skiing at Levels 5 to 9, taught by top women instructors. Four-day package includes video, lift ticket, Continental breakfast, spa activities and banquet; special lodging rates available.

Special Programs

Guided Skiing: Hosts offer free ski tours of the mountain daily at 10:00 A.M. and 1:00 P.M. Meets under the "Free Guided Skiing Tour" sign at Snowbird Plaza.

Sunrise Tram: Strong intermediate and advanced skiers can ski from the tram with a mountain host before regular morning opening. Available Christmas through Easter, weather permitting, for an additional cost, including Continental breakfast. Reservations required; **(801) 742-2222, Ext. 4135.**

Fun Run: Top-to-bottom route marked with easily visible orange ball–topped stakes for skiers looking for an easier way down the mountain. The route changes daily, depending on weather and snow conditions permitting.

Junior's Seniors: See "Advanced and Specialty Programs," above.

For Families
Nonskiing Children

Nursery: Licensed day care for ages 6 weeks to 3 years. Indoor nursery and age- and weather-appropriate outdoor play. Day and evening babysitting also available by prior arrangement for lodging guests. Located at the Cliff Lodge. Reservations required; **(801) 742-2222, Ext. 5026.**

Camp Snowbird: Located in the Cliff Lodge, for children 3 to 12. Full-day programs in conjunction with ski school's children's programs (see below). Reservations required.

Skiing Children

Chickadees: Two children ages 3 to 4 per instructor in 1¼-hour Level 1 and 2 classes. Lunch and day care also available through Camp Snowbird in the Cliff Lodge, which offers nonskiing activities for children ages 3 to 12. Reservations required.

Super Class: Full-day program for children ages 5 and older at Levels 1 to 9. Lunch and supervision available at Cliff Lodge Children's Center.

Snowboarding: Same program as adult classes (but youngsters usually progress faster), with

Photo courtesy Alta Ski Resort

requirement that youngsters ages 8 to 15 pre-register in the Alpine Room at Snowbird Center before 10:00 A.M. for all-day classes and before 1:00 P.M. for half-day afternoon classes.

Teens

Teen Super Classes: Full-day program for children ages 5 and older at Levels 1 to 9.
Wings for Teens: Similar program for advanced skiers 8 to 15 years old, available Christmas through Easter.

Noteworthy

The Chickadee slope is Snowbird's kiddie classic, but the new Baby Thunder area largely steals its thunder with isolated and very easy terrain and a children's ski-through theme area called the Kids Fun Park. Snowbird also signed on early with Ske-Cology program, a cooperative effort between the ski area and the U.S. Forest Service to introduce children to the wondrous mountain environment, its plants, its animals and its fragility. Ske-Cology terrain is also at the Baby Thunder area. But these amenities pale in comparison to Snowbird's outstanding offers for free use of all chairlifts for children ages 12 and under, one per skiing (or snowboarding) adult.

For Racers

NASTAR Race Clinic: 2½-hour afternoon workshop for Levels 6 to 9, meeting at Big Emma Corral.
NASTAR: Tuesdays, Thursdays, Fridays and Saturdays from 10:30 A.M. to 2:30 P.M. at the Big Emma Race Arena. **The Race Department (801) 742-2222, Ext. 5170**.
Coin-Op Racing: Available weekdays from 9:30 A.M. to 3:30 P.M. at the Big Emma Race Arena.

Nordic Skiing

There is no cross-country facility within the narrow confines of Little Cottonwood Canyon. The closest is at the Solitude Nordic Center in Big Cottonwood, one canyon over (see that chapter, page 213).

Off-Piste Skiing

The Utah Interconnect, a guided multi-area program using Alpine equipment, is a backcountry experience par excellence. See the Park City chapter, page 191. Note that the four-area tour, which starts at Snowbird, is scheduled Tuesday, Thursday and Saturday.

Heli-Skiing

Wasatch Powderbird Guides' office and helipad near Snowbird's Entrance 4 overlooks the Snowbird Resort, for one of the Rockies' two most convenient heli-operations (the other is at Panorama, BC, in case you're wondering). Powderbirds flies to nearly a dozen venues in the Wasatch. Fat skis recommended, and reservations necessary. Powderbirds maintains an office in the Cliff Lodge. **P.O. Box 920057, Snowbird, UT 84092; (801) 742-2800, (801) 783-5678.**

WHERE TO STAY

Alta

Alta Reservation Service, (801) 942-0404.

Lodges

Alta Lodge

A contender for "America's ultimate ski lodge" honors. Returning guests dominate. Great atmosphere. Fireplace lounge is one of the most congenial in skiing. Accommodations for 115 guests, from old-style dorms at a relative bargain to extremely comfortable, in fact, nigh-luxurious rooms with private baths at a price. Modified American Plan (MAP) lodge, known for fine, hearty food. Big-screen TV in common areas. Daily housekeeping, children's program, full breakfast and dinner included. Dining room, lounge, hot tubs, sauna, guest laundry, ski storage. **Alta, UT 84092; (800) 707-ALTA, (801) 742-3500.**

Alta Peruvian Lodge

Accommodations from dorms to two-bedroom suites in somewhat rustic lodge that rambles charmingly. TV in common areas. Daily housekeeping, three meals included in packages, complimentary resort shuttle. Outdoor pool, outdoor hot tub, dining room, liquor store, private club, recreation room, game room, ski shop, rental shop, ski storage, guest laundry. **Alta, UT 84092; (800) 453-8488, (801) 742-3000.**

Goldminer's Daughter

Old-style Alta lodge, with accommodations from quad-occupancy dorms with bath (but no TV) to several sizes of bedrooms and a one-bedroom suite, all with TV and private bath. Friendly and informal. Top-floor dining room with great views. MAP accommodations, breakfast and dinner included. Daily housekeeping. Lodge guests get first choice of equipment from rental shop. Dining room, lounge/bar, game room, ski lockers, guest laundry, ski shop. **Alta, UT 84092; (800) 453-4573, (801) 742-2300.**

Rustler Lodge

Elegant atmosphere, but with traditional Alta absence of pretension. MAP accommodations from men-only dorm for four to suite with living room with king-size bed. Dining room known for excellent food and views to match. Daily housekeeping, free shuttle to Snowbird, children's program offered during holiday season. Outdoor pool, sauna, hot tub, fireplace lounge, liquor store. **Alta, UT 84092; (800) 451-5223, (801) 742-2200.**

Snowpine Lodge

Alta's oldest and smallest lodge. Home-like and relaxed. MAP lodging from dorms with bunks to rooms with queen-size or twin beds with private bath. Daily housekeeping, breakfast and dinner included. Dining room, outdoor hot tub, sauna. **Alta, UT 84092; (801) 742-2000.**

Snowbird

Snowbird Central Reservations, (800) 453-3000. Note that Snowbird operates all of the lodging at the resort. Central reservations books packages, including airfare, ground transportation and lodging.

The Cliff Lodge is the largest and most luxurious, with accommodations from limited dorm space to luxurious two-bedroom suites. Its east wing is crowned by the world-class Cliff Spa with a full selection of health and beauty facilities and services, massage and huge rooftop hot tub and pool. It also offers room service, bell staff and valet services, 24-hour front desk, three restaurants and two lounges, on-site children's center, retail shops, guest laundry and an outdoor downstairs pool popular with youngsters. **The Lodge at Snowbird, The Inn** and the **Iron Blosam Lodge** are condominium-style lodges with accommodations from lock-off bedrooms to studios and one-bedroom loft units with kitchens and fireplaces. Condominium facilities include saunas, heated pools and guest laundry facilities. Each, except The Inn, has an on-site restaurant and lounge. The Iron Blosam has a game room and separate health spa. The address for all Snowbird lodgings is **Snowbird, UT 84092.**

Little Cottonwood Canyon

Condominiums

Blackjack Condominiums

Located between the two resorts. Ski-in/ski-out from Snowbird on the Blackjack Run; ski-in from Alta on Westward Ho. Fireplace units from studios to three bedrooms. Ridge-top location with great views. Warm and cozy, yet contemporary and well equipped. Common lounge area, game room, guest laundry on each floor, sauna. **Alta, UT 84092; (800) 343-0347, (801) 742-3200.**

Hellgate Condominiums

Fully equipped studio to five-bedroom condos between Alta and Snowbird. Each with mountain view, fireplace. Garage (not remarkable elsewhere) merits mention because of huge snowfalls. Complimentary van to both ski areas, guest laundry. **Alta, UT 84092; (801) 742-2020.**

Sugarplum Townhouses

Huge (up to six bedrooms) with ultra-luxury European-style decor, exquisite appointments and fabulous views. Features include marble fireplaces in living room and master bedroom, floor-to-ceiling living room window, breakfast nook, private redwood hot tub and attached garage. Nearby are Village at Sugarplum Condominiums, with two- and three-bedroom units (some with lofts) and all with cathedral ceilings, stone fireplaces, Jennaire kitchens, private whirlpool tubs and sauna. **Canyon Services, P.O. Box 92005, Snowbird, UT 94092; (800) 562-2888, (801) 943-1842.**

The View Condominiums

Deluxe ski-in/ski-out from Alta; view of Snowbird. One- to three-bedroom units, each with fireplace, full kitchen, Jacuzzi tub and spacious living room. Hot tub, ski lockers, common lounge area. **Alta, UT 84092; (800) 274-7172, (801) 277-7172.**

Salt Lake City

Salt Lake City offers a huge range of accommodations including lovely B&B inns, "ma-and-pa" motels, chain hotels and motels in all price ranges and condominiums. UTA buses comb the city to bring skiers to Little Cottonwood Canyon. For a listing of hotels, restaurants and activities contact the **Salt Lake Convention and Visitors Bureau, (800) 541-4955, (801) 521-2822.**

DINING OUT

Alta

Alta lodges, which provide meal plans for guests, usually accept outside dinner guests on a space-available basis. See phone numbers above. Otherwise, Alta offers but one place to have dinner.

The Shallow Shaft

A mine-theme decor and a perennially popular steak-and-seafood menu. Moderate prices. Reservations accepted. **(801) 742-2177.**

Snowbird

All Snowbird restaurants have discounts for children 12 and younger and accept Bird Bucks available at hotel and restaurant front desks. These come in $1 to $50 denominations, and are like easy-to-use gift certificates. Call **(801) 742-2222** for all Snowbird restaurants (except for Royce's Restaurant). Each restaurant has its own extension (see below).

The Aerie

Stylish restaurant serves Continental cuisine and spectacular views. Breakfast buffet or à la carte.

Seafood and prime rib featured at dinner. Reservations suggested. **Cliff Lodge, Snowbird. Level 10, Ext. 5500.**

The Atrium

Light fare in the Cliff Lodge's spectacular 11-story atrium. Light breakfasts, lunches, espresso and après-ski snacks. **Cliff Lodge, Snowbird. Level B, Ext. 5300.**

Birdfeeder

Quick breakfast, lunch or après-ski burger or hot dog. **Snowbird Center, Snowbird. Level 3, Ext. 4232.**

Forklift

Family restaurant serving breakfast, lunch and dinner. Most popular meat and vegetarian entrées plus new Chinese menu in the evening, all at very reasonable prices. **Snowbird Center, Snowbird. Level 3, Ext. 4100.**

Lodge Club

Mediterranean-influenced bistro menu and an elegant atmosphere with wonderful views. Reservations suggested. **Lodge at Snowbird, Pool Level, Snowbird. Ext. 3042.**

Mexican Keyhole

Mexican and American favorites, including soups, salads, sandwiches, burgers at lunch and dinner. Casual and fun. **Cliff Lodge, Snowbird. Level A, Ext. 5100.**

Pier 49 San Francisco Sourdough Pizza

The name says it all. By the slice and takeout available too. **Snowbird Center, Snowbird. Level 2, Ext. 4076.**

Royce's Restaurant

Fine dining in a sporty setting. Located at the Canyon Racquet Club. Not at the resort, but down in the canyon, 10 miles from Snowbird; **(801) 943-1044.**

Spa Cafe

Sprightly garden atmosphere and enforced healthful snacking on soups, fresh-squeezed juices, protein drinks, fresh-baked muffins, yogurt and such. **Cliff Lodge, Snowbird. Level 10, Ext. 5970.**

Steak Pit

Skier-pleasing hearty steak and seafood dinners. **Snowbird Center, Level 1, Ext. 4060.**

Wildflower Ristorante

Northern Italian dinners at moderate prices. Soups, pasta, popular entrees and great desserts. Reservations are suggested. **Iron Blosam, Level 3, Ext. 1042.**

NIGHTLIFE

Having expended their energies trekking to and skiing the powder, Alta skiers tend to go easy on the après-ski. The main activities are languishing in a hot tub or in front of a roaring fire. Those who must party do so in one of the lodge lounges or at The Shallow Shaft.

At Snowbird, the Forklift next to the tram at Snowbird Center is the immediate after-skiing center. An ample selection of happy-hour appetizers and drinks plus two big-screen TVs for ski videos and sportscasts keep people occupied. At the Cliff Lodge, the Atrium serves slightly heartier afternoon fare (burgers, chicken wings and the like), and also tunes its TV to what's hot in the sporting world. The Mexican Keyhole does Mexican and American munchies for famished skiers. The Lodge Club has excellent appetizers and a roaring fireplace, while the Aerie Lounge and Sushi Bar in the Cliff Lodge have appetizers and a piano player—and both are fine for après-ski and later in the evening. The Comedy Circuit in Snowbird Center does the post-ski routine and also has comedians and variety entertainers on tap; shows nightly except Monday; Warren Miller movies, Adventure Lecture Series presentations, Murder-Mystery Dinner Theatre and Party Nights for Teens are scheduled through the season. Children ages 3 and older can join the fun at the Kids' Club Night Out in the **Children's Center** several nights a week; reservations are required, **(801) 742-2222, Ext. 4080.** Vacationers can purchase a temporary membership to The Club at Snowbird for evening activities of the resort.

For more information, contact **Alta Ski Lifts, Inc., Alta, UT 84092, (801) 742-3333; Snowbird Ski & Summer Resort, Snowbird, UT 84092, (801) 742-2222.**

Snowbird's huge 125-passenger tram climbs nearly 3,000 feet in 7$^1/_2$ minutes—a real express ride to Utah's most glorious powder.

Photo by Snowbird Photo/Snowbird Ski Corp.

BIG COTTONWOOD CANYON

BACKDROP

This long, deep and incredibly scenic canyon between the Parley's Canyon and the Park City ski areas and Little Cottonwood, where fabled Alta and Snowbird are located, has been a local "secret" for a long time. Pocketed at the end of the canyon, Solitude and Brighton are low-key, low-cost alternatives to their better-known neighbors in the Wasatch Range. Limited lodging at and near Brighton and a new, rather ambitious $10 million resort development, called the Village at Solitude, are there for vacationers who want to stay near the slopes. However, Solitude and Brighton are essentially commuter areas. Salt Lake City is astonishingly close (even downtown and the airport are less than 30 miles), so they are an outstanding choice for skiers with an urban base. They are also an easy day trip from nearby resorts for vacation variety.

THE LAY OF THE LAND

Big Cottonwood Canyon is the longest of three canyons just southeast of Salt Lake City which among them boast seven incredible ski areas. The lower portion of the Big Cottonwood is a narrow corridor through dramatic rock walls with wilderness on both sides. The Mt. Olympus and Twin Peaks Wilderness designations mean that skiers headed for Solitude and Brighton will always enjoy a pristine gateway. Farther up, the canyon widens into a gentler glacier-formed valley. The base areas of the two mountains are just a couple of miles apart, and at various times in the past, they have made it easy for people to ski between them and even formerly offered interchangeable lift tickets. You can ski between them on the Solbright Trail, a giant arc from the top of Solitude's Summit Chair toward Brighton's Mt. Millicent and back to the Solitude base. Most recently the two areas have cooperated with a Big Cottonwood lift ticket, good at both.

GETTING THERE

From Salt Lake City, take I-215 to Utah Route 210 and the 6200 South exit. Follow this highway south to Exit 6 (Route 190, which is the Big Cottonwood road. **UTA** public buses, **(801) BUS-INFO,** have frequent service from the large parking lot at the mouth of the canyon, with connections from various parts of the city. Solitude is 12 miles up. In addition to UTA, **Lewis Bros. Stages,** **(801) 359-8677,** operates daily between Big Cottonwood and both downtown Salt Lake City and Park City. **Daytrips, (801) 649-TAXI,** also has Park City service.

THE SKIING

Solitude

212 Profile

This long-time Salt Lake City favorite ski area is located in a wide spot along Little Cottonwood Canyon—well, sort of a wide spot—with three lift bases and two day parking lots. Even before you reach the first lot, you'll see the Eagle Express lift. It is the speedy mainline to a mountain sector called Inspiration, namesake of a wide handsome signature run. The Eagle Express climbs to the top of Eagle Ridge and the most accessible portions of Solitude's noteworthy blue-square runs and some black diamonds as well. In addition to Inspiration, you'll find such admirable cruisers as Rumble, Grumble, Stumble and Serenity—trail names reminding some skiers of a

With the addition of lodging at the base, Solitude is graduating from being just a day area.

Mountain Stats— Solitude

Resort elevation 8,200 feet
Top of highest lift 10,035 feet
Bottom of lowest lift 7,988 feet
Total vertical 2,047 feet
Longest run 3½ miles
Average annual snowfall 450 inches
Ski season late October or early November to late April
Lifts 1 high-speed quad chairlift, 2 triples, 4 doubles
Capacity 11,200 skiers per hour
Terrain 63 trails and 3 bowls, 1,200 acres (20% beginner and novice, 50% intermediate, 30% advanced and expert)
Snowmaking more than 80 acres (18 runs)
Mountain dining The Roundhouse, Sunshine Grill
Snow reports (801) 536-5777
Note In 1995–96, Solitude instituted electronic ticketing and a variety of flexible lift-ticket options.

takeoff on four of Snow White's seven dwarfs—start with dark blue pitches and moderate quickly to solid blue squares. Their width and pitch make them excellent for powder tyros learning to handle the fluffy stuff. Sunshine Bowl, Olympia Bowl and Gary's Glade provide similar terrain farther along Eagle Ridge. Nestled at the confluence of these trails is the Roundhouse. This was Solitude's first building, and the recently renovated landmark at mid-mountain features panoramic canyon views, meal service and a great deck for sunny days.

Continue up the road and you'll come to the high end of the lower (and larger) day lot and the base of the Moonbeam II chair. Together with the nearby Link chairlift, it opens an exemplary novice area as well as serves as headquarters for the Solitude's children's facilities, a second base, the nucleus of the village and the bottom of three more chairlifts. The Apex double complements the Moonbeam II and serves some slightly harder trails.

The Powderhorn base is now considered the main one. The new day lodge, called the Last Chance Mining Camp, is the nucleus of recent resort development. Of the three lifts at this base, the Powderhorn chair offers the most for

Photo by Hal Louchhem/Solitude Ski Resort

advanced skiers, rising to the peak of Eagle Ridge to its most difficult pitches. A series of broad chutes and open glades—Diamond Lake, Concord, Paradise and others—funnel down toward the Roundhouse side, while really steep glades such as Middle Slope, Milk Run and Cirque are on the other side. If you want to stay with the steep and deep, you'll probably scoot up the Summit Chair, which provides the best access to the Headwall Forest and the most phenomenal chutes of Honeycomb Canyon. The Sunrise lift, the third at the uppermost base, serves a small web of mix-and-match trails for all ability levels.

If Big Cottonwood Canyon and its two areas have remained out of Utah's touristic mainstream, Honeycomb Canyon is out of Big Cottonwood's mainstream. This steep-walled valley "behind" Eagle Ridge (and therefore also reachable from the Eagle Express and Powderhorn chairs) has tremendous vertical and some 400 acres of incredible snow and really steep skiing. Never-groomed single and double black diamonds are emblazoned on chutes and glades on both sides of the canyon, and the return via on long ski-out to the Eagle Express base means it is never crowded. Hotshots seem to prefer other, more accessible but less interesting parts of the mountain.

Snowboarding

Solitude tiptoed into the snowboarding, first permitting it just three days a week, then extending it to four and finally welcoming riders seven days a week. Solitude's excellent beginner terrain is good for learning snowboarding too, and specialty workshops are available through the ski school. The tree-studded steeps off the Summit Chair appeal to advanced snowboarders.

Ski School Programs

For details on all adult programs, call **(800) 748-4SKI, Ext. 5730.**

Introductory Programs

Learn to Ski Package: Morning or afternoon two-hour lesson and all-day beginner lift ticket, with day-two option. Reservations recommended.
Solitude Ski Days: Two-for-one pricing for lift tickets, lessons, and rentals; generally around the first week in December.

Advanced and Specialty Programs
Adult Group Lessons: Half-day and full-day options for all ability levels.
Improvement Plus Workshop: All-day lesson with all-day lift ticket and rental equipment for Level 5 and up. Reservations recommended.
"Private" Lessons: Booked from 1-hour to 6-hour, all-day classes. Two rate scales, 1 to 3 skiers and 4 to 6 skiers, which is more like a group than a private. Reduced rate for First Track class (9 to 10 A.M.).
Women's Day Workshops: Series of four 2-hour lessons available from early January; includes lift class and free use of coin-op race course.
Seniors' Racing: Workshops beginning in November.

For Families
Skiing Children
Moonbeam Learning Center: Full-day program with lessons, lunch, supervision and age-appropriate indoor play. SKIwee for ages 4 to 7; Quad Squad for ages 8 to 12. Half-day option too. Learn-to-Ski beginner special. Reservations recommended. Children's Troll Village is the terrain garden with a Norwegian mythology theme.

213

Noteworthy

Solitude offers free skiing to age 10 and a junior lift ticket for ages 11 to 13. The area also sells a beginner-only lift pass.

Nordic Skiing

Solitude is the only Wasatch ski area with adjacent cross-country facilities. Access to the **Solitude Nordic Center** and its 20 kilometers of prepared trails is just beyond the Powderhorn base area. The trails are on the easy to intermediate side and exceptionally scenic. Buena Vista is a delightful blue-square route that snakes from the top of the Sunshine lift through a great open meadow to the trail network; the cross-country trail pass is valid on this chair. In addition to the normal rentals, snack bar and complement of classes and workshops in cross-country skiing and telemarking, the center operates a trailside yurt for dining and even overnight tours. Day tours into the backcountry are offered on request. For information, **(800) 748-4SKI, Ext. 5774.**

Photo courtesy Solitude Ski Resort

The mix of mountain chalets, Utah snow and sunshine is a formula for great skiing and riding.

²¹⁴ Brighton

Profile

One of the real oddities about Utah skiing is how underrated Brighton is. Older than Alta, with more snow than any of the Park City areas, a greater lift capacity than Snowbird and the highest base elevation in the Wasatch, its reputation is mainly local. Economical lift tickets and enticing learn-to-ski pricing have given it a reputation as the place locals learn to ski before moving on, but with aggressive terrain expansion, lift improvements and a toe-dipping market among ski vacationers, this is changing. The only less-than-impressive statistic is the vertical drop—a Wasatch modest 1,745 feet—but hey, you can only make one turn at a time anyway. Mt. Majestic and Mt. Millicent, two of the mountains at the head of Big Cottonwood, were once lightly developed as separate ski areas. They merged in 1963 and are now owned by the family company which owns Michigan's Boyne Country resorts and Montana's Big Sky, but the origin as two-from-one remains clear from the layout.

The access road loops past the Mt. Millicent base, with two lifts, a small day lodge, and minimal parking before widening into a huge parking lot with a shiny new day lodge and the loading areas for four lifts nearby. The modest area with the ambitious name of Mt. Majestic has grown into the bigger "half" of the substantial parcel now called Brighton. From the old Majestic double chair (and from the parallel Crest triple which rises higher), you can ski broad cruisers—wide slopes, generously cut trails, a few little cross-overs. You'll find a few green circles and a couple of black diamonds, but mainly, this is intermediate heaven. You can keep riding the Snake Creek chair, which unloads at mnemonic Snake Creek Pass, if you want to ski just the upper central part of the mountain and its further choice of novice and intermediate trails cut through the trees.

This big area with unbeatable views now rates more than two-thirds of its terrain for intermediate and advanced skiers. The Great Western high-speed quad angles off to the left of the base, climbing high on Clayton Peak. The top is right about at treeline, offering a dazzling choice of fall-away pitches, chutes and glades. A dozen routes and trails are shown on the map, but the mix-and-match possibilities are far greater. You can follow the ridge on one side to such gnarly open steeps as Clark's Roost and Rein's Run, or head the other way and drop off into whatever combination of length, pitch, tree census and number of people ahead of you appeals.

Knowledgeable locals often stick to the Mt. Millicent side, with its traditional slow lifts and grandiose open terrain. To get there from the main area, you need to hang a hard left from the lower Majestic runs, find a trail called the Millicent Access and follow it past the snowcat garage. Mt. Millicent is sort of like the terrain served by the Majestic chair—on steroids. There's a commendable variety of terrain, including long novice runs with a true big-mountain feel to gut-sucking steeps. Chutes, bowls and radical drop-offs where young skiers and snowboarders like to catch air abound. The Millicent double is the summit chair. From it, there are but two intermediate options. Everything else is big black-diamond terrain. Scree Slope is as dramatic and demanding a bowl as you'll find anywhere in the Wasatch, and if you ski the entire Interconnect route from the Park City end (see page 191), you'll use the Evergreen lift toward Twin Lakes Pass and the fabled traverse to Alta known as Highway to Heaven.

Snowboarding

While other Utah areas were still dithering over whether to allow snowboarding (a number still don't), Brighton dusted off the welcome mat. The fact that the ski school calls itself the Brighton Ski and Snowboard School tells part of the story. The fact that the area builds at least two half-pipes off the Majestic chair and grooms them daily tells the rest of the story. But snowboarders, as always, write their own tales too. Skilled free-riders have taken to Mt. Millicent like cat fur to black slacks. This lesser of Brighton's two mountains in terms of lifts, lodges and other accouterments is rich in the kinds wild natural features and incredible powder that snowboarders love. This peak, which has been likened to a grand natural terrain garden, has gotten popular especially with riders that Brighton's next lift will probably be a replacement for one of Millicent's slow-moving relics.

Ski School Programs

Introductory Programs

The Intro Package: Twice-daily ski and snowboard packages, including instruction, lift ticket and rental equipment.
The Works Package: Ski and snowboard instruction, all-area lift pass and rental equipment for novice and intermediate skiers.

Advanced and Specialty Programs

Adult Parallel Workshops: High-level clinic for advanced skiers.
Women's Workshops: For women and taught by women.

Special Programs

Mountain Hosts: Complimentary mountain tours by volunteer hosts.

Noteworthy

Children 10 and under ski free every day. In addition, Brighton offers a bargain beginner lift ticket.

Mountain Stats— Brighton

Top of highest lift 10,500 feet
Bottom of lowest lift 8,755 feet
Total vertical 1,745 feet (2,000 hike-accessible feet)
Longest run 3 miles
Average annual snowfall 500 inches
Ski season mid-November to late April
Lifts 2 high-speed quad chairlifts, 2 triples, 3 doubles
Capacity 10,100 skiers per hour
Terrain 64 trails, 850 acres (21% beginner and novice, 40% intermediate, 39% advanced and expert)
Snowmaking 200 acres
Night skiing 18 runs, 200 acres; nightly except Sunday from mid-December to early April
Snow reports (801) 943-8309

For Families
Skiing Children
Kinderski: Half- and full-day lessons with lunch and rental-equipment options for ages 4 to 7. Classes limited to six or fewer. Older children go into regular class with their age and skill peers.

WHERE TO STAY

Big Cottonwood Canyon has minimal lodging. In addition to those below, Salt Lake City's variety and abundance are a really good alternative. For information (but not reservations), call **Salt Lake City Convention and Visitors Bureau, (800) 541-4955, (801) 521-2822.**

Brighton Chalets

Private cabins with full kitchens and fireplaces; some with whirlpool tubs. Across from lifts. Tranquil and economical. Game room with pool and pingpong tables. **1750 East 9800 South, Sandy, UT 84092; (800) 748-4824, (801) 942-8824.**

Brighton Lodge

Basic ski accommodations in 20-room lodge. Motel style and ski lodge ambiance. Vague Alpine look. Ski-in/ski-out. Rooms, suite and hostel accommodations. Great Ski Week packages (four days or longer) include lodging, Continental breakfast and lift tickets. Two children 10 and under stay and ski free with each paying adult. Outdoor pool, hot tub. Daily housekeeping. **Brighton, UT 84121; (800) 873-5512.**

The Creekside at Solitude
The first 18-unit building in the Village at Solitude opened for the 1995–96 ski season. Deluxe one-, two- and three-bedroom condos. Restaurant, lounge, hot tub. **Big Cottonwood Canyon, Solitude, UT 84121; (801) 536-5700.**

Das Alpen Haus
European-style B&B inn. Four rooms with private baths; two with shared bath. Romantic and luxurious, with touches like down pillows and comforters and terry robes. Walking distance from lifts. Sauna, library and living room with fireplaces. Daily housekeeping, deluxe breakfast daily. **Star Route, Brighton, UT 84121; (801) 649-0565.**

Home Away from Home
Home-style cabins and chalets in Big Cottonwood Canyon. Accommodate from 2 to 25. Fully equipped and well appointed. Moderate and functional to luxurious. **5060 S. Mile High Dr., Salt Lake City, UT 84124; (801) 272-0965.**

216

Inn at Solitude
Deluxe new 46-room lodge. Nicely appointed and well located. Close to lifts. Lounge, fitness center, outdoor heated pool. Daily housekeeping. **Big Cottonwood Canyon, Solitude, UT 84121; (800) 745-4754, (801) 536-5700.**

DINING OUT

Alpine Rose
Cafeteria-style breakfast and lunch, plus dinner when there's night skiing. Unpretentious and filling fare. Nightly specials. Located in old lodge, behind Brighton Center. **Brighton Ski Area; (801) 532-4731.**

Creekside Restaurant
Bright new hotel restaurant. Contemporary style in decor and food. Pizza from wood-burning oven and varied pastas are specialties. Moderately priced. **Creekside at Solitude, Solitude; (801) 536-5787.**

Molly Green's
Pub-style private club (Utah-style, with temporary visitor "memberships" available) upstairs in old-fashioned A-frame lodge. Varied dishes; nightly specials. Bar service. Occasional live entertainment. **Brighton Ski Area; (801) 532-4731.**

Roundhouse Sleighride Dinner
Snowcat-pulled sleigh ferries 40 passengers to historic and scenic restaurant at 9,000 feet. Twenty-foot ceiling and huge central fireplace. Panoramic view of canyon and ski area. Five-course gourmet dinner. Menu changes weekly. Specialties include spring rolls, ahi tuna peppersteak, rack of lamb, sea scallops and prime rib. Prix fixe. Offered Thursday through Saturday evenings. Reservations required. Full bar service; BYO wine (with corkage charge). **Solitude Ski Area; (801) 534-1400.**

The Yurt
Groups of up to 16 cross-country to a heated yurt. Beginner skiers can handle it; no children under 8. Five-course meal, rental equipment, guide and gratuity for one price. Rustic setting with gourmet fare. Offered Fridays, Saturdays and holiday periods. Reservations required. BYO wine permitted. **Solitude Ski Area; (801) 534-1400.**

NIGHTLIFE

Each Big Cottonwood ski area has its own après-ski spots. At Solitude, the Last Chance Mining Camp is open sporadically and features local brews and mountain views, and the new lounge at the Creekside gained fans practically as soon as it opened. Brighton's Molly Green's and Solitude's Thirsty Squirrel Club at the base of the Apex lift are private clubs. Both are popular with visitors and locals alike.

For more information, contact **Solitude Ski Resort, 1200 Big Cottonwood Canyon, Solitude, UT 84121; (800) 748-4754** (U.S. only), **(801) 534-1400. Brighton Ski Resort, Star Route, Brighton, UT 84121; (800) 873-5512, (801) 532-4731.**

THE OGDEN AREAS

Photo by Richard Cheski/Powder Mountain Ski Resort

BACKDROP

If you're looking for marvelous, uncrowded skiing and value-filled lodging, dining and entertainment, you can't do much better than skiing Snowbasin and Powder Mountain from a base in Ogden. As the designated site for the speed events during the 2002 Winter Olympics, Snowbasin will be getting plenty of attention in the coming years. It's been a sleeper until now—a big bold ski area with stunning scenery and tremendous snow. It and nearby Powder Mountain, a beguiling family-run ski area, are big enough to appeal to vacationers, while tiny Nordic Valley, the ski hill closest to town, is skied mainly by locals.

Ogden was once an important railroad center. The city, an Olympic skating venue, is restoring many of the buildings in its historic center. A little-known charmer, Ogden offers much of the character and many of the trappings of a ski town but without high resort prices.

THE LAY OF THE LAND

Ogden sits on a broad apron of land with the Great Salt Lake to the west and the soaring Wasatch Range to the east. Access to the ski areas is via Ogden Canyon and then Ogden Valley on the east side of the Wasatch. Both areas nestle in high basins, reached via long winding access roads. The combination of temperate Ogden and two ski areas so safely above the normal snowline means that snowmaking is unnecessary. Snowbasin is surrounded by dramatic soaring peaks, while Powder Mountain is draped across of a huge hump-backed massif, with long-distance views rather than in-your-face high-mountain scenery.

GETTING THERE

Ogden is 35 miles north of Salt Lake City via I-15. Take the 12th St. exit for downtown and Ogden Canyon. You'll need a car to drive between the city and the ski areas, so renting at the airport is smart strategy. However, airport transfers are available via **Rocky Mountain Transportation,**

(800) 397-0773; Classic Limo, (801) 322-1266 in Salt Lake City, (801) 393-4055 in Ogden, and **Rocky Mountain Super Express, (800) 678-2360, (801) 328-2360,** and rental cars are available in Ogden as well. I-15 and I-84 intersect just south of Ogden, for easy north-south and east-west road access. Amtrak stops in Ogden's downtown Union Station, **(800) USA-RAIL,** and **Greyhound, (801) 394-5573,** has a terminal nearby.

From Ogden, drive east through Ogden Canyon on Route 39, which is a national designated Scenic Byway. At Pineview Reservoir, either go straight on Route 226 Snowbasin (17 miles from Ogden) or turn left on Route 158 for Powder Mountain (19 miles). If you're looking at a regional map, you'll find the ski areas on opposite sides of the reservoir. From Salt Lake City, you can reach them more directly via I-15 north to I-84 east to the Mt. Green-Huntsville exit, then Utah 167, also known as Trappers Loop, to Route 226 for **218** Snowbasin or the turnoff at Eden onto the Powder Mountain access road. Future plans call for a direct link between Trappers Loop and Snowbasin.

THE SKIING

Snowbasin

Profile

If you want to sample a low-key, laid-back ski area with sensational terrain and fabulous scenery, go to Snowbasin as soon as possible. If you prefer skiing at a place with international renown and sleek upgrades, wait a few years. Snowbasin, one of Utah's many well-kept secrets, is slated to host the most glamorous ski events of the 2002 Winter Olympics: the men's and women's downhill and Super G races. Before the Olympics, there will be at least one new major lift, probably better base facilities and perhaps even some slopeside housing. The lift will have to climb to the start of the men's downhill course on Allen Peak, and it will extend the lift-served vertical and vastly expand the inbounds terrain. Even within its current dimensions, Snowbasin is a good-sized, gritty and uncrowded area with huge

Mountain Stats— Snowbasin

Top of highest lift 8,800 feet
Bottom of lowest lift 6,400 feet
Total vertical 2,400 feet
Longest run 2½ miles
Average annual snowfall 400 inches
Ski season Thanksgiving to early April
Lifts 3 triple chairlifts, 1 double
Capacity 7,400 skiers per hour
Terrain 39 trails, 1,800 acres (20% beginner and novice, 50% intermediate, 30% advanced and expert)
Snow reports (801) 399-0198

snowfalls and real high-mountain thrills and high-mountain hazards. In key spots below slide zones, controlled by an avalanche-savvy patrol, trees poke out of the snow at angles nature never intended. In their sapling stages, they were bowled over by slides, subsequent winters reinforced their growth pattern and the result is a weird fun-house kind of glade skiing.

For now, pre-Olympic Snowbasin remains purely and simply a very fine ski area, offering sustenance to powder-hungry skiers but no condiments or other extras. Its terrain radiates from a very modest base area to broad sweep of skiing acreage arrayed beneath arc of dramatic summits—Strawberry, DeMoisey, Needles, Mt. Ogden and Allen Peak. Two long lifts climb the spines of two main ridges, two upper-mountain chairs access generous bowls that funnel into U-shaped gullies between them and a beginner lift beside the base serves an outstanding teaching slope. You can ski virtually anywhere along the two main ridges, which are muscular as the steaks served in some of Ogden's most popular restaurants, as well as the three adjacent drainages. The real options, however, are more abundant and the terrain more complex than the trail map would suggest.

You'll find some great warm-up cruisers off the Becker chairlift. It angles up from base to a flat spot high along the eastern perimeter, where you'll see panoramic views and the great tempting snowfields of Strawberry Bowl beyond the area's "sign line." When the powder is high and the snow is secure, you might be seduced into canning the warmup and following locals' tracks into the Strawberry Bowl. But don't let the untracked deep inspire you to venture too far beyond the tracks, unless you're ready for a long, long slog back to the lifts. Someday, there will probably be resort development and more lifts and runs in the four more big drainages. For now, you can follow the locals as far as they traverse or drop directly into sweet little cruiser called Philpot Ridge on one side or a steep powder-holding tree run called Sunshine Bowl or the somewhat milder version called Willow Springs on the other. All of them eventually end on one of the Becker side's easy roads and provide a belated warmup after all. School Hill is now just a run-out, but it was the site of one of the two original rope tows at what is now Snowbasin.

Novices can keep doing laps riding the Becker chair and skiing plenty of long, mild runs, but better skiers use it as a connector to the Middle Bowl chair. Of the truly steep runs and less harrowing ones threading through the sparse trees, Little Chicago and adjacent Grizzly command respect. Mapmakers found a way to create two named runs, but locals refer to this duo and the divine and dizzying powder shots between and beside them as The Cirque. Trail 119 and Pork Barrel at the base of the dramatic rock outcropping known as the Needles, combine stunning scenery and challenging skiing in equal measure. This section looks so little on the map yet feels like such big-mountain skiing, which is Middle Bowl's most distinctive quality.

Like the Becker chair, the Wildcat lift serves both as a transfer lift to an upper-mountain chair and high terrain and as direct access to lower runs. But where Becker serves mostly relatively easy runs, Wildcat's are tougher. The signature run is Wildcat Bowl, which isn't a true bowl but a great scoop in the draining between the big ridges. Misnomer or not, it is a grandiose blue run that grooms into a sensational cruiser. On the other side of the ridge, Chicken Springs is Wildcat Bowl's mirror image. Many skiers are so captivated that they ski this blue-square boulevard all the way down the gully time after time. From the top of the Wildcat chair, you can also slide down to the Porcupine lift, which accesses a wide open bowl, and small bowls within the big one,

that in many ways are the essence of Snowbasin. Porky unloads on a tree-free bulge high on the bowl. Open glades up top, tight trees lower down, sudden drop-offs, powder chutes and smooth meadows are sprinkled with abandon and generosity. You can follow the area boundary markers and drop into the Chicken Springs drainage through the Ogden Chutes, where you'll find untracked patches days after a storm. From the top of Porky there is but one easy bailout run for those who are up there by mistake or just for the scenery, but the vast majority of this Alpine-style acreage is for good skiers. Some runs are marked blue, and some are marked black, but that seems more a function of whim or conditions than a flawless comparison. Most of it isn't marked at all, which invites the kind of follow-your-nose exploration that characterizes Snowbasin.

If the inbounds skiing is impressive in terms of scale and variety, the terrain beyond the "sign line" ups the options. When the patrol signals that conditions are stable, those willing to traverse or hike can find an unsurpassed abundance of off-piste skiing. In addition to Strawberry Park and its easy-access skiing, huge bowls above Porky and Middle Bowl invite the powder-crazed. You can traverse to the west and climb to a the huge snowfield under the John Paul peak, or you can get a jump on the Olympians by climbing up to the top of men's downhill on Allen Peak or the of the women's downhill on a high saddle ignominiously called No Name. Want to bet that by 2002, it will have been christened with a real name?

No-frills facilities make Powder Mountain an unsung bargain.

Photo by Richard Cheski/Powder Mountain Ski Resort

Snowboarding

Snowbasin is one of those mountains that seems to have waited for snowboarding to be invented. The abundance of chutes, gullies, trees and jumps and the long-lingering powder stashes make it a natural terrain garden. Anything skiers can do, riders do with a little more freedom, and anywhere skiers go, riders do too. The Littlecat chairlift is an generous learning slope, sheltered from down-rushing traffic and broad enough for new riders and skiers to practice without getting tangled up with each other. All levels of snowboarding have been woven into the instruction program.

Ski School Programs

Reservations are recommended for all ski school programs; **(801) 399-1146.**

Introductory Programs

First Time on Skis: One-day program with two two-hour lessons, rental equipment and Littlecat beginner lift ticket. Available for ages 7 and older. **Learn to Ski:** Two-day program with two two-hour lessons each day, rental equipment and Littlecat beginner lift ticket. Available for ages 7 and older.
First Time on Boards: One-day program with two two-hour lessons, rental equipment and Littlecat beginner lift ticket. Available for ages 10 and older.
Learn to Board: Two-day program with two two-hour lessons each day, rental equipment and Littlecat beginner lift ticket. Available for ages 10 and older.

Advanced and Specialty Programs

Ski Continuation: One-day program with two two-hour lessons, rental equipment, and all-lifts ticket. Available for ages 7 and older.

For Families
Skiing Children

Littlecat Kids: All-day program for 4- to 6-year-olds, including rental equipment, Littlecat lift ticket, lunch and supervision. Maximum of four children per class. Half-day version available mornings or afternoons, as above, but with cookie break instead of lunch.
Wildcat Kids: All-day program with lifts, all-lifts ticket and lunch for ages 6 and above who can at least ski from the Becker chair.

Powder Mountain

Profile

For deep-snow addicts and pernicious skiers, Powder Mountain is heaven. For geographical perfectionists, it is northeast of Eden. It is huge and complex, with a unique layout that takes a lot of figuring out and even some real getting used to. The trail map is more a hint than a guide to the great expanses and low lift capacity that make for a near-pristine skiing experience. There's grooming for those you want it, but the abundance, variety and complexity of the mountain means that most people can't possibly explore it all in a week.

You don't ski numbers, but when the stats are as impressive as Powder Mountain's, they merit showcasing. Just two chairlifts cover most of the 1,600 acres, an area so vast that long roads and occasional surface lifts are required to ski from one end to another. And additional another 2,400 acres comprise of beyond-the-ropes terrain of various kinds includes designated out-of-bounds sections which you can ski or snowboard to the access road and return via complimentary shuttle bus, plus 1,200 off-piste acres where you'll get hauled back by snowmobile and an equally vast parcel accessible to those outfitted with Alpine touring gear. But whichever way you like your backcountry experience, just think that the in-bounds and out-of-bounds acreage is by far the greatest in Utah.

Despite the grandiose dimensions of Powder Mountain's skiing, the area is little known outside the greater Ogden area, and its infrastructure remains astonishingly modest. As you wind up the 5½-mile access road, you'll first pass the shuttle pick up points for designated off-piste routes and then the Sundown beginner area. It is laid out like a separate little ski area with a base lodge, a good little teaching hill, some neat novice and intermediate trails and a couple of advanced runs. Sundown is Powder Mountain's night-skiing area too, so some locals with demanding day jobs probably never ski anything but this little complex. Sundown also accesses the smaller of the two sections officially designated as Powder Country but known by locals as "the backside." You can drop off the green run called Confidence into an untamed mix of snowfields and steeps, where you'll need both go-for-it-confidence and skill to reach the shuttle pickup.

After driving past a sprinkling of vacation homes, you finally come to parking lot and main base lodge. But surprise of surprises, there's no lift loading area anywhere in sight. You have to ski from the lodge to the bottom of the Timberline chair, and from there, you have to sidle over to the Hidden Lake chair. Though it is a vintage double, it accesses the heart of Powder Mountain's terrain and therefore must be considered the main lift. Timberline angles up the side of one ridge, and Hidden Lake, whose liftline is virtually plumb-line north-south, climbs to the top of a second and culminates at Powder Mountain's highest point. Each chairlift has terrain of all kinds. There are easy runs at the bottoms of the two big drainages that comprise the bulk of the inbounds terrain. There are challenging ones down the steepest sides of the gully walls. And there are mid-level runs wherever the land contours most hospitably. A lot of such intermediate hospitality is abundant off the Hidden Lake chair. In fact, the entire vast western drainage is devoted to some of the finest low-end cruising you'll find anywhere.

The Timberline chair, the shorter of the two, is the magic carpet to much of Powder Mountain's most easily accessible challenging terrain. The vertical may not be impressive, but you need to ski hard to dominate such steeps as Exterminator, Dynamite and Hidden Valley on one side of the lift or Sun Slope or Powder Chamber on the other. All are marked on the map, but the surrounding knolls and knobs, and trees and powder stashes escalate the experience. Although there are a few black diamonds on the trail markers at Hidden Valley, when the powder is fresh, the snow is flying, the visibility low, the

Mountain Stats— Powder Mountain

Resort elevation (main lodge and parking lot) 8,250 feet
Top of highest lift 8,900 feet
Bottom of lowest lift 7,600 feet
Total vertical 1,300 feet (1,980 feet to Powder Country shuttle pickup)
Longest run 3 miles
Average annual snowfall 500 inches
Ski season mid-November to mid-April
Lifts 1 triple chairlift, 2 doubles, 2 platterpulls, 2 tows
Capacity 6,350 skiers per hour
Terrain 47 trails, 1,600 lift-served acres (10% beginner and novice, 60% intermediate, 30% advanced and expert); 1,200 acres of snowcat skiing and 1,200 backcountry acres
Night skiing nightly except Sundays
Mountain dining Hidden Lake Lodge at the top of the Hidden Lake lift
Snow reports (801) 745-3772

light flat, trees tighten or some combination, green runs ski like blues and blues turn charcoal gray. The truly tough stuff is all off-piste, and there's more of it surrounding the main area than off Sundown. Powder Mountain's adventure skiing is what sets it apart from anything else in Utah. You can do it on the cheap, skiing the easy

Powder Mountain has a nifty night-skiing operation.

Lodge Trail from the Hidden Lake chair and dropping into the other section of Powder Country. You'll end up at the shuttle pickup, roughly across the street from the sector of Powder Country off the Sundown chair. You can sign up for cat skiing or hook up with an Alpine touring group and explore the huge, untracked forests and snowfields beyond even the car boundary.

Snowboarding

Like neighboring Snowbasin, Powder Mountain has such abundant natural features and such outstanding snow that it's as good for snowboarding as for skiing. The Powder Country shuttle usually has more snowboarding passengers than skiers, and the area has also installed a half-pipe between the Hidden Lake Run and Whiskey Springs to add another dimension to riders' options.

Snowcat Skiing

222 The Meadow Express is a snowcat that accesses the steep, ungroomed expanses of Cobabe Canyon on a pay-per-ride basis. Bluebell and Side Kick, Pow Wow and Gunslinger, Proving Ground and Buckshot are among the named runs falling away from the steep ridges that wall in Cobabe Canyon, but they merely hint at the variety of glades, gullies and powder pockets you can ski. Cat tows also haul skiers back to lifts from numerous steep glades and chutes below the Hidden Lake lift's lower terminal. The terrain tends to be challenging without being extreme.

Ski School Programs

Introductory Programs
Learn to Ski: Lesson and rental package, offered daily.
Powder Mountain Super Package: Weekend and holiday package with ski lesson and choice of rental equipment or Sundown lift ticket. For ages 8 and older.

Advanced and Specialty Programs
SheSkis: Women's classes, Sundays and Tuesdays.

For Families
Skiing Children
Powderkids: Classes for ages 4 to 5 and 6 to 12.
Powder Mountain Super Package: Available for ages 8 and over.

Nordic Skiing

There is no marked and groomed cross-country skiing at Powder Mountain or Snowbasin, but Powder's full and half-day Alpine tours into the backcountry offer some of the most spectacular Nordic opportunities in the Rockies. Randonée equipment, which allows for free-heel and fixed-heel options depending on whether you are climbing or skiing downhill, and climbing skins are available for rent. Call the ski area for details and reservations. The **Ogden Nature Center**'s trails are popular for snowshoeing and cross-country skiing. It is closed from mid-December to January 2. **(801) 621-7595.**

A Few Words About Nordic Valley

Vacationers can hardly imagine more skiing for less money than at Snowbasin and Powder Mountain, but thrifty locals also recognize the value of little Nordic Valley. This 1,200 vertical-foot, two-chairlift ski area is a mighty midget. The appeals are really inexpensive season passes and lift tickets, day and night skiing (with rates lowered for families, students and dating twosomes various nights of the week) and an aggressive recreational racing program. Since its elevation is far lower than its bigger neighbors, vacationers might find it a good option when a storm, low visibility or a cold snap hits the high country. **(801) 745-3511, (801) 476-8027.**

WHERE TO STAY

At and Near the Mountains

Columbine Inn
Small slopeside complex next to Powder Mountain's main lodge. Hotel rooms have refrigerator, microwave and coffee maker. Larger units have full kitchens. Well appointed and reasonably priced. Recently remodeled units, many with fireplace and balcony. Popular with families. Daily housekeeping (complete on request). **P.O. Box**

450, Eden, UT 84310; (801) 745-3772, Ext. 146, (801) 745-1414.

Jackson Fork Inn

Former dairy barn, now with new life as restaurant with eight upstairs lodge rooms, five with in-room Jacuzzi tubs. Rooms newly constructed and with eclectic furnishings, like staying in a friend's spare room. Close to ski areas. Leashed pets permitted for an additional charge. Restaurant, lounge. Complimentary Continental breakfast, daily housekeeping. **7435 East 900 South, Hwy 39, Huntsville, UT 84317; (800) 255-0672, (801) 745-0051.**

Powder Ridge Village

Adjacent to Powder Mountain slopes. Ski-in/ski-out and outstanding views. Spacious one- and two-bedroom units, some larger ones with loft and/or Jacuzzi tub. **MTA Resorts, 36 N. Wolf Creek Dr., Eden, UT 84310; (800) 272-UTAH, (801) 531-9011.**

Snowberry Inn

Lovely log lodge with wide views. Five rooms, each with private bath. In valley, short drive from ski areas. Ski packages. Daily housekeeping, full breakfast. Outdoor hot tub, billiard room, TV room. **1315 N. Hwy 158, P.O. Box 795, Eden, UT 84310; (801) 745-2634.**

Wolf Creek Resort

One building of timeshares, one of condos at the bottom of the Powder Mountain access road. Built for golf and available for winter rentals. Well-appointed one-bedroom to two-bedroom-plus-loft units, all with full kitchens and gas-log fireplace. Sauna, whirlpool, weight room, racquetball court. Three reservations services handle different units:
Wolf Creek Resort, Wolf Creek Dr., Eden, UT 84310; (800) 933-9653, (801) 745-0222.
Skinners, Inc., 3615 N. Wolf Creek Dr., Eden, UT 84310; (800) 345-8824, (801) 745-2621.
Wolf Lodge MTA Resorts, 36 N. Wolf Creek Dr., Eden, UT 84310; (800) 272-UTAH, (801) 531-9011.

Ogden

For information and reservations, contact the **Ogden-Weber Chamber of Commerce, (800) ALL-UTAH;** reservations through **Utah Reservations, (800) 554-2741.**

Luxury Accommodations

Radisson Suite Hotel Ogden

Landmark hotel with 146 recently refurbished suites. Outstanding downtown location, overlooking park and near shops and entertainment. Amenities in all or some rooms include hair dryer, coffee maker, microwave, wet bar and/or refrigerator, free HBO. Ski packages. Restaurant, lounge, private club, exercise room. Daily housekeeping, room service, 24-hour front desk, bell staff, complimentary buffet breakfast. **2510 Washington Blvd., Ogden, UT 84401; (801) 627-1900, (800) 333-3333** for Radisson reservations.

Mid-Priced Accommodations

High Country Inn

A 110-room motor inn, with bridal and executive suites. Just off I-15. Restaurant, free HBO, VCR and video rentals, outdoor heated pool, Jacuzzi, exercise room, tanning bed, guest laundry, ski storage and waxing facilities. Daily housekeeping, 24-hour front desk. **1335 W. 12th St., Ogden, UT 84404; (800) 594-8979, (801) 394-9474.**

Holiday Inn Ogden

Comfortable motor in with 109 recently renovated rooms, some poolside. Ski and B&B packages. Atrium recreation area with indoor heated swimming pool, whirlpool and fitness center. Restaurant, private club, guest laundry. Daily housekeeping, 24-hour front desk. **3306 Washington Blvd., Ogden, UT 84401; (800) 999-6841, (801) 399-5671, (800) HOL-IDAY** for Holiday Inn reservations.

Ogden Park Hotel

Largest hotel in town, with 287 rooms. Motor inn convenience but with excellent downtown location. Restaurant, lounge, private club, fitness center, indoor pool and hot tub, beauty parlor and massage service on site. Children 18 and under free in parents' room. Twenty-four-hour front desk and room service, daily housekeeping, laundry, complimentary local and 800 calls, complimentary poolside cocktails and hors d'oeuvres Monday through Thursday evenings, complimentary buffet breakfast on some rates. **247 24th St., Ogden, UT 84401; (800) 421-7599, (801) 627-1190.**

Economy Accommodations

Motel 6
Economical motor hotel (truck parking available). Has 110 rooms, some with Jacuzzi tub. Restaurant, club, outdoor heated pool. Twenty-four-hour front desk, daily housekeeping, complimentary coffee in lobby. **1500 W. Riverdale, Riverdale, UT 84405; (801) 627-2880.**

Sleep Inn
Functional 66-room motel. Children free in parents' room; generous senior discounts. Most rooms non-smoking. Complimentary Continental breakfast and local phone calls, daily housekeeping. Hot tub, in-room VCR with satellite TV and video rentals available. **1155 South 1700 West, Ogden, UT 84404; (801) 731-6500.**

224

DINING OUT

The City Club
Private club, with transient memberships available, played in the key of Beatles. Sleek and spacious upstairs restaurant and pub. High ceiling, light wood and soaring spirits prevail. Socialize with locals who socialize with each other. **264 Historic 25th St., Ogden; (801) 392-4447.**

The Daily Grind
Sprightly and modern cafe and restaurant, open for breakfast, lunch and dinner. Espresso bar, good sandwiches and dinner specials. **252 Historic 25th St., Ogden; (801) 629-0818.**

Ebenezer's Restaurant & Brew Pub
Casual, light-hearted spot for prime rib, seafood, ribs, sandwiches, salads and, of course, microbrews. Open daily for lunch and dinner. Earlybird specials until 6:00 P.M. **4286 Riverdale Rd., Ogden; (801) 394-0302.**

La Ferrovia
A taste of Italy in informal, red-check-tablecloth downtown setting. Lunch and dinner, with such Neapolitan specialties as calzone, lasagne and pasta. **234 Historic 25th St., Ogden; (801) 394-8628,**

Gray Cliff Lodge
Delightful restaurant in scenic Ogden Canyon location. In business since 1945. Trout, lamb, steaks and prime rib are specialties. Locals love the cinnamon rolls and distinctive oatmeal pie. Lunch and dinner on weekdays; Saturday dinner only, and all-you-can-eat Sunday brunch and early supper. Closed Mondays. **508 Ogden Canyon, Ogden; (801) 392-6775.**

The Greenery
Original health spa and pool next to natural hot springs. Now large informal eatery featuring soups, salads and sandwiches. Their Mormon muffin, Hedda Gobbler and Marco Polo are famous around town. Huge gift shop with unique items and bowling center in old indoor swimming-pool area from the property's spa days. Lunch and dinner daily. **Mouth of Ogden Canyon, Ogden; (801) 392-1777.**

Jackson Fork Inn
Spacious country-style restaurant convenient to slopes. Knotty-pine coziness. Steak, chicken, seafood and pasta dinners (all including soup and salad), plus Sunday brunch. **7345 East 900 South, Huntsville; (801) 745-0051.**

Jeremiah's Restaurant
Lively place serving huge portions at breakfast, lunch and dinner. Mountain Man decor. Soup and salad bar. Cajun specialties, buffalo, megaburgers, prime rib and seafood featured. **High Country Inn, 1335 W. 12th St., Ogden; (801) 394-3273.**

The Prairie Schooner
One of Ogden's two huge, themed steakhouses (The Timbermine is the other). Booths topped with canopies replicating covered wagons parked in a desert setting. Steaks and prime rib are main fare, but sandwiches, chicken and seafood also served. Open at lunch and dinner. **445 Park Blvd., Ogden; (801) 627-6171.**

Roosters 25th St. Brewing Co.

Trendy and stylish downtown brew pub, located in a wonderfully adapted historic building and filled with interesting metal art and fun artifacts. Excellent assortment of beer and ale, plus food as up-to-the-minute as the decor. Oak and wrought iron furniture is really unique. Gourmet pizza, designer pasta and creative American fare. Bar and dining downstairs, plus balcony seating. Open daily, lunch though dinner and late-night supper. **253 Historic 25th St., Ogden; (801) 627-6171.**

Star Noodle Parlor

May not be the finest Chinese food the world has ever seen, but huge landmark neon dragon sign is best in Utah. Oriental and American seafood, steaks, stir fries and combination dishes. Take-out too. **225 Historic 25th St., Ogden; (801) 394-6331.**

The Timbermine

Huge restaurant and steakhouse, filled with antiques and memorabilia. Barbecue chicken and rib specials Mondays through Wednesdays. Main dining room has mining theme. Funky and fun. Always busy, but rarely too busy to get everyone seated, reservations or not. Suitable for large parties. Lounge. Open for dinner nightly. **1701 Park Blvd., Ogden; (801) 393-2155.**

Union Grill

Delightful restaurant overlooking the tracks in wonderful Union Station location. Historic and nostalgic, with fine food too. Open from lunch through dinner daily except Sunday. **2501 Wall Ave., Ogden; (801) 621-2830.**

NIGHTLIFE

No beer or alcohol is served at Snowbasin, so thirsty skiers stop at the Hill Haus for a cold one. Powder Mountain skiers can pause for a drink at the Powder Keg in the main lodge before heading down the hill. But no matter where you ski, no trip to the Ogden area is complete without at least one visit to the Huntsville. Its main claim to fame is the Shooting Star Saloon, established in 1879 and allegedly Utah's oldest continuously serving beer bar. Any place that managed to circumvent the hurdles of both Mormon influence and Prohibition is something of a shrine. Foaming brew, century-old oak back bar, pool table, wooden booths buffed to a patina by years of beers and some of the most readable restroom graffiti (both his and hers) make this a must. Chris's is a huge and lively spot, with flowing beer, pool, munchies, gas (for the car, but perhaps also from the beer and munchies) and even a snowmobile rental operation. For a totally different sort of after-ski opportunity, you can stop at the Trappist Monastery, officially known as the Abbey of Our Lady of the Holy Trinity. The brothers welcome visitors—Catholics and non-Catholics—to its tranquil reception area, church and grounds daily except Sunday from 12:00 to 5:00 P.M. Quiet reflection can bring even the most juiced-up skier down from a powder high.

If you get back from the slopes early enough, you can still browse the delightful boutiques on Historic 25th St., the antique shops concentrated near Union Station and the stores in the Ogden City Mall, an indoor shopping center that combines a downtown location with suburban-style layout. Jeremiah's and Roosters are good bets for beverages and a lively evening scene. Several in-town spots have live entertainment: acoustic music Friday and Saturday evenings at The Daily Grind, rock and roll at the Gray Moose, country at the Tamarack, miscellaneous at Brewsky's and jazz at The Zippers. The City Club is tops with Ogden yuppies, while the Sports Page is for fans who groove on big-screen TV sports. Slightly out of town and incongruously in Motel 6, Club Nadir is the latest hot spot for Ogden's young crowd. Most nightspots are private clubs, with temporary memberships available for visitors. Weber State University's home games and activities on The Ice Sheet, which will be one of the 2002 Olympic venues, are other diversions.

For more information, contact **Ogden-Weber Chamber of Commerce, 2501 Wall St., Ogden, UT 84401, (800) ALL-UTAH, (801) 627-8288, fax (801) 399-0783; Powder Mountain, P.O. Box 450, Eden, UT 84310, (801) 745-3772; Snowbasin, P.O. Box 460, Huntsville, UT 84317, (801) 399-1135.**

SUNDANCE

BACKDROP

Sundance owes its renown to Robert Redford, who has owned it since 1968, and its tranquil beauty to his notions of what a ski resort ought to be. This exceptionally scenic spot at the foot of Mt. Timpanogos is more hideaway than Hollywood—not surprising given the actor's ecological agenda and his feelings about public figures' entitlement to private lives. The land has been likened to a semi-wilderness, if there is such a thing, and Redford's stewardship has been a more protective than a development-oriented one. The ski area has been expanded to a point where it is a worthy multiday destination, yet the resort takes up just 50 of Sundance's 4,000 acres, and the ski terrain itself is a modest 450 acres.

226

While snow depths on the mountain never approach other Utah meccas, Sundance's complicated quilt of trails, slopes, bowls, glades and headwalls tossed across several ridges and the valleys creates a mid-size area that skis bigger than 41 runs and just three lifts would suggest. Since Sundance is off-course from the parallel canyons of Little Cottonwood, Big Cottonwood and Parley's to the north and a little farther from Salt Lake City, liftlines are virtually nonexistent—despite low ticket prices. The modest lift capacity and virtual absence of crowds mean that new snow tends to last, so when there is new powder, it is as good as anyplace else in the state.

Redford himself refers to the resort as a "community," one that combines the outdoors with the arts. The community is tiny, with just 200 full-time residents. The resort can house only about 240 guests (thereby more than doubling the "population" when there's a head on every pillow), and even on Saturdays when Provo and Brigham Young University skiers are on the mountain, you're more likely to spot Redford than a real liftline. Subtle yet memorable architecture, music, art and artifacts generously displayed are as important as the lifts and downhill trails and small cross-country network. The resort is the home of the Sundance Institute, a noteworthy workshop for independent filmmakers, composers, playwrights and choreographers, and of the Institute for Resource Management, which seeks practical solutions to the often conflicting needs of resource development and preservation.

What makes Sundance really special for the visiting skier are the accommodations—precious private chalets (called "mountain homes") and condominium units (called "Sundance cottages") that make you feel as if special friends have let you use their place in the mountains. Country singer Juice Newton's apartment, which is in the rental pool, is decorated with some of her musical memorabilia and her husband's polo trophies. The homes range from intimate cabins to understated baronial mini-mansions, and the condos are so cleverly tucked into the spruce, pines and aspens that they feel more private than clustered. Most are within walking distance of the lifts and of the Reception Center, restaurants and shops. It's a Ralph Lauren kind of a place, infused with understated country elegance. Rusticity, Southwestern art, tranquility, creativity and fine food are words and phrases that Sundance regulars associate with this unusual resort.

THE LAY OF THE LAND

It's simple, really. Sundance consists of a huddle of pristine accommodations sprinkled through—and almost disappearing into—the woods off a narrow two-lane canyon road. There is a small complex of public buildings, including two restaurants, a general store, conference facilities, rehearsal hall and film screening room. Very nearby is the ski area base, from which one quad chairlift rises to terrain that is up and mostly out of sight. In fact, though it is at the foot of 11,750-foot Mt. Timpanogos, one of the Wasatch's loftiest summits, the peak is not visible from Sundance either. While Provo is conveniently nearby, few ski resorts display such a tenuous real-life link to the closest town. When you go to Sundance, your instincts are to be enfolded by it, not to reach out beyond it.

GETTING THERE

Sundance is 50 miles south of Salt Lake City and 15 miles north of Provo. From Salt Lake City, the fastest route is via I-80 east, I-15 south, Utah 52 east, Utah 189 north and finally Utah 92 into Provo Canyon. The Scenic Alpine Loop (I-80, I-15 and Route 92) takes longer but is exceptionally beautiful. For Salt Lake City International Airport information, see the "Park City" chapter in this book. Transfers between the airport and Sundance are provided by the resort and by **Rocky Mountain Super Express, (800) 678-2360, (801) 328-2360** and **Lewis Bros. Stages, (800) 826-5344, (801) 826-5844.**

PROFILE

Rays Lift, a new quad, climbs from the tiny base area up the side of a typical Wasatch ridge, with a mid-station, both for loading and unloading, so that high-intermediate and better skiers can stay on the upper part of the ski area without long, flat runouts at the bottom, and novices can ski just that kind of terrain. The top station is on the ridge's sloping shoulder with the loading area of Arrowhead just beyond. A short catwalk leads to the Flathead chair, which angles up one side of a second peak that is set back behind the first. These juxtaposed lifts, offset from one another and rarely in sight of each other, give Sundance an illusion of greater size than its statistics indicate. The view from the top of each lift is different, yet each is as breathtaking as anything in Utah.

The lower mountain provides ideal learning and improving slopes for novices and intermediates, and Bearclaw from the top of Arrowhead, Roundup below it along the area boundary and Maverick off Ray's are real cruising runs. Nevertheless, Sundance is by and large a challenging little area. With steep-faced bowls such as Bishop's and Grizzly and other runs such as Mar-

Photo by Hughes Martin/Sundance Ski Resort

mot Gulch, Maverick and Buntline, which are wide enough to ski in a bowl-like fashion, Sundance boasts fantastic powder possibilities. Although the runs down the ridges are oriented to get the sun at least part of the day, the area essentially is north-facing, protecting some of the powder from the lethal thaw-freeze cycle, which can be a real problem when new snow hasn't been groomed down or skier-packed. There is some tree skiing as well, notably in glades beside Bishop's Bowl and some of the upper-mountain steeps are excellent mogul drops.

Amy's Ridge under the Arrowhead chair is a typical Sundance mixture. It starts out looking for all the world like a broad intermediate cruiser, and even Wildflower and James, the short runs that feed off the west side into Bearclaw, are easily skiable blues. All of a sudden, the feeder runs become plunges. Quickdraw, Hawkeye and Junior's Run are black as the ace of spades. Even reasonably mild Amy's Ridge bends to the right, turning into the meaner blacker Grizzly Ridge. It's telling that the headwall runout is called Tombstone. Below the ridge is Grizzly Bowl, itself clad in an outlaw's black diamond.

SKI SCHOOL PROGRAMS

The Ski School Desk is located next to the **Creekside Lodge, (801) 377-4700, Ext. 275.**

Introductory Program

Learn-to-Ski Program: Special bargain instruction, lift and equipment rental program.

Advanced and Specialty Programs

Recreational Performance Package: Two-day clinics with classroom instruction, on-hill coaching and indoor workshops. Focuses on personal athletic development.

For Families

Skiing Children

Children's Ski School: Full-day programs of class lessons, lifts and lunch for ages 6 to 12. Private instruction available for younger children. No day care, but private in-room nanny can be booked on 24-hour notice; 3-hour minimum.

NORDIC SKIING

With just 14 kilometers of marked trails, the **Sundance Nordic Center**—like the resort

itself—is small but special. The impeccably groomed trails wind through the Elk Meadows Preserve at the base of Mt. Timpanogos. The Nordic Center also puts on guided torchlight ski and snowshoe tours on Wednesday and Friday nights. Rental equipment and lessons are available, **(801) 225-4107.** Additional nearby touring terrain is at **Wasatch Mountain State Park, near Midway, (801) 654-1791.** Backcountry touring is in the Strawberry Valley.

WHERE TO STAY

Sundance

Seventy Sundance cottages (11 of them built in 1996), which are one- to three-bedroom apartments, and 10 larger "mountain homes," which are individual chalets with up to five bedrooms, are managed by the Sundance Resort. All lodgings are privately owned and decorated in distinctive and personal styles, and all have central housekeeping. There is a central check-in in the new Creekside Lodge and equal access to all resort facilities. A bell staff is available to assist with luggage. Full breakfast is served in the restaurant, complimentary to all overnight guests, and Continental breakfast and après-ski refreshments are served in the lounge of the old Reception Center, where video rentals are also available. Each cottage and home has a washer and dryer. A beautician, hairdresser and masseur from Provo make house calls at Sundance. For reservations, call **(800) 892-1600, (801) 225-4107.**

Provo

Best Western Cottontree Inn

Fine motor inn with 80 rooms, many with a river view and recently redecorated. New indoor pool. Fifteen minutes from Sundance. AAA Three Diamond recipient. Daily housekeeping, 24-hour front desk. Restaurants, indoor pool, hot tub, video rentals. **2230 N. University Parkway, Provo, UT 84604; (800) 662-6886, (801) 373-7044, (800) 528-1234** for Best Western reservations.

The Provo Park Hotel

AAA Four Diamond hotel, still known locally known as "The Excelsior." Has 242 well-appointed rooms, yet very reasonable rates. Fifteen minutes from Sundance. Daily housekeeping, 24-hour front desk, complimentary van to Sundance, valet service, concierge. Restaurant, club, fitness center, pool, hot tub. **101 West 100 North, Provo, UT 84601; (800) 777-7144, (801) 377-4700.**

DINING OUT

Foundry Grill

Breakfast, lunch and dinner in an informal new bistro-style restaurant, built in 1996. Big sandwiches at lunch. Mostly American fare, from Dungeness crab cakes to Utah trout. Southwestern specialties too. Designated low-fat, low-sodium items. Sundance Institute photographic art on walls. **(801) 225-4107, Ext. 214.**

Tree Room

Fine dining in exquisite restaurant decorated with Native American art, antiques and Butch Cassidy and the Sundance Kid and other Redford cinematic memorabilia. Dinner only. Small menu of carefully selected, creatively prepared items. Featured are fresh seafood, poultry, game birds and steaks. Pricey—but worth it. Fine wine list. Reservations required. **(801) 225-4107, Ext. 214.**

NIGHTLIFE

Very limited, but then people don't go to Sundance to party. Day skiers hang around the new Owl Bar for a short while after the lifts close, while resort guests partake of gentle wine-and-cheese après-ski before a roaring fire in the Reception Center parlor. With all accommodations in cottages, cabins and chalets, evenings tend to be tranquil and private. In fact, guests often prefer to order from the in-room menu. Dinner service starts at 5:00 P.M. in both Sundance restaurants, so many people just have a cocktail before eating. Films from the Sundance Festival and

Mountain Stats—
Sundance

Resort elevation 6,100 feet
Top of highest lift 8,250 feet
Bottom of lowest lift 6,100 feet
Total vertical 2,150 feet
Longest run 2 miles
Average annual snowfall 320 inches
Ski season mid-December to mid-April
Lifts 1 quad chairlift, 2 triples
Capacity 5,800 skiers per hour
Terrain 41 trails, 450 acres (20% beginner and novice, 40% intermediate, 40% advanced and expert)
Mountain dining Bearclaw's Cabin at the top of the Arrowhead chair
Snow reports (801) 225-4100

Robert Redford's private collection are shown in with the Institute Screening Room Friday and Saturday evenings most of the ski season. Those who must party join the locals at the Picasso's Club in the Provo Park Hotel. Since BYU is a Mormon university, Provo doesn't have the amount of high life that a college town normally would, though university-related and cultural activities abound.

For more information, contact **Sundance, RR #3, Box A-l, Sundance, UT 84064; (800) 892-1600, (801) 225-4107.**

Tranquillity is the year-round watchword at this secluded mountain haven.

Photo by Hughes Martin/Sundance Ski Resort

230

FARMINGTON

522
Red River
Taos Ski Valley
TAOS
285
84
Ski Santa Fe
SANTA FE
40

ALBUQUERQUE

RATON
64
Angel Fire
25

54

NEW MEXICO

25
380
48
Ski Apache
RUIDOSO
ALAMOGORDO
10
LAS CRUCES
ROSWELL
70
380

New Mexico

Photo by Ken Gallard/Taos Ski Valley

231

TAOS

BACKDROP

The town of Taos, New Mexico, ranks with Santa Fe as a major regional artistic and culinary capital and repository for the greatest concentration of B&B inns in the Southwest, with exceptional skiing at a vest-pocket resort 18 miles and light years away. The resort, known officially as Taos Ski Valley, is located high and deep in the spectacular Sangre de Cristo range. This forested hideaway is renowned for fabulous snow and free-fall slopes. Resembling an eclectic corner of the Alps magically transported to the edge of the desert, Taos Ski Valley is awash with continental ambiance yet blanketed with Rocky Mountain powder. Founded in 1955 by the late Ernie Blake, the ski valley is still family-run, remaining one of the most personal of all ski resorts, where small eccentricities of layout or operations are viewed as endearing quirks, not as impositions on the skiing public. A handful of lodges nestled at the base of the lifts offer comfortable accommodations, congenial atmosphere and first-rate cuisine. Skiers return year after year with the regularity of Capistrano swallows.

The Ernie Blake Ski School ranks as one of the best in the land, enrolling more guests in lessons than any other—three-quarters of them in high-level classes. If you spend a week at Taos, your daily routine will be breakfast, ski your legs off in a fast-moving morning class, recoup at lunch, put your skills into practice in the afternoon, enjoy a delicious dinner and wind up with a mellow, civilized evening. A week of that routine, and you'll end up feeling relaxed and skiing better than you ever have in your life. And, if you are like the rest of the skiing swallows, you'll make a reservation for the next year before you leave.

On July 1, 1996, the Village of Taos Ski Valley officially incorporated as New Mexico's 100th municipality. It is the ultimate company town, because it is truly a ski resort, nothing more. It isn't even a ski and snowboard resort, for this is one of the small number of ski areas in the West were snowboards are not permitted. There are more ski shops than restaurants but no skating rinks, swimming pools, tennis courts, dance clubs, fancy boutiques, museums or any of the other trappings that escalate ski towns into four-seasons resorts. It's just as well that Taos doesn't aspire to such scale, because there's no room for all that anyway in a tight little cul-de-sac at the end of the canyon. The town of Taos more than compensates for anything that might be missing at the ski valley. With adobe-style buildings inspired by the 1,000-year-old Taos Pueblo, the country's oldest continuously inhabited community, Taos is a legitimate multicultural center. It combines the Spanish, Native American and Anglo in a way that has long inspired artists, writers and craftsmen. The entirety of Taos—Euro-flavored ski resort, Rocky Mountain snow, classic Southwestern town, ancient Indian pueblo—has assumed a mythic identity, expanding the skiing experience to include culture, cuisine and history. It's an unbeatable combination.

THE LAY OF THE LAND

The town of Taos and Taos Ski Valley are connected by an 18-mile-long, two-lane umbilical cord, which starts in a desert distinguished by red earth, sagebrush and arroyos and climbs through Taos Canyon into a tight mountain valley where the deep snows of winter eventually melt into rushing Alpine streams. A downtown ticket office sells lift tickets and books ski school programs. Day and evening shuttles connect town and mountain; special free buses run Tuesdays and Thursdays for ski valley guests to spend an evening in town, and shops and galleries make a point of staying open longer to accommodate skiers. Taos Ski Valley is a small walk-about complex of buildings, parking lots and lanes. A multilevel resort center and a hodgepodge of small lodges nestle at the base of the lifts. Nothing was planned in the modern sense. Taos Ski Valley just grew, but this spontaneous development works surprisingly well.

232

GETTING THERE

Direct and connecting flights into Albuquerque International Airport are operated by several airlines, and rental cars are available. Bus and van operators are **Faust's Transportation, (505) 758-3410** and **Enchanted Circle Tour & Coaches, (505) 754-3154.** Taos Municipal Airport is the local general aviation field. Taos Ski Valley's Edelweiss Hotel operates **Edelweiss Air, (800) 458-8754, (505) 776-2301,** an FAA-approved air shuttle between Albuquerque and Taos for hotel guests and other ski valley guests.

The 173-mile drive from Albuquerque takes about four hours via I-25 north to New Mexico 84 and 68 to the town of Taos. It is exceptionally scenic and also allows a sightseeing or dining detour to Santa Fe. From Denver the distance is 281 miles and the driving time about five hours via I-25 south, US 160 west, Colorado 159 south and New Mexico 522. New Mexico Route 150 leads from Taos up the canyon to the ski valley.

PROFILE

The skiing at Taos is as multifaceted as at any other resort in the Rockies. Based on statistics, Taos would seem to be a mid-size ski area, but it skis big. It has a reputation for challenge, but its secret gentler side is surprisingly beguiling. The ski terrain is complex and subtle, like an origami mountain. You see just a bit at a time, with new vistas, textures and challenges constantly unfolding. A long ridge sloping off the shoulder of 12,481-foot Kachina Peak creates a huge basin, distinguished by steep chutes, grandiose snowfields and dense stands of trees. In the middle of this cirque is a forested subpeak.

All but a handful of runs are out of sight of the resort. Al's Run directly under the main chair is an arrow-straight free fall that is about as steep and bump-studded as a ski run can get. It is also the first bit of terrain that you see, prompting the late Ernie Blake to erect a now-famous sign at the bottom of the lifts reading "Don't panic! You are looking at 1/90th of Taos Ski Valley. We have many easy

Photo by Ken Gallard/Taos Ski Valley

Inside Taos

runs too." All this is true, but unease, if not outright panic, is a common emotion that wells up in skiers taking their first look at Al's. This intimidating vertical parcel has solidified Taos's fame as a super-tough mountain, but it makes it look as if the challenge lies in the bumps. In reality, Taos's black diamonds tend to adorn more than those bottom-of-the-mountain bump runs. They mark breathtaking chutes, snowy paths cascading from the ridges on top and demanding glades below that give Taos an unbeatable edge with experts.

To reach any place on the mountain requires riding over Al's via Lifts #1 or #5, rising like adjacent elevators from the resort center to a rounded crown topping the subpeak, which has a steep side and a gentle one. Some people stay on the subpeak's true cut-through-the-woods trails. They tend to be uncrowded, though a ride up from the base is required each time. A few iron-legged show-offs ski Al's Run itself, but most skiers merely think about it and wish they dared. There are other bumped-up steeps like Spencer's Bowl, Inferno, Showdown and Snakedance, mercifully out of sight of the lifts. The gentle side is where a good portion of Taos's easier terrain is found. The green-circle and blue-square trails share no single personality, for some are wide, some narrow, some have long steady pitches, others undulate over constantly changing terrain, some are straight, others curve gently. But taken together, they are sudden comfort for novices and intermediates—as well as anyone intimidated by the sight of Al's or simply smart enough to want to warm up.

234

A short shot to the right from the top of #1 and #5 leads to the bottoms of another set of parallel chairlifts, which climb to another plateau. There you'll find the Ski Patrol headquarters—and tellingly, probably an avalanche dog cavorting in the snow. You must pass this spot en route to the fabled high chutes, which are reached through control gates and wear double diamonds with the regal naturalness of Princess Diana donning a tiara. You can head either to the right along West Basin Ridge or to the left along Highline Ridge until you reach the entrances to the chutes. Taos-style double diamonds abound on both sides, but these legendary ultra-pitches would perhaps merit triples at most areas. When there's new snow, and the patrol gives the go, the powder hogs hit those chutes, which are packed with powder that provides steep-and-deep skiing as good as it gets. Most mountains' chutes are hemmed in by rock walls, and expert slopes are bracketed by trees, but at Taos, these slim free falls often have both: heart-stopping cliffs on both sides with trees growing in the cracks in the rocks. Confined to corridor narrowness, the snow gets tracked out fast, so first in equals first tracks.

From West Basin Ridge, you can leap into Fabian, Oster, Staufenberg or Szdarsky, or stay on the traverse to the perpendicular couloirs named after Taos's early lodges: St. Bernard, Thunderbird, Hondo. If you keep going as far as possible, you reach Wonder Bowl, which is wider but not a whole lot easier than the chutes. They all feed into the broad trough called West Basin, an easy-skiing blue. If instead you climb Highline Ridge, the choice is Hidalgo, Juarez or Niños, steep runs chopped out of the forest. Twin Trees Chute, on the far end, spills into Kachina and Hunziker Bowl for a long, uncommonly varied expert run.

Of course, you can ski steeps without hiking or climbing or even passing through control gates. On the east side of the main mountain, Bob's Run, Sir Arnold Lunn and especially Walkyrie's Chute are lift-accessed knee-knockers. Curvaceous and plunging like a pinup's neckline, Lorelei seduces experts. Honeysuckle, the single green-circle route from the upper lifts, serves the runout from the Highline Ridge chutes and is the only access from the summit to delightful novice and intermediate runs. Nestled into the east side of the mountain, this sector catches the morning sun and is both varied and interesting. Many intermediates spend days riding Chair #7 and happily skiing Maxie's, Lone Star, Totemoff and Lower Honeysuckle in various combinations. Beyond, on the far eastern end of the area under the brow of another, even steeper ridge off Kachina Peak, is a group of wide-open, near-bowl snowfields. Returning to the base from any of this ample terrain requires a long cruise down Rubezahl, a road skirting the lower mountain. Since there is a restaurant at the bottom of Chair #4, skiers tend not to do "Rube" till the end of the day unless returning to one of the lodges for lunch.

Taos is one of the premier mountains in the country for unremitting challenge, and its ski school keeps attracting advanced skiers who want to become even better. But no one was born skiing the steeps, and the Ernie Blake Ski School is also adept at jump-starting beginners, goosing them to an intermediate level and giving them the confidence to set their sights on Al's, the chutes or the glades. Taos doesn't neglect youngsters either. Kinderkäfig was one of the earliest children's ski schools in the country that truly helped young skiers achieve their own potential, and it also was a pioneer in providing classes just for teenagers. The last gap in family facilities was filled with the recent addition of an infant day-care facility and expansion of the toddler center.

SKI SCHOOL PROGRAMS

The **Ernie Blake Ski School** is one of the country's best; it encourages full-week programs. For information on ski classes and child care, call the ski school at **(505) 776-2291.**

Introductory Program

YellowBird Program: Specially priced morning and afternoon lessons, two hours each. Free lift ticket. Rental equipment option.

Advanced and Specialty Programs

Super Ski Week: The premier Taos experience, consisting of six days of morning and afternoon lessons focusing on advanced skiing (moguls, adventure skiing and technical aspects) and racing at all levels, plus video. Pre-Christmas and January only.

Ski-Better-Week: Same as above, but with morning class only. All ability levels. Available all season long, with six-day version beginning on Sunday and five-day program beginning on Monday and continuing through Friday. Low, Value and Regular Season pricing.

Masters Ski Weeks: Designed for skiers 50 and older who want challenge. Not watered-down classes, but setting in which experienced, older skiers are with their peers rather than much younger classmates. Includes half-day classes, lift tickets, video analysis and NASTAR race. Maximum of seven skiers in a group. Offered several times throughout the winter.

Women's Ski Weeks: Classes by women and for women of all ability levels. Includes half-day group lessons, lift tickets, video analysis and NASTAR race. Maximum of seven skiers in a group. Offered several times throughout the winter.

Women's Weekends: Two days' lifts, six hours of classes and video analysis.

235

Mogul Workshops: Five days on Taos's fabled bump runs with two hours of instruction per day, lift tickets, lunches, video analysis and seminars. Classes limited to five people. Given several times during the ski season.

Mogul Mini Workshop: Three-day version of above, with five hours of classes per day and a maximum of four skiers per group.

Special Programs

Ski Guides: Two hours of guided skiing to Taos's hidden powder spots and "secret" runs. Maximum group of eight.

For Families

Nonskiing children

Kinderkäfig: A three-level, 18,000-square-foot, opened in 1994–95 as the headquarters for the resort's well-regarded children's programs. It features drive-to drop-off, award-winning child-friendly interior design and lifts in an isolated area right outside the door. Children's lift tickets, rental equipment, lunch area and a small accessories shop are at the Kinderkäfig. Reservations are required for all Kinderkäfig programs.

Bébékare: Full-day program for infants ages 6 weeks to 1 year. Hourly, half-day and full-day options.

Kinderkare: Full-day program for children ages 1 and 2, including lunch and snacks, in new "toddler-designed" facility.

Skiing Children

Junior Elite I: All-day program of ski lessons, snowplay, indoor play, crafts and lunch for children ages 3 to 6. Reservations recommended.

Junior Elite II: Full-day program of lifts, ski lessons and lunch for children ages 7 to 12.

Teens

Teen Super Ski Weeks: Classes grouped by age and ability for 14- to 17-year-olds, given during school holiday periods.

NORDIC SKIING

There is no traditional cross-country skiing at Taos. The nearest cross-country center is Enchanted Forest near Red River (see Red River chapter), but ample backcountry skiing is in the Wheeler Wilderness Area and elsewhere in the **Carson National Forest; (505) 758-2911.** Amole Canyon, on New Mexico 518, 12 miles south of Taos, has marked trails that comprise the most extensive system in the immediate area.

Noteworthy

In addition to an exceptionally child-friendly environment on and off the mountain, the ski area has designated several green-circle and blue-square runs as slow-skiing zones.

The **Taos County Chamber of Commerce** issues a booklet called the *Kid's Guide to Taos,* which covers such local topics as Native American culture, cowboys, pioneers, art, natural history and other subjects from a youngster's point of view. It is not a ski guide, but it does provide additional diversion to ski-vacationing youngsters. It's free. **(800) 732-8267.**

Taos Mountain Outfitters, 114 S. Plaza, Taos, NM 87571; (505) 758-9292, is the top local source for Nordic information and rentals. The shop-sponsored Nordic Ski Club grooms about 9 miles of Amole Canyon's route network. Nordic and Alpine touring gear, information and tours are also available from

Los Rios River Runners, P.O. Box 2734, Taos, NM 87511; (505) 776-8854

Native Sons Adventures, P.O. Box 6144, Paseo del Pueblo Sur, Taos, NM 87571; (800) 743-7559, (505) 758-1167

WHERE TO STAY

Agencies handling reservations at the ski valley, in town and in between include

Affordable Accommodations & Tours, (800) 290-5384, (505) 751-1292

Rosslyn Reservations, (800) 764-3366, (505) 751-1088

Ski Central Reservations, (800) 238-2829, (505) 758-9550

Taos Valley Resort Assn., (800) 776-8111, (505) 776-2233

Taos Central Reservations, (800) 821-2437, (505) 758-9767

Taos Bed & Breakfast Assn., (800) 876-7857, (505) 758-4747

Taos Ski Valley

In the context of Taos Ski Valley, "luxury" must be defined as comfortable and charming accommodations rather than spacious and opulent ones in inns that are owner-operated and offer excellent food and exceptional hospitality. Prices may seem high for the size and scale of the lodgings, but the price of a room buys exemplary personal care. In the case of Taos's traditional ski-week packages, meals are included in the package price.

Luxury Accommodations

Hotel Edelweiss

Slopeside inn, under new ownership and refurbished in 1995 and partially destroyed by fire in

April 1996. Owners rebuilding. Previously, 11 rooms with king or queen beds, down comforters and mountain country decor. Outstanding breakfasts, exceptional lunches and dinners. Après-ski mecca. Tradition decreed that television is available only in common area; hotel also manages several nearby two-bedroom condominiums, each with kitchen, balcony and fireplace and runs commuter air service to Taos Municipal Airport. Ski week packages. Daily housekeeping, massage available. Restaurant, fireplace lounge, outdoor hot tub in gazebo, sauna, sundeck. **P.O. Box 83, Taos Ski Valley, NM 87525; (800) 458-8754, (505) 776-2301.**

The Inn at Snakedance
Total remodel and expansion of the Hondo Lodge, Taos Ski Valley's oldest inn. The original stone building now houses restaurant. Thirty-four of the 60 rooms have stone fireplaces; all have cable TV, telephone, small refrigerators and bar sinks. Ski week packages available, but inn also accepts short stays (less than a week). Breakfast included, but it's the only ski valley hotel without a mandatory meal plan (it prides itself on flexibility). Nonsmoking hotel. Restaurant, lounge, indoor hot tub, sauna, exercise room, sundeck, library with fireplace. Daily housekeeping, attended ski check room, bell service. **P.O. Box 89, Taos Ski Valley, NM 87525; (800) 322-9815, (505) 776-2277.**

St. Bernard Hotel & Condominiums
Classic 28-room lodge, renowned for fine food and ultimate Taos tradition. Run by ski school technical director Jean Mayer. All-inclusive packages (three meals, lifts, lodging). Après-ski, children's activities. Daily housekeeping. Also, 12 luxurious two-bedroom, two-bath condo units. **P.O. Box 88, Taos Ski Valley, Taos, NM 87525; (505) 776-2251** (hotel), **(800) 306-4135, (505) 776-7506** (condos).

Mid-Priced Accommodations
Innsbruck Lodge & Condos
Chalet-style, family-friendly lodge with hotel rooms and suites with kitchens. Most casual and least expensive resort lodge. Breakfast included. Ski packages. Daily housekeeping. Hot tub, game room. **P.O. Box 82, Taos Ski Valley, NM 87525; (800) 243-5253, (505) 776-2313.**

Thunderbird Lodge
Thirty-two-unit lodge perched on a hill overlooking the slopes. Known valley-wide for excellent breakfasts and Sunday buffet, as well as fine lunches, dinners and wine list. Daily housekeeping, massage. Hot tub, sauna. **P.O. Box 87, Taos Ski Valley, NM 87525; (800) 776-2279, (505) 776-2280.**

Condominiums
Alpine Village Suites
Twenty-three luxury suites accommodating from two to six guests; some can be connected. Kitchenette units with balconies, fireplaces, hand-carved contemporary Southwestern furniture and tiled baths. Isolated from other Ski Valley buildings and surrounded by evergreens, but just a short walk from the lifts. Packages available. Restaurant, bar and two ski shops in complex. Daily housekeeping, ski lockers. **P.O. Box 2719, Taos, NM 87571; (800) 576-2666, (505) 776-8540.**

Kandahar Condominiums
Four ski-in/ski-out buildings terraced into steep hill with great views of resort and slopes. Simple decor but up-to-date amenities. Eighteen one- and two-bedroom units with full kitchens (including microwaves and ice makers), TV and stereo. Packages. Hot tub, steamroom. **P.O. Box 72, Taos Ski Valley, NM 87525; (800) 756-2226, (505) 776-2226.**

Powderhorn Condominiums
Taos Ski Valley's newest condos, featuring combination of European and Southwestern decor. Cheerful colors; real tile floors. Hotel rooms, studios and one- and two-bedroom suites. Daily rates (except at Christmas), plus weekly rates and packages. Daily housekeeping. **P.O. Box 69, Taos Ski Valley, NM 87525; (800) 776-2346, (505) 776-2341.**

Rio Hondo Condominiums
Eighteen two- to four-bedroom luxury apartments with fireplace, full kitchen, phone, TV, stereo, private balcony. Lifts across the road; ski back to the door. Ski packages. Only booked for Saturday-to-Saturday stays in high season; low season flexible. Daily housekeeping. Outdoor hot tub, sauna, ski storage, guest laundry. **P.O. Box 81, Taos Ski Valley, NM 87525; (505) 776-2646.**

Sierra del Sol Condominiums

Newly renovated fireplace condos. Short walk to the resort center and lifts. Thirty-two studio to two-bedroom units, each with kitchen, fireplace and balcony overlooking river. Daily housekeeping. Two indoor hot tubs, sauna, guest laundry. **P.O. Box 84, Taos Ski Valley, NM 87525; (800) 523-3954, (505) 776-2981.**

Twining Condominiums

Studios and two-bedroom loft units, each with full kitchen, fireplace, balcony and attractive furnishings. Ski packages. Twining also manages 20 private homes in the ski valley, all within walking distance of lifts. Linen and towel service every third day. Indoor hot tub, sauna. **P.O. Box 696, Taos Ski Valley, NM 87525; (800) 828-2472, (505) 776-8873.**

Taos Canyon

238

An address of "Ski Valley Rd." or "Route 150" means the property is directly on the access road.

Luxury Accommodations

Salsa Del Salto

Excellent 10-room B&B in the foothills, overlooking Taos Mesa. About equidistant from town and ski valley. Each room different, but all with finely crafted New Mexican furniture, king-size beds and down comforters. Elegant master suite with fireplace and private entrance. Large lobby fireplace. Daily housekeeping, gourmet breakfast, afternoon hors d'oeuvres. Heated pool, hot tub. **P.O. Box 1468, El Prado, NM 87529; (800) 530-3097, (505) 776-2422.**

Mid-Priced Accommodations

Amizette Inn

Twelve-room inn, $1^{1}/_{2}$ miles from ski valley and adjacent to Wheeler Wilderness Area. Rooms with one or two queen-size beds; also, private and romantic studio rooms. Modified American Plan and ski packages available. One child five or younger can stay free in parents' room. Daily housekeeping, full breakfast and dinner. Hot tub, sauna. **P.O. Box 756, Taos Ski Valley, Taos, NM 87525. (800) 446-TAOS, (505) 776-2451.**

Austing Haus Hotel

Largest and tallest post-and-beam timber building in the United States but decorated with a European touch. Twenty-four spacious and immaculate rooms (owner repaints annually), many with fireplaces. Most rooms with queen-size beds; some with additional loft sleeping space. Located $1^{1}/_{2}$ miles from the ski area. Also, Stream Side Suite units across the street, with fireplaces and kitchens. MAP and ski packages available. Daily housekeeping. Restaurant, indoor hot tub. Austing Haus also manages several fully equipped private chalets accommodating groups of up to 12; housekeeping for an additional charge on chalet rentals. **P.O. Box 8, Taos Ski Valley, NM 87525; (800) 748-2932, (505) 776-2649.**

Economy Accommodations

Abominable Snowmansion

Budget "bunk-and-breakfast" dorm lodging for 76. Six dorms with wide beds, large closets, lavatories, shower rooms and dressing areas. Ideal for young solo travelers. Two-story common room with fireplace, music, games, piano and other tools for socializing. Breakfast and dinner served family style. Nine miles from ski area in Arroyo Seco. **476 State Rd. 150, P.O. Box 3271, Taos, NM 87571; (505) 776-8298.**

Condominiums

Hacienda de Valdez

Lovely and well-appointed Southwestern-style units in the Sangre de Cristo foothills 8 miles from the ski valley, 12 miles from town. Spanish tiles, fireplaces, balconies and sundecks with great views. Housekeeping, outdoor hot tub. **P.O. Box 5651, Taos, NM 87571; (800) 837-2218, (505) 776-2218.**

Quail Ridge Inn Resort

Well-appointed adobe-style resort complex with 110 attractive units. Condos range from lock-off rooms to multi-bedroom suites, all with fireplaces and full kitchens. Casitas are two-level townhouses with two bedrooms, two baths, washer and dryer and other extras. Great views. Twelve miles from ski valley. Ski packages. Daily housekeeping. Huge outdoor heated pool, fitness center, indoor tennis, racquetball, squash, restaurant, lounge, shops, guest laundry. **P.O. Box 707, Taos, NM 87571; (800) 624-4448, (505) 776-2211.**

Taos East Condominiums
Eleven pleasant condos in woodsy, mountain style surrounded by the Carson National Forest, $3^1/2$ miles from ski valley. Efficiency to four-bedroom units with fireplace. Hot tub, guest laundry. Daily housekeeping. **P.O. Box 567, Taos Ski Valley, NM 87525; (800) 238-SNOW, (505) 776-2271.**

Taos

Luxury Accommodations
Adobe & Pines Inn
Atmospheric seven-room B&B in 165-year-old adobe home, nestled among the pines on Taos's outskirts. Tranquil and romantic. Each room has a private entrance and kiva fireplace, one with two-person soaking tub and dry Swedish sauna, one with two-person whirlpool tub and one with one-person whirlpool tub. Two casitas have two gas-burning fireplaces and whirlpool tubs. No smoking indoors; no children ages 12 or younger. Daily housekeeping, full gourmet breakfast. **P.O. Box 837, Rancho de Taos, NM 87557; (800) 723-8267, (505) 751-0947.**

Casa de las Chimeneas
Just four ultra-luxurious guest quarters set in a spectacular garden, one a suite with library sitting room. Kiva fireplaces, Talavera tile and deluxe bed and bath linens abound. Exceptional breakfasts, daily housekeeping, complimentary hors d'oeuvres. Outdoor hot tub. **P.O. Box 5303, Taos, NM 87571; (505) 758-4777.**

Fechin Inn
Elegant new 85-room hotel, two blocks from Taos Plaza and adjacent to Kit Carson Park. Some suites. Many rooms with kiva fireplaces, private patios or balconies. Two-story adobe building on the beautiful grounds of the Fechin Institute, built in the 1920s and now on the National Register of Historic Places. Interior features bold ornamental designs in the tradition of artist Nicolai Fechin. Authentic Southwestern Pueblo style, with custom-design furnishings and hand-carved woodwork. Daily housekeeping, 24-hour front desk, elegant buffet breakfast included. Bar and lounge areas, exercise room, outdoor hot tub. **227 Paseo de Pueblo Norte, Taos, NM 87571; (800) 811-2933, (505) 751-1000.**

The Historic Taos Inn
Landmark 39-room hotel just steps from the town plaza. Listed on National Register of Historic Places. Two-story lobby, built around an old community well, known as "the town's living room." Library is popular meeting place for local artists, guests. Antique-filled, exquisite and full of tradition. Unique rooms are individually decorated but each has adobe fireplace, hand-loomed bedspreads, original art and locally crafted furniture in a flawless Southwestern style. Daily housekeeping, après-ski refreshments. Greenhouse room with hot tub, restaurant, lobby bar. **125 Paseo del Pueblo Norte, Taos, NM 87571; (800) TAOS-INN, (505) 758-2233.**

Mid-Priced Accommodations
Brooks Street Inn
Six-room B&B with charm, humor and imagination. Private or shared bath. Fireside evenings. Mornings with breakfasts, including Czech, Lithuanian and Mexican specialties. Main house and additional guest house on spacious grounds. Walking distance to Plaza. No smoking or children ages 15 or younger. Daily housekeeping, full breakfast. **P.O. Box 4954, Taos, NM 87571; (505) 758-1489.**

Casa Benavides
Elegant 31-room complex one block from Taos Plaza. Main house was once artist's residence; several buildings in complex including the six-room Miramon House, on the National Register of Historic Places. Charming rooms with custom and antique furnishings and skylights; some with private patios. Non-smoking; no children. Daily housekeeping, full breakfast. Two outdoor hot tubs. **137 Kit Carson Rd., Taos, NM 87571; (505) 758-1772.**

Casa Europa
Adobe inn appointed with fine furnishings, original artwork and fine architectural details combining

Southwestern style and modern European craftsmanship. Five spacious rooms, some with private whirlpool bath or kiva fireplace. Located just outside of town. Daily housekeeping, gourmet breakfast, afternoon hors d'oeuvres. Spa, art gallery. **P.O. Box 157, Upper Ranchitos Rd., Taos, NM 87571; (505) 758-9798.**

Holiday Inn Don Fernando de Taos

Pueblo-style resort hotel 1 mile south of the Plaza. Contemporary interpretation of historic style. Built on site of historic Don Fernando Hotel. Now 126 modern rooms in several price categories. Lavish happy-hour buffet on weeknights. Art in lobby. Daily housekeeping, 24-hour front desk, Taos Airport shuttle. Restaurant, lounge, hot tub, tennis. **1005 Paseo del Pueblo Sur, P.O. Drawer V, Taos, NM 87571; (800) 759-2736, (505) 758-4444, (800) HOL-IDAY for** Holiday Inn reservations.

Kachina Lodge

Large 118-room resort hotel on spacious site close to town. Taos-style furniture with Southwestern paintings. Navajo Living Room a cozy hideaway for games or relaxing by the fireplace. Entertainment many nights in large cabaret. Children 12 and younger stay free in parents' room. Best Western affiliate. AAA Three Diamond winner. Daily housekeeping, 24-hour front desk. Restaurants, lounge, Olympic-size pool, hot tub. **P.O. Box NN, Taos, NM 87571; (800) 522-4462, (505) 758-2275, (800) 528-1234 for** Best Western reservations.

Quality Inn

Motor inn with 99 rooms with king-size or two double queen-size beds. Public areas with fireplaces, Southwestern arts and crafts on display. Suitable for families. Ski packages. Daily housekeeping, room service, 24-hour front desk. Heated outdoor pool, hot tub, restaurant, lounge. **1043 Paseo del Pueblo Sur, P.O. Box 2319, Taos, NM 87571; (800) 845-0648, (505) 758-2200, (800) 228-5151 for** Quality Inn reservations.

Rancho Ramada at Taos

Contemporary 124-room hotel. Spacious accommodations and public areas. Fireplace lounge located just south of town. Daily housekeeping, room service, 24-hour front desk. Indoor pool, hot tub, restaurant, lounge. **P.O. Box 6257, Taos, NM 87571; (800) 659-TAOS, (505) 758-2900, (800) 2-RAMADA for** Ramada Inn reservations.

The Ruby Slipper

Whimsical, romantic B&B with rooms named after characters from *The Wizard of Oz*. Seven rooms, some with private entrances. Handsome and interesting furnishings. No smoking. Daily housekeeping, natural-foods breakfasts, hot tub. **416 La Lomita, P.O. Box 2069, Taos, NM 87571; (505) 758-0613.**

Sagebrush Inn

Built in 1929 during the Pueblo-Mission era, the original inn is awash with the charm and patina of recent Southwestern history. First blush of adapted pueblo architecture has aged gracefully and attractively and is furnished with authentic Navajo rugs, rare pottery, antiques and paintings. Many of the 79 rooms and suites have fireplaces. Cuisine is award-winning. Nightly entertainment. Sagebrush Village is a new section of condo suites sleeping up to six, all with fireplaces and two bathrooms. Three Stars from Mobil. Daily housekeeping, 24-hour front desk. Pool, tennis courts, two hot tubs, restaurant, lounge. **1508 Paseo del Pueblo Sur, P.O. Box 557, Taos, NM 87571; (800) 428-3626, (505) 758-2254.**

Sun God Lodge

Well-priced 55-room motel with good in-room amenities, including TV with VCR, coffee maker with gourmet coffee and kiva fireplace. Some suites with kitchenettes. Attractive, built around a courtyard on spacious grounds. Handmade Southwestern-style furniture and Taos art. Senior discounts and ski packages. One mile south of Taos Plaza. Daily housekeeping. Hot tub. **819 Paseo del Pueblo Sur, P.O. Box 1713, Taos, NM 87571; (800) 821-2437, (505) 758-3162.**

Economy Accommodations

Harrison's Bed and Breakfast

Budget-watchers' B&B, with some rooms with shared baths and some connecting. Located west of town, with fine views. Daily housekeeping, breakfast. **Millicent Rogers Museum Rd., P.O. Box 242, Taos, NM 87571; (505) 758-2630.**

Indian Hills Inn
Economical downtown motel two blocks from the Plaza. Thirty new rooms and 30 remodeled older ones. Daily housekeeping, complimentary coffee, continental breakfast included. Guest barbecue. **233 Paseo del Pueblo Sur, Taos, NM 85751; (800) 444-2346, (505) 758-4293.**

The Plum Tree
AYH (American Youth Hostel) affiliated hostel and B&B between Taos and Santa Fe; therefore, good choice for skiers who want to sample both ski areas or explore northern New Mexico as well as ski. Friendly budget inn with dorms for women, bunkhouse for men, domes, private rooms for couples. Bring sleeping bag or rent linens for small fee. Light breakfast. Common kitchen for guests' use. **P.O. Box A-1, Pilar, NM 87531; (800) 678-PLUM, (505) 758-4696.**

Taos Motel
Comfortable and commodious 28-room motel with double beds. Two doors from family restaurant. Children 12 and younger stay free in parents' room. Ski packages available. Daily housekeeping, staff member on site 24 hours, complimentary coffee. **P.O. Box 729VG, Ranchos de Taos, NM 87557; (800) 323-6009, (505) 758-2524.**

Condominiums

Sonterra Condominiums
Bright, contemporary condo units furnished in New Mexican style. All with private patios and some with kiva fireplaces. Pueblo-style complex built around inner courtyard. Quiet, yet just four blocks from the Plaza. **P.O. Box 5244, Taos, NM 57571; (505) 758-7989.**

Property management companies handling Taos area condos include
Craig Management Co., (800) 800-4SKI, (505) 776-5710
Premiere Properties, (800) 987-8423, (505) 776-8045
Taos Vacation Rentals, (800) 788-TAOS, (505) 758-5700

DINING OUT

Taos Ski Valley

The Bavarian
Austrian and Bavarian specialties. Good spot at the bottom of Chair 4, accessible on skis, four-wheel drive vehicle or complimentary shuttle. Excellent stop for hearty ski lunches, including cold platters, soups, goulash and hot entrées. Après-ski spot. Prix fixe dinner, with welcome cocktail and menu rotating nightly. Excellent desserts. Dinner reservations suggested. **Taos Ski Valley; (505) 751-6661.**

Dolomite
Hand-tossed pizza with wonderful toppings at lunch and dinner. Available by the pie or by the slice. Fresh pasta and fresh-baked breads and desserts. Beer, wine and cappuccino—and live jazz Mondays through Thursdays. Daily specials. Also light breakfasts and rich coffees. Delivery within valley. Across from Thunderbird Lodge. **Taos Ski Valley; (505) 776-1868.**

Hondo Restaurant
Spacious and congenial hotel dining room, located in the renovated original Hondo Lodge that's the nucleus of the Inn at Snakedance. Buffet breakfast, lunches and good dinners. Creative menu offering classic Continental favorites and creative contemporary dishes. Excellent wine list; Wednesday wine dinners pair food and wine. Live entertainment on the mild and mellow side. Adjacent outdoor deck serves grilled meats and poultry, salads and light fare. Reservations recommended. **Inn at Snakedance, Taos Ski Valley; (505) 776-2277.**

Hotel Edelweiss
Since terrible fire in April 1996, hotel and its dining room being rebuilt. Check, but previously welcomed non-guests to join house guests for à la carte breakfast, lunch and exceptional dinner. Weekly rotating menu. Saturday Grand Buffet features varied appetizers, salads, entrées and

241

desserts. Other nights offer four-course dinners with choices of appetizers, entrées and desserts. Vegetarian dishes always available. Excellent wine list. Children's menu on request. Non-smoking restaurant. **Hotel Edelweiss, Taos Ski Valley; (505) 776-2301, Ext. 197.**

Rhoda's Restaurant
Sitdown restaurant in main base lodge. Lunch and dinner overlooking Al's Run. Eclectic menu, strong on hefty midday sandwiches and Omaha Angus steaks at dinner. Poultry, seafood and vegetarian selections also available. Daily specials. Homemade desserts. Full bar, plus good wine and microbrew selections. Children's menu. Dinner served until 8:30 P.M. Reservations accepted. **Taos Ski Valley; (505) 776-2005.**

Tim's Stray Dog Cantina
Good for hearty skiers' breakfast, including burritos, pancakes and *papas y chile*. Easy stroll from slopes for lunch. Shines after the lifts close. Lively cantina-style bar dinner with Mexican-American accent. Margaritas, beer and wine and excellent munchies. Dinner ranges from Cilantro Chicken to cheeseburgers; served until 9:00 P.M. Good desserts. Affordable and fun. **Cottams Alpine Village, Taos Ski Valley; (505) 776-2894.**

Downtown, Taos Canyon and Surrounding Areas

Apple Tree Inn
Four cozy dining rooms with piñon-burning fireplaces in historic adobe home. Charming and intimate. Seafood, salads, pasta and Mexican specialties. Nightly specials. Espresso bar. Excellent desserts. Excellent wine list (winner of Wine Spectator Award for Excellence); domestic and imported beers. Lunch, dinner and Sunday brunch. Reservations recommended. **123 Bent St., Taos; (505) 758-1900.**

Austing Haus
Restaurant's Glass Dining Room, spacious yet cozy, with fine atmosphere and a Continental flair. Favored close by "escape" from Taos Ski Valley. Game, seafood, rack of lamb, roast duck and interesting pastas are specialties, with wine list match. Also, extensive beer selection. Strudel is the top

dessert choice. Located 1 1/2 miles from Taos Ski Valley. Reservations recommended. **Ski Valley Rd., Amizette, Taos; (505) 776-2649.**

Bent Street Deli and Cafe
Something for everyone, and at every time of day too. Good breakfasts, light lunches and dinners from light to not. Soups, salads, sandwiches and terrific desserts, plus good pasta, seafood, and vegetarian entrées. Inspirations from many cuisines, including Japanese, Indian, Greek, Italian and Spanish. Moderate prices. Heated patio. Beer and wine. Skiers' lunches to go are available. Closed Sunday. **120 Bent St., Taos; (505) 758-5787.**

Casa Cordova
Continental cuisine in lovely, traditional restaurant, a Taos classic since 1961. A place for special dinners. Atmospheric, elegant and humane. Uses only organically grown produce, chemical-free beef, free-range chicken, veal from naturally fed calves and farm-raised seafood. Variety of pastas. Half-portions available. Coffee and dessert served in the comfortable, loungelike bar. Closed Sunday. Reservations recommended. **Ski Valley Rd., Arroyo Seco; (505) 776-2500.**

Casa Fresen Bakery
Almost obligatory stop from town to the ski valley for excellent baked goods and specialty coffees, to eat in or take out. Good place to wait out heavy after-ski traffic with coffee and pastry. Also packs fine fare for picnicking on the mountain. **Ski Valley Rd., Arroyo Seco; (505) 776-2969.**

Doc Martin's
Hotel restaurant serving breakfast, lunch and dinner. Atmospheric gem, serving contemporary and traditional Southwestern specialties. Innovative way with seafood and game. Daily chef's specials. Breakfast, lunch and dinner. Excellent value for fine food and unsurpassed ambiance. Award-winning wine list, good beer selection and full bar. Dinner reservations recommended. **Historic Taos Inn, 125 Paseo del Pueblo Norte, Taos; (505) 758-2233.**

Don Fernando's
Sprightly setting and specials in large hotel restaurant. Daily specials and themes. Salad bar at lunch and big happy-hour buffet on weekdays.

Lotsa Pasta on Thursday nights, Friday Seafood Extravaganza and Cattleman's Club Prime Rib on Saturday. Sunday brunch. Children's menu. Reservations accepted. **Holiday Inn, 1005 Paseo del Pueblo Sur, Taos; (505) 758-4444.**

Eske's Brew Pub

Great unfiltered and unpasteurized beer on tap, fine entertainment and lively scene sprinkled through several small rooms. Good pub food (and trendy healthy fare too). Range is from Tabouleh Salad to Bangers and Mashers. Beer-Battered Club Sandwich a must for hungry souls who can't get too much brew. Moderate prices. **106 Des Georges Ln., Taos; (505) 758-1517.**

Fred's Place

Home cooking—as cooked in northern New Mexico homes. *Carne adovada, horno chicos, calabacitas,* blue corn enchiladas and other interesting and unusual specialties. Lavish New Mexican plates contain one specialty or a combo, with pinto beans, Spanish rice or posole—and a sopapilla. Sandwiches for unadventurous Anglos. Dinner nightly except Sunday. **332 Paseo del Pueblo Sur, Taos; (505) 758-0514.**

Hopi Dining Room

Casual yet elegant hotel dining room. Leisurely dining when you want it; quick service when you need it. Varied cuisine, but emphasis is on New Mexican specialties. Children's menu. Lunch buffet and dinner. Impressive Sunday brunch buffet. **Kachina Lodge, 413 North Pueblo Rd.,Taos; (505) 758-2275.**

La Luna Ristorante

Traditional Italian dishes, including a dozen pastas and sauces. Manicotti, gnocchi and lasagne featured. Gourmet pizzas from wood-burning oven. Freshly made bread and desserts. Pleasant and casual atmosphere, welcoming to families. Moderate prices. Weekday lunches and nightly dinner. **223 Paseo del Pueblo Sur, Taos; (505) 751-0023.**

Lambert's of Taos

Contemporary American cuisine in sleek attractive setting. Dinner menu changes nightly, but many grilled dishes are always offered. Lamb, a specialty, prepared in various creative ways. Outstanding desserts. Nightly dinner and weekday lunch. Beer and wine, by the bottle or by the

243

The St. Francis de Assisi mission church in Ranchos de Taos, New Mexico, is probably one of the most photographed and painted churches in the United States. Its thickly buttressed adobe walls, once used for defense, are evidence of the mission style of architecture brought to this country by the Spanish conquistadores.

Photo by Ken Gallard/Taos Ski Valley

glass. Dinner reservations recommended. **309 Paseo del Pueblo Sur, Taos; (505) 758-1009.**

Los Vaqueros Steak House

Favorite dinner spot for grilled meats and prime rib, but New Mexican, Tex-Mex and seafood dishes also offered. Full bar and wine list. Children's menu. Nightly entertainment. **Sagebrush Inn, Paseo del Pueblo Sur, Taos; (505) 758-2254.**

Marciano's Ristoranti

Quiet, simple atmosphere. Homemade pasta specialties, chicken, fish and desserts. Italian specialties with a Continental flair. Nightly except Tuesday. Beer, wine and espresso—all select and special. Reservations recommended. **La Placita and Ledoux St., Taos; (505) 751-0805.**

Ogelvie's Bar & Grille

Overlooking the Plaza. Traditional and regional cuisine, including pasta, seafood and aged Angus beef. Varied appetizer menu. Light and healthy specials also offered. Lunch and dinner. Live music in the lounge. Reservations accepted. **Taos Plaza; (505) 758-8866.**

Renegade Cafe

Imaginative breakfasts, hearty enough to launch a ski day. Salads, sandwiches and other light lunches. Italian-accented Southwestern specialties served at dinner, along with good steak and seafood. Muffins, pastries and desserts baked on premises. Good wine selection. **Quail Ridge Inn, Ski Valley Rd., Taos; (505) 776-1777.**

Roberto's

Three dining rooms in 150-year-old building. Local versions of Spanish food, made from scratch and very creative. Authentic and excellent. Skiers' favorite for atmosphere, food, fun. Located across from Kit Carson Museum. Reservations recommended. **Kit Carson Rd., Taos; (505) 758-2434.**

Shogun

New Japanese restaurant and sushi bar. Open daily from 11:00 A.M. to 11:00 P.M. for tempura, teriyaki, sushi and other Japanese specialties. **321 Paseo del Pueblo Sur, Taos; (505) 758-7645.**

Tapas de Taos Cafe

Taos's first taqueria, but with a multicultural twist. Appetizers from the world's cuisines served until 11:00 P.M. Espresso, fruit drinks and nonalcoholic wines and beers. Also, Mexican combo platters and grill specialties. Lunch on weekdays, dinner nightly except Sunday and weekend brunch with salsa bar. Children's menu. Live and recorded music and sophisticated setting. Reservations not accepted. **136 Bent St., Taos; (505) 758-9670.**

Tim's Chile Connection

Big busy place serving Mexican food. Famous for red and green chile. Terrific bar, serves everything from don't-miss margaritas to top-dollar brandy. Also home of the Taos Brewery. Entertainment. Lunch, dinner and late-night bar menu. Moderate prices. Located at mile marker number one en route from town. **Ski Valley Rd., Taos; (505) 776-8787.**

Trading Post Cafe

New Italian restaurant with good renditions of popular favorites—and popular prices too. Located in a historic trading post, which was once the largest general store in the Taos area and the de facto community center of Rancho de Taos. Some meat, some poultry and lots of pasta. Dinner nightly. **4179 State Road 68, Rancho de Taos; (505) 758-5089.**

Villa Fontana

Fine dining in lovely, romantic restaurant filled with art and atmosphere. Award-winning northern Italian cuisine and outstanding service. Also seasonal game such as venison, duck and pheasant. Even local wild mushrooms. Fine wine list. Winner of 1994 DiRoNa award; AAA Four Diamonds. Closed Sunday. Reservations recommended. **Hwy 522, 5 miles north of Taos; (505) 758-5800.**

Wild & Natural Cafe

Southwestern specialties in creative low-fat, vegetarian and vegan versions. Outstanding meatless chile. Espresso bar. Local beer and organic wine. "Monkey Meals" for children. Takeout available. Breakfast, lunch and dinner, except Sunday. **812B Paseo del Pueblo Norte, Taos; (505) 751-0480.**

NIGHTLIFE

Less is more when it comes to nightlife at Taos Ski Valley because most skiers are so wasted (or at least enervated) that late nights hold little appeal. Early après-ski starts at The Bavarian at the base of Lift 4. When the slopes close, it shifts to the Martini Tree Bar in the resort center and spreads around the valley. Tim's Stray Dog Cantina is young and lively. The St. Bernard, the Edelweiss, the Inn at Snakedance and the Thunderbird are restrained. Live music includes rock, jazz and more classical than at any other ski resort, usually ending at a fairly civilized hour. Sometimes entertainment is limited to congenial cocktails and ski movies. The Dolomite, essentially a pizza place, has live jazz Monday through Thursday evenings.

Down-valley, Casa Cordova and Villa Fontana do a quiet, refined cocktail hour. Tim's Chile Connection makes no effort at refinement but is fun. It's got a big-screen TV and all the associated merriment, especially when a Big Game is on. The larger downtown hotels put on good happy-hour buffets. Another popular activity in town involves exploring Taos's outstanding shops and galleries, which are at a level achieved in few ski towns. Mixing the two, some of the galleries even offer après-ski refreshments several nights a week.

Try the Susan Wilder Fine Art Cafe for such a blend. More in the customary after-ski mode, the Historic Taos Inn's Adobe Bar is the traditional place to see and be seen. This congenial, social place with live jazz, folk or country in the lobby or the bar several nights a week; the adjacent Library, where drinks are also served, is quieter. Later, you're also likely to find some action and often live entertainment at Ogelvie's, Rancho Ramada's Fireside Cafe, Holiday Inn's Fernando's Hideaway and the Stakeout. Add dancing to the roster at the Hacienda Inn, Kachina Lodge's Zuni Lounge and Sagebrush Inn, the latter known for good country music. Old Martinez Hall in Rancho de Taos and El Taqueño also have dancing on some nights. Artsy locals stop at the Caffe Tazza on Kit Carson Rd., for touring folksingers and an open mike every Saturday evening where poets, musicians and singers can perform. There's live jazz every Sunday at La Luna.

For more information, contact **Taos Ski Valley, Inc., P.O. Box 90, Taos Ski Valley, NM 87525; (505) 776-2291, fax (505) 776-8596; Taos Valley Resort Assn., P.O. Box 85, Taos Ski Valley, NM 87525; (800) 776-1111, (505) 776-2233; Taos County Chamber of Commerce, P.O. Drawer 1, Taos, NM 87571; (800) 732-TAOS, (505) 758-3874.**

SKI SANTA FE

BACKDROP

New Mexico skiers treasure Ski Santa Fe, but many out-of-staters don't even know the city has skiing. And that's their loss, for it provides one of the truly unique winter vacation experiences in the Rockies. As a town, Santa Fe is like Taos but more so. As a ski area, Ski Santa Fe is like Taos Ski Valley but less so. This means you can combine skiing in the normally benign New Mexican climate with an excursion into the art, history, cuisine and culture of the Southwest. It's just that, at Santa Fe, you'll find more hotels, restaurants, shops and galleries but less (and less challenging) ski terrain than at Taos and no slope-side accommodations at all. The experience is similar; you'll just have to decide on the balance that suits you best.

Since off-season is winter, bargain rates and packages are offered by many lodgings. This in itself is stunning, since fully one-third of the city's lodging rooms are rated in the luxury category, and its small inns rank among the best in the West. Even the finest restaurants are less crowded, as are galleries and shops (and there may even be sales). In terms of statistics Ski Santa Fe won't make your jaw drop, but the ski area is complex and varied, and when you consider the opportunity to ski on a congenial mountain and explore one of America's most desirable towns, the modest numbers don't really matter at all.

THE LAY OF THE LAND

High in the mountains 16 miles northeast of the temperate desert city of adobe, Ski Santa Fe is an Alpine aerie snaring more than 225 inches of snow a year. It is essentially a day-skiing area, but since Santa Fe is such an attractive tourist mecca year-round, it becomes a minor-league ski destination. The city of Santa Fe, New Mexico's capital, is built around a traditional Spanish colonial plaza, which remains the center of activities as it in centuries past (though the activities certainly have changed). Since the ski area is some distance from town, it maintains a convenient ticket outlet and ski and snowboard retail, rental and repair shop in town at the corner of Wyoming and Menaul Streets, **(505) 292-4401.** The ski area is at the end of a scenic road that winds steeply past deep forests (mostly evergreens but including one of northern New Mexico's grandest stands of aspen) to a white world. You won't need to drive around Santa Fe, a compact little city surrounding the historic Plaza, but if you do rent a car for the mountain commute, make sure it is "skierized." Frequent morning and afternoon ski shuttles between the main hotels and the ski area are operated by **Shuttlejack, Inc.** Reservations are required before 3:00 P.M. the previous day, **(505) 982-4311.**

GETTING THERE

Albuquerque International Airport, the nearest major gateway, is just 65 miles to the south. Rental cars are available, and **Shuttlejack, Inc.,** runs 10 scheduled buses a day between the airport and Santa Fe, with stops at major hotels (reservations required), **(505) 982-4311.** Santa Fe Regional Airport handles private planes. Shuttles also meet **Amtrak's Southwest Chief** between Chicago and Los Angeles, which stops in Lamy, 16 miles from Santa Fe, **(800) USA-RAIL.** Santa Fe is right off I-25 or US 84/285. **Greyhound/Trailways/TNM&O Coaches** have daily buses to Santa Fe from all four compass directions, **(505) 471-0008.**

PROFILE

At the base of the area you will find parking lots and a spacious day lodge that looks like a giant chalet but, in approved Santa Fe fashion, is called La Casa. Close by is the Chipmunk Corner Children's Center offering day care and snowplay for pre-skiers and ski instruction for youngsters ages 3 and older, using a private little surface lift for tiny beginners. From there, the Santa Fe Super Chief quad climbs over broad, gentle slopes that fan out into a wide cirque. The ski terrain is shaped rather like a funnel. The slopes on the lower mountain are the runout from the upper mountain but, since they are mild enough for beginners, two chairlifts and a surface lift are available for those wishing to ski just this terrain. Off to one side is a charming terrain garden called Adventure Land, open to children and the adults who accompany them.

The Tesuque Peak triple chairlift climbs from the spot where the "funnel" flares out to a high point on the ridge that forms the cirque. Easy intermediate routes lead in either direction—Gayway to the right and Sunset to the left. Runs for all abilities appear on the trail map, but for all practical purposes, the challenging upper mountain actually boasts more acreage among the trees than on the marked runs. The Gayway or west side consists of grand skiing among stunted timberline trees that create dramatic visuals as well as an unusual form of open-glade skiing. Parachute is a marked black trail in the midst of this sector, but it is just a suggestion. You might ski here for hours and pick a different line each time. The Sierra chairlift and the Santa Fe Super Chief unload farther out and lower down, accessing novice and intermediate trails that cut through thicker trees. Skiers comfortable in the backcountry also use this side of the mountain to reach Big Tesuque Bowl, a grandiose cirque that eventually steepens and closes in to provide outstanding glade skiing. It is a long, long run that ends along the ski-area access highway below the base of the lifts. If you ski it, you'll need to arrange for a vehicle to transport you back to the base.

Roadrunner under the Tesuque Peak triple exhibits the open-glade characteristics of the Gayway side, but everything off to the left or east of that is tighter, steeper and more genuinely demanding. The trees below Sunset are just about as close as those off the Sierra and Santa Fe lifts, but the terrain is a lot more sheer and rugged, and advanced skiers are more likely to be

Inside Ski Santa Fe

drawn to, not put off by, the thought of skiing it. You can ski Roadrunner to Easter Bowl, First Tracks, Avalanche Bowl, Desperado and Double Eagle—precipitous routes through the trees. Or you can follow Sunset to the black diamond of your choice—Pipeline, Molly Hogan, Tequila Sunrise, Wizard and Columbine. These trails are steep and sinewy, beefed up with snowy downspouts, bruising boulders and twisty bump sections. The forest is dense on this entire face of the cirque, adding to the options and the challenges. These runs all open into Alpine Bowl, a wide valley dotted with "real," rather than stunted, trees for more open-glade skiing. When there's new snow, this is a good place to find it.

A master plan in circulation at this writing could boost Ski Santa Fe higher in the rankings of midsize ski areas. Various alternatives have been considered, including the resurrection of the Alpine side with a new chairlift, expansion above Sunset, the addition of a new surface lift into Spruce Bowl on the west and the addition of more beginner facilities. No decision has been made as to what might be permitted and when.

SNOWBOARDING

With its big-bowl feeling and excellent gladed steeps, Ski Santa Fe could just as easily have been called Snowboard Santa Fe as well. There is no better riding in the southern Rockies than through the trees of Tequila Sunrise and The Burn, and snowboarders—perhaps more than skiers—are willing to undertake an excursion into the Tesuque area. Now Ski Santa Fe builds a jib park as soon as snow conditions permit and hosts snowboarding as well as ski competitions.

SKI SCHOOL PROGRAMS

Introductory Programs

Never Ever Skier Package: Beginner lift ticket and four hours of lessons for skiers and snowboarders.
Second Day Package: All-lift ticket and four hours of lessons.
Seasoned Beginner Skiers: Three Monday afternoons of lifts, lessons and rentals for new skiers ages 50 and older.

Advanced and Specialty Programs

Moguls & Powder: Bump-skiing workshop, with powder coaching when conditions dictate.
Snowboard Workshop: Two all-day sessions, beginner to expert, including lifts, and discounts on rentals.
Telemark Workshops: Two days of lifts and five hours of lessons from visiting PSIA Nordic Downhill Demonstration Team member.

For Families

Chipmunk Corner Children's Center: Comprehensive child care for infants and children. Hours are 8:30 A.M. to 4:30 P.M., **(505) 988-9636.**

Nonskiing Children

Tiny Chips: All-day nursery and day care for children ages 2 months to 3 years. Children separated by age. Snacks and lunch included for toddlers. Reservations required.
Little Chips Snow Play: Indoor activities, ski play, movies and naps plus up to one hour of morning and afternoon snowplay for non-skiers ages 3 to 5 years.

Kids bundled up for a day in the snow and sun.

Photo courtesy Ski Santa Fe

Skiing Children

Little Chips I Can Ski: Two hours of morning ski lessons, plus indoor activities for children ages 3 to 5 years. Includes rental equipment, snacks and lunch. Children in this age group who can demonstrate the ability to stop and turn competently may be enrolled in the Chipito Lunch Package.

Chipito Lunch Package: Two two-hour lessons, all-day lift tickets, snacks and lunch for children ages 5 and 6. Rental equipment additional.

Chipmunks Package: Two-hour morning and afternoon lessons, snacks and lunch for children ages 7 to 9. Rental equipment additional.

Saturday Shredders: Lifts and snowboarding lessons for all ability levels on eight consecutive Saturday sessions for children ages 9 to 17.

Teens

Santa Fe Adventure Team: For advanced skiers (but not racers) ages 13 to 17 who want to challenge themselves in the steeps, bumps and powders. Safety is stressed. Eight consecutive Saturday sessions.

FOR RACERS

NASTAR: Thursday through Sunday all season long.

NASTAR Race Clinic: Half- and full-day options.

Fall Race Camp: One-, two- and three-day versions (skiers may enroll in any or all days). For racing skiers ages 12 years to adult. Held in early December.

Recreational Race Program: For racers ages 7 to 17. See "For Families" section, under "Skiing Children."

NORDIC SKIING

The Norski Ski Club of Santa Fe grooms a 4^1/$_2$-kilometer track near the Santa Fe Ski Area, and the Albuquerque-based New Mexico Ski Touring Club maintains a larger trail system in the Jemez Mountains and offers one or two organized tours

---

Mountain Stats—
Ski Santa Fe

Resort elevation 7,000 feet (city)
Top of highest lift 12,000 feet
Bottom of lowest lift 10,350 feet
Total vertical 1,650 feet
Longest run 3 miles
Average annual snowfall 225 inches
Ski season Thanksgiving through early April
Lifts 1 quad chairlift, 1 triple, 2 doubles, 1 Poma, 2 Mitey-Mite tows
Capacity 7,300 skiers per hour
Terrain 590 acres, 38 runs (20% beginner and novice, 40% intermediate, 40% advanced and expert)
Snowmaking 30%
Mountain dining Totemoff's Bar & Grill at mid-mountain (top of Sierra chairlift, bottom of Tesuque Peak chair)
Snow reports (505) 983-9155, (505) 857-8977

each weekend around Santa Fe, **(505) 821-0309.** There are lots of Nordic skiing opportunities in the **Santa Fe National Forest, (505) 988-6940.** A year-round outfitter called **Southwest Adventure Group** offers guides and other services, **(505) 988-7453.** It also has a year-round walk-in office at Sanbusco Market Center, 500 Montezuma. **Ten Thousand Waves,** a Japanese health spa, offers cross-country skiing instruction and guided ski tours, **(505) 988-1047.**

WHERE TO STAY

Central reservations services include **Bed & Breakfast of New Mexico, (505) 982-3332; Santa Fe Central Reservations, (800) 776-SNOW** and **Santa Fe Hotel Hotline, (800) 338-6877.**

Luxury Accommodations

Hotel St. Francis

Luxurious classic hotel with charm and elegance from the roaring twenties. Listed on the National Register of Historic Places. Eighty-two charming rooms. Antique furnishings. Outstanding, old-world service. Award-winner. Afternoon tea in the lobby is an elegant treat. Ski packages. Daily housekeeping, 24-hour front desk, concierge, room service, bell staff, valet. Restaurant, lounge. **210 Don Gaspar Ave., Santa Fe, NM 87501; (800) 666-5700, (505) 983-5700.**

Inn of the Anasazi

Award-winning and highly regarded hotel with 59 luxurious and attractive rooms. Excellent downtown location. Pets accepted. Daily housekeeping. Restaurant, lounge. **113 Washington Ave., Santa Fe, NM 87501; (800) 688-8100, (505) 988-3030.**

Inn of the Governors

Surprisingly intimate for 100-room hotel. Stylish Southwestern furniture and folk art. Many rooms with kiva fireplaces, private balconies, mini-bars. Two blocks from the Plaza. Nightly entertainment in Mañana Bar. Ski packages. Daily housekeeping, room service, 24-hour front desk, complimentary newspaper and coffee. Restaurant, lounge, outdoor pool. **Alameda at Don Gaspar, Santa Fe, NM 87501; (800) 234-4534, (505) 982-4333.**

La Posada de Santa Fe

Gracious and romantic 116-room hotel, just two blocks from the Plaza but set on 6 acres. Many units with fireplaces, some with kitchenettes. Guests can use Fort Marcy Sports Complex, a full health spa. Ski packages. Daily housekeeping, 24-hour front desk, room service, concierge, restaurant, lounge. **330 E. Palace Ave., Santa Fe, NM 87501; (800) 727-5276, (505) 986-0000.**

Preston House

Luxuriously, attractively furnished 15-room B&B. Fine in-town location. Ski packages. Daily housekeeping, breakfast. **106 Faithway, Santa Fe, NM 97501; (505) 982-3465.**

Mid-Priced Accommodations

Days Inn

Attractive 96-room inn. Eight room types, from economical to luxurious two-room suite with in-room whirlpool tub. Non-smoking rooms available. South of town. Daily housekeeping, complimentary Continental breakfast. Indoor pool, hot tub, restaurant adjacent. **3650 Cerrillos Rd.,**

250

Santa Fe, NM 87501; (505) 438-3822, (800) 325-2525 for Days Inn reservations.

Grant Corner Inn

One of Santa Fe's nicest B&B inns. Wonderful 13-room inn, two blocks from Plaza. Antique furnishings. Private and shared baths. Hospitable and charming. Ski packages. Daily housekeeping, gourmet breakfast, afternoon wine. **122 Grant Ave., Santa Fe, NM 87501; (505) 983-6678.**

Hotel Plaza Real

Newly built and finely designed hotel in traditional style. Most of the 56 rooms have fireplaces and French doors leading to small patio or balcony. A few rooms have whirlpool tubs. Ski packages. Daily housekeeping, 24-hour front desk, complimentary Continental breakfast. **125 Washington Ave., Santa Fe, NM 87501; (800) 279-REAL, (505) 988-4900.**

Inn at Loretto

Well-located, full-service hotel with 136 spacious rooms. Adjoins historic chapel. Daily housekeeping, room service, 24-hour front desk, bell staff. Restaurant, lounge, shops, outdoor pool. **211 Old Santa Fe Trail, Santa Fe, NM 87501; (800) 727-5531, (505) 988-5531, (800) 327-0200 for InterContinental reservations.**

Luxury Inn

Semi-suite hotel (divider between sitting area and sleeping area with king-size bed). Remote-control TV. Daily housekeeping, Continental breakfast. Pool, hot tub. **3752 Cerrillos Rd., Santa Fe, NM 87501; (505) 473-0567.**

Marriott's Residence Inn

All-suite hotel with 120 attractive kitchenette units. Studios sleep three; penthouses up to six. Pets accepted. Daily housekeeping, 24-hour front desk, complimentary breakfast buffet, social hour Monday through Thursday evenings. Three hot tubs, sport court, tennis. **1698 Galisteo, Santa Fe, NM 87501; (505) 788-3131, (800) 331-3131 for Marriott reservations.**

Quality Inn

Well-priced 99-room motor inn a short drive from downtown. Family plan; children 18 and younger stay free or receive discount for adjoining rooms. Daily housekeeping, 24-hour front desk. Outdoor pool, restaurant, lounge, playground. **3011 Cerrillos Rd., Santa Fe, NM 87501; (505) 471-1211, (800) 228-5151** for Quality Inn reservations.

Radisson Santa Fe

Attractive contemporary 133-unit hotel. On north side of town, with city views. Units from hotel rooms to two-bedroom suites. Live entertainment on weekends in Petroglyph Bar. Guests have complimentary use of Santa Fe Spa, next door. Daily housekeeping, 24-hour front desk, courtesy van to downtown, bell staff. Restaurant, lounge, outdoor hot tub. **750 N. St. Francis Dr., Santa Fe, NM 87501; (505) 982-5591, (800) 333-3333** for Radisson reservations.

Territorial Inn

Lovely 10-room B&B one block from the Plaza. Sophisticated and delightful. No children under 10. Daily housekeeping, breakfast, hot tub. **215 Washington Ave., Santa Fe, NM 87501; (505) 989-7737.**

Economy Accommodations

Budget Inn

Comfortable, 160-room downtown hotel at reasonable prices. AAA and Mobil rated. Daily housekeeping, 24-hour front desk. Restaurants, pool. **725 Cerrillos Rd., Santa Fe, NM 87501; (800) 288-7600, (505) 982-5952.**

Desert Chateau Motel

Ten-room motel, seven with kitchenettes. Well-located near center of town. Pets accepted. Daily housekeeping. **1622 Cerrillos Rd., Santa Fe, NM 87501; (505) 983-7976.**

Park Inn

Good choice for families; children 16 and younger stay free. Attractive rates for 83 good-sized rooms. In-room coffee. Daily housekeeping, Continental breakfast available, 24-hour front desk, bell service. Ski packages. **2900 Cerrillos Rd., Santa Fe, NM 87501; (800) 279-0894, (505) 473-4281.**

Traditional farolitos adorn buildings around the Plaza during the holiday season, and the length of Canyon Road on Christmas Eve.

Photo by Mark Nohl

Plaza TraveLodge

Forty-eight-room hotel with good location and moderate prices. Ski packages. Daily housekeeping. Heated pool. **646 Cerrillos Rd., Santa Fe, NM 87501; (505) 982-3551; (800) 255-3050** for TraveLodge reservations.

Santa Fe Youth Hostel

True budget accommodations for the young and young-at-heart traveler. Fifteen dorm rooms. Kitchen privileges. **1412 Cerrillos Rd., Santa Fe, NM 87501; (505) 988-1153, (505) 983-9896.**

Condominiums

Campanilla Compound

Thirty-eight one- and two-bedroom adobe units four blocks from the Plaza. Charming and well-furnished. Available for weekend, week or longer stays. **334 Otero St., Santa Fe, NM 87501; (800) 825-9700, (505) 988-7585.**

Cielo Grande

252 Opulent contemporary condominiums. One- and two-bedroom units, all with balconies, hot tubs, fireplaces. Hilltop location. Restaurant, lounge, pool, health spa. **750 N. St. Francis Dr., Santa Fe, NM 87501; (800) 441-5591, (505) 982-5591.**

Fort Marcy Compound Suites

Studios and one-, two- and three-bedroom units with different layouts in three downtown complexes: the 90-unit Fort Marcy Suite Hotel, 19-unit Las Palomas and 12-unit 527 Santa Fe. All with kitchens, fireplaces, televisions with VCRs; some hotel service. Moderate prices. Ski packages. Daily housekeeping, Continental breakfast. Heated indoor pool, hot tub, fitness facilities, guest laundry. **320 Artist Rd., Santa Fe, NM 87501; (505) 98-CONDO.**

DINING OUT

The Bishop's Lodge

Classic American and Continental cuisine as well as New Mexican specialties. Excellent luncheon buffet and even better Sunday buffet. Five minutes north of town. Reservations recommended. **Bishop's Lodge Rd., Santa Fe; (800) 732-2240, (505) 983-6377.**

La Casa Sena

Famous green chili chicken enchiladas and almost-as-famous trout baked in clay. Other northern New Mexican and Continental specialties. Lunch and dinner. Live entertainment in the Cantina. **125 E. Palace, Santa Fe; (505) 988-9232.**

La Choza

Casual Southwestern dining in old adobe ranch house. Local hangout. **905 Alarid St., Santa Fe; (505) 982-0909.**

India Palace

A delicious taste of old India in an area where the influences of "new India" predominate. Excellent food and pleasing atmosphere. **227 Don Gaspar, Santa Fe; (505) 986-5859.**

Maria's New Mexican Kitchen

Old Santa Fe incarnate. Old recipes prepared by local cooks. Homemade tortillas, Mexican beer and wonderful margaritas. Moderate prices. Lunch and dinner. **555 W. Cordova Rd., Santa Fe; (505) 983-7929.**

Natural Cafe

Healthy versions of international cuisine from Chinese to Chimayo. No red meat, but excellent vegetarian, seafood and organic chicken dishes. Wine and beer. Lunch and dinner. Dinner reservations are recommended. **1494 Cerrillos Rd., Santa Fe; (505) 983-1411.**

El Nido

Local hangout for seafood and steaks. More than 60 years in business. Full bar and good wine list. Atmosphere more authentic than touristic. **State Rd. 590 and 591, Santa Fe; (505) 988-4340.**

Old Mexico Grill

Regional "Old Mexico" specialties in casual restaurant. Mexican beers. Full bar. **2434 Cerrillos Rd., Santa Fe; (505) 473-0338.**

The Palace Restaurant & Saloon

Contemporary renditions of northern Italian and other Continental dishes. Piano player holds forth with "saloon" entertainment. Reservations accepted. **142 W. Palace Ave., Santa Fe; (505) 982-9891.**

Piñon Grill

Located in the 250-year-old Casa de Ortiz. Atmospheric and intimate. Known for ribs, Kansas City beef, seafood, salads and more. Reservations recommended. **Hilton of Santa Fe, 100 Sandoval St., Santa Fe; (505) 988-2811, Ext. 410.**

Rancho de Chimayo

Old hacienda, pleasingly tucked into the mountains north of town. Family-run purveyor of fine New Mexican cuisine. **State Rd. 520, Santa Fe; (505) 984-2100.**

Sakura

Japanese specialties. Pleasant setting. Beer and wine. Lunch and dinner (except Sunday). **321 W. San Francisco St., Santa Fe; (505) 983-5353.**

Santacafe

Contemporary cafe in 200-year-old Padre Gallegos House. Seasonal menus with dishes derived from many cuisines. Many locals consider this the best in town. Weekday lunch; nightly dinner. Reservations recommended. **231 Washington Ave., Santa Fe; (505) 984-1788.**

The Shed

Santa Fe classic located in a 17th-century hacienda. Owner/chef specializes in fine northern New Mexican cuisine. **113$^{1}/_{2}$ E. Palace Ave., Santa Fe; (505) 982-9030.**

Vanessie of Santa Fe

Sophisticated piano accompaniment to traditional favorites such as steak, rack of lamb, chicken and fish. Art on the walls. Full bar service. **434 W. San Francisco St., Santa Fe; (505) 982-9966.**

NIGHTLIFE

Santa Fe is at once urban, Spanish and sophisticated, with nearly 200 restaurants. Nightlife tends to center around the finest and most distinctive ones, some of which have live entertainment during all or part of the week. The same is true for the larger hotels, which offer fine lounges, often with entertainment and perhaps even dancing. Visitors can enjoy early-evening shopping and gallery-hopping, movies and simply promenading around the Plaza and surrounding streets of America's oldest capital city, founded in 1610. The Santa Fe Music Hall is a dinner theater that serves a four-course meal, puts on an original musical production and also features a sports bar. Chamber music at the Loretto Chapel or Santuario de Guadelupe, the Garson Theatre on the College of Santa Fe campus, the New Mexico Repertory Theatre at the Armory for the Arts, ProMusica, the Santa Fe Symphony, Desert Chorale and Santa Fe Community Orchestra are among the cultural opportunities available between September and May for locals and "off-season" visitors. For those who like gambling and bingo, the 24-hour-a-day Camel Rock Casino on Tesuque Tribal Lands about 10 minutes north of Santa Fe is appealing. More than any other ski destination, Santa Fe merits a day or two off skis to shop, visit museums, sightsee and drink in the ambiance of this lovely city at its uncrowded, low-season best.

For more information, contact **Ski Santa Fe, 1210 Luisa St., Santa Fe, NM 87501, (505) 983-9155** (downtown office), **(505) 982-4429** (ski area); **Santa Fe Convention & Visitors Bureau, P.O. Box 909, Santa Fe, NM 87504-0909; (800) 777-CITY, (505) 984-6760.**

RED RIVER

BACKDROP

There are bigger mountains than the Red River Ski Area and bigger fancier resorts than the town of Red River, but nowhere will you find a place that is simply as much fun. It just doesn't take itself too seriously, and it's more a place to kick back. The terrain is lighthearted yet interesting, and the people are on the slopes to enjoy themselves—whether on skis, snowboard or snowskates. Instructors in the huge and popular ski school teach with a rare degree of exuberance. Fun events permeate the calendar, on the mountain and in town. You'll be more likely to find a Wiffle golf competition than hardcore downhill racing, and visitors display more après-ski enthusiasm than a universal compulsion to get in just one more run.

The century-old former mining town retains its western-style aw-shucks, cowboy-hat ambiance (with an obligatory sprinkling of pseudo-Alpine chalets thrown in so you know you're in a mountain resort). Log cabin lodgings, brightly painted false-front buildings, and classic "mom-and-pop" motels, shops and eating places prevail. It's miles and miles to the nearest restaurant or motel chain, and the town is all the richer for the absence of America's cookie-cutter side. As important to many visitors as the skiing itself, and befitting a resort whose main clientele comes from Texas, Red River is famous for partying that never stops. Budget-friendliness doesn't stop either. Lift tickets, lodging, meals and entertainment are on the economy side, and except for key holiday periods, Red River's midweek, multiday packages rank among the best deals in the southern Rockies.

THE LAY OF THE LAND

Red River is a quaint former mining town in small mountain valley surrounded by ponderosa pine, aspen and spruce forest. It is a compact, stroll-about community, with two lifts just a block from the heart of the main drag and an astonishing 90 percent of the lodgings within walking distance of the lifts. The skiing starts where the sidewalks end, convenience matched by few ski towns in the Rockies.

GETTING THERE

Red River is 160 miles from Albuquerque, 105 miles from Santa Fe and 37 miles from Taos. Car rentals are available in Albuquerque. Take I-25 north to Santa Fe, and New Mexico 68 north to Taos. From there, you can either take New Mexico 522 north to Questa and Route 38 east to Red River, or continue east on New Mexico 64 and then north and west on Route 38. If you drive from Taos to Red River in one direction and return the other way, you will have completed the scenic Enchanted Circle Route. Airport shuttles from Albuquerque are available through **Enchanted Circle Tour & Coaches, (505) 754-3154.**

PROFILE

Although there is in-town lift access to Red River, beginners don't get to enjoy it. New skiers need to thread their way up a small road to the main base area, with day lodge, ski school, day care and, most important, the easiest terrain. The Blue chair (a real beginner double claiming to be "the shortest, lowest, slowest, unscariest lift in America"), the Gold chair (a higher, faster triple) and a small fenced-off nursery slope are within shouting distance of the day lodge. If you're a better skier, you might use Gold chair to boomerang back downhill to the Red chair, with a midstation load just for such purposes. Or you can also go directly to either the Red or Copper chair, the two that are just at the edge of town. For years the Red chair (at $1\frac{1}{2}$ miles is New Mexico's second-longest), was the area's big lift which meant that it sometimes spawned big lines. But when the Copper chair was added in 1993–94, some of the pressure came off the

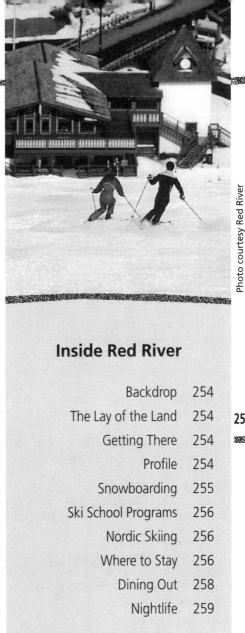

older lift and Red River recaptured its reputation as uncrowded. Some trails are straightforward and easy to find and easy to ski. Others are challenging, and some even require knowing which cut-off to take, which outcropping to skirt or which little midmountain hill to climb.

Between them, the Red and Copper chairlifts access the entire steep frontside. Still, trail cutting was clever, and you can find every kind of run that can be cut through dense woods: trails like Cowpoke's Cruise and Broadway bulldozed and groomed to ballroom width and smoothness, mellow mid-range runs like Boom Town and No Name, which is equally suitable for traversing low intermediates and rocketing advanced skiers, and true gut-gripping steeps. Maverick is a short shot, which is good for testing your ski legs before embarking on longer pitches. You need to do a little prospecting to find Mine Shaft, which is tucked around a corner and up a little hill, and because it requires a short climb, gets less traffic and holds new snow well. Bad Medicine is Red River's steepest run, and Linton's Leap its newest black-diamond run, which is easy to find under the Copper chair. If you can ski Catskinner to Airplane to Landstrip, Red River's black-diamond daisy chain, with no problems, you can consider yourself a very good skier.

Red River's backside runs are far gentler and more sheltered. If you follow a ridgetop run called Re-Run from the summit, you can select from two chairlifts serving two sides of a high ridge and two different types of terrain. You'll first get to the top station of the Green chair, which accesses gentle and exceptionally pretty runs lacing through large stands of aspen that dapple the snow in a beguiling pattern of light and shadow. This is also where you'll find the outstanding children's terrain garden. Keep going and you'll reach the Silver chair, Red River's only upper-mountain triple, and trails that are somewhat more challenging. This neat division enables skiers on the cusp to move up from green-circle runs to more difficult terrain to see how they do, or recent graduates to the blue-square realm to retreat and regroup on the blues. From the summit, two long novice-caliber roads snake down the frontside, which is necessary when all the mid-level skiing is over the top and in the back.

Inside Red River

SNOWBOARDING

Snowboards and snowskates are welcome at Red River. The combination of wide runs, consistent fall-line terrain and commendable steeps on the frontside and snowboardable glades on the backside suits riders well.

SKI SCHOOL PROGRAMS

For information and reservations, call the **Ski School Hot Line, (505) 754-2223.**

Introductory Program
First Time Skier: 1¹/₂-hour beginner class (Level 1); classes given in morning and afternoon sessions.

Advanced and Specialty Programs
Parallel Breakthrough: For novice to intermediate skiers (Levels 2 to 5) looking to move from a wedge to a parallel turn. Meets at Red River Ski Lodge.

Style & Technique Workshop: Afternoon workshop for intermediate and advanced skiers (Levels 4 to 9) focusing on skills to make skiers more elegant, graceful and competent. Meets at Red River Ski Lodge.

Bump Workshop: Afternoon classes for Levels 7 to 9 on mogul technique. Meets at Ski Tip Restaurant.

Steeps: Challenging afternoon workshop for Levels 8 and 9 on black-diamond skills. Meets at Ski Tip Restaurant.

Racer Tune-Up: Intense gate-training workshop, offered Tuesdays, Thursdays and Sundays for Levels 5 through 9. Meets at Ski Tip Restaurant.

For Families
The new Youth Ski Center is headquarters for children's programs. For day care and children's program reservations, call **Ski School Hot Line, (505) 754-2223.**

Nonskiing Children
Buckaroo Child Care: Half- and full-day care and play for ages 6 months to 4 years. Located in the Youth Ski Center. Reservations are accepted for all periods, strongly recommended for holidays and other peak periods.

Skiing Children
Kinderplay: Morning and afternoon lessons for ages 4 and 5, with supervision and lunch. Rental equipment option.

Kinderski: All-day program with morning and afternoon lesson and lunch, or half-day lesson, for ages 6 through 10. Rental equipment option.

Mountain Stats— Red River

Resort elevation 8,750 feet
Top of highest lift 10,350 feet
Bottom of lowest lift 8,750 feet
Total vertical 1,600 feet
Longest run 2 miles
Average annual snowfall 200 inches
Ski season Thanksgiving to the end of March
Lifts 2 triple chairlifts, 4 doubles, 1 tow
Capacity 7,920 skiers per hour
Terrain 58 trails, 220 acres (31% beginner and novice, 38% intermediate, 31% advanced and expert)
Snowmaking 75%
Mountain dining Ski Tip at the summit
Snow reports (505) 754-2220

NORDIC SKIING

Enchanted Forest, New Mexico's largest cross-country center, is 3¹/₂ miles east of downtown Red River. More than 30 kilometers of trails wind through deep forests and across meadows, groomed for classic skiing and skating, and offering great views of the Wheeler and Latier Wilderness areas and several peaks and valleys. With a congenial warming hut, a full instruction program, patrol and calendar full of special events, it offers many of the amenities of a downhill area—but without the lifts and at a much lower cost. **(505) 754-2374, (505) 754-2240.**

WHERE TO STAY

Most lodges offer ski packages, and many participate in the Kids Ski Free/Stay Free promotion on stays of three days or longer. For information and further referrals, call the **Red River Chamber of Commerce, (800) 348-6444.**

Mid-Priced Accommodations
Alpine Lodge
Forty-five-unit chalet-style complex across from the Red chair, with lodge room, apartment and

cabin accommodations. AAA rated and senior discounts. In-room phones—no big deal elsewhere, but unusual in Red River. Daily housekeeping. Restaurant, lounge, hot tub, guest laundry. **P.O. Box 67, Red River, NM 87558; (800) 525-2333, (505) 754-2952.**

The Lodge at Red River

Local charm leader. Delightfully restored Main Street lodge, with 27 antique-filled, wood-paneled rooms. Restaurant, lobby bar, fireplace, guest library and entertainment center. Daily housekeeping. **P.O. Box 189, Red River, NM 87558; (800) 915-6343, (505) 754-6280.**

Ponderosa Lodge

Homey one- to five-bedroom wood-paneled suites with fireplaces and kitchens. AAA-rated. In-room phones. On a hillside, overlooking town. Pets permitted. Sauna, spa, guest laundry. Daily housekeeping. **P.O. Box 528, Red River, NM 87558; (800) 336-RSVP, (505) 754-2988.**

Terrace Towers Lodge

Cutely decorated lodge with hearts emblazoned on fences, shutters and elsewhere. One-bedroom apartments. Three blocks from lift. Hot tub. Daily housekeeping. **P.O. Box 149, Red River, NM 87558; (800) 695-6343, (505) 754-2962.**

El Western Lodge

Ski-in/ski-out at base of the Copper chair. Rustic log-cabin ambiance. Sixteen spacious lodge rooms and eight two-bedroom cabins with kitchen and fireplace. Deluxe guest house for 8 to 16, suitable for families and groups. Daily housekeeping. Hot tub, coin laundry. **P.O. Box 589, Red River, NM 87558; (800) 548-5713, (505) 754-2272.**

Economy Accommodations

Arrowhead Lodge

One-story motel-style building with 19 one- to three-bedroom units, most with kitchens and some with fireplaces. Located close to the ski area day lodge, easy walk to lifts. **P.O. Box 261, Red River, NM 87558; (800) 299-6547, (505) 754-2255.**

Black Mountain Lodge

Ten kitchenette units, all with enclosed ski racks and some with fireplaces. Ski-in/ski-out. Daily housekeeping. Glass-enclosed hot tub, large game room. **P.O. Box 787, Red River, NM 87558; (800) 825-2469, (505) 754-2469.**

Golden Eagle Lodge

Recently renovated chalet-style lodge nestled in the trees. Twenty one- and two-bedroom units, some with fireplace and/or kitchen. Daily housekeeping. **P.O. Box 869, Red River, NM 87558; (800) 621-4046, (505) 754-2227.**

Lazy Miner Lodge

Cute western-style lodge on Main Street, two blocks from lifts. One-, two- and three-bedroom apartments, most with kitchens and/or fireplaces. In-room phones and coffee pot. Schmidlapp's Ice Cream Parlor downstairs. Daily housekeeping. Glass-enclosed hot tub. **P.O. Box 836, Red River, NM 87558; (800) 766-4637, (505) 754-6444.**

Pioneer Lodge

Central location, half a block from the lift. Cabin-style accommodations with fireplaces and kitchens. Pets permitted. Hot tub, game room. Daily housekeeping. **P.O. Box 550, Red River, NM 87558; (800) 542-0154, (505) 754-2291.**

Silver Spur Mountain Lodge

Ski-in/ski-out. Efficiency apartments, two-bedroom cabins (some with fireplaces), one-bedroom suites and RV hookups. Some of the least expensive rooms in town. Daily housekeeping. **P.O. Box 174, Red River, NM 87558; (800) 545-8372, (505) 754-2378.**

Sportsman's Lodge

Rustic, low-slung motel with one- and two-bedroom kitchenette units and motel rooms with fireplaces. In-room phones. Pets permitted. Daily housekeeping. Game room. **P.O. Box 175, Red River, NM 87558; (800) 367-7329, (505) 754-2273.**

Noteworthy

Red River participates in the Ski 3 discount card with Taos Ski Valley and Angel Fire.

Timberline Lodge

Two-story, family-owned and family-friendly motel. Motel rooms; some kitchen facilities. Next to Community House; close to river and lifts. Daily housekeeping. **P.O. Box 9, Red River, NM 87558; (800) 284-0899, (505) 754-6114.**

Condominiums

Caribel Condos

Thirty-two one- and two-bedroom condominiums with fireplaces and full kitchens. Some motel-style rooms also available. On spacious grounds, one block from lift and Main Street. Senior discounts. In-room phones, guest laundry, heated pool. Daily housekeeping. **P.O. Box 590, Red River, NM 87558; (800) 237-7310, (505) 754-2313.**

Edelweiss

Comfortable condos with fully equipped kitchens, fireplaces and phones. Heated pool, sauna, guest laundry. Daily housekeeping. **P.O. Box 730, Red River, NM 87558; (800) 445-6077, (505) 754-2942.**

Eisenhut

Luxurious and spacious three- and four-bedroom condominiums, with fireplaces, full kitchens and two bathrooms. Walking distance to lifts. senior discounts. Outdoor heated pool, hot tub, game room, guest laundry. Daily housekeeping. **P.O. Box 305, Red River, NM 87558; (800) 222-3488, (505) 754-2326.**

Lifts West

Eighty-three contemporary condos built around three-story atrium lobby with giant stone fireplace and shops. Front desk and other hotel-style facilities. AAA-rated. In-room phones. Ski lockers, heated indoor pool, two hot tubs, restaurant. **P.O. Box 330, Red River, NM 87558; (800) 221-8159, (505) 754-2778.**

Valley Condominiums

Twenty-three two-bedroom fireplace units and one five-bedroom behemoth suitable for large, extended family group. Creekside location. In-room phones. Restaurant, hot tub. **P.O. Box 309, Red River, NM 87558; (800) 333-2398, (505) 754-2403.**

Woodlands

Streamside location at the foot of the mountains. Fireplace units. In-room phones. Daily housekeeping. Heated pool, guest laundry. **P.O. Box 279, Red River, NM 87558; (800) 762-6469.**

Rentals of townhouses, cabins and private homes are handled by
Bandanna Red River Properties, (800) 521-4389, (505) 754-2949
Red River Real Estate, (800) 453-3498, (505) 754-2459
Reservations Unlimited, (800) 545-6415, (505) 754-6415

Noteworthy

The Moon Star Mining Camp boasts wonderful hidden trails threaded through the trees off the Green chair. These children's favorites include such theme areas as Fort McCows, Animals of the Forest, Tree House, Indian Village and Hoop-de-Doo Haven. The entire Gold and Blue chair areas, the bottom of the Red chair and the Green Acres trail under the Green chair are designated slow-skiing zones. Children 12 and under may participate in free races on Gold Rush Hill every Saturday, with prizes awarded by age category.

Many Red River lodgings participate in **Kids Ski Free/Stay Free** offers on packages of three days or longer with a paying adult; call **(800) 331-SNOW** for details.

DINING OUT

Angelina's

Southwestern specialties, grilled trout, steak and sandwiches. Big soup and salad bar. Lunch and dinner served. Children's menu. Casual. **Main St., Red River; (505) 754-2211.**

Brett's Homestead Steakhouse

Relaxed, homelike restaurant. Great steaks, prime rib, seafood and trout. Children's menu.

258

Sizable wine list. Reservations recommended. **West Main** at **High Cost Trail, Red River; (505) 754-6136.**

Lodge at Red River
Pleasant lodge dining room serving breakfast, lunch and dinner. Popular American and international dishes. Nightly all-you-can-eat specials. **Main St., Red River; (505) 754-6280.**

Sundance Restaurant
Mexican and New Mexican specialties. Stuffed sopapillas, fajitas and chilies relleños, plus steak. Children's menu. Drink specialty is frozen wine margarita; domestic and imported wines and beers served too. Children's menu. **High St., Red River; (505) 754-2971.**

Texas Red's Steakhouse & Saloon
Lively drinking and dining place right on Main Street. Established in 1967 and cranking ever since. Dinner reservations recommended. **Main St., Red River; (505) 754-2922.**

NIGHTLIFE

The party-hardy Texans flock to this funky resort town for fun in the sun (and after it sets too). Après-ski starts at the Lifthouse at the bottom of the Red chair. This popular bar pours copious amounts of beer, as well as such special drinks as spiked hot apple pie, coffee and hot chocolate. The action moves, virtually undiminished, to the center of town, just a block away where it's easy to slide into the scene with terrific bands, big dance floors and happy folks taking advantage of both. The Motherlode, Texas Red's and Bull o' the Woods see a good bit of evening action—as does

This aerial view of the Red River Ski resort shows just one aspect of the ski area's layout.

anyplace with a TV and a few barstools when the Cowboys, the Oilers or any other Texas pro team is playing. Families head for the Playhouse at the Black Mountain Lodge, featuring video games, ping pong, air hockey and other diversions.

One of skiing's great traditions, a torchlight parade, takes place at 7:00 P.M. on Christmas Eve, New Year's Eve and every Saturday during the ski season, far more frequently than any other Rockies resort. Torch-bearing skiers glide down beside the Red chair. The slow-flowing glow of their lights is visible from all over town, but the Lifthouse provides the best vantage point. Party time is just about anytime, but the revelry really cranks up during Mardi Gras. While the world is descending on New Orleans for its pre-Lenten bacchanalia, Louisianans and their sympathizers are enjoying Red River's version. Masquerade balls, Cajun music and a parade now and then highlight the festivities.

For more information, contact **Red River Ski Area, P.O. Box 9000, Red River, NM 87558; (505) 754-2382,** or **Red River Chamber of Commerce, P.O. Box 870, Red River, NM 87558; (800) 348-6444.**

259

ANGEL FIRE

BACKDROP

Angel Fire is a ski and golf resort with few frills and no pretensions. Skiers may be drawn by modest prices, but those who stay and ski and often return are also delighted with the low-key, friendly atmosphere and the emphasis on family skiing and family vacationing. After years of financial problems, with stability at last and the kind of investment that various generations of managers have said is needed for new lifts and other improvements, Angel Fire's appeals should continue to grow.

260 THE LAY OF THE LAND

Angel Fire is a year-round resort development perched in a saucer-sided trough on the side of a mountain in the Sangre de Cristo Range in the area of Wheeler Peak, New Mexico's highest mountain. The Moreno Valley's broad, flat expanse spreads below and Agua Fria Peak rises above the resort, which itself was once ranchland. The open space that is a legacy of the valley's ranching era, surrounding pine woods and snow-covered slopes form the landscape. Angel Fire Village includes shops, restaurants and services, with the ski area base at the top of the hill. The ski runs drape across a wide portion of a complex mountain. The main base area is at the resort itself, while a smaller, auxiliary base on the backside of the mountain can be reached by a long road up a side valley.

GETTING THERE

Angel Fire is 150 miles northeast of Albuquerque. Take I-25 north to Santa Fe, then US 84/185 north to Española, New Mexico 68 east to Taos, New Mexico 64 east and then New Mexico 434 south to Angel Fire. Transportation between Albuquerque and Angel Fire is available from **Enchanted Circle Tour & Coaches, (505) 754-3154,** and **Faust's Transportation, (505) 758-3410, (505) 377-3400 in Angel Fire.** You don't need a car at the resort, where a shuttle operates throughout the village from 8:00 A.M. to 9:00 P.M. for a nominal fee.

PROFILE

Angel Fire's ski terrain is something like an iceberg. The "tip" that is visible from the base is but a tiny portion of what is hidden out of sight above. When you look up the hill from the resort base, you can see some beginner terrain, two chairlifts (referred to as #1 and #2) and two wide slopes. The scene is more reminiscent of a Midwestern ski area than a Rocky Mountain one, and the immediate thought that springs into mind is, "Is that all?" The frontside, though indeed modest, makes for wonderful teaching and recreational racing terrain. And no, that isn't all—not by a longshot. To get to the majority of the terrain, you have to ski down a small slope to the chairlift serving the majority of Angel Fire's frontside runs and its entire Back Basin. This lift is now a high-speed quad climbing up the side of the mountain and paring to under ten minutes a ride that used to take nearly half an hour on two chairs.

Photo courtesy Angel Fire Resort

Angel Fire got a new lease on life with new owners in 1996.

The new quad chair makes it feasible to explore the front of the mountain and actually get in a lot of runs. The trails are varied, interesting and exceptionally pretty, but with the old slow chairs, they were way underskied. Once you get off the quad, New Mexico's first express chair, you can show off on a steep liftline slash directly below called Upper Domino, or you can drop into another black diamond option called Sluice Box. But if you ski off to the right, as most people do, you'll reach a long road called Headin' Home. This scenic sensuous green-circle enables even novices to ski from the top. It also accesses a great range of wonderful intermediate trails. Some are wide cruisers. Others are narrow paths. Some are nice manageable glades. The upper ones feed back to the liftline, where it tames down from black to blue. About halfway down the mountain, a few additional green-circle options become available. The terrain on this part of the mountain is interesting and varied, and the absence of that old tedious lift ride should notch it up on the popularity charts.

If you ski over a knoll from the top of the quad, you'll reach an ultra-gentle mountaintop run called Angel Food. Novices can stay here for hours, practicing on a this wide slope and riding Lift #3. But Angel Food also feeds skiers into the Back Basin. If you have true expert blood in your veins, try the radical run called Hell's Bells, and if that blood is racing, drop your ski tips into Maxwell's Grant, Silver Chute, Angel's Plunge. This trio may not be as challenging as Taos's steepest, but they match or surpass most other black-diamond trails in the state. The Back Basin isn't all radical, however. You can traverse from the top of Lift #3 along Highway and take your pick of greens and blues, with only a couple of blacks thrown in for good measure. Hully Gully, Arriva and Motherlode are among the wonderful mid-level cruisers on this sector of the ski area. The name Back Basin carries strong implications as to how this terrain fits into the scheme of things, an impression skiers riding lifts and skiing over from the resort base also get. It looks

Photo courtesy Angel Fire Resort

Inside Angel Fire

and feels like the backside of the ski area, but in fact, the Back Basin's bottom is an additional base area. A road leads up from the valley, and you'll find a parking area and day lodge—sort of like finding a flag planted on the bottom of an iceberg.

SNOWBOARDING

At this writing, a frontside snowboard park between Exhibition and Gusto Grande is in the works, with access from the top of #2 and the new quad. In addition, a popular two-race slalom competition and a thrilling banked slalom race have put Angel Fire on riders' maps.

SKI SCHOOL PROGRAMS

Introductory Program

Beginner Special: Lift tickets, rentals, and two $1^3/4$-hour group lessons. Meet at the Village Haus

Young shovel racer prepares to enter the "little scoops" division of Angel Fire's world Shovel Race Championships. Photo courtesy Angel Fire Resort

Mountain Stats— Angel Fire

Resort elevation 8,600 feet
Top of highest lift 10,650 feet
Bottom of lowest lift 8,600 feet
Total vertical 2,050 feet
Longest run 3.2 miles
Average annual snowfall 210 inches
Ski season late November through early April
Lifts 1 high-speed quad chairlift, 4 doubles, 1 tow
Capacity 8,100 skiers per hour
Terrain 58 trails, 391 acres (33% beginner and novice, 59% intermediate, 8% advanced and expert)
Snowmaking 50% of trails
Snow reports (505) 377-4222, (800) 633-7463, Ext. 4222
Note Half-day ticket begins at noon.

---

base. Guarantee that first-time adult skier will be able to ride beginner chairlift and do linked wedge turns; lesson can be repeated at no charge until this is accomplished.

Advanced and Specialty Programs

Skiers Special: Morning or afternoon classes of all ability levels, packaged to include all-lifts ticket and all-day rentals.

For Racers

Pole Bangers Race Clinics: Available on group or private lesson basis at the bottom of the NASTAR hill.

For Families

Nonskiing Children

Angel Fire Day Camp: Day care for ages 6 weeks to skiing age. Charges by the hour (more for tots in diapers, less for those out of diapers). Parents must supply full cold lunch; no facilities available for heating food. Nursery is located across from fire station. Reservations recommended.

Skiing Children

Children's Skiing Center: Full-day and afternoon SKIwee and MINIrider programs for ages 3 to 12, including lift tickets, rentals, instruction, supervision, lunch and snacks. Reduction if child has own equipment. Children's Center is located at the bottom of Lift #4. Reservations recommended. Children enrolled in five-day program pay for four days and get fifth day free. Children ages 3 to 5 advance according to their ability and energy. Program guarantees that children ages 6 and over will be able to ride chairlifts comfortably and ski from the top of the mountain.

NORDIC SKIING

At this writing, the closest track skiing is at Enchanted Forest (see Red River chapter, page 256), but Nordies with their own gear do ski on the Angel Fire Golf Course, which once was also used as a cross-country center with set tracks and other facilities. In the first couple of seasons under the new regime, skiers with their own cross-country gear can still use the golf course, but no facilities exist. Angel Fire's expansion plan includes a comprehensive Nordic center on the backside. It will probably include rentals, instruction and groomed trails. The earliest it could be in place is for the 1997–98 ski season.

Noteworthy

Dream Catcher is Angel Fire's new beginner area, on the frontside's far right, featuring a wide open slope of extreme gentleness and a double chairllift. It is not accessible from above, so downbound traffic does not interfere with new skiers' first turns. The ski school offers guarantee features, as outlined above. Angel Fire has designated several slow-skiing areas. Seniors 65 and older ski free.

WHERE TO STAY

Angel Fire can be booked through the ski area's reservation service at **(800) 633-7463.**

Mid-Priced Accommodations

Barbara's Bed & Breakfast
Four-room B&B, all with fireplaces and private baths. Three miles from ski area. Guest laundry, full breakfast, daily housekeeping. **P.O. Box 12, Angel Fire, NM 87710; (800) 847-9779, (505) 377-6529.**

Elkhorn Lodge
Two-story cedar building. Elegant 15-room lodge, with some suites. Four blocks from lifts. Daily housekeeping, restaurant. **P.O. Box 274, Angel Fire, NM 87710; (505) 377-2811.**

Hill House Bed & Breakfast
Two rooms with private baths in owner's home. Can be converted into commodious suite sleeping up to 12. Known for excellent baked goods at breakfast. **P.O. Box 793, Angel Fire, NM 87710; (800) 621-2965, (505) 377-6055.**

The Legends Hotel
Slopeside hotel, with 157 rooms, at the bottom of **263** Lifts #1 and #2. Simple and contemporary decor with a hint of Southwestern inspiration. Centerpiece of resort development. Restaurants, lounge, shops, game room, multilevel spa complex with indoor pool, hot tub, exercise equipment, game room. Twenty-four-hour front desk, daily housekeeping, room service. **P.O. Drawer B, Angel Fire, NM 87710; (800) 633-7463, (505) 377-6401.**

Mountain Creek Bed & Breakfast
Located between Angel Fire and Taos and convenient for skiers who want to sample both areas. Two private rooms with fireplaces. Additional kitchenette unit. Located on 5 acres, bordering on Carson National Forest. Hot tub, full breakfast, daily housekeeping. Massage and yoga available. **Route 1, Box 49, Taos, NM, 87571; (800) 717-4695, (505) 751-TAOS.**

Condominiums and Homes

Angel Fire Property Management
Resort's property management department. Handles 115 private homes and condominiums. All with kitchens, some with fireplaces. Access to The Legends Hotel's swimming pool, hot tub and other facilities included in rates. Ski packages.

Two-night minimum on weekend arrivals. **P.O. Drawer B, Angel Fire, NM 87710; (800) 633-7463, (505) 377-6401.**

Four Seasons Property Management
Forty-five condominiums and private homes. Many with fireplaces, some with guest laundry or washer and dryer and/or hot tub. Pets permitted in some. Packages. **P.O. Box 430, Angel Fire, NM 87710; (800) 888-6062, (505) 377-6062.**

Pinetree Commons
Twenty-three condo units near lifts. All with kitchens, washer and dryer and fireplaces. Pets permitted. Ski packages. **Angel Fire, NM 87710; (800) 477-3616, (505) 377-3616.**

ReMax of Angel Fire
Property Management
Ten homes and condos, all with kitchens and some with fireplaces and washer/dryer. Two-night minimum. **P.O. Box 639, Angel Fire, NM 87710; (800) 884-6640, (505) 377-3999.**

264

Resort Properties of Angel Fire
Manages 115 homes and condominiums, all with kitchens and some with fireplace, washer and dryer, hot tub, and/or sauna. Two-night minimum (five at Christmas). **P.O. Box 829, Angel Fire, NM 87710; (800) 338-2589, (505) 377-2312.**

The Legends Hotel at the base of Angel Fire offers guests convenient ski-in/ski-out accommodations.

Photo courtesy Angel Fire Resort

DINING OUT

Angel Fire Country Club
Golf course restaurant opened weekends in 1995-96, with weekday and perhaps expanded service to follow. An instant fixture on Angel Fire's dining scene. Stylish and contemporary cuisine, with all the implied creativity and presentation. Complex pasta creations and other signature entrées. Clubby lodgelike ambiance. Reservations recommended. **Angel Fire Golf Course, Angel Fire; (505) 377-4271.**

Bandana's
Open and spacious dining room with good views. Upstairs eatery serving Mexican fare, chicken-fried steak and other popular dishes at dinner. Family favorite. Beer and wine also available. **Village Center, Angel Fire; (505) 377-3115.**

Elkhorn Lodge Restaurant
Spacious restaurant with western look. Rock floor and wood-beamed ceiling. Breakfast, lunch and dinner. American and Mexican dishes, with a fine-dining flair. Offers the gamut from game to vegetarian specialties. **Hwy 434, Angel Fire; (505) 377-2811.**

The Mill
Main hotel restaurant, serving three meals a day. Informal and pleasant. Light and hearty breakfast classics; salads, sandwiches and Mexican favorites at lunch, and light or more substantial fare at dinner. Takeout available. Beer, wine and cocktails served. **The Legends Hotel, Angel Fire; (505) 377-6401.**

Morning, Noon & Night
Bakery and deli serving interesting specialty menu. Excellent baked goods, deli sandwiches and gourmet coffee drinks featured. Sometimes live entertainment. **Hwy 434, Angel Fire; (505) 377-6845.**

Pizza Stop
Family-friendly dispensary of pizza, sandwiches, spaghetti and stromboli. Delivery available within village. Beer and wine. Senior citizens' discount. Open daily except Tuesdays for lunch and dinner. **Village Center, Angel Fire; (505) 377-6340.**

Rocky Mountain Barbecue & Grill

Full line of hickory-smoked barbecue. Half-pound burgers, chicken-fried steak and Mexican specialties. Also, vegetarian items. Children's menu. **Hwy 434, Angel Fire; (505) 377-2763.**

Springers

Lovely dining room at The Legends Hotel, serving popular beef, lamb, pasta, Mexican and seafood entrées. Also, chef's choice selections, including Cornish hen, rack of lamb or chateaubriand for two, veal piccata and lobster tail. Salad bar. Children's menu. Beer, wine and cocktail service. Reservations recommended. **The Legends Hotel, Angel Fire; (505) 377-6401.**

Zebadiah's

Breakfast, lunch and dinner in publike restaurant. Long bar and casual table service. Good Mexican food, sandwiches, soup and salad bar, steak and chicken. **Hwy 434, Angel Fire; (505) 377-6358.**

NIGHTLIFE

Après-ski starts at the Village Haus Restaurant and Bar, at the main base, and at Mother Mogul's at the bottom of Lift #6 in the Back Basin. There's live entertainment weekends and holidays at the Village Haus. You can catch some of the spillover action without the booze element at the Siberian Espresso & Tea House on the deck next to Lift #2. Specialty coffees, soft drinks, fresh baked goods and even ice cream are served—and are great on warm spring afternoons. Annie O's in the Legends Hotel features sporting events on a big-screen television and often live entertainment too. The game room in the covered walkway between the hotel and the ski area is called The Legendary Arena. It's more than just a hangout, putting on weekly contests for games and prizes, including sports memorabilia, for skill in popular video games. Bring plenty of quarters. Down on Hwy 434, Zebadiah's Lounge has a full bar, big-screen TV and often live entertainment, and Morning, Noon & Night may also have live entertainment to go with their gourmet coffees and delicious baked goods. The relaxing lounge at the Angel Fire Country Club on the golf course is opening in winter for the first time for the 1996–97 ski season.

For more information, contact **Angel Fire Resort, P.O. Drawer B, Angel Fire, NM 87710; (800) 633-7463, (505) 377-6401; Angel Fire Chamber of Commerce, P.O. Box 547, Angel Fire, NM 87710; (800) 446-8117, (505) 377-6661.**

SKI APACHE

ridge. The base facilities are those of a simple day-trip area, with lifts rising from pine-covered lower slopes to the tree-free summit at an 11,500-foot elevation.

BACKDROP

Ski Apache is distinctive in several ways. Closer to El Paso than to Denver, Albuquerque or any other traditional gateway to Rocky Mountain skiing, it is America's southernmost major ski area. It also is the only ski resort in the country owned and operated by an Indian tribe, and it is uniquely situated partly in the Lincoln National Forest and partly on Mescalero Apache land. It has New Mexico's greatest hourly lift capacity, including the state's only gondola. Most of the accommodations are in the town of Ruidoso, a classic mountain getaway, with eclectic architecture and a benign year-round climate that is cooler than the coast, desert or the Plains in summer, is near skiing but gets little snow in winter and is beautiful throughout the year. Prices are moderate, and economical lift-lodging packages abound. An option to staying in Ruidoso is the Inn of the Mountain Gods, a sprawling convention-style hotel on reservation land. It is decorated with Native American themes, and if you like to gamble, you'll find the hotel's on-site casino a convenient diversion.

266

THE LAY OF THE LAND

Ruidoso nestles in an east-west mountain valley, rich in nature's landscaping of ponderosa and piñon pine and very temperate in climate. This sizable town has many shops, galleries, restaurants and a large number of cabin accommodations. Upper Canyon on the west end of town is the heart of Ruidoso's original and traditional vacation lodgings. Sudderth Drive is the main street, and Mechem Drive heads up toward the ski area. Sierra Blanca Peak, cresting at 12,003 feet over sea level, is a huge mountain roughly north of town. It looms high over the surrounding countryside, with Ski Apache on its mighty north

GETTING THERE

Ruidoso is 130 miles north of El Paso via US 54 north and US 70, and 195 miles south of Albuquerque via I-25 or US 40 to Carrizozo, then US 380 east, to New Mexico 37 south to Alto, and New Mexico 48 into town. Rental cars are available at both airports. Since the town sprawls, a car is useful, but you can get along without one if you are staying at the Inn of the Mountain Gods or at a central spot in Ruidoso. You can reach the town via **Greyhound New Mexico Transit, (505) 257-2660.** To get from Ruidoso to Ski Apache, take Hwy 48 north for 6 miles, then Hwy 532, also called Ski Run Rd., 12 miles west to the base. To avoid this hairpinny road and too many drivers inexperienced and ill-equipped for mountain driving, it's often worth paying for transportation. **S&S Shuttle** runs morning and afternoon buses with stops along Sudderth or Mechem Drives, two main Ruidoso thoroughfares, and en route to the mountain. Reservations required (before 10:00 P.M. the night before), **(505) 378-4456.**

PROFILE

Ski Apache's base area looks simple and standard (a big parking lot, a miscellany of service buildings, beginner slopes and the loading zones for three major lifts), but it is merely a prelude to a large and complex ski area. Two long, steep-sided ridges, one broad gully between them and a vast, 200-acre mountaintop bowl provide a lot of skiing. Because the area is so attractive to new and occasional skiers, Ski Apache's many steep runs remain astonishingly uncrowded, even during peak times.

The four-passenger gondola is literally the king of the hill, rising up the spine of the main ridge to a plateau at the end of a ridge. The see-

forever view from the mountaintop lodge is of Ruidoso's forested valley, the vast Tularosa Basin, and the shimmering White Sands desert. Distant mountains line the horizon, while the summit proper of Sierra Blanca Peak looms some 600 feet higher. The near view is of a good chunk of Ski Apache's terrain. As you look downhill to the right, you'll see the vastness of Apache Bowl. There's not a tree on the upper sections, and just a few brave and hardy pines are sprinkled on the slope partway down. If you want to lap the bowl, keep riding the #6 triple. You don't have to be an expert for this bowl, however. Its moderate, steady pitch makes it suitable for strong intermediates, but the crenulated and textured terrain keeps it interesting for experts too. The Apache Bowl runout, a long cruiser called Deep Freeze, follows the gully all the way to the base.

The greatest concentration of pure expert runs is the procession of steep trails, chutes and glades cascading down the other side of the ridge. You can drop into the likes of Wild Onion, Incredible, The Terrible, Screaming Eagle and Roy's Run. These steeps, which on any given day may be powdery, bumpy, chopped or recently groomed, but the mountain does let at least two trails mogul up. If you like this sector but prefer a little less challenge, you can explore half-a-dozen intermediate runs on the high end of the ridge. Novices ski the Sierra Blanca Trail, an easy road swooping down this side from the summit, and better skiers can use it as a midway drop-in or bail-out from the steeps. All these runs eventually end up in Moonshine Gully, which is very long, very wide and very easy—and leads back to the lifts. If this section of Ski Apache is your cup of tea, you can ride the #1 triple chair over and over.

Elk Ridge, whose upper reaches form one side of Apache Bowl, is the ski area's newest section. The #8 chairlift, a fixed-grip quad, covers about half the potential vertical on this ridge. The runs down into a smaller gully aren't long, but compensate in pitch and width. The attractive day lodge at the base of the Elk chair at first seems out of the way, but it is so pleasant that it's worth skiing this part of the area around midday. As is the case with the upper mountain, Elk Ridge just

Inside Ski Apache

doesn't get the crowds, because it's beyond the ability of Ski Apache's legions of beginners. The place where you will find hordes is a hillock called Capitan, which is between the main and Elk areas. If you can ignore the traffic, you'll find it one of Ski Apache's delightful surprises. It's 475 vertical feet of fun—wide as a football field and steadily pitched for warm-ups, short confidence-building cruising or a quick last run at the end of a perfect day.

SNOWBOARDING

Ski Apache allows snowboarding and offers lessons for all abilities. Apache Bowl is unquestionably the riders' favorite. Sparse trees, dips, snow humps and no flats make for great riding. Even better, imprinted on the bowl's 200 acres are wonderful natural half-pipes, which are actually snow-laden erosion lines that in summer are 20 to 30 feet deep. Upper Deep Freeze, the bowl's runout, has a similar quality and is great for snowboarding too.

268

SKI SCHOOL PROGRAMS

Introductory Program

First Time Beginner Special: Free lift ticket with purchase of beginner lesson. Available for skiers and snowboarders. Staggered lesson times, starting at 9:30 A.M. Half-day and two-day options. All packages with or without rental equipment. Available for ages 6 and above.

Noteworthy

Children's group lessons are held at the same time as adults', enabling parents and children to ski together before and after their classes. Children 5 and under receive a free one-day lift ticket if they are enrolled in a private lesson.

Mountain Stats— Ski Apache

Resort elevation 6,800 feet (Ruidoso)
Top of highest lift 11,500 feet
Bottom of lowest lift 9,600 feet
Total vertical 1,900 feet
Longest run 2.7 miles
Average annual snowfall 185 inches
Ski season Thanksgiving to Easter
Lifts one 4-passenger gondola, 2 quad chairlifts, 5 triples, 1 double, 1 tow
Capacity 15,300 skiers per hour
Terrain 53 trails, 750 acres (20% beginner and novice, 35% intermediate, 45% advanced and expert)
Snowmaking lower $1/3$ of the mountain
Mountain dining Gazebo Snack Bar at the top of the gondola; Lookout Snack Bar at the top of the Apache Bowl lift
Snow reports (505) 257-9001

Advanced and Specialty Programs

Master Classes: For nonbeginner skiers and snowboarders. Offered daily.
Women's Seminars: Eight-week program of weekly classes for women, taught by women.
Men's Master Seminars: Same program, for men.

Special Programs

Ski Tips for the Master Skier: Free tips from an instructor, given a 9:15 A.M. on Saturday and Sunday mornings.

For Families

Nonskiing Children
No nursery or day care at Ski Apache. Guests are referred to **Tender Tots, (505) 257-5784,** in Ruidoso. Accepts infants and up. Reservations required for infants, requested for ages 2 and older.

Skiing Children
Kiddie Corral: Full-day program with lifts, instruction, supervision and lunch for 4- and 5-year-olds. Optional rental equipment at modest add-on. First-come, first-served. Capacity of indoor facility doubled for 1996–97 season.

Children's Classes: Regular ski classes, grouped by age and ability, for ages 6 and above.

HANDICAPPED SKIING

Ski Apache offers instruction for physically handicapped, developmentally disabled or visually impaired skiers.

NORDIC SKIING

No cross-country centers are found near Ruidoso, but there are several touring routes on Forest Service roads, which are not groomed but are easy to follow. The most popular is along the Buck Mountain Road, with access from the same canyon as Ski Apache, with the Crest Trail and Monjeau Roads as runners-up.

Noteworthy

Ski school and many area services staffed with Spanish-speaking employees. Free overnight storage for equipment rented from the area's ski and snowboard shops.

WHERE TO STAY

For information and referrals, call **(800) 253-2255.**

Luxury Accommodations

The Enchantment Inn

Adobe-style inn is Ruidoso's most luxurious hotel. Eighty comfortable rooms, including 29 suites with spa tubs and kitchenettes. Southwestern decor. Restaurant, lounge, indoor pool, hot tub. Daily housekeeping, room service. **307 Hwy 70 West, Ruidoso, NM 88340; (800) 435-0280, (505) 378-4051.**

Inn of the Mountain Gods

Large and rather lavish hotel complex, with 253 rooms in several buildings. Southwestern and Native American decor. Only $3^1/2$ miles southwest of town. Ski packages. Daily housekeeping, 24-hour front desk, bell staff, room service. Restaurant, lounge, casino, card room, video arcade, shops, fireplace lobby, outdoor heated pool, saunas. **P.O. Box 26, Mescalero, NM 88340; (800) 545-9011, (505) 257-5141.**

Mid-Priced Accommodations

Carrizo Lodge

Landmark lodge on Carrizo Canyon Rd., bordering Mescalero Apache Reservation. Hotel rooms, suites and condominiums. Hot tubs, sauna, fitness facilities, outdoor heated pool, restaurant, lounge. Midweek special rates. Daily housekeeping. **P.O. Drawer A, Ruidoso, NM 88345; (800) 227-1224, (505) 257-9131.**

High Country Lodge Cabins

Four miles north of Ruidoso and 12 miles from ski area. Thirty-two two-bedroom cabins, each with kitchen, wood-burning fireplace and free wood. Pets permitted. Ski packages. Indoor heated pool, spa, sauna, guest laundry, video arcade, tennis court, playground. Daily housekeeping at additional charge. **P.O. Box 137, Alto, NM 88312; (800) 845-7265, (505) 336-4321.**

Innsbruck Lodge

Forty-eight-room motor inn. Downtown location, adjacent to well-equipped City Park. Pets permitted. Children under 10 free in parents' room. Hot tub. Complimentary coffee, daily housekeeping. **601 Sudderth Dr., Ruidoso, NM 88345; (505) 257-4071.**

La Junta Guest Ranch

Family-owned mountaintop resort on seven acres with outstanding views of Sierra Blanca Peak. Ten cabin-style units, each with wood-burning fireplace and well-equipped kitchenette. "Cajun country home" decor, including touches like hand-stitched patchwork quilts on the beds and handsome wall hangings. Fireplace lobby. Secluded location, 6 miles north of town and 1 mile in from the main highway. Dining room. **146 Geneva, P.O. Box 139, Alto, NM 88312; (800) 443-8423, (505) 336-8423.**

Scandia Chalet

Charming B&B inn, with one loft suite with private Jacuzzi, two bedrooms that share a bath, and a two-bedroom cottage suitable for families. Glass atrium with fireplace. Located 8 miles from Ruidoso and 2 miles from Ski Apache access road; shuttle stops at the intersection. Welcome refreshments, après-ski refreshments, gourmet breakfast, daily housekeeping. **P.O. Box 835, Alto, NM 88312; (505) 336-7741.**

Swiss Chalet Inn

Large hotel and conference center. Great views. Alpine decor. Some rooms with steam saunas. Ski packages. Restaurant, lounge, indoor pool. **1451 Mechem Dr., Hwy 48 North, Ruidoso, NM 88345; (800) 47-SWISS, (505) 258-3333, (800) 528-1234 for Best Western reservations.**

Track & Ski Lodge

Motel rooms and five two-story chalets with large decks, fireplaces and kitchens. Set on eight acres. Located $1^{1}/2$ miles from Ski Run Rd. turn-off. **Hwy 48 N. at Airport Rd., Alto, NM 88312; (800) 687-0620, (505) 336-4240.**

Village Lodge

Thirty-two one-bedroom suites with fireplace (free firewood), wet bar and microwave. Exterior is traditional and timbered, interior is contemporary, and setting is amid the pines. Centrally located. AAA rated. Hot tub, barbecue grill. Daily housekeeping. **1000 Mechem Dr., Ruidoso, NM 88345; (800) 722-8779, (303) 258-5442.**

Economy Accommodations

Sitzmark Chalet

Comfortable family lodgings, with microwaves and refrigerators. Reasonable and convenient. Daily housekeeping. **627 Sudderth Dr., Ruidoso, NM 88345; (800) 658-9494, (505) 257-4140.**

Condominiums

Condotel

Has 160 units, some with fireplace and/or kitchen. Pets permitted. Ski packages. **P.O. Box 4450, 1103 Mechem Dr., Ruidoso, NM 88345; (800) 545-9027, (505) 258-5200.**

Fairway Meadows

Centrally located, well-priced units with fireplaces and washers and dryers. Ski packages. **P.O. Box 2428, Ruidoso, NM 88345; (800) 545-9013, (505) 257-4019.**

Innsbrook Village

Condo complex 2 miles from downtown, near Cedar Creek. Units range from one-bedroom mini-suites to four-bedroom, four-bath luxury apartments. Full kitchens and wood-burning fireplaces. All individually decorated and moderately priced. **Hwy 48 North, 146 Geneva, Ruidoso, NM 88345; (800) 284-0294, (505) 258-5441.**

Tiara del Sol

Twenty-three time-share units at motel prices. One to three bedrooms, each with full kitchen and a washer and dryer. Located on top of Camelot Mountain. Midweek cleaning on request. Indoor pool, hot tub, game room. **P.O. Box 3148, Ruidoso, NM 88345; (800) 777-8932, (505) 257-9232.**

Rentals of privately owned condos, cabins, townhouses and homes are handled by **Aspen Real Estate, (800) 657-8990, (505) 257-9057 Four Seasons Property Management, (800) 822-257, (505) 257-9171 Lela Easter Realtors, (800) 530-4597, (505) 257-7313 Lookout Management, (800) 545-5137, (505) 257-5064 International Vacation Owner Services, (800) 545-9017, (505) 257-9600 Gary Lynch Realty, (505) 257-4011 Ruidoso Properties, (800) 687-2596, (505) 257-4057 SDC Realtors, (800) 626-9213, (505) 257-5111**

DINING OUT

Ahna-Michelle's Restaurant

Charming hotel restaurant in scenic setting with spectacular views. Swiss and Italian specialties. German buffet on Friday evenings. Prime rib buffet on Saturdays. Lounge. **Swiss Chalet Inn,**

270

1451 Mechem Dr., Alto Crest; (505) 258-3333.

Casa Blanca

Hilltop restaurant and cantina, serving continuously from 11 A.M. to 10 P.M. daily. Specializes in beef (rather than pork) green chili, fajitas, quesadillas and other Mexican dishes, plus burgers and steak (chicken-fried and otherwise). Reservations for large parties suggested. **501 Mechem Dr., Ruidoso; (505) 257-2495.**

Che Bella

Cozy setting with simple and tasteful European decor. Northern Italian cuisine at moderate prices. Veal, poultry and seafood featured, plus gourmet pizzas. Good selection of wine and beer. Closed Tuesdays. **Sudderth Dr. and Mechem Dr., Ruidoso; (505) 257-7540.**

D 2 Ranch

Sleighride to warm tent with open fireplace. Hot dogs, hot cider, hot chocolate and coffee. BYO wine. Couples only. Reservations required. **N. Hwy 48, Gavalin Canyon, Ruidoso; (505) 257-7836.**

The InnCredible Restaurant

Huge glassed-in dining room sparkles at night with thousands of tiny lights. Fine food with Southwestern and European accents. Hot rocks cooking a special. Fondue too. Atmosphere is casual. Wednesday night lobster specials. Steak, prime rib, barbecued ribs, pasta, lamb and more with wine list to match. Lunch and dinner. Reservations recommended. **Hwy 48 N., Alto Village; (505) 336-4312.**

La Lorraine

A stylish and delicious corner of France on the streets of New Mexico. Well established and highly praised by local connoisseurs. Reservations recommended. **2523 Sudderth Dr., Ruidoso; (505) 257-2954.**

Marie LaVeaux

American steakhouse with a French name. Seafood is also a specialty. Courts skiers. Popular bar. Dinner seven evenings a week until 10:30 P.M. **1314 Mechem Dr., Ruidoso; (505) 258-3764.**

Michelena's Italian Restaurant

Family restaurant with casual dining and takeout options. Pizza, pasta and more. Daily specials at lunch and dinner, plus several sampler plates. Home-baked bread. Beer and wine served. **2703 Sudderth Dr., Ruidoso; (505) 257-5753.**

Screaming Eagle Restaurant

Hotel restaurant at the Enchantment Inn. Contemporary decor. Friendly and informal. Specializes in American and Mexican dishes. **307 Hwy 70 West, Ruidoso; (505) 378-0280.**

NIGHTLIFE

The Inn Credible Saloon, between Ski Run Rd. and town, sure gets a lot of after-ski attention and offers weekend entertainment. Hotel pubs like Ol' Barry's Tavern at the Swiss Chalet Inn and the Screaming Eagle Lounge in the Enchantment Inn get their share of evening action. The Eagle often has live entertainment. Casa Blanca's cantina serves good nachos and margaritas, and the Sports Bar at the Marie LaVeaux Restaurant rocks at happy hour and when there's a good game on. The Winners Circle has a horseracing theme and cooks when the ponies are running at Ruidoso Downs, but it's a top nightspot during ski season too. A band plays mostly country and western, with some rock Thursday through Sunday nights. Show up Friday, Saturday or Sunday afternoons if you want to get into the pool tournament. Wednesday is karaoke night. Gamblers flock to the casino at the Inn of the Mountain Gods to try their luck at bingo and video slots and at live poker in the Ina Da Card Room.

Ruidoso has many shops and galleries, often with western themes, making shopping, window shopping and browsing a popular diversion. Half-hour sleighrides or carriage rides on local streets is a way for families to dip into the ways of the past. Check what's happening at the Ruidoso Civic Center, the Ruidoso Little Theater and Eastern New Mexico University.

For more information, contact **Ski Apache, P.O. Box 220, Ruidoso, NM 88345; (505) 336-4356; Ruidoso Valley Chamber of Commerce, P.O. Box 698, Ruidoso, NM 88345; (800) 253-2255, (505) 257-7395.**

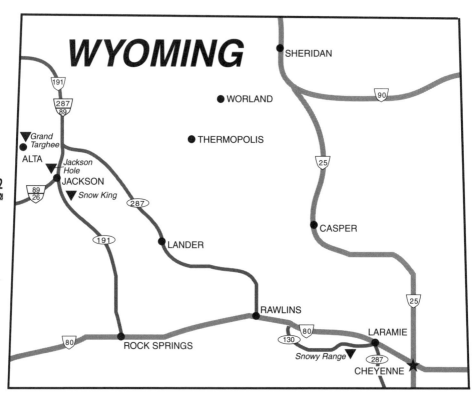

272

Wyoming

Photo by Bob Woodall/Wade McCoy

JACKSON HOLE

BACKDROP

The northwestern corner of Wyoming presents a combination of scenic wilderness and rustic western flavor that is comforting to locals and compelling to visitors. Even in the context of the Rockies, this is big, beautiful country with two national parks adjoined by two national forests in three states plus ranches with elbow room, a small population of cowboys and other frontier-mentality iconoclasts and a growing group of well-heeled owners of lavish vacation homes. **274** Plunked into the middle of this contradiction of wilderness, cowpoke culture and wealth is yet another disparate element, a world-class ski mountain called Jackson Hole. Located in the splendid Teton Range, it was for years the United States's only ski area with a vertical exceeding 4,000 feet—and it remains the only one with a steady, continuous and totally unrelenting vertical that great.

In this age of political correctness and non-gender-specific references, it's a risky throwback to describe a ski area as masculine, but that's the way Jackson Hole comes across. Such adjectives as beefy, brawny, broad-shouldered and rugged come to mind. It has a lot of acreage but not a lot of lift capacity. Its weather can be clouds that generously plaster the slopes and chutes and bowls and woods with classic Rocky Mountain powder, wind that can sift it into the trees or sun that can melt and pack it into goo—sometimes all on the same day. Skiers tend to speak of Jackson Hole with the reverence accorded to mountains that are especially challenging, a reputation that management is trying to tame. Summer contouring and winter snow grooming have been undertaken to mellow the mountain to levels more skiers find comfortable. This has prompted locals to paste "Stop the Brutal Grooming" stickers on their bumpers, and even with a quarter of a million dollars per recent summer pumped into making the beast more docile, it skis almost as tough as ever.

Jackson Hole is huge, and no matter how management has tried to tame the mountain—whether with summer rock blasting, winter winch-cat grooming or a fine children's facility—it's wild and steep and offers uncrowded skiing. Because of the difficulty of the terrain, the vagaries of snow conditions and the people it attracts, the level of skiing ability is as high as any in the land. One of skiing's badges (or, more accurately, belt buckles) of merit is a 14-karat belt buckle awarded to skiers who have logged 1,000,000 vertical feet at Jackson (silver and bronze buckles are for 500,000 and 300,000 vertical feet respectively). Even skiers tallying 100,000 or 150,000 vertical feet in any given week get a "Ski the Big One" pin and certificate—an easy goal to shoot for.

Of special note is the Ski Three Program, a multi-area ticket to Jackson Hole and Snow King (both described in this chapter) and Grand Targhee (covered in a separate chapter). Vouchers can be redeemed for a day of skiing at Jackson Hole, a lift ticket at Snow King and dinner at Rafferty's Restaurant or Grand Targhee Express bus transportation to and a lift ticket at Grand Targhee. You can obtain a voucher book through any of the three participating ski areas or via Jackson Hole Central Reservations.

As a winter tourist destination, Jackson's appeals are unparalleled. A sleighride in the 25,000-acre National Elk Refuge, where up to 10,000 head spend the winter, is a must. Visiting Yellowstone by snowcat (you drive), snowcoach (you are driven) or on touring skis (nobody drives) is in many ways more exciting and direct than joining the summer hordes. Old Faithful and hundreds of other thermal ponds, geysers and hot mudpots are even more dramatic steaming out of the snowy landscape, and the chances of seeing wildlife are greater than in the summer. The region also has more opportunities for such non-Alpine-ski diversions as cross-country skiing, snowmobiling, flightseeing and dogsledding than any other Rockies resort. Since the town of Jackson is set up for huge summer tourist traffic, its many motels and inns drop their rates

dramatically in winter. There is good dining, terrific nightlife and neat shops selling wares from standard-issue T-shirts and touristic kitsch to authentic western apparel and quality crafts. Jackson has also become a notable center for western art, meaning that the artistic spirit, as well as the physical and natural, can be attended to.

THE LAY OF THE LAND

Jackson Hole is located on the east-facing flank of the Tetons, overlooking the broad, flat Snake River Valley and the Gros Ventre Range beyond. Teton Village is a small built-for-skiing resort at the base of Jackson Hole's lifts. The town of Jackson, 12 miles southeast of the ski resort, is flooded with tens of thousands of summer visitors—some driving through, some stopping—heading just a short way north to Grand Teton and Yellowstone National Parks. In winter, it manages to retain the flavor of the West. You can stay at the mountain resort, but you'll probably want to spend a good part of your evenings in town, or you can stay in town, knowing that you will have to commute daily to the mountain. This is made possible by **START,** the public bus that makes frequent low-cost runs between Jackson and Teton Village, with intermediary stops, **(307) 733-4521.** The complimentary Village Shuttle runs between Teton Village condominiums and the base of the tram during the day and evening.

GETTING THERE

Jackson Hole Airport, 10 miles north of Jackson, has service from Boise, Chicago, Dallas, Denver, Salt Lake City and Seattle. Vans, taxis and rental cars are available. While air service is good and getting better, Jackson Hole's remoteness dictates that very few skiers drive. It's 275 arduous miles and about five hours from Salt Lake City via I-15 north to US 89 north to US 26/89. Denver is 530 even more arduous miles and 10 hours via I-25 north (or US 287 north) to US 80 west, then US 191 and US 189/191 north.

Inside Jackson Hole

PROFILE

Almost any way you measure it, Jackson Hole is one of the true giants of American skiing. It is the place where the concept of the double-black diamond (or, more precisely, a red exclamation

Resort elevation 6,311 feet
Top of highest lift 10,450 feet
Bottom of lowest lift 6,311 feet
Total vertical 4,139 feet
Longest run 4.7 miles
Average annual snowfall 384 inches
Ski season early December to early April
Lifts 1 aerial tram, 1 high-speed quad chairlift, 2 fixed-grip quads, 1 triple, 3 doubles, 1 platterpull
Capacity 9,000 skiers per hour
Terrain 2,500 acres, 62 runs (10% beginner and novice, 40% intermediate, 50% advanced and expert)
Snowmaking 75 acres
Mountain dining Corbet's Cabin with limited food service (breakfast, lunch and snacks) at the top of the tram, Shades at Thunder at the base of the Thunder lift (lunch and snacks) and Casper Restaurant in Casper Bowl (Continental breakfast and lunch)
Snow reports (800) DEEP-SNO

mark in a yellow triangle) was devised to indicate terrain beyond the black diamond. Its vertical is so tremendous that temperatures and snow conditions can be radically different between top and bottom. Its skiable acreage, equal to two Breckenridges or nearly five Aspen Mountains, in all of the Rockies, is exceeded only by Vail, Steamboat and Snowmass. Jackson Hole's vertical is like putting Purgatory on top of Winter Park. Yet its lift capacity is about half that of Boyne Mountain, a Michigan ski hill with just 17 runs on a modest 450-foot vertical. All these numbers and comparisons translate into an enormous amount of skiing with no lines and an occasional "got-the-mountain-to-myself" feeling.

Rendezvous Peak, Jackson Hole's main attraction, is a huge, steep-flanked massif ranking as the mightiest all-around mountain in the land. It gives Jackson Hole its reputation as a macho mountain—with good reason. Except for a handful of upper intermediate blue runs and another handful of harrowing chutes of super-duper double blacks, Rendezvous is a sea of single-diamond steepness. By itself, Rendezvous's acreage is counted in four figures, its pitch in high doubles and its trails in the dozens.

Jackson Hole's 60-passenger tram climbs the entire 4,139 vertical feet in just 12 minutes and serves as the main transport to this precipitous paradise. In the context of the Rocky Mountains, the 4,000-feet-plus elevation gain is a climb through three distinct life zones in less than a quarter of an hour. In the context of skiing, it's the difference between a cozy middle-aged mountain village in a civilized valley and a raw summit 10,450 feet above sea level. The temperature differences and snow conditions between the two are often dramatic—perhaps really cold and blustery at the summit and mild in the valley or, when there's an air inversion, just the opposite. You also have the option of a series of chairlifts and traverses to the top, which takes a lot longer and is more cumbersome, enabling the area to add a couple of bucks extra for each tram ride to the lift ticket.

Five substantial bowls are scooped out of the upper part of Rendezvous Peak. Rendezvous Bowl, just below the tram's summit station, has the best-known name. Its steep initial drop-off,

steady ongoing pitch and simply sublime skiing when snow and visibility conditions are favorable make it a goal in its own right. Sublette Ridge emerges below this highest bowl, with Cheyenne Bowl to the south and Laramie Bowl to the north. These are both tough and tricky, as is the Pepi's Run along the top of Sublette Ridge. Most people choose either the ridge or a bowl, but daring experts can ski the Alta Chutes, a series of side-by-side free-fall plunges deep into Laramie Bowl. South Pass Traverse is a blue bail-out leading to easier skiing. The Upper Sublette Ridge quad chairlift lets you ski Laramie Bowl or the Alta Chutes. Riding this lift plus the Rendezvous Bowl platterpull takes about the same amount of time as the tram, but the lines are far shorter and, if the snow is uneven, the good stuff is always at the top. If you do want to ski to the bottom, you have a choice of steep expert runs that comprise the lower frontside of this massive mountain. North and South Colter Ridge, Buffalo Bowl between them, Rawlins Bowl and Lower Sublette Ridge provide great texture and variety—snowfields, trees, drainages—all steep and never crowded.

Instead of Laramie Bowl, you might choose Cheyenne Bowl. It is another broad, steep parcel—a long, luscious and in parts relatively protected trough. Rendezvous Traverse isn't a mellow road in the normal sense but a steepish route along the rims of Rendezvous and Cheyenne Bowls leading to the famous Hobacks, which rank near the top in the hierarchy of great powder slopes. Long and steep and steady as anything on this extraordinary mountain, the Hobacks are the place to be if you're strong and gutsy and a tiger in deep snow. This abundance of terrain—from Rendezvous Bowl, Cheyenne and Laramie Bowls below to the Hobacks way off in the lower eastern corner—would comprise enough black diamonds to give boasting rights to most ski areas, but, at Jackson Hole, that's just what you'll find south of the tram.

North of the tramline are sections so precipitous that they are perennially closed due to extreme avalanche hazard. The East Ridge Traverse, arguably the only double-black "traverse" in the Rockies, and a harrowing run simply called Downhill skirt these high-hazard areas and lead to some terrain that's safe but still even closer to plumb-vertical than the Alta Chutes. Foremost is Corbet's Couloir, steep as an elevator shaft and nearly as frightening, with an image as the most death-defying run on Rendezvous Peak and perhaps in the land. Skiers with hearts of steel and legs of iron, or perhaps simply no sense at all, can leap into a vertical patch of snow that doesn't seem much bigger than a phone booth—two walls of rock, one of air and one of snow (that's the one you're supposed to ski) and then "flattens" to a 50-degree slope. The good news is that you can ski Corbet's without the legs to leap; the bad news is that you better have biceps like Arnold Schwarzenegger's, because the second option is to be lowered into the precipitous chute by rope. The option that most skiers choose, however, is not to ski Corbet's at all.

Even such other dual-diamond alternatives as the Expert Chutes, the Tower Three Chute (named after its location relative to the tram tower) and Paint Brush are easier than Corbet's. The single diamonds of Downhill, which is the most famous

track down a bowl called the Cirque, or the narrow trail called Thunder pale into skiability by mortals in comparison. And Gros Ventre, dropping off the ridge and following the bottom of the wide drainage along Rendezvous's northern slope, wears a Jacksonian shade of blue and is as comforting as a cup of hot tea to a skier who has tackled Rendezvous's colossal steeps.

No matter how accurately these awesome precipices confirm Jackson Hole's reputation for unrelenting challenge, the area offers an abundance of intermediate runs too. The entire northern part of the ski area—a lower peak called Apres Vous and the broad drainage that separates it from Rendezvous—is awash with blue squares. The mid-level terrain demonstrates respectable scale and variety. With separate chairlifts on the upper and lower mountain, skiers can select the portion of Apres Vous that best suits their skills. The lower slopes in the Teewinot section, true green novice runs, are now served by the resort's first high-speed quad **277** chairlift. It is somehow fitting that Jackson Hole would install its high-speed lift on novice terrain, perhaps to give new skiers more practice runs per day and get them off those greens as soon as possible.

Apres Vous's upper ones are blue with a few blacks, notably the little-known tree skiing in the Moran Woods, on Moran Face and Upper Teewinot. You can take the Togwotee Pass Traverse over to the Crystal Springs/Casper Bowl sector, which spreads in the generous dip between the Rendezvous and Apres Vous. Crystal Springs, the lower portion, has very easy beginner runs (another chairlift serves just those) and relatively steep glade skiing, while Casper Bowl above is mostly intermediate. Relativity kicks in here, for only in contrast to the mass of Rendezvous Peak does this part of Jackson Hole seem modest. In reality, its five lifts, more than two dozen trails and 2,170 feet of vertical would be a significant ski mountain in other parts of the country.

No matter how many improvements and upgrades are ultimately made, Jackson will never become a crowded mountain. Its sheer size, its truly rugged terrain and weather and its distance from any substantial population center set it apart from all other major Rockies resorts. It's big and brutish, which is a major part of its appeal and renown, yet it is a surprisingly gentle giant that offers something for all skiers—and boasting rights for those who have skied there.

SNOWBOARDING

Snowboarders have taken to Jackson's grandeur and challenge as if it were their own invention. Like the skiers who have been drawn to Jackson Hole for decades, local riders tend to be really, really good—and really, really tough. You'll find them strutting their stuff in Thunder Bowl, jibbing and pack riding on Gros Ventre (which they've nicknamed "The Track") and getting air anywhere and any way they can, which at Jackson Hole is lots of spots that skiers often pass by.

SNOWCAT AND HELICOPTER SKIING

The Jackson area is the rare, make that unique, resort in the U.S. Rockies offering both snowcat and helicopter access to the backcountry for expert skiers and snowboarders seeking adventure. Grand Targhee offers the cat skiing (see that chapter), **High Mountain Helicopter Skiing, (307) 733-3274,** departs from the Jackson Hole Ski Area into the Snake River Range and the Palisades south of Jackson. With guides' tips on powder skiing and fat skis, intermediates can handle a heliday. Snowboarders are welcome and heli-riding in increasing numbers. The basic fee is for six runs averaging 2,000 vertical feet, with additional runs available based on weather and each group's wishes. Groups average eight or nine runs per day.

SKI SCHOOL PROGRAMS

Tickets for all adult programs are available in the **Jackson Hole Ski School Chalet, (307) 739-2686.**

Introductory Programs

Beginner Lessons: Jackson Hole, being as big and tough a mountain as it is, considers Level 1 (first time on skis, basic gliding, wedge turning and control on easiest runs) to Level 4 (controlled wedge with parallel finish) to be a green-circle level skiers. Available half-day, full-day or multiday.

Snowboard Program: Beginner snowboard instruction.

Advanced and Specialty Programs

Group lessons: Level 5 (ability to bring skis parallel at the finish of turns on all green runs) to Level 9 (strong parallel skier in bumps, powder and steeps, skiing most black runs comfortably). Available half-day, full-day or multiday.

Snowboard Program: Intermediate and advanced instruction.

Mountain Experience (MX): Challenge of skiing powder, steeps and isolated runs; for Level 8 and above. Four hours for three or more students; three hours for minimum of two students. Reservations recommended.

Rise to the Occasion with Pepi Stiegler: Two hours of skiing with Olympic gold medalist Pepi Stiegler, brunch and personal photo. Reservations required.

Coffee 'N' Coombs: Coffee, carbo-loading and two-hour private clinic with two-time World Extreme Skiing Champion Doug Coombs. Reservations required.

Steep Skiing and Steep Snowboarding Camps: World Extreme Champions Doug Coombs and Emily Gladstone-Coombs coach dynamic big-mountain skiing experience. Level 8 or higher. Pro riders coach the snowboard version. Three-day camps, offered several times a season.

Women's Camp: Jackson's top female instructors teach women in three-day camp. Includes welcome party, lectures and awards banquet. Offered in late January.

Special Programs

Alpine Ski Guides: Personalized guide service for advanced skiers looking for Jackson's best terrain and snow. Reservations recommended.

Ski with Pepi: Ski free with Olympic gold, silver and bronze medalist and Jackson Hole Ski School director Pepi Stiegler. Monday through Friday at 1:30 P.M. at the top of the Casper lift.

Ski Hosts: Complimentary mountain tours from the top of Rendezvous Mountain every hour on the hour. Also, mountain orientation at 9:30 A.M. daily.

Go for the Gold: Honor system rewarding skiers who ski 100,000 to 150,000 vertical feet in a week or up to 1,000,000 vertical feet cumulatively.

For Families

Kids' Ranch is the children's facility, housing licensed day care and junior ski school programs. Hours are from 8:30 A.M. to 4:30 P.M. Reservations required for all programs, **(307) 739-2691.**

Nonskiing Children

Tenderfoots: Infant and toddler nursery with day care for ages 2 to 18 months.

Wranglers: Child care for ages 19 months through nonskiing 5-year-olds. Full-day program includes lunch, snacks and indoor and outdoor play, as appropriate for age and weather.

Skiing Children

Rough Riders: Introductory one-on-one basics for 3- to 5-year-olds in conjunction with day care program. Lunch and snacks included; equipment additional.

MiniMeisters: Group lessons for children ages 3 to 5 who can stop and turn; operates in conjunction with the day care program and includes lunch, snacks and Eagle's Rest lift ticket. Equipment is additional.

Noteworthy

Jackson Hole and Snow King both extend children's rates through age 14 (at many areas, it's still 12). Jackson offers a chairlift-only ticket which is less expensive than one which includes the tram.

You can rent cribs, high chairs, playpens and other baby needs from the local franchise of Baby's Away, (307) 733-0387.

SKIwee: Group lessons for ages 6 to 13. Available on half-, full- or multiday packages. All-day program includes lunch at Solitude Cabin.

Teens

Teen Clinic: Half- and full-day classes for teens, available during peak school holiday periods.

FOR RACERS

Race Camp: Five-day racing camp offered in mid-December, with coaches assembled by Olympic gold medalist Pepi Stiegler.

NASTAR: Tuesdays, Thursdays and Sundays at 1:00 P.M. Register at Casper Restaurant from 10 A.M. Super-NASTAR Sundays at 10:30 A.M., with sign-ups beginning at 9:30 A.M.

HANDICAPPED SKIING 279

Adaptive Skiing: Program for people with disabilities. Uses adaptive equipment and specifically trained instructors. Available by the full or half day. Lessons include lift ticket. Reservations recommended.

NORDIC SKIING

Jackson is the self-proclaimed "big one" of Alpine skiing—and it could claim that honor in Nordic circles too. Simply stated, the greater Jackson area has more and better cross-country skiing and ski-touring than any other place in the Rockies. With several touring centers (each with groomed trails, instruction and rental equipment), endless backcountry skiing on public lands and two Alpine areas that welcome telemarkers, Jackson is a Nordic hotbed. The Teton Track Ticket is a bargain, enabling you to ski twice at each of the region's touring centers.

The **Jackson Hole Nordic Ski Center**, headquartered right at Teton Village, has 17 kilometers of groomed trails for diagonal and skating technique and a complete rental and instruction

Wyoming

program, half- and full-day naturalist-guided backcountry tours to Teton National Park and Teton Pass, **(307) 733-2292, Ext. 710. Spring Creek Ranch**'s 10 kilometers comprise the country's only system laid out around the travel patterns of the local deer population, and you may well see wildlife along the trails, **(307) 733-8833. Teton Pines Ski Center** is golf-course skiing with 12 kilometers of trails, a health club and even child care, **(307) 733-7004.**

The region offers free skiing on all manner of public lands—unplowed roads, trails and meadows, with elevation gains and steepnesses for most ability levels. Among the popular backcountry opportunities you'll hear about from locals are Bradley and Taggert Lakes, Cache Creek, Jenny Lake, Moose/Wilson Road, Shadow Mountain, Snake River Dike and Signal Mountain. Teton Pass Ridge is especially popular with telemarkers. Abundant touring terrain exists in two national parks, which are worthy winter destinations in their own right. In addition to skiing (and winter camping) on your own, you can join a ranger-led moonlight tour in Teton National Park or interpretive tours in Yellowstone. Yellowstone has an especially large and still growing network of marked touring trails and plentiful backcountry skiing, and the Mammoth Hot Spring Hotel and Old Faithful Snow Lodge are now open in winter. For details, contact the appropriate national forest and park offices: **Grand Teton National Park, (307) 733-3399; Yellowstone National Park, (307) 344-7381; Bridger-Teton National Forest, (307) 739-5500, (307) 733-2664** for 24-hour **Avalanche Hotline;** and **Targhee National Forest, (208) 624-3151.**

SNOW KING

Profile

Visitors from the around the world come to Jackson to ski Jackson Hole, but locals are as likely to step into their bindings at Snow King. This simple area is skiing the way it used to be. Located just

Mountain Stats— Snow King

Resort elevation 6,237 feet
Top of highest lift 7,808 feet
Bottom of lowest lift 6,237
Total vertical 1,571 feet
Ski season early December to early April
Longest run 9/10 mile
Average annual snowfall 250 inches per year
Snowmaking 110 acres
Lifts 1 triple chairlift, 2 doubles, 1 surface tow
Capacity 4,000 skiers per hour
Night skiing Tuesdays through Saturdays, 4:30 to 8:30 P.M., on 110 acres
Terrain 17 runs, 400 acres (15% beginner and novice, 25% intermediate, 60% advanced and expert)
Snowmaking 110 acres
Snow reports (307) 733-5200

six blocks from Jackson's Town Square, the ski hill was founded in 1939, making it one of the Rockies' oldest. Traditionally and unsubtly laid out, its two chairlifts and one tow rise to different elevations on the front face with the easy terrain at the bottom, the intermediate in the middle and the difficult stuff on top. There are wide fall-line trails of varying pitches, a green circle switchback route called Slow Trail (no mistaking the intention) and some steeps sufficient for slalom or real mogul skiing. Sixty percent of the terrain is groomed, but 40 percent isn't, so the skiing and snow conditions do cover a big-mountain range.

Snow King's ski school is surprisingly well-regarded among its peers. The area's lift tickets are much cheaper than Jackson's. The biggest bargain is a ticket for the tow only (great for very little children and shaky beginners who want just a small practice slope), hourly tickets and twi-night and night skiing is available Tuesday through Saturday. The resort also has a new children's center and a snowboard park. Were it not the closest neighbor of the mightiest ski area in the country, Snow King would feel bigger. It's that Jackson relativity kicking in again.

WHERE TO STAY

Jackson Hole Central Reservations, P.O. Box 2618, Jackson Hole, WY 83001; (800) 443-6931, (307) 733-4005; Jackson Hole Bed & Breakfast Assn., (800) 542-2632.

Teton Village
Luxury Accommodations
Alpenhof Lodge
Full-service, Alpine-style lodge within short walk of lifts. Rustic yet elegant. Forty-one bedrooms with king-size beds, many with balconies. AAA Three Diamond property. Award-winning restaurant. Ski packages. Daily housekeeping, room service, valet service. Outdoor heated pool, hot tub, sauna, two restaurants, lounge, guest laundry, game room, ski lockers. **P.O. Box 288, Teton Village, WY 83025; (800) 732-3244, (307) 733-3242.**

Mid-Priced Accommodations
Crystal Springs Inn
Comfortable rooms with queen- or twin-size beds on main level and twin beds in the loft. In-room refrigerators. Good value. Ski packages. Daily housekeeping, valet service. Guest laundry, ski lockers. **P.O. Box 250, Teton Village, WY 83025; (307) 733-4423.**

Inn at Jackson Hole
Distinctive 123-room inn, 60 of them new and the rest recently remodeled. Well-furnished rooms, all sleeping up to four people, some with fireplaces, lofts or kitchenettes. AAA rated and Best Western affiliated. Children 14 and younger stay free in parents' room. Ski packages. Daily housekeeping, room service, 24-hour front desk. Outdoor heated pool, sauna, hot tubs, restaurant, lounge, ski lockers. **P.O. Box 328, Teton Village, WY 83025; (800) 842-7666, (307) 733-2311; (800) 528-1234 for Best Western reservations.**

Sojourner Inn
Teton Village's largest hotel, with 98 rooms. King- and queen-size beds. Ski-in/ski-out hotel. Ski packages. Daily housekeeping, room service. Pool, hot tub, sauna, game room, two restaurants, two lounges, ski lockers, guest laundry. **P.O. Box 348, Teton Village, WY 83025; (800) 445-4655, (307) 733-3657.**

Village Center Inn
Sixteen newly remodeled studios to two-bedroom units, all with full kitchens. Located next to the tram base. Daily housekeeping. Ski packages. Shops, cafe and deli in building. Guest laundry. **P.O. Box 310, Teton Village, WY 83025; (800) 735-8342, (307) 733-3155.**

Economy Accommodations
Hostel
The Motel 6 of Teton Village—frill-free comfort at a budget price. Informal and fun. Perpetually popular with young crowd. Ski packages. Daily housekeeping. Lower lounge and game room with fireplace and TV, ski-waxing room, ski lockers, guest laundry. **P.O. Box 546, Teton Village, WY 83025; (307) 733-2311.**

Condominiums
Teton Village Condominiums
A variety of condos from studios to four bedrooms. Also chalets and houses with three to six bedrooms. Individually owned and furnished. Styles and locations vary. All have fireplaces and kitchens. Laundry facilities and hot tubs and/or outdoor heated pool are on-site or nearby. All are within a mile of the lifts. Housekeeping service is on a limited basis. Children ages 14 and younger stay free in some units. The most luxurious complexes are Snowridge, Timber Ridge, Tram Tower and Wind River. The mid-price, mid-level ones are Eagles Rest, Four Seasons, Nez Perce, Sleeping Indian, Teewinot, Tensleep/Gros Ventre and Whiteridge. The simplest is La Choumine. **P.O. Box 249, Teton Village, WY 83025; (800) 443-6840, (307) 733-4610.**

Jackson and Surrounding Area
Luxury Accommodations
Rusty Parrot Lodge
Fine 31-room lodge with handcrafted furniture (including lodgepole-pine beds), goose-down

281

comforters, oversized baths. Some rooms with fireplace, balcony and/or whirlpool. Wyoming's only Four Star, Four Diamond hotel open year-round. Ski packages. Daily housekeeping, breakfast included. Hot tub, ski lockers. **P.O. Box 1657, 175 N. Jackson St., Jackson, WY 83001; (800) 458-2004, (307) 733-2000.**

Mid-Priced Accommodations

Cowboy Village Resort
Complex with 57 individual log cabins with kitchenettes and other comforts. Close to Town Square. Ski packages. Housekeeping service. Two hot tubs. **P.O. Box 1747, 120 S. Flat Creek Dr., Jackson, WY 83001; (800) 962-4988, (307) 733-3121.**

Days Inn of Jackson Hole
New and very nicely appointed motel. Rooms have remote-control TV and in-room coffee; some with microwave and refrigerator. Ski packages. Located 1 1/2 miles south of town on START route. Daily housekeeping, Continental breakfast included, free local calls, overnight ski tuning available. Hot tub, sauna, boot and glove dryers. **1280 W. Broadway, Jackson, WY 83001; (307) 739-9010, (800) DAYS-INN** for Days Inn reservations.

Snow King Resort
Full-service resort with 250 rooms and condos. Outstanding facilities at reasonable rates. All amenities and services. Located at base of Snow King ski area, six blocks from Town Square. Ski packages. Daily housekeeping, room service, 24-hour front desk, bell service, airport shuttle, ski shuttle. Swimming pool, hot tub, sauna, ski area game room, restaurant, cocktail lounge. **P.O. Box SKI, 400 E. Snow King Ave., Jackson, WY 83001; (800) 522-KING, (307) 733-5200.**

Sundance Inn
Cozy motel operating on B&B plan. Just 1 1/2 blocks from Town Square. Twenty-eight rooms, individually and casually decorated. Friendly, affordable and owner-operated. Daily housekeeping, Continental breakfast, afternoon social hour. **P.O. Box I, 135 W. Broadway, Jackson, WY 83001; (307) 733-3444.**

Teton Tree House Bed & Breakfast
Owned by veteran Teton guides. Four-story inn on forested mountainside. Large rooms with excellent views. Eight miles from resort. Daily housekeeping. Hot tub, game room. **P.O. Box 550, Wilson, WY 83014; (307) 733-3233.**

Virginian Lodge
Sizable lodge with 158 rooms, including eight deluxe Jacuzzi suites. Located on shuttle route between town and ski area. Pets permitted. Ski packages. Daily housekeeping, 24-hour front desk. Pool, restaurant, guest laundry, liquor store. **P.O. Box 1052, Jackson, WY 83001; (800) 262-4999, (307) 733-2792.**

The Wort Hotel
Historic downtown hotel. Great public spaces. Large, comfortable rooms. Central location—and hub of activity. AAA rated with Four Diamonds. Ski packages. Daily housekeeping, 24-hour front desk, bell staff, room service, airport shuttle, complimentary western-style breakfast. Restaurant, lounge, ski lockers. **P.O. Box 69, Jackson, WY 83001; (800) 322-2727, (307) 733-2190.**

Economy Accommodations

Antler Motel
Large motel with 100 units, some with fireplaces. TV with HBO. One block from Town Square and close to Snow King. Ski packages. Daily housekeeping. Hot tub, sauna. **P.O. Box 575, 43 W. Pearl St., Jackson, WY 83001; (800) 522-2406, (307) 733-2535.**

Anvil Motel
New motel close to Town Square. Queen-size beds. Remote-control TVs. Some two-room family suites. Some units with whirlpool tubs. Daily housekeeping. Outdoor hot tub. **P.O. Box 468, 215 N. Cable, Jackson, WY 83001; (800) 234-4507, (307) 733-3668.**

The Bunkhouse
Ultra-bargain dorm accommodations in downtown Jackson. Showers additional to nightly rate. Lounge, kitchen, guest laundry, ski lockers. **P.O. Box 486, 215 N. Cache St., Jackson, WY 83001; (307) 733-3668.**

49'er Inn
Rooms, studios and 30 new fireplace suites. Central location, near shops and restaurants and on shuttle route. Daily housekeeping. Indoor and outdoor hot tubs, sauna. **P.O. Box 1948, 330 W. Pearl St., Jackson, WY 83001; (800) 451-2980, (307) 733-7550.**

Hitching Post Lodge
Economy in-town motel. Quiet location. Daily housekeeping, complimentary coffee. Heated pool. **P.O. Box 521, 460 E. Broadway, Jackson, WY 83001; (307) 733-2606.**

Parkway Inn
Reasonably priced inn with 38 rooms, 12 suites, many furnished with antiques. Non-smoking. Three blocks from Town Square. Ski packages. Daily housekeeping. Indoor pool, two hot tubs, exercise gym. **P.O. Box 494, Jackson, WY 83001; (307) 733-3143.**

Rawhide Motel
Well-appointed motel two blocks from Town Square. Spacious rooms. Lodgepole-pine furniture. Children 8 and younger stay free in parents' room. Ski packages. Daily housekeeping. **P.O. Box 3289, 75 S. Millward St., Jackson, WY 83001; (307) 733-1216.**

Super 8 Motel
Economy chain motel with non-smoking rooms available. Located south of town. Daily housekeeping, 24-hour front desk. **P.O. Box 1382, 750 S. Hwy 89, Jackson, WY 83001; (307) 733-6833, (800) 800-8000** for Super 8 reservations.

Trapper Motel
Comfortable motel close to town center. Good quality and value. START bus across the street. Queen-size beds, some rooms with refrigerators. Ski packages. Three Diamonds from AAA. Daily housekeeping. Two hot tubs, guest laundry, ski-waxing room. **P.O. Box 1712, 235 N. Cache St., Jackson, WY 83001; (800) 341-8000, (307) 733-2648.**

Condominiums
The Aspens
Extremely comfortable and well-appointed homes and condos with one to four bedrooms, some with lofts and all with fireplace, full kitchen and washer and dryer. Four miles to ski resort. Membership to on-site athletic club available for additional fee (policy may change in the future with club membership included with all or some vacation rentals). Housekeeping differs according to property management company policies for various units. Athletic club, indoor hot tub, sauna, restaurant, liquor store, grocery store, post office. BBC Property Management, Jackson Hole Property Management and Village Property Management handle units at The Aspens.

Jackson Hole Lodge
One- and two-bedroom condo units, fully equipped, including washer and dryer. Also motel. Three blocks from center of town. Daily housekeeping. Indoor pool, hot tubs, sauna. **P.O. Box 1805, 420 W. Broadway, Jackson, WY 83001; (307) 733-2992.**

Jackson Hole Racquet Club Resort
Elegant and well-appointed complex with units ranging from studios to four bedrooms. Each unit has full kitchen, washer and dryer and fireplace. Four miles from Teton Village. Limited housekeeping, complimentary ski shuttle. Sauna, hot tub, fitness center, indoor courts, restaurant, lounge, convenience store, cross-country skiing. **P.O. Box 3647, Jackson, WY 83001; (800) 443-8616, (307) 733-3990.**

Spring Creek Resort
Grandiose spread a thousand feet above the valley floor. Charming, elegantly rustic units. Kitchenettes. Great views. Exceptional restaurant. Surrounded by wildlife sanctuary. Wyoming's only full year-round resort with AAA Four Diamond rating. Ski packages. Daily housekeeping, complimentary airport and ski shuttle, 24-hour front desk, room service, bell staff. Restaurant, lounge, hot tub, cross-country facilities. **P.O. Box 3154, Spring Gulch Rd., Jackson, WY 83001; (800) 443-6139, (307) 833-8833.**

Other property management companies handling condominiums and homes in the Jackson area include
BBC Property Management, (800) 735-8310, (307) 733-6170
Ely & Assoc. of Jackson Hole, (800) 735-8310, (307) 733-8604
Teton Village Property Management (800) 443-6840

283

DINING OUT

Teton Village

Alpenhof Dining Room
Atmospheric four-star restaurant with lots of German dishes and game specialties. Tableside preparation of classic dishes, some flambée. Salmon en Croute, Beef Wellington, Tournedos Diane and Elk and Caribou Diane for two. All entrées include soup or salad, vegetable and starch. Sublime rolls and pastries. Children's menu. Breakfast, lunch and dinner. Dinner reservations recommended. **Alpenhof Lodge, Teton Village**; (307) 733-3242.

Dietrich's Bistro
Casual hotel restaurant, counterpoint to fancier Alpenhof Dining Room. Tops for après-ski. Appetizers include Smoked Duck Spring Rolls, Sesame Chicken Tenders and Wild Game Sausage—enough, with a salad, for a light meal. Entrées include Wild Game Loaf, Mountain Man Stew, Osso Buco and nightly seafood special. Fine desserts. Espresso and cappuccino. Open daily for lunch and dinner. **Alpenhof Lodge, Teton Village**; (307) 733-3242.

284

Jenny Leigh's Dining Room
Lovely ambiance. Hotel restaurant serving breakfast, lunch and dinner. At dinner, impressive wild game selection, including elk, moose, buffalo and boar. Also serves steaks, veal, pasta. Good wine list. Full bar. Takeout available. Reservations recommended. **The Inn at Jackson Hole, Teton Village**; (307) 733-7102.

Mangy Moose Saloon
Lively restaurant, nearly as old as the resort but eternal favorite of the young. Lunch, plus light dinners and heftier ones. Steak, prime rib, seafood, chicken and pasta featured; also stir-fry cooking. Salad bar. Children's menu. Peanut butter and coconut pies are favorite desserts. **Mangy Moose Bldg., Teton Village**; (307) 733-4913.

Rocky Mountain Oyster
Casual, easy-on-the-wallet family spot. "Bullish breakfasts," including all-you-can-drink coffee. New York–style pizza by the slice or by the pie.

Homemade soups, big sandwiches and burgers, chili and fresh-baked desserts. Takeout available. **Mangy Moose Bldg., Teton Village**; (307) 733-5525.

The Village Steak & Pasta House
Long-time Teton Village steak place gone contemporary with new pasta component. Carnivores love quality beef plus lamb, pork, elk, buffalo, chicken, ribs and seafood specialties. Design your own pasta recipe with choice of sauce and topping ingredients. Pizza with secret crust recipe. Salad bar. Friday fondue night. Lounge adjacent. Also serves breakfast and lunch. **Sojourner Inn, Teton Village**; (307) 733-3657.

Jackson and Surrounding Area

The Acadian House
Cajun fare in the shadow of the Tetons. Chicken, seafood, gumbo and étouffée. Crawfish in season. Veggie plates, spicy over rice or Creole-style over pasta. Grilled ribeye, blackened on request. Nightly specials. Lunch Tuesday through Friday; dinner nightly. All dinners with house salad or excellent gumbo, plus vegetable and starch. Takeout available. Reservations recommended. **1140 Hwy 22** (junction of Hwy 89), between **Jackson** and **Teton Village**; (307) 739-1269.

Anthony's Italian Restaurant
Seafood, pasta, veal and chicken in both the northern and southern Italian modes. Many meatless pasta specialties. Soup, salad and garlic bread with all dinners. Cocktails, beer and wine. Children's menu. **62 S. Glenwood St., Jackson**; (307) 733-3717.

Bar-T-Five
Sleighride dinner to historic pioneer cabin. Two rides nightly, departing at 5:00 and 7:00 P.M. Singin' Cowboys provide entertainment. Price reduced for children under 10. Reservations required. **Corral** at **Cache Creek Rd.**, 1 mile east of Town Square; (307) 733-5386.

The Blue Lion
Quaint cottage atmosphere. Game, lamb, veal and seafood prepared with flair. Creative adaptations

from elk Wellington to tempeh crepes. Nightly fish specials. Excellent desserts. Full bar and extensive wine list. Children's menu. Takeout available. Reservations accepted. **160 N. Millward St., Jackson; (307) 733-3912.**

Bubba's Bar-B-Que

Hearty western specialties including ribs, pork, turkey and chicken, all richly accompanied by potatoes, beans and such. Combo plates for the undecided. Broiled beef or chicken with salad for dieters. Big (or smaller half) orders of wings and Shrimp à La Bubba available after 5:00 P.M. Salad bar. Children's menu. Breakfast too. **515 W. Broadway, Jackson; (307) 733-2288.**

The Bunnery

Great breakfasts and lunches, and now early dinners too (until 9:00 P.M.). Omelettes, eggs and whole-grain energy food to start the day. Hefty sandwiches and some Mexican dishes later. Home-baked breads and pastries daily. Seniors' discount. Daily specials. Kid's Korner menu. Nonsmoking restaurant. Beer, wine, gourmet soda and specialty coffees. **Hole-in-the-Wall Mall, 130 N. Cache St.; (307) 733-5474.**

Cadillac Grille

Fun-filled and funky art deco decor and creative and well-prepared American dishes, including game, beef, veal and really fresh seafood. Menu changes daily. Eclectic offerings such as Stuffed Dakota Pheasant with Boisenberry Sauce and Dumplings, Bleu Cheese Tournedos and Fresh Ahi Tuna Grilled with Mango Salsa. Good bar and excellent wine list, especially from American wineries. Takeout available. Reservations advised. **55 N. Cache St., Jackson; (307) 733-3279.**

Calico Pizza Parlor

Recently renovated restaurant, serving simple and specialty pies, interesting pastas, sauté and salads. Good night spot, but also suitable for families. Beer, wine and cocktails. Takeout available. **Teton Village Rd., Jackson; (307) 733-2460.**

Gouloff's

Creative fare "in the spirit of the Rocky Mountains." Self-defined western cuisine, including Bridger Duck, Tournedos Santa Fe and Sierra Madre Lamb. All dinners include homemade

bread, salad and more. Excellent and interesting soups. Dinner nightly. Reservations recommended. **Teton Village Rd., Jackson; (307) 733-1886.**

The Granary

Elegant contemporary restaurant serving lunch and dinner. Atmospheric and excellent. Outstanding views. Original and imaginative dishes, including Game Chili, Black Angus New York with Pinenut Leek Butter and Smoked Turkey Croissant. Menu changes nightly. Top dollar and top quality. Fine wine list and excellent desserts. Dinner reservations requested. Sleighride dinners also available. **Spring Creek Resort, Jackson; (307) 733-8833.**

Jedidiah's Original House of Sourdough

Generous lunches and dinners (here called "supper") in hunting lodge setting. Various cuts of steak and Single Barrel and Double Barrel Prime Rib. Game, chicken, seafood and even pasta primavera for non-red-meat types. Nightly game specials. Steaks and suppers served with soup or salad sourdough bread, vegetable and choice of potatoes. Sourdough desserts include carrot cake and brownies. Dinner reservations suggested. **135 E. Broadway, Jackson; (307) 733-5671.**

J.J.'s Silver Dollar Bar & Grill

Notable après-ski hot spot also serves breakfast, lunch and dinner. Good steaks and prime rib, plain or fancy. Game also featured. Lively and fun for the whole evening. **Wort Hotel, 50 N. Glenwood St.; (307) 733-2190.**

Riders join skiers on Jackson's steeps. Photo by Bob Woodall and Wade McCoy

285

Lame Duck Chinese Restaurant

All-purpose and very popular Oriental restaurant, with Chinese dishes from various regions plus sushi and sashimi. Full bar; exotic drinks and sake are the specialties. Private tearooms. Children's menu. Free transportation anywhere in town. Takeout available. Reservations accepted. **680 E. Broadway, Jackson; (307) 733-4311.**

Million Dollar Cowboy Steakhouse

Big downstairs restaurant, once a Mexican mecca and now an upscale steakhouse. Various cuts of beef, plus good selection of game and seafood, including a nightly special. Light fare too for lighter appetites. Full bar. Reservations recommended. Downstairs in the **Million Dollar Cowboy Bar, Town Square, Jackson; (307) 733-4790.**

LeJay's Sportsman's Cafe

Jackson's 24-hour-a-day eatery. Big country breakfasts, served any time. Popular burgers and choice steaks and ribs of various cuts, all with salad bar, vegetable, potato and rolls. Hearty dinners, including steak specials on Friday and prime rib on Saturday evenings. Salad bar. Children's and senior citizens' menu. **Glenwood and Pearl Sts., Jackson; (307) 733-3110.**

286

Louie's Steak & Seafood

Log cabin provides charming and traditional atmosphere. Continental and American dishes, including the Wyoming Wellington. Seafood specials. Cocktails and full wine list. Dinner nightly. Reservations accepted. **175 N. Center St., Jackson; (307) 733-6803.**

Winter horseback riding is a popular activity in the Jackson Hole area. Photo by Bob Woodall/Wade McCoy.

Mountain High Pizza Pie

Skiers' special all-you-can-eat pizza buffet, Monday through Friday evenings, including a large drink for a small price. Also, build-your-own pizzas with choice of crusts and toppings, available in small and large sizes. Also, calzone, stromboli, sausage roll, gyro sandwiches, subs and salads. Bottled beer and wine by the glass. Open daily from early lunch through late dinner. All-day delivery. Takeout available. **120 W. Broadway, Jackson; (307) 733-3646.**

Nani's Genuine Pasta House

European flavor to the place, Italian flavor to the food. Many regional dishes, including nightly specials. Well-conceived and well-prepared gourmet fare at moderate to high prices. Good wine list. Dinner nightly. Takeout available. Reservations recommended. **El Rancho Motel, 240 N. Glenwood St., Jackson; (307) 733-3888.**

Off Broadway

Innovative entrées, including interesting renditions of popular pastas, seafood, poultry, meat and game, such as Wild Game Stuffed Manicotti with Fresh Herb Tomato Sauce, Thai Steamed Seafood with Ginger Sauce and Tournedos Gorgonzola. Wonderful desserts. Fresh-ground coffee. Cocktails, beer and good wine list. Moderate prices for the trendy nature of the place and inventiveness of the food preparation. Non-smoking restaurant. Reservations accepted. **30 King St., Jackson; (307) 733-9777.**

Rafferty's

Good Continental, regional and classic American specialties in resort hotel's fine dining room. Fresh seafood, aged beef and a lovely atmosphere with beamed ceiling, low lights and gleaming glassware and silver. Sunday brunch. Reservations recommended (in fact, highly recommended for brunch). **Snow King Resort, 400 E. King Ave., Jackson; (307) 733-5200.**

Snake River Grille

Fine new restaurant serving stylish food, including excellent appetizers, interesting pasta and dinners centered around fresh seafood, meat and chicken. Also, pizzas in terrific combinations from wood-burning oven. Small luncheon menu with entrées, sandwiches and salads. Reservations suggested. **Town Square, Jackson; (307) 733-0557.**

Stiegler's

Warm and cozy Austrian atmosphere. Continental dinner specialties, many from the Alpine region (East Tyrolean carp, liver dumpling soup, Wienerschnitzel and terrific Austrian pastries). Light Copper Bar menu too. One of the resort's sophisticated spots. Children's menu. Open nightly except Monday. Reservations recommended. **Jackson Hole Racquet Club, Teton Village Rd., Jackson; (307) 733-1071.**

Sweetwater Restaurant

Light lunches (soups, sandwiches, pita pockets and such). Dinners are more elaborate—lamb, seafood and mesquite-grilled specialties. Excellent desserts, including some Austrian treats. Cocktails, wines. Takeout available. Dinner reservations recommended. **King and Pearl Sts., Jackson; (307) 733-3553.**

Teton Pines

European-inspired preparation of meat, game, chicken and seafood. Known for fine sauces. House specialties include steaks, chicken veal and seafood, all done well. Reasonable prices and big portions. Weekday lunch and dinner nightly except Sunday. Children's menu. Reservations recommended. **Teton Village Rd., Jackson; (307) 733-1005.**

Vista Grande

Long-popular Mexican restaurant and bar. Margaritas and chips to start, good Mexican food to follow. Authentic and adapted dishes, all excellent. Large and small portions of most selections, and combination plates too. Better desserts than most Mexican places offer. A few American dishes for the timid. Children's menu. Takeout available. **Teton Village Rd., Jackson; (307) 733-6964.**

NIGHTLIFE

Après-ski starts at Teton Village, with the youngest crowd at the Mangy Moose (loud, lively and fun) or Sojourner's Rendezvous Lounge & Pub (good hors d'oeuvres, largest beer selection in Teton Village, two pool tables, big-screen TV, drink specials), while the somewhat older and slightly more subdued group heads for Dietrich's Bar & Bistro (appetizers and pizza till 11:00 P.M., casual dinners, ski movies and big-screen sports TV) at the Alpenhof or Beaver Dick's Saloon (beer by the yard, bar menu, big-screen sports TV) at the Inn at Jackson Hole. These spots all remain popular throughout the evening. Located between the resort and town, the Calico Pizza Parlor has a pool table and dart board while Stiegler's has a far more restrained ambiance.

In town, the two musts are J.J.'s Silver Dollar Saloon in the Wort Hotel and the Million Dollar Cowboy Bar around the corner. Both are lively, loud and lots of fun. There are other nightspots in Jackson, but those two are the top. The former is noted for the hundreds of silver dollars embedded in the bar top and the latter for saddle-shaped bar stools. Sharing such western atmosphere is the Stagecoach Bar in Wilson, with weekly dancing to the Stagecoach Band, which has played there every Sunday evening since February 16, 1969. The Silver King Resort's Shady Lady Saloon has good drinks and a congenial atmosphere. The latter has happy hour, a roaring fire and live entertainment. Jackson Hole Pub & Brewery, the area's first brew pub, is a hit for congenial drinking and casual dining.

For more information, contact **Jackson Hole Ski Corp., P.O. Box 290, Teton Village, WY 83025, (307) 733-2292; Jackson Hole Visitors Council, P.O. Box 982, Jackson Hole, WY 83001, (800) 782-0011** or **Jackson Hole Chamber of Commerce, P.O. Box E, Jackson, WY 83001, (307) 733-3316.**

GRAND TARGHEE

BACKDROP

Set against the majestic Tetons on the Wyoming-Idaho border, Grand Targhee, Wyoming, offers more skiing with less infrastructure than almost any other area. Just three chairlifts on two adjacent mountains and a vest-pocket resort are really all there is. Granted, that ski area sprawls over 1,500 acres on 2,200 vertical feet and, if that isn't enough, you can always sign on for a day of snowcat skiing on another 1,500 acres with a few hundred more vertical feet. But, for fussy purists, only one number counts, and that's snowfall. That's where Targhee shines, snaring more than 500 inches a year and putting it into the rarefied big leagues with Utah's Snowbird and Alta. Yet this powder haven is so laid-back that Harrison Ford, who has a home over the hill in Jackson, and Jill Clayburgh, who doesn't, created less of a stir than the snowcat driver picking up a powder-tour group.

Targhee is a place to ski your buns off, kick back, relax and ignore the world. A hot night on the town is driving down to Driggs, Idaho, for a pizza. The tiny resort has replaced a reputation for seamless powder for its old bare-bones image that kept many skiers from vacationing there. With award-winning architect Mory Bergmeyer, a fugitive from the Boston rat race, at the helm, Targhee's new construction, renovations and even redecoration are first-rate. Targhee's new style can be described as a "mountain monumental," with rough-hewn lodgepoles, natural stone and stucco. The upgrades started with the refurbishment of primitive motel-style lodges with Bergmeyer's pieces prompting a side business mail-ordering lodgepole furniture. Most people first ski Grand Targhee on day trips from Jackson Hole by car or Targhee Express Bus, and many return—seduced by the prices, the powder and

the privacy. Mory Bergmeyer is 6-foot-4 and rangy—and he has envisioned a ski resort built to his dimensions. He plans lifts reaching into the present snowcat-served area and base development expanded from the present teensy-weensy to just a little bigger—something that would still be compact. The plans are ambitious, especially for a family-owned, noncorporate business. Even as the grand master plan (now approved) painfully wound its way through maze of federal, state and local approvals, Targhee's prime purpose remained snow and the pleasures it affords, and the ski resort retains the feeling of an intimate jewel in the Tetons where great skiing, moderate prices and a laid-back friendliness prevail.

THE LAY OF THE LAND

Grand Targhee is located at the end of the road that climbs out of Idaho's pancake-flat Teton River Valley. One of the greatest contrasts in skiing is the drive from Driggs, a farm town in the midst of Idaho potato country that is only reluctantly stirring to a skiing bear, straight to the west flank of the Tetons. Accessed from Idaho but in Wyoming with a 6-mile margin, Grand Targhee shows a distinctly Alpine face. Set on a wooded mountainside with jagged peaks in the background, it is the quintessential hideaway.

The resort is often defined by what it isn't—unsophisticated, unpretentious, inexpensive. But it's noteworthy that no one ever calls it uninteresting or unfriendly. The base area (describing it as a village, at this point, is still hyperbole) consists of three lodges and two pleasant log cabins (one that serves as the Kids' Club and the other as Nordic center). The Rendezvous Lodge features dining, entertainment and shops under one roof, and the new Powder Scouts Headquarters is the center for older children's lessons and activities. Everything, including the lifts, is a short walk to everything else. With such compactness, it is exceptional for families, who also get good multiday deals on lodging and lifts, and with expansive skiing and Grand Teton soaring to 13,770 feet as a backdrop—assuming that the snow lets up enough for you to see it—Grand Targhee provides an unsurpassed combination of enormity and intimacy.

GETTING THERE

Grand Targhee is 42 miles northwest of Jackson, Wyoming, and 87 miles northeast of Idaho Falls. Both have scheduled air service from various major cities. Driggs's own airport, just 13 miles from the resort, can handle charter flights and private aircraft. Grand Targhee's van provides transportation between any of the airports and the resorts; on multiday packages, children 14 and younger are free. If you drive, you will find Grand Targhee 290 miles from Salt Lake City, via 15 north to US 26 east, Idaho 33 north to Driggs, then 12 miles up the mountain road to the resort.

PROFILE

The resort's whole name, Grand Targhee Ski & Summer Resort, is almost as long as a thumbnail description of the place: half a dozen buildings at the base of a 2,200-vertical-foot ski area. Its slogan, "Snow from Heaven Not Hoses," alludes to the average annual snowfall of 42 feet. Even when all 444 guests who can be accommodated at the base, a busload or two from Jackson and the entire day-skiing population of metropolitan Driggs are on the mountain, it doesn't begin to crowd 1,500 acres of lift-served ski terrain or even to create lift lines on the three chairlifts. Taking a page from neighboring Jackson Hole's book, if you join Targhee's Vertical Club and manage a cumulative 100,000 feet, you'll get a special hat, free airport shuttle and a hefty discount off your next snowcat trip.

Only about one-fifth of Targhee's terrain is groomed into European-style pistes. The rest of the snow is left as nature laid it on the slopes. With so much acreage skied by so few people, some fresh snow normally lasts from storm to storm. The 40-plus named runs have more to do with the fact that trail maps look funny without them than to limit where you actually might ski. With the exception of a band of off-limits cliffs, Targhee's premise is, if you can see it, you can ski it—and what you see and ski is three ridges, a pair of wide bowls and endless acres of generous

Inside Grand Targhee

glades. Actually, the forestation is thicker than you might suspect, for the snow is so deep that the small trees are buried, the medium-size ones poke up like frail saplings and only the big guys look like real trees.

Resort elevation 8,000 feet
Top of highest lift 10,200 feet
Bottom of lowest lift 8,000 feet
Total vertical 2,200 feet (more than 2,800 feet with snowcat)
Longest run 2 1/2 miles
Average annual snowfall 500 inches
Ski season mid-November to mid-April
Lifts 1 high-speed detachable quad chairlift, 1 fixed-grip quad, 1 double, 2 surface tows
Capacity 140,000 skiers per season
Terrain 46 runs, 1,500 lift-served acres (10% beginner and novice, 70% intermediate, 20% advanced and expert); 20 runs, 1,500 snowcat-served acres (all intermediate, advanced and expert)
Snow reports (307) 353-2300

A beginner tow and two chairlifts are just steps from the base. The Shoshone novice chair, now a quad, climbs 365 vertical feet up a neat little hill peppered with widely spaced trees. The Bannock chair, which is now a high-speed quad, covers nearly a 1 1/4 miles with a 2,200-foot vertical, rising along a ridge to the summit. The massive cirque it serves is rilled with named routes that cascade down generously scooped-out bowls. Long traverses embrace Targhee's lift-served terrain. Powderhounds ski south along the ridge, following Teton Traverse into such snow-holding chutes as Lost Groomer's, while mid-level cruising skiers, and experts on an ego trip, barrel down immaculate snowfields in the cusp of the bowl. To the north of the Bannock unloading area is the traverse to Sitting Bull Ridge. Intermediates ski the crest of the ridge, while experts hit more north-facing chutes. Those who can resist the temptation to plunge into such enticing terrain keep going to Chief Joseph Bowl, one of the best blue-square runs in all the Rockies.

Continuing toward the northern area boundary is the third chairlift, Blackfoot, rising 1,200 vertical feet to what many skiers consider the essence of Grand Targhee—hundreds of acres of open slopes where trees are sprinkled like confetti and the untracked powder snow lingers and lingers. The small but loyal cadre of Targhee regulars feels this north end, where the slope is steeper and the tracks are even fewer, offers the best skiing of all—actually, the best in-bounds skiing of all.

SNOWBOARDING

If snowboarders had a heaven, it would be Grand Targhee. There is a permanent half-pipe right next to the Dream Catcher high-speed quad. Wide open terrain, great steeps (and equally great gentle terrain for learners) and best of all, that abundant powder is what riders treasure most. The absence of skiing crowds (or crowds of any sort) is also a plus, for while skiers and snowboarders have largely learned to accommodate each others' styles and needs, riders do like to have a lot of terrain to work.

SNOWCAT SKIING

You can sign on for some of the finest snowcat skiing in the Rockies, which takes place by the half or full day on a wonderfully contoured, blissfully powdery, oddly named mountain called Peaked Mountain. More often than not, this mountain is blanketed with an extravagance of downy-light snow, and the snowcat is the only conveyance other than a helicopter that makes the dream of powder skiing a reality. The cat ferries just a dozen skiers at a time—10 guests and two guides—to an additional 1,500 acres with 20 named routes which ups the vertical to runs of 2,600, 2,800 or very occasionally 3,000 feet, depending on snow conditions and the group's stamina and ability. A confident intermediate with a solid stance, a willingness to go for it and fat skis can find no better place to learn to ski powder than on Peaked's steady, fall-line runs of moderate pitch and uncommon width under the tutelage of Targhee instructors, who are practiced in teaching people to handle the fluff—including what the resort calls the Ultimate Powder lesson for those who need it. But veteran and newly minted powderhounds alike believe a day of snowcat skiing is akin to being in heaven—and so do snowboarders, for whom Peaked Mountain absolutely ranks as a peak experience.

SKI SCHOOL PROGRAMS

Advanced and Specialty Programs

Egan and DesLauriers Brothers Advanced Ski Clinics: Upper-level workshop with ski-film stars Dan and John Egan and Rob and Eric DesLauriers. Available a few times during the season.
Women's Ski Clinics: Available in January and March, under the direction of Pat Campbell, Targhee's new ski school director.
Ultimate Powder Lessons: Half-day lesson on the snowcat with an instructor.

For Families

Nonskiing Children

The old Kids' Club building is now a dedicated nursery and day-care facility, with play, nap and eating areas for infants, toddlers and pre-schoolers.
Baby's Club: Full- or half-day care for infants and toddlers ages 3 or younger and non-skiers to age 5. Discount for second child, same family. Open Saturday evening for with hourly child care. Reservations required, **(800) TARGHEE.**

Skiing Children

The Kids' Club building is the home base for children 5 and younger, where you can arrange for children's ski school, rentals and day care, if necessary to supplement ski lessons. Reservations recommended. **(800) 827-4433.** The new Powder Scouts headquarters is for ages 6 and older, with ski instruction, gear storage, lunch and other activities.

Noteworthy

Free Skiing: Children 5 and younger ski free at all times. Also, children 14 and younger stay and ski free per paid adult on packages of three nights or longer.

Kid's Club Ski Lessons: Group half-day or private lessons for children ages 5 to 7. May be combined with Kids' Club supervision.
Powder Scouts: Group half-day and full-day lessons for children ages 7 and older.

FOR RACERS

NASTAR: Tuesday, Friday and Saturday

NORDIC SKIING

The Targhee Nordic Center has 15 kilometers of groomed trails, including tracks and a skating lane. It may be not much in terms of mileage, but the views, the variety and the snow conditions would do a bigger facility proud. The ski school offers instruction in track, skiing and skating skills, as well as telemarking. Ample backcountry opportunities exist in the Tetons. **Rendezvous Ski Tours,** headquartered in nearby Victor, offers day tours, hut trips and even backcountry tours. They range from easy instructional or photographic tours in and near Teton National Park to the gonzo Teton Traverse all the way to the Jackson Hole ski area. **219 Highland Way, Victor, ID 83455; (208) 787-2906.**

WHERE TO STAY

Grand Targhee

Grand Targhee Ski & Summer Resort, (800) TARGHEE. Address for entire resort is **P.O. Box SKI, Alta, WY 83422.** The resort's complete new spa and fitness center features outdoor heated pool, outdoor hot tub and indoor hot tub for all guests. Packages of three days, three nights or longer include lift tickets and discounts on other resort activities.

Wyoming

Mid-Priced and Economy Accommodations

Targhee & Teewinot Lodges
Recently redecorated and attractive, but still functional and price-worthy. Rooms have two queen-size beds. Public space with adobe fireplaces. Daily housekeeping, complimentary coffee, bell service.

Condominiums

Sioux Lodge
Upgraded condos. Studios have one queen-size bed and one bunk bed, sleeping four. Loft units have one double bed, one bunk bed and one queen-size sleep-sofa and accommodate up to six. Two-bedroom units have two queen-size beds and two sets of bunk beds and sleep up to eight. All have kitchenettes, fireplaces and balconies.

Driggs, Victor and Alta

Mid-Priced Accommodations

Best Western Teton West
Biggest motel in Driggs with 40 units, some with kitchenettes. Pets allowed. Daily housekeeping.

Hot tub. **476 N. Main St., P.O. Box 780, Driggs, ID 83422; (208) 354-2363, (800) 528-1234** for Best Western reservations.

High Country Comforts
Five-acre ranch $1 1/2$ miles from access road. Huge yet intimate log lodge with big fireplace in living room. Four rooms with shared baths. Niceties include flannel sheets and down comforters. Quiet, secluded and remote. Daily housekeeping, full country-style breakfast. Bar area, outdoor hot tub. **Route 1, Box 3720, Alta, WY, via Driggs, ID 83422; (307) 353-8560.**

The Teton Teepee
Old-time ski lodge 7 miles from Targhee. Friendly and family-run. Has 22 private rooms and dorms for 52 skiers. Small but cute rooms have private baths and queen-size beds. Soaring central lounge with fireplace, bar and dining area. Meals served family-style. Special rates for children and teens. Modified American Plan packages include breakfast and dinner, beverages, Targhee lift tickets, ski shuttle. Shuttle to Jackson Hole and region's airports for extra fee. Daily housekeeping, breakfast and dinner, courtesy shuttle to lifts. Outdoor hot tub, game room, TV room, ski

An expert skier plunges off a cornice into one of Targhee's generous glades. Photo by Willaim Sallaz Duomo

shop. **Route 1, Box 3475, Alta, WY, via Driggs, ID 83422; (307) 353-8176.**

Economy Accommodations

Pines Motel
Simple, nine-unit motel. Super-bargain rates. **105 S. Main St., P.O. Box 117, Driggs, ID 83422; (208) 354-2774.**

Timberline Motel
Economy 22-room motel 20 miles from resort. Located at junction of Hwys 31 and 33. **P.O. Box 157, Victor, ID 83455; (208) 787-2772.**

Noteworthy
Ski Three is a noteworthy package combining Jackson Hole and Grand Targhee, Jackson Hole or Snow King Resort, with several extras. Book through any resort. (See Jackson Hole chapter, page 274, for details.)

DINING OUT

Martin's Sleigh Ride Dinner
Short ride to nearby yurt. Choice of steak or chicken with hearty western fixins served family-style. BYO wine, beer or booze. Two seatings nightly. Entertaining and fun. Reservations through Grand Targhee Activity Center in the Retail Building or by dialing Ext. 1355 from your room.

The Wizard of Za
Fine pizzas, from classics to creative. Available daily. Takeout or delivered by room service. **Rendezvous Base Lodge, Grand Targhee; (307) 353-2300.**

Wild Bill's Grille de Border
Cafeteria-style breakfasts, including fresh baked goods, and such lunches as grilled sandwiches, burgers and pizza. Salad bar. **Rendezvous Base Lodge, Grand Targhee; (307) 353-2300.**

Skadi's
Attractive high-ceilinged restaurant. Eclectic menu. Good quality and interesting. Moderate prices. Friendly service. Children's menu. **Rendezvous Base Lodge, Grand Targhee; (307) 353-2300.**

Snorkels
Pastries, espresso and deli fare. **Retail Building, Grand Targhee; (307) 353-2300.**

Trap Bar
Light food at lunch and dinner. Loud, live entertainment. No kids. South-facing deck and outdoor barbecue when the weather's right. **Retail Building, Grand Targhee; (307) 353-2304.**

293

NIGHTLIFE

There's the Trap Bar and the Trap Bar and the Trap Bar and ... . As Targhee's only nightspot, it seems to feel that the volume and enthusiasm generated by several ought to be encapsulated in one. The music is live and loud, the beer and liquor flow and the merriment is genuine. Ski Weekers have an evening agenda to plug into: wine and cheese on Mondays, movie classics on Tuesdays and Thursdays, casino night on Wednesdays and bingo night on Fridays, all included in the package. Teens have their own turf in the rear of the Wizard of Za pizza restaurant in the Rendezvous Base Lodge with video games, pool, pinball and a cool CD jukebox. (Driggs, being a largely Mormon farming community, doesn't offer much in the way of nightlife.)

For more information, contact **Grand Targhee Ski & Summer Resort, P.O. Box SKI, Alta, WY 83422; (800) TAR-GHEE, (307) 353-2300.**

SNOWY RANGE

BACKDROP

The world may ski at Jackson Hole, but Wyoming skis at Snowy Range. This agreeable little ski area is 32 miles from Laramie (population 27,000, plus 12,000 students at the University of Wyoming) and 75 miles from Cheyenne (population 50,000), the state capital. These census figures are significant only because these are the two largest cities in the state that ranks ninth in land area but 50th in population with fewer than 500,000 inhabitants. By contrast, world-famous Jackson Hole is diagonally across more than 400 lonely miles of Wyoming from where the largest concentration of its people live. In addition to being convenient, Snowy Range provides the kind of skiing that people complain has been lost. Anybody who rues the crowds and costs and complications of big-time resorts clearly has never been skiing in southern Wyoming.

THE LAY OF THE LAND

Snowy Range is simplicity itself. The base area is a sprinkling of the kind of A-frames they don't make anymore. The day lodge is the Papa Bear-size A-frame; the Mama-Bear size one is the children's ski school and the lift shacks are Baby Bear-size A-frames, but the reality is that they're all just right because such buildings from the past keep prices low in the present. The area is set just east of Medicine Bow Pass, which is where the Continental Divide has its easternmost thrust. You drive into the close-in parking lot, buy a very inexpensive lift ticket and go skiing. Period. It's skiing in a time warp. Heck, even getting to Snowy Range is a time warp. The only settlement you pass is Centennial, a hamlet that's half-

hippie-hokey with drop-city dwellings and junked cars and half-touristic with a handful of cafes, bars, convenience stores and motels.

GETTING THERE

Laramie, in southeastern Wyoming just off I-80, is an old-fashioned town built as a Union Pacific boomtown. Most accommodations are located there. To reach the ski area, you drive through the glorious Centennial Valley on Wyoming 130, a scenic byway. The ski area is 5 miles from the town of Centennial. Laramie's Brees Field Airport has had on-again, off-again commercial air service with connections through Denver. Amtrak and Greyhound also serve the city.

PROFILE

Snowy Range's lifts are few and simple, and the area is laid out so that you can get from the bottom of any lift from the top of any other, which is something few giants can boast. You'll want ski around, since the terrain is surprisingly varied and interesting, and if you move from one mountain sector to another, you'll feel as if you are at a much larger ski area. Snowy Range sits in a powder pocket. Snow clouds roll in from the northwest, collide with an upslope on the front face, and deposit their load onto the ski terrain. In fact, Snowy Range claims to have its own little weather system. When there's not a patch of snow on the ground in Laramie or even in Centennial, the clouds are often thick over the ski area, sprinkling new flakes on top of the last snowfall.

Of the three lifts visible from the base area, the double chair called Virginian, after the Owen Wister opus, is the main chair. It serves beguiling boulevards, consistently pitched and as comforting as hot chocolate with marshmallow topping after a cold childhood afternoon on the sledding hill. Easy-street skiing. Warmup-ville. Bring on the novices. Invite the whole family. Cruisarama. The next lift over, on your right as you are looking uphill, is a double chairlift, installed in 1996

Photo courtesy Snowy Range

to replace the T-bar, the area's original lift. The runs it serves are reminiscent of classic Eastern terrain with western snow. Laramie, Overland, Bronco and Boomerang are a quartet of steep trails threaded through the woods, alternating spunky little pitches that bump up with gather-yourself-together flats between them. Until snowmaking was added to these runs, they were as narrow as they were steep, but now they've been widened too. The old T-bar liftline is the newest in this cluster of challenging runs. Snowy Range apparently has more tree skiing than it does tree skiers, because the snow in those woods is often virtually untracked for days after a storm. From the top of the lift, you can slide to a group of chutes west of the cut trails, stopping in a clearing to admire Medicine Bow Peak, at over 12,000 feet the highest point in this part of Wyoming. The chutes are nicknamed Woodchuck, Rock Chuck, RPM and Lost Cohones; the tight trees, mandatory turns and occasional under-growth make it easy to infer how the latter might have gotten its name.

Locals refer to the terrain off these two chair-lifts as Snowy Range, while Corner Mountain on the far left end of the ski area is the newer—and a precursor of what make be in the future. To get there, you can either take the Pioneer beginner chair and follow a green-circle trail called 22 to Lower Drifter or ski from the top of the Virginian via Upper Drifter, Drifter and Lower Drifter. With a triple chairlift and half a dozen runs from easy blues to moderate blacks, Corner Mountain is a haven for intermediate skiers who enjoy the sweeping trails and expansive views. (A nifty piece of trivia is that Corner Mountain isn't called that on any topographical map. It got that name because the true Corner Mountain is visible from the ski trails.)

Also visible off the backside are Horseshoe and Libby Creek beyond, two drainages on Snowy Range's development wish list. Build-out to this dimension would up Snowy Range's vertical by a hair, but more importantly, would provide slopeside lodging for up to 500 skiers. Expanding into Libby Creek would, in a large sense, also bring skiing full circle. An old-time ski area called Libby Creek once operated one drainage over from the present ski area. It was a formidable place with an

Inside Snowy Range

old mine-hoist lift and super-steep terrain (up to a 37 percent grade). In 1959, when Route 130 was relocated, Libby Creek closed and Snowy Range opened with the T-bar and somewhat gentler ter-rain than Libby Creek had offered. The current owners tripled the acreage and doubled the num-ber of lifts with the Pioneer beginner slope and a chairlift in 1985 and Corner Mountain and its triple chair a year later. Skiing at Horseshoe and Libby Creek may be in the future, but for the present, Snowy Range remains a congenial, old-fashioned oasis and the top choice for budget-conscious skiers from Wyoming, plus Nebraska and northern Colorado.

SNOWBOARDING

You'll see lots of riders on the half-pipe on the lower portion of "old" Snowy Range, but many more are on the black-diamond runs off the new chair. The widening of these trails has made them appealing to the swoop-and-turn technique favored by some riders, while the contiguous trees draw the short-turn, obstacle-jumping contingent.

296 SKI SCHOOL PROGRAMS

Introductory Programs

Learn to Ski: Lessons, rentals and Pioneer beginner chairlift ticket.
Learn to Snowboard: Lessons, rentals and Pioneer beginner chairlift ticket.

Advanced and Specialty Programs

All Area Packages: All-area lift ticket, 1$\frac{1}{2}$-hour lesson and rental ski or snowboard equipment.

For Families

Skiing Children

Skiasauruas Club: Instruction for ages 3 to 7, with all-day supervision and lunch available; optional equipment rental.
Ski Whiz Club: Instruction for ages 8 to 12, with all-day supervision and lunch available; optional equipment rental.

NORDIC SKIING

There are two nearby cross-country centers. Medicine Bow National Forest has 10 main trails

Mountain Stats—
Snowy Range

Resort elevation 9,200 feet (base area)
Top of highest lift 9,880 feet
Bottom of lowest lift 8,990 feet
Total vertical 990 feet
Longest run 1.9 miles
Average annual snowfall 250 inches
Ski season mid-November through mid-April
Lifts 1 triple chairlift, 3 double chairs
Capacity 5,400 skiers per hour
Terrain 25 trails, 100 acres (25% beginner and novice, 50% intermediate, 25% advanced and expert)
Snowmaking 65% coverage
Snow reports (307) 745-5750

and several shorter connectors through the Snowy Range mountains from several trailheads. Some are groomed, others are marked and there are additional opportunities for backcountry skiing. Pole Mountain's 13 miles of machine-groomed trails start at the Upper Tie City winter campground and parking lot off Happy Jack Road and wind through the Curt Gowdy State Park in four main loops. Telemark enthusiasts flock to the challenging old Libby Creek area, accessible from the Green Rock Picnic Area trailhead. For information, check with the **Medicine Bow National Forest Supervisor, (307) 745-8971.**

WHERE TO STAY

Reservations: **(800) GO-2-SNOW.**

Centennial

Mid-Priced Accommodations

Brooklyn Lodge

Spacious log lodge nestled in spruce and pine forest. Located on scenic site at 10,200 feet, off Hwy 130. Two rooms, decorated with western charm. Children permitted only when parties rent both rooms. Friday and Saturday must be booked together. Living room with large stone fireplace. Non-smoking inn. Full or Continental breakfast, optional box lunch on advance request. **P.O. Box 292, Centennial, WY 82055; (307) 742-6916, (307) 745-7874.**

Vee Bar Guest Ranch

Picturesque and authentic spread in the Centennial Valley, 21 miles from Laramie and 10 miles from Snowy Range. Accommodations in six duplex suites and three cabins, finely restored and furnished with western antiques. Rustic ranch house with cozy lobby and atmospheric dining room. Operates on B&B plan during ski season, with full breakfast daily included and Friday and Saturday night dinners at additional cost. Horseback riding and/or sleighrides sometimes available. Daily housekeeping. Outdoor hot tub. **2091 Hwy 130, Laramie, WY 82070; (800) 788-4630, (307) 745-7036.**

Noteworthy

Children 5 and under ski free. A low-cost ticket for the Pioneer chair is available for older children and adults.

Economy Accommodations

Friendly Motel

Simple budget motel. Ten rooms, all with two double beds and private bath and shower. Adjacent grocery and convenience store, lounge. Pets permitted. Daily housekeeping. **P.O. Box 195, Hwy 130, Centennial, WY 82055; (307) 452-6033.**

Old Corral Motor Hotel

Tourist landmark motel with 15 simple and functional rooms, plus large adjacent restaurant and entertainment complex. Children 13 and under free in parents' room. Pets permitted. Daily housekeeping, B&B plan option. **P.O. Box 277, 1750 Hwy 130, Centennial, WY 82055; (800) 678-2024, (307) 745-5918.**

Snowy Mountain Lodge

Former University of Wyoming Science Camp. Now guest lodge with winterized cabins, each accommodating as few as two to as many as

eight people. Also, bargain bunkhouse for 25. Secluded location, one-third mile beyond Hwy 130 winter closure. Lodge operates Snow Rover shuttle to road and to ski area. Restaurant, lounge. **3474 Hwy 130, P.O. Box 151, Centennial, WY 82055; (307) 742-SNOW.**

Laramie

Mid-Priced Accommodations

Annie Moore's Guest House

Built in 1910 and operated for years as a ladies' boarding house. Now charming home-style B&B inn close to the university campus. Six rooms (four with personal sinks) and two baths. Spacious sunroom with television. Kitchen privileges. Non-smoking inn. Generous Continental breakfast, daily housekeeping. **819 University Ave., Cheyenne, WY 82070; (800) 552-8992, (307) 721-4177.**

Foster's Country Inn

Large full-service motor inn with 112 units, just off I-80. Some non-smoking rooms. Children free in parents' room. Twenty-four hour front desk, room service, daily housekeeping. Twenty-four-hour restaurant, indoor pool, spa. **P.O. Box 580, 1561 Snowy Range Rd., Laramie, WY 82070; (800) 526-5145, (307) 742-8371, (800) 528-1234** for Best Western reservations.

Prairie Breeze

Victorian mansion, once the home of the University of Wyoming president, and now a charming B&B. Six rooms (four with personal in-room sinks). **718 Ivinson Ave., Laramie, WY 82070; (307) 745-5482.**

Economy Accommodations

Holiday Inn

A 100-room motor inn at Laramie's major highway intersection of I-80 and US 287. Some non-smoking rooms. Basic motel rooms, but some hotel-style amenities and services. Children free in parents' room. Pets permitted. Restaurant, lounge and sports bar, indoor pool, spa, 24-hour front desk. **2313 Soldier Spring Rd., Laramie, WY 82070; (800) 526-5245, (307) 742-6611; (800) HOL-IDAY** for Holiday Inn reservations.

Laramie Travel Inn
Budget lodging, with 28 rooms, some non-smoking. Adjacent to restaurant. Daily housekeeping, complimentary in-room coffee. **262 N. Third St., Laramie, WY 82070; (800) 227-5430, (307) 745-4853.**

Sunset Inn
Fifty-one-room motel located three blocks from I-80. Some kitchenette units. AAA and senior discounts; children stay free in parents' room. Pets permitted. Continental breakfast, daily housekeeping, hot tub. **1004 S. Third St., Laramie, WY 82070; (307) 742-3741.**

Super 8 Motel
Budget chain motel, just off I-80. Forty-two rooms, some non-smoking. Guest laundry. Complimentary coffee, daily housekeeping. **I-80 and Curtis St., Laramie, WY 82070; (307) 745-8901; (800) 800-8000** for Super 8 reservations.

298

DINING OUT

The Beanery
Bargain Mexican and American food. Daily breakfast to early dinner (closes Sundays at noon). **2-58 Snowy Range Rd., Laramie; (307) 742-0869.**

The classic A-frame school of ski area architecture is alive and thriving at Snowy Range. Photo by Claire Walter

Bowman Pub & Brewing Co.
New brew pub, featuring unique beer and ale. Casual atmosphere. Pub-style specialties served at reasonable prices. Also, gourmet baked goods. Open from early lunch to late dinner. Children's menu. **320 S. Second St., Laramie; (307) 742-3349.**

Cafe Jacques
Trendy downtown bistro in historic building. Innovative American and eclectic dishes. Seafood, pasta and steaks featured. Also wines (by the bottle or by the glass), beer and cocktails. Reservations accepted. **216 Grand, Laramie; (307) 742-5522.**

Cafe Olé
Lively spot for filling Mexican fare. Good margaritas. Children's menu. Convenient to motel row. Takeout available. Open daily from lunch through dinner. **519 Boswell, Laramie; (307) 742-8383.**

Jeffrey's Bistro
Fine dining and natural foods in happy harmony. Laramie's best salads. Lunch and dinner Monday through Saturday; Sunday brunch. **123 Ivinson Ave., Laramie; (307) 742-0744.**

Jeffrey's Too
Espresso and light fare, served continuously from breakfast to after-dinner, around the corner from Jeffrey's Bistro (see above). **116 S. Second St., Laramie; (307) 742-0744.**

The Laramie Stage Stop
Three restaurants under one roof. The Rails, The Eatin' House and The Red Room. Cocktails. **109 S. Third St., Laramie; (307) 745-6433.**

The Old Corral
Sprawling steakhouse serving hearty meals "with all the trimmings." Informal and fun. Family-friendly. Open nightly for dinner. Lounge and entertainment. **2750 Hwy 130, Centennial; (307) 745-5918.**

Outrider Cafe
Casual restaurant for breakfast (served 24 hours a day), lunch and dinner. Basic favorites such as burgers, sandwiches, steak, chicken, spaghetti and a few Mexican dishes. Fountain treats, Good children's menu. Takeout available. **Curtis St. and I-80, Laramie; (307) 745-9008.**

The Roundhouse Restaurant
Family dining with a railroad theme. Moderate prices. Steak and prime rib featured. Lounge. **1560 N. Third St., Laramie; (307) 721-2017.**

Vee Bar Guest Ranch
Dinners served Friday and Saturday nights in rustic and charming Centennial Valley ranch. Choice of about nine entrées, including steak, shrimp and trout. Full bar. Reservations required. **2091 Hwy 130, Centennial Valley; (800) 788-4630, (307) 745-7036.**

Winger's
Casual American restaurant. Best known for Buffalo chicken wings, but also serves good ribs and has fresh fruit and salad bar. Cocktails. **3626 Grand Ave., Laramie; (307) 742-4999.**

NIGHTLIFE

Centennial is the first stop for after-ski activities, with a choice between the Trading Post Saloon and the Old Water Hole Saloon at The Old Corral. Both have full bar service, munchies and sometimes live entertainment. The Laramie Stage Stop's Muddy Gap Saloon, the Depot Lounge and the Buckhorn & Parlor Car are in-town equivalents. The Buckhorn dates back to the 1890s and is Laramie's oldest saloon, with a bullet hole in the mirror behind the bar from some long-ago altercation and such believe-it-or-not bric-a-brac as a two-headed colt and dwarf calf. A newer one is Bogie's Tavern in the Holiday Inn (the hotel restaurant is, predictably, called Bacall's). The Bowman Pub & Brewing Co. brews quality ales and is open really late for the thirsty and hungry. Cafe Jacques is a with-it downtown bar and grill, featuring three dozen imported and domestic premium beers. Wood Landing is a country bar with a great following among locals and students. Its wooden dance floor was built on railroad car springs and really rocks. You might also take a brisk stroll through Laramie's historic downtown—and brisk is the way you'll probably want to do your strolling in winter—and stop in at the growing number of interesting shops and art galleries. Taking in evening activities at the University of Wyoming or the Laramie Plains Civic Center is also a good way to spend your off-slope hours.

For more information, contact **Snowy Range, 1420 Thomes, Laramie, WY 82070, (307) 745-5750; Laramie Area Chamber of Commerce, 800 S. Third St., Laramie, WY 82070, (800) 445-5303, (307) 745-7339.**

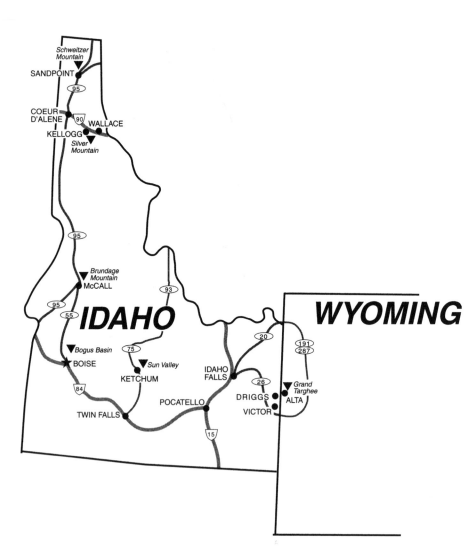

Idaho

Photo courtesy Sun Valley Ski Resort

301

SUN VALLEY

BACKDROP

Set in the middle-of-nowhere sheep country of central Idaho, with the magnificent Sawtooth Range as a backdrop, Sun Valley debuted in 1936 as America's first built-for-skiing resort. Over the years, skiing changed from glamorous and simple to demanding and complex. Sun Valley maintained its edge by developing a huge, complex peak called Bald Mountain, the unrivaled giant of Idaho skiing—and one of the biggest mountains in all the Rockies. Other ski areas come up with dandy skiable acreage and impressive statistics, but none tops Sun Valley in sustained vertical or steady challenge. Baldy continues to attract some of America's best skiers—bad bumpers, persnickety powderhounds and solid veterans who tame the mountain with run after run of high-speed GS turns. Other ski resorts sign on medal-winning ski stars. Sun Valley grows them; Olympic medalists Gretchen Fraser, Christin Cooper and Picabo Street are also local talent.

After six decades in skiing's big time, Sun Valley is still up there—like the aging beauty who's recently had a lift here, a tuck there, a color highlight someplace else and somehow manages to look better than ever. More than any other resort, Sun Valley combines the best of the old and the best of the new—new lifts and snowmaking, but old-time glamour, holiday traditions and unsurpassed overall cachet. Other than the magnificent mountains and the wonderful white that falls upon them, Sun Valley's most enduring element is the classy Sun Valley Lodge, with the glamorous Duchin Lounge, legendary Lodge Dining Room and hallways lined with photographs of the famous who have visited both.

Baldy, the beacon around which everything else revolves, remains a revered giant among ski mountains, and the resort—which comprises both Sun Valley and Ketchum—remains a mecca too. The Ketchum–Sun Valley area also offers exceptional cross-country terrain, backcountry

302

excursions, heli-skiing and a panoply of non-ski sports, yet—like Aspen—it is synonymous with big-mountain, lift-served skiing and a fine lifestyle. With air access only by commuter flights to nearby Hailey and no sizable drive-market city at all nearby, Sun Valley and Ketchum are awkward to reach, so it is testimonial to the joint appeals of town, mountain and resort that so many people who could afford to ski anywhere still prefer Sun Valley.

THE LAY OF THE LAND

Ketchum is a traditional western town, with streets laid in a grid pattern in the flat land between two streams. West of town is Bald Mountain, which is where most folks who say they are skiing Sun Valley actually ski. The ski terrain is accessible from River Run, on the outskirts of town, where significant base development has recently taken place, but many people commute around the mountain to the Warm Springs side, where a resort village has taken shape, slowly but surely. Northeast of downtown is the resort known as Sun Valley, comprising the Sun Valley Lodge, Inn and Condominiums, the Mall and the famous outdoor ice rink where Sonja Henie twirled in *Sun Valley Serenade*. Off on a side road east of Ketchum is Dollar Mountain, Sun Valley's beginner hill, and on its backside are the slopes of Elkhorn. Behind this two-faced ski complex is Elkhorn Resort, a sizable condominium and townhome community with its own small central mall. Lift tickets are sold at the Baldy and Dollar bases as well as at the Sun Valley Village Sports Center, the latter open until 7:00 P.M.

GETTING THERE

Commuter planes fly into Hailey's Friedman Memorial Airport. Other carriers operating larger aircraft serve Twin Falls (82 miles, 1½ hours), Idaho Falls (155 miles, three hours) and Boise (154 miles, three hours). Rental cars are available at all airports, and **Sun Valley Stages** provides daily scheduled bus service from Boise,

(800) 821-9064, (208) 622-4200. Salt Lake City is 292 miles (5½ hours) via I-15 north, I-84 west and Idaho Route 75 north. Ironically, for a resort built by the Union Pacific to promote rail travel, the nearest Amtrak station is in Shoshone, more than 40 miles away.

Complimentary Sun Valley buses, which are yellow, connect Sun Valley Village with Baldy and Dollar from 8:30 A.M. to 4:30 P.M. daily. Elkhorn operates complimentary morning and afternoon ski shuttles between the resort and the lifts. There are also free shuttle buses between the Sun Valley Village (Mall area) and condominiums, though they are within easy walking distance. KART buses, which are blue, run by the municipality and also free, connect the ski areas, the resort and Ketchum, running from early morning until midnight. If you take your own car to ski, bear in mind that parking is extremely limited (and costly).

THE SKIING

Bald Mountain

Profile

One of only a handful of American ski mountains with a vertical drop exceeding 3,000 feet, Baldy dominates Idaho skiing, both physically and psychically. It is so complex that for years its trails were mapped in four separate panels. In the cold clutch of deep winter, the best strategy is to launch your skiing day on the River Run side, where two of the quads perform a high-speed hoist. Start with the River Run and then shift over to the Lookout Express for a speedy approach to skiing. A good initial target is the east-facing cruising runs of Seattle Ridge. That's where you'll find Baldy's most endearing terrain, including Gretchen's Gold and Christin's Silver. They honor two local women and the Olympic medals they won—respectively, gold in 1948 by Gretchen Fraser and silver in 1984 by Christin Cooper. Wide and super-groomed, Seattle Ridge's trails are gentle enough for relatively new skiers but fast and fun for better ones to warm up on.

After that, or instead if there's fresh powder, it's great to head for the steeper slopes off the

Inside Sun Valley

Idaho

Christmas, Exhibition and Cold Springs lifts and ultimately to eight fabulous mountaintop bowls. The huge cirque between Seattle Ridge and Christmas Ridge is crenulated into bowls of various steepnesses, ranging from Broadway Face and adjacent Sigi's Bowl, which are quite mild, to Lookout, Easter and Little Easter Bowls, which are more than just passingly steep. Christmas Bowl is the most demanding; with steep sides and monster moguls in the trough, there is no opportunity to bail out. Easter, Lookout and Mayday start steep as well, but they soon tame down—which is not to say they are easy skiing, just less than hair-raising. Visually and experientially, this is the most Alpine section of Baldy, for the trees are sparse, the views are wide-ranging and lifts rising in various directions are visible from many spots. Also, and more significantly, you can ski anywhere. When the snow is blowing and the visibility is low, or the snow is no longer new, the bowls aren't the most fun you'll ever have on skis. But when the powder wells up around your legs and you are engulfed by the uncrowded vastness of Baldy's bowls, there is absolutely no better skiing in the northern Rockies.

304

When seeking words to describe the bowls and the views from the high ridges, expansive, massive, wide and immense are the broad sort of adjectives that come to mind. But when you focus on some of the mountain's infamous trails, you seek tight words like steep, confining, twisting, and challenging—for as expansive as the area is on high, the lower mountain narrows and angles

With a massive mountain and huge trackage, Sun Valley offers excellent Alpine and Nordic facilities.

more sharply into near-razorback ridges and drainages. Olympic, Holiday, Inhibition and especially Exhibition are superlative mogul slopes on the River Run side—and Sun Valley's gifted bump skiers ply their thigh-frying trade on these incredible mogul runs. Ski them tentatively and you're a tourist. Ski them respectably and you'll gain approval of hot-skiing young locals. Ski them with real skill and aggression, and they might invite you to move to town.

In the afternoon, when the sun has kissed the Warm Springs side, its long, sinuous runs live up to their name. The Challenger is North America's max-vertical quad, traveling more than 3,000 feet in just 10 minutes. With the absence of lines and the fast ride, strong skiers often can make three round-trips an hour on Warm Springs's 3,144-foot vertical—a potential of 80,000 feet in a day. Consider that a good day's heli-skiing is 10,000 vertical feet and a great week is 100,000, and you begin to get a notion of how much skiing the Challenger really allows. The astonishing top-to-bottom runs, some wearing blue squares and others black diamonds, are among the best and most steadily pitched super-cruisers in the

Photo courtesy Sun Valley Ski Resort

Rockies. When you get a rhythm working, you might find yourself GS-ing a thousand or more vertical feet down the mountain before your legs start to demand a break. Greyhawk, Baldy's third high-speed lift, parallels the lower third of the Challenger chair, accessing the much-used race courses on the lower mountain and serving as a standby in case the long quad is down. A long lazy catwalk meanders down the Warm Springs side, enabling even novices to zigzag down this tremendous mountain face. It is here, on the steady steeps of Warm Springs, that Sun Valley honors its latest skiing heroine: Picabo's Street, the black-to-blue liftline run next to the Flying Squirrel Chair, commends the achievement of Picabo Street, 1994 Olympic silver medalist and two-time (at this writing) World Cup downhill champion.

Dollar Mountain

Profile

Dollar Mountain, the 628-vertical-foot beginner hill, would rank as a destination resort in the Midwest. It is essentially a seamless, treeless snowfield on which to learn, to practice, to gain confidence. Sun Valley's famous ski school, very traditional and very Austrian in the best sense, is in legion here, patiently, professionally and perfectly teaching the foundation of solid skiing techniques. Many of Sun Valley's 175 ski instructors work with beginners and small children, coaxing them onto Dollar's three gentle lifts and down the manicured white blanket draped over the hill's gentle contours. When the sun is high, tree-free Dollar Mountain is like a snow-covered dune—brilliant, inviting and arguably the best novice hill in the Rocky Mountains. Baldy lift tickets may be used on Dollar Mountain, but much less expensive Dollar-only tickets are also available. Elkhorn access is via Dollar's backside. Many skiers also assume that Dollar was the site of Sun Valley's—and the world's—first chairlift, but the assumption is wrong. The original lift climbed up what is now a field on the other side of the resort; its towers are still visible.

Mountain Stats— Dollar Mountain

Resort elevation 6,010 feet
Top of highest lift 6,638 feet
Bottom of lowest lift 6,010 feet
Total vertical 628 feet
Longest run ½ mile
Average annual snowfall 150 inches
Lifts 1 triple chair, 3 double chairs
Capacity 4,800 skiers per hour
Terrain 13 runs, 127 acres (all beginner to low intermediate)
Snowmaking portable snowguns, maximum 75%
Snow reports (800) 635-4150

SNOWBOARDING

What could be more appealing to a snowboarder than a big, beefy mountain with a lot of fall-line terrain? Very little, and snowboarders have taken to Baldy with fervor. They are welcome everywhere except on Christin's Silver and Southern Comfort on Seattle Ridge. Sometimes, there may be additional early-season restrictions. Dollar Mountain's broad flanks are idyllic learning terrain for snowboarders, and since a Dollar-only lift ticket costs less than one good also on Baldy, it is an economical practice area too.

SKI SCHOOL PROGRAMS

Classes can be booked and lessons purchased at the Sun Valley Sports Center in Sun Valley Village, Dollar Mountain's Dollar Cabin and at ski school desks in the Lookout Restaurant, Warm Springs Lodge and River Run Plaza, all at Baldy. For information, call **Sun Valley Ski School, (208) 622-2248.**

Introductory Programs

Adult Clinics: Sun Valley's name for its group lessons. Beginners and low-intermediates meet at Dollar Mountain's Dollar Cabin at 9:45 A.M. daily.

Snowboarding: Beginner and up, meet at Dollar Cabin daily at 9:45 A.M.

Advanced and Specialty Programs

Adult Clinics: Intermediate to advanced skiers meet for class lessons at Baldy's Lookout Restaurant at 9:45 A.M. daily.

Women's Clinic: Two-, three- and five-day workshops for intermediate to expert women skiers, taught by women.

Snowboarding: All levels meet daily at Dollar Mountain's Dollar Cabin at 9:45 A.M. Lessons on Baldy by appointment.

Special Programs

Ski With a Forest Ranger: Tours of Bald Mountain meet every Thursday and Saturday at 10:30 A.M. and 1:30 P.M. at the Lookout Restaurant ski school desk.

For Families

Nonskiing Children

Children's Playschool: Located at the Sun Valley Mall. Day care for children ages 6 months to 5 years. Can be combined with Alpine or Nordic instruction for children 4 and older. For reservations and information, call (208) 622-2288.

Other child-care options for non-skiers include **A Child's Place, (208) 726-3240,** and **Elkhorn Children's Center, (800) 622-4101, (208) 622-4104.**

Skiing Children

Introduction to Skiing: New one-hour class for first-time skiers ages 3 and 4. Also known as PeeWee program. Given at Dollar Mountain. Can be combined with Playschool.

SKIWee: Nationally franchised classes for beginners 4 years and older. Held at Dollar Mountain. Lunch supervised but additional cost.

Children's Classes: Beginners to low intermediates, aged 5 to 12, meet at Dollar Cabin.

Baldy Bears: Daily classes on Baldy for intermediate and advanced skiers ages 7 to 12. Lunch supervised but at additional cost.

Noteworthy

Sun Valley offers free skiing to children ages two to 12 sharing parents' lodging at a Sun Valley Company hotel or condominium during selected weeks.

There are slow-skiing zones on Baldy, but Dollar Mountain is a good bet for small skiers, new skiers and, most of all, small beginners. As a bonus, the Dollar Mountain lift ticket is less expensive than a Baldy ticket. If you are traveling with a wee one and need a crib, playpen, high chair or other baby and toddler equipment, you can rent from the Sun Valley outpost of **Baby's Away, (208) 788-7582.**

FOR RACERS

Race Clinic: Three hours of daily racing workshop for adults. Offered for one to five days.

Master's Race Clinic: For good skiers who want to work seriously on racing technique. Offered Monday through Friday after Christmas.

NASTAR: Held at noon on Tuesday, Thursday and Friday on Lower Warm Springs. Sign up at the race window at the Warm Springs base.

HELI-SKIING

Sun Valley Heli-Ski runs full-day tours into a 750-square-mile area of the Pioneer, Smoky and Boulder ranges. Groups average five runs and about 10,000 vertical feet per day. The company's Powder Primer package is a more relaxed two- or three-run outing, suitable for first-time heli-skiers and riders. Intermediate and better ability level is best suited, and fat skis are included in all programs. In addition, telemark tours, trips to remote valley floors for cross-country skiers and even overnight yurt trips can be arranged.

Contact **Sun Valley Heli-Ski Guides, P.O. Box 978, Sun Valley, ID 83353; (208) 622-3108.**

NORDIC SKIING

With more than 175 kilometers of track and skating lanes, hut-to-hut tours and backcountry experiences, Sun Valley and its vicinity rank among North America's top centers for Nordic skiing. Four cross-country centers, all with instruction, rentals and food service, draw skiers from Sun Valley, but one of the country's best is right at the resort. **The Sun Valley Nordic Center, (208) 622-2250,** located in Sun Valley Village, offers 40 kilometers of meticulous tracks and groomed trails. It is known for its exceptional ski school, which among other firsts pioneered "tiny tracks," close-set tracks for small children ages 3 and older beside adult tracks, a children's terrain garden and special ski instruction for youngsters as well. One of the most popular excursions, even for occasional cross-country skiers, is the 3-kilometer track to Trail Creek Cabin, past the Hemingway Memorial. The cabin serves hearty lunches and is a rustic charmer. Telemark instruction is given by Nordic instructors at Dollar Mountain, and guided ski tours in the Sawtooth National Recreation Area (see below) can also be arranged.

The other three are farther afield but are worth the commute: **Busterback Ranch,** 40 miles north of Ketchum, **(208) 774-2217; Idaho Rocky Mountain Ranch,** 50 miles north of Ketchum, **(208) 774-3544; Galena Lodge,** 24 miles north of Ketchum. Galena sends a shuttle to pick up skiers at Ketchum for a day of cross-country skiing on 50 kilometers of groomed trails; there is a charge, and reservations are required, **(208) 726-4010.** It also offers various classes, including introduction sessions to classical skiing and skating to a series of Ladies' Days. **Town & Country Scenic Tours** runs shuttles to both Galena and Busterback, **(208) 726-7109.** Guide services specializing in regional backcountry experiences including yurts for overnights are **Sun Valley Trekking, (208)** **788-9585,** and **Sawtooth Mountain Guides** based in Stanley, **(208) 774-3324.** A free trail map and guide to all sorts of touring options and special events is available from the **Sun Valley Nordic Assn., P.O. Box 2420, Sun Valley, ID 83353; (800) 634-3347.**

There are also several popular wilderness excursions in the **Sawtooth National Recreation Area,** 8 miles north of Ketchum, with trails that are marked and occasionally groomed and a visitor center but no commercial services, **(208) 726-7672.** Some of the best backcountry opportunities are an hour or more from Sun Valley, but the country is so beautiful that the drive is a joy (of course, barring a major snowstorm). Stanley Lake is the backcountry marked with a green circle: mostly flat terrain and virtually no avalanche danger. The route to Redfish Lake is a slightly darker green, while the stretch continuing to Lower Bench Lake is for intermediate and advanced skiers. So are the routes to Hell Roaring Lake and Silver Creek Ridge.

WHERE TO STAY

Sun Valley–Ketchum Chamber of Commerce Reservations, (800) 634-3347, (208) 726-3423; Sun Valley Company Reservations, (800) 786-8259 (SUN-VALY), (208) 622-4111.

Luxury Accommodations

The Knob Hill Inn

Large for a chalet but small for a hotel. Intimate, exquisite inn with charming rooms and luxurious fireplace suites. Austrian furniture, down comforters and other fine decorative touches. Located on a hillside with lovely views. Daily housekeeping, gourmet breakfast. Two restaurants, indoor swimming pool, whirlpool, sauna, workout room. **960 N. Main St., Ketchum 83340; (800) 526-8010, (208) 726-8010.**

The Pinnacle Inn

Fine new condo-hotel at the base of Warm Springs (formerly Lift Haven Inn). One of two hotels on Warm Springs side. B&B format.

Rooms combinable into suites, all with VCR and options, including spa tubs, extra bathrooms, decks. Country French decor. Daily housekeeping, full breakfast. Outdoor hot tub, restaurant, lounge, ski shop. **P.O. Box 2259, Sun Valley, ID 83353; (800) 255-3391, (208) 726-5700.**

Sun Valley Inn

Slightly less prepossessing sibling of Sun Valley Lodge, at other end of Mall. Children 17 and younger stay free in parents' room. Ski packages. Daily housekeeping, 24-hour front desk, bell service, concierge, room service, valet, complimentary airport and ski shuttles. Outdoor hot pool, cafeteria, lounge. **Sun Valley, ID 83353; (800) 786-8259 (SUN-VALY), (208) 622-4111.**

Sun Valley Lodge

This is the original Sun Valley. Great history and tradition, updated to modern luxury hotel levels. Fine decor, especially in the more deluxe rooms. Public spaces adorned with fantastic historical and nostalgic photographs. Famous fancy restaurant, informal restaurant and cocktail lounge. Exceptionally competent and caring staff, accustomed to providing top service. Anchors Mall. Daily housekeeping, nightly turndown service, 24-hour front desk, concierge, bell staff, room service, valet, complimentary airport and ski shuttles. Restaurant, lounge, beauty salon, massage, game room, bowling, ski storage, outdoor hot tub. **Sun Valley, ID 83353; (800) 786-8259 (SUN-VALY), (208) 622-2144.**

Mid-Priced Accommodations

Best Western Christiana Motor Lodge

Thirty-eight-room lodge on Sun Valley Rd. Some units with fireplace and/or kitchenette. Family rates. Ski packages. Daily housekeeping, Continental breakfast. Outdoor hot tub, coffee room. **P.O. Box 2196, Ketchum, ID 83340; (800) 535-3241, (208) 726-3351, (800) 528-1234** for Best Western reservations.

Best Western Tyrolean Inn

Comfortable and well-equipped 58-room lodge near River Run lifts. Refrigerators and/or whirlpool tubs in some rooms. Austrian-style decor. Ski packages. Daily housekeeping, Continental breakfast included. Hot tub, sauna, game room. **P.O. Box 202, Ketchum ID 83340; (800) 333-**7912, (208) 726-5336, (800) 528-1234 for Best Western reservations.

The Christophe

Forty-room condo-hotel, halfway between downtown Ketchum and River Run lifts. All suites and some rooms with two-person spa tub. Eclectic contemporary decor. High end of mid-price properties. Housekeeping by arrangement, management can set up and guide backcountry tours and other excursions. Outdoor hot tub. **351 Second Ave. South, Ketchum, ID 83340; (800) 521-2515, (208) 726-5601.**

Clarion Hotel Sun Valley

Contemporary downtown inn with 58 rooms, some with fireplaces. Southwestern-influenced decor with custom pine furnishings. Main Street Ketchum location—despite mailing address. Daily housekeeping, breakfast included. Outdoor heated pool, hot tub (planned for 1997–98). **P.O. Box 660, Sun Valley, ID 83353; (800) 262-4833, (208) 726-5900.**

Heidelberg Inn

Well-regarded 30-room inn, rated by AAA and Mobil. Some kitchenette units. Pets permitted. Located on Warm Springs Rd. Ski packages. Family rates. AAA discount. Daily housekeeping, VCR and film rentals. Hot tub, sauna, pool, guest laundry. **P.O. Box 304, Ketchum, ID 83340; (800) 284-4863, (208) 726-5361.**

Idaho Country Inn

Spacious 10-room inn on high knoll between Ketchum and Sun Valley. Each room different, with discreetly and tastefully executed Idaho themes—rodeo, Native American, wagon days, willow and the like. Top rooms are upper end of mid-price range. Exquisite furnishings and handmade quilts. Each room with remote-control TV and small refrigerator. Great views, especially from Sun Room where ample breakfast is served. Non-smoking inn. Daily housekeeping, full breakfast, hot tub. **P.O. Box 2355, Sun Valley, ID 83353; (208) 726-1019.**

River Street Inn

Lovely all-suite B&B in Ketchum, close to shops and restaurants. Nine suites. Located on Trail Creek. Ski packages. Daily housekeeping,

308

breakfast, Japanese soaking tubs. **P.O. Box 182, Ketchum, ID 83340; (208) 726-3611.**

Tamarack Lodge
Pleasant 27-room motor inn. All rooms with refrigerators, microwaves, fireplaces and/or mountain views. Located on Sun Valley Rd., a short walk from town. Ski packages. Daily housekeeping, courtesy coffee. Indoor pool, hot tub. **P.O. Box 2000, Ketchum, ID 83340; (800) 521-5379, (208) 726-3344.**

Economy Accommodations

Bald Mountain Lodge
Comfortable 30-unit lodge on Main St. Suitable for families. Some units with kitchens. Units sleep up to six. Built in 1929, before Sun Valley, as hot springs lodge; now listed on National Register of Historic Places. Pets permitted. Daily housekeeping. **P.O. Box 426, Ketchum, ID 83340; (208) 726-9963.**

Ketchum Korral Motor Lodge
Simple property. Conventional rooms and cabins with kitchens and fireplaces. Main St. location. Daily housekeeping, hot tub, guest laundry. **P.O. Box 2241, Ketchum, ID 83340; (208) 726-3510.**

Lift Tower Lodge
Economy 14-room lodge with views of Baldy. In-room refrigerators. Ski packages. Daily housekeeping, free Continental breakfast, hot tub. **P.O. Box 185, Ketchum, ID 83340; (800) 462-8646, (208) 726-5163.**

Condominiums

Elkhorn Resort
Village-style development of hotel-type lodge but mainly condos and homes. Self-contained resort offering accommodations from hotel rooms to multibedroom apartments. Lodge rooms include hotel rooms to two-bedroom suites. Condos from studios to three bedrooms. Shops and entertainment in small village core. AAA Four Diamond awardee. Children 12 and younger stay free in parents' room; kids ski free during much of the ski season too. Ski and special-occasion packages. Daily housekeeping, complimentary Continental breakfast and après-ski refreshments (deluxe lodge rooms only), 24-hour front desk. **P.O.**

Box 6009, Sun Valley, ID 83354; (800) ELK-HORN, (800) 355-4676, (208) 622-4511.**

Sun Valley Condominiums
Condominiums of all sizes within walking distance of mall. Accessible to all Sun Valley Village shops, services and facilities. Spacious and individually decorated. Lodge apartments and Wildflower are sized from hotel-type bedroom to three bedrooms. Villager I and II, Atelier, Snow Creek, Dollar Meadow and Cottonwood have studio to four-bedroom configurations. There are also cottages under the same management. Children 11 and under stay free in parents' room; those 17 and younger stay and ski free except at peak holidays. **Sun Valley, ID 83353; (800) 786-8259 (SUN-VALY), (208) 622-4111.**

Companies managing and/or handling reservations for assorted condominiums, chalets and homes include
High Country, (800) 726-7076, (208) 726-1256
Mountain Resorts, (208) 726-9344, (208) 726-9344
Peak Investment Properties, (800) 245-6443, (208) 726-0110
Premier Resorts at Sun Valley, (800) 635-4444
Sun Valley Area Reservations, (800) 635-1076 out of state, (208) 726-3660
Sun Valley Lodge & Property Management, (800) SUN-VALY, (208) 622-4111
Amenities and housekeeping policies vary, and some companies offer lift/lodging packages too.

DINING OUT

Baldy's Bistro
Open for breakfast from 6:00 A.M., for late-night meals until 3:00 A.M. and continuously for lunch, dinner or mealtimes of your own devising. High-quality ingredients and innovative preparation at all times. Smoke-free environment. Upscale billiards club too. **271 Main St. Ketchum; (208) 726-2267.**

Buffalo Cafe
Rustic-style log cabin with decidedly un-rustic food. Oatmeal pancakes, *huevos ranchero* and an

assortment of omelettes lead the breakfast list, but locals come in for the budget breakfast special. Excellent sandwiches and salads on deck for lunch. New dinner menu includes daily pasta special, jerked ribs, gourmet salads in dinnerlike portions and gourmet buffalo burgers. Children's coloring menu. Wines by the glass and specialty beers. **320 East Ave. North, Ketchum; (208) 726-9795.**

Cafe at the Brewery
Serves "refined pub grub" from various cuisines in casual setting. Roasted Garlic Cream Cheese with Focaccia is splendid counterpoint to excellent microbrews. Homemade chicken pot pie and bratwurst, Thai Curry Pasta and Roasted Vegetable Quesadillas are examples. Also, innovative versions of traditional soups, salads, sandwiches and pizza. Steaks, chops, seafood and Mexican specialties too. Excellent desserts and specialty coffees. Open daily for lunch and dinner. Sunday brunch menu. **202 N. Main St., Hailey; (208) 788-0805.**

310

Chandler's Restaurant
Creative American cuisine served nightly at dinner. Specialties include fresh seafood, homemade pasta and excellent desserts. Nightly prix fixe dinner. Elegant and romantic cabin ambiance. Excellent wines. Reservations suggested. **Trail Creek Village, 200 S. Main St. Ketchum; (208) 726-1776.**

China Pepper
Upscale Oriental cuisine, including interesting and delicious Szechuan, Hunan and Thai fare. Unusual dishes, such as Tiger Rolls and Stuffed Salmon. Five Spice Ice Cream is a must at dinner's end. Fireside dining. Reservations accepted. **The 511 Building, Sixth** and **Washington, Ketchum; (208) 726-0959.**

Desperado's Mexican Restaurant
Desperate for Mexican food? Desperado's makes it—and makes it well. Popular dishes, toppable with four kinds of salsa. Open daily from lunch to dinner time. Beer and wine. Moderate prices. Daily specials. Children's menu. Open daily except Sunday from early lunch through dinner. Takeout available. **211 Fourth St., Ketchum; (208) 726-3068.**

Felix's Restaurant
Lovely restaurant in equally lovely inn. Hillside location, high-style cuisine and service. Mediterranean lamb shanks, rack of lamb, pasta du jour and other interesting and authentic dishes featured. Excellent wine cellar. Dinner only. Reservations "appreciated." **Knob Hill Inn, 960 N. Main St., Ketchum; (208) 726-1166.**

Gretchen's
Informal restaurant in Sun Valley Lodge. Breakfast, lunch and dinner. Dinners include full meals such as Idaho beef, lamb and salmon. Salads and pastas also offered. Dinner reservations recommended. **Sun Valley Lodge, Sun Valley; (208) 622-2144, (208) 622-2097.**

Grumpy's
Inexpensive food. Burgers (including famous fowl burger) and sandwiches for lunch or dinner. Warm Springs Rd., Ketchum. (No phone.)

A Hungarian Radish
Mid-priced purveyor of creative and popular contemporary dishes, from escargots or lobster strudel to start, beef Wellington or interesting pastas as an entrée to killer desserts such as chocolate bag of mousse. Lunch menu has similar style but is lighter. Takeout available. Reservations recommended. **Trail Creek Village, Ketchum; (208) 726-8468.**

Ketchum Grill
Casual in food style and ambiance. Pleasant bistro-style restaurant with modern American fare. Great and interesting appetizers, pizza, pasta and entrées, all reasonably priced. Dinner nightly. Reservations accepted. **520 East Ave., Ketchum; (208) 726-4660.**

Knob Hill Cafe

Charming hotel restaurant with limited hours and limitless quality. Sumptuous buffet breakfast for inn-guests and outsiders. European pastries and coffees in the morning, after skiing or to take out. Breakfast daily except Sunday; Sunday brunch. **Knob Hill Inn, 960 N. Main St., Ketchum; (208) 726-1166.**

The Konditorei

Long-standing favorite for hearty breakfasts, light lunches and good dinners as well as Austrian-inspired pastry any time. Moderate prices and informal family-friendly atmosphere. Takeout available. **Sun Valley Mall, Sun Valley; (208) 622-2235.**

The Lodge Dining Room

One of the Rockies' most elegant restaurants. Fine Continental fare, exquisitely prepared and presented. Fabled "white-glove service" intimidates some guests and has been moderated. Trio plays for dancing. Closest to forties supper club ambiance in modern American skiing. Not-to-be-missed treat. Sunday brunch opulent and delicious (worth missing anything but a powder day). Reservations strongly recommended. **Sun Valley Lodge, Sun Valley; (208) 622-2150, (208) 622-2097.**

Mama Inez

New Mexican meals (lunch and dinner). Mama's *Carnitas, Spanish Chicken Mole*, Chicken Jalapeño and seafood specials. Various chilis. Vegan specials. Smaller portions for *niños* too. Open for lunch daily except Saturday and dinner seven evenings a week. **Seventh St.** and **Warm Springs Rd., Ketchum; (208) 726-4213.**

Michel's Christiania Restaurant

Atmospheric fine-dining restaurant, serving Sun Valley since 1959. Glass-walled chalet contains high-ceilinged dining room. Michel Rudigoz's menu changes daily, but accent is traditional French cuisine, specializing in Steak au Poivre, veal, lamb and pasta. Home-baked breads and outstanding desserts. Appetizers and light suppers also served at the adjacent Olympic Bar. Open nightly. Reservations requested. **Sun Valley Rd.** and **Walnut Ave., Ketchum; (208) 726-3388.**

The Ore House

Casual and convenient Sun Valley Mall location. Long-standing favorite. Best known for steaks but also offers stir fry, chicken, fresh seafood and vegetarian specials. Excellent salad bar. Nightly specials (including dessert of the evening). Cocktails, beer, wine and entertainment. Reservations accepted. **Sun Valley Mall, Sun Valley; (208) 622-4363.**

Panda Chinese Restaurant

Ever-popular Chinese specialties from various regions. Reasonable prices. Resort outpost of popular Boise eatery. Weekday lunches; nightly dinners. Reservations accepted. **515 N. East Ave., Ketchum; (208) 726-3591.**

Perry's

Inexpensive breakfast, lunch and early dinner offerings. Casual. Kids' menu. **131 W. Fourth St., Ketchum; (208) 726-7703.**

The Pioneer Saloon

The downtown place for prime rib—or steaks, shellfish, chicken, pork and various combinations. Full bar plus beer and wine. Reservations not accepted. **308 N. Main St., Ketchum; (208) 726-3139, (208) 726-3149.**

The Ram

Cozy spot for pasta, chargrilled chops and steaks, salads and other popular fare. Entertainment. Dinner reservations recommended. **Sun Valley Inn, Sun Valley; (208) 622-2225, (208) 622-2097.**

The Sawtooth Club

Delicious food in stylish restaurant. Mesquite-grilled steaks, chops, poultry and healthy pasta dishes featured. Soups, salads and sandwiches also offered. Cocktails, wine and beer in fireplace lounge. Congenial dining. Reservations recommended. **201 S. Main St., Ketchum; (208) 726-5233.**

Something Special

Popular caterer now has sit-down bistro. Appetizers, seafood, chicken, sandwiches, steaks, ribs and special desserts all available. Lunch and dinner daily. Takeout and delivery available. **Fifth** and **Washington, Ketchum; (208) 726-7247.**

Sun Valley Wine Company

Excellent wine bar and restaurant. Ever-changing menu always has soups, salads, gourmet pizzas, fruit and cheese selections, pâtés and lovely desserts—all designed to match the wines, champagnes and beers of the day. **300 N. Leadville Ave., Ketchum; (208) 726-2442.**

Tequila Joe's

Boisterous Mexican lunches and dinners. Moderate prices. Lunch, dinner, full bar and entertainment. Takeout available. Reservations accepted. **Elkhorn Lodge, Elkhorn; (208) 622-4511, Ext. 1157.**

Trail Creek Cabin

Country cabin with short menu of classic American fare such as barbecued ribs, prime rib, broasted chicken and Idaho trout. Casual, family-style service. Open for lunch and dinner. Lounge, fireplace and light-hearted easy entertainment. Good selection of wines and full bar too. Ski in on cross-country skis, drive in or take a sleighride to dinner. Sleighs leave the Sun Valley Inn hourly between 6:00 and 9:00 P.M. Reservations recommended for dinner, required for sleighride. **Trail Creek Rd., Sun Valley; (208) 622-2135, (208) 622-2097.**

312

Warm Springs Ranch Restaurant

An ageless Sun Valley tradition. Large and varied menu. Lots of beef, pork and lamb, plus seafood and mountain trout. Burgers too. Regular dinners include sizable entrée portions, salad, starch and sourdough scones. Petite dinners are scaled down. Children's menu also offered. Open for dinner nightly. Reservations requested. **Warm Springs Rd., Ketchum; (208) 726-2609.**

A Winter's Feast

Reach a traditional yurt on a horsedrawn sleigh, cross-country skis or snowshoes. Five-course full dinners centered around four entrée choices—filet mignon, salmon, rack of lamb or pork roast. Each entrée interestingly prepared and perfectly accompanied by appropriate appetizer, salad, soup, sauce, vegetable and starch. Fresh specialty breads too. Each dinner ends with an appropriate dessert, plus specialty coffees and teas. Wine selections such as yurt-dwelling Mongolians could never envision; corkage fee if you BYO wine. Limited seating; reservations mandatory. **P.O. Box 2456, Ketchum, ID 83340; (208) 726-5775.**

NIGHTLIFE

Even more than most resorts, Sun Valley's places may change names, ownership and ambiance, but there is always a wealth of choices after the lifts close. The first strains of après-ski activity crank up at both areas, notably at the glamorous Warm Springs Lodge and River Run Lodge, both of which have equal measures of music and merriment. The Baldy Base Club and Apples also rev up in the fading afternoon light with live entertainment.

Not much later, the Mall swings into action. Mike Murphy's irreverent one-man show in the Ram Bar at the Sun Valley Inn begins at 5:00 P.M. The legendary Joe Cannon performed at the Ram for years, and now Murphy has stepped in to fill his spot—still one of the best after-ski acts in the Rockies. Those who prefer real European-style après-ski fork into pastry at The Konditorei. The nearby Ore House has live entertainment on weekends. The Duchin Lounge in the Lodge is elegant and restrained, and a gourmet dinner with dancing is one of the classiest ways to spend a special evening.

The Elkhorn Saloon always attracts its share of the action with live entertainment and dancing. Lately the Vuarnettes, Creekside alumnae with a following in the manner of Cannon and Murphy, have been performing at Whiskey Jacques downtown. This wild place is a perennial magnet for the young crowd that likes to party loud and dance a lot, starting with happy hour and finishing in the wee hours when the last of the nine big-screen televisions is turned off. Baldy's Bistro, with good spirits (both the liquid and emotional sorts) and upscale billiards, even serves a late-night menu until 3:00 A.M.

More refined styles have crept into Ketchum's western firmanet too. Gourmet coffees in trendy cafes, wine bars and microbrews are the Ketchum of today. The Cafe at the Brewery taps into good microbrews, and The Olympic Bar, decorated with likenesses of the skiing champions chef Michel Rudigoz coached before he traded in his ski hat for a chef's tocque, where after-ski drinks and light bistro-style food are served. The Sawtooth Club has a western-style bar and roaring fire, while the Sun Valley Wine Company serves excellent and varied wines and champagne by the glass or bottle (and beers too) and matches food to the vintages and brews, also in a classy fireplace setting. The arts also play a major part in Sun Valley–Ketchum nightlife. The Sun Valley Center for the Arts and Humanities underwrites music, dance, film and visual arts programs, and the Sun Valley Gallery Assn. sponsors a gallery evening one Friday of each month.

Bruce Willis has, as the locals say fliply, been "buying up Hailey." That's an exaggeration, but the actor, who maintains a local home, has bought The Liberty Theater and other important downtown buildings, setting off a renaissance. Among his developments is The Mint, a fine restaurant and nightspot that has been booking the kinds of musical acts that previously only appeared in bigger cities or real resorts, and skiers have been commuting to dance or just be part of the new scene.

For more information, contact **Sun Valley, Sun Valley, ID 83353; (208) 622-4111; Sun Valley–Ketchum Chamber of Commerce, P.O. Box 2420, Sun Valley, ID 83353; (800) 634-3347, (208) 726-3423.**

SCHWEITZER MOUNTAIN

BACKDROP

Schweitzer Mountain is Idaho's second-largest ski area in terms of vertical and capacity, but with some 2,300 acres, it is the state's leader in terms of skiable terrain, comprising 55 cut runs and hundreds of acres of open bowls and glades. Located in the Selkirk Mountains, a range whose British Columbian portion—like the Bugaboos and the Monashees beyond—is known for heli-skiing, the resort is just 60 miles from the Canadian border. It's sort of at the end of the road as far as skiing the U.S. Rockies goes. It has long been one of the biggest local ski areas in the West. That's all changing—and changing fast. Now halfway through an ambitious 10-year, $100 million expansion program to catapult it into the big time by the turn of the century, Schweitzer boasts northern Idaho's first high-speed quad chair and a classy new slopeside hotel. Because it is at the end of a serpentine 9-mile access road, Schweitzer Mountain Resort—with an accent here on the resort part—strives to provide on-site diversions for vacationers. As the village continues to take shape and more destination skiers discover the expansive mountain and ample snow, there will be more and more of these and full resort facilities for them to enjoy.

THE LAY OF THE LAND

The nascent village at the base of Schweitzer, locally pronounced "Sweitzer," presently consists of an expansive day lodge and the hotel, the nucleus of a projected village development for nearly 4,000 overnight guests. The new Schweitzer Mountain Resort was designed by Ecosign Mountain Recreation Planners, the Canadian firm responsible for award-winning Whistler Village, British Columbia. A new mountaintop restaurant, 350 condominium units, 70 private homes, two more lifts and 19 additional trails are anticipated by the year 2000. Sandpoint, a popular summer resort on Lake Pend Oreille, is 11 miles away and still provides the lion's share of the accommodations and nightlife for vacationing skiers. Nearly half the distance is a curvaceous access road which was widened, paved, shortened and generally tamed early in the development game but remains more terrifying than seductive to those timid about mountain driving.

GETTING THERE

Sandpoint is 75 miles northeast of Spokane via I-90 east to Hwy 95 north and 45 miles from Coeur d'Alene via Hwy 95 north, and the resort is 11 miles north of town. Spokane International Airport has flights on major national and regional carriers, while commuter service goes into Coeur d'Alene Airport. Rental cars are available at both airports, and ground transfers are available with 24-hour notice. **Amtrak's** Empire Builder serves Sandpoint, and the local airport accommodates private planes.

PROFILE

Schweitzer Mountain is one of those ski areas that give ski mapmakers gray hair. This undulating massif is composed of two long, intersecting ridges with skiing in all compass directions. The ski area's front side, known as Schweitzer Basin, is a big, sparsely wooded cirque. The back side, known as Colburn Basin, is an even bigger basin with lots of trees. A small beginner hill lies out of the mainstream below the base area—out of sight and, mostly, out of mind, for Schweitzer's vastness and challenge on high are a potent draw for good skiers. The ski area's topography permits access to such widespread terrain via relatively few chairlifts (just five plus the beginner

314

lift) because there are runs along the crest from all the chairs. You unload, tack to the left or right until you see the run that looks good and plunge right in.

At the few other ski areas that even have true open bowls, these snowy treasures tend to be way up and back and out of the way and bothersome to reach. At Schweitzer Mountain, where the base is quite high and the timberline is rather low, a big, beautiful bowl is up close and easy to reach. Chair 1 climbs straight up from the Headquarters day lodge to one of the most expansive bowls in the Rockies. The frontside segments neatly into a steep cirque and a medium difficult run-out below, and Chair 1's midstation enables intermediates to ski the wide runout trails through the woods (and allows night skiing there as well) and experts to play the powder game on high. Schweitzer, like other northern Rockies resorts, gets Pacific Northwest weather and wet snow, but it also racks up its share of classic Rocky Mountain fluff. In new snow, the Schweitzer side is a deep-snow paradise, and in spring, the corn snow just doesn't get any better. The Face and Upper Sam's Alley are perpendicular snowfields near the chair, while vast South Bowl beyond provides acres and acres of challenge on six side-by-side chutes, cornices and more steep faces.

Headwall is a north-facing plunge into the broad drainage between the Chair 1 terrain and the sector served by the Great Escape lift. Locals claim Headwall and Upper Stiles across the way have Schweitzer's best powder. While many skiers use the Great Escape high-speed quad to reach the backside, it and the Sunnyside chairlift near Schweitzer's eastern edge combine to offer lots of terrain for good skiers. Steep, steadily canted slopes, cut trails and stands of trees from generously spaced to barely skiable all wear black diamonds. This is tough skiing too, but the 1,280-foot vertical doesn't measure up to other mountain sectors, so many experts don't bother with it.

As enormous and diverse as the Schweitzer side is, the Colburn side is even bigger and more varied on a greater vertical. It's primarily a north-facing cirque nestled in the embrace of a long, long ridge. Another intersecting ridge down the middle of Colburn's Basin in effect divides the big

Inside Schweitzer Mountain

cirque into two smaller ones, and these, in turn, are textured with smaller bowls, chutes, headwalls, knobs and valleys. You can drop into the backside from the mountaintop runs stretching in both directions from the Great Escape quad or the Sunnyside double, and you can come back up again via Timber Cruiser or Snow Ghost double chairlifts, veering off from each other to opposite sides of the basin. Colburn consists of trails on the ridge crests, open snowfields on top, glades of various steepnesses down the sides and a baker's dozen trails—semi-steep and groomed or very steep and mogully—wherever someone has chosen to cut them. The Snow Ghost chair rides up a high ridge dividing the Colburn Basin into two drainages. From the top, you can see Lake Pend Oreille glimmering below, as well as the Selkirk and Cabinet Ranges forming a grand panorama, stretching into three states and Canada.

The chair accesses Snow Ghost and Kaniksu, a pair of blue-square trails on the spine of the ridge. But it is also the ride to the steep. Just beside the chair, you'll find Downhill Trail, a free-fall into the bowl that even good recreational skiers do with a lot of checking. The racers who launch themselves out of the start house onto this Nor-Am downhill course take it nearly straight, a double black just thinking about it. Big Timber is nearly as demanding, and the North Side Powder Chutes beyond are a steep stretch of **316** conifers, clearings and corridors packed with soft snow. These terrifying, terrific expert runs, unofficially nicknamed Siberia because they are at the farthest reaches of Schweitzer's in-bounds terrain, gentle into a drainage laced with long, lush, tree-lined intermediate trails. If the black diamonds are off-putting, you can use Snow Ghost's midway station to unload and ski only the blues.

On the other side of the lift you'll find more challenge in North Bowl, as near-vertical as it is expansive on the horizontal. If you take pleasure in skiing sheer precipices as long as you have generous room to turn, this is a slope to love. Nearby go-for-broke free-falls include Whiplash, Chute the Moon, Debbie Sue and Toomey's Run, cut in 1995 and received with great acclaim by Schweitzer's hardcore skiers and riders. All these blacks funnel into Vagabond, a blue-square boulevard back to the lifts.

Timber Cruiser is the chair on Colburn's other side, the one that's wooded top to bottom but, in parts, is just as steep. If you want to ski more blues, you'll find lots of them off this chair. If you want moguls, you'll find them here too on Revenge and No Joke, which bump up with the best. The trees here are generally too tight for comfort, but the cut trails are sinuous and inviting. Cathedral Aisli is a true-blue alternative to Zip Down,

Resort elevation 4,700 feet
Top of highest lift 6,400 feet
Bottom of lowest lift 3,394 feet
Total vertical 2,406 feet
Longest run 2.7 miles
Average annual snowfall 300 inches
Ski season Thanksgiving through early April
Lifts 1 high-speed quad chairlift, 5 doubles
Capacity 7,092 skiers per hour
Terrain 2,350 acres; 55 runs (20% beginner and novice, 40% intermediate, 40% advanced and expert)
Snowmaking 14 acres
Night skiing off Chairs 1 and 2, Thursday through Saturday and holiday weeks
Mountain dining Outback Inn, bottom of Timber Cruiser chair
Snow reports (208) 263-9562

a more challenging black. You have to ski from the high point on the ridge to the bottom of the Timber Cruise chairlift to enjoy Schweitzer's entire vertical, but even the runs with less than the max in vertical offer the max in variety and skiing quality.

SNOWBOARDING

Schweitzer worked with local riders, members of the club called Stormriders, to create an "air-raising" haven of half-pipes, jibs, jumps, bumps, walls and slides on the Sparkle run off the Midway chairlift. Most of the mountain is congenial to snowboarders, especially the trees, chutes and gullies on the upper sections of both bowls.

SKI SCHOOL PROGRAMS
Introductory Programs

Ski It to Believe It: Three two-hour lessons, three-day beginner lift ticket and three-day rental equipment. Special dates; reservations required.

Beginner Skills: Group lessons, rental equipment and beginner lift ticket for children and adults.

No Excuses, No Regrets, No Kidding: Three consecutive days of lessons, lift tickets and rentals to introduce newcomers to skiing.

Learn to Shred: Beginner lesson, board rental and beginner lift ticket for children and adults.

Advanced and Specialty Programs

The Skier's Edge: Series of three intermediate lessons and three-day lift; rental package optional. Special dates; advance reservations are required.

Intermediate Skills: Group lesson and all-mountain lift ticket.

Shred Mo' Betta: Intermediate snowboard lesson and all-mountain lift ticket; rental board option.

Advanced Riding Clinic: Covers advanced riding, including extreme terrain and gates. Available Saturdays at 1:20 P.M.

Women's Ski Series: Six three-hour classes for intermediate and expert skiers. Select six out of eight Wednesdays in January and February.

Women's Super Saturday: Classes by women for women of intermediate and higher ability. Includes all-day lesson, lunch and video on specific Saturday.

For Families

Nonskiing Children

Kinder Kamp: Day care for children ages 3 months to nonskiing 11-year-olds. Open daily for full-day and half-day care and weekend evenings. Reservations required for toddlers, recommended for infants, **(800) 831-8810, (208) 263-9555.**

Skiing Children

Kinder Kamp on the Mountain: Full day of lessons, indoor play, supervision and lunch for ages 3½ to 6; rental equipment and lunch additional.

Mogul Mice: Group lessons, lunch and supervision for children ages 5 through 11. Full day, including lift ticket and lunch, or half day including lift ticket.

Tenderboots: Three days of beginner instruction on consecutive Saturdays or Sundays for youngsters ages 6 to 17. Includes beginner lift tickets, group lessons and rentals. Advance reservations required for special dates.

Diamond Cutters: Series of two classes a day in freestyle skiing or snowboarding over six consecutive weeks for skiers ages 8 to 15. Advance reservations are required for special dates.

Noteworthy

Beginner Skills, The Skier's Edge and Intermediate Edge for skiers and Learn to Shred and Shred Mo' Betta for snowboarders are available for ages 6 and up. All are group lessons. Enchanted Forest Terrain Garden is the ski-learning center for beginners in the Kinder Kamp on the Mountain and Mogul Mice programs. Schweitzer also has established a slow-skiing zone on the mountain.

Kids Ski and Stay Free program enables children ages 7 to 12 to ski and stay free when parents purchase a minimum four-day, four-night package at a participating lodging property. Children ages 6 and younger ski free at all times; youngsters 7 to 17 and college students with an ID to ski on a low-priced junior ticket, and lower-mountain lift tickets are also available for new skiers.

317

A lone skier negotiates the North Bowl at Schweitzer Mountain Resort with Lake Pend Oreille and the distant peaks of Montana forming the dramatic backdrop.

Photo by Dick O'Neill

FOR RACERS

NASTAR: Saturday and Sunday at 1:00 P.M. and Thursday at 2:00 P.M.
Coin-Op Racing: Set up Wednesday through Friday from 11:00 A.M. to 2:00 P.M. on the NASTAR course.

NORDIC SKIING

Schweitzer's 8 kilometers of groomed trails begin at the bottom of the Great Escape. Use of traditional tracks and skating trails is free. The ski school offers cross-country and telemark lessons. The scenic Selkirks offer numerous backcountry options. Priest Lake's 10½-mile Hanna Flats Trail is more than 50 miles from Sandpoint, but it's flat and therefore the best beginner trail around. The Lost Lake Loop from Garfield Bay to Mineral Point is nearly 9 miles and suitable for novice and intermediate skiers. The **Sandpoint Ranger District** has maps, **(208) 263-5111. Round Lake State Park,** 10 miles south of Sandpoint, has a 3-mile ski trail with ice skating at the end; there is a fee, **(208) 263-3489. Farragut State Park,** 25 miles south of Sandpoint on Lake Pend Oreille, grooms a 9.4-mile trail system; **(208) 683-2425.** To the north, the Snow Creek Recreation Area between Sandpoint and Bonner's Ferry offers numerous marked trails for different ability levels, including a groomed one to Cook's Lake. Some must be shared with snowmobilers. Information is available from **Bonner's Ferry Ranger District,** **(208) 267-5561.**

WHERE TO STAY

Schweitzer Mountain Central Reservations, **(800) 831-8810.**

Schweitzer Mountain Resort

Luxury Accommodations

Green Gables Lodge
Sparkling lodge, built in 1991. Each of the 82 rooms has two queen-size beds. Also, efficiency rooms with one queen-size bed, one sleep sofa, a refrigerator and basic cooking appliances. Family suites combine one of each. Some Jacuzzi units are available. Ski-in/ski-out. Daily housekeeping. New pool complex built into the hillside, with heated decks, large outdoor pool, three hot tubs and cabana with change rooms and showers. Restaurant, lounge, shops. **Schweitzer Mountain Resort, P.O. Box 815, Sandpoint, ID 83864; (800) 831-8810, (208) 265-0257.**

Condominiums and Homes

Nine condo complexes are currently at the resort. Highland Village (3 and 4 bedrooms), Wildflower at Crystal Springs (2 and 3 bedrooms), Pinnacle Ridge (2 bedrooms) and Crystal Run (2 bedrooms) are the most luxurious. All three are ski-in/ski-out and offer hot tub or sauna access. Creekside is almost up there but is within walking distance of a ski trail and without hot tub/sauna feature. Wildflower (1 to 3 bedrooms, walk to ski run) and Schweitzer Creek (2 and 3 bedrooms, ski-to) are next in line. Alpine and Die Schmetterling are both budget groupings of simple studios accommodating up to six; both are within walking distance of a ski trail. All have fireplaces. The newest additions are The Peaks and The Glades (luxurious 3- and 4-bedroom, individually decorated townhomes) and The Cabins (charming 3-bedroom fireplace cabins), all with great views. For reservations call **(800) 831-8810.**

Sandpoint

Sandpoint Central Reservations, P.O. Box 1933, Sandpoint, ID 83864; (800) 876-8921, (208) 263-6921.

Mid-Priced Accommodations

Angel of the Lake Bed & Breakfast
Delightful, economical four-bedroom B&B on Lake Pend Oreille. Recently redecorated with antiques recreating spirit from various motion pictures. Two rooms with private bath, two share. Daily housekeeping, full gourmet breakfast, après-ski refreshments, outdoor hot tub with lake views. **410 Railroad Ave., Sandpoint, ID 83864; (800) 872-0616, (208) 263-0816.**

Connie's Best Western Motor Inn

Top Sandpoint motel, with 53 comfortable and well-appointed rooms. Also, two-room suite with wet bar, fireplace and private hot tub. Some family suites. Convenient to restaurants, shops. Ski packages. Daily housekeeping. Indoor swimming pool, hot tub, sauna, restaurant, lounge. **323 N. Third Ave., Sandpoint, ID 83864; (800) 282-0660, (208) 263-9581, (800) 528-1234** for Best Western reservations.

Edgewater Resort Motor Inn

Lakefront motel with water views from all 55 rooms. Most with two double beds. Some suites with fireplace or whirlpool tubs. Daily housekeeping, room service. Hot tub, sauna, restaurant, lounge. **56 Bridge St., Sandpoint, ID 83864; (800) 635-2534, (208) 263-3194.**

LakeSide Inn

Sixty spacious balcony rooms, some kitchenette suites. Water views. AAA rated. Ski packages. Children 12 and under free in parents' room. Daily housekeeping, complimentary Continental breakfast, free pickup from airport or Amtrak station, free local transportation, ski shuttle available. Indoor and outdoor hot tubs, sauna. **106 Bridge St., Sandpoint, ID 83864; (800) 543-8126, (208) 263-3717.**

Sandpoint Quality Inn

Sprawling 57-room motor inn, some with kitchenette. Close to restaurants and shops. AAA rated. Family rates. Ski packages. Daily housekeeping, room service, complimentary newspaper delivered to door. Indoor pool, hot tub, guest laundry, restaurant, night club. **807 N. Fifth Ave., Sandpoint, ID 83864; (800) 635-2534, (208) 263-2111, (800) 228-5151** for Quality Inn reservations.

Economy Accommodations

Best Spa Motel

Twenty-one-room motel with good location and at good value. Walk to lake or town. Daily housekeeping. Indoor hot tub, sauna. **521 N. Third Ave., Sandpoint, ID 83864; (208) 263-3532.**

K-2 Motel

Eighteen-room motel, some family units with kitchens. Close to restaurants. Daily housekeeping.

Hot tub. **501 N. Fourth Ave., Sandpoint, ID 83864; (208) 263-3441.**

S&W Motel

Budget motel with 10 kitchenette units with queen-size beds. Senior discounts. Daily housekeeping. Guest laundry. **3480 Hwy 200 East, Sandpoint, ID 83864; (208) 263-5979.**

Super 8 Motel

Sixty-one-unit economy motel with extra-long double beds or queens. Ski packages. Daily housekeeping, free coffee, free local calls, 24-hour front desk, indoor hot tub. **Hwy 95 North, Sandpoint, ID 83864; (208) 263-2210; (800) 800-8000** for Super 8 reservations.

Condominiums

Pend Oreille Shores Resort

Timeshare complex with one- and two-bedroom units with full kitchens, fireplaces and VCRs (video rentals on site). Nightly and weekly rentals available. Guest privileges at Pend Oreille Shores Athletic Club, with weights, racquetball, indoor swimming pool, tanning booth, sauna, indoor tennis, steamroom and indoor and outdoor Jacuzzis. **1250 Hwy 200, Hope, ID 83836; (208) 264-5828.**

In-town and lakeside condos are managed by **R&L Property Management, (208) 263-4033** and **TKE Vacation Rentals, (800) 765-5539, (208) 263-5539.**

DINING OUT

Connie's Cafe

Affordable family meals at breakfast, lunch and dinner. Counter service or dining room. Dinner specials. **Best Western, 323 Cedar St., Sandpoint; (208) 263-9581.**

Eichardt's Pub

Casual and friendly spot with something for every taste. Steaks, burgers, pasta, sandwiches, Mexican and healthful specialties. Daily lunch and dinner specials. Fresh seafood on weekends. Fireplace. Live entertainment. Takeout available. **212 Cedar St., Sandpoint; (208) 263-0833.**

Fifth Avenue Restaurant

Cozy, informal restaurant serving breakfast, lunch and dinner. Varied menu, including steaks, stir fries, vegetarian and Mexican and Italian food. Daily seafood specials. Weekend prime rib specials. Cocktails. Children's menu. **Quality Inn, 807 N. Fifth Ave., Sandpoint; (208) 263-0596.**

The Garden Restaurant

Atmospheric restaurant in rambling lake-view building. Fine food and good service. Seafood, poultry and pastas. Salad bar. Lunch, dinner and Sunday brunch. Cocktails, wine and beer. Reservations recommended. **15 E. Lake St., Sandpoint; (208) 263-5187.**

Hydra Restaurant

Reasonably priced dinners; lunch buffet Tuesday through Friday; Sunday brunch. Fresh fish, creative pasta and prime rib featured. Nightly specials. Sixty-item salad bar. **115 Lake St., Sandpoint; (208) 263-7123.**

Ivano's

Italian restaurant in quaint side-street building. Charming and gracious atmosphere. Veal, chicken, pasta and seafood, all prepared with northern Italian flair. Dinner only. Cocktails, beer and wines. Reservations recommended. **124 S. Second Ave., Sandpoint; (208) 263-0211.**

Jean's Northwest Bar & Grill

Affordable but excellent Northwest-style dining at resort hotel. Continental-style sautéed specialties, entrée-size salads, steaks and seafood. Cocktails. Breakfast also served. Dinner reservations suggested. **Green Gables Lodge, Schweitzer Mountain Resort; (208) 265-0257.**

Longhorn Barbecue

Family-friendly spot for reasonable breakfast, lunch and dinner, daily except Monday. Barbecued and charbroiled meats a specialty. Salads too. Cocktails, beer and wine. Takeout available. **1382 Hwy 95 South, Sandpoint; (208) 263-5064.**

Panhandler Pies

Home-style cooking and on-site baking. Soups, special steaks, stir fries, lasagne and pies, pies, pies. Breakfast, lunch and dinner. **120 S. First Ave., Sandpoint; (208) 263-2912.**

Pastime Cafe

Informal and inexpensive. Mexican specials and other favorites too. Breakfast, lunch and dinner. Open 24 hours on Fridays and Saturdays. Takeout available. **207 N. First Ave., Sandpoint; (208) 263-2019.**

Second Avenue Pizza

Pizza and calzone. Friendly service. Lunch and dinner. Takeout available. **215 S. Second St., Sandpoint; (208) 263-9321.**

Swan's Landing

Waterfront cocktails and dining. Après-ski specials. Fine Northwest cuisine, seafood and steaks. Casual dining room, made atmospheric with massive stone fireplace and waterfall. Reservations suggested. South end of **Long Bridge, Sandpoint; (208) 265-2000.**

NIGHTLIFE

The Headquarters base lodge glows with the first after-ski flush. Taps is a popular watering hole with live music on weekends. The Ski Patrol has a beer there Wednesdays at 5:00 P.M.; free beer and slide show or video presentation. The nearby Keg Lounge gets a young, noisy crowd. Jimmie's at Green Gables is a newer lounge that doesn't yet have the same regular following. Ski-weekers are encouraged to create that following by joining the Ski School Wine & Cheese Party, kicking off the week every Monday at 4:30 P.M.

In Sandpoint, Eichardt's Pub & Grill starts with après-ski and stays active through the evening. The pub offers 25 varieties of beer and specialty drinks. It has become Sandpoint's newest hangout for the young hip ski and snowboard crowd. There's something going on every night:

ski movies, reggae or other music. There's always a dart board, live music and merriment. Bugatti's features 70 beers, including microbrews from the Northwest, a dart board and a friendly atmosphere. Every night is "Open Mike Night," and there's live music Friday and Saturday nights. Kamloops has Burrito Night on Tuesday and Spaghetti Night on Wednesday when children are welcome, then it's nightly music (live on Friday and Saturday) and dancing—and bye-bye kids. The 219 Lounge, Mitzy's and P.J.'s all have big-screen televisions. P.J.'s also has pool and darts. The ski resort and several other local companies sponsor a midweek Ski Party with movies, music and prizes one Thursday a month at different spots in town; check with the resort for the dates.

Moviegoers have a better selection at Schweitzer/Sandpoint than at most resorts. At the mountain, free movies are shown at Headquarters every Saturday evening. In town, Cinema 4 West has four screens and current hits. Classic and contemporary films are screened irregularly throughout the winter at the historic Panida Theater.

For more information, contact **Schweitzer Mountain Resort, P.O. Box 815, Sandpoint, ID 83864; (208) 263-9555; Sandpoint Chamber of Commerce, P.O. Box 928, Sandpoint, ID 83864; (800) 800-2106, (208) 263-2161.**

Snow-clad trees and great views of Lake Pend Oreille from the high-speed quad at Schweitzer Mountain Resort.

321

Photo by Scott Spiker/Schweitzer Mountain Resort

BRUNDAGE MOUNTAIN

BACKDROP

Brundage Mountain is one of those Rocky Mountain treasures: a good-size ski area with a bargain lift ticket, coupled with reasonably priced accommodations in a quaint town—and amazingly accessible to a good airport. This low-key family mountain is just outside of McCall on the shore of Payette Lake in Idaho. With downhill and cross-country racers on the U.S. Ski Team during 8 out of the last 12 Winter Olympics, McCall is one of the towns that calls itself Ski Town U.S.A. (the other contender is Steamboat Springs, Colorado). McCall's most successful racer was Jean Saubert, who won silver and bronze medals at the 1964 Olympics, equaling the combined achievements of her better-known teammates Billy Kidd and Jimmie Heuga, but she has since preferred to stay out of skiing's limelight. McCall is also primarily a summer resort, whose lodges and motels charge low ski-season rates. Its Winter Carnival, normally over the week bridging the end of January and the beginning of February, is known for immensely creative snow sculptures and a variety of special events. It's one of the best in the Rockies—and if there is just one time you choose to visit McCall and ski Brundage, that ought to be it.

THE LAY OF THE LAND

McCall nestles in the lush mountains of southwestern Idaho, close to the Oregon border. Brundage is an easy 8-mile drive northwest of town. Closer to town is the Little Ski Hill, a community-run area with 405 vertical feet of Alpine skiing and cross-country terrain.

GETTING THERE

McCall is a scenic 100-mile drive north of Boise, via Route 55, which is served by several major carriers. Rental cars are available, and **Mountain High, (800) 590-3495, (208) 634-3495,** operates shuttle service every day of the week. Private aircraft may use the McCall Airport, just outside of town.

PROFILE

Brundage's three dozen cut and groomed runs down the west-facing mountain range from steep, narrow liftlines to ballroom-wide slopes for beginning skiers. A platterpull rises partway up the mountain to a web of easy isolated runs. A new triple chairlift is dedicated to the Easy Street beginner area and offers appropriately easy access to children headquartered at the Kids' Center. A pair of parallel chairlifts go all the way to the top. Two ridge runs, a steep one to the left and a super-gentle traverse to the right of the chairs, access all of the trails. The most popular, just to the left of the chairs, is Main Street, which is too long to be a "slope" but too wide to be a "trail." Dotted with trees on top but opening to freeway width below, Main Street is dream skiing. Just beyond Main Street the slope steepens. North, North Boundary, Northwest Passage and Upper Slobovia are snow-holding steeps tucked into the mountain's northern corner.

If you follow the easy traverse to the right, you will come first to Alpine, then Alpine Glades and Bee Line, which is all commendable intermediate turf, and finally to the unloading area of Brundage's Centennial Lift, a triple built for the 1990–91 season, which upped the mountain's vertical, increased the skiable acreage by nearly a third and provided more trails for all ability levels. But the area's glory lies in the trees, where powder lingers. Huge ponderosa pines grow on Brundage's slopes, forming sensational snow-holding glades—tight or narrow, steep or mellow, popular or hidden. There are ski areas with much more impressive annual snowfall, but if you judge by the staying power of the powder on this little-trafficked mountain and the silky smoothness of the groomed terrain, Brundage can claim four aces when it comes to its normal snow quality.

SNOWBOARDING

With great tree skiing and often powder to match, Brundage doesn't need a special snowboard facility to keep riders happy. Hidden Valley, a high run on the farthest corner of the mountain, is a special favorite with snowboarders.

SNOWCAT SKIING

In 1990–91, Brundage inaugurated CatSki, guided snowcat tours on the east side of the mountain. This program has been so successful that it has grown every year since and now has expanded north of the lift-served ski area too. In all, the CatSki terrain stretches across 19,000 backcountry acres. East-side runs down everything from open bowls to ski film-style chutes that average 800 to 1,100 feet of vertical, while the more recently opened north-side runs are as long as 2,000 vertical feet. One group racked up a vertical record of 21,000 vertical feet of powder skiing during the 1995–96 season, which would be considered two good days' worth of heli-skiing. Typically, groups of six visitors and two guides tend to get in 8 to 10 runs a day, and half-day trips are also available. Participants should be fall-line skiers able to ski most runs and have some powder experience, and to make the day easier and more fun, Brundage's rental shop discounts fat skis for CatSki participants and the ski school offers a special CatSki Workshop with on-the-job training in powder skiing.

SKI SCHOOL PROGRAMS

Introductory Programs

First Time Beginners' Special: Learn-to-ski

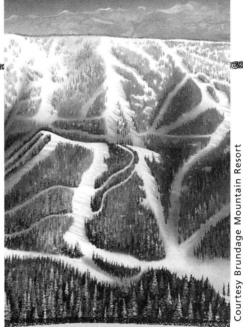

Courtesy Brundage Mountain Resort

week with special rates for instruction, Easy Street lift ticket and rentals. Offered daily, with one or two lessons per day for children 7 and older through adults.

Low Impact Snowboard Lesson: No more than two people in the class, available daily at noon.

Ski Week: Five-day traditional lift-and-lesson

package for ages 13 and older. One-a-day or two-a-day lesson options. Midweek only, except Christmas week.

Advanced and Specialty Programs

Flex Lesson Card: Four or more lessons at a discount.

The Daily Workshop: Topic of the day clinic-style instruction for skiers ages 18 and older who ski at an E or F Level. Available daily at 10:30 A.M.

CatSki Workshop: Powder lessons in conjunction with CatSki program (see page 323).

Custom Workshop: Design your own workshop. Available for groups of four or more.

One-Run Tuneup: Low-cost lesson, available daily at 9:30, to work on one thorny problem or technical sticking spot.

Silverstreakers: Wednesday program for skiers 50 and older of all ability levels.

Ladies' Day: Thursday women's program for skiers and snowboarders.

324 Sunday Snowboard Series: Series of three mid-winter snowboard lessons for adults.

Ski Week: Five-day traditional lift-and-lesson package for ages 13 and older. One-a-day or two-a-day lesson options. Midweek only, except Christmas week.

For Families

Brundage's Kid's Center offers all-day programs for children from 6 weeks to 10 years. For information and reservations, call **(206) 634-7462.**

Nonskiing Children

Bunny Hutch: Full- and half-day care for children ages 6 months to non-skiing pre-schoolers. Half-day, full-day and hourly rates. Family rate for additional children. The children's ski school operates in conjunction with day care for children taking lessons. Reservations recommended.

Skiing Children

Tiny Tracks: One half-hour private lesson for 3-year-olds.

Brundage Snow Cats: Instruction program for all abilities levels, ages 4 to 6. Options are lessons-only (two 1½-hour classes per day; 1-hour class if fewer than three children in a class) or lessons plus day care.

Brundage Bombers: For beginning to advanced skiers, aged 6 to 12. Also available after school or in a series of 10 Saturdays or Sundays for local and/or area children.

Noteworthy

Children 6 and under ski free at all times. In addition to the child's ticket for ages 7 to 12, Brundage offers a junior ticket for ages 13 to 18. There is also an Easy Street chairlift and platterpull ticket that is considerably less than the all-lifts version. For season passholders, there are child, family, junior, college student and grandparent add-on tickets.

NORDIC SKIING

The McCall area offers excellent cross-country terrain. There are 50 kilometers of top-flight trails, instruction and a day lodge at the Little Ski Hill just outside of town; **(208) 634-5691. Ponderosa State Park** has 15 kilometers of groomed tracks and skating lanes—and exceptionally scenic views; **(208) 634-2164.** There are also ample backcountry opportunities, including miles of logging roads. For a brochure, write to the **McCall Nordic Ski Council, P.O. Box 4396, McCall, ID 83638.**

WHERE TO STAY

Mid-Priced Accommodations

Best Western McCall
Well-equipped 79-room motel, each with microwave, refrigerator and hair dryer. Ski packages. Daily housekeeping, 24-hour front desk. Indoor swimming pool, hot tub. **P.O. Box 4297, McCall, ID 83638; (208) 634-6300, (800) 528-1234** for Best Western reservations.

The Chateau Bed & Breakfast
Victorian B&B with three moderately priced rooms, shared bath and one private spa suite including champagne. Antique furnishings, down comforters but a very modern TV with HBO and VCR. Cozy sitting room. Daily housekeeping, breakfast. **803 N. Third St., McCall, ID 83638; (208) 634-4196.**

Hotel McCall
Restored historic hotel. Heart of town but with lake views. Twenty-two rooms with phones and TV (not to be assumed in McCall budget properties). Lovely decor with antique furnishings, fresh flowers and other personal touches. Non-smoking property. Ski packages. Daily housekeeping; complimentary breakfast, après-ski refreshments and bedtime cookies and milk. **P.O. Box 1778, McCall, ID 83638; (208) 634-8105.**

The 1920 House
B&B inn with three lovely rooms with shared baths in home built by owners of local lumber mill and furnished with owners' family antiques. Homelike, warm and comfortable. Sitting room with lake view, nicknamed "night-owl room," with teakettle, cookies, games. Fireplace living room; library. Daily housekeeping, full breakfast, après-ski tea or sherry. Ski storage. **143 E. Lake St., P.O. Box 1716, McCall, ID 83638; (208) 634-4661.**

Mountain Stats—Brundage Mountain

Resort elevation 5,021 feet (McCall)
Top of highest lift 7,640 feet
Bottom of lowest lift 5,840 feet
Total vertical 1,800 feet
Longest run 2 miles
Average annual snowfall 300 inches
Ski season Thanksgiving to mid-April
Lifts 2 triple chairlifts, 2 doubles, 1 platterpull, 1 handle tow
Capacity 4,425 skiers per hour
Terrain 36 runs, 1,300 acres (20% beginner and novice, 55% intermediate, 25% advanced and expert)
Snow reports (208) 634-5650

Northwest Passage Bed & Breakfast   325
Built in 1938 for the *Northwest Passage* film crew, now beautifully decorated B&B in a country Victorian style. Six rooms, all with private baths, one master suite, one honeymoon suite and one apartment with kitchen. Situated on five acres with mountain views from every window. Beautiful common area with fireplace. Daily housekeeping, full breakfast, complimentary wine in the evening. **P.O. Box 4208, McCall, ID 83638; (800) 597-6658, (208) 634-5349.**

Shore Lodge
McCall's biggest, best appointed resort property, recently renovated to the tune of $3 million. Lakeside lodge with 115 rooms of various sizes. Ample public rooms and amenities. Daily housekeeping, 24-hour front desk, room service, bell staff. Spa, pool, racquetball, weight room, restaurant, lounge, coffee shop. **P.O. Box 1006, McCall, ID 83638; (800) 657-6464, (208) 634-2244.**

Economy Accommodations

Brundage Bungalows
Cozy cabins with complete kitchens and TV with VCR. Serene setting. Great views of Payette Lake and beyond. **308 W. Lake St., McCall, ID 83638; (208) 634-8573.**

Brundage Inn

Closest motel to Brundage Mountain. Clean, cozy motel. Some family units with kitchenettes. All rooms with phone, cable TV and individual climate control. Daily housekeeping, complimentary coffee. **P.O. Box 734, McCall, ID 83638; (208) 634-2344.**

Riverside Motel & Condos

Fine motel rooms with queen beds. Also, fully equipped two-bedroom condos. Located on Payette River with lake views. Ski packages. Daily housekeeping (motel). Hot tub. **P.O. Box 746, McCall, ID 83638; (800) 326-5610, (208) 634-5610.**

Scandia Inn Motel & Cabin

Clean motel in log cabin style, surrounded by pine trees. Rooms with queen beds. Walking distance to shops and restaurants. Long-time McCall institution. Non-smoking rooms available. Daily housekeeping. Finnish sauna. **P. O. Box 746, McCall, ID 83638; (208) 634-7394.**

Woodsman Motel

Large downtown budget motel with 63 rooms. Popular with snowmobilers as well as skiers. Daily housekeeping. Cafe. **P.O. Box 884, McCall, ID 83638; (208) 634-7671.**

Condominiums

Fircrest Condominiums

New downtown condos within walking distance of shops and restaurants. One-, two- and three-bedroom units with fully equipped kitchens, cable TV and ski lockers. Contemporary decor. Linen exchange upon request. **P.O. Box 1978, McCall, ID 83638; (208) 634-4528.**

Mill Park Condos

Spacious and well-furnished units—McCall's most luxurious. Each with Jenn-aire range, whirlpool tub, microwave, fireplace, washer and dryer and garage. With just eight two- and three-bedroom units, the feeling is private. Located on the lake. Great views too. Guests get midweek discount on lift tickets. **P.O. Box 1062, McCall, ID 83638; (800) 888-7544, (208) 634-4151.**

Companies providing management and reservations services for condos, cabins and homes in the area include

Clark Property Rentals, (208) 634-7766
Engen Real Estate, (208) 634-2114
Johnson & Co., (208) 634-7134
Jan Kangus Accommodations Services, (800) 551-8234, (208) 634-7766
McCall Vacations, (800) 799-3880, (208) 634-7056

DINING OUT

Bev's Cottage Cafe

Breakfast, lunch and dinner in pleasant place. Home-baked goods. Espresso menu. **801 N. Third St., McCall; (208) 634-7964.**

Blue Moon Outfitters Winter Culinary Adventure

Ski, with a guide, 1 mile to a backcountry yurt on the shore of Payette Lake in Ponderosa State Park. Gourmet five-course dinner, including hot beverages. BYO wine or beer. Less expensive and more adventurous than typical sleighride dinner. Equipment needed, cross-country skis (additional) and headlamps (supplied). Reservations required. **McCall; (208) 634-3111.**

Harvest Moon Deli

Deli-style breakfast, lunch and dinner. Store stocked with prepared and gourmet specialty foods, coffee, tea, wine and scrumptious freshly baked pastries. Eat-in or takeout. **1135 Lake St., McCall; (208) 634-5578.**

The Huckleberry

Innovative Northwest cuisine, plus pasta, served for dinner. Homemade soups. Omelettes and other breakfast favorites. Lunch too. One of McCall's special spots. **402 North Third St., McCall; 634-8477.**

Lardo Grill & Saloon

Lively saloon and casual restaurant. Huge portions appreciated by hardworking local loggers and miners and hard-skiing visitors. Italian dishes and char-grilled burgers, plus complete bar service. **600 W. Lake St., McCall; (208) 634-8191.**

The Mill

McCall's atmosphere leader. Antiques and memorabilia to look at. Prime rib, seafood and steak to dine on. Specialty drinks, cocktails and wines. Reservations accepted. Located **"beside the Mill,"** McCall; **(208) 634-4441.**

The Narrows Restaurant
Lovely lake views and Northwestern cuisine in this hotel restaurant. Good wine list. **Shore Lodge, McCall; (208) 634-2244.**

The Pancake House
Breakfast and lunch. Big portions. Bargain prices. Home baking, especially cinnamon rolls, a well-loved treat. Takeout available. **209 N. Third St., McCall; (208) 634-5849.**

Panda on the Lake
Chinese restaurant serving Mandarin, Szechuan and Hunan specialties at lunch and dinner. Lower-level restaurant with near-fish-eye view of lake. Full bar. Takeout available. **317 East Lake Street, McCall; (208) 634-2266.**

Romano's
Italian-American food in a historic lakeside building. Comfortable and homey. Cocktails, wine and beer. Children's menu. **203 Lake St., McCall; (208) 634-4396.**

Smoky Mountain Pizza
Low prices. Family-friendly pizza purveyor. Large selection of beer on tap. **504 W. Lake St., McCall; (208) 634-7185.**

Si Bueno Mexican Restaurant & Rodrigo's Cantina
Tex-Mex comes north—plus steaks and seafood at Si Bueno. Adjacent cantina is lively and fun. Atmospheric. Children's menu. Takeout available. Off **Rte. 55** at **McCall Airport; (208) 634-2128.**

NIGHTLIFE

McCall hardly qualifies as a hot spot, though typical après-ski conviviality takes place in the base lodge, where beer, wine and snacks are available. In town, Rodrigo's Cantina serves good margaritas of all flavors and potencies and has an official happy hour with munchies on weekday evenings in the new cocktail lounge. Lardo's Saloon and Sportsmen's Bar are pretty lively. Lardo's especially gets local miners and loggers. The Mill has live music and dancing on weekends. Smoky Mountain Pizza puts on the best evening face for families and young folks, with a large selection of beers on tap, video games and a pool table. Located in the biggest resort hotel in town, the Shore Lodge's Narrows Lounge and Restaurant also is popular, often with a pianist presiding. **327** Out on Hwy 55, the McCall Brewing Company is the latest draw, with handcrafted microbrews as well as good food. Some people just head for Zim's Hot Springs to unkink in a natural pool—and a game room for the youngsters who never seem to get kinked up from skiing.

For more information, contact **Brundage Mountain, P.O. Box 1062, McCall, ID 83633; (800) 888-7544, (208) 634-4151; McCall Area Chamber of Commerce & Visitor's Bureau, P.O. Box D, McCall, ID 83638; (208) 634-7631.**

SILVER MOUNTAIN

BACKDROP

The most intriguing offering on the Rocky Mountain skiing menu is Silver Mountain, the only new large-scale ski area on the western American firmament. This modern ski area, which debuted in 1990–91, brought new life to a down-at-the-heels mining town that could, until then, charitably be called shabby. Kellogg itself is not in a snowbelt, so the world's longest gondola climbs from a fantastic, quasi-Tyrolean base terminal over mountainous mine tailings to a ski area high above.

THE LAY OF THE LAND

I-90 is a concrete ribbon across Idaho's slim panhandle. Beside the highway is Kellogg, where the gondola's bottom terminal is found. There is no on-mountain lodging yet, though a village has been part of the plan—and may be still, or again. Kellogg started with a few rather simple motels, added a handful of interesting new B&B inns and then condominiums and is undergoing a real renaissance. Wallace, 15 minutes to the east, has more options for overnighting and dining. Many visitors still happily stay at the opulent Coeur d'Alene Resort, a scenic half-hour drive to the west, which offers attractive ski packages. The area is now promotionally referred to as the Silver Valley.

GETTING THERE

Silver Mountain is directly off I-90, 70 miles east of Spokane International Airport, served by major airlines, and Amtrak. Sometimes there are commuter flights to Coeur d'Alene Airport. **Silver Shuttle Service, (208) 783-1234, operates** transportation from both cities and also handles the local ski shuttle in Kellogg. Silver Mountain is within reasonable driving distance from other cities, approximately 2 hours from Missoula, Montana; 5½ hours from Seattle and 7 hours from Calgary.

PROFILE

A high-speed gondola, Idaho's first and the world's longest (3.1 miles), travels in 19 minutes from an ore town to a new mountain aerie with broad vistas and clear air. Technically, it would be possible to credit Silver Mountain with a 4,000 base-to-summit vertical, but unless and until snowmaking is installed on a trail back to town, the true skiable vertical is nearly 2,200 feet—which isn't bad at all. There is a fairytale quality to Silver Mountain—not just the "living-happily-ever-after aspect" initially promised by its developers, but the whole look of the place. The bottom and top gondola terminals, done in a fanciful Alpine derivative style, between them offer eating facilities and other services you would normally find at a ski area base. Fifty runs, served by five new chairlifts, spread over two mountains behind, above and below the gondola summit. Silver Mountain today includes all the runs of a long-defunct local ski hill called Silverhorn (and before that, Jackass Ski Area) on Wardner Peak and new ones in a contemporary mix of wide, easily groomable trails and narrower, steeper, more traditional ones on adjacent Kellogg Peak. With some 32,000 acres of private land, other peaks beyond could eventually be developed.

The Mountain Haus perches on a plateau near the area's eastern boundary. It has a curious but rather nice feeling of being the portal to the skiing yet somehow being apart from it. From the lodge, you can see Kellogg Peak's upper runs and the upper chairlift, but you can't ski to the lodge from anywhere. Skiers reach it via lift from all directions—the gondola from the frontside, a short quad chair from the hollow between upper

Kellogg and the Mountain Haus plateau from another and a longer triple chair out of Kellogg's lower runs from a third. As you approach this monumental chateau in the sky, you get a rare sense of approaching an important building, and when you leave and step into your skis, you really feel as if you are going skiing as opposed to going to board a ski lift and eventually going skiing. It's a subtle distinction but one that separates Silver Mountain from almost every other ski area around.

Kellogg's upper runs are an inviting criss-cross of solid blue-square runs on a respectable vertical of more than 1,000 feet. Interestingly laid out with numerous mix-and-match possibilities and immaculately groomed, Kellogg is the average skier's dream skiing. This is also the terrain that has, at times, been lighted for night skiing and conceivably might be again. The trails range from short shots like Junction to long roads like Heaven, the aptly named perimeter run that offers super cruising with views to match. You can ride Chair 2, a triple, and play around upper Kellogg for hours, and if you want to sample a black diamond, Quicksilver and the top section of Steep & Deep provide a taste. If you drop off the back, you get more than a taste of a black diamond; you get a full plate. Just off the summit is The North Face, a huge stand of trees clinging to an ultra-steep slope that are spaced just sufficiently to enable skiers to snake through but close enough to be scary. Double black is the color of North Face—and the shade suits this perpendicular powder glade just fine. If it's bumps you want, bumps you'll get off Sky Way Ridge. Marked with a single diamond to scare off shaky intermediates, it is the route to Sunset, a heavily moguled super-steep snowfield and a couple of trails that are equally bumped up but far narrower.

Lower Kellogg, a wooded bowl below the Mountain Haus elevation, has a handful of easy-skiing novice trails and intermediate cruisers, but it is best known for its own bump runs. Terrible Edith, Paymaster, Collateral under Chair 3, Saddle Back and the bottom of Rendezvous are rarely groomed and always great magnets for the rubber-kneed.

Inside Silver Mountain

While Kellogg's runs ski in a suitably contemporary way, Wardner is a combination of new planned runs and quirky old trails and slopes from its previous incarnation. You can reach Wardner via either Sky Way Ridge from the top of Kellogg or from Centennial, a blue-square boulevard in the cusp of the drainage between the two peaks. Wardner is a something-for-everyone (except raw beginners) mountain. Silver Mountain's longest chairlift, Chair 4 (nearly a mile long and 1,874 vertical feet), has a midstation so that intermediates can ski just the moderately pitched top section, bump maniacs the bottom and skilled skiers who like it both ways the whole works. Wardner's most challenging terrain is on both sides of the steep-walled ridge to the west of Chair 4. Take Morning Star, a dive-bomber snowfield, or Solitude, a web of lacy powder shots, both canted back toward the lift and you've found some of the best open steeps around. Drop off the ridge's backside into Silver Basin, which is difficult tree and chute skiing by any standard, or ski the Meadows or Sheer Bliss for open slope skiing with breathtaking pitches. Either way, you've aced some of the best black-diamond terrain in northern Idaho.

Resort elevation 2,300 feet
Top of highest lift 6,300 feet
Bottom of lowest lift 2,300 feet (gondola), 4,126 feet (Chair 4)
Total vertical 4,000 feet (summit to gondola base, snow conditions permitting); 2,200 (normally skiable)
Longest run 2½ miles (normally skiable)
Average annual snowfall 320 inches
Ski season mid-November to mid-April
Lifts one 8-passenger gondola, 1 quad chairlift, 2 triples, 2 doubles
Capacity 7,400 skiers per hour
Terrain 1,500 acres, 50 runs (15% beginner and novice, 45% intermediate, 40% advanced and expert); 2,000 acres including off-piste
Snowmaking 150 acres
Mountain dining Mountain Haus at the gondola summit
Snow reports (208) 783-1111

330 SKI SCHOOL PROGRAMS

Introductory Program

Skiing 101: Learn-to-ski program, including all-day lift ticket, three-hour group lesson and rental equipment. Two-tier pricing (less during midweek). Also, available as five-lesson package guaranteeing the ability to come down from the top of Kellogg Peak by the end of program.

From Kellogg Peak, you can see Wardner Peak—and vice versa.

Advanced and Specialty Program

Advanced Workshop: Clinics available to intermediate and advanced skiers, including bumps, steeps, racing and telemark sessions. Available on selected weekends and holidays.

For Families
Skiing Children
Minors' Camp: Introduction to skiing and indoor activities for children ages 3 to 5. Half- and full-day options, the latter with lunch.
SKIwee: Franchised children's teaching program for children ages 6 to 10. Offered as part of half- or full-day program, the latter including lunch.

FOR RACERS

NASTAR: Weekdays and holidays.

Photo courtesy Silver Mountain

NORDIC SKIING

The Hale Fish Hatchery near Mullan and Lookout Pass trails are marked for cross-country skiing and snowshoeing. Lookout Mountain is a small ski area, and cross-country skiers can arrange to ride the chairlift to reach Nordic trails.

WHERE TO STAY

Silver Valley Bed & Breakfast Association operates as a **Silver Valley Central Reservations System, (800) 443-3505, (208) 556-1178; Kellogg Chamber of Commerce, (208) 784-0821,** has information but does not offer a reservations service.

Kellogg and Vicinity

Mid-Priced Accommodations

The Doctor's Inn
B&B just off Main Street. Just two second-floor luxury suites with private baths. Hospitable and relaxing. Non-smoking inn. Children permitted. Ski packages. Daily housekeeping, Continental breakfast included. Sitting room with fireplace, outdoor hot tub. **118 W. Mill St., Kellogg, ID 83837; (208) 783-9110.**

The McKinley Inn
Built in the early 1900s as the Connel Hotel, now a delightful eight-room inn, each with private bath. All rooms decorated with different themes and all non-smoking. Restful private parlor; adjacent balcony with gondola view. Three blocks from gondola base. Antique car collection and gift shop on premises. Daily housekeeping, breakfast included. Restaurant, lounge. **210 McKinley Ave., Kellogg, ID 83837; (208) 786-7771.**

Mountain View Cabins
Cozy and comfortable cabins with fireplaces and luxurious feather beds. Full kitchens, microwaves, barbecues and private patios with all. Hot tub. **410 Main St., Kellogg, ID 83837; (208) 786-1310.**

Silverhorn Motor Inn
Bavarian-style motel. Forty well-appointed rooms with queen-size beds. Six blocks from gondola. Ski packages. Daily housekeeping. Hot tub, restaurant, ski wax room, guest laundry, gift shop. **609 W. Cameron Ave., Kellogg, ID 83837; (800) 437-6437, (208) 783-1151.**

Sterling Silver Bed & Breakfast
Romantic inn with two rooms, luxuriously appointed with down comforters and lovely furnishings. One room best suited for a couple, but one can accommodate children too. Serene sitting room with Victorian chairs and soft music. No smoking. Ski packages. Morning coffee service to the door, gourmet breakfast, daily housekeeping, dinner available from owner/chefs by reservation. Private deck with outdoor hot tub. **101 W. Mission Ave., Kellogg, ID 83837; (208) 783-4551.**

Super 8 Motel
Sixty rooms, including family suites. Excellent location, close to gondola terminal. Children 12 and under stay free. Daily housekeeping, complimentary coffee, 24-hour front desk, complimentary Continental breakfast. Indoor heated pool, spa, guest laundry, ski storage. **608 Bunker Ave., Kellogg, ID 83837; (800) 785-5443, (208) 783-1234; (800) 800-8000** for Super 8 reservations.

Ward's Sunshine House
Luxurious "executive retreat" at moderate price. Rented on different plans according to demand, from individual rooms or suites, with or without breakfast or other meal plan. Living area with two fireplaces, full kitchen and two bedrooms on each of three levels. Each bedroom with double bed plus other sleeping area. Semiprivate baths. Hot tub, sauna, game room with pool table and table tennis. **Big Creek, Kellogg, ID 83837; (800) 800-6181, (208) 783-0371.**

Economy Accommodations

Kellogg Hostel
Basic lodging for budget-minded travelers. Dorms for four to six, plus some family rooms. Accommodates total of 40 guests. Kitchen privileges. Several common areas, including game room and TV/VCR room. **834 W. McKinley Ave., Kellogg, ID 83837; (208) 783-4171.**

Rio Club
Skiing on the cheap in this bare-bones inn. Four rooms with beds for one or two. Roof over your

Idaho

head; you do the rest. No linens; bring your sleeping bag. **203 McKinley Ave., Kellogg, ID 83837; (208) 786-0761.**

The Sands
Recently remodeled 15-unit hotel. Located just off I-90, 2 miles from Silver Mountain. Daily housekeeping. Restaurant, lounge, hot tub. **605 Washington Ave., Smelterville, ID 83868; (208) 343-2533.**

Sunshine Inn
Sixteen spartan rooms for budget-watchers. Pets permitted for extra charge. On-site restaurant open 24 hours a day. Daily housekeeping. Restaurant, lounge. **301 W. Cameron Ave., Kellogg, ID 83837; (208) 784-1186.**

Trail Motel
Kellogg's ultra-budget motel with 23 small recently remodeled rooms. TV and phone in each room. Daily housekeeping. **206 W. Cameron Ave., Kellogg, ID 83837; (208) 784-1161.**

Condominiums

Silver Ridge Mountain Lodge Condominiums
One and two-bedroom suites, near the river and across I-90 from the gondola terminal and downtown. All units with full kitchen, microwave, washer and dryer and balcony or patio. Daily housekeeping, Continental breakfast included. Outdoor hot tub. **410 Main St., Kellogg, ID 83837; (208) 786-1310.**

Rentals of fully equipped houses in and around Kellogg are available through **Kellogg Vacation Homes, (800) 435-2558, (208) 786-4261 Silver M Property Management, (800) 621-2963, (208) 784-1166 Valley Investment Properties, (208) 786-2241**
The Silver Valley also offers direct short-term rentals of "ski houses" for families and small groups.
Scott's Inn (two-bedroom, two-bath apartment), **(208) 786-8581**
Kellogg's Coziest Mountain Chalet (accommodates two to four people, in town, hot tub, cable TV), **(208) 786-4261**

Silber Berg Haus (A-frame near gondola, accommodates up to eight people), **(208) 784-7551**
Wardner Ski House (large fully equipped kitchen, two minutes' drive to gondola, accommodates six to eight), **(208) 784-5841**

Coeur d'Alene
Coeur d'Alene Lodging Assn., **(208) 667-7765.**

Luxury Accommodations
Coeur d'Alene Resort
One of the Northwest's leading resorts, frequently honored with assorted hospitality and culinary awards. Worth the commute over the Fourth of July Pass. Full-service hotel with 358 rooms and all amenities. All rooms good, but the 173 Lake Tower units are best, with great views and splashy decor. Knockout penthouses for the terminally rich. Mainly a summer resort with great off-season prices and ski packages in winter. Daily housekeeping, 24-hour front desk, room service, bell staff, valet, ski shuttle. Indoor pool, hot tub, sauna, fitness facilities, racquetball, indoor computerized golf, bowling, restaurants, lounge, adjacent shopping mall. **Second** and **Front Sts., Coeur d'Alene, ID 83814-1941; (800) 688-5253, (208) 765-4000.**

Mid-Priced Accommodations
Bennett Bay Inn
Twenty units, both traditional rooms and four unique spa suites. Some kitchenettes. Lakeside location. **E. 5144 I-90, Coeur d'Alene, ID 83814; (800) 368-8609, (208) 664-6168.**

Comfort Inn
Fifty-one-room motor inn, 21 with kitchen facilities and 60 percent non-smoking. Seven spa suites. Children 18 and younger stay free in parents' room. Perkins restaurant adjacent with hotel charge privileges. Ski packages. Daily housekeeping, complimentary Continental breakfast, complimentary evening snack. Outdoor covered pool, whirlpool, sauna, playground. **280 W. Appleway, Coeur d'Alene, ID 83814; (208) 765-5500 (800) 4-CHOICE** for Comfort Inn reservations.

Holiday Inn Resort

Up-market motor inn with 122 rooms, some non-smoking. Pets allowed. Children 18 and younger stay free in parents' room. Winner of Superior Hotel Award from Holiday Inn worldwide three years in a row. Ski packages. Daily housekeeping, 24-hour front desk, room service, bell staff, VIP transport to Silver Mountain. Outdoor pool, restaurant, lounge. **414 W. Appleway, Coeur d'Alene, ID 83814; (208) 765-3200, (800) HOL-IDAY** for Holiday Inn reservations.

Economy Accommodations

Pines Resort Motel

Well-appointed motel with 55 units, including two-room family suites. Good value. Ski packages and student discounts. Daily housekeeping, indoor pool, hot tub, restaurant, lounge. **1422 Northwest Blvd., Coeur d'Alene, ID 83814; (208) 664-8244.**

Wallace

Mid-Priced Accommodations

The Historic Jameson

Built in 1889 as "The Jameson Steak, Billiard Hall & Hotel." Carefully restored as a B&B inn. All rooms are charming, mostly with shared baths. Located in center of town. Ski packages. Guests have privileges at the Best Western's pool, exercise room, hot tub, sauna and steamroom. Daily housekeeping, breakfast. Restaurant, lounge. **304 Sixth St., Wallace, ID 83873; (800) N-IDA-FUN, (208) 556-1554.**

21 Bank Street

Eighty-year-old former convent now a charming B&B. Each room individually decorated. Shared baths. Children over 12 welcome. Sitting room with fireplace. Non-smoking inn. Ski packages. Daily housekeeping, full breakfast included, dinner available with reservations. **21 Bank St., Wallace, ID 83873; (208) 752-1292.**

The Wallace Inn/Best Western

Wallace's largest inn with 63 rooms and four suites. Well-appointed. Daily housekeeping, pool, hot tub, steamroom, exercise room, restaurant, lounge. **100 Front St., Wallace, ID 83873;** **(208) 752-1252, (800) 528-1234** for Best Western reservations.

Economy Accommodations

Molly B. Damm Motel

Seventeen-room budget motel. Kitchenette units with two beds at bargain multiday rates. Pets permitted. **371 Hwy 10, Wallace, ID 83873; (208) 556-4391.**

Ryan Hotel

Clean rooms, reasonable prices and spirit of historic Wallace. Twelve rooms with private baths. **608 Cedar, Wallace, ID 83873; (208) 753-6001.**

DINING OUT

Kellogg

Broken Wheel

Casual place for breakfast, lunch and dinner. Friday Neptune Night (seafood special), Saturday (sirloin steak or BBQ rib special) and Fried Chicken Sunday (just what it claims). Salad bar. Open daily except Sunday. **102 E. Cameron Ave., Kellogg; (208) 784-0601.**

Fred's

Breakfast and light fare. Deli sandwiches, salads, soups and chili. Favored by off-hours eaters; open from 6:00 A.M. to midnight daily. **113 McKinley Ave., Kellogg; (208) 783-0091.**

Humdinger Drive-In

Hankering after the '50s? Relive the feeling in this home-town drive-in, serving milkshakes, burgers, chicken, fish and fries seven days a week. **205 Hill St., Kellogg; (208) 786-7395.**

Kopper Keg

Family favorites such as pizza, chicken and burgers. Breakfast too. **2 S. Division St., Kellogg; (208) 786-9221.**

Meister Burger

In 1950s-style care where you can watch burgers being grilled across from your counter seat. Fresh-ground beef, homemade pies, old-fashioned fountain treats and the house specialty called the

Green River. Open for lunch and early supper. Budget eatery. **116 W. McKinley Ave., Kellogg; (208) 783-5691.**

Patrick's

Kellogg's classiest. Atmospheric and stylish. Affordably elegant with tablecloths, candles and well-prepared, nicely served dinners. Steaks, pastas and seafood. House specialty combining all: Steak Patrick (tenderloin filet wrapped in bacon, smothered in crabmeat and topped with béarnaise sauce). Beer, wine and cocktails in Victorian parlor. Reservations accepted. **The Inn, 305 S. Division St., Kellogg; (208) 786-2311.**

Sam's Restaurant

Full menu at breakfast, lunch and dinner seven days a week. Economy pricing. Casual eating. **711 W. Cameron, Kellogg; (208) 784-761.**

Timbers Restaurant & Bar

Stylish yet casual full-service restaurant at base of Silver Mountain gondola. Convenient for skiers' breakfasts. Also serves lunch and dinner. Specialties are the most popular Mexican and American dishes. **Silver Mountain, Kellogg; (208) 783-1111.**

Wah Hing

Family-style dinners from Chinese and American menus. Appetizers, combination dinners and Asian specialties. Open for lunch and dinner, except Monday. **215 McKinnley Ave., Kellogg; (208) 783-3181.**

Zany's Pizza

Sleek spot for good pizza, gourmet sandwiches, pasta and salads. Also, good beer selection, featuring microbrews and Kellogg's best selection of appetizers and munchies. **105 McKinkley Ave., Kellogg; (208) 784-1144.**

Coeur d'Alene

Beverly's

Most highly regarded restaurant in this part of Idaho. Fine dining, especially known for Northwestern specialties prepared and served with Continental flair. Lake views from huge windows, sixth-floor location. Award-winning restaurant for food and service. Light jazz and acoustic guitar. Cocktails and fine wine list. Reservations recommended. **Coeur d'Alene Resort; (208) 765-4000.**

NIGHTLIFE

Moguls in the Mountain Haus has a convivial, spirited atmosphere and live entertainment. More merriment is at the Timbers Bar and Gondola Cafe, both at the base. In Kellogg, Zany's Underground, Patrick's Inn and the Broken Wheel's cocktail lounge are good gathering places for après-ski drinks. Jason's Snowshoe Inn is lovely and restrained. The Sunshine Inn Lounge has live entertainment on weekends. The Sands in Smelterville has a sports bar with giant-screen television. If you're en route back to Coeur d'Alene, the Enaville Resort (known over the years as The Snakepit, Josie's, Clark Hotel and some unprintable names) has been a landmark for a century. It offers food, drink and authentic congeniality. It's located 1 1/2 miles up the Coeur d'Alene River Rd. from Exit 43 off I-90 and is worth the detour. In the lakeside town, the Coeur d'Alene Resort ranks as tops for nightlife—as for everything else in town. The Lobby Cafe is a busy and stylish spot for a drink, while Whisper's is the quiet lounge for a romantic and flirtatious evening. Beverly's Lounge adjacent to the fine-dining restaurant of the same name features mellow music such as light jazz and acoustic guitar. Foxie's in the Holiday Inn is fun, with live entertainment with the resort's only karaoke machine. In Wallace, the top spot is the Jameson's gorgeous old-style saloon, whose monumental back bar is a natural gathering spot for the sociables.

For more information, contact **Silver Mountain, 610 Bunker Ave., Kellogg, ID 83837; (208) 783-1111; Kellogg Chamber Tourist Information, 712 W. Cameron Ave., Kellogg, ID 83837; (208) 784-0821; Wallace Chamber of Commerce, P.O. Box 1167, Wallace, ID 83873; (208) 753-7151; Coeur d'Alene Convention & Visitors Bureau, P.O. Box 1088, Coeur d'Alene, ID 83814; (800) 232-4968, (208) 664-0587.**

BOGUS BASIN

Photo courtesy Bogus Basin

BACKDROP

Boise thinks it has Bogus Basin all to itself, and so, in a real sense, it does. This interesting mid-size mountain is visible from Idaho's capital city, and it's so close that residents have to think twice about traveling any farther to ski, but with limited on-mountain facilities and a harrowing access road, it has remained largely undiscovered by skiers and snowboarders outside of the immediate region.

The area finally jumpstarted its 20-year master plan in 1996 with the long-awaited replacement of one old double with a high-speed detachable quad. With it came a huge new beginner area, a good thing for the ski area where booming Boise learns to ski. The result of the slow-growth pattern, however, is an economical ski destination which can easily be combined with accommodations in an interesting and worthwhile little city. Located on a broad plain some 3,000 feet lower than the ski area, Boise boasts a temperate climate where you can mix golf, tennis, shirtsleeve jogging and other outdoor pursuits with skiing. For sometime skiers and mixed groups of skiers and nonskiers, it's a combination that's hard to beat.

THE LAY OF THE LAND

Bogus Basin is one of the most accessible ski areas in the Rocky Mountain West, located just 16 miles northeast of Boise and 22 miles both from I-84 and the airport. The distance is modest, but it can be slow going—about a 45-minute drive up a hairy hundred-hairpin access road.

GETTING THERE

Boise Airport is served by national and regional airlines, and rental cars are available. You can drive to Boise (I-84 is the closest), take **Amtrak,**

(800) USA-RAIL or arrive on the bus at **Boise Bus Depot, (208) 343-3681,** with a choice of Greyhound Winnemucca Stages and Sun Valley Stages. **Boise Urban Stages** (acronym BUS, in case you didn't notice) provides transportation around the city, **(208) 336-1010.**

PROFILE

Bogus Basin's "last name" describes the area's frontside, which consists of a broad basin with skiing on either side of the Bogus Creek Lodge. But it has an appropriate "first name" too. The "basin" actually has lifts and skiable terrain on all sides of its main mountain, a rounded summit called Shafer Butte, meaning that thinking of the skiing as being limited to the basin is a "bogus" and far too modest image. Fortunately, there's nothing bogus about the skiing. The terrain is interesting, and when conditions are right, the area can provide a first-rate experience at a very modest cost.

The area's two summits, Shafer Butte and Deer Point, are connected by a long ridge with lifts and trails cascading down both faces of each, as well as the "ends" for real wrap-around skiing. The trail census is overly modest as well, for Bogus Basin is a ski-anywhere mountain, with some of the truest open slope and best tree skiing around. The 2,000 skiable acres is a better measure of what's really available for skiing and snowboarding. The Bogus Creek Lodge, the area's large day lodge, nestles in the cusp of the basin and provides the most direct access to the easiest terrain as well as to night skiing. The Deer Point double chairlift, which became a quad in 1996–97, rises nearly 900 feet to a saddle from which you can access terrain on both sides. With the new lift came a new beginner area, 1,600 feet long and 300 feet wide—of really flat terrain. That's several football fields worth of light green. This Front Side includes a variety of tree-studded trails and slopes, ranging from a gentle downhill drift called Mambo Meadows to a steep open slope that is simply known as Bowl. Intermediates may elect to stay on the Showcase chairlift, which serves lovely nearby blue-square

Mountain Stats— Bogus Basin

Resort elevation 6,800 feet (Pioneer Lodge)
Top of highest lift 7,600 feet
Bottom of lowest lift 5,800 feet
Total vertical 1,800 feet
Longest run 1½ miles
Average annual snowfall 250 inches
Ski season Thanksgiving to mid-April
Lifts 1 high-speed quad chairlift, 6 doubles, 3 surface tows
Capacity 7,400 skiers per hour
Terrain 46 trails, 2,000 acres (22% beginner and novice, 45% intermediate, 33% advanced and expert)
Snowmaking 75 to 80 acres (15% of the cut runs)
Night skiing nightly from 4:00 to 10:00 P.M. on 15 slopes
Snow reports (208) 342-2100

terrain. An option is the backside of Deer Point, riding the Bitterroot lift and skiing the likes of Sleepy Hollow, Lazy Mary or Bitterroot Basin.

The Morning Star chair rises gently in the other direction from the Bogus Creek Lodge, accessing additional ultra-easy terrain and unloading above the Pioneer Lodge, which offers mid-mountain accommodations. Novices and very small children can ski the interesting wooded Morning Star runs all day and never get bored, while advanced skiers can drop into the Back Side via the War Eagle Cat Track, which is marked with a black diamond because it's long and because there's no reason for anyone scared of black diamonds to be on this side of the mountain.

The Back Side, directly served only by the Pine Creek chairlift and therefore never crowded, is complex and interesting, and even really good, strong skiers and snowboarders can explore for days without retracing their tracks. Marked runs just tell a fraction of the Back Side's tale, and that tale is of steeps and bumps and leaps and jumps. The real story, however, is told by the trees. Even more than the Front Side, Bogus's Back Side is defined by gladed slopes, both wide open and tight woods, which provide interest and challenge. The trail map may point you to Wildcat,

Nugget, Lightning, Paradise and the like, but you'll want to follow the locals (or locals' tracks) to discover such open secrets as Nugget Meadows or Wildcat Meadows, great glades all—greater still on a powder day—and Waterfall, a tight, steep run that cascades down two frozen waterfalls. You'll probably also want to follow some locals out, because the terrain gets a tad tricky and brushy near the Pine Creek chair's 5,800-foot bottom station.

SNOWBOARDING

Bogus Basin's snowboard park is located just off the Morning Star run and the half-pipe is in the Bowl. The trees, glades and wide open terrain is ideal for snowboarding, and the only downside to riding at Bogus Basin is the long cat tracks that link the Front Side and Back Side, and most riders are willing to pedal, hike or hitch on a ski-pole tow to get past the trouble spots.

Photo courtesy Bogus Basin Resort

SKI SCHOOL PROGRAMS

Introductory Programs

Learn to Ski: Multiday program with two lessons a day for beginners.

Advanced and Specialty Programs

Mountain Experience: Daily guided skiing with an instructor for advanced and expert skiers.

For Families

Nonskiing Children

Bogus Basin Day Care: For nonskiers ages 6 months to 5 years. Available by the hour. Free child care when parent(s) enroll in two-hour private lesson or group lesson.

Skiing Children

Mogul Mouse: Full-day program of ski instruction, supervised day care for ages 3 to 5. Lunch not included or supervised. For ages 5 and over, kids can bring or buy lunch, which will be supervised.

Noteworthy

A low-cost lift ticket for Bitterroot Basin is suitable for families with young children, and preschoolers ski free as well.

337

FOR RACERS

NASTAR: Four times a week. Coin-operated citizens' race course also available.

NORDIC SKIING

Twenty-seven kilometers of groomed and trackset cross-country trails are accessible from a trailhead just off the access road, including 2 kilometers of new trails. Options range from a 5-kilometer two-way road that skirts the bottom of the ski area to a difficult 4-kilometer loop with significant up- and downhills. Pioneer Inn guests may use the trails free; for others, there is a small charge.

WHERE TO STAY

Luxury Accommodations

Red Lion Hotel, Riverside

Boise's luxury leader with 304 rooms and many amenities. Located on Boise River and Greenbelt.

Idaho

Pets permitted. Senior discounts. Twenty-four-hour front desk, daily housekeeping, room, bell and valet service. Restaurants, lounge, sports bar, fitness center. **1401 Lusk, Boise, ID 83706; (800) 547-8010, (208) 343-1871.**

Statehouse Inn
Comfortable mid-rise hotel, located across from the Boise Convention Centre. Eighty-eight well-appointed, attractive rooms, including Jacuzzi suites. In-room computer-fax lines and televisions with video cassette players. Twenty-four-hour front desk, daily housekeeping, complimentary airport transfers, free local phone calls, room service. Restaurant, lounge, fitness facilities, spa. **981 Grove St., Boise, ID 83702; (800) 243-4622, (208) 342-4622.**

Mid-Priced Accommodations
Idaho Heritage Inn
Traditional B&B inn located six blocks from downtown and close to Greenbelt (bicycles available). Six rooms, all with private baths. Graceful home (a former governor's mansion and once Senator Frank Church's home) built in 1904 and listed on National Register of Historic Places. Charming and tasteful non-smoking inn, furnished with antiques. Daily housekeeping, full gourmet breakfast, complimentary evening wine. **109 W. Idaho, Boise, ID 83702;(208) 342-8066.**

Idanha Hotel
Landmark Victorian hotel, built in 1901. Forty-five rooms done with period furnishings. Some suites and kitchenette units. Atmospheric and special. Listed on National Register of Historic Places. Daily housekeeping, complimentary continental breakfast. Restaurant, lounge. **928 Main St., Boise, ID 83702; (208) 342-3611.**

Pioneer Inn
Ski-in/ski-out lodging mid-mountain at Bogus Basin. Close to all resort services. Seventy individually decorated, condo-style rooms from hotel rooms to one-bedroom units. Some units with kitchenettes and/or fireplaces. Ski packages. Mid-stay housekeeping on stays of five nights or longer (more often or additional towel change extra surcharge), complimentary grocery shopping service, complimentary use of laundry

facilities. Restaurant, lounge, whirlpool, sauna, game room, ski lockers. **2405 Bogus Basin Rd., Boise, ID 83701; (800) 367-4397, (208) 332-5100.**

Shilo Inn Riverside
Recently remodeled 112-room inn on Greenbelt, close to downtown. Some non-smoking rooms. Daily housekeeping, complimentary daily newspaper, continental breakfast included, free airport shuttle, free local phone calls. Indoor swimming pool, spa, sauna, steamroom, fitness center, guest laundry. **3031 Main St., Boise, ID 83702; (800) 222-2244, (208) 344-3521.**

Economy Accommodations
Sunliner Motel
Twenty-five-room frill-free budget motel with oversized beds. Daily housekeeping. **3433 Chinden Blvd., Boise, ID 83714; (208) 344-7647.**

DINING OUT

Amore
Top-rated Italian restaurant, known for generous antipasto selection, good pasta, rich desserts and good wine list. Weekday lunches and nightly dinners served. Reservations recommended. **921 W. Jefferson, Boise; (208) 343-6435.**

Angell's Bar and Grill
Award-winning Boise favorite, known for salmon, pasta and steak. Good service and excellent wine list. Open for lunch and dinner. Reservations

accepted. **Ninth** and **Main Sts., Boise; (208) 342-4900.**

Lock, Stock & Barrel

Popular steakhouse, serving Boise carnivores for nearly two decades. Known for handcarved steaks and prime rib. Fresh grilled fish available as well. Nightly food and drink specials. All-you-can-eat salad bar. Wine bar and good beer selection. Reservations recommended. **4705 Emerald, Boise; (208) 336-4266.**

The New Gamekeeper

Trendy restaurant, featuring tableside preparation of popular continental favorites such as Steak Diane, Scampi, Cherries Jubilee, Crêpes Suzette and others. Also, good venison, steak and poultry. Weekday lunch and nightly dinner served. Reservations suggested. **Owyhee Plaza Hotel, 1109 Main St., Boise; (208) 343-4611.**

Onati

Boise's only Basque restaurant, reflecting the traditional cuisine of an important cultural group in this part of Idaho. Lamb is the specialty, as expected from a shepherding tradition. Also, excellent soups and salads and good wine list. Weekday lunches and nightly dinners. **3544 Chinned Blvd., Boise; (208) 343-6464.**

Singapore Sam's

Steaks, seafood, salads and international specialties with a Pacific Rim cast, served nightly for dinner and lunch daily except Sunday. Casual dining and pleasant surroundings. Imported and microbrewed beers, plus wines and cocktails. Located in historic 8th Street Marketplace. **370 S. Eighth St., Boise; (208) 389-2241.**

Table Rock Brewpub

Cheerful and bustling restaurant serving full lunch and dinner menu. Popular pub food and heartier fare. Short stroll from downtown.

Brewery tours available. Weekday lunches and service nightly until midnight (10:00 P.M. on Sundays). Children's menu. **705 Fulton St., Boise; (208) 342-0944.**

NIGHTLIFE

With night skiing seven days a week, nightlife is often on the slopes—or at least at slopeside. When enough is enough, the Firewater Saloon at the Pioneer Inn tends to be the first stop. In town, the top restaurants and hotels all have cocktail lounges, but the Bitter Creek Ale House, Harrison House and Table Rock Brew Pub are the top draws these days. The Main Street Bistro also ranks as a sociable place. Lock, Stock & Barrel's lounge opens daily at 4:00, with a wine bar, more than 30 imported and microbrewed beers and also nightly entertainment. The Flicks is the name of Boise's in-town two-screen movie emporium which tends to show specialty, foreign and art films, and Rick's Cafe American a good place for a drink, an espresso or a light meal before, after or instead of the cinema. Singapore Sam's has live entertainment some nights. Brando's is quieter, with an upscale tearoom ambiance (English afternoon tea is a treat if you're off the mountain early) and a piano bar that continues into the evening. Because Boise is a real city (and a capital one at that), there's also a cultural side to nightlife, including Ballet Idaho, the Boise Philharmonic and the Boise Opera Company.

For more information, write or call **Bogus Basin, 2405 Bogus Basin Rd., Boise, ID 83702; (800) 367-4397, (208) 332-5100; Boise Convention & Visitors Bureau, P.O. Box 2106, Boise, ID 83701; (800) 635-6235, (208) 344-7777.**

Montana

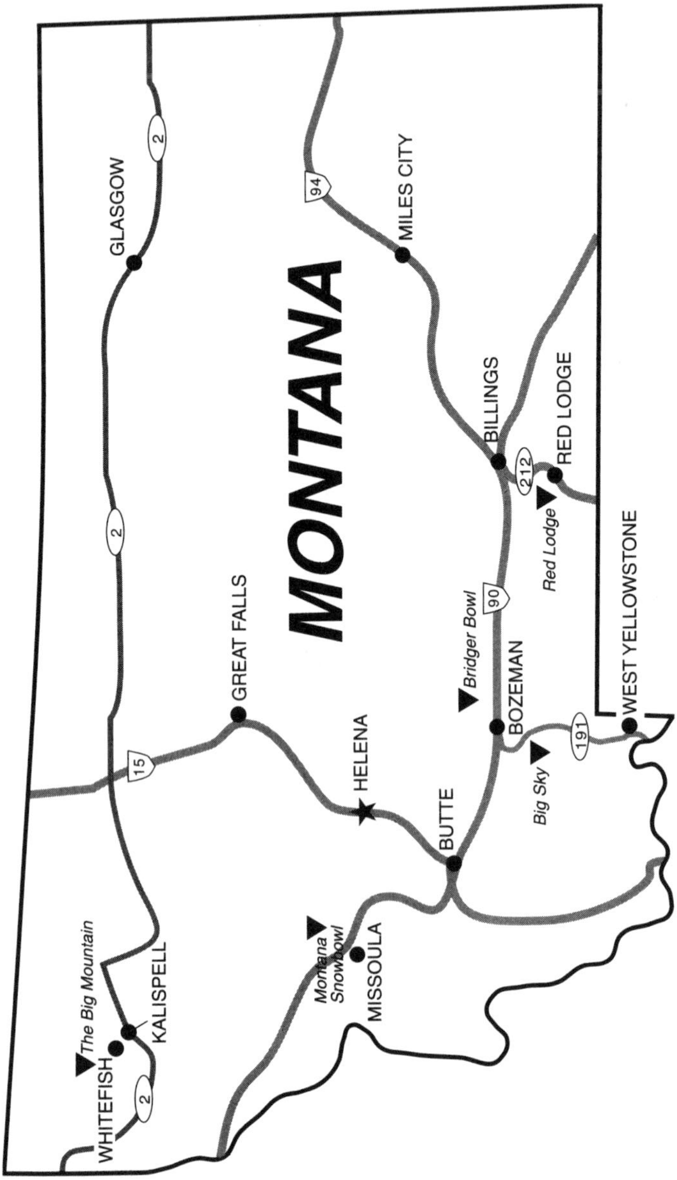
MONTANA
GLASGOW
MILES CITY
BILLINGS
RED LODGE
Red Lodge
WEST YELLOWSTONE
GREAT FALLS
HELENA
Bridger Bowl
BOZEMAN
Big Sky
BUTTE
Montana Snowbowl
MISSOULA
The Big Mountain
KALISPELL
WHITEFISH
2
94
212
90
191
15

Montana

341

BIG SKY

BACKDROP

Big Sky, in southwestern Montana, is on the brink of the big time. As a ski area, it is one of the handful on the continent with more than 4,000 feet of vertical drop. The most significant recent (1995–96) on-mountain development is a very small tram to the top of a very large mountain, upping Big Sky's skiable terrain by 1,200 acres and giving it bragging rights as the first ski area in the United States to stretch to a higher vertical than Jackson Hole. The most significant recent (1996–97) resort development is the much-needed expansion and slicking-up of what had become a rather tacky indoor mall. As a resort, it is a tad sophisticated, though. Still, beneath the increasingly glossy veneer, Big Sky retains an aw-shucks friendliness, with dinner at the Best Western in the valley still considered one of the finest around.

342

The resort is set against Lone Mountain soaring skyward to 11,166 feet and dominating the Gallatin River Valley, as compelling a landmark peak as the Matterhorn in its realm. With the addition of the tram, Lone Mountain is now a ski mountain too—and what a challenging parcel it is, a peak to slide on, look at, admire. The expansiveness of Montana, the proximity to Yellowstone National Park and the splendor of the immediate surroundings all combine to imbue Big Sky with a special flavor. It is a place where you will find a mixture of close-by rugged wilderness and civilized resort living, as well as the open sky that inspired the resort's name and the intimacy of the way in which it developed. Off the beaten path, yet accessible from most of the country, Big Sky has steadily, persistently and engagingly come into its own as one of the top draws in the Rockies.

THE LAY OF THE LAND

The skiing component of the Big Sky Ski & Summer Resort lies at the end of a 7-mile access boulevard—so wide and well-contoured that calling it an access road would be an injustice—between the Gallatin River Canyon and the lifts. There are two resort centers. The private homes, townhomes and condominium complexes comprising Meadow Village closer to the canyon have special appeal for golfers but are less convenient for skiers, for whom the best locale is Mountain Village. Set right at the base of the lifts, this is where you will find the main lodge, several condominium complexes and a few restaurants—most within easy walking distance. Big Sky's skiing is split between two neighboring mountains—Lone and Andesite—that share the single base area. A side road between Meadow and Mountain Villages veers off to Lone Mountain Ranch, a notable guest ranch and cross-country ski center. Complimentary shuttles operate every half hour between Mountain Village, Meadow Village and canyon locations.

GETTING THERE

Big Sky is 43 miles south of Bozeman, Montana, with commercial flights to Gallatin Field. Rental cars are available, and Big Sky's shuttle meets all major flights during the ski season. From Bozeman, take US 191 south to the resort. You won't need a car at the resort. The Huntley Lodge bell service runs on-demand intraresort transportation, and SnowExpres operates free buses between the upper and lower villages from 7:00 A.M. to 11:00 P.M.

PROFILE

Lone Mountain, the higher, larger and more varied of Big Sky's two peaks, has a beginner chair, a new high-speed quad and a slightly shopworn gondola climbing two-thirds of the way up and a gee-whiz tram to the tippy-top that escalates Big Sky from the big time into the pantheon of truly major ski areas. A small tram. A huge, steep area. Every five minutes, just 15 skiers and snowboarders step onto their boards and launch

themselves onto terrain that until recently only the intrepid and strong hiked to. It's a scenario unmatched anywhere else on this side of the Atlantic.

The lower portion of the mountain offers mostly novice and intermediate trails sliced through the trees. Of them, Mr. K is an especially pretty fall-line novice run that flows with the contours of the terrain like a finger of hot fudge down a scoop of ice cream. Andesite, pretty and varied and a sizable ski hill configured in the modern mode, brings skiers closer to what Big Sky is all about, but the upper portion of Lone Mountain is where the picture comes into the sharpest focus.

The high, white world at the top of this fabulous mountain is the defining ski element of the Big Sky experience. The lift-served terrain tops a huge, treeless bowl that looks like a crater with one side blown out. With an average of more than 400 inches of snow a year, this cirque provides some of the best deep-snow skiing in the West. You can stay on the Lone Peak triple, Big Sky's upper-mountain chairlift rising to 9,800 feet, and ski nothing but The Bowl. Its steep sides and seamless cover entice lovers of deep midwinter snow and spring corn—and those who can handle mashed potatoes or crud or windpack on occasion. It looks enormous and skis even bigger. You can ski it in a variety of ways, traversing a little or a lot or simply angling into the snowfield at various spots for a different line with each run.

The front side of the bowl is somewhat steeper and far rockier. Until the tram went in, the upper reaches of Lone Peak were the private province of powderhounds who climbed to a series of chutes etched into the steep and rocky upper mountain. Ironed-legged expert skiers worked their way up to the A–Z Chutes for the reward of skiing down. Now you can do it for the price of a lift ticket—if you have the nerve for rock-rimmed chutes of gut-grabbing steepness.

Even the easiest run from the top is a black diamond cascading down Lone Peak's massive South Face. It's called Liberty Bowl, and actually referring to it as a "run" is charitable. Actually it is a very demanding route marked by stakes in the snow. It never gets groomed, so you may find powder or bumps or crud or corn or some com-

Inside Big Sky

bination any time you ski it. The other South Face runs are even hairier. Thunder, Lightning and Tohelluride drop off the tip of a steep ridge, and the Dictator Chutes (Lenin, Marx and Castro's Shoulder, whose 50-degree pitch makes it Big Sky's steepest) are carved into it. Dirt Bag Wall's very name evokes an image of on-the-edge verticality and gnarliness, and Dakota Territory is so far from the lifts, even by Montana standards, that it might as well be in the Dakotas. These South Face runs spill into the Shedhorn area, a web of truly lovely intermediate and advanced trails and tree skiing too, but coming—as they do—after Lone Peak, skiing them is anticlimactic.

There's plenty of black-diamond turf below the summit steeps too, for huge tracts can be reached by a traverse off the triple chair. Some of the easiest to get to and hardest to ski are off the east-facing ridge that forms The Bowl's northern wall. Big Rock Tongue, Little Rock Tongue, Moonlight Basin, Midnight Basin and Nashville Basin were once hike-in bowls and chutes too, but since they have been lift accessed, they now offer mogul skiing as well as powder. The prodigious snow is a big part, but not the only part, of what makes skiing Big Sky so compelling. On clear days, when the snow clouds aren't dumping their load, the nonstop views from the upper reaches of Lone Mountain of the Spanish Peaks in the Lee Metcalf Wilderness to the Beartooth and Absaroka Ranges and even Wyoming's Tetons are among the northern Rockies' finest. The panoramas are enough to make even the most die-hard skiers stop and take notice.

344

Most skiers find Lone Mountain summit intimidating (but anyone can take the tram up and back and simply drink in the view), and many even find The Bowl's easiest runs to be too much. Some prefer the shelter of the trees when the snow is falling hard and piling deep on the upper

Big Sky offers ski school programs and racing instruction classes for skiers of all ages and kids 10 and under ski free.

Mountain Stats— Big Sky

Resort elevation 7,500 feet
Top of highest lift 11,150 feet
Bottom of lowest lift 6,970 feet
Total vertical 4,180 feet
Longest run 3 miles
Average annual snowfall 400 inches
Ski season Thanksgiving to early April
Lifts one 15-passenger tram, one 4-passenger gondola, 3 high-speed quad chairlifts, 1 fixed-grip quad, 3 triples, 3 doubles, 4 surface tows
Capacity 17,180 skiers per hour
Terrain 75 runs, 3,500 acres (10% beginner and novice, 47% intermediate, 43% advanced and expert)
Snowmaking 10 to 15% of the trails
Snow reports (406) 995-5900

slopes, and some just are happier at a lower altitude. For all of them, Andesite is ideal. This is Big Sky's all-round gentler peak, angling off from the Lone Mountain lifts and providing 1,900 vertical feet of wonderful skiing on generously cut trails of all levels. The Ram Charger, a high-speed quad chairlift, is one of Andesite's three lifts climbing three mountain sides and meeting at the top. Ambush, a frontside cruiser under the Ram Charger, sets the Andesite style for wide runs and consistent fall-line pitches. Novices can spend hours on the sunny, gentle trails served by the Southern Comfort triple chairlift and take Pacifier back to the village when they're done. The Thunder Wolf quad has the greatest vertical and serves some truly terrific upper-end yet most manageable runs. The runs off Mad Wolf are where newly minted intermediate skiers rack up mileage and find confidence and where experts seek out glades and mogul runs that are more sheltered than Challenger's yet demand attention and skill. Big Horn is a super-wide cruiser that rarely fails to delight. The often-bumped-up liftline run called Mad Wolf and the immaculate snowfield called Elk Park Meadows are also options.

Montana is booming, and Big Sky is on the crest of the boom. Two new chairs, all the way around the mountain from Shedhorn and Andes-

Photo courtesy Big Sky Ski & Summer Resort

ite, were installed and a handful of runs were cut as a ski-in/ski-out sales feature of expensive building lots. The Pony Express triple is simply a real estate chair, with green and easy blue runs, but the Iron Horse quad accesses some legitimately interesting terrain, especially when combined with the old Challenger double chair which limbs to Lone Mountain's steep, sloping shoulder. There's a rather neat balance to all this. Long before there was a lift to the top of Lone Peak, Challenger was the lift the best skiers rode, serving steep gullies and hidden bowls. The overall name for this side of the mountain is Moonlight Basin, and to have Challenger representing the old Big Sky ski area and the Powder Express representing the new Big Sky resort development roughly on the same part of the mountain ties everything together into one nice, neat Moonlit package.

SNOWBOARDING

Since extreme terrain and snowboarding go together like peanut butter and jelly, the Lone Peak tram seems to have been installed just for the pleasure of the best riders around. Andesite provides some excellent easy snowboarding terrain. This complex area includes scoopy drainages which resemble natural half-pipes, and in fact, a run now called the Natural Half Pipe has become a favorite of snowboarders.

SKI SCHOOL PROGRAMS

Introductory Programs

Learn to Ski Package: Economical surface-tow ticket, half-day lesson and equipment rentals for adult beginners.
Beginner Group Snowboarding Lesson: Offered daily at 9:45 A.M.

Advanced and Specialty Programs

Powder Sessions: Twice-daily classes (9:45 A.M. and 2:00 P.M.) in skiing powder, conditions permitting. For parallel skiers.

Master the Moguls: Daily class in bump skiing for new and experienced mogul skiers. Available afternoons at 2:00 P.M.
Style Workshop: Emphasis is on elegant form and technique, as well as skiing with less effort. Offered every afternoon at 2:00 P.M.
Rent a Ski Instructor Mountain Tour: Ski the mountain and get pointers en route. Requires at least five skiers of 13 and older at stem-christie level or above.
Seasoned Skier Guided Tours: Tours and tips to familiarize strong intermediates and higher with Challenger and Lone Peak areas. Available for the full day (six hours, meeting at 9:00 A.M.) or half day (three hours, meeting at 9:00 or noon). Reservations required.
Hot Shot Clinics: Ski the steepest of the steepest with some of Big Sky's most experienced pros. Three hours, meeting at 1:15 P.M. Advance reservations required.
Lone Peak Ski Camp: Three days of challenge on Big Sky's highest, toughest terrain. Includes **345** instructor/guide fees and use of avalanche transmitter and shovel pack. Available three times a season to skiers ages 14 and older. Reservations required.
Great Ski Week: Traditional five-day ski week on comprehensive package including deluxe accommodations, daily breakfast, lifts, lessons, social activities and more. Available for all levels. Group stays together and skis with same instructor all week. Also available in children's version.

For Families

Big Sky's mid-'90s base redo includes a fine new children's center, with nursery, kids' ski school, rentals and other facilities under one roof.

Nonskiing Children
Playcare Center: Two programs, one for infants under 18 months and the other for toddlers from 18 months to nonskiing preschoolers. Montana law requires proof of immunization for children in day care, which can be faxed in advance to **(406) 995-3286**. Open daily from 8:30 A.M. to 4:00 P.M.

Skiing Children
Small Fry Try: Introduction to skiing for first-timers ages 3 and 4.

Big Sky Ski Camp: Full-day program, including lunch. Group classes divided by age and ability for skiers ages 4 to 14. Daily on- and off-slope activities scheduled including ice cream social, skis-on treasure hunt and search for jumps and bumps.

Teens

Teen Program: Classes for 14- to 16-year-olds, skiing with "cool" guides.

Hot Shot Clinics and Lone Peak Advanced Ski Camp: Available to high-level skiers ages 14 and older.

Noteworthy

Up to two children to age 10 ski free per paying adult every day of the season. Junior lift tickets in effect for ages 11 to 16.

FOR RACERS

Racing Clinics: Classes focusing on competitive racing. Two-person minimum.

NORDIC SKIING

Lone Mountain Ranch's cross-country center boasts 50 miles of well-groomed trails for all ability levels, divided into upper and lower loops, and a free morning and afternoon shuttle now takes skiers to the upper trails. (Siberia, the highest-altitude trail, is rated tops by picky locals.) Trail use is free to ranch guests and economical for others. The ranch's cross-country center also has instruction and a complete rental and ski shop. Lone Mountain also offers excellent guided ski tours, including Yellowstone National Park, **(406) 995-4644.**

Yellowstone by Ski is an exclusive multiday program led by expert cross-country guides and naturalists, run by a tour organizer called **Off the Beaten Path,** which specializes in unique and personalized mountain adventures, **(406) 586-1311.** The closest corner of Yellowstone National Park is just 18 miles from Big Sky, providing independent as well as guided backcountry skiing into this natural wonderland, with Specimen Creek in the park's northwest corner being both beautiful and not overly demanding. For information on trails and conditions, call **Yellowstone National Park, (307) 344-7381.** Locals have also come to love the Lee Metcalf Wilderness, notably the Fan Creek Trail and Bacon Rind Creek Trail in the Upper Gallatin area.

WHERE TO STAY

Big Sky Ski & Summer Resort, Big Sky Reservations, (800) 548-4486. Unless otherwise stated, the address for all resort accommodations is **P.O. Box 160001, Big Sky, MT 59716.**

Big Sky

Luxury Accommodations

The Huntley Lodge/Shoshone Condominium Hotel

Luxury accommodations—with qualifications. Two properties sharing lobby, restaurant and other public spaces. Lodge has 200 recently renovated rooms, some with mountain views, two double beds and refrigerators. Condo wing is more luxurious with 94 spacious, well-decorated one-bedroom and loft units with gas fireplaces, kitchens and small balconies. Conference Center adjacent to both. Daily housekeeping, 24-hour front desk, bell service, room service, concierge. Restaurant, lounge, indoor/outdoor pool, hot tub, fitness center, shops, guest laundry, game room; **(406) 995-4211.**

Lone Mountain Ranch

Memorable family-run rustic resort with charm and class. Big, beautiful spread with quaint cabin accommodations and spacious new log lodge with sensational views and private outdoor hot tub. Located between Mountain and Meadow Villages. Fine cuisine; even better ambiance.

"Winter Ranch Vacations" are full packages for seven nights, including three excellent meals a day, served family style. Children 2 and younger stay free in parents' room; rate reductions for children to age 12. Daily housekeeping, airport and ski shuttle. Restaurant, lounge, cross-country center, outdoor hot tub, massage available. **P.O. Box 69, Big Sky, MT 59716; (800) 514-4644, (406) 995-4644.**

River Rock Lodge
European boutique-style inn with 29 deluxe rooms, one a suite. Natural log and river rock lodge set decorative tone, and magnificent high-ceilinged lobby reflects it perfectly. Rustic western furnishings. Located in Meadow Village, 6 miles from lifts. Children 12 and under stay free in parents' room. Smoke-free inn. Daily housekeeping, continental breakfast included. **3080 Pine Dr., P.O. Box 160700, Big Sky, MT 59716; (800) 995-9966, (406) 995-2295.**

Condominiums

Arrowhead
Luxurious and spacious chalet-style units at the base of the Silverknife trail on Andesite Mountain. Ski-in/ski-out convenience, plus broad valley views. Each unit is a separate building. Three- and four-bedroom units have private hot tubs, washers and dryers and full kitchens with microwaves.

BeaverHead
Luxurious two- and three-bedroom townhouse-style units with private balconies. Ski-in/ski-out location at the base of the White Wing run. Largest has four bedrooms, loft and five bathrooms and accommodate up to 10. Private hot tub, washer and dryer and full kitchen with microwave featured.

BigHorn
Newest complex on the mountain. Ski-in/ski-out location near Bear Back pomalift. Spacious three-bedroom units with private garages and washer and dryer.

Hill Condominiums
Functional smaller condos ¹/₄ mile from the lifts. All are studios, with or without lofts.

Lake Condominiums
Two- and three-bedroom condos, some with lofts. Located on shore of Lake Levinsky, ¹/₄ mile from lifts. Each with washer and dryer; some with lofts and/or microwaves. Complex has outdoor pool and hot tub.

SkyCrest
Well-furnished units with two to four bedrooms with loft. All with private whirlpool, sun room or balcony. Located ¹/₂ mile from lifts, perched on a hill with spectacular views of Mountain Village and Lone Mountain.

StillWater
Studio to two-bedroom units with balconies and fireplaces. A short walk to lifts. Each building has guest laundry. Guests may use pool facilities at nearby Huntley Lodge.

Companies handling condominium and private home rentals at Big Sky and environs include **Big Sky Chalet Rentals, (800) 845-4428,** **(406) 995-2665**
Big Sky Condominium Management, (800) 831-3509, (406) 995-4560
Big Sky Resort Condominium Management, (406) 995-4211
Big Sky Vacation Properties, (406) 995-4891
Golden Eagle Management, (800) 548-4488, (406) 995-4800
River Rock Accommodations Management, (800) 995-9966, (406) 995-2295
Triple Creek Realty and Management, (800) 548-4632, (406) 995-2316 (Mountain Village), **(406) 995-4847** (Gallatin Canyon)

A pair of snowmobilers get a good look at some of the local American Bison population.

Photo courtesy Big Sky Ski & Summer Resort

Gallatin River Canyon

Mid-Priced Accommodations

Best Western Buck's T-4 Lodge

Seventy-five comfortable, moderately priced rooms with queen-size beds and six deluxe suites. Forty non-smoking rooms. Lodge is 1 mile south of Big Sky entrance. Ski packages. Daily housekeeping, 24-hour front desk, bell service, room service, in-room coffeemakers, VCR and movie rental. Two restaurants, lounge, game room, two large outdoor hot tubs. **P.O. Box 160279, Big Sky, MT 59716; (800) 822-4484, (406) 995-4111, (800) 528-1234 for** Best Western reservations.

Rainbow Ranch Lodge

Rustic lodge 5 miles south of Big Sky entrance. Hot tub, game room, restaurant. **42950 Gallatin Rd., Gallatin Gateway, MT 59730; (406) 995-4132, (406) 995-4552.**

348 320 Ranch

Western-style resort complex 12 miles south of Big Sky Rd. Modern cabins, most with kitchenettes, including 12 new units on banks of Gallatin River. Daily housekeeping. Restaurant, lounge. **205 Buffalo Horn Creek, Gallatin Gateway, MT 59716; (800) 243-0320, (406) 995-4283.**

DINING OUT

Buck's T-4 Dining Room

Surprisingly sophisticated fare for a motor-inn dining room serving traditional western dishes, game, veal, steaks and seafood. Informal setting. Complimentary evening dining shuttle for Big Sky resort guests. Fine wine list. Breakfast also served. Adjacent Buck's Grill, for inexpensive family fare. Burgers, fried chicken, pizza and salad bar. Takeout available. Dinner reservations suggested for dining room. **US Hwy 191,** 1 mile from Big Sky entrance; **(406) 995-4111.**

Cafe Edelweiss

Austrian and German cuisine and delightful continental atmosphere. American dishes also offered. Imported wines and beers. Full bar. Lunch and dinner. Reservations suggested. **Meadow Village, Big Sky; (406) 995-4665.**

First Place Restaurant

Intimate and romantic. Creative American and continental cuisine. Baked Brie in Puff Pastry with Red Wine Butter is outstanding appetizer. Sets tone for seafood, steaks, veal and game specialties, all especially well prepared. Nightly specials. Good wine list (especially California) and desserts. Reservations suggested. **Meadow Shopping Center, Meadow Village, Big Sky; (406) 995-4244.**

Huntley Lodge Dining Room

Attractive, high-ceilinged room with a little nostalgic '50s feeling. Big buffet breakfast with hot and cold sections, plus made-to-order omelettes. Lights dim at dinner. Some Continental and many popular American offerings, with dinner entrées heavily drawn from the meat department. All accompanied by soup or salad, starch, vegetable and bread. Good selection of wines. Dynamite Sunday brunch too. Dinner reservations recommended. **Huntley Lodge, Big Sky; (406) 995-5783.**

Lone Mountain Ranch Dining Room

Spectacular non-smoking restaurant, serving well prepared, generous portions. Breakfast, buffet lunch and dinner. Also, sleighride dinner in North Fork Cabin, with beef and chicken served, plus western entertainment. Reservations required for dinner both on the sleighride and in the dining room. **Lone Mountain Ranch, Big Sky; (406) 995-4644.**

Rainbow Ranch

"The West May Be Wild, but It's Not Uncivilized," is the restaurant motto. Civilization equals beef tenderloin, veal chop, fresh salmon, grilled lamb, venison and other temptations, all prepared with flair and sophistication. Also, nightly vegetarian special. Lovely dining room, with no smoking. Reservations suggested. **US Hwy 191,** 5 miles south of Big Sky entrance; **(406) 885-4132.**

Rocco's

Mixture of Mexican and Italian fare, so it's the place of choice if one wants pasta, the other fajitas. Terrific happy hour and good margaritas. Casual atmosphere. Various nightly specials. Reservations accepted. **Big Sky; (406) 995-4200.**

Scissorbills

Breakfast, lunch and dinner served in casual restaurant and bar. Breakfast is breakfast. Other times, soup and salad bar, sandwiches, burgers, steaks, chicken and fish. Casual but sophisticated atmosphere. Wine bar with Big Sky's largest champagne selection. Terrific happy hour, often with live entertainment. **Arrowhead Mall, Big Sky; (406) 995-4933.**

320 Ranch Restaurant

Steak, seafood and nightly specials. Old West atmosphere. Fireplace. **205 Buffalo Horn Creek, Gallatin Canyon; (406) 995-4283.**

Twin Panda

Lunch and dinner, eat in or takeout. Whatever your style, it's Chinese from the two pandas. **Arrowhead Mall, Big Sky; (406) 995-2625.**

Uncle Milkie's

Casual atmosphere and casual food. From-scratch pizza with choice of four sauces. Subs, broasted chicken and salads. Also, 10 draft beers, cocktails and fun. Open daily at 4:00; delivery from 5:00 to 10:00. Takeout too. **West Fork Retail Bldg., Meadow Village, Big Sky; (406) 995-2900.**

Whiskey Jack

Lively, spacious restaurant, newly renovated. Ski-in lunch and big patio for sunny days. Good dinner in casual atmosphere. Eclectic menu. Good appetizers. Moderate prices. **Mountain Mall, Big Sky; (406) 995-4211, ext. 2293.**

NIGHTLIFE

Après-ski tends to be congenial and lively rather than wild and out-of-hand. Happy hour starts at Mountain Village and keeps going long enough for most skiers who have tackled more than 3,000 vertical feet of mountain. Chet's Bar in the Huntley Lodge, Scissorbills Bar & Grill in the Arrowhead Mall and M. R. Hummer's, the Caboose and the recently expanded and rebuilt Whiskey Jack Restaurant & Bar, all in the Mountain Mall, start early and keep going. Other good choices are Rocco's, Uncle Milkie's in the West Fork Retail Building and the Half Moon Saloon, on Hwy 191, 3 miles south of the Big Sky entrance. Among them you'll find music, food and general merriment (which may include such diversions as live entertainment, pool, coin-operated gambling, ski movies and sports on big-screen TV). "Montana atmosphere" is nurtured off campus, where ultrainformality and western motifs prevail. The two bars at Buck's T-4 Lodge, Corral Bar, 320 Ranch bar and the Half Moon Saloon snare lots of action—locals included. Occasionally, the Yellowstone Conference Center adjacent to the Huntley Lodge is used for theatrical or musical performances.

For more information, contact **Big Sky Ski & Summer Resort, P.O. Box 160001, Big Sky, MT 59716, (800) 548-4486, (406) 995-4211.**

BRIDGER BOWL

BACKDROP

Bozeman, Montana, a lively college town, has also become one of America's trendy new lifestyle centers. Bridger Bowl is its local ski hill. Though not by any stretch a resort, the duo offers a great deal to visiting skiers. Bridger's 2,000 vertical feet, reputation for great snow conditions and absence of crowds make it one heck of a hill. The proximity of a good airport and a major east-west interstate highway, the abundance of economical in-town accommodations and ample evening activities—even if not in the common notion of après-ski—make it a value-laden ski-vacation destination as well. Though best known for exemplary advanced and expert terrain, Bridger's pricing and policies encourage beginners and families, plus easy access make it a good bet the budget-conscious. Named after Jim Bridger, a noted explorer of the Rocky Mountains, the ski area likes to retain the rough-and-ready flavor of the real West with few frills and fabulous snow.

THE LAY OF THE LAND

Located in the mnemonic Bridger Mountains, Bridger Bowl has a traditional day-skiing layout with ample parking and base-area facilities. A few simple condominiums skirt the property, but most visitors choose to stay in town.

GETTING THERE

National and regional airlines fly to Gallatin Field from several major western and Midwestern cities. The local airport is roughly a 30-minute drive from the ski area. Auto access is via I-90, which skirts the northern edge of Bozeman. The ski area is 16 easy miles northeast of downtown via scenic Bridger Canyon. The low-cost Motel Shuttle operates daily along Main Street and the motel strip just off I-90, stopping at all properties that offer Bridger packages.

PROFILE

From a skier's viewpoint, Bridger Bowl could be named Bridger Ridge, for the ski terrain is imposed on a long, essentially east-facing ridge, or Bridger Bowls, because two big bowls comprise much of the upper portion of that ridge. The lifts and runs fan out in a V-shape from the compact base, with the easiest filling in the point of the V and ample and excellently groomed novice and intermediate terrain along the V's arms. The upper midsection between the two arms is the most challenging of the lift-served terrain, while the climbs to snowfields above the lifts are the steepest of all. Bridger Bowl comes into its own for upper-level skiers. Like other ski areas, it describes its green runs as "easiest" but refers to the blues as "moderately difficult" and the blacks as "more difficult." The double blacks are "most difficult," which translates into "watch out!"

The very bottom of the mountain is beginnerville—long, wide runs of gentle pitch and comforting proximity to the day lodge—and the midsection and northern slopes are the next step up. Tiny tots and brand new skiers ride the Virginia City chair (there's a bargain ticket just for this lift). Then, it's on to the Alpine chair and its long green and blue trails along the area's northern perimeter. To reach any of the advanced terrain, you can take the new Powder Park quad or the Virginia City double and ski to one of three upper lifts—Pierre's Knob to the left, Bridger essentially straight ahead, or Deer Park in the middle. The Pierre's Knob chair at the southern edge of the area offers a handful of green and blue trails and a couple of blacks, and experts ride it and then climb to the Fingers, a quartet of steep powder chutes.

If you choose the Bridger chair, you'll find some of Montana's best black-diamond skiing.

From the upper section of the lift, you'll see North Bowl to your right and first Deer Park and then South Bowl to your left. The two bowls scooped out of "Bridger Ridge" and the rocky dividers separating them provide great terrain and even better snow. This section of the mountain is a symphony of roads and catwalks with drop-offs into bowls and snow-holding cracks in granite cliffs turn into skiable chutes. If your knees and your head are geared for bumps, ride Deer Park chairlift to 1,100 vertical of marvelous moguls. Slide into North or South Bowl to ski perpendicular powder marked with black diamonds or plunge down Avalanche Gulch, rated yellow for "most difficult," Bridger-style, and a bear by anyone's standards. When you need some R&R, the newly rebuilt Deer Park Chalet offers expanded food service and a fireplace to relax by.

Experts gravitate to Bridger Bowl just to ski the Ridge, whose acreage ups the area's total by 50 percent—and all of it seems close to vertical. If you are hearty and hardy and hungry for out-of-bounds skiing, you can check out with the patrol at the top of the Bridger chair and climb nearly 600 feet straight up to the Ridge's crest. The path is steep, and it's one of those exercises in frustration to toe into the snow step by step by arduous step as an occasional patroller zips up the incline on a rope tow that the public is prohibited from riding. Once on top, the agony of the climb will melt into the ecstasy of the skiing. You'll feel as if all of Montana is at your feet and that some of the most extreme terrain in the northern Rockies is dropping away under your skis.

The easiest of the Ridge terrain lies just south of the rope tow on the Nose, a large snowfield with high-Alpine snow conditions. It has the outback flavor without the supreme difficulty, and it is a good choice if you want to ski the Ridge just once for the experience. By contrast, keep traversing to Colter's Crawl, which is as far south on the ridge as you may ski, and you'll find yourself in a harrowing downhill situation. You don't have to traverse at all to come to precipitous terrain. Immediately north of the rope tow are two sets of chutes cut through the cliff band along upper North Bowl. Skiing any one of them is like putting yourself through a snowy needle's eye. Sometimes a Great Notion is a steep, narrow couloir

Photo courtesy Bridger Bowl

Inside Bridger Bowl

with a dramatic entrance around a rock spire. One Flew Over the Cuckoo's Nest is the monkey in the middle, while Stupor Couloir must be entered via a tricky double traverse. If you continue traversing northward, you'll come to Chutes 1 through 7, consecutively numbered from the north. Chutes 3 to 7 also feed into North Bowl, while 1 and 2 lead into Bridger Gully.

You can also keep going into Upper Bridger Gully itself, entering it straight and sane or in from the side and mad-skier steep. Heavenly

Photo courtesy Bridger Bowl

A skier carves a turn through fresh snow on The Ridge of one of Bridger's renowned bowls.

Blue, usually blanketed by heavenly white, and Angel Dust are reasonable routes into Bridger Gully, but the Virtues, dropping off the chasm's south wall, are beyond steep. Barely skiable, these abysses are the area's truest extreme terrain. Hidden Gully, the last inbounds drainage to the north, is deep, scenic and a little easier than Bridger Gully. It holds the snow especially long, since impatient skiers can't be bothered with the long traverse to the far end of the Ridge. Hidden Gully is manageably steep rather than terrifying, yet with untracked snow and outback conditions, it is challenging enough. The reward for having done it is dropping into a hoot-and-holler snowfield called The Apron that widens turn after ego-building turn, and ends at the top of the Alpine lift. When you reach such lift-served runs as North Meadows Road, Porcupine and Limestone, a trio of green-circle runs populated by slow-moving novices skiing careful turns, you quickly return to the reality of mere-mortal skiing after the challenge and ethereal powder off the Ridge. If you've burned yourself out, you can join the new skiers on the easy runs off Alpine. If you've still got something left, try the Three Bears. A line of trees just above them serve as nature's snow fencing and dump oceans of powder into these three drops. Mama Bear, Papa Bear and Baby Bear were named according to their depth and consequent volume of snow—and any one of them is a suitable cap to the Ridge.

SNOWBOARDING

Just as Bridger Bowl attracts a high level of skier, its regular corps of snowboarders tend to

be very, very good, and The Ridge is where you'll find most of the them.

SKI SCHOOL PROGRAMS

Introductory Programs

Early Bird Learn-to-Ski: All-day beginner lift ticket, four hours of class lessons and equipment-rental option, for ages 7 and above, available early December weekends.
Early Board: Snowboarding equivalent of Early Bird.
Invitation to Ski: Season-long introduction package, including beginner lift ticket, two-hour class lesson and rental equipment for ages 7 and above.

Advanced and Specialty Programs

Technique Tune-Up: Four-hour workshop for intermediate and advanced skiers, available early December weekends.
Mountain Experience: All-lifts ticket, 1½-hour group lesson and optional rental equipment for beginning wedge turners through advanced skiers, ages 7 and above.
Wednesday Workshop: Adult Alpine skiing, snowboarding and telemarking workshops for adults. Two four-week sessions, with optional equipment rental.
For Women Only: Thursday morning women's classes. Two four-week sessions, with optional equipment rental and optional fifth workshop.

Special Programs

Mountain Tour: Free mountain tour; sign up at reservations desk.
Ridge Tour: Ski the Ridge with an instructor. For strong advanced skiers and experts only. Avalanche orientation required.

For Families

Nonskiing Children
Playcare: Nursery from 18 months to 6 years. Age-appropriate indoor play, crafts and snowplay. Full- and half-day options, with low-cost lunch also available. Reservations required for 18 to 24 months and recommended for older children; **(800) 223-9609, (406) 586-1518.**

Skiing Children

Mom/Dad and Me: Private instruction and full-day's rental equipment for children ages 3 and 4, with parent(s) on hand to encourage and learn to work with child.

First Tracks: Morning and afternoon ski lesson for ages 4 to 6, including Playcare, lunch and lifts. Full-day and half-day options; rental equipment available. Reservations required.

Mogul Mice: Two four-day weekend sessions for ages 4 to 6, with lessons plus lift ticket and rental options.

Mitey Mites and Development Team: Two four-day weekend sessions for ages 7 to 12, including morning and afternoon lessons, plus lift ticket and rental options.

Team Extreme: Two four-day weekend sessions for hot-skiing 9- to 13-year-olds, including morning and afternoon lessons and optional 10-ticket lift option for those without season passes.

Noteworthy

Children's lift tickets for ages 12 and under are especially economical, costing less than half of the adult rate. In addition, a low-priced lift ticket for just the Virginia City beginner lift is offered.

HANDICAPPED SKIING

Eagle Mount: Program equipped for people even with severe physical and developmental disabilities. One-on-one or even two-on-one ski instruction and adaptive equipment. Video filmed at Bridger Bowl available on request; **(406) 587-8221.**

NORDIC SKIING

The **Bohart Ranch,** next to Bridger Bowl, grooms 25 to 30 kilometers of cross-country trails and offers instruction and rental equipment; **(406) 586-9070.** The ranch's biathlon range is open for year-round training and competition, meaning

Mountain Stats—
Bridger Bowl

Resort elevation 6,100 feet (4,793 feet, city of Bozeman)
Top of highest lift 8,100 feet
Bottom of lowest lift 6,100 feet
Total vertical 2,000 feet (2,500 including the Ridge)
Longest run 2½ miles
Average annual snowfall 350 inches
Ski season weekends from Thanksgiving, then daily from second weekend in December through first weekend in April (both beginning and end somewhat flexible, depending on when holidays fall and on snow conditions)
Lifts 1 fixed-grip chairlift, 5 doubles
Capacity 7,300 skiers per hour
Terrain 51 runs, 800 lift-served acres (25% beginner and novice, 35% intermediate, 40% advanced and expert), plus 400 acres on The Ridge (all advanced and expert)
Snowmaking 25 acres of high-traffic areas
Mountain dining Deer Park Chalet at the top of the Virginia City lift
Snow reports (406) 586-2389

353

that top athletes may put on a good show of skiing and shooting. Packages including three days of Alpine skiing at Bridger and two days at Bohart, including rentals and instruction, are available; **(800) 223-9609, (406) 586-1518.** Lindley Park, entirely within the city, features trails groomed for diagonal skiing and skating. Marked touring trails for all abilities in the Bozeman area include Stone Creek, Bozeman Creek or New World Gulch to Mystic Lake and Hyalite Reservoir.

Off the Beaten Path is a Bozeman-based travel service specializing in environmentally oriented backcountry trips; **(406) 586-1311.** The **Bridger Ski Foundation** has extensive information on Nordic skiing in the region; **(406) 587-2445.** Several backcountry cabins in the Gallatin National Forest are available for overnight rentals to backcountry skiers and snowshoers; for information, contact the **Bozeman Ranger District, (406) 587-6920. Yellowstone National Park** to the south is also a major center for cross-country skiers, though the most popular sections are not at the park's northern end; information is available from **(307) 344-7381.**

WHERE TO STAY

Many Bozeman properties offer special skier rates and packages. Midweek and off-peak (just after New Year through mid-February) ski-and-stay packages of three days or longer are particularly economical in all price ranges. **Bridger Bowl Central Reservations, (800) 223-9609; (406) 586-1518.**

Luxury Accommodations

Gallatin Gateway Inn

Beautifully renovated railroad hotel, on the National Register of Historic Places. Twenty-five rooms furnished with contemporary pieces; public spaces have antiques. Not expensive in what is considered off-season, but upscale atmosphere and dining compared with other Bozeman area lodgings. Twelve miles south of Bozeman (perfect for combining Bridger and Big Sky in one trip). Worth the commute to skiing for lovers of history and atmosphere. Restaurant known for lovely ambiance and fine cuisine. Ski packages. Daily housekeeping, 24-hour front desk. Hot tub, restaurant, lounge. **P.O. Box 376, Gallatin Gateway, MT 59730; (800) 676-3522, (406) 763-4672.**

Lindley House

Victorian mansion, listed on the National Register of Historic Places. Elegant and romantic B&B inn with seven delightful rooms. Convenient location, two blocks south of Main Street. Totally remodeled (a three-year project). Gleaming floors, natural woodwork and French wallpapers. Antique furnishings include some iron beds from historic Yellowstone National Park lodgings. Full gourmet breakfast, complimentary carafe of wine in each room, brandy nightcap on request, daily housekeeping. Outdoor hot tub and deck. **202 Lindley Pl., Bozeman, MT 59715; (800) 787-8404, (406) 587-8403.**

Voss Inn

Beautifully restored Italianate mansion built in 1883, now a B&B inn, in historic district within walking distance of downtown restaurants and shops. Six rooms all with hardwood floors, Victorian antiques, brass beds and private baths with antique clawfoot tubs. Telephones in rooms; television and piano are only in guest parlor. Daily housekeeping, full breakfast served at two seatings (7:30 and 8:30 A.M.) or room service, afternoon tea. **319 S. Willson Ave., Bozeman, MT 59715; (406) 587-0982.**

Mid-Priced Accommodations

GranTree Inn

Self-contained property with many extras. Recent refurbishments include recarpeting all 103 rooms. Ski packages. Daily housekeeping, 24-hour front desk, complimentary airport shuttle. Indoor pool, hot tub, restaurant, coffee shop, lounge with casino room, guest laundry, game room, ski storage. **1325 N. Seventh Ave., Bozeman, MT 59715; (800) 624-5865, (406) 587-5261, (800) 528-1234** for Best Western reservations.

Holiday Inn

Large motor inn, with 158 recently remodeled rooms, including two with Jacuzzi tubs. Children stay free in parents' room and eat free. Complimentary airport shuttle, 24-hour front desk, daily housekeeping. Special skier rates include complimentary breakfast in hotel restaurant, complimentary cocktail and free movie per stay. Restaurant, lounge, indoor swimming pool, hot tub, fitness equipment, game room, guest laundry, ski storage. **5 Baxter Ln., Bozeman, MT 59715; (800) 366-5101, (406) 587-4413, (800) HOL-IDAY** for Holiday Inn reservations.

Kirk Hill Bed & Breakfast

Lovely ranch-style inn at mouth of Hyalite Canyon, 6 miles south of Bozeman. Close to cross-country and snowmobile trails and also Kirk Hill Nature Trail, and one-half hour's drive from Bridger. Three guest rooms share two bathrooms. Daily housekeeping, continental breakfast included. **7960 S. 19th Rd., Bozeman, MT 59715; (800) 240-3929, (406) 586-3939.**

Silver Forest Inn

Charming and rustic log-hewn inn set in pine grove, close to ski-area access road. Five queen-bedded bedrooms, two with private tub and shower and three with shared baths. Turret Room has splendid panorama of Bridger Range. Ski packages, including discount lift-ticket coupons for three-night stays. Entire inn (sleeping 10) is available for group rental. Daily housekeeping, full breakfast. Also contact Silver Forest Inn for adjacent Flaming Arrow Lodge, suitable for functions or groups of up to 10. Hot tub. **15325 Bridger Canyon Rd., Bozeman, MT 59715; (406) 586-l882.**

Torch & Toes

Colonial revival home and carriage house in Bon Ton Historic District. Three quaint upstairs rooms, all with private bath. Furnished in combination of antiques and contemporary pieces. Also, carriage house suitable for families. Within walking distance of downtown. Daily housekeeping, full gourmet breakfast. **319 S. Third Ave., Bozeman, MT 59715; (406) 586-7285.**

Economy Accommodations

Bozeman Inn

Functional inn with traditional decor. Fifty recently remodeled rooms and one luxury executive suite. Non-smoking rooms available. Free local phone calls. Skier rates. Daily housekeeping, free continental breakfast, airport shuttle. Restaurant, lounge, sauna, hot tub, guest laundry. **1235 N. Seventh Ave., Bozeman, MT 59715; (800) 648-7515, (406) 587-3176.**

Comfort Inn

One of the many motor inns along Bozeman's "motel row." Skier rates. Daily housekeeping, complimentary continental breakfast. Indoor pool, hot tubs, sauna, fitness room. **1370 N. Seventh Ave., Bozeman, MT 59715; (800) 587-3833, (406) 587-2322.**

Continental Motor Inn

Economical motel, close to town and near restaurants and entertainment. Skier rates. Daily housekeeping, complimentary continental breakfast. Hot tub. **1224 E. Main St., Bozeman, MT 59715; (800) 221-1886, (406) 587-9231.**

Days Inn of Bozeman

Eighty rooms on two floors, including some non-smoking rooms. A-Plus rated by Days Inn. Skier rates. Daily housekeeping, complimentary continental breakfast. Hot tub, sauna, fitness equipment, free HBO and local phone calls, plug-in heaters for cars, restaurant and lounge adjacent. **1321 N. Seventh Ave., Bozeman, MT 59715; (406) 587-5251, (800) 325-2525** for Days Inn reservations.

Fairfield Inn

Local outpost of Marriott's economy chain. Children under 18 free in parents' room. Daily housekeeping, 24-hour front desk, free continental breakfast, local phone calls and HBO. Indoor pool, hot tub. **828 Wheat Dr., Bozeman, MT 59715; (406) 587-2222, (800) 228-2800** for Fairfield Inn reservations.

Western Heritage Inn

Hotel rooms, suites and family suites, some non-smoking. Relaxing lobby area. Skier rates. Daily housekeeping, complimentary light breakfast. Ski storage, hot tub, fitness equipment, steamroom, guest laundry. **1200 E. Main St., Bozeman, MT 59715; (800) 877-1094, (406) 586-8534.**

Condominiums

On-mountain lodging includes the Alpenhaus, which accommodates up to 14 guests, plus a variety of simple cabins and A-frames. The Bridger Pines condo complex has units with master bedroom with one or two beds, sleeping loft, two baths, sleep-sofa and kitchen. **15792 Bridger Canyon Rd., Bozeman, MT 59715; (406) 587-3096.**

DINING OUT

Banana Bay

Some south-of-the-border dishes, some Cajun adaptations. All sprightly and contemporary. Full bar. Weekday lunches; nightly dinner. **Main Mall, Bozeman; (406) 587-0484.**

The Baxter
Monumental space in historic hotel. Indoor fountain, two-story-high ceiling and balcony dining. Contains two restaurants, Bacchus Pub and Pasta Company. Breakfast, lunch and dinner. All-you-can-eat soup, bread and salad bar. Imported beers, good wine selection and cocktails. Reservations accepted. **105 W. Main St., Bozeman; (406) 586-1314.**

Bridger Bar-B-Q & Grill
Lively downtown dispensary for breakfast, lunch and dinner. Charbroiled steaks and burgers, plus great hickory-smoked ribs, pork, beef, chicken, turkey and seafood satisfy most tastes. Extensive beer and wine menus. Cellar billiards hall is popular evening hangout. **101 E. Main St., Bozeman; (406) 586-1071.**

Cantrell's Food & Spirits
Holiday Inn's restaurant with mid-priced breakfast, lunch, dinner and Sunday brunch offerings for all tastes. Dinner menu features meat, poultry, seafood and combos thereof. Pasta and salad entrées too. Daily specials. **Holiday Inn, 5 Baxter Ln., Bozeman; (406) 587-4561.**

356

Casa Sanchez
Fun restaurant in small house near campus. Family-run since 1980. Good Mexican food, especially the fajitas. Big menu with all the standards plus daily specials. Imported beers and wines. Homemade desserts and specialty coffees. Takeout available. Reservations accepted. **719 S. Ninth St., Bozeman; (406) 586-4516.**

Colombo's Pizza & Pasta
Family-owned place for stick-to-the-ribs pasta, pizza and hot and cold sandwiches. Reasonably priced and popular with kids of all ages. Specializes in pizza for all tastes and philosophies, from vegetarians who order the Very Veggie Pizza to meat eaters who go for the More Meat Pizza with four versions of animal flesh and extra cheese. Preparation as low in salt and fat as possible for Italian fare. Beer and wine. Takeout and delivery

available. **10th & College, Bozeman; (406) 587-5544.**

The Crystal Bar
Breakfast and burgers in terrific downtown spot. Wednesday burger specials from 5 to 8 P.M. are great deal. Beers and merriment—but not at breakfast. **123 E. Main St., Bozeman; (406) 587-2888.**

Donna Marie's
Casual place with home-style cooking. Open at lunch and dinner, with daily specials. Family cafe. **1104 E. Main St., Bozeman; (406) 585-9550.**

Gallatin Gateway Inn
One of Montana's top restaurants. Outstanding ambiance and cuisine. High prices, high quality. Outstanding wine list. Top service. Twelve miles from Bozeman. Reservations recommended. **US Hwy 191, Gallatin Gateway; (406) 763-4672.**

It's Greek to Me
Economy eat-in, takeout or delivery. Satisfying food with Greek accent. Open for lunch and dinner, except Sunday. **16 N. Ninth Ave., Bozeman; (406) 586-0176.**

John Bozeman's Bistro
Homemade soups, updated continental cuisine and fabulous desserts. Lunch, dinner and Sunday brunch. Excellent wine list and good selection of microbrews. Located in downtown historic building. Montana artwork on the walls. Cozy and intimate. Dinner reservations recommended. **242 E. Main St., Bozeman; (406) 587-4100.**

O'Brien's Restaurant
Downtown restaurant. Elegant atmosphere. Best known for steaks. Good wine list. Reservations accepted. **312 E. Main St., Bozeman; (406) 587-3973.**

Spanish Peaks Brewery & Cafe
New hot spot in town. Art deco look. Brew pub serving gourmet pizzas, pastas and own beers. Imbibers do not live by beer alone, inspiring good wine and coffee selections too. Large and lively. Lunch and dinner. **120 N. 7th Ave., Bozeman; (406) 585-2296.**

NIGHTLIFE

The closest approximation of traditional après-ski occurs right at Bridger Bowl. In the late afternoon, you'll find some on-mountain conviviality at the rustic Deer Park Chalet; the beer party moves outdoors in the spring when it's warm. Skiers also congregate at the bar in Jimmy B's in the Jim Bridger Lodge, the day lodge at the base. Thereafter, nightlife moves off the mountain. Some of it takes on the flavor of a college town rather than a ski town, with lively hangouts around the Montana State University campus.

The Leaf & Bean Coffee House serves a fine selection of gourmet coffees and fresh baked goods in a satisfying, artsy setting. There's even live music weekends and Monday evenings. Also, some of the hotel and motel lounges and restaurants offer happy hour, including weeknights at the Crystal Bar and nightly at Cantrell's in the Holiday Inn. The GranTree Inn's lounge has a congenial atmosphere and includes casino games. The Crystal Bar draws a young crowd for burgers, plus pool and conviviality. Montana Fats in the basement of the Bridger Bar-B-Q & Grill is a high-energy winner. This Bozeman hot spot serves 90 imported and domestic beers and wines and a mean selection of munchies, plus pool, darts and casino games. During the winter rodeo, there's a cowboy overlay to the scene as well. Bozeman boasts an increasing array of movies, concerts, plays and collegiate sporting events.

For more information, contact **Bridger Bowl, 15795 Bridger Canyon Rd., Bozeman, MT 59715; (800) 223-9609, (406) 586-1518; Bozeman Area Chamber of Commerce, 1205 E. Main St., P.O. Box B, Bozeman, MT 59715; (800) 228-4224, (406) 586-5421.**

MONTANA SNOWBOWL

BACKDROP

In the pantheon of unsung ski areas, this low-key, laid-back local hill outside of the college town of Missoula ranks high. An impressive vertical plus substantial and very challenging terrain, but a simple infrastructure and few lifts make Montana Snowbowl a truly old-style mountain. The loyal cadre of local regulars who appreciate the friendly laid-back atmosphere and low prices hope it stays that way. Despite the fact that the area has been around since the early '60s and was even the site of the U.S. National Alpine Championships in 1967, word of Snowbowl's huge and demanding skiing has leaked out slowly. A few University of Montana alumni who appear to have majored (or at least minored) in skiing occasionally spread the word to a wider world, but people often don't believe what a big, tough mountain it is. Southbound Canadians comprise a significant share of the destination market, and occasionally, skiers from Seattle, Spokane or other points west make the effort to find adventure in western Montana. But mainly Snowbowl remains a locally owned, locally skied area.

Some people from Missoula learn to ski there because it's the bigger and more prestigious of the two hometown hills (the other is the Marshall Ski Area, 7 miles east of the city, while Snowbowl is farther out and to the west). It is such a hardcore ski area that the nursery for nonskiing children closed due to lack of demand. Parents get even little kids on snow as soon as possible. Those who learn at Snowbowl have ample incentive to improve fast, because the steep, rugged area offers little for perpetual cruising skiers. Snowbowl regulars, dedicated mountain folk, are an eclectic mix of highly skilled Alpine skiers, telemarkers and snowboarders in fairly even

proportions. There is even a pod of "gelände" jumpers—practitioners of a somewhat arcane activity which involves leaping, in Alpine equipment, off a jump in a quest for style and distance (200 feet off Snowbowl's 55-meter jump is common). Snowbowl, in short, is a ski area for people who like to meet challenge in their own way.

THE LAY OF THE LAND

The Montana Snowbowl base is stuffed into a narrow funnel of a valley in the northern reaches of the Bitterroot range. The ski terrain starts at a tiny base area and flares out into the vast arc that forms the head of the valley. The 30,000-acre Rattlesnake Wilderness is northeast of the ski-area boundary, and views from the top extend south over the Bitterroots and north to the Flathead Indian Reservation, the Bob Marshall Wilderness and occasionally Glacier National Park.

GETTING THERE

Missoula County International Airport, 5 miles west of the city, is a good facility with national and regional air carrier service but more capacity than it has thus far needed. **Greyhound, Bitterroot Stages, Intermountain** and **Rimrock Stages** provide bus service from various points, **(406) 549-2339.** The city also boasts several I-90 exits for east-west road travelers. The ski area is 12 miles northwest of town, off the Reserve Street exit of I-90 and ultimately 3 miles up a twisty access road.

PROFILE

Montana Snowbowl is one of those ski areas that time forgot (a few years ago, they undertook a major upgrade by replacing an old double chairlift with a newer but nevertheless used double from Big Sky), but it is also one that skiers long remember. The base facilities are, well,

basic: a parking lot that overflows on weekends and a cluster of spartan buildings whose style is A-frame-plus-add-ons. Family owned and run and not heavily capitalized, substantial character-changing "improvements" are unlikely. When you look up to the left, you'll see a teaching slope served by a T-bar and one of the country's few remaining *geländesprung* hills ("gelande" is an American corruption of that German tongue-twister), while straight ahead, you'll see a very small and very mild tow-served beginner slope and a double from Big Sky chairlift heading somewhere in the direction of the stratosphere.

This Snowbowl's mainline lift, directly accessing the prodigious frontside vertical and big-time steeps which are collectively called the Bowl Runs. With 2,600 feet of continuous and very challenging vertical, it is truly a skier's mountain noteworthy for heavy-duty glades and gulches, cliffy drop-offs and iffy detours, secret powder shots and splendid hidden spots. The liftline run is the combination of Grizzly to Grizzly Chute, a big vertical-foot duo of consistent pitch that is steep enough to send all but the most stalwart back to the lodge for another espresso and a transfusion of nerve. This route is marked with a single black diamond, perhaps reflecting Snowbowl's overall terseness of style, but elsewhere, it would surely be a double black. Oh yes, there are a couple of dozen cut trails, some of which are actually groomed, but that just isn't Snowbowl's major appeal.

The Lavelle Creek runs on Snowbowl's backside are shorter, wider and significantly easier than the Bowl runs. You reach them by taking Missoula Magic from the top of the Grizzly chair to the bottom of the Lavelle chair, the higher lift, which unloads at 7,600 feet. Its another 326 feet to Point Six, which is the highest inbounds spot and the access to some of the longest-lingering powder. No matter how tempting, the powder pockets below Point Six probably aren't the best bet for a Snowbowl first-timer to begin exploring the area. Far better is a warmup run from the top of the Lavelle chair back to the base. A long road curves along the areas eastern boundary and is a fine way to get a sense of the area's grand scale and get your ski legs under you. It starts with a very flat portion called the North Dakota Down-

Inside Montana Snowbowl

hill, but it steepens slightly from green to true blue and changes its name to Paradise. You may want to take it all the way back to the base, or you may be tempted by one of the occasional black-diamond trails and constant access to the chutes and glades that are Snowbowl's soul.

Skiing Snowbowl's longest, steepest routes requires riding both chairs, and it's just as well that both are of the original non-high-speed variety, because you have time to rest on what is as demanding and exhausting mountain as it is a divine and exhilarating one. Relatively open, straightforward steeps like Big Sky, West Ridge, West Bowls and East Bowls are marked on the map and comprise the main named runs and are the core of the area, but in truth, they are only a fraction of what's skiable. You'll probably never find Red Bud Ridge, China Bowl, the Door, the Meadows or any of the other unmarked treasures unless you stumble on them, hire an instructor or follow a local to the off-piste glory. The Snowbowl cake is frosted with a sprinkling of bump runs, which mogul up more from lack of serious grooming than from constant traffic. If you can handle these untamed, front-of-the-mountain steeps, you've found your own paradise.

If the frontside is too humbling, the Lavelle Runs offer an easier, arguably more civilized skiing option. They are mostly marked with blue squares (Hot Fudge even wears a green circle). **360** Long perimeter combination routes such as North Dakota Downhill/Paradise and Hot Fudge/Spartan Second Thought considerably up the paper census of intermediate runs, but there is no all-green-circle way from the summit to the base. In fact, a sign at the top pointedly tells tyros: "Easiest Way Down—the Chair." Remember, you don't ski paper, and Montana Snowbowl's untamed steeps which do not go into these calculations are really what make it so unique and so enticing to good skiers and snowboarders.

Mountain Stats—
Montana Snowbowl

Resort elevation 3,205 feet (city of Missoula)
Top of highest lift 7,600 feet
Bottom of lowest lift 4,990 feet
Total vertical 2,610 feet
Longest run 3 miles
Average annual snowfall 300 inches
Ski season Thanksgiving to early April
Lifts 2 double chairlifts, 1 T-bar, 1 beginner tow
Capacity 3,400 skiers per hour
Terrain 30 trails, 900 acres (20% beginner and novice, 40% intermediate, 40% advanced and expert)
Snowmaking only at base area, including Sunrise Bowl, rope-tow slope and outruns of the Bowl, Longhorn and Paradise
Night skiing Wednesday and Thursday nights
Mountain dining Grizzly Chalet at the top of the Grizzly lift
Snow reports (406) 549-9777
Note ski area closed Tuesdays

SNOWBOARDING

The area has a half-pipe, but most of this stunningly steep mountain with all kids of natural jumps, hits and transitions make it splendid riding terrain. The major caution is to stay off the North Dakota Downhill, which can be a real slog on a snowboard.

SKI SCHOOL PROGRAMS

Introductory Programs

Learn to Ski: Economical lift, lesson and rental package.
Free Lesson Day: Free mini-lessons, one day in mid-December for all ages and abilities.

For Racers

Racing Clinics: Missoula Ski Education Foundation runs clinics at Snowbowl.

Noteworthy

Montana Snowbowl sells a T-bar-only ticket, offers free skiing to children 6 and under with a skiing parent and has a reduced student ticket for those who have outgrown the child limit of 12 and are in school.

For Families

Skiing Children

Pandas: Ski instruction for ages 3 to 6.

NORDIC SKIING

There is no cross-country ski area nearby. The nearest are at the top of Lolo Pass and at Lolo Hot Springs, 35 miles south of Missoula, which grooms 10 kilometers of its 200 kilometers of winter recreation trails. Information on the abundant regional backcountry opportunities is available from the **U.S. Forest Service Regional Office, (406) 329-3511.**

WHERE TO STAY

Bozeman lodging reservations are available by calling **(800) 869-7666.**

Luxury Accommodations

Goldsmith's Inn

Three gorgeous rooms and three suites, all with private baths (one suite with Jacuzzi tub). Turn-of-century charm. Located on Clark Fork River, close to downtown and university. Full breakfast, daily housekeeping. **809 E. Front St., Missoula, MT 59802; (406) 721-6732.**

Gracenote Garden

Lyrical and lovely inn—with music as the civilized theme. Two rooms with private baths. Daily housekeeping, full breakfast. **1558 S. Sixth St., Missoula, MT 59802; (406) 543-3480.**

Mid-Priced Accommodations

Campus Inn

Eighty-one-room motel, close to shopping and university. Pets permitted. Daily housekeeping, complimentary airport shuttle. Heated pool, hot tub, game room, plug-in heaters for cars. **744 E. Broadway, Missoula, MT 59802; (800) 232-8013, (406) 549-5134.**

Holiday Inn Parkside

Large in-town motor hotel with 200 attractive rooms and suites, many with views of Clark Fork River. Children free in parents' room. Pets permitted. Ski packages. Twenty-four-hour front desk, room service, daily housekeeping, complimentary airport shuttle. Indoor swimming pool, health spa, sauna, game room, restaurant, lounge. **200 S. Pattee, Missoula, MT 59802; (800) 824-4536, (406) 421-8550, (800) HOL-IDAY** for Holiday Inn reservations.

Southgate Inn

One of the area's better-equipped motor inns. Eighty-one hotel rooms and family units. Children 12 and under free in parents' room. Some non-smoking rooms. Pets permitted. Restaurant next door. Ski packages. Daily housekeeping, continental breakfast included, courtesy airport shuttle. Hot tub, sauna, exercise room. **3530 Brooks St., Missoula, MT 59802; (800) 247-2616, (406) 251-2250.**

Economy Accommodations

Birchwood Hostel

Missoula's youth hostel, with budget rates. Twenty-two beds in four bunkrooms; one private room. Bring sleeping bag or rent linens. Guest laundry, full kitchen facilities for guests' use. Reservations suggested. **600 S. Orange St., Missoula, MT 59802; (406) 728-9799.**

4B's Inn

Two local motor inns, the one just off I-90 being the closest accommodation to Snowbowl. Each has children-free policy, indoor swimming pool, solarium, spa, plug-in heaters for cars, daily housekeeping, ski packages. Both with or near restaurants. AAA approved. Reservations for both, **(800) 272-9500. Hwy 93 & Reserve, Missoula, MT 59802; (406) 251-2665; I-90 & Reserve, Missoula, MT 59802; (406) 542-7550.**

Snowbowl's skiers and riders are an aggressive, gutsy lot.
Photo by Jean Arthur/Montana Snowbowl

The Inn on Broadway

Reasonably priced motel close to Snowbowl exit off I-90. Children free in parents' room. Ski packages. Pets permitted. Daily housekeeping, airport shuttle service. Restaurant, lounge, pool, spa. **1609 W. Broadway, Missoula, MT 59802; (800) 286-2316, (406) 543-7231.**

Ruby's Reserve Street Inn

AAA-rated motor inn, with 128 rooms. Senior discount. Ski packages. Daily housekeeping, complimentary continental breakfast, plug-in heaters for cars. Hot tub, sauna, restaurant, lounge, casino. **4825 N. Reserve St., Missoula, MT 59802; (800) 221-2057, (406) 721-0900.**

ThunderBird Motel

Twenty-six-room motel close to Snowbowl exit off I-90. Rooms and family suites, some with kitchen facilities, some non-smoking and some with water beds. Pets permitted. Ski packages. Daily housekeeping, complimentary continental breakfast, airport shuttle. Indoor lap pool, hot tub, sauna, guest laundry, plug-in heaters for cars. **1009 E. Broadway, Missoula, MT 59802; (800) 952-2400, (406) 543-7251.**

362

DINING OUT

Alley Cat Grill

Downtown charmer in alley off Main Street. Creative cuisine and pleasing, contemporary decor. Nightly fish special, plus steaks, seafood and chicken. Reservations accepted. **125½ Main St., Missoula; (406) 728-3535.**

Casa Pablo's

Popular Mexican restaurant. Green chili is local favorite, plus good renditions of such standards as burritos, enchiladas and tacos. Major margaritas. Service from lunch (early enough for brunch on weekdays) through late dinner. Accepts reservations for eight or more. **147 W. Broadway, Missoula; (406) 721-3854.**

Golden Pheasant

Long-running Chinese restaurant (established in 1941), with full bar and dine-in or takeout options. Specializes in Chinese barbecued pork. Chef makes own noodles. Szechuan duck is tops. Classic and simple Chinese decor. Accepts reservations. **318 N. Higgins, Missoula; (406) 728-9953.**

McKay's on the River

Riverside restaurant in Hellgate Canyon, overlooking Clark Fork River. Appetizers and grill menu for those wanting lighter fare. Prime rib, steak, seafood, pasta and poultry. Daily lunch and dinner specials. Breakfast also served. Reservations accepted. Lounge. **1111 E. Broadway, Missoula; (406) 728-0098.**

The Mustard Seed

Light airy decor, with jazzy Oriental art. Contemporary cuisine in casual setting. Amalgam of Chinese, Japanese and Polynesian influences, geared to American palates. Only uses fresh vegetables and makes from-scratch sauces. Fine wines and beers. Desserts way beyond canned litchis and fortune cookies. Reservations accepted only for large parties. **419 W. Front St., Missoula; (406) 728-7825.**

New Pacific Grill

Located in historic Northern Pacific Building. Huge, high-ceiling dining room divided into three sections with frosted-glass dividers. Huge windows. Casual atmosphere but fine dining. Weekday lunches and nightly dinners. Specialties are seafood, plus some beef and chicken choices. Extensive appetizer menu. Cocktails and beer. Reservations accepted. **100 E. Railroad Ave., Missoula; (406) 542-3353.**

Press Box

Busy in-town place, which crackles from early breakfast (six bargain specialties every day) through late dinner. Pizza, steak and prime rib are top dinner choices. Lots of entertainment too. **835 E. Broadway, Missoula; (406) 721-1212.**

Shack Restaurant

Large and filling breakfasts. Omelets are excellent. Also, freshly prepared lunch and dinner. Dinner specials have continental influences. Seafood a plus. In-town eatery with moderate prices. Espresso, wine and beer. Takeout available. Reservations accepted, but not required, for dinner. **222 W. Main St., Missoula; (406) 549-9903.**

Zimorino's Red Pies Over Montana
New York–style pizza and other popular Italian fare, including pasta, veal and chicken. Wine and beer. Dinner nightly. **424 N. Higgins, Missoula; (406) 549-7434.**

NIGHTLIFE

If you haven't caught the locals on the lifts or the hill, you'll find a lively bunch at The Last Run Inn, a busy base-area bar. With night skiing Thursday and Friday nights, après-ski runs well past 9:00 P.M. The Rhinoceros does a terrific happy hour, with pitcher specials and two-for-one drinks, 11 beers on tap out of an impressive inventory of 23 imports and 19 domestic microbrews, and live music Monday through Thursday evenings. The Iron Horse Brew Pub in the North Pacific Building offers hand-crafted German-style lager beers, with service until 2:00 A.M. An equally late-night spot is Casa Pablo's Ritz Lounge. The Top Hat has music seven nights a week—blues, bluegrass, reggae or country. Wednesday night carries a modest cover charge, but free beer is poured from 10:00 P.M. to midnight. The Press Box is a noisy sports bar with 13 big-screen televisions, pool and video games.

Games of chance—mostly mechanized poker, keno and slots—are a popular diversion in Montana. There is no shortage of opportunities to dump your money into a machine in greater Missoula. The city abounds with casinos of various sizes, but they provide other after-dark diversion too. All serve at least beer and wine. Others have full bar service and perhaps live entertainment and even dancing. Some places serve food, from light munchies to full meals. Missoula casinos include the Airport Restaurant & Lounge at Jackson Bell Field, Duelin' Dalton's, The Edgewater in the Village Red Lion, Flippers, Gay Nineties Lounge, R.J. Grin's, Harry David's, Heidelhaus, the Iron Horse, Joker's Wild, The Limelight in the EconoLodge, Lucky Strike Casino Restaurant, Maxwell's, McKay's on the River, Montana's in the Holiday Inn, Press Box, The Rhinoceros, Santorono's and Westside Lanes.

Downtown Missoula offers good shops, art galleries, restaurants and nightspots, but if it's just too cold at night to cruise the streets, the city also has an indoor shopping mall with more than a hundred shops. The University of Montana offers a variety of spectator sports, including basketball, and such cultural entertainment as concerts, drama and dance. You may luck upon a Missoula Symphony Orchestra and Chorale concert or a play put on by the Montana Repertory Theatre, the state's only equity company.

For more information, contact **Montana Snowbowl, 1700 Snowbowl Rd., Missoula, MT 59802, (406) 549-9777; Missoula Convention & Visitors Bureau, 825 Front St., P.O. Box 7577, Missoula, MT 59807-7577, (800) 526-3465, (406) 543-6623.**

THE BIG MOUNTAIN

BACKDROP

One of the great sights in skiing is getting off a plane in Kalispell or a train in Whitefish—both in the plainlike Flathead Valley—and seeing The Big Mountain, seemingly right there. By day, white ski runs are etched through dark woods. After sunset, night-skiing lights shine through the inky blackness and make the mountain seem even closer. You know this oddly named mountain is some miles away, but in the clear air, it seems just out of touching distance. You want to race to the lifts, clap on your boots and discover for yourself what this mystery mountain in northwestern Montana is like—and why it has been garnering so much national attention.

364

Ski areas elsewhere dwarf The Big Mountain by several significant measures—vertical, lift capacity, number of runs and snowfall. But northern Montana's snowy showplace, which yields to few in terms of skiable acreage or absence of crowds, truly lives up to its name in the way it skis. And it has begun attracting national attention. With celebrities "discovering" Montana, the state overall has developed new cachet as well, which has also rubbed off on its northernmost major ski area.

The Big Mountain looms above the valley like a lift-served sentinel, but it is intimately linked with all that lies below, because that's where most of the lodging and diversions are found. The modest base facility still suffices, but with the surge in The Big Mountain's popularity, more substantial resort development is under way. Development may seem slow to outsiders, but it has perhaps come a tad too quickly for the patient ranchers and other locals who have steadfastly supported this mammoth ski area for half a century but no longer have it to themselves. The Big Mountain is maturing and attracting a wide clientele, a situation that promises only to escalate when the ambitious base development has been accomplished and a significant resort takes shape.

The Big Mountain is way up north, closer to the Canadian border than to anything else. It's also west of the Continental Divide, which usually ensures a relatively mild ocean-influenced climate. Daytime temperatures in the 20s are common, but occasionally a misdirected Arctic front comes in and drops the bottom out of the mercury. When a snowstorm squalls in or a heavy mist wells up from the lakes or the thermometer simply threatens to bottom out, the locals may be prepared but visiting skiers often opt for a day on skinny skis, shopping, hot tubbing or power napping. One of the beauties of The Big Mountain is that the skiing is superb; another is that the liftlines are still so short and the ticket prices so low that you don't feel as if you are wasting a lot if you opt out of skiing for a day or two of your vacation.

THE LAY OF THE LAND

The Big Mountain lies 8 miles north of Whitefish via a winding access road and 60 miles south of the Canadian border with little but splendid scenery between. Scattered below the ski area and concentrated more densely right around the lifts are lodges, condominiums and chalets. While housing up to 1,500 guests, which is a respectable capacity, they lack the flavor of an inviting village. The Nordic Center is headquartered right at the lift base, which makes it convenient for skiing, but for dining and entertainment, valley lodgings still offer more. Skiers also stay as far away as Kalispell, 15 miles south of Whitefish, via Route 93, the north-south highway through the valley. The Flathead Valley has long been a popular summer mecca with strong regional appeal. The namesake Flathead Lake is the largest natural freshwater lake west of the Mississippi, and the valley lies just 32 miles west of Glacier National Park, a much-visited wonder abutting the Canadian border. The valley is not really a quick drive from any major U.S. metropolis (though Calgary is "just" six hours or so away, and the resort has turned remoteness into a benefit by at one point promoting itself as "conveniently in the middle of nowhere").

GETTING THERE

Glacier Park International Airport in Kalispell, 19 miles away, has scheduled daily flights from such cities as Minneapolis, Salt Lake City, Billings, Missoula, Portland, Seattle and Spokane. Rental cars are available. **Amtrak's Empire Builder** between Chicago and Seattle/Portland stops daily in Whitefish, both east- and westbound, **(800) USA-RAIL.** The **Whitefish Area Rapid Transit** (acronym WART, intentional or not) handles transfers from both the airport and the Amtrak station and also operates ski and evening shuttles between Whitefish and The Big Mountain, **(406) 862-3501.** I-90, the closest freeway, is more than 130 miles to the south; take US Hwy 93 north to reach the resort.

PROFILE

Although it has a mid-size 2,400-foot vertical and just nine lifts, The Big Mountain's overall size (4,040 acres on the U.S. Forest Service permit, all but 40 acres skiable) and the complexity of its trails and off-piste skiing do justice to its name. The base area, officially called the Mountain Village, is compact, but the ski terrain is anything but. It sprawls and spreads and winds all over the beefy mountain. The timberline at this latitude is just below the 7,000-foot summit—on the sunny south side anyway—making for abundant go-anywhere tree-free slopes on high. The runs below often approach slope width and most of the glades between them are accessible too, and sometimes it seems as if there are as many skiers and snowboarders in the trees as on the runs. With so much terrain to slide upon and so few people, especially experts, to do so, powder can last for days in some places.

If you stand at the base and look up at the south-facing terrain, which is cumulatively called

the Valley Side, you see the novice section to the left (or west) and the main mountain to the right. The novice area, which is actually a sloping shoulder off the higher peak, has three lifts and a tow. There's a comforting congeniality and apartness to the easier trails, which are immaculately groomed and lighted for night skiing. The main mountain has mostly intermediate and advanced frontside terrain accessed by a high-speed chair, which is the only one visible from the base, and three conventional-speed chairs which are out of sight. The Glacier Chaser, Montana's first high-speed quad, beelines off to the right from the base area, reaching the summit in just seven minutes. Near the top, the ride takes on a surreal beauty, for at timberline the snow packs onto the widely spaced, gnarly trees near the top to create wondrous "ghosts" standing on the upper slopes as eerie white sentinels.

Below these phantasmagoric formations, frontside skiing is like sailing on a great white sea. You have a choice of cruisers wide as football fields, mega-slopes that are like tilted carrier decks, both deep and shallow drainages and abundant tree skiing. Because of the area's vastness and low traffic, the one challenge that is relatively lacking is lots of bumps. With so few skiers and those dispersed in search of powder—boot-top, knee-high, hip-deep or whatever—the bumps just don't build as they do on other large mountains.

The Glacier Chaser and two other chairlifts meet at The Big Mountain's summit, climbing from three directions. The Glacier Chaser, of course, comes up the frontside. The North Slope chair rises up from the backside, while the Glacier View quad chair, serving just the upper mountain, angles in from the east. The cut trails, open snowfields and more obvious glades on the frontside runs are the most straightforward and most heavily trafficked. Ptarmigan Bowl, just west of the Glacier Chaser, stretches to the area boundary—steep, steady and inviting. As the trees thicken, intermediate runs arc wide through them while black-diamond powder shots and glades beckon advanced skiers.

Toni Matt, a blue-square run, ought to be skied at least once as homage to the legendary Austrian racer who was the only man ever to schuss the Headwall at Tuckerman Ravine on Mt. Washington, New Hampshire. He traveled west to found the ski school at The Big Mountain. Hard-skiing powderhounds might ski Matt just once as an honor, but intermediates can knock out mileage with run after blissful run on this wonderful boulevard. The nearby Big Ravine

366

Mountain Stats—
The Big Mountain

Resort elevation 4,800 feet
Top of highest lift 7,000 feet
Bottom of lowest lift 4,600 feet
Total vertical 2,400 feet
Longest run 2½ miles
Average annual snowfall 300 inches
Ski season Thanksgiving to early April
Lifts 1 high-speed quad chairlift/gondola combination, 1 fixed-grip quad, 4 triples, 1 double, 1 T-bar, 1 platterpull
Capacity 12,000 skiers per hour
Terrain 63 trails (25% beginner and novice, 55% intermediate, 20% advanced and expert trails); total of 4,000 acres (off-piste is nearly all advanced and expert)
Snowmaking 60 acres
Night skiing Wednesday through Sunday, from 4:30 to 9:00 P.M., December through mid-March; day tickets valid for night skiing
Mountain dining Summit House on the top of the mountain, Ski Hut at the base of the Great Northern chair
Snow reports (406) 862-SNOW

is an astonishingly wide, gracefully curved top-to-bottom intermediate run stretching first around the ridgetop and then shooting along the fall line to the base. Young studs like to jump the Big Drift alongside the Big Ravine, but mainly, it's a cruiser of stupendous dimensions. Big Medicine parallel to the Big Ravine is a long, steepish, snow-catching basin that usually offers the best powder on the frontside.

The Glacier View chair by itself is relatively short, but by combining it with Chair 4 on the lower mountain, you can ski the entire vertical with two lift rides and a traverse between them. Glacier View lets skiers play in the powder of the upper snowfields, gullies and hanging walls, while Great Northern accesses the incredible clefts, beguiling glades and occasional clearings below. North Bowl, Hogan's and Hogan's East are upper-intermediate routes on the east side of the mountain, but they're basically bait for powder skiers. Around the side, The Big Mountain hollows out into a large horseshoe shape. The Faults are on one end, East Rim is on the other and everything in between is available—always steep, usually soft and never, never crowded. Ski the Cornice to a snow-holding gully such as Fault 1, Fault 2 or No Name, spill out into a steep clearing called Haskil Slide, follow a local powderhound into Movie Land and when you're done, you'll think you've just skied paradise. A long road leads back to the Great Northern chair and reality.

The North Slope is The Big Mountain's backside and the newest sector. Because it is sheltered from the drying sun, this face is timbered all the way to the top, thick with evergreens and exceptionally beautiful with the best views toward the high peaks of Glacier National Park and the Continental Divide. Caribou is an easy road winding to the bottom of the lift, but most of the North Slope is otherwise for better skiers. Three of the four delightful intermediate runs get most of the traffic. Blue-clad Goat Haunt, Whitetail and Silvertip are trails cut through the trees, expanding to create a broad drainage with a natural half-pipe near the bottom. Grey Wolf, the intermediate run, arcs around the perimeter with a feeling of isolation and woodsy tranquility. Between these intermediate runs is the North Slope's steepest face. Marmot, Black Bear and Bighorn are drop-off trails, but the trees and powder shots between them are also skiable. If and when The Big Mountain expands even more, it will occur on another peak adjacent to the North Slope.

SNOWBOARDING

Snowboarders and The Big Mountain are a fine pair. Riders love to explore and find hidden spots that aren't on every skiers' itinerary, and the mountain, with so few closed areas and such great trees, invites such exploration. George's Gorge on the North Slopes and Snowboard Ranch on the frontside off Chair 2 have quarter-pipes, ridges, table tops, slides and other features. The high bowls and snowfields are primo for snowboarding, and the North Bowl funnels into a natural half-pipe.

SNOWCAT SKIING

Someday The Big Mountain may put lifts into Flower Point and Caribou, both east of the summit, but meanwhile the area runs a snowcat back there. Four hours of cat skiing usually yields five to six runs. The cat will operate for groups of four or more and can take seven and a guide. You need to be an intermediate or advanced skier or snowboarder. The Big Mountain's cat operation is traditionally one of the least expensive in the Rockies (you must also have a lift ticket to reach the snowcat pickup area). For information or reservations, call **(800) 858-5439, (406) 862-2909.**

SKI SCHOOL PROGRAMS

Big Mountain Ski School, (406) 862-2909, (406) 862-2910.

Introductory Programs
Hassle Free, Learn to Ski: Free two-hour beginner lesson with purchase of adult beginner lift ticket, or free beginner lift ticket with purchase of first-timer lesson.
Tenderfoot Chair: Half-day, morning or afternoon classes.

Advanced and Specialty Programs
Afternoon Workshops: Two-hour lessons for intermediate and advanced skiers.
Sunday Clinics: Discounted bump and snowboard clinics offered on alternate Sundays, in addition to regular instruction in those skills.
Snowcat Powder Skiing Lessons: Afternoon sessions, weather permitting, for three and a half hours with an instructor and a snowcat.
The Big Mountain Guides: Midday mountain intro. Two hours; cost is comparable to a lesson.
Women's Clinic: Annual three-day clinic, offered a couple of times a winter, for women and by women.

For Families
Nonskiing Children
Kiddie Korner: For nonskiing children of all ages, includes day care and optional ski instruction for

367

children ages 4 and older at an additional cost. Lunches may be provided by parents or purchased for an additional fee. Open daily from 9:00 A.M. to 5:00 P.M. Reservations required for nonwalking infants and suggested for all others, **(406) 862-1999.**

Skiing Children
Kiddie Korner Skiing: Instruction combined with Kiddie Korner day care and is optional for young tots.
Beginner Tot: Private lessons required for youngsters under 4.
Half Pints: Group instruction for children ages 4 to 6.
Rough Riders: Morning and afternoon lessons, 2½ hours each, for children ages 6 to 12. Optional supervised lunches are also available.

Teens
Adventures of The Big Mountain: Adventure skiing and mountain exploration offered during peak school vacation periods. Two-hour classes, morning and afternoon, meet between the Hellroaring chair and the T-bar.

368

Noteworthy
The Big Mountain offers free skiing for youngsters 6 and under, children's tickets for ages 7 to 18. Also, Dog Sled Adventures provides free dogsled rides for children between 2:00 P.M. and 4:00 P.M., Tuesday and Saturday; depart from dog sign near bottom of Glacier Chaser.

FOR RACERS

Race Clinics: Two hours, Wednesday afternoons.
NASTAR: For information, call **(406) 862-2912, (406) 862-2913.**

HANDICAPPED SKIING

DREAM: Big Mountain Disabled Skier Program, (406) 852-1998.

NORDIC SKIING

The **Big Mountain Nordic Center** trail system is modest in size, but it is secluded, and deer and elk are frequently seen along the trail. Ten kilometers of groomed trails start right at the resort base, and instruction in classical skiing or skating and rental equipment are available. The single-set track and a 14-foot skating lane are both extremely well maintained, **(406) 862-2946.**

Down in the valley, the **Glacier Nordic Touring Center** near the Grouse Mountain Lodge has 13½ kilometers of mostly golf-course skiing and is particularly suited to new skiers. Of that, 5 kilometers are lighted for night touring, and instruction and rental equipment are also available, **(406) 862-4369.** Farther afield, the **Izaak Walton Inn** in Essex has 30 kilometers of marked, groomed tracks, instruction and rental equipment, but it is especially noteworthy for its guided backcountry tours into **Glacier National Park, (406) 888-5700.** Virtually all of the park's hiking trails double as marked but ungroomed touring trails in winter. Many of the most storied sights such as McDonald Falls, Sacred Dancing Cascade and Garden Wall are accessible, and the chances of seeing wildlife are great. Strong backcountry skiers might consider a two-day ski along the Going to the Sun Road, which is closed to vehicles in winter. It requires snow camping at midway, **(406) 888-5441.**

WHERE TO STAY

The Big Mountain Central Reservations, (800) 858-5439, (406) 862-1900.

The Big Mountain Village
Mid-Priced Accommodations
Kandahar Lodge
Lovely lodge with 48 rooms from studios to two-room suites. Hotel rooms have two queen-size beds. Beamed ceilings, oak furniture and tasteful decor provide European charm and ambiance. Some kitchenette, spa and loft units. Walk to lifts;

ski back to lodge. Children 12 and younger stay free in parents' room. Meal package plans available. Ski packages. Daily housekeeping, morning room service, 24-hour front desk, complimentary van to lifts. Restaurant, two hot tubs, sauna, guest laundry, two ski-and-boot rooms. **P.O. Box 1659, Whitefish, MT 59937; (406) 862-6098.**

Economy Accommodations

Alpinglow Inn
Unprepossessing 54-room lodge. Most rooms sleep up to six, good for budget-minded groups and families. Lively. Restaurant serves three meals daily. Walk to lifts and other village lodges and lounges. Children 12 and younger stay free in parents' room (one child per adult). Meal plans available. Daily housekeeping, complimentary morning coffee, 24-hour front desk. Restaurant, ski lockers, two outdoor hot tubs, saunas, guest laundry. **P.O. Box 1770, Whitefish, MT 59937; (406) 862-6966.**

Hibernation House
Economy B&B. Walk to lifts; ski back. Family rooms each have queen-size bed and bunk beds. TV and phones in lobby. Daily housekeeping, breakfast. Hot tub, game room, ski storage, guest laundry. **P.O. Box 1400, Whitefish, MT 59937; (406) 862-3511.**

Condominiums

Anapurna Properties
Sixty-two individually decorated condominiums accommodating from 2 to 10. All units within walking distance to Chair 6. Children 12 and younger stay free when sharing parents' unit. Midweek housekeeping, indoor pool, 15 hot tubs. **P.O. Box 55, Whitefish, MT 59937; (800) 243-7547, (406) 862-3687.**

Edelweiss Condominiums
Forty-nine fully furnished luxury condos with fireplaces (wood provided) and balconies or patios. Studios to two-bedroom, two-bath units in a contemporary style. Closest lodging to Glacier Chaser. Midweek housekeeping for stays of longer than five days, complimentary nightly ski and snowboard waxing, nightly wine and cheese parties. Indoor hot tub, sauna, guest laundry.

P.O. Box 846, Whitefish, MT 59937; (800) 228-8260, (406) 862-5252.

Whitefish

Whitefish Chamber of Commerce, (406) 862-3501.

Luxury Accommodations
Grouse Mountain Lodge
Full resort with fine amenities and services 1 mile from town of Whitefish. Spacious rooms and attractive public space, decorated in a cross between American western and country English. Huge river-rock fireplace in lobby. Ski packages. Daily housekeeping, 24-hour front desk, bell service, complimentary airport or Amtrak shuttle. Indoor pool, hot tub, sauna, restaurant, lounge, card room with gambling machines, cross-country skiing. **1205 Hwy 93 West, Whitefish, MT 59937; (800) 321-8822, (406) 862-3000.**

Mid-Priced Accommodations
Best Western Rocky Mountain Lodge
Newly expanded and totally renovated 79-room motor inn. Twelve suites with fireplace and/or in-room Jacuzzi. Attractive and well-appointed. Daily housekeeping, 24-hour front desk, continental breakfast included, complimentary airport or Amtrak transfers. Outdoor heated pool, hot tub. **6510 Hwy 93 South, Whitefish, MT 59937; (800) 862-2569, (406) 862-2569, (800) 528-1234** for Best Western reservations.

Downtowner Motel & Health Club
The motor inn for the fitness-oriented skier. Thirteen rooms, two non-smoking. Health club in building free to motel guests. One block to Main St. and two blocks to Amtrak station. Daily housekeeping, 24-hour front desk, complimentary continental breakfast, free local phone calls. Health club, sauna, hot tub, racquetball court, weight room. **224 Spokane Ave., Whitefish, MT 59937; (406) 862-2535.**

Duck Inn Lodge
Large cedar lodge with 10 rooms each with fireplace, balcony and large bath. European charm and great river and mountain views. Car rental and lodging packages available.

Daily housekeeping, continental breakfast included. Indoor Jacuzzi. **1305 Columbia Ave., Whitefish, 59937; (800) 344-2377, (406) 862-3825.**

The Garden Wall Inn
Charming five-room B&B in fine old Whitefish home. Five rooms, three with private baths. House built in 1920s with antique furnishings from that period. Opulent full breakfasts, with special-blended coffee and own baking. No TV in the inn; shared phone. Wake up with coffee delivered to room, après-ski sherry in front of the fireplace, daily housekeeping. **504 Spokane Ave., Whitefish, MT 59937; (406) 862-3440.**

Good Medicine Lodge
Classic Montana lodge built of rough-hewn cedar. Rustic charm. Rooms with private baths, custom lodge-pole beds, balconies and mountain views. Daily housekeeping, full breakfast included. Outdoor spa, guest laundry, ski room. **537 Wisconsin Ave., Whitefish, MT 59937; (406) 860-5488.**

370

Economy Accommodations

Allen's Motel
Reasonably priced, centrally located motel just south of town; short walk to restaurants and shops. Eighteen rooms, some with kitchens available. Pets OK. Daily housekeeping. **6540 Hwy 93 South, Whitefish, MT 59937; (406) 862-3995.**

Condominiums

Bay Point Estates
Fifty-one condominiums on Whitefish Lake. Contemporary design and individual decor. Wonderful views. Ski packages. Midweek housekeeping for stays of five days or longer. Indoor pool, two hot tubs, sauna, game room. **P.O. Box 35, Whitefish, MT 59937; (800) 327-2108, (406) 862-2331.**

Crestwood Condominiums
Attractive condos for up to six people. Fireplace and washer and dryer in each unit. Guest membership to Downtowner Health Club. Outskirts of town. Ski packages. Complimentary shuttle service, pool, hot tubs. **P.O. Box 1000, Whitefish, MT 59937; (406) 862-7574.**

Ptarmigan Village
Condos and chalets on mountain access road. All units with lofts. Knotty pine rusticity. Individually decorated, well-furnished and casual. All with fireplace or wood stove. Three miles from lifts. Housekeeping every three days. Indoor pool, hot tub, sauna. **P.O. Box 458, Whitefish, MT 59937; (406) 862-3594.**

Whitefish Property Management, (406) 862-2578, specializes in home and condominium rentals on Whitefish Lake.

It is also possible to stay in Kalispell, 15 miles south of Whitefish; some properties even have ski packages. For information, contact the **Kalispell Chamber of Commerce, (406) 758-2800,** or the **Flathead Convention & Visitors Assn., (800) 543-3105, (406) 756-9091.**

DINING OUT

Buffalo Cafe
Fun and friendly. "The Liars Club Doesn't Meet Here Every Morning," proclaims a sign. Hearty food, from traditional to invented specialties. Casual oil-cloth "elegance." Big breakfasts; burgers and Mexican lunches later. **307 E. Second St., Whitefish; (406) 862-BUFF.**

Cafe Kandahar
Charming and classy restaurant. Knotty-pine rusticity with a continental overlay. Good food and ambiance. BYO wine or beer. Dinner reservations accepted. **Kandahar Lodge, Mountain Village; (406) 862-6098.**

Dos Amigos
Start with the Macho Nacho and work up to bodacious Mexican and Southwestern dishes, seafood or steaks. Imported beers, wines. Affordable and atmospheric. Located between town and mountain. Children's menu. Reservations accepted. Takeout available. **Wisconsin Ave., Whitefish; (406) 862-9994.**

Glacier Grande
Family-pleasing dinners, including Southwestern specialties, Italian pastas and seafood. Entertainment, including appearances by nationally

known musicians. **10 Central Ave., Whitefish; (406) 862-9400.**

Logan's

Fine food well presented in lovely, high-ceiling dining room. American and continental specialties. Wine list. Reservations accepted. **Grouse Mountain Lodge, 1205 Hwy 93 West, Whitefish; (406) 862-3000.**

Moguls Bar & Grille

Formerly the Mountain Haus, but recently redecorated and renamed. Base-of-mountain purveyor of breakfast, lunch and dinner specialties. Trendy and eclectic fare. Espresso bar. Après-ski and entertainment too. **Mountain Village; (406) 862-1980.**

The Place

Antiques and memorabilia fill this nostalgic saloon. Casual. Super Nachos suffice for some appetites. For others, wide range of popular items, including pizza, chicken, ribs, seafood, steaks and sandwiches. Thursday spaghetti night. Lunch and dinner. Children's menu. Takeout available. **845 Wisconsin, Whitefish; (406) 862-4500.**

The Remington

Large restaurant, cafe, casino and dance hall. Basic but good food. Steaks, burgers, chicken and seafood—and lots of fun. **130 Central Ave., Whitefish; (406) 862-0017.**

The Summit House

Protective gondolas replace open chairs for nighttime dinner ride Wednesday and Saturday evenings. Casual atmosphere but sparkling views. Buffet-style service with ethnic themes, changing weekly. Reservations accepted. **The Big Mountain; (406) 862-1971.**

Whitefish Lake Restaurant

Soaring, roaring fireplace and white linen. Fine dining in upscale rusticity. Excellent wine selection. Reservations recommended. **Hwy 93 West, Whitefish; (406) 862-5285.**

NIGHTLIFE

With Calgary the closest drive-market city, you know that the nightlife is full of Canadian enthusiasm, raucous good cheer and free-flowing brewskis. It starts at the mountain—or more accurately, way up on the mountain, with cocktails at The Summit House. At the base, Moguls Bar & Grille is a hot spot on the après-ski scene with live entertainment every night and good drinks and snacks. It's the spot for Powder Hour every Monday and ski movies on Tuesday. The Bierstube is a rockin' classic ski bar with live entertainment some nights. The Bierstube hosts the ski patrol's Frabert Award with a free keg of beer given to the "Clod of the Week." Hellroaring Saloon is great for after-ski munchies and drinks. Hellroaring shows ski movies, made by famous filmmakers or The Big Mountain's video crew. They share equally in the early action—and with night skiing Wednesday through Saturday evenings until 10:00 P.M., that early action can last quite long.

If you want kicked-back entertainment till whenever, head down the road to Whitefish. The Great Northern Bar has dancing and other diver- **371** sions, and the Bulldog Saloon is a good sports bar. The Glacier Grande has name acts from all over the country, and Logan's at the Grouse Mountain Lodge has mellow music and dancing to easy-listening and Top-40 numbers five nights a week. No matter what, you must party at The Palace. Noisy, crowded and filled with a mix of skiers and locals, it's a classic. You'll find flowing pitchers of beer tapped by great bartenders, two pool tables and a variety of video game machines.

A number of spots have limited-stakes gambling, generally keno and poker, and of them, enthusiastic players seem to like the Remington, which has live poker, video keno and poker, country-and-western music and even dinner. Best Bet is a less atmospheric restaurant and casino complex. That's culture of a sort, but for the other kind, the Glacier Orchestra and Chorale performs during the winter, and other ballet and theatrical performances are also on the calendar.

For more information, contact **The Big Mountain Ski & Summer Resort, P.O. Box 1400, Whitefish, MT 59937, (800) 858-5439, (406) 862-1900; Whitefish Chamber of Commerce, P.O. Box 1120, Whitefish, MT 59937, (406) 862-3501.**

RED LODGE

BACKDROP

When you wander down the wide main street of Red Lodge, you can imagine John Wayne or Gary Cooper moseying along across the way, for the town is steeped in genuine westernness. It nestles in a valley that was once the summer encampment of the Crow Indians, whose "red lodges," or clay-coated teepees, gave the town its name. A large and totally authentic teepee at the ski area's base is the resort's signature, and "meet me at the teepee" is a common suggestion for an on-slope rendezvous. In the decades before the completion of the Beartooth Highway connecting it to Cooke City and Yellowstone National Park, it was by turns a coal mining and cattle and sheep ranching community at the end of the road. Red Lodge still maintains a general western ambiance, but the long winters, steady snow and stereotypical big sky overhead combine to give it a specific Montana overlay. Many of the picturesque buildings lining a six-block stretch of Broadway have been listed on the National Register of Historic Places. Red Lodge is a real town, with resort facilities but without a resort persona, and the existence of a growing ski area just up the road adds to its appeal as a low-key, economical place to ski.

372

THE LAY OF THE LAND

The town of Red Lodge is one of the most beautifully situated in southwestern Montana. It is the northern gateway to the rugged and beautiful Beartooth Mountains. Granite Peak, at 12,799 feet Montana's highest mountain, is less than 10 crow-flight miles away. The Red Lodge Ski Area is in a snow pocket 6 miles from town, with ski terrain draped over 9,516-foot Grizzly Peak and incredible mountain views to the west and the south.

GETTING THERE

Red Lodge is 60 miles (a little over a one-hour drive) southwest of Billings, Montana's largest city, via US 212. The state's great concentration of passenger flights come into Billings Logan International Airport, and rental cars are available. **Greyhound** has service to the downtown bus station, **(800) 231-2222.** I-90 crosses just south of the city and offers excellent east-west highway connections. Low-cost shuttle buses connect the town and mountain, both named Red Lodge.

PROFILE

Red Lodge's layout is a ski-area classic. It has a simple and functional base area and the easiest terrain at the bottom, the majority of the most difficult runs at the top, and the mid-range runs scattered about on two ridges and a deeply etched valley. On the whole, this beefy mountain boasts a medley steeps and flats and hollows and gullies. The first of these adjacent drainages to be brought into Red Lodge's lift-served skiing fold is Cole Creek, with the long-awaited construction of two new lifts for the 1996–97 ski season. This expansion doubles the skiable terrain and complicates the layout, but it promotes a modest mountain into the ranks of the solidly mid-sized. Red Lodge is escalating into a resort community too, with a new subdivision called Red Lodge Mountain Village, a golf course and other four-seasons amenities 1 mile west of downtown.

Red Lodge Mountain itself is in transition, but for now, the main, simple base area with three lifts remains the portal to all of the skiing. Beginners still have a large area called Miami Beach, sheltered both from speeding expert skiers and from the weather, with a chairlift and as fine a learning slope as you'll find in the Rockies. Eventually ski-in/ski-out lodging will be developed at Miami Beach, which will change the nature of this part of the ski area. A triple chair from the base climbs to a knob, from which you can look at

Photo by Gordon Wilstie/Red Lodge

or ski into Cole Creek, warm up on a nice web of mainly easy and moderate terrain or ski to one of the mid-mountain-loading chairs to reach the challenging summit runs. A high-speed base-to-summit lift is also planned, which will eliminate the need to ride two chairs to the top. But old chairs or new, the summit offers grandiose views, a couple of splendid intermediate routes to the bottom and a rousing dose of truly challenging skiing. If you want a black-diamond sampler, you can ski a trio of shortish, steepish topside pitches called 1st Street, 2nd Street and 3rd Street, but if you crave real steeps, you won't find a better place than the Drainage. You can get to this gully-washing pitch via such glade runs as Intimidation, East Parks and West Parks, or you can drop your tips into it directly from the top of the Grizzly Peak chair. If you just want to ski the steeps, board the Midway Express (an "express" lift in name only, but in reality a regular double chair) out of the drainage and then the Grizzly chair back to the summit. A pair of big cruisers called Lazy M and Barriers arc around the southern portion of the currently developed area and aim back toward the concentration of runs in the center. Lazy M, named after a cattle brand, is Red Lodge's longest run and a real classic.

You can keep riding the main triple and even another nearby double to ski these center runs, for this dense web of relatively short but nicely varied terrain remain Red Lodge's core skiing. Slow-skiing areas, wide and gentle slopes, a handful of perfectly pitched medium runs and just a couple of steep parts make this varied section ski like a mini-area within a larger one. They are close enough to the base to make them ideal on those frosty Montana days when you might want to go inside every now and then to warm the chill out of your bones. Once an off-piste section, the addition of lift service to Cole Creek expands Red Lodge's top-end skiing. This beautiful bowl distinguished by rock outcroppings and cliff bands has sprouted 10 new trails—five intermediate and five expert—plus glades and extreme chutes, served by a pair of high-speed quads, which may be away from the base area but combine adrenaline-pumping skiing with fast lift rides.

Inside Red Lodge

SNOWBOARDING

Red Lodge builds a terrain garden on Cariboo and sometimes has a half-pipe too. Snowboarders themselves occasionally build hits and obstacles on Lower Miami Beach. Strong riders love the trees off the Drainage, and some of the new Cole Creek terrain will probably be hot for this cool crowd as well. The entire mountain is congenial for snowboarding, with the exception of the flat traverse from the top of Chair 1 to Tipi Trail.

SKI SCHOOL PROGRAMS

Introductory Programs

Beginners Ski and Snowboarding Packages: Low-cost package with novice lift ticket, two-hour lesson and all-day rentals. Available for never-ever skiers age 7 and older.

Advanced and Specialty Programs

Skiers and Snowboarding Packages: All-day, all-lifts ticket and two-hour lesson; snowboard version includes board.

Special Programs

Mountain Hosts conduct complimentary mountain tours daily at 10:00 A.M., meeting at the bottom of the triple chair.

374

For Families

Nonskiing Children

The Mountain Nursery: New day-care center for ages 6 months to 4 years. Older children taken outside for snowplay, depending on weather. Immunization records and reservations required.

Skiing Children

SKIwee: Classes for 3- to 6-year-olds, half day or full day with lunch.
Teepee Creepers: All-day program for 7- to 12-year-olds, including lunch. Ski and snowboarding options.

NORDIC SKIING

The **Red Lodge Nordic Center** is 2 miles west of Red Lodge. Most trails are easy and are machine-groomed for diagonal and skating. Rentals and instruction are available, including beginner packages with trail pass, rentals and lessons. It is also a popular venue for skiing in the light of a full moon. For information, call **(406) 425-1070.**

If you don't need rental equipment and don't

Mountain Stats— Red Lodge

Resort elevation 5,555 feet
Top of highest lift 9,146 feet
Bottom of lowest lift 7,100 feet
Total vertical 2,350 feet
Longest run 2½ miles
Average annual snowfall 250 inches
Ski season Thanksgiving to mid-April
Lifts 2 high-speed quad chairlifts, 1 triple, 4 doubles, 1 handle tow
Capacity 10,690 skiers per hour
Terrain 45 trails, 1,000 acres (15% beginner and novice, 55% intermediate, 30% advanced and expert)
Snowmaking 40%
Mountain dining Midway Chalet at the base of the Grizzly chair
Snow reports (406) 446-2610

insist on groomed trails, you have a choice of three loops totaling more than 30 miles of marked trails south of Red Lodge. Silver Run, 5 miles up the West Fork of Rock Creek, has three loops, ranging from an easy 4-kilometer trail to a challenging 11-kilometer route. Parkside located on Rock Creek's Main Fork has two—a 5-kilometer and a 9-kilometer trail, with backcountry access. Lake Fork also has two short loops, 3 and 5 kilometers respectively, and access to the adjacent Absaroka-Beartooth Wilderness. If you have time for just one Nordic tour, make it to Silver Falls, a special place with magnificent views. Other Nordic options include the 2-mile Palisade Trail between the Palisades Campground and the ski area, and 8-mile-long West Fork Road, which is unplowed, but which skiers share with snowmobilers.

WHERE TO STAY

Reservations are available through **Red Lodge Central Reservations, (800) 444-8977.**

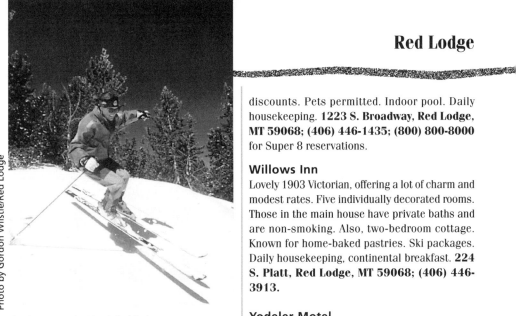

Photo by Gordon Wiltsie/Red Lodge

Catching air at laid-back Red Lodge.

Luxury Accommodations

The Pollard

Red Lodge's most distinctive and distinguished hotel. Excellent downtown location. Moderately priced by standards of other resort towns. Historic landmark (Buffalo Bill stayed there), lovingly and charmingly restored. Ski packages. Forty non-smoking rooms and suites with in-room whirlpool tubs, balconies and/or adjacent sitting rooms. Fitness facilities, racquetball court, hot tub, saunas, restaurant, lounge. Daily housekeeping. **2 N. Broadway, Red Lodge, MT 59068; (800) POLLARD, (406) 466-0001.**

Mid-Priced Accommodations

Best Western LuPine Inn

Low-rise motor inn, with 46 simple and functional rooms in various configurations, including kitchenette units, rooms with Jacuzzi tubs, and connecting units for families. Some rooms non-smoking. Pets accepted. Ski packages. Indoor heated pool, whirlpool, game room, guest laundry, ski waxing room. Daily housekeeping. **P.O. Box 30, 702 Hauser, Red Lodge, MT 59068; (406) 446-1321, (800) 528-1234** for Best Western reservations.

Economy Accommodations

Super 8

Fifty-room economy chain motel, including large family units. Some rooms non-smoking. Senior discounts. Pets permitted. Indoor pool. Daily housekeeping. **1223 S. Broadway, Red Lodge, MT 59068; (406) 446-1435; (800) 800-8000** for Super 8 reservations.

Willows Inn

Lovely 1903 Victorian, offering a lot of charm and modest rates. Five individually decorated rooms. Those in the main house have private baths and are non-smoking. Also, two-bedroom cottage. Known for home-baked pastries. Ski packages. Daily housekeeping, continental breakfast. **224 S. Platt, Red Lodge, MT 59068; (406) 446-3913.**

Yodeler Motel

Simple and functional motel close to downtown. Twenty-two large family rooms, some with kitchenettes and some with in-room steambaths. Honeymoon suite. Ski packages. AAA rated. Outdoor hot tub. Daily housekeeping. **P.O. Box 1336, 601 S. Broadway, Red Lodge, MT 59068; (406) 446-1435.**

Condominiums and Homes

Cheateau Rouge

Sporty and well-appointed 24-unit complex, styled like linked A-frames. One-bedroom units with kitchenette and breakfast nook; two-bedroom units with full kitchen, fireplace and dining room. Located south of town. Ski packages. Daily housekeeping, complimentary coffee. Indoor pool, Jacuzzi, exercise facility. **P.O. Box 3410, Red Lodge, MT 59068; (800) 926-1601. (406) 446-1601.**

Pitcher Guest Houses

One historic four-bedroom home and one three-bedroom log home, both tastefully and distinctively furnished. Two one-bedroom log cabins. Homelike and personal. **P.O. Box 3450, Red Lodge, MT 59068; (406) 446-2859.**

Red Lodging

Creekside cabins, Victorian homes, farmhouses, condominiums and townhomes, some with fireplaces, hot tubs and other amenities. Largest home accommodates up to 10 people. **16½ N. Broadway, P.O. Box 1477, Red Lodge, MT 59068; (406) 445-1272.**

Rock Creek Resort

Attractive and secluded resort complex at the approach to Beartooth Pass, 4½ miles south of town. Eighty-four units in lodge and condo buildings. Beartooth Lodge has 33 suites with kitchenettes, fireplaces and balconies. Grizzly Condos are one- and two-bedroom apartments with full kitchens and fireplaces. Fitness center, hot tub, sauna, indoor swimming pool, restaurant, lounge. **Route 2, Box 3500, Red Lodge, MT 59068; (406) 446-1111.**

Other property management firms include **Coal Creek Realty & Property Management** (private homes only), **(406) 446-2266 Grizzly Peak Realty, (406) 446-3030 H Bar S Real Estate, (800) 596-2449, (406) 446-3535**

DINING OUT

376

Bear Creek Saloon

Take a short drive to Bear Creek and stop at this congenial dispensary for popular Mexican dishes. The back bar is 140 years old, and the pool table is an antique too. Open Friday, Saturday and Sunday evenings. **Hwy 308, Bear Creek; (406) 446-3481.**

Beartooth Wagon & Sleigh Rides

Chuckwagon dinner around a roaring fire. Roast beef, baked beans, macaroni salad and brown-

Red Lodge shows off its rugged beauty.

Photo by Gordon Wilstie/Red Lodge

ies. Steaming hot chocolate. BYO wine or other alcoholic beverages. Available for groups of 10 or more; reservations required. **(406) 446-2179.**

Bogart's

Mostly Mexican meals (and pizza too). Memorabilia and antiques in this eclectic downtown restaurant. Good margaritas. Lunch and dinner daily. **11 S. Broadway, Red Lodge; (406) 446-1784.**

Brown Bear Inn

Saloon and restaurant, 15 minutes from Red Lodge. Steak, prime rib and lots of casual fun are the specialties. Serves daily from early lunch through late dinner. Reservations accepted. Full bar. **2 N. First St., Roberts; (406) 445-2318.**

Old Piney Dell

Charming streamside restaurant, grown from a log cabin built by a homesteader in the 1920s. Steak, seafood, lamb and poultry served. Cozy atmosphere and lovely views. **Rock Creek Resort, Red Lodge; (406) 446-1196.**

P. D. McKinney's

Casual restaurant, just south of downtown. Popular with—and catering to—families. Great breakfasts and lunches. Sourdough pancakes are a specialty; good omelettes too. Charbroiled burgers. Kids' menu at both meals. **407 S. Broadway, Red Lodge; (406) 446-1250.**

The Pollard Dining Room

Delightful restaurant in restored hotel. Fine dining, eclectic and creative menu and great atmosphere. Prelude to dinner can be drinks by the fireplace and postlude can be dessert and coffee in the History Room. Game, seafood and poultry that is smoked, grilled and prepared in other contemporary, creative ways. Wine list. **2 N. Broadway, Red Lodge; (406) 466-0001.**

Ranch House Restaurant

Lunch and dinner served. Best known for steak, chicken and seafood dinners. Prime rib on Friday, Saturday and Sunday evenings. Beer and wine. Stretch out evening at adjacent casino. Located behind **Red Lodge Drug, Red Lodge; (406) 446-1011.**

Willy Pitchers

Casual and pleasant restaurant in historic downtown building. Contemporary cuisine and crayons on the table for trendy pre-food pastime, amusing for all ages. Lunch, dinner and Sunday brunch. All-you-can-eat pasta night a major hit. Also known especially for great appetizers and desserts. Full bar, plus wine and beer selections. **17 S. Broadway, Red Lodge; (406) 446-1717.**

NIGHTLIFE

The Willow Creek Saloon, which locals persist in calling the Bierstube, at the base of the mountain snares the early after-ski crowd. Beers, drinks, munchies and even light meals are available. When the present base complex is replaced by a new main lodge, probably in 1997, management promises another Willow Creek Saloon. In town, drinks are served at The Pollard, Willy Pitchers and the Ranch Restaurant, which also has low-stakes poker. Families like Ten Pin Alley, which offers bowling, video games, poker and other diversions in addition to dining. There's sometimes live entertainment at Snow Creek and Natali's, both downtown. The Trapper Room at the Rock Creek Resort is also popular. For the ultimate in funky fun, check out the Bear Creek Saloon. In addition to such mundane amusements as karaoke, you might luck out and be there in time for the weekend iguana races, complete with sports betting.

For more information, contact **Red Lodge Mountain Resort, P.O. Box 750, Red Lodge, MT 59068, (406) 446-2610; Red Lodge Chamber of Commerce, Red Lodge, MT 59068, (406) 446-1718.**

377

Kids test their ski legs with a Red Lodge instructor.

Photo by Gordon Wilstie/Red Lodge

Alberta

378

ALBERTA

ALBERTA

Photo courtesy Banff/Lake Louise Tourism Bureau

379

THE BANFF AREAS

BACKDROP

The tourist town of Banff and the resort center of Lake Louise, nestled in the heart of Banff National Park, rank among western Canada's leading summer attractions. The town's setting is breathtaking and its facilities unsurpassed, as attested by hordes of visitors from all over the world who jam in to stretch their legs after driving through the park, ride the scenic Sulphur Mountain Gondola, work Banff's busy shopping district, restock their traveling larder and photograph each other beside the improbably blue waters of Lake Louise. Winter is off-season, but you'd never think so from the traffic to three ski areas within an hour's drive of Banff and each other. Skiers and snowboarders from Calgary, the Plains provinces, the United States and abroad treasure the terrain at Lake Louise Ski Area, Sunshine and Norquay, as well as the amenities and infrastructure offered by a major tourist center.

Twofold financial benefits are simply the economical icing on the multitiered cake that is Banff/Lake Louise skiing: first, for U.S. skiers, is the strength of the American versus the Canadian dollar and second is that winter is considered low season in this high-powered summer resort area. Today, there is nothing modest about the Banff and Lake Louise area—except the price. The skiing is immodestly vast and varied, and the resort amenities rank with the best and most comprehensive in the world. Three mountains, accessible individually or via the Ski Banff/Lake Louise lift pass and linked by convenient shuttle buses, and some of the best lodging, dining, shopping, off-slope activities and nightlife of any ski resort on the planet make this a destination to visit and revisit.

THE LAY OF THE LAND

The historic Canadian Pacific rail line and, more significantly these days, the TransCanada Highway bore through Banff National Park, and it is the rare traveler who does not stop in Banff. The town is located on the Bow River. Banff Avenue, the vibrant main street, forms the nucleus of a genuine downtown, with abundant accommodations, shops, restaurants and nightspots on both sides and spilling over onto adjacent streets. The majestic Banff Springs Hotel dominates a hill just north of the downtown center. Mt. Norquay, Banff's hometown hill, is located up a winding access road south of town. The highway swings northwestward from Banff, leading to the turnoffs first to Sunshine Village and then to Lake Louise. Sunshine, whose gondola base is 11 miles (16 kilometers) from Banff, is a self-contained resort with limited on-mountain lodging, but neither Norquay nor Lake Louise has ski-in/ski-out accommodations. In fact, the Lake Louise resort facilities and the Lake Louise ski area are on opposite sides of the TransCanada Highway, 35 miles (58 kilometers) from Banff. The Chateau Lake Louise maintains sole possession of prime lakeview property, while Lake Louise Village, a short ride downhill and closer to the highway, is more an agglomeration of lodging properties and a handful of hops than anything truly resembling a town, so if you are looking for a lot of off-slope options close to the place you're staying, Banff will be your choice.

GETTING THERE

Banff is about 83 miles (130 kilometers) from Calgary, Alberta's largest city and site of the 1988 Winter Olympics, and 10 miles (16 kilometers) west of the Banff National Park entrance gate. Calgary International Airport is serviced by Canadian and international carriers. Rental cars are available from major national, international and local agencies. Motorcoach services between the airport and Banff/Lake Louise are operated by **Brewster Transportation, (403) 762-6700, (403) 221-8284** in Calgary, and **Laidlaw Transportation, (800) 661-4946, (403) 762-9102. Greyhound** of Canada also services the Banff/Lake Louise area, **(403) 762-6767** in Banff, **(403) 265-9111** in Calgary.

A car can be useful but is not necessary. Many Banff accommodations are within walking distance of town (there's a free in-town shuttle system too), and buses run from Banff to all three ski areas and between Lake Louise's hotels and its namesake ski area. Ski buses to all three areas are free for holders of any tri-area, multiday ticket, including participants in the Banff Club Ski program, and some of the larger hotels additionally run their own complimentary shuttle services.

Photo by Bill Marsh/Lake Louise

THE SKIING

Lake Louise

Profile

Lake Louise's base complex, which was extensively rebuilt and expanded in 1996 but is still modest by the standards of other major ski areas, gives just the barest hint of the area's incredible expanse and astonishing variety of terrain. At the base, you'll find a rather standard assortment of facilities: day lodge with food service and other services, children's slope, beginner hill and three chairlifts climbing to somewhere on high. "Somewhere" turns out to be a great realm of wide boulevards, seductive glades and huge expanses of steep-walled, tree-free bowls that make this one of North America's best-kept secrets for advanced and expert skiers and riders. With 4,000 acres draped over four mountain faces on a commendable vertical, it ranks as Alberta's largest ski area and one of the biggest in Canada as well. Once you get the hang of the convoluted layout, which requires three separate trail maps to depict accurately, this complex mountain becomes surprisingly user-friendly, with skiing in every compass direction and at many altitudes and at least one easy and one challenging run from each lift.

Inside the Banff Areas

381

Lake Louise's 1,000-acre South Face is a mix of cut lower runs that boast snowmaking and are frequently groomed (including the Men's Downhill and Ladies' Downhill, used for World Cup and other top-level competitions) and gladed upper slopes that are steeper and more rugged. On a

Mountain Stats—
Lake Louise

Top of highest lift 8,500 feet (2,591 meters)
Bottom of lowest lift 5,400 feet (1,646 meters)
Total vertical 3,100 feet (1,445 meters)
Longest run 5 miles (8 kilometers)
Average annual snowfall 144 inches (366 centimeters)
Ski season early November to mid-May
Lifts 2 high-speed quad chairlifts, 1 fixed-grip quad, 2 triples, 3 doubles, 1 platterpull, 1 T-bar, 1 children's tow
Capacity 15,499 skiers per hour
Terrain 77 trails, 4,000 acres (25% beginner and novice, 45% intermediate, 30% advanced and expert)
Snowmaking 40% or 1,600 acres (2,200 vertical feet)
Mountain dining Whitehorn Lodge near the bottom of the Eagle chair, Temple Lodge at the base of the Larch and Ptarmigan chairs
Snow reports (800) 258-SNOW, (403) 522-3555 at ski area, (403) 244-6665 in Calgary

them is solid blue. There are some marked pistes here, but basically, this upper mountain is a symphony of hanging walls, open glades and surprising U-troughed chutes that are especially tempting on cold Canadian mornings, for the sun first kisses the eastern and southern exposures.

If you're after powder or even steeper steeps, however, you won't devote a turn to the frontside but will drop directly into the Back Bowls. Bearing the same name and exuding the same sense of grandiosity as their opposite numbers at Vail, these vast white basins are always challenging and never crowded. Courageous low intermediates can get a lick of the bowls by skiing a road called Saddleback from the Top of the World quad, or stronger intermediates can pick their way down Boomerang from the Summit Platter, but essentially black diamonds—singles and doubles—prevail. Because of limited lift access, there never are true crowds in the Back Bowls, meaning that untracked snow lasts astonishingly long. The double-diamond gut-wrenchers closest to the Paradise chair—ER3, Swede's and North Cornice—get the most attention. They are as radical as anything you'll find in the Rockies, and it is an indication of the skill of local skiers and riders that as many people tackle them as do. Such long single-diamond steeps off the top of the platter as Brown Shirt, Ridge Run and Whitehorn I get less attention, because of the cumbersome roundtrip that involves a runout called Pika to the Paradise or Ptarmigan chair for a ride to the ridgetop, dropping into the frontside and making your way back to the platter.

If you're into open chutes and headwalls, the Paradise chair has your name on it. If you prefer tree-lined chutes, steep trails and fall-away glades, Ptarmigan is the lift you'll want to ride, and Exhibition Trees, Ptarmigan Chutes, Exhibition Chutes, Exhibition Glades and Pika Trees comprise the kind of challenging terrain you'll want to explore. When you're out of gas, you can pop into the Temple Lodge, nestled into a small valley on the backside of the ski area. After refueling, you can knock your socks off on Ptarmigan again or explore the fascinating and varied terrain off the Larch chair. For groups of mixed ability, it's hard to do better than the Larch area, with more than 1,200 vertical feet and runs ranging from a trio of

plateau near the top of the Friendly Glacier Express, you'll find the Whitehorn Lodge and just below is the Eagle chair base station. This lift serves some of Lake Louise's nicest novice and intermediate trails, as well as a few good tree shots like Eagle Flight and STM that are marked with black diamonds and are a good introduction to that level of terrain.

The South Face's appeals are great for new skiers, early in the season when you really need to be on snowmaking runs or when the light is flat and tree-lined trails are just the ticket, but the outback territory, which is not visible from the frontside, is where Lake Louise really shines. To reach it from the base, you can either ride the Olympic chair to the Summit Platter, a black-diamond lift that has many riders hanging on with their toenails, or the Glacier Express to the Top of the World Express. The former unloads high on Mt. Whitehorn and the latter along the ridge that slopes off Whitehorn's eastern shoulder. You take a few runs on the upper frontside, which cannot be confused as warmups because the easiest of green-circle runs to the double-black-diamond opus called Lookout Chutes. If you ski no other Larch run, make it the Rock Garden. Reached by a slim traverse, Rock Garden starts with a fall-away headwall and quickly widens to a scoop-shaped slope peppered with large boulders. You can dart around these boulders, remnants from an old slide, for one of the more surrealistic experiences. From the Larch area, you can return to the South Side or Back Bowls via the Ptarmigan chair or ski out on a long, long road that takes you back to the base.

Snowboarding

Lake Louise's wide-ranging terrain appeals to free riders, especially those inclined to riding among the trees and playing on the steeps. There's a snowboard park off the Wiwaxy run near the top of the Olympic chair, but essentially, the entirety of this huge area is one humongous snowboard park.

Photo by Mark Gallup/Lake Louise

Lake Louise's backside steeps are the peer of any of the continent—and the views are sensational too.

Ski School Programs

The general ski school number is **(403) 522-2951.** Ski school information and reservations can also be made at the **Whiskyjack Lodge, (403) 522-3555, Chateau Lake Louise, (403) 522-3511, Ext. 1211,** and **Wilson Mountain Sports** in **Lake Louise Village, (403) 522-3636.**

Introductory Programs
Guaranteed Learn to Ski: Beginners' special including 1-hour morning lesson, full-day lift ticket for Sunny T-bar and rental equipment, with additional afternoon lesson free if new skier is not satisfied with his or her progress.
Lake Louise Ski Week: Beginner version of the following program, starting on Mondays.
Discover Snowboarding: Beginner lift ticket, lesson, board and boot rental and half-price coupon for future lesson. Offered twice daily by the Lake Louise Snowboard School.

Advanced and Specialty Programs
Turn & Burn Clinics: 2 1/4-hour afternoon clinics for advanced and expert skiers, focusing on bumps, powder, crud, steeps and racing.
Hourglass Clinics: Two-hour clinic using shaped skis, designed to help skiers break out of the intermediate rut.

Lake Louise Ski Week: Classic ski week, and 3-, 4- and 5-day versions available, with 2 3/4 hours of daily group lessons and guided skiing, video workshop, dual slalom fun race and après-ski reception. Optional torchlight parade with dinner.
CSIA Courses: Canadian Ski Instructors' Alliance Level 1 course offered once a month, November through April.
Lauralee Bowie Ski Adventures: Two- and three-day improvement programs designed for intermediate and advanced skiers; **(888) 263-6666, (604) 689-7444** for information and reservations.

Special Programs
Ski Friends: Free mountain tours led by volunteer hosts, departing daily at 9:30, 10:30 and 1:00 from the north end of Whiskyjack Lodge.

For Families
With the 1996 expansion of Lake Louise's base facilities, children's services moved into larger, better quarters.

Nonskiing Children
Nursery: Programs for babies from 18 days to 18 months and toddlers from 18 to 35 months. Three-hour minimum stay. Reservations required for infants 18 months and younger, requested for others.

Skiing Children
Day Care: Informal supervised day care and a choice of one or two 1-hour lessons daily. Uses beginner lifts and special children's area, with kids' lift and outdoor play.

Noteworthy

In addition to bargain children's lift tickets for ages 7 to 12, a teen ticket for ages 13 to 17 is available for less than the cost of an adult ticket. Children under 6 ski free. The Alpha Play Station, isolated and with its own slow lift, is designed for very young skiers making their first turns. Lake Louise has designated slow skiing zones off the Eagle and Glacier chairlifts.

The Banff/Canmore franchise of **Baby's Away** rents cribs, high chairs, playpens and other supplies, **(403) 678-4380.**

Lake Louise's grandeur comprises just a part of the greater Banff scene.

Photo by Pat Morrow/Lake Louise

Kids Ski: Ski classes for ages 7 to 12. Children in full-day program get free lift ticket; morning-only participants need children's lift ticket. Optional supervised lunch on full-day program.

Teens
Teen Ski: Morning, afternoon or full-day program for ages 13 to 19, available second weekend in December to second weekend in January and again mid-February to late March.

For Racers

NASTAR: Open daily at the NASTAR Race Centre.

Sunshine Village

Profile
Sunshine Village could, with equal justification, be called Sensational Village or Snowfall Village. Located at the top of a 6-passenger transport gondola, Sunshine is an intimate group of small buildings surrounded by lifts and ski runs, a unique layout which is simply fabulous. The huge congenial bowl that for years comprised the totality of Sunshine's skiing was supplemented in 1995–96 with the addition of Goat's Eye Mountain, which offers the kind and scope of challenge that the resort previously lacked and underscores the resort's sensational side. With the highest resort elevation in the Canadian Rockies (the gondola doesn't count in terms of run-after-run skiability) and at least twice the average annual snowfall of just about every other ski area in the range, Sunshine packs a powder wallop that is rarely matched and never surpassed. But Sunshine is an apt name too—at least when the snow isn't falling and the full solar force plays over the mountains.

Whether you are day skiing or checking in, your introduction to Sunshine Village will be the bustling gondola terminal in a deep, dark valley. No scene in North America so perfectly mimics the Alps: pull into a small, congested parking lot next to a feeder lift that is reached by climbing a long flight of stairs, followed by a quarter-hour ride to a sunny plateau, where the village is located. It's like going from one world to another. Day skiers either disembark from the gondola at the new Goat's Eye station, a 10-minute ride, or continue to the village, a car-free gem, which

384

Mountain Stats—
Sunshine Village

Resort elevation 7,082 feet (2,160 meters)
Top of highest lift 8,954 feet (2,730 meters)
Bottom of lowest lift 5,440 feet (1,658 meters)
Total vertical 3,514 feet (1,070 meters)
Longest run 5 miles (8 kilometers)
Average annual snowfall 360 inches (9 meters)
Ski season mid-November to late May
Lifts one 6-passenger gondola, 3 high-speed quad chairlifts, 1 triple, 4 doubles, 2 T-bars, 2 beginner tows
Capacity 19,200 skiers per hour
Terrain 85 trails, 2,200 acres (20% beginner and novice, 55% intermediate, 25% advanced and expert)
Mountain dining Sunshine Village day lodge atop the gondola station with deli, cafeteria, saloon and pub and snack shop at the Old Sunshine Lodge; Goat's Eye lodge with food service at the base of the Goat's Eye chair
Snow reports (403) 762-6543 (Banff), **(403) 277-SNOW** (Calgary)

Photo courtesy Sunshine Village Ski Resort

Sunset at Sunshine Village with a grandiose panorama.

bustles while day skiers are around but quiets to surreal tranquillity in the evening. Then, the feeling of a private mountain retreat is palpable.

The village is located in the cusp of a natural bowl with skiing around the compass. The WaWa T-bar serves east-facing terrain that catches the morning sun and is a good way to start the day. Novices can ski a long run called Meadow Park, intermediates cruise down WaWa Bowl or Tincan Alley and advanced skiers shoot such steeps as Birdcage and Star Trek. On powder days, the Strawberry and Standish chairs, climbing up behind the village to the upper portions of Mt. Standish, serve north-facing runs where the fresh snow lingers longer. The new Strawberry Park quad also accesses the Assiniboine T-bar which leads to a huge amount of gentle green-circle and blue-square terrain that covers a large expanse of the lower bowl. Facing primarily southwest, these easy runs warm up by mid-morning and stay that way well into the afternoon.

But the most exhilarating part of the bowl is the vast arc that defines the classic Sunshine experience: wide open terrain and sensational views. Access to this prime parcel is first via the Angel high-speed quad which climbs from the village nearly two-thirds of the way up the bowl and then over to the Great Divide double chair for one of the most scenic lift rides in the Rockies and the only interprovincial one. The lift climbs to the top of Lookout Mountain on the Continental Divide, crossing the Alberta–British Columbia line in the process. Another option from a clearing not far from the village is the TeePee Town double chair. You can use it to reach the Great Divide chair, but it's most popular with skiers and riders who like to dance down a ten-pack of fall-away steeps and chutes that earn their black diamonds both on the bases of pitch and bumps. When the clouds are hanging low and the snow is falling, you'll be wise to avoid the high, tree-free slopes that stretch across the bowl on either side of the Great Divide lift, but when the sun is out and the sky is blue, you'd be foolish to ski anywhere else. You can ski a few marked and groomed pistes etched into the snow, but you can also pick your own line, skimming over snowfields, through gullies and over little air-catching lips. You'll find a few genuine steeps up high, but acres and acres of sublime mid-level slopes—and even a long green all the way from the top. When the sun is out and Sunshine lives up to its name, you won't find any better skiing than these fabulous open slopes.

To reach Goat's Eye from the village, you either need to download on the gondola or take the Fireweed T-bar to a road that leads to Sunshine's new prized parcel. Goat's Eye is like an area within an area, featuring a new day lodge and Canada's swiftest high-speed chair. The top of Goat's is wide open, much like Lookout Mountain—only steeper. Halfway down, rock walls appear and so do trees. The open terrain quickly funnels into just seven cut trails that steepen perceptibly. You'll find blue-square options like Chicken, Sergei's Shortcut and The Big Woody, but lower Goat's Eye is double-black-diamond steeps, in a sense like the lower Lookout runs, off the TeePee Town chair—only steeper. Free Fall and Hell's Kitchen are arrow-straight, skydiver steep pitches that are as gnarly as they come. The double blacks boast an average 48-degree pitch, and the single blacks like After-burner and Gladerunner don't feel much milder. Only four can be groomed by winch cat; the others are simply too steep.

Goat's Eye is not only challenging, but it is beautiful too. Named for a distinctive rock formation with

A skier goes through the "goat's eye," an unusual rock formation on a slope at Sunshine Village.

a hole in it that resembles a goat's head, this new area holds the potential for additional development. Picnic tables on a spectacular overlook called Scurfield Point, after the family that owns the area, signal what might eventually be the site for a mountain restaurant. Casual skiers and most vacationers didn't need the likes of Goat's Eye, but for hard-skiing Calgarians who make a day trip out of Banff area and eat black diamonds before lunch, both the new challenge and the shortened gondola ride make Sunshine legitimate competition to Lake Louise and its awe-inspiring steeps. At the end of the day, you can either ride the gondola down or join the hordes cruising, skidding, sliding or really carving down the 2 1/2-mile-long ski-out to the parking lot.

Snowboarding

Riders love Sunshine's wide open terrain and challenging steeps. The gondola provides easier access from the village to the Goat's Eye area than taking the long, super-flat road called Juniper and then riding the T-bar.

Ski School Programs

For information and advance bookings for adults' and children's programs, call **(403) 762-6560.**

Introductory Programs

Never Ever Package: Low-cost lift, lesson and rental package. Register at the Spoke N Edge at the gondola base by 10:00 A.M. for program that runs from 10:30 to 1:00 P.M.

Advanced and Specialty Programs

Ski Improvement Clinics: All levels from low intermediate up. Available for ages 13 and over.
Short Turn Clinic: 1 1/2-hour group lessons for intermediate and advanced skiers, focusing on groomed terrain, moguls and racing.
Dave Irwin's Master Ski Camps: Three-day camps for intermediate and advanced skiers. Directed by former World Cup downhill star Dave Irwin and held on Goat's Eye Mountain. For information and reservations, call **(800) 661-1676.**

Special Program

Free Guided Mountain Tours: Meets daily at 10:30 A.M. and 1:00 P.M. from Sunshine Village.

386

Photo courtesy Sunshine Village Ski Resort

For Families
Nonskiing Children
Kids Kampus Daycare: For nonskiers, ages 19 months to 6 years. Open from 8:30 A.M. to 4:30 P.M. Can be booked by the hour with lunch option. Reservations recommended, **(403) 762-6560.**

Skiing Children
Kids Kampus: Wee Angels ski lessons available for children from age 3 enrolled in Kids Kampus.
Wee Angels: 1½-hour afternoon beginner lesson for 3- to 5-year-olds. Includes use of skis and boots.
Ski Angels: Fun classes, divided by age and ability, for beginning, novice and intermediate skiers ages 6 to 12. Half-day and full-day programs with lunch.
Young Devils: Ages 6 to 12, all levels, available half or full day, with or without lunch.

Banff Mt. Norquay

Profile

Banff's underrated hometown hill is one of western Canada's classic ski areas, yet it has been overshadowed and eclipsed by its giant neighbors and struggled in recent years both financially and in name. It has long ranked as one of the Rocky Mountains' mighty midgets, conveniently located, packing a lot of challenge into relatively modest-sized terrain. Long called Mt. Norquay and respected as a challenging little ski area, previous owners expanded it by putting in lifts on an adjacent and easier sector and renamed it Mystic Ridge Norquay. In 1995, a new owner group took over the ski area, maintaining its family and racing orientation and trying to solidify the niche it has long maintained. Loyalists, who persist in calling it Norquay, no matter who owns it and how they want to market it, don't need to be convinced of its charms. Visitors, who can ski it on Banff/Lake Louise multiday tickets or with the Banff Club Ski program, find it convenient for mixing a half day on the slopes with a half day in town, for a morning ski before departing for Calgary and a late-afternoon or evening flight or simply as a congenial change of pace.

The area's long-standing reputation for challenge is based on the first runs you see upon approaching the area: a quintet of super-steep,

Mountain Stats—
Banff Mt. Norquay

Top of highest lift 7,000 feet (2,133 meters)
Bottom of lowest lift 5,350 feet (1,636 meters)
Total vertical 1,650 feet (497 meters)
Longest run 3/4 mile (1.2 kilometers)
Average annual snowfall 120 inches (300 centimeters)
Ski season early December to mid-April
Lifts 1 high-speed quad chairlift, 1 fixed-grip quad, 2 double chairs, 1 platterpull, 1 beginner tow
Capacity 6,300 skiers per hour
Terrain 25 trails, 160 acres (11% beginner and novice, 45% intermediate, 44% advanced and expert)
Snowmaking 90%
Night skiing off the Cascade and Sundance lifts, Wednesdays from 4:00 to 9:00 P.M. (perhaps additional nights in the future)
Snow reports (403) 762-4421 (Banff), **(403) 221-8259** (Calgary)

387

mogul-studded freefalls served by the old Norquay double chair. Hardcore Norquay regulars pull into the upper parking lot and rarely visit the rest of the mountain. For them, no runs anywhere can match Upper Lone Pine and Gun Run, a dynamite black-diamond duo as demanding as any trails in the Rockies. Memorial Bowl isn't a bowl at all but a generous, consistent swath with an average 34-degree pitch that rarely feels the blade of a snowcat. Even North American, the easiest of these runs, legitimately earns its black diamond.

This terrain is truly formidable, but three more chairs climb up roughly parallel, stepped-back parallel ridges and serve the area's mid-level runs. Anyone who continues to the lower parking lot, just a bit deeper into the valley, comes upon the main base area, the welcome gateway to this more benign terrain. In addition to a small, sheltered beginner slope, you'll find the Cascade double chair, which itself accesses some fine blue-square slopes, a good intro-to-black-diamonds mogul field called Temptation and traverses to the short Spirit double chair and

Noteworthy

While many ski schools have cut their group lessons to 1 1/2 or 1 3/4 hours, Norquay maintains the traditional two-hour lesson format.

the long Mystic Express quad way beyond. Because it lies deep in a valley under some very steep summits, this terrain has a really rugged and interesting feeling. Lying below the true Mystic Ridge of the topographic maps, the skiable terrain was cut from forested ridges, sidewalls, chutes and deep gullies. The easiest run you'll find here is a long cruiser called Banshee that is a real blue, but most of the blue squares come in pairs, signifying more challenge than "intermediate" would indicate. Lower Excalibur, Illusion and Knight Flight are graced with double blue squares and are tough enough for many skiers. Because it lies below the really steep ridge, avalanche control on the upper sections of these runs is as assiduous as at larger, higher areas with above-treeline skiing, and in fact, portions of the intermediate trails called Imp and Bruno's Gully are frequently closed because of slide hazard.

Still, most of the blue-square runs off the Mystic Express march down the hill in a cavalcade of real cruising pleasure. Knight Flight and Banshee are long, lush runs with interesting contours and curves. Black Magic, K-Proof and Excalibur are black-diamond runs close to the liftline that are best for skiers and riders who aren't quite up to ultrachallenging terrain served by the Norquay chair but want something darker than blue. When conditions are right, experts can also drop into the Sun Chutes and a rocket ride down the gully floor.

The shorter runs off the Spirit quad nestled on a neat little hill rank between the breathtaking steeps of the old Norquay terrain and the sinuous outback trails of the newer Mystic Ridge development. Many skiers use Spirit as a linchpin between two more prepossessing sectors, but they have charm of their own. Wide, relatively uncrowded

and graciously cut, they are ideal for groups of casual skiers and families just looking for easy going—and the congeniality of a quad chairlift for the ride back up.

Snowboarding

Most of Norquay's slopes and trails make for excellent riding, though some of the traverses between the lifts can be tedious. The area has carved a sensational 700-foot-long half-pipe out of the snow beside the Cascade chair, and the old T-bar line on the side of the Phantom trail off the Spirit quad makes for some great riding too. A reduced-rate Cascade lift ticket is available. Solidifying Norquay's commitment to snowboarding is the Unlimited Snowboard School, which offers a commendable selection of introductory and advanced programs for adults and children. Off-piste free-riding, freestyle, extreme riding and high pro freecarving are among the upper-level specialties offered.

Ski School Programs

For information or reservations for **Ski School** programs, call **(403) 762-4421**; for details on snowboarding instruction, call the **Unlimited Snowboard School** at **(403) 762-8208** (Norquay), **(403) 762-3725** (Banff).

Introductory Programs

Learn to Ski: Lift ticket, two-hour lesson and equipment rental package, available in economical day and night versions.

Discover Skiing: Intense introductory package with Saturday and Sunday lift tickets, eight hours of lessons and equipment rental.

First Tracks: Introduction to snowboarding given by the Unlimited Snowboard School, with three-hour lesson only or packaged with rental equipment options. Offered during the day and on Wednesday evenings.

Advanced and Specialty Programs

Ski Improvement Clinics: Two-hour group lesson for all ability levels. Maximum of eight skiers per group.

Unlimited Snowboard School: Specialty programs for riders of all levels, including intro, Two Timer for second-day adult snowboarders and true advanced skills.

For Families
Nonskiing Children
Kid's Place: Day care for ages 19 months to 6 years, with optional lessons for ages 3 to 6. Open from 9:00 A.M. to 4:00 P.M. Reservations required.

Skiing Children
Ski & Play: Fun-filled entry-level classes for ages 3 to 6.

Mini-Mites: Introduction to skiing for ages 4 and 5. One-hour lessons offered four times daily for eight weeks. Also offered for three consecutive days in spring.

Discover Skiing: Two-hour introductory lessons, Cascade lift ticket and rental equipment for ages 6 to 12.

Club Adventure: Half-day or full-day class with optional lunch for ages 6 to 12.

Kids Ski Camps: Multiday programs during school vacations for ages 6 to 12.

Rec Training: Ten Sundays of introduction to racing for ages 6 to 12.

Kids' Board Camps: Two-day snowboarding camps with maximum of four youngsters for ages 7 to 13.

Nordic Skiing

As you'd expect of ski centers surrounded by national parkland, Nordic options abound in the area. Eight trailheads surround the Banff Townsite and access routes from basic to difficult. Some 50 miles of the most varied marked and/or groomed and trackset trails surround Lake Louise, ranging from ultra-easy paths across the lake's frozen surface to mountain touring routes with significant challenge and vertical. Eight trailheads surround Banff, including Forty Mile

Aerial view of Banff Mt. Norquay's famous front face.

Creek, accessible directly from Norquay's base. Details and trail maps are available from **Information Centres** at **224 Banff Avenue** in **Banff, (403) 762-4256,** and **Lake Louise Village** next to Samson Mall, **(403) 522-5833.** Guided cross-country ski and snowshoe tours are organized by **White Mountain Adventures, (403) 678-4099,** and **Michele's Cross-Country Ski Tours & Lessons** at the Post Hotel in Lake Louise, **(403) 522-3989.**

But the greatest treat for touring skiers are excursions to the region's distinctive backcountry lodges. From the fringes of the Lake Louise Ski Area near the Temple Lodge, it's roughly a 7-mile (11-kilometer) ski-in to Skoki Lodge. This historic and rustic backcountry cabin was built in 1930 (the "new" wing dates from 1936), and it still is unburdened by electricity or running water. You'll cross Boulder Pass and Deception Pass, which present steep ascents on the way up and rollicking descents on the downside. You can ski to Skoki for afternoon tea and pastries, or you can book an overnight in this splendid retreat and even ski to Marlin Lake or Red Deer Lakes. For reservations, **Skoki Lodge, P.O. Box 5, Lake Louise, AB T0L 1E0; (403) 522-3555.**

From the Red Earth trailhead, 12 miles (18 kilometers) west of Banff, you can ski 9 miles (13 kilometers) to Shadow Lake Lodge, once a Canadian Pacific Railroad rest house, now a rustic lodge accommodating up to 24 backcountry skiers in the main house and cozy log cabins which also serves afternoon tea and meals. It is also

389

Noteworthy

The heady decisions about where to ski can be made by Banff Club Ski, a long-popular package that includes three or five days of skiing or snowboarding in a small group and with an instructor/guide, liftline priority, a special dinner and a variety of other services. Club Ski goes to Lake Louise Mondays and Thursdays, Sunshine Village Tuesdays and Fridays and Banff Mt. Norquay Wednesdays, which happens to be dinner and night-skiing night. In addition to the adult program, Club Ski Jr. is offered for youngsters from 6 to 12, combining the individual ski areas' children's ski schools with complimentary bus transportation. The programs can be booked at any of the three areas' ski school desks, at the Ski Banff/Lake Louise offices in the Banff Avenue Mall (225 Banff Avenue), at the Banff Springs Hotel or Chateau Lake Louise and other hotels in the area. You can also call **(403) 762-4561.**

possible to ski in from Sunshine Village, Egypt Lake or Highway 93. For reservations, **Shadow Lake Lodge, P.O. Box 954, Banff, AB T0L 0C0; (403) 762-5454.**

Heli-Skiing

There is no heli-skiing directly in Banff National Park, but operators from Canmore (see Kananaskis Country chapter) to Panorama aggressively market one-day and multiday trips to Banff and Lake Louise guests. Much of the heli-skiing actually takes place across the border in British Columbia, which requires a commute from Banff. Heli-skiing operators seeking clients among Banff skiers and snowboarders include **Canadian Mountain Holidays,** headquartered in Banff but operating in nine areas from the Adamants to Valemont, **(403) 762-7100; R.K. Heli-ski Panorama, (403) 762-3771** (Banff), **(250) 342-3889** (Invermere), and **Mike Wiegele Helicopter Skiing** in Blue River, **(250) 673-8381.**

WHERE TO STAY

Banff

Luxury Accommodations

Banff Caribou Lodge

Stylish new lodge with 200 well-appointed rooms (65 non-smoking), including seven loft suites and 29 balcony rooms. Located about a 10-minute walk from downtown. Hotel offers Caribou Ski School program, including personalized ski session, transportation to ski areas and liftline priority. Children 16 and under stay free in parents' room. Ski packages. Daily housekeeping, bell service, same-day laundry service, massage. Restaurant, lounge, whirlpool, steamroom, saunas, exercise equipment. **521 Banff Ave., P.O. Box 279, Banff, AB T0L 0C0; (800) 563-8764, (403) 762-5887.**

Banff Park Lodge

Sporty four-star ski hotel in great location, half-block from downtown. Contemporary luxury lodge with 210 spacious and well-appointed rooms, some non-smoking and some with fireplaces. Moderate winter rates. Daily housekeeping, 24-hour front desk, bell and room service. Indoor swimming pool, fitness facilities, sauna, hot tub, two restaurants, lounge, retail shops adjacent. **222 Lynx St., Banff, AB T0L 0C0; (800) 661-9266, (403) 762-4433.**

Banff Springs Hotel

Flagship of the CP Hotel chain and the first among equals in the realm of luxury ski hotels. One of the most magnificent hotels in all the Rockies and a tourist attraction in its own right. Turreted landmark, opened in 1888, overlooking Banff. Nicknamed "Castle in the Snow." Award-winning hotel (including being named one of the 20 best non-U.S. hotels in the world by *Condé Nast Traveler.* Recently renovated and restored with magnificent, opulently furnished public spaces and 817 rooms in many categories, from modest singles and doubles to monumental suites with private in-room whirlpool tubs. On site is Solace, outstanding $12 million health and beauty spa built in 1995, featuring men's and women's fireplace lounges, indoor and outdoor heated pools, children's wading pool, private and coed solariums, three cascading mineral whirlpools, men's and women's saunas, whirlpools and inhalation pools, aerobic studio and classes, cardio and strength conditioning area, massage therapy, beauty and body treatments, personal fitness training, nutritional and fitness consultations and more. Ski, spa, combined and other packages. Daily housekeeping, 24-hour front desk, ski storage, room service, bell staff, valet parking, laundry and dry cleaning services, complimentary town and Norquay shuttle. Spa (as detailed above), shopping arcades with 50 shops (including ski, ice skating and snowshoe rentals), 17 restaurants and lounges, game area, bowling lanes, indoor miniature golf, outdoor ice skating rink. **P.O Box 960, Banff, AB T0L 0C0; (403) 762-2211, (800) 441-4141** for CP Hotels reservations.

Buffalo Mountain Lodge

Lovely and well-appointed retreat, with 85 guest units, including rooms and loft or balcony suites and private chalets, some with kitchens or kitchenettes and all with gas-log or wood-burning fireplaces. Hand-hewn log lodge construction and custom country furnishings, including down-filled duvets and feather pillows. Complimentary in-room coffeemakers. Secluded and tranquil, on nine wooded acres overlooking Banff Townsite. Daily housekeeping, daily firewood stocking, bell staff. Restaurant, lobby bar, whirlpool, steamroom. **Tunnel Mountain Rd., P.O. Box 1326, Banff, AB T0L 0C0; (800) 661-1367, (403) 762-2400.**

Dynasty Inn

Well designed and furnished new hotel, with 95 attractive rooms ranging from hotel rooms to loft suites. Some non-smoking, some with Jacuzzi tub and/or gas fireplace. Most with balconies. Daily housekeeping, bell staff. Whirlpool, sauna, steamroom, ski storage. **501 Banff Ave., P.O. Box 1018, Banff, AB T0L 0C0; (800) 667-1464, (403) 762-8844.**

Rimrock Resort Hotel

Stylish new hotel with 345 well-appointed rooms (including 41 suites) with mini-bars and other amenities. Fine public spaces in grand building that was well conceived and attractively decorated

in a contemporary and elegant manner. Top restaurant on site. Daily housekeeping, 24-hour front desk, 24-hour room service, valet, concierge, complimentary town and ski shuttle. Two restaurants, two lounges, indoor swimming pool, health and fitness center, business center, hot tub, sauna. **Mountain Ave., P.O. Box 1800, Banff, AB T0L 0C0; (800) 661-1587, (403) 762-3356, (403) 265-5110** in Calgary.

Mid-Priced Accommodations

Banff International Hotel

Downtown hotel with 125 spacious, comfortable rooms at moderate prices. Some rooms non-smoking. Contemporary mountain chalet style. Family units. In-room mini-bars. Daily housekeeping. Restaurant, lounge, whirlpool. **333 Banff Ave., P.O. Box 1040, Banff, AB T0L 0C0; (800) 665-5666, (403) 762-5666.**

Banff Ptarmigan Inn

Convenient downtown hotel with 145 European-style rooms with variety of bed configurations from one double to two queens or one queen and two singles. Thirty-two non-smoking rooms and 33 balcony rooms. All rooms with complimentary in-room coffee, down-filled duvets and TV with in-room movies. Children 16 and under stay free in parents' room. Ski packages. Daily housekeeping, same-day laundry service, massage. Restaurant (featuring economical all-you-can-eat skiers' buffet), lounge (serving complimentary after-ski beverages and snacks), ski lockers, waxing and tuning room, ski shop, gift shop, exercise facility, hot tub, sauna. **337 Banff Ave., P.O. Box 1840, Banff, AB T0L 0C0; (800) 661-8310, (403) 762-2207.**

Bow View Motor Lodge

Unprepossessing, moderately priced motor lodge with quiet riverside location just two blocks from downtown. Fifty-seven rooms, most with balconies and some non-smoking. Daily housekeeping, room service. Coffee shop, whirlpool, sauna. **228 Bow Ave., P.O. Box 339, Banff, AB T0L 0C0; (800) 661-1565, (403) 762-8093.**

Inns of Banff

One hundred eighty sizable rooms, some non-smoking and some with balconies, in attractive, well-located complex close to downtown. Twenty-four-hour front desk, daily housekeeping. Outdoor heated swimming pool, hot tub, sauna, restaurant, lounge, ski shop. **600 Banff Ave., P.O. Box 1077, Banff, AB T0L 0C0; (800) 661-1272, (403) 762-2261.**

Mount Royal Hotel
Well-equipped, block-long 136-room hotel in the center of Banff. Comfortable rooms, some non-smoking. Twenty-four-hour front desk, daily housekeeping. Restaurant, lounge, whirlpool, sauna, fitness facilities. **138 Banff Ave., Banff, AB T0L 0C0; (800) 267-3035, (403) 762-3331.**

Economy Accommodations

Banff International Hostel
Private and shared accommodations for 154 thrifty skiers, including rooms for two to six and also some family/couple rooms. Located 3 kilometers from town center. Use of self-serve kitchen and lounge area with fireplace. Non-smoking hostel. Ski packages. Cafe, ski workroom, laundry facilities. **Tunnel Mountain Rd., P.O. Box 1358, Banff, AB T0L 0C0; (800) 363-0096, (403) 762-6204, (403) 762-4122.**

392

Banff Voyager Inn
Economical 88-room motor inn close to downtown. Daily housekeeping. Restaurant, lounge, sauna, whirlpool, outdoor pool. **555 Banff Ave., P.O. Box 1540, Banff, AB T0L 0C0; (800) 879-1991, (403) 762-3301.**

Blue Mountain Lodge
Beautifully renovated turn-of-the-century lodge close to town, now a ten-room B&B inn. Some rooms with private, some with shared baths. No smoking. Kitchen privileges. Daily housekeeping, healthy breakfasts. **327 Caribou St., P.O. Box 2733, Banff, AB T0L 0C0; (403) 762-5134.**

King Edward Hotel
Recently renovated 21-room downtown hotel with exceptional convenience to shopping, dining and nightlife. Some rooms smoke-free. Daily housekeeping, room service. **137 Banff Ave., P.O. Box 8000, Banff, AB T0L 0C0; (800) 344-4232, (403) 762-2202.**

Y Mountain Lodge
Operated by the YWCA and one of the Rockies' best values. Clean and comfortable coed accommodations for 40, including private rooms with or without private bath, family rooms and dorms. Hearty, homemade and inexpensive meals also available in cafe. Smoke-free. Ski packages. Riverside location, 1 1/2 blocks from downtown. **102 Spray Ave., P.O. Box 520, Banff, AB T0L 0C0; (800) 813-4138, (403) 762-3560.**

Condominiums

Douglas Fir Resort & Chalets
Family-friendly resort, 133 spacious condo-style units. Full-kitchens and wood-burning fireplaces. Excellent sports and recreational facilities, including the only indoor waterslides in the Canadian Rockies. Indoor pool, fitness facilities, sauna, whirlpool. Located a short drive from town. **Tunnel Mountain Rd., P.O. Box 1228, Banff, AB T0L 0C0; (800) 267-8774, (800) 661-9267, (403) 762-5591.**

Lake Louise

Information and reservations, **(800) 258-SNOW.**

Luxury Accommodations

Chateau Lake Louise
Extraordinary hotel in even better location at the end of Lake Louise. Excellent views of lake, Victoria Glacier and surrounding mountains, plus fine services and top-notch facilities. Total renovation completed in 1990. Huge public spaces and 515 spacious rooms, many with lake or mountain panoramas. Nearly half non-smoking rooms. Distinctive and memorable hotel. Daily housekeeping, 24-hour front desk, ski storage, room service, bell staff, valet parking, laundry and dry cleaning services. complimentary ski shuttle. Restaurants, lounges, 35 shops, health club, heated indoor swimming pool, steamroom, whirlpool, on-site ice skating and cross-country skiing. **Lake Louise, AB T0L 1E0; (403) 522-3511, (800) 441-4141** for CP Hotels reservations.

Post Hotel
A quaint corner of Europe in a Rocky Mountain setting. Spacious log lodge and private cabins.

Ambiance is at once rustic and elegant. Ninety-five rooms including split-level suites, all well-appointed and many with stunning views. Some rooms with kitchens, many with whirlpool tubs. Beautifully furnished with solid Canadian pine furniture and down-filled comforters. Member of prestigious Relais & Chateaux group. Five minutes from the slopes; cross-country trails outside the door. Daily housekeeping, 24-hour front desk, afternoon tea served in the lobby. Dining room, lounge. **200 Pipestone Rd., P.O. Box 69, Lake Louise, AB T0L 1E0; (800) 661-1586, (403) 522-3595, (403) 265-4900** in Calgary.

Mid-Priced Accommodations

Deer Lodge

A lot of quaintness and character for the money. Fine, moderately priced mountain resort, grown from a 1921 teahouse, winterized and restored in 1988. Quiet and charming retreat, with 73 rooms, all with private baths, antique and custom furniture and down comforters on all the beds— but no in-room television and few in-room phones. Beautiful stone fireplace in main lobby. Daily housekeeping. Rooftop hot tub. **109 Lake Louise Dr., P.O. Box 100, Lake Louise, AB T0L 1E0; (800) 661-1595, (403) 522-3747, (403) 237-8173** in Calgary.

Lake Louise Inn

Attractive and comfortable five-building complex with 221 rooms, recently expanded to include 36 condo-style units with kitchenettes and/or fireplaces. Many hotel and chalet rooms, some poolside and some with lofts. Closest lodging to Lake Louise Ski Area. Daily housekeeping, 24-hour front desk. Children 16 and under stay free in parents' room. Two restaurants, two lounges, indoor pool, whirlpool, sauna, guest laundry, ski storage and workshop. **210 Village Rd., P.O. Box 209, Lake Louise, AB T0L 1E0; (800) 661-9237, (403) 522-3791.**

Economy Accommodations

Lake Louise International Hostel

Newly expanded hostel accommodation for 150 thrifty guests, including 2-, 4- and 6-bed rooms plus 25 family/couple rooms with private washrooms and hot showers. Reading lounge with stone fireplace and open beamed ceiling. Cafe/restaurant, guest laundry, ski workshop, sauna, game room. **Village Rd., P.O. Box 115, Lake Louise, AB T0L 1E0; (403) 522-2200.**

Sunshine Village

Sunshine Inn

The Banff area's only ski-in/ski-out hotel. Center of action by day but tranquil and quiet in the evening. Grown from Sunshine's original log lodge to cozy 85-room hotel. Accommodations include hotel rooms, chalet-style fireplace rooms and suites, some with private Jacuzzis. Family favorite. Ski packages. Daily housekeeping, bell staff. Restaurant, lounge, outdoor hot pool, sauna. **P.O. Box 1510, Sunshine Village, Banff, AB T0L 0C0; (800) 661-1676, (403) 762-6555.**

Elsewhere

Emerald Lake Lodge

Historic lodge in Yoho National Park, beautifully restored in 1986. Secluded and romantic setting and spectacular lakeside location. Off the beaten path for Alpine purists—40 kilometers (25 miles) to Lake Louise—but ideal for winter retreat with shuttle service to Lake Louise Ski Area, on-site cross-country and snowshoeing and utter tranquillity and beauty. Eighty-five rooms in 24 cabin-style buildings, each with lake views, wood-burning fieldstone fireplace, in-room coffee-makers and lovely country-style furnishings. Cozy bar is an 1890 Yukon original, and award-winning chef specializes in Rocky Mountain cuisine served in atmospheric dining room. Daily housekeeping, bell service, daily firewood stocking. Restaurant, lounge, exercise equipment, sauna, outdoor hot tub. **P.O. Box 10, Field, BC V0A 1G0; (800) 663-8338, (250) 343-6724.**

West Louise Lodge

Affordable lodge, located 9 miles (16 kilometers) west of Lake Louise. Twenty-one double rooms and five suites with loft bedroom, wood-burning fireplace and separate living room. Ski packages include daily breakfast. Daily housekeeping. Dining room, lounge, swimming pool, sauna. **Field, BC V0A 1G0; (250) 343-6311.**

DINING OUT

Banff

Athena's Pizza & Spaghetti House
Casual downtown restaurant, popular with budget-watchers and families. Pizza, steaks, ribs and well-known Italian dishes dominate. Lunch and dinner. Free delivery in Banff. **112 Banff Ave., Banff; (403) 760-3030.**

Barberry Coast
Lively spot starting at early lunch (11:00 A.M.) and winding down with dancing till very, very late (2:00 A.M.). Variety of hot tapas. Made-from-scratch pastas and pizzas. Sandwiches and burgers too. Children's menu. All dishes available for takeout (no extra charge) or delivery (slight additional charge). Good happy hour and nightly entertainment. **229 Banff Ave., Banff; (403) 762-4616.**

394 Buffalo Mountain Lodge Dining Room
Gorgeous restaurant with high, beamed ceiling and elegant country furnishings. Innovative yet hearty cuisine, featuring fresh ingredients and interesting combinations. Fine soups, homemade breads, freshly baked pastries and excellent desserts compliment interesting entrées based on traditional French and newer California traditions. Smoke-free restaurant. Fine wine list. Reservations recommended. **Buffalo Mountain Lodge, Tunnel Mountain Rd., Banff; (403) 762-2400.**

Bumper's Beef House
Alberta beef is king in this merry steakery. Prime rib, steaks of various sorts, salmon and all-you-can-eat salad bar make for a hearty dinner. Lounge. Reservations recommended. **603 Banff Ave., Banff; (403) 762-2622.**

The Caboose
Railroadiana and popular dishes, including Rocky Mountain trout, steak, lobster, prime rib and crab. Self-service salad cart. Lounge. Open nightly for dinner. Reservations suggested. **Railroad Depot, Elk and Lynx Sts., Banff; (403) 762-3622, (403) 762-2102.**

The Chinook
Hotel's family restaurant, serving breakfast, lunch and dinner. Regional and contemporary Italian cuisine at dinner. Popular Friday buffet from 5:00 to 9:30 P.M. with antipasto, salad selection, weekly seafood, poultry and meat specials, pasta bar, pizza bar and Italian ices and other specialty desserts. Children 5 and under free; discounts for older kids and seniors. **Banff Park Lodge, 222 Lynx St., Banff; (403) 762-4433.**

Coyote's Deli & Grill
The Southwest, Alberta-style, which means Southwest plus fresh pasta. Breakfast, lunch and dinner in pleasant, casual setting. Tortilla Soup, Smoked Chicken Pizza, Black Bean Chili with Striploin and Asiago, and Spinach Fettuccini with Mushrooms and Prosciutto trendily highlight the menu. Non-smoking restaurant. Takeout available. Dinner reservations accepted. **206 Caribou St., Banff; (403) 762-3963.**

Earls
Quality and freshness at moderate prices. Upstairs location and pleasing atmosphere. Selections for light eaters and gluttons alike. Good drinks and appetizers, gourmet burgers, fresh pasta, steak, chicken and home-baked desserts. **229 Banff Ave., Banff; (403) 762-4414.**

Giorgio's Trattoria
Contemporary Italian dining emporium, featuring pizza from a wood-burning oven and pasta in an array of flavors. Relaxing and moderately priced restaurant serving dinner only. Reservations accepted for parties of six or more. **219 Banff Ave., Banff; (403) 762-5114.**

Grizzly House
Romantic and atmospheric restaurant catering to hungry hedonists. Private dining rooms for two (and for four or six). Choice of 14 fondues, including meat, cheese, dessert and exotic (e.g., alligator or rattlesnake) versions. Open daily from 11:30 A.M. to midnight. Hundred-wine list. Reservations recommended. **207 Banff Ave., Banff; (403) 762-4055.**

Joe Btfsplk's Diner
Classic '50s-style diner with black-and-white tile floor, jukebox and ever-popular classics "like Mom used to make," served at breakfast (but not too early, starting at 8:00), lunch and dinner. Light fare and full meals. Children's menu. Cocktails. **221 Banff Ave., Banff; (403) 762-5529.**

Le Beaujolais

Banff's fine French restaurant. Atmospheric upstairs restaurant with excellent French food and classic service and excellent wine list. Open nightly for dinner. Reservations recommended. **212 Buffalo St., Banff; (403) 762-2712.**

Melissa's

Home cooking, Canadian-style. Rustic and cozy dining room inside a timbered vaguely English-country-looking building. Breakfast, lunch and dinner. Reservations accepted. **218 Lynx St., Banff; (403) 762-5511.**

Norquay Dining Room

Hearty breakfasts, light lunches and full-course Canadian and Italian dinners in downtown hotel restaurant. Friendly and hospitable. **Mt. Royal Hotel, 138 Banff Ave., Banff; (403) 762-3331.**

Paris's Restaurant

Established in 1903 and boasts of being Banff's oldest family restaurant. Name notwithstanding, not French but generally popular resort dishes, such as German specialties, steak, seafood and chicken. Live lobster. Soup and salad bar. Open for light lunches and full or light dinners. Cocktails. Reservations welcomed. **114 Banff Ave., Banff; (403) 762-3554.**

Pavilion Restaurant

Attractive hotel restaurant with an Italian accent. Known for antipasto buffet and varied pasta entrées. Open nightly for dinner. Reservations recommended. **Banff Springs Hotel, Banff; (403) 762-6860** before 5:00 P.M., **(403) 762-2211** after 5:00.

Primrose Restaurant

Stylish cafe-style hotel restaurant open continuously for breakfast, lunch, dinner, Sunday brunch and light snacks. Establishing a rep for popular Pasta Wednesdays, featuring salad bar and create-your-own pasta dishes. Fine desserts and good wine list. Excellent service, trendy cuisine and soft music at all times. Reservations recommended. **Rimrock Hotel, Sulphur Mountain Rd., Banff; (403) 762-3356.**

Ristorante Classico

Atmospheric hotel restaurant specializing in northern Italian cuisine. Elegant and charming dinner spot. Excellent views of Bow River Valley. Fine wine selection. Reservations recommended. **Rimrock Hotel, Sulphur Mountain Rd., Banff; (403) 762-3356.**

Rob Roy Dining Room

Elegant hotel restaurant, with gourmet meals and tableside preparation. Attentive service. Nightly dancing. Reservations strongly recommended. **Banff Springs Hotel, Banff; (403) 762-6860** before 5:00 P.M., **(403) 762-2211** after 5:00.

Smitty's

Family restaurant serving pancakes and waffles from 6:30 A.M. and steaks, chicken and burger favorites until 9:00 P.M. Reasonable prices and casual atmosphere. Cocktails. Children's and seniors' menus. **227 Banff Ave., Banff; (403) 762-2533.**

Sukiyaki House

Good Japanese restaurant, frequented by homesick visitors from Tokyo as well as North Americans and Europeans who want authenticity. Fresh sushi from fine sushi bar, plus steaks, beef, seafood, chicken and excellent noodle dishes. Large restaurant in convenient upstairs location. **Park Avenue Mall, 221 Banff Ave., Banff; (403) 762-2002.**

Ticino

Outstanding Swiss-Italian restaurant. Recently relocated but a Banff tradition for over 20 years. Cozy atmosphere and quality food, with wine list to match. Nightly prix fixe specials, plus fondue. Children's menu. Reservations recommended. **High Country Inn, 415 Banff Ave., Banff; (403) 762-3848.**

Lake Louise

Baker Creek Bistro

Fine dining in out-of-the-way rustic setting. Country ambiance. **Bow Valley Pkwy, Lake Louise; (403) 522-2182.**

Edelweiss Dining Room

Main hotel dining room, featuring excellent continental and Canadian specialties in elegant setting. Prepossessing architectural scale, with food "designed" to match. Reservations recommended. **Chateau Lake Louise, Lake Louise; (403) 522-3511.**

Mt. Fairview Dining Room

Lovely hotel restaurant, known for interesting and well-presented Rocky Mountain cuisine. Appetizers include Game Platter, Crisp Phyllo Tart of Wild Mushrooms and Salmon Leek Chowder. Entrées include game, free-range chicken, pork, beef and veal, all well prepared and beautifully presented. Desserts range from modest Trio of Cranberry Sorbets to waistline-expanding Rich Chocolate Cake with Preserved Black Berries. Excellent wine list, including dessert wines. Also open for breakfast and lunch. Dinner reservations recommended. **Deer Lodge, 109 Lake Louise Dr., Lake Louise; (403) 522-3747.**

Poppy Room Family Restaurant

Breakfast, lunch and early dinner (only until 7:30 P.M.) in informal hotel dining room. Sure-fire pleasing menus for youngsters and adults. **Chateau Lake Louise, Lake Louise; (403) 522-3511.**

Village Grill and Bar

Family restaurant serving breakfast, lunch and dinner. Chinese and Western food available at moderate prices. Open daily from 8:00 A.M. to 1:00 A.M. **Samson Mall, Lake Louise; (403) 522-3879.**

Walliser Stube

Intimate little bistro and wine bar, serving Swiss-style light meals and dinners. Open weeknight evenings and from noon on weekends. Good wine list and pleasant, continental atmosphere. Reservations recommended. **Chateau Lake Louise, Lake Louise; (403) 522-3511.**

Sunshine Village

Eagle's Nest Dining Room

Full-service restaurant in the Sunshine Inn, with more casual Chimney Corner Lounge adjacent for light meals and bar service. Open from 7:00 A.M. to 10:00 P.M., serving breakfast, lunch and dinner. Known for large portions and friendly service. Pleasant and convenient for resort guests. **Sunshine Inn, Sunshine Village; (403) 762-6500.**

NIGHTLIFE

Après-ski typically kicks off slopeside, especially on weekends when the Calgary crowd unwinds before heading home (Banff-dwellers are more likely to bolt for the buses as soon as the lifts close). Whenever sunshine and temperatures permit, the outdoor deck at Lake Louise's base sees immediate after-ski crowds, and with the redevelopment of the base, another spot will have materialized by the time the 1996–97 ski season cranks up. Trapper Bill's gets the first wave at Sunshine, followed by the WD Saloon which does a good happy hour business and later the Chimney Corner Lounge. From Norquay, you can ski to the Timberline Lodge which does a good happy hour with hot and cold drink specials and a free ride to town afterwards.

With more than a hundred restaurants, lounges and bars, Banff ranks as one of the most lavishly endowed after-ski resorts on the continent, but for many visitors, the evening activity of choice is shopping, shopping and more shopping. Banff Avenue, the town's lively main street, is lined with purveyors of everything from opulent furs to funky T-shirts. When temperatures drop, you can continue your browsing and buying at 10 indoor shopping malls downtown as well as concentrations of fine stores in the big hotels. You don't have to spend big to enjoy the bounty, for window shopping is free. **Banff Centre** hosts cultural and entertainment events including art exhibitions, lectures and educational programs and musical, dance and dramatic performances of all sorts, **St. Julien Rd., Banff, AB T0L 0C0; (403) 762-6100.**

In town, the most active spots are The Keg, The Rose & Crown, Magpie and Stump and Wild Bill's Legendary Saloon. Tommy's Neighborhood Pub has different two-for-one happy hour specials every night of the week from 4:00 to 9:00 and again from midnight to 2:00. Earls does Margarita Mondays, Wing Wednesdays and good non-themed after-ski the other days of the week. The Buffalo Paddock is a downstairs pub in the Mt. Royal Hotel with cocktails, light fare, billiards, darts, karaoke, off-track betting, video lottery and games galore. If there's a reggae group in town, you'll probably find them at Sherwood's, while the Barberry Coast books mostly good groups and offers nightly dancing. Alternative music and the young crowd it draws are most likely at Eddie's Back Alley. There's nightly piano entertainment at the Banff Park Lodge's Terrace and pool in many local pubs plus at King Eddy Billiards. Last call is at 2:00 in the late-night meccas.

Up at the Banff Springs Hotel, you can choose your style, including cocktails in the Rundle Lounge, dining and dancing in the baronial Rob Roy Dining Room, mingling at the sports bar called the Whiskey Creek Saloon or partying at The Works with music from the '50s to the '70s, big-screen TV and ample pub-type diversions. The Rimrock's Larkspur Lounge offers light meals, plus fireplace coziness and great Bow Valley views, and the Juniper Lounge is also congenial. In the quiet aerie of Sunshine Village, nightly activities are planned for adults and families, and the Chimney Corner Inn is a pleasant spot till midnight.

In Lake Louise Village, Charlie Two's Pub and the Saddleback Lounge are the best bets, with dancing at the former and live entertainment on weekends at the latter. The Outpost Pub in the Post Hotel cranks up on weekends at noon and at 4:30 midweek and is open until midnight. The hotel also serves a lovely afternoon tea from 2:00 to 5:00 P.M. daily. The Chateau Lake Louise offers a variety of watering holes, ranging from the coffee shop to the Glacier Saloon, a nightclub that cooks into the wee hours. The Chateau Lake Louise also organizes a weekly calendar of optional evening activities, some free and some not. Activities are geared for ski-weekers and kickoff with a Skiers' Reception at the Glacier Saloon. Midweek activities include a torchlight dinner and ski-down at Lake Louise's slopes on Monday nights, sports night at Charlie Two's or a sleighride on Tuesdays, Wild Bill's Western Ski Race or a choice of after-ski or skating parties on Wednesdays, a reception on Thursdays and a Ski Week Wind-Up Party and Kids' Night on Fridays. Saturday also brings the choice of movie night at Charlie Two's, a romantic dinner in a vintage railcar, a skating party or kids' party.

For more information, contact

Lake Louise Ski Area/Skiing Louise, 1550 Eighth St. SW, Ste. 505, Calgary, AB T2R 1K1; (403) 522-3555, fax (403) 522-2095
Sunshine Village, P.O. Box 1510, Banff, AB T0L 0C0; (403) 762-6500, fax (403) 762-6513
Banff Mt. Norquay, P.O. Box 219, Banff, AB T0L 0C0, (403) 762-4421, fax (403) 762-8133
Banff/Lake Louise Tourism Bureau, P.O. Box 1298, Banff, AB T0L 0C0; (403) 762-8421, fax (403) 762-8545
Banff Visitor Information Centre, 224 Banff Ave., Banff, AB T0L 0C0; (403) 762-8421

MARMOT BASIN

BACKDROP

The Canadian Rockies' northernmost ski resort is a two-fer: a very neat ski area called Marmot Basin and the beguiling town of Jasper. The appeals for visiting skiers and snowboarders include fabulous, usually uncrowded slopes, the knock-out scenery of the Far North and the sense of winter isolation in a very busy summer destination. Jasper Townsite, as the community is officially called, lies in the northern third of namesake Jasper National Park, the largest of the contiguous national parks and wilderness areas in the Canadian Rockies. The region's sharp-peaked granitic mountains striated in shades of gray provide unsurpassed scenery which is as grand in the winter as in the summer, but the atmosphere changes with the seasons. During the warm months, Jasper is loaded with sightseeing tourists, wildlife is scarce and prices are high. In winter, the tourists are all but gone, there's not a day when you don't spot some elk or deer right in town and to make things even better, prices drop to rockbottom. Although the thermometer often dips into the bottom of the scale too, the low-key friendly community doesn't hibernate but rather comes into its own as a beguiling ski town. This is a place where you'll most likely bundle up in your warmest clothing, don your face mask and crank up your boot heaters to ski and enjoy this casual, friendly and extremely economical ski destination.

THE LAY OF THE LAND

The town of Jasper nestles in a generous valley where the Miette River flows into the Athabasca. Lovely lakes surround the town, which lies at a comfortable 3,500 feet, and the ski area is 19 kilometers (about 12 miles) to the south. The access road is a hairpin-laden twister that gains most of the 2,000-foot elevation difference between town and ski area. Marmot Basin itself lies within Jasper National Park boundaries.

GETTING THERE

Jasper is 362 kilometers (234 miles) west of the provincial capital of Edmonton, which is served by major Canadian air carriers. Rental cars are available. **Greyhound Bus Lines, (403) 852-3926** in Jasper or **(403) 421-4211** in Edmonton, or **VIA Rail, (800) 561-8630,** connect Edmonton and Jasper. The drive along Hwy 16, also known as the Yellowhead Highway, is one of Alberta's scenic routes. Another popular option is to combine Jasper/Marmot with the Banff area, flying into Calgary and out of Edmonton or vice versa. The drive between the two resorts is 330 kilometers (190 miles) over the Icefields Parkway, one of the most scenic drives in North America. Once in Jasper, you don't need a car for most activities. If you stay in town, you'll find it compact enough for walk-around shopping and dining, and **Heritage Tours, (403) 852-5154,** operates daily buses between the town and the area. Jasper Park Lodge guests ride the resort's own shuttle.

PROFILE

Marmot's last name is Basin, quite appropriate for this vast cirque. However, when you're skiing it, the feeling is more "mountain"—a genuine mountain with a pointed summit, several subsidiary peaks and a collection of awe-inspiring slopes, scarps, cliffs, rock bands, walls and chutes. Perhaps it's fair to say that it looks and feels like a concave rather than a convex mountain, with all the dimension and complexity such an analogy implies. The terrain is spectacular, both visually and in the way it skis. While more than a third of the runs are suitable for low-level skiers, the image skiers carry of Marmot Basin is of high, steep, open slopes buried in more powder than the modest 160-inch annual snowfall would imply.

The ski area's infrastructure is simple and functional. The base facilities—a spare day lodge, ample nearby parking, and the loading areas for three lifts—don't begin to hint at the grandeur above. If the weather is dicey, you'll probably stick to a pair of parallel chairs, the Eagle Express quad and Tranquilizer double, which access the lower mountain. Configured in a drop-off and roll-away pattern, such major runs as Slash, Spillway, Liftline and Dromedary start off with enough pitch to sprout major moguls and enough width for comfort, but then suddenly level out to green-circle runouts. Slow Poke is a traverse that enables novices using the School House T-bar and Easy Street to ski to all of these lower runs.

You can ski the bottom when Arctic winds are howling, when visibility on the higher slopes is low or when it's just so cold that you like to be able to pop into the day lodge to warm up. The Caribou chair, just above the T-bar, is the exception that proves the rule. It is not a lower or mid-mountain lift, but rather one that directly accesses a handful of intermediate cruising runs and more demanding mogul trails. This lift is especially popular with locals, who are happy to start and finish their skiing right at the upper parking lot.

Both the Eagle Express and Tranquilizer chairs unload on a sort of mid-mountain "shelf" which separates the exposed upper terrain from lower mountain. Here you'll find the spacious Paradise Chalet serves rather like the base for the upper mountain. It perches between the unloading area of the Eagle and Tranquilizer chairs from below and the loading areas of the Triple chair and the Kiefer T-bar. These two timberline lifts access the lion's share of the open slopes and generous glades for which Marmot Basin is known. They rise through thinning trees to great snowfields and meet at a dramatic point high on a scenic subpeak called Caribou Ridge. By itself, this middle section of the mountain would comprise a beguiling little ski area with big views. While this terrain looks dramatic and has a real mountain feel, much of it is as suitable for solid intermediates (and even for confident novices on one run) as for more advanced skiers. Exhibition

Photo courtesy Marmot Basin

Inside Marmot Basin

is a well-named beneath-the-lift bumper, while Kiefer's Dream is for those who prefer not to be seen, and Caribou Knoll is a hideaway open glade that remains one of Marmot's less-trafficked secrets.

The Knob chair accesses roughly the top third of the mountain, which boasts the lion's share of the expert terrain: the highest tree-free bowls, most substantial snowfields, gnarliest chutes and beefiest ridges. These features etched into the basin's steep upper sections draw really good skiers and snowboarders, but rarely so many that the snow gets skied out quickly. This is legitimate expert territory, where pitch, topography, snow conditions and weather all add to the challenge. The Knob Traverse snakes across the gentlest possible route on the upper mountain and enables intermediates to sample the beauty and thrill of the top, but really, it's high-end territory. If you are an advanced skier ready to test yourself on a true black diamond, you might start on Charlie's Bowl, which is truly steep but relatively short. If you're satisfied with your way of handling it, you can go for longer black diamonds. Charlie's and the neighboring Dupres Bowl and Dupres Chutes comprise as splendid a spread of lift-served powder terrain as can be found in the Rockies, and Knob Hill and Knob Bowl, which are closer to the chair, build into bad bumps. Experts with energy in addition to a high level of skill can add to the adventure by climbing an additional 500 feet to the summit and skiing Upper Basin or Peak Run.

If you're partial to tree skiing, you can cruise the High Traverse from the top of the Knob chair to Ridge run and Chalet Slope, a pair of demanding glades which skiers like and snowboarders love. Thunder Bowl is as much a tilted plateau as it is a bowl, while Eagle East is in fact a huge bowl with a hump in the middle. A sizable portion of the terrain off the Knob chair will be closed anytime that avalanche danger exists, relegating experts to bump runs below, but the tradeoff is that the powder lasts for days after a storm in these challenging precincts. Marmot Basin's steep slide-prone territory includes everything off the Knob chair, both the Eagle East area on the perimeter of the lower mountain and all the high slopes and bowls on top. The fact that much of this high terrain can be closed due to avalanche danger, minimal visibility or both seems just to add to Marmot's mystique.

SNOWBOARDING

Local snowboarders create a short sweet snowboard park just above the mid-mountain lodge, but with such an abundance of chutes, trees and natural half-pipe, Marmot Basin is practically one huge snowboard playground. Novice and intermediate riders stick to the green and blue runs in the area's mid-section and to the glades between the trails, while advanced and expert riders join their skiing colleagues off the Knob chair. Hiking to the summit doesn't bother them, but the High Traverse can be high frustration when the snow is deep. Therefore, they either shoot the steeps of Dupres or Charlie's, or simply walk to the top of Chalet Slope and ride the little bumps, drainages and dipsy-doodle gullies through the trees.

SKI SCHOOL PROGRAMS

Introductory Programs

Never Skied Before: Beginner package including rental equipment for new skiers age 6 and over.

Never Boarded Before: Comparable package for beginner snowboarders, with rental equipment.

Advanced and Specialty Programs

Ski Improvement Week: Monday through Friday program with daily two-hour clinic, fun race, video session and night out in Jasper.
Ladies' Day: Lifts, two-hour clinic and lunch, every Friday.

Special Program

Mountain Tours: Complimentary meet-the-mountain tours available several times a week. Check with Guest Services for meeting place and time.

For Families

Nonskiing Children

Little Rascals Nursery: Supervised play center for children ages 19 months to 5 years. Reservations recommended. One-hour introduction to skiing lesson and rental equipment available at an additional cost.
The Wishing Well: Supervised activities for nonskiing children ages 4 to 12 staying at the Jasper Park Lodge.

Skiing Children

Never Skied Before: Beginner group lessons including rental equipment for new skiers age 6 and over.
Children's Clinics: Group classes for ages 6 and older. Marmot Basin requires 4- or 5-year-olds who have never skied before to take private lessons, but preschoolers who have skied and can ride a lift are accepted in group classes.
Ski Improvement Week: Available for juniors age 6 to 12.
Snowboard Clinics: All levels.

NORDIC SKIING

The Jasper Park Lodge's groomed, 25-kilometer (about 18-mile) trail system includes easy routes around Lac Beauvert and the golf course and connects to marked trails through adjacent forests. Abundant Nordic skiing is also available in

Photo courtesy Marmot Basin

Marmot Basin's Charlie's Bowl offers experts powder skiing on very steep terrain.

Noteworthy

Marmot Basin reduces lift ticket prices from the full adult rates for full-time students to age 25, youths 13 to 17, juniors 6 to 12 and seniors 65 and older. Marmot Mites age 6 and under ski free. In addition, Jasper in January is a 16-day fun-filled festival featuring reduced-rate lift tickets and in-town activities.

Jasper National Park. The closest trails to town, with trailheads at Pyramid Bench and Whistlers Campground, offer easy to moderate groomed loops of medium length. The Athabasca Whirlpool trailhead, 20 kilometers (12 miles) south of Jasper, accesses several easy to moderate trails, both of the loop and the out-and-back variety, plus shelters, privies and other backcountry conveniences. Maligne Lake is 48 kilometers (about 27 miles) from Jasper, with five loop trails ranging from the 3.5-mile Lake Trail, which is very easy, to the more challenging 12-kilometer Evelyn Creek Trail. Telemarkers love the nearby Bald Hills area. The park visitors center at **500**

Connaught Dr. in central Jasper has maps and details; **(403) 852-6176.**

HELI-SKIING

The closest operator, **Robson Heli-Magic,** offers day skiing in the Mt. Robson–Valemount area about an hour west of Jasper on about 1,500 square kilometers of gladed, wooded and open terrain, suitable for strong intermediate to expert skiers. **Hwy 5 North, P.O. Box 18, Valemount, BC V0E 2Z0; (403) 852-6052** in Jasper.

WHERE TO STAY

For lodging information and packages including lift tickets, contact **Jasper Tourism and Commerce, P.O. Box 98, Jasper, AB T0E 1E0; (403) 852-3858.** Reservations for lodges and private homes can be made through **Reservations Jasper, P.O. Box 1840, Jasper, AB T0E 1E0; (403) 852-5488,** fax **(403) 852-5489.**

Luxury Accommodations

Charlton's Chateau Jasper

Award-winning hotel with 112 deluxe rooms and seven luxurious suites with private Jacuzzi tubs. Some accommodations non-smoking. Tasteful and subdued decor. Resort-type facilities and services. Dining room, lounge, indoor pool, whirlpool spa. Daily housekeeping, bell and room service. **96 Geikie St., P.O. Box 1418, Jasper, AB T0E 1E0; (800) 661-9323** in Canada, **(403) 852-5644.**

Jasper Park Lodge

Outstanding resort complex on 903 secluded acres on the outskirts of Jasper. Operated by CP Hotels, Canada's leading luxury hotel chain. Excellent facilities and services. All 442 rooms have been renovated since 1990. Accommodations in main lodge and in charming cedar or log cottages, many with lake views and/or fireplace. Packages such as Ski For Free (an early-season package featuring two complimentary lift tickets for each room night), Scrooge Package (also early season which includes breakfast and dinner at the hotel, lunch at the mountain and lift ticket) and Jasper in January (bargain rates for accommodations and lift ticket). For families, children's menus in all hotel restaurants and free lodging for youngsters 18 and younger sharing parents' room. Outdoor skating and cross-country skiing on site (rental equipment available), four restaurants, two lounges, nightclub, cafe, heated outdoor pool, game room, exercise room, health club, hot tub, sauna, steamroom. Private shuttle to Marmot Basin, daily housekeeping, bell and room service, 24-hour front desk, concierge, ski storage. **P.O. Box, Jasper, AB T0E 1E0; (800) 465-SKIS** in Alberta, **(403) 852-3301, (800) 441-4141** for CP Hotels reservations.

Mid-Priced Accommodations

Amethyst Lodge

Quiet location near center of town. Ninety-seven rooms, some non-smoking, some with balconies. No charge for children under 15. Pets permitted. Ski packages. Outdoor hot tub, restaurant, lounge. Daily housekeeping. **P.O. Box 1200, Jasper, AB T0E 1E0; (800) 661-9935, (403) 852-3394.**

Jasper Inn

Spacious rooms with stylish contemporary furnishings. Suites with kitchenettes and fireplaces, and deluxe suites also with private Jacuzzi tubs. Ski packages. Children to 17 free. Restaurant, lounge, indoor pool, exercise room, whirlpool,

Paradise Chalet at Marmot Basin

Photo courtesy Marmot Basin

sauna, steamroom, ski room, guest laundry. Daily housekeeping. **98 Geikie St., P.O. Box 879, Jasper, AB T0E 1E0; (800) 661-1933** in western Canada, **(403) 425-9784** in Edmonton, **(403) 852-4461.**

Lobstick Lodge

Lodge renovated in 1994. Restaurant redone in 1996. Has 138 sizable rooms, some kitchen units. Ski packages and family plans with children to age 15 free. Indoor pool, indoor and outdoor hot tubs, sauna, guest laundry. **P.O. Box 1200, Jasper, AB T0E 1E0; (800) 661-9317, (403) 852-4431.**

Marmot Lodge

Casual, contemporary 109-room lodge, some with kitchens and fireplaces. Ski packages and family rates, with children to 15 free. Indoor pool, whirlpool, sauna, restaurant, fireplace, lounge. Daily housekeeping. **P.O. Box 1200, Jasper, AB T0E 1E0; (800) 661-6521, (403) 852-4471.**

Mt. Robson Inn

Luxurious 76-room inn. Executive suites with whirlpool tubs. Some non-smoking rooms. Art deco inspiration to furnishings. Ski packages. Restaurant, ski lockers, outdoor hot tubs. Daily housekeeping, room service. VCR and movie rentals. **P.O. Box 88, Jasper, AB T0E 1E0; (800) 587-3327, (403) 852-3327.**

Sawridge Hotel Jasper

Recently redecorated hotel with rooms surrounding an indoor atrium with three-story fireplace. Ski packages, including breakfast and gratuities. Children to 16 free. Restaurant, cafe, fitness and massage center, hot tub, sauna, plug-in engine heaters. Daily housekeeping, room service. **82 Connaught Dr., P.O. Box 282, Jasper, AB T0E 1E0; (800) 661-6427, (403) 852-5111.**

Whistlers Inn

European-style hotel with 41 rooms. Located across from rail and bus station. Children to age 12 free. Ski packages. Restaurant, pub, hot tub, ski lockers. Daily housekeeping. **P.O. Box 250, Jasper, AB T0E 1E0; (800) 282-9919, (403) 852-2261.**

Economy Accommodations

Astoria Hotel

Centrally located hotel with 35 recently refurbished guest rooms with mini-fridge. Eccentric exterior with four steep gables. Guests have privileges at the nearby Aquatic Centre. Ski packages and B&B option. Children to age 18 free in parents' room. Restaurant, lounge. Daily housekeeping. **404 Connaught Ave., P.O. Box 1710, Jasper, AB T0E 1E0; (800) 661-7343** in western Canada, **(403) 852-3351.**

Athabasca Hotel

Hotel in the heart of town with 60 rooms of various sizes and degrees of luxury, from shared-bath basics to sizable, well-appointed Victorian-style charmers, all at reasonable rates. Some non-smoking rooms. Lively spot. Children to age 12 free. Ski packages. On-site restaurant, cappuccino bar, nightclub. Daily housekeeping, room service. **510 Patricia St., P.O. Box 1420, Jasper, AB T0E 1E0; (800) 563-9859, (403) 852-3386.** 403

Private Homes

Jasper boasts a large inventory of extremely economical rooms in private homes. A list of licensed accommodations in homes inspected and approved by the Canadian Parks Service for compliance with health, fire and building code regulations is available from the **Jasper Home Accommodation Association, P.O. Box 758, Jasper, AB T0E 1E0.** The association's brochure details such information as number of rooms, bed and bath arrangements, availability of kitchen facilities, and each home's phone number, but the association does not handle reservations.

DINING OUT

Beauvallon Dining Room

Award-winning hotel restaurant in Chateau Jasper serving breakfast, lunch and dinner daily. Continental adaptations of steaks, chops, veal and pasta. Moderately priced, all-you-can-eat

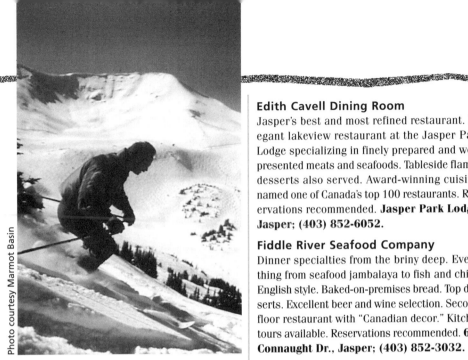

Blue skies and vast terrain are typical of Marmot Basin and the Canadian Rockies.

Saturday evening buffet is ample feast with beef, barbecue, pasta, salads, cheeses and desserts. Sunday brunch also outstanding. Children 7 to 12 eat cheap, and those 6 and under eat free. Reservations recommended. **Chateau Jasper, 96 Geikie St., Jasper; (403) 852-5644.**

Beauvert Dining Room

Continental restaurant, serving lunch and dinner. Less formal than Edith Cavell Dining Room, but sophisticated, tasteful and somewhat less expensive. Reservations recommended. **Jasper Park Lodge, Jasper; (403) 852-6052.**

Coco's Cafe

Casual spot for full breakfasts, light lunches, soups and salads. Excellent for budget-watching non-smokers. **608 Patricia St., Jasper; (403) 852-4550.**

Dining through the Snow

Progressive dinner via horsedrawn sleigh every Wednesday evening. Welcome reception at the gallery, soup and salad at the Amethyst, entrée at the Jasper Inn and dessert and coffee at Something Else. Set menu, but dietary requirements can be met with advance reservation. Children are charged for the sleighride and may select from the children's menu at the Jasper Inn. Reservations required. **(403) 852-3152.**

Edith Cavell Dining Room

Jasper's best and most refined restaurant. Elegant lakeview restaurant at the Jasper Park Lodge specializing in finely prepared and well-presented meats and seafoods. Tableside flambé desserts also served. Award-winning cuisine; named one of Canada's top 100 restaurants. Reservations recommended. **Jasper Park Lodge, Jasper; (403) 852-6052.**

Fiddle River Seafood Company

Dinner specialties from the briny deep. Everything from seafood jambalaya to fish and chips, English style. Baked-on-premises bread. Top desserts. Excellent beer and wine selection. Second-floor restaurant with "Canadian decor." Kitchen tours available. Reservations recommended. **622 Connaught Dr., Jasper; (403) 852-3032.**

Miss Italia Ristorante

The day starts with a big breakfast, works through lunch and ends with Italian specialties derived from various regions of Italy: Venice, Sicily, Florence and southern Italy. Daily specials. Informal look. **Patricia Centre, second floor, Jasper; (403) 852-4002.**

O'Shea's

Homey, lively atmosphere in hotel restaurant. Meal service starts with breakfast, ranging from hearty skillet-cooked entrées to healthy granola, yogurt and fruit sundaes. Burgers, pasta, stir-fries, steak and seafood available at lunch and dinner. **Athabasca Hotel, 510 Prince St., Jasper; (403) 852-4229.**

Palisades Restaurant
Relaxed greenhouse setting for eclectic dining. Steaks, seafood, Greek and Italian favorites and barbecue. Children's menu. Full-course dinners, plus lunch to late supper service. **Pine Ave.** off **Connaught Dr., Jasper; (403) 852-5222.**

Papa George's
Jasper tradition since 1924. Casual eatery serving breakfast, lunch and dinner. Medley menu includes pasta, burgers, soups, salads, sandwiches, European entrées, vegetarian specials and desserts, all at moderate prices. Reservations accepted. **Astoria Hotel, 404 Connaught Dr., Jasper; (403) 852-3351.**

Something Else Restaurant
Recently renovated restaurant with a sprightly atmosphere and a vaguely Mediterranean theme. Great grazing from appetizer menu, Greek, Italian and other European specialties. Also, mesquite-broiled meats, a sprinkling of Cajun dishes and the ubiquitous pizza. Lunch and dinner. Open until midnight. Free delivery to local hotels. **621 Patricia St., Jasper; (403) 852-3850.**

Tokyo Tom's Place
Sushi bar, *ozashinki* booths and table seating for Japanese fare any way you like it. Combination dinners and à la carte dining. Also live lobster and fresh crab specialties. Lunch and dinner. (Tokyo Tom's also operates Jasper Park Lodge's sushi bar.) Dinner reservations recommended. **410 Connaught Dr., Jasper; (403) 852-3780.**

Tonquin Prime Rib Village
Alberta beef lovers' paradise, known for excellent prime rib. Also, seafood and poultry for those who shy away from red meat. Homemade Italian-style bread and desserts. Children's menu. Breakfast also served. **Juniper St., Jasper; (403) 852-4966.**

Walter's Dining Room
Top restaurant in the Sawbridge Hotel. Steaks, pasta, stir-fries, sandwiches and daily specials with a Continental or Canadian accent. Breakfast buffet served weekends. Candlelight dinners. Reservations recommended. **Sawbridge Hotel, 82 Connaught Dr., Jasper; (403) 852-5111.**

NIGHTLIFE

Locals often like to have a quick slopeside nip at Charlie's Lounge and The Nook at the base area, but most of the après-ski takes place in town. Happy hour is in high gear at the Dead Dog in the Astoria Hotel, Nick's Bar, the Whistler Stop and Buckles. The latter doles out free popcorn and bargain wings, shooters, pints and a lethal drink known as Buckles Beer Margarita. On the mellower side, Walter's in the Sawridge Hotel has a quiet fireside lounge serving drink specials and fondue. You'll find big-screen TV, drinks and perhaps such other diversions as darts, shuffleboard or pool at the Dead Dog, Jasper Inn, Nick's Bar, Room With a View Lobby Lounge in the Amethyst Lodge and the Whistle Stop in the Whistler Inn. Jasper Pizza Place also has pool tables. For a quieter, more refined option, try the Bonhomme Lounge in the Chateau Jasper where a harpist plays Wednesday through Sunday evenings. The fireside lounge at Echoes in the Marmot Lodge may also have live entertainment. Tokyo Tom's has a karaoke bar, which could be called semi-live entertainment. You can find top-forty music or oldies, often with dancing, at The Night Club in the Athabasca Hotel, Champs in the Sawridge, The Moose's Nook and City Tent, both in the Jasper Park Lodge. Probably the liveliest scene in town is at Atha-B, the nightclub in the Athabasca Hotel, with live bands, dancing, pool and video games.

For more information, contact **Marmot Basin Ski-Lifts Ltd., P.O. Box 1300, Jasper, AB T0E 1E0, (403) 852-3816, fax (403) 852-3533; Jasper Park Chamber of Commerce, P.O. Box 98, Jasper, AB T0E 1E0, (403) 852-3858,** fax **(403) 852-4932.**

KANANASKIS COUNTRY

BACKDROP

Kananaskis Country is the main gateway to the Canadian Rockies. Scarcely an hour from Calgary's booming western suburbs, it is nevertheless an authentic ski country outpost with two significant Alpine ski areas and western Canada's finest Nordic area. The Canmore Nordic Centre is one of North America's top cross-country areas, and the two Alpine areas, which are a half-hour drive apart and offer interchangeable lift tickets, are a real study in contrast.

Nakiska, one of the continent's first truly modern ski mountains, was computer-designed also for the 1988 Winter Olympics to provide the most interesting ski trails and fastest racing courses on a thickly forested mountain. It instantly became a world skiing showcase with the latest in lift and snowmaking technology. Fortress Mountain, a quirky, high-altitude ski area assembled by a group of Calgary locals rather than laid out, is one of the Rockies' unsung treasures with gorgeous scenery, abundant snow and the kind of friendly informality that is hard to come by today. It retains much of the casual approach to skiing which is becoming as rare in Canada as in the United States. As the 1990s wind down, Fortress remains a place that time and progress forgot. There's an ambitious master plan called Fortress 2000, calling for resort trappings beyond those its founders could have envisioned, but Calgary loyalists and the occasional visitor to this beguiling ski area rather hope that the plan won't be implemented too soon.

For the moment, the two Alpine areas balance each other perfectly in personality and terrain. Nakiska offers immensely easy access, peerless trail skiing and a true-blue racing heritage. Fortress Mountain, whose base elevation is just 500 feet lower than Nakiska's summit, is noteworthy for wide, ski-anywhere terrain that draws bumpers, boarders and just plain folks who prefer free-form skiing. Nakiska and Fortress Mountain now issue a fully interchangeable lift ticket, and because they are now under the same ownership as giant Lake Louise, north of Banff, they will probably ultimately offer multiday, multimountain tickets as well. The lodging at Nakiska and Fortress are minimal, but booming Canmore makes a great bedroom community with easy right-off-the-highway access and excellent values in accommodations, dining and entertainment. Not only is Canmore close to Calgary, but it is also shockingly close to the higher-rent district of Banff, so the opportunity to base there and ski either the Kananaskis areas or those around provides an excellent value for a vacation or a long weekend.

THE LAY OF THE LAND

Nakiska and Fortress Mountain are located on the west side of the long, deep valley carved by the Kananaskis River, south of the TransCanada Highway. The Nakiska ski area and Kananaskis Village, which is not a true village but rather three fine lodgings surrounding a skating rink, require a long walk or a short drive. Fortress Mountain is self-contained but isolated. Canmore is a bustling community that sits in a wide spot in the broader Bow River Valley, west of the Kananaskis Country exit.

GETTING THERE

From Calgary, drive west on the TransCanada Highway to Kananaskis Country. Hwy 40 accesses both Alpine areas. Nakiska is 90 kilometers (55 miles) from Calgary, and Fortress Mountain is 27 kilometers (about 18 miles) farther. The Canmore exit is past the Nakiska/Fortress Mountain interchange. Regular bus service operates from Calgary seven days a week and from Banff on weekdays; for information, call **(403) 591-7777.** For skiers staying in Canmore and wishing to sample the Banff/Lake Louise areas, **Canmore Ski Bus** makes daily runs; **(403) 678-6282.** Canmore is on the main Canadian Pacific

rail line, and as the town shifts from a resort community into a commuter exurb of Calgary, eventual passenger train service might return.

THE SKIING

Nakiska

Profile

When it comes to traditional trail skiing, there's no better choice than Nakiska. This easy-to-get-to and easy-to-get-around mountain is well laid out, which perhaps leads less to romantic prose than to practical, pleasurable skiing. Good planning shows from the time you disembark at Port Nakiska. It's but a short walk across the flats from the skier drop-off area to the lifts and the base facilities, a layout that is ideal for families or anyone else who would prefer to ski than to encounter slippery slopes, bothersome stairs or confusion. Because it is so logical, Nakiska can operate most days with just two main lifts and two for new skiers, which keeps lift prices modest. Furthermore, the easiest runs from each chair are the farthest to the right (as you unload), progressing to the most difficult at the far left. Whether this was planned or whether it was simply the unforeseen by-product of computer design is impossible to determine, and not really important, but it is great. Cut to follow the mountain's contours, they are more varied and more interesting than its modest 230 acres would suggest. Roads and traverses are kept to a bare minimum, which maximizes the skiing.

At the base, you'll find a sheltered beginner slope and two main lifts, one of which operates just when weekend or holiday crowds demand it, that ferry skiers to the heart of the runs. The Silver chair shoots straight up the mountain, accessing Nakiska's best cruising trails. Wide, beautifully shaped, and well-groomed runs like North Axe, Mighty Peace and Maverick invite wide, swooping high-speed turns. Eye-Opener loses part of its generous width to the well-used recreational racing center, while Legacy, one of just two black-diamond runs off the Silver chair,

Inside Kananaskis Country

is frequently taken over by the Kananaskis Alpine Ski Club and other serious racing teams.

From the top of the Silver chair, you angle back down to the Gold chair and to Nakiska's formidable topside steeps. Ranging from Whoop-Up, the dark gray slope off to the right, to Eagle Tail and Bobtail, the double-black duo stacked one above the other to the left, the Gold chair's steep fall-line runs will keep you on your toes. Some are partially groomed, so you can bail out or ease into the moguls, while others are left to mound massive moguls. If you prefer trees to bumps, a new gladed section is bound to appeal. Because

Mountain Stats—
Nakiska

Resort elevation 4,945 feet (1,525 meters)
Top of highest lift 7,415 feet (2,260 meters)
Bottom of lowest lift 4,922 feet (1,500 meters)
Total vertical 2,493 feet (760 meters)
Longest run 2 miles (3.2 kilometers)
Average annual snowfall 90 inches (225 centimeters)
Ski season early December to mid-April
Lifts 2 detachable quad chairlifts, 1 triple, 1 double, 1 handle tow
Capacity 8,620 skiers per hour
Terrain 30 trails and one 45-acre glade, 230 acres (16% beginner and novice, 70% intermediate, 14% advanced and expert)
Snowmaking 85% of the area
Mountain dining Mid-Mountain Lodge
Snow reports (403) 229-3288

Nakiska's trees are formidably dense, even so close to the treeline, four mini-trails have been cut through them. They develop hoot-and-holler rolls and funny little pitches to delight young skiers and snowboarders, but again, Nakiska offers an option. It's Mapmaker, the solitary easy road from the summit which zigzags through the gladed section, so again, you can plunge in or escape without committing to the entire tree section. At busy periods, the Olympic chair is cranked up which provides additional access to Gold country, but the short, steep summit Poma above the Gold chair is not open to the public. Built to haul racers to the start of the men's Olympic downhill, it leads into bighorn sheep territory and is now used only by the patrol for avalanche control work. Avalanches aren't even an issue for riders of the Bronze chair, a low-to-the-ground double which accesses the area's excellent, sheltered novice trails. Wide and immaculately groomed, these runs have all been designated as slow-skiing areas.

The downhill races are the glamour events of Alpine skiing, and if you ski the women's downhill (North Axe) and the men's (Eagle Trail, Bobtail and North Axe) nonstop, you'll get a glimmer of what the world's best skiers accomplish—and they hardly turn. Nakiska will long bask in Olympic glory, but modifications since 1988 have been directly toward making the mountain more user-friendly for all ability levels. Among Calgarians, Nakiska has suffered from a reputation for having more trails on the map than truly skiable, for grooming too much, while at the same time having too little terrain for low intermediate skiers. While the focus used to be on snowmaking runs, natural-snow terrain is now also targeted. Current management's goal is to open all the terrain that shows on the map. This includes a steep, wide slope called Bear Paw, which was once a bighorn sheep area but which the sheep no longer use. Also, they've regraded some of the runs and built new detours around some of the steep pitches, and also, they're now into partial grooming, leaving sides of some trails mogully while grooming the mid-sections.

Snowboarding

Despite its Alpine pedigree, Nakiska draws carving riders who love the fall-line runs, the new Glades, and the fact that the mountain requires minimal traversing. The free riders are all on the Bronze chair, which access the area's generous half-pipe, jumps and walls. An additional plus is the inexpensive lift ticket for this novice chair. Snowboard lessons are big at what can no longer simply be called the ski school, because it offers a menu of children's and adult snowboard classes and even Canadian Snowboard Instructors Alliance certification courses.

Ski School Programs

The ski school offers a traditional mix of class and private instruction for all levels of skiing and snowboarding.

Special Programs
Free Guided Tours: Mountain orientation daily at 10:30 A.M. and 1:30 P.M.

For Families
Nonskiing Children
Day Care: Spacious center with a capacity for 35 children ages 19 months to 6 years. Adjacent fenced outdoor snowplay yard. Theme days, including Farm Day, PJ Day, Zoo Day and such holidays as Valentine's Day. Hourly rates available, with two-hour minimum. Reservations required on weekends; recommended on weekdays.

Ski School: Ski classes for ages 3 to 12; snowboarding for older children.

Fortress Mountain

Profile

You really need to see (or better yet, ski) Fortress to believe it. After you've wound your way up a steep access road whose hairpins bear numbered signs so that management can find a car that's been reported to have stalled or slipped off the road, you end up in a high wide bowl of grandiose proportions and real beauty. The ski area's vertical isn't impressive and its facilities are truly basic, but the terrain is way beyond the bush leagues. At what would have to be called the resort center, you'll find a parking lot, an odd rambling day lodge, which includes a simple hotel, the rental shop/ski school building, two T-bars and a chairlift that swoops riders out of a valley to the top of a long, white ridge. The huddle of perky new condos perched on a nearby hill look incongruous, even out of place, at an area whose main lodge is kind of a peaked pentagon with oddball extensions, a shape that belies easy description.

On-slope facilities are as basic as the "resort" infrastructure. Nothing that immediately hits your eye hints at the spectacular and varied terrain Fortress offers, both lift-accessed and snowcat-served. The area grooms but doesn't overgroom the open bowls, knock-out glades and steep-walled gullies that comprise this unpretentious area. The lifts look primitive but remain functional, so no one seems to care. They rise up on two sides of two valleys, and while you can get into the nub of the terrain two ways, the most eye-popping way to experience Fortress is to

Mountain Stats—
Fortress Mountain

Resort elevation 6,970 feet (2,293 meters)
Top of highest lift 7,775 feet (2,557 meters)
Bottom of lowest lift 6,692 feet (2,201 meters)
Total vertical 1,083 feet (356 meters)
Longest run 1 1/4 miles (2 kilometers)
Average annual snowfall 248 inches (630 centimeters)
Ski season early November through late April
Lifts 1 triple chairlift, 2 doubles, 3 T-bars
Capacity 7,000 skiers per hour
Terrain 31 named runs plus extensive open snowfields, glades and chutes; 328 acres (20% beginner and novice, 55% intermediate, 25% advanced and expert)
Snowmaking 60% of the trails
Snow reports (403) 245-4909

head down a novice run from the lodge to the Canadian chairlift. This triple is the one visible from the parking lot. It climbs a ridge that looks like an uptilted field of white, onto which are etched a quartet of straight-shot gullies and a breathtaking slope called Raceway which is wide enough for a half-pipe, a mogul course and a couple of slalom courses with space left over. Of the gullies, Fortress tends to groom two frequently, one occasionally and one never, so that you can pick the texture of your steeps. If you prefer not to ski these frontside pitches, just sidle down the Ridge Trail till you find something easier or drop off the backside to the core of the ski area. This broad basin is dominated by the squared-off namesake summit of Fortress Mountain, and it offers terrain to match the scenery.

Lovely blue-square runs lace through thin glades, again offering a choice of skiing the trees or not. From the bottom of the drainage, you can take the Backside double chair back up or board the Farside double up the next mountain. Here you'll find everything from a sensationally wide novice run called Canterbury Tale to a high traverse leading to such gut-popping chutes as Coliseum and Cauldron. While trails show on the trail map, there's plenty of skiing between the marked routes, and because of Fortress's

Noteworthy

Sheltered beginner tow, and Bronze chair built low-to-the-ground for small children. Various-priced lift tickets for adults, youth/student, senior and child, with free skiing to age 5.

Photo by Alec Pytlowany

Built for the '88 Olympics, Nakiska passes the test of time.

relatively low lift capacity and sparse midweek traffic, powder lingers and lingers. Fortress has a couple of curious lifts, especially the Curved T-bar, which isn't so much curved as routed in a continuous, up-and-over skewed diamond. The leg nearest the lodge serves as the main beginner lift, while the leg up from the backside returns skiers and riders to the front of the area.

Snowboarding

Fortress's frontside half-pipe is almost superfluous, for the area's knock-out gullies, chutes and knobs offer abundant natural snowboarding terrain. Devil's Gulch, for instance, is marked on the trail map with an innocuous blue square, but it is not a ski trail so much as a humongous natural half-pipe with high banks, wall shots and air-raising kickers.

Snowcat Skiing

Fortress offers what can be called "snowcat-assisted" skiing, which means that snowcats are used to ferry guided groups back to the lifts, a time-saving system that works because the skiing is just beyond the area's boundary. It is on six sections, which range from moderately steep to incredibly challenging. The South Chutes are reached by a long traverse from the top of the triple chair. Wall Street and the Canterbury

Chutes are beyond the ropes of the main bowl. Fortress Lake, The Graces and The Artisans are all off various portions of the Farside's backside. The north-facing Artisans hold light snow so you can find powder days after a storm. The cat skiing season is generally from early February through April. Half- and full-day tours including breakfast and two guides are offered. Advance reservations are required, **(403) 591-7108** or fax **(403) 591-7133**.

Ski School Programs

Introductory Programs
Discover Skiing: First-timer's package available Saturday or Sunday morning or afternoon, including ski or snowboarding lesson, full-day rental and T-bar ticket. Available for children 6 and over and adults.

Advanced and Specialty Programs
Daily Specials: In addition to normal lessons at various levels, ski school offers daily specials including bump, powder and snowboard carving clinics.

Special Program
Free Guided Tours: Mountain orientation daily at 10:30 A.M. and 1:30 P.M.

For Families
Nonskiing Children
Day Care: Supervised indoor and outdoor program for ages 6 months to 6 years. Basic indoor playroom, but older children are taken outdoors to play. Open Thursdays through Sundays. Hourly rates available, with two-hour minimum. Reservations accepted for full-day spots.

Skiing Children
Ski and Snowboard Lessons: Ski lessons from age 3; snowboard lessons from age 6. Reservations required for non-holiday periods.

Nordic Skiing

Built for the '88 Olympics, the Canmore Nordic Centre's huge and immaculate, 65-kilometer trail system and topflight base facilities put it in a class by itself when it comes to cross-country skiing. The trails range from virtually flat to extremely challenging, both for skating lanes and classical skiing. The first-rate ski area-style day lodge features a cafeteria that dishes up hearty and healthy fare. Canmore also has a ski school and rentals, night-lit trails, biathlon range and a team training facility. A trail use fee is charged. **Canmore Nordic Centre, P.O. Box 1979, Canmore, AB T0L 0M0; (403) 678-2400.**

Forty kilometers of free, groomed and trackset trails lace through the dense woods around Ribbon Creek, one of the main tributaries of the Kananaskis River. The system is directly accessible from the Nakiska base area, as well as from highway trailheads. Another 15 kilometers is nearby, but there is no direct link because an avalanche zone lies between the two sections. For information, call **(403) 673-3663.** Other nearby Nordic loops include 20 kilometers of racing and touring trails at Mt. Shark, 90 kilometers of groomed and trackset trails at Peter Hougheed Provincial Park and 30 kilometers of more sporadically groomed trails in the Smith-Dorrien system; for information, call **(403) 591-7222.**

Guided cross-country ski tours can be booked through the **Canadian School of Mountaineering** in Canmore, which offers traditional and glacier tours, **(403) 678-4134; Excursions West** which teaches Nordic skiing and offers backcountry tours, **(403) 678-6837; Mirage Adventure Tours** in the Lodge at Kananaskis in Kananaskis Village, **(403) 591-7773,** and **White Mountain Tours,** which guides ski tours and ice walks, **(403) 678-4099. Canmore's Nordic Ski**

Institute specializes in telemarking clinics and camps, **(403) 678-4102.**

Heli-Skiing

Canmore-based **Assiniboine Heli-Tours, (403) 678-5459,** and **Canmore Helicopters, (403) 678-4802,** offer heli-skiing packages of various types, from half-day to multiday options.

WHERE TO STAY

Ski Kananaskis Reservations, (800) 258-7669.

Nakiska

Luxury Accommodations

The Lodge at Kananaskis and Hotel Kananaskis

Adjacent luxury properties, developed for the 1988 Olympics. Jointly operated by top-of-the-line CP Hotels & Resorts. With 251 rooms, the Lodge is larger and contains more of the facilities. The Hotel has 68 rooms and suites, all with wet bars and balconies, whirlpool tubs and/or fireplaces; more deluxe and intimate. All rooms have On Command, which offers video games and pay-per-view movies. All bathrooms have hair dryers, alarm clocks, mini-bars and coffee machines. Restaurants, lounges, shops, full fitness center, indoor swimming pool, indoor/outdoor whirlpool, saunas, beauty salon, massage, game room, video arcade in Lodge, all for both Lodge and Hotel guests; smaller fitness facility, whirlpool, saunas in Hotel accessible only to its own guests. Ski Escape packages. Twenty-four-hour front desk, ski check, bell and room service, daily housekeeping, nightly turndown service. **Kananaskis Village, AB T0L 2H0; (403) 591-7711, (403) 271-0459** in Calgary, **(800) 441-1414** for CP Hotel reservations.

Mid-Priced Accommodations

Kananaskis Inn

Modern 68-room inn sharing Kananaskis Village location with Lodge at Kananaskis and Hotel Kananaskis. Many rooms with gas fireplaces and

411

Silky snow and open slopes at Fortress and other Canadian mountains.

kitchenettes; some loft rooms and connecting rooms. Children 18 and under free in parents' room. Ski packages. Indoor pool, whirlpool, steamroom, exercise room, restaurant, lounge, ski lockers, plug-in engine heaters. Daily housekeeping, 24-hour front desk. **Kananaskis Village, AB T0L 2H0; (403) 591-7500, (800) 528-1234** for Best Western Reservations.

Fortress Mountain

The reservations phone numbers for all lodging are **(800) 258-SNOW, (403) 591-7108** and **(403) 264-7133.** The fax number is **(403) 591-7133.**

Economy Accommodations

Fortress Mountain Lodge
Basic hotel rooms with private baths arranged on two floors around the main lodge's "atrium," with the signature Copper Hearth as the centerpiece. Minimal services but exceptional convenience. Lodge's East Wing also offers dorm-style bunkrooms which can be booked with or without bedding, towels, and pillows. Lodge has food service (breakfast, lunch and dinner), game room and sometimes entertainment.

Condominiums

First eight ski-in/ski-out units completed in December 1995. Three bedrooms, sleeping up to 10, with two-and-a-half baths and separate tub

412

and shower room. Up to two dozen more slated for 1996–97 season, with on-going construction thereafter. All have full kitchens and fireplaces.

Canmore
Mid-Priced Accommodations

Chateau Canmore
New suite hotel with 26 standard, loft, one- and two-bedroom units, all with two televisions, VCR, separate living room with sofa bed, fireplace, refrigerator and microwave. Larger suites have washer and dryer; chalets have full kitchens. Deluxe king-bedded loft suites offer jetted tubs, nightly turn-down service and upgraded amenities. Restaurant, fitness center, indoor swimming pool, outdoor hot tub. Twenty-four-hour front desk, daily housekeeping. **Hwy 1A, 1720 Bow Valley Trail, P.O. Box 3451, Canmore, AB T0L 0M0; (403) 678-6699, (800) 228-5151** for Quality Inn reservations.

Georgetown Inn
Fourteen rooms, all with private baths and individually decorated in a distinctive and romantic style, with down duvets, abundant pillows and thick towels. Daily housekeeping, traditional English breakfast. **1101 Bow Valley Trail, P.O. Box 3327, Canmore, AB T0L 0M0; (403) 678-3439.**

Green Gables Inn
Sprawling 61-room motor inn, convenient to Alpine and Nordic skiing and town. Recently redecorated. Some rooms with fireplaces, Jacuzzi tubs and/or kitchenettes. Some luxury suites, including honeymoon suite in windmill. Non-smoking rooms available. Children under 18 free in parents' room. Restaurant, lounge, fitness center, outdoor hot tub, in-room refrigerators, hair dryers, continental breakfast, complimentary in-room coffee and tea. Daily housekeeping. **1602 Second Ave., P.O. Box 250, Canmore, AB T0L 0M0; (800) 661-2133, (403) 678-5488; (800) 528-1234** for Best Western reservations.

Greenwood Inn
New inn, Canmore's biggest and most luxurious, with 190 well-appointed rooms. Contemporary styling. Luxury suites with fireplaces, steam showers and Jacuzzi tubs. Spacious public areas.

Children to age 16 stay free in parents' room. Ski packages. Restaurant, lounge, hot tub, sauna. Twenty-four-hour front desk, room service. **511 Bow Valley Trail, Hwy 1A, Canmore, AB T0L 0M0; (800) 263-3625, (403) 678-3625.**

Rocky Mountain Ski Lodge
Eighty-two units, including lodge rooms, loft units in several buildings, and one- and two-bedroom apartment units. Some rooms with fireplace or kitchen. Owned by Swiss-born guide and his family and very ski oriented. Ski packages. Sauna, hot tub, social room with fireplace, wax room. Daily housekeeping, free local phone calls. **1711 Mountain Ave., P.O. Box 3000, Canmore, AB T0L 0M0; (800) 665-6111, (403) 678-5445.**

Rundle Mountain Motel & Gasthaus
Sprawling complex combining rustic charm and European warmth and style. Tree-shaded property feels secluded despite proximity to highway. Options from standard motel rooms to commodious suites with kitchens and fireplaces and cedar log cabins, some with kitchens. More than 50 percent non-smoking. Ski packages. Indoor pool, whirlpool, restaurant, wax room. **Hwy 1A, Mountain Ave., Canmore, AB T0L 0M0; (403) 678-5322.**

Economy Accommodations

Akai Motel
Forty-three recently redecorated rooms, some with kitchenettes. Located between Canmore and Banff National Park gate. Daily housekeeping. **1717 Mountain Ave., P.O. Box 687, Canmore, AB T0L 0M0; (403) 678-4664.**

Bow Valley Motel
Two-story motel located at the edge of downtown. Twenty-five rooms, including some family suites with kitchenettes and separate living area. Ski packages. Outdoor hot tub, complimentary in-room coffee and tea, coin laundry adjacent, plug-ins for cars. Daily housekeeping. **P.O. Box 231, Canmore, AB T0L 0M0; (403) 678-5085.**

Condominiums

Canmore Regency Suites
New complex of two- and three-bedroom suites with full kitchens. Non-smoking units. **1206 Bow Valley Trail, Hwy 1A, Canmore, AB T0L 0M0; (800) 386-7248, (403) 678-3799.**

Private Homes
Canmore boasts an abundance of moderately priced private homes inspected and licensed by the town. Those B&B plans range from a 1913 riverside log structure to contemporary homes with excellent mountain views. Most have private baths, though several are shared. Some have fireplaces, hot tubs and/or saunas. Most serve a full breakfast. Some welcome children, and a few even accept pets. Most are smoke-free. The free Canmore–Bow Valley Bed & Breakfast Association Guide is available from the **Canmore-Kananaskis Chamber of Commerce, (403) 678-4094.**

DINING OUT

Kananaskis Village

Brady's Market
European-style cafe that serves as casual dining spot. Ambiance reminiscent of the Mediterranean. Tapas and oyster bar are popular. Specializes in Spanish and Argentinian wines. **Lodge at Kananaskis, Kananaskis Village; (403) 591-7711, Ext. 51.**

Fireside Lounge
Intimate and cozy lounge, also serving wine, flaming coffees and selection from fresh pasta bar. **Hotel Kananaskis, Kananaskis Village; (403) 591-7711, Ext. 51.**

L'Escapade Dining Room
Elegant and romantic dining room with fine food, great wine and atmosphere. Basically Canadian food focus, with northern Italian or other specialty cuisines featured during theme weeks. Excellent wine list. Formal yet friendly service. Live piano. Reservations required. **Hotel Kananaskis, Kananaskis Village; (403) 591-7711, Ext. 51.**

Peaks Dining Room
Sprightly and attractive hotel dining room, serving breakfast and dinner. Hotel's "family dining room," but with pleasant ambiance and sophisticated

decor. View of ice sculptures on patio. Beef the specialty, but seafood, pasta and vegetable strudel for variety. Also, Saturday night western buffet and Sunday brunch. Reservations required. **Lodge at Kananaskis, Kananaskis Village; (403) 591-7711, Ext. 51.**

Canmore

Boccalino Grotto
Charming Italian-Swiss restaurant, serving gourmet pizza, pasta and Swiss specialties. Fine food and notable wine list. Children's menu. Dinners nightly except Monday. Reservations recommended. **838 Tenth St., Canmore; (403) 678-6424.**

Canmore Rose & Crown
English pub fare, including steak and kidney pie, shepherd's pie and fish and chips. Casual and friendly. Children's menu. **749 Railway Ave., Canmore; (403) 678-5168.**

414

Chez François
Breakfast, brunch, lunch and dinner served daily. Dinners heavy on French specialties, pasta and seafood. Children's menu. Dinner reservations recommended. **Green Gables Inn, Bow Valley Trail, Hwy 1A, Canmore; (403) 678-6111.**

Des Alpes
Swiss-French restaurant with fine food and cozy atmosphere. Chalet style. Meats and game are specialties. Dinner nightly except Wednesday. Handmade chocolates. Reservations recommended. **702 Tenth St., Canmore; (403) 678-6878.**

The Drake Inn
Friendly and moderately priced pub and restaurant. Lunch and dinner. Kid-friendly. **909 Railway Ave., Canmore; (403) 678-5131.**

Famous Chinese Restaurant
Recently expanded, with new glassed-in patio. Western music, Eastern food. Extensive menu, including Szechuan and Beijing specialties. Ginger Beef and Salt-and-Pepper Seafood are specialties. Open for lunch and dinner, daily except Monday. **629 Eighth St., Canmore; (403) 678-9531, (403) 678-9535.**

Faro's
Downtown family restaurant. Authentic Greek specialties, plus pizza, pasta and charbroiled meats. Children's menu. Senior citizens' discounts. Takeout and delivery too. Open daily. **837 Eighth St., Canmore; (403) 678-2234, (403) 678-2263.**

Fireside Inn
Friendly, newly renovated eatery. Home-cooked family favorites, made from scratch. Sunday brunch. Buffet dinners. Open daily from breakfast through dinner. Reservations accepted. **718 Eighth St., Canmore; (403) 678-9570.**

Georgetown Inn
Cozy restaurant with mining memorabilia and English specialties. Dinner served nightly except Mondays. **1101 Bow Valley Trail, Hwy 1A, Canmore; (403) 678-3439.**

Peppermill Restaurant
Swiss and other Continental fare at moderate prices. Pepper steak considered a house specialty. Warm and cozy atmosphere. Locals' special-occasion favorite. Daily specials. Open nightly except Tuesday. Reservations recommended. **726 Ninth St., Canmore; (403) 678-2292.**

Rundle Mountain Gasthaus Restaurant
German and barbecue specialties, in happy contrast. Dinner served nightly except Tuesdays. Reservations recommended. **1723 Mountain Ave., Canmore; (403) 678-5000.**

Sam Bucca's
Red-and-white-checked-tablecloth bistro as casual backdrop for Italian cuisine. Specialty pizzas. Also, breakfast and lunch. Children's menu. Reservations accepted. **Greenwood Inn, 511 Bow Valley Trail, Canmore; (403) 678-3625, Ext. 416.**

Santa Lucia Italian Restaurant
Pizza, pasta, subs and other casual food, plus Italian meat and poultry dishes. Family-friendly. Daily lunch and dinner specials. Takeout and delivery too. **714 Eighth St., Canmore; (403) 678-3414.**

Sherwood House

Pizzas, light meals, burgers, sandwiches and popular appetizers in informal log building. Service to 10:00 P.M. and pizza until midnight daily. Also, Saturday and Sunday brunch. Free delivery. Reservations accepted. **Eighth & Main Sts., Canmore; (403) 678-5211** for reservations, **(403) 678-6422** for delivery.

Sinclair's

Casual yet innovative restaurant in new Victorian-style building. Excellent salads, unusual pastas, gourmet pizza, creative side dishes, hot pots and regular steaks and such for the less adventuresome. Lunch specials, including soup-and-salad combos. **637 Eighth St., Canmore; (403) 678-5370.**

Vienna Restaurant

Open from early lunch through late dinner daily. Austrian specialties served at dinner. Burgers and sandwiches at lunch. *Germütlichkeit*-filled restaurant. Children's menu. Dinner reservations recommended. **722 Eighth St., Canmore; (403) 678-4485.**

NIGHTLIFE

After-ski at both Nakiska and Fortress starts at the respective day lodges. Nakiska's upstairs Finish Line Lounge is a bright, loft-ceilinged gathering spot where the fire crackles, the beer flows, the nachos are piled high and sports dominate on television. Fortress's gathering place is the Copper Hearth, the center of the lodge which, astonishingly, was a black-tie dining room in the ski area's early years. Kananaskis Village's hotels offer a choice of locales. The Bighorn Lounge in the Lodge at Kananaskis is the liveliest spot, with cocktails including nightly drink specials, good hors d'oeuvres, live entertainment and karaoke. Recently redecorated in a ranch style, the lounge attracts an international clientele that likes the western theme. Over in the quieter Hotel Kananaskis, you can relax by the fire in the aptly named Fireside Lounge or add dancing to your elegant dinner at L'Escapade. Woody's Pub in the Kananaskis Inn has a rather English atmosphere, thanks to the steady games of pool and darts.

Canmore offers a wide choice of places to wile away some evening hours. The Sherwood House has to be considered the top locals' spot. It has a rundlestone fireplace, big-screen TV and often live entertainment. At the Greenwood Inn, Sam Bucca's Lounge often draws a lively crowd, while the wine bar attracts a more subdued clientele. Legend's Pub in the Canmore Lodge has it all: live and DJ entertainment, dancing, pool, darts and video games. You'll find the pub spirit and perhaps live entertainment at The Drake Inn and the Canmore Rose & Crown, so named to distinguish it from its Banff namesake. The Miner's Lamp Pub in the Georgetown Inn is a congenial gathering spot and serves premium beers on tap. The Fireside Inn's big-screen TV attracts a crowd for major sports events, as does the Dog 'N Duck Pub in the new Chateau Canmore. For early après-ski of a non-alcoholic kind, try the Cappuccino Bar in the Nakiska day lodge or, in Canmore, the Coffee Mine Tenth Street Bistro & Cafe where climbers and mountaineers hang out or Blends for cappuccino, great sweets and a delightful smoke-free cafe setting.

For more information, contact **Ski Kananaskis** (for information on Nakiska and Fortress Mountain), **1550 Eighth St. SW, Ste. 505, Calgary, AB T2R 1K1, (403) 229-3637,** fax **(403) 244-3774; Kananaskis Information, P.O. Box 280, Canmore, AB T0L 0M0, (403) 678-5508.**

BRITISH
COLUMBIA

416

Sun Peaks
GOLDEN
1
97
KAMLOOPS
Silver Star
Panorama
1
5
97
VERNON
KELOWNA
93
95
Big White
CRANBROOK
3
VANCOUVER
7
97
3
1
3
95 93

British Columbia

Photo by Don Weixl/Silver Star

PANORAMA

BACKDROP

Panorama is the ski resort of the Purcell Range, which puts it as close as you can get to the birthplace of Canadian heli-skiing. In fact, Canadian Mountain Holidays, which pioneered the concept of heli-skiing, established its first base in nearby Radium Hot Springs. This can be translated into reliable snow and weather that's as consistent as one can expect in the mountains. Panorama has built a reputation as a purist's place to ski. The mountain is big, with both superbly groomed cruising trails and outstanding ungroomed steeps. The season's snowfall totals may not be impressive, but because there are no crowds, grooming is excellent and snowmaking coverage is substantial, ski conditions tend to be very good. The powder even lasts longer that you might expect. In addition to doorstep Alpine skiing, a small but exquisite cross-country trail system and a top helicopter skiing operation are right at the resort.

When you stand at the Panorama summit and drink in the priceless Rocky Mountain views to Mt. Nelson and other high peaks, you know that the resort was well named, but from other vantage points, it could just as well have been called Deception Mountain. On clear days, you can easily see the very summit from the bottom of the lifts. As you look up, the mountain doesn't seem as if it could possibly rise 4,300 vertical feet. Panorama's topography creates this optical illusion. It's an illusion reinforced by the trail map. When you study it, the ski area seems quite compact, but that's an illusion too. It results from the artist's trick to scrunch a large ski area onto a small piece of paper. The best way to get a sense of its size is to ski Panorama. Your muscles will help you realized how much ground you cover. Another good perspective comes from the Nordic network. When you look back up at the mountain from the cross-country trails, you see how large the ski area really is.

What reinforces this ski-intensive experience is that a very small ski resort nestles at the base of this very large ski mountain. Skiers from Calgary, which is the closest large city, have to pass the Kananaskis Valley and the three areas of Banff/Lake Louise and cross through two national parks to reach Panorama, and the truth is that most don't bother. The result is excellent ski terrain, unsurpassed scenery and minimal crowds, even on weekends.

THE LAY OF THE LAND

An 18-kilometer (11-mile) access road winds from Invermere to Panorama, a multilevel resort with ski-in/ski-out or walk-to-the-slopes hotel and condominium accommodations and homesites in the surrounding woods. IntraWest, the mammoth resort developer which runs Blackcomb, B.C.; Tremblant, P.Q.; Stratton, VT; and Snowshoe, WV, also owns Panorama. As the heralded developer of Whistler Village and now River Run at Keystone, CO, and redeveloper of the base villages at Tremblant and Stratton, IntraWest is redesigning, expanding and vitalizing Panorama's off-slope facilities as well. Panorama's walk-around development means a car is not necessary, but for those with small children or who simply don't like a lot of stairs, a frequent, free shuttle stops at lodgings at various levels and lifts.

GETTING THERE

From Calgary, it is 282 kilometers (181 miles) via the TransCanada Highway through Banff and Kootenay National Parks, then south 10 kilometers (just over 6 miles) on Hwy 93/95 to Invermere, and west up an 18-kilometer (11-mile) access road directly to the resort. In favorable weather and road conditions, this gorgeous ride takes roughly 3 1/2 hours. Panorama packages vacations that include accommodations, lifts and transportation from Calgary. Once at the resort, you won't need a car.

PROFILE

Panorama's wedding cakelike setbacks segment naturally, with the easiest terrain at the bottom and the most challenging at the top. Wrapped around a single-peak mountain is excellent trail skiing, fabulous steep glades and even a mid-mountain snowfield that is paradise on a powder day. Because the area is broad at the base, steepening and tapering a true summit on top, the skiing becomes both simpler and more challenging the higher up you go. At the same time, most of the runs follow the fall line, providing a very pure skiing experience. Panorama not only looks and skis the way many people think an area ought to be, but it boasts Canada's second-highest vertical too. Its 4,300 feet follow Whistler and Blackcomb, the neighboring mega-mountains across the province in western British Columbia, which for such statistical comparisons Panorama management considers to be one ski destination. You could argue about whether that actually makes Panorama the country's second- or third-highest ski area, but either way, it has considerable bragging rights.

The European Quadzilla high-speed quad is the only way for anyone but bottom-dwelling beginners to access dozens of trails. It rises quickly up nearly half the area's vertical, and it is stunning to think that in the area's early days, it was a long, long T-bar. The lower section of the mountain offers great cruising, and if you just like non-stops on green-circle and blue-square freeways with minimal lift riding, you can really rack up your vertical footage on the lower mountain. Horseshoe and Hoggsflats are easy, Old Timer and Powder Trail are somewhat more challenging and the race area at the bottom of Showoff, appropriately visible to Quadzilla riders, is great for gate-runners. Angling off from Old Timer is the entrance to a black-diamond short shot called Hay Fever, and angling off that in a way that's easy to overlook is the entrance to the Cliff Glade. This double black is a real surprise because Panorama's lower slopes are so thickly forested that you never would expect to be able to ski the trees.

The quad unloads on a little plateau, which gives you your first serious choice. You can either

traverse to a completely different part of the mountain or continue skyward. If you decide on the former, you'll wind partway around the mountain on the Triple Traverse, appropriately, to the Sunbird triple chair area. Offset from the main runs, this section has an isolated feeling of being a ski area within an area. With a different exposure, the condition of the snow and even the look of the mountain are different. Fritz's, Whiskey Jack and the liftline run called Sunbird are perfect long runs for advanced skiers, while Heaven Can Wait and Little Dipper are good intermediate options and Out Rider is a swooping novice run. If you decide instead to ride higher on the Horizon double chair, you'll find the best of Panorama's fall-line runs. There are more mid-level cruisers, Skyline and Rollercoaster, and some outstanding bump runs, Downhill, Tacky, Liftline and Cow's Face. Like the bottom-of-the-mountain offerings but with more pitch and more moguls, these Panorama crankers appeal to folks who simply like to ski.

If you're game for another lift ride, the Champagne T-bar presents you with yet another choice. You can ski some short, steep runs or pick your way through the thinning (well, slightly thinning) trees or angle over on another traverse. From here, it's all black-diamond territory. You can take a long steep trail called Schober's Dream and drop into any one of the challenging glades on this part of the mountain. Hideaway, the first and longest glade, is a cooperative effort between Panorama and a logging company called Crestbrook Forestry Industries which could become a ski-industry model for the right way to harvest trees from a ski mountain. If you have the patience to continue along Schober's, you'll find terrific tree skiing in Black Door, Stump Farm and Alive. The latter, named because the movie *Alive!*, though set in the Andes, was filmed nearby, spills into an open snowfield called Hopeful Sun Bowl. It's very wide but not to steep, and on a powder day it's heavenly. On a mountain so thick with trees, this grandiose expanse comes across as a special treat.

The real prize for experts perches atop Panorama, reached by the Summit T-bar which rises to guess-where and provides some of the most challenging skiing in the Canadian Rockies. Roy's Run and Top of the World, the easy ways down, are marked with single diamonds, and though they are steep knee-crankers, at least one of them might be smoothed out. Outer Limits, Tree Time and Tight Spots, a trio of double-diamond

420

glades that pack the snow for days after a dump. The gut-gripping chutes accessible though a summit gate make you wonder why Panorama doesn't find a way to mark a third diamond on the trail sign. The slope, which appears to be more a mogul farm than a ski run, plunges off the summit. Once you've picked your way through monster bumps, you are confronted with a combination of bumps and jack pines, and when you've made your way through that minefield, you find yourself on top of a cliff. Gutsy experts follow gravity down the chutes etched into these cliff bands, while skiers and riders more conscious of their mortality cut way over to the right to a steep glade. At the bottom of the cliff, the terrain again tames down to a 200-acre double diamond area called Extreme Dream. A stand of tamaracks burned in a long-ago fire is one of nature's special sculpture gardens, and the snow seems to last and last. For skiers and snowboarders who seek a pure adventure experience, but without the cost of heli-skiing or the arduousness of the backcountry, Panorama does indeed fulfill a dream—one with few distractions or interruptions.

Mountain Stats— Panorama

Resort elevation 3,550 feet (1,082 meters)
Top of highest lift 7,850 feet (2,393 meters)
Bottom of lowest lift 3,450 feet (1,052 meters)
Total vertical 4,300 feet (1,311 meters)
Longest run 2.8 miles (4½ kilometers)
Average annual snowfall 110 inches (279 centimeters)
Ski season mid-December to mid-April
Lifts 1 high-speed quad chairlift, 1 triple, 2 doubles, 2 T-bars, 1 platterpull, 1 beginner tow
Capacity 7,600 skiers per hour
Terrain 55 trails (20% beginner and novice, 55% intermediate, 25% advanced and expert), 1,600 acres
Snowmaking 1,000 acres
Mountain dining Cappuccino Hut at the top of the Horizon chair
Snow reports (250) 342-6941

SNOWBOARDING

With minimal traversing, Panorama is an excellent carver's area. Along the left side of Rollercoaster and Whiskey Jack is a unique snowboarder's route, which takes advantage of the natural terrain and has hit stations and even jumps to add interest for free riders. Not surprisingly, the glades, cliffs and chutes draw most of the really good snowboarders.

SKI SCHOOL PROGRAMS

Introductory Programs

Tortoise Club: Six hours of instruction for beginners.
Snowboard Day Club: Three hours of instruction and rental board for juniors or adults.

Advanced and Specialty Programs

Tortoise Club: Six hours of instruction for novices and intermediates.
Ski Canada Magazine Workshops: Two-day clinics with Heather Bilodeau, who devised a Skill Drill program with guaranteed results.

From the base, Panorama doesn't seem like a 4,000-foot ski mountain—but it is.

Special Program
Mountain Friend Ski Tours: Free mountain tours daily at 10:00 A.M. and 1:00 P.M., except Tuesday and Wednesday.

For Families
Nonskiing Children
Snowbirds Child Care: Child care and snowplay for ages 18 months and older. Also handles evening babysitter requests.

Skiing Children
Children's Adventure Club: Daily four-hour ski program for ages 5 to 12. Includes terrain garden, leadership skills and report card. Three-day option also available.

Noteworthy
Panorama schedules Super Family Ski Weeks with special activities at excellent values. Throughout the winter, the resort also sells a bargain lift ticket for ages 6 and under and also has various reductions for juniors ages 7 to 12, teens ages 13 to 18 and seniors 65 and over.

421

NORDIC SKIING

A Panorama lift ticket includes free use of the resort's 22 kilometers of Nordic ski trails, which are groomed for classic skiing or skating. Rental equipment is available at the Nordic Centre in the Heli-Plex, a short walk from the accommodations. With the impending development of a golf course, some of the cross-country trail will be rerouted, but the distance and variety from novice to quite advanced should remain roughly the same. Twelve kilometers of trails called **Natural Bridge/Cross River** are accessible from Radium Hot Springs and are trackset for classic skiing; **(250) 342-4200,** but this region, with its steep mountains and avalanche chutes, is not a major backcountry skiing area.

HELI-SKIING

Panorama is at the southern end of Canada's heli-skiing belt, which stretches all the way north to Revelstoke. Of all major Alpine resorts, however, Panorama has the closest ties to a chopper operation. R.K. flies from its own Heli-Plex right at Panorama, so its day trips are easy to dovetail into resort skiing. You can book your heli-skiing trip in advance along with your Panorama package. Eleven-person groups of intermediate, advanced and expert ability are grouped for thrilling day trips over nearly 660 square miles in the Purcell Range, where the guides have scouted out more than 120 runs. **R.K. Heli-Skiing, P.O. Box 695, Invermere, BC V0A 1K0; (800) 661-6060** from the United States; **(250) 342-3889.** If you don't prebook, you can mosey down to the Heli-Plex, chat with the guides and determine whether it's right for you.

422

WHERE TO STAY

Panorama

Panorama is a self-contained resort with accommodations from hotel rooms in the Pine Inn and Europa Lodge, which are at the base of the Quadzilla chair, and studio and one- and two-bedroom condos in the nearby Toby Creek Lodge and Horsethief Lodge. All hotel rooms have daily

Panorama nestles in the heart of Canada's prime heli-skiing country.

Photo by Scott Rowed/Panorama

housekeeping and include access to the hot tubs and a fitness center in the Europa Lodge. All condominiums have wood-burning fireplaces and full kitchens with dishwasher. Additional outdoor hot tubs and a large communal outdoor grill where guests can barbecue their own favorites, are available to condo guests. The largest units sleep up to eight people. Guest laundries are in the Horsethief and Toby Creek Lodges. The central reservations offices operates as a resort-wide front desk and is staffed 24 hours a day. Information and reservations for all resort lodging, **(800) 663-2929.**

Columbia River Valley

The resort of Radium Hot Springs and the hamlet of Invermere, both down in the Columbia River Valley, offer options for skiers who prefer a small town to the isolation of a pure ski resort. Winter rates at all the accommodations are budget to moderate, and all offer ski packages including Panorama lift tickets. For information, but not reservations, contact **Invermere Tourist Information, P.O. Box 1019, Invermere, BC V0A 1K0; (250) 342-2844,** fax **(250) 342-2844,** or **Radium Hot Springs Tourism Information, P.O. Box 225, Radium Hot Springs, BC V0A 1M0; (250) 347-9331,** fax **(250) 347-9127.**

DINING OUT

Panorama

Starbird Family Dining Room
Breakfast, lunch and dinner in casual slopeside restaurant. Daily specials at all meals and weekend breakfast buffet. Varied menu, with light to full meals and snacks. Child-friendly, with children's menu and an especially tolerant wait staff. **Pine Inn Hotel, Panorama; (250) 342-6941.**

T-Bar and Grill
Lively eating and entertainment spot specializing in Tex-Mex food. Daily lunch and dinner specials. Wednesday evening dinner theater. Children must be out of restaurant by 9:00 P.M. **Pine Inn Hotel, Panorama; (250) 342-6941.**

Toby Creek Dining Room

Panorama's finest restaurant in a spacious dining room. Large fireplace, high ceiling, dim lights and candlelight atmosphere. Interesting European-Oriental combinations. Excellent desserts and specialty coffees. Management says "children welcome," but small fry would be happier elsewhere. Reservations recommended. **Toby Creek Lodge, Panorama; (250) 342-6941, Ext. 343.**

Invermere

For guests who want to sample Invermere dining without the access-road hassle, a free bus departs from Panorama's central registration area every Monday evening at 6:15.

NIGHTLIFE

The T-Bar and Grill in the Europa Lodge, the Starbird Lounge in the Pine Inn Hotel, the Strathcona Pub in the Horsethief Lodge and the Fireside Piano Lounge in the Toby Creek Lodge are the places to go for traditional after-ski and evening entertainment, which is quite a selection for so modest a resort. The Glacier Night Club, also in the Europa Lodge, is Panorama's late-night spot, with music and dancing as long as your legs hold out.

Panorama also puts some kind of special entertainment together every night of the week. Some events are free; others are on a fee basis. These include family activities such as casino night, mini-golf and other activities crossing the age range. There are also special children's and teen activities, plus adult events such as wine tastings, comedy and "dating game" entertainment and "bar Olympics." Evening cross-country skiing and sleighrides are popular. Panorama's buses also go to Invermere and Radium Hot Springs one evening each week so that guests can check out the valley.

For more information, contact **Panorama Resort, Panorama, BC V0A 1T0; (800) 663-2929, (250) 342-6941, fax (250) 342-3395.**

423

SILVER STAR

BACKDROP

Silver Star is more about high spirits than high living. On a cheerfulness scale of 1 to 10, it practically leaps off the chart. This delightful resort greets the world with a shamelessly painted face. As you drive toward the village center, the first house that hits your eye is a mauvey purple nouveau Victorian, its gingerbread trimmed in gold, sky blue and forest green. And that's only the beginning. In the village center you'll find western-style false-front buildings, board sidewalks and turn-of-the-century details that are meant to invoke images of an old mining town, but done in a palette of brilliant colors that old miners couldn't have imagined. In the surrounding resort, you'll find fanciful homes done in even more startling color combinations, reminiscent of San Francisco's "painted ladies"—and with more light-hearted humor than homeowners by the Bay manage. The scale of the resort is modest, but a few buildings pack a walloping impact when they are so clever and harmonious. The resort's indoor swimming pool, for instance, is signed "Doc Simmons Swim and Soak." The firehouse looks like an old-fashioned hose company. One hotel has its outdoor hot tub under the replica of a water tower.

But you don't come to Silver Star simply to see. You come to ski, and the terrain surrounding the smile-invoking village is wonderful as well. The close-in runs offer lots of options for little kids and new skiers. There are cruisers aplenty and an entire adjacent mountain that is full of genuine challenge. The Nordic facilities are right on a par with the Alpine terrain—and are perhaps even better known among knowledgeable skiers. Silver Star offers big-time skiing coupled with small-resort compactness and convenience, all in an unremittingly delightful atmosphere.

THE LAY OF THE LAND

Silver Star is in a high basin above the Okanagan Valley town of Vernon. It is separated from suburban sprawl by a long, sinuous access road that, in part, passes through Silver Star Provincial Park. The resort center is laid out to replicate a Wild West town, but instead of hitching posts and horses on a dusty street, there are ski racks and pedestrians on a snowy promenade. It's a compact village where even young children can be given a long rein. Primary access to the ski runs are at the head of main street, just behind the ski-school building, which not surprisingly looks just like a one-room schoolhouse, but there's skiing all around the village. In addition to the resort center, private chalets from simple A-frames to elaborate Victorians dot the hilly residential development known as The Knoll, and a splendid new condominium appropriately called Grandview continues the turn-of-the-century theme and offers commanding views of the Valhalla and Monashee Ranges. Most have either direct ski-in/ski-out access or are just a quick walk from the nearest slope or skiway.

GETTING THERE

The nearest airport is Kelowna, 55 kilometers (24 miles) south of Vernon, with flights from Calgary, Toronto and Vancouver. Rental cars are available, but since you won't need a vehicle at the area, you can arrange for airport transfers from **Jim's Limo & Delivery, (250) 542-6119.** (Jim's also has a deal to pick up phone-in grocery orders from Butcher Boy's market in Vernon for condo-dwelling vacationers who don't find the resort's small convenience store to have a sufficient selection.) Take Hwy 97 north to Vernon, turn east on 48th Ave., pass Jim Attridge Sports whose big sign reads, "Honk If You Ski" and wind your way 18 kilometers (11 miles) up to the resort. **Greyhound Lines of Canada, (800) 661-8747, (604) 662-3222,** has service to Vernon.

PROFILE

Silver Star's ski terrain unfolds like a paper fan. When you think you've figured it out, you come to the next crease, unfold it a little more and find yet more skiing. Directly beside the village is a broad slope and a chairlift loading area. You can board the chair and ride to the summit or ski down the slope called Milky Way to the Vance Creek quad, which rises almost to the summit. From the top, you have a choice. One option is the main face, where you'll find some really beguiling terrain that doesn't get overskied simply because the return to the lifts takes some time and is awkward. Drop left off the ridge, and you find yourself on Attridge Face, which locals love because it has few trees, ample challenge and a good chance of powder. Continue along the Attridge Access and you'll find a selection of runs arrayed like a hand of playing cards. The "Bus Runs"— Bus Back, Outback and Fastback—drop into a low drainage that is now a ski-out to the lifts, but once, Silver Star ran a shuttle down the road to retrieve skiers who had tackled this black-diamond trio. Solitude, Lone Star and Interlude are easier but, like the Bus Runs, are interesting for their varied pitch and tempting tree skiing. The runout leads back to a T-bar from which you can ski back down to either the Summit chair or the quad.

The other option from the village is to ski over the bridge across the resort access road to the Silver Queen chair. This slow-moving beginner chair is favored by children's classes but also accesses Silver Star's ski-in/ski-out homes. If you're feeling puckish, you can take Aberdeen Skiway, with or without a shortcut on Rollercoaster, and end up back at the bottom of the quad. It's fun to circumnavigate the village center this way simply because so few North American resorts offer a real circuit. Silver Star's upcoming expansion, perhaps in 1998–99, will continue in this direction, with a new high-speed quad to be called the Silver Woods Express, several steadily pitched intermediate runs with a snow-holding northeast exposure and about 500 feet of additional vertical.

There was a time when good skiers dismissed Silver Star as "Bambi Basin" and sought their

Inside Silver Star

thrills elsewhere. No more. The Putnam Creek sector, which is one mountain over and set back from the main area, tests the mettle of advanced and expert skiers and snowboarders. And if you're strong and tireless, you too will take Far

Out or Main Street over to Putnam Creek. While Vance Creek and the rest of the front part of the ski area come across as wide and squat, practically everything on the Putnam Creek side is long and steep, giving you the sense of threading your way down a very challenging mountain. Add to the difficulty a largely northern exposure, which is great for keeping the snow dry.

In addition to looking and skiing totally different from the frontside, Putnam Creek is a surprisingly large parcel set far back from the main mountain with access and egress via long roads leading to a conglomeration of several ridges and drainages. One green-circle trail looping around the perimeter is called Aunt Gladys under the premise that "it's easy enough for your Aunt Gladys," but in general, the Putnam Creek's ridge tops are dark blue runs of fine width, while steep, steeper and hold-your-hat steep trails drop away precipitously to the bottom. One trail intersection is nicknamed The Orchard, perhaps because **426** you have to pick which run you'll take: Doognog, Wise Men, Headwall and Quicksilver on one side of the lift; Where's Bob, Black Pine, Gowabunga and Free Fall on the other. Patrollers at the lift's mid-station, ready to help the injured or bail out those who simply have miscalculated what Bambi Basin has now become.

Silver Star's fanciful Victorian look provides a cheery and congenial setting for extremely varied terrain.

Photo by Don Weixl/Silver Star

SNOWBOARDING

A generous portion of Big Dipper beside the Yellow chair, an auxiliary lift for peak times, has been turned into a large snowboard park, but riders love the whole mountain (though they don't always appreciate the long flats to and from Vance Creek).

SKI SCHOOL PROGRAMS

Reservations are recommended for all ski-week programs and available for others; **(250) 558-6065.**

Introductory Programs

Discover Skiing: Beginner lift ticket, all-day equipment rental and 1½-hour ski lesson, with classes three times daily.
Discover Snowboarding: Same as above for snowboarders.
First Step Snowboard Camp: For first-time snowboarders, including lunch, video and other extras.
Ski Week: Five days of daily 1½-hour lessons, plus fun race. All levels.

Advanced and Specialty Programs

Woman's Way: Two-day camps for women, taught by women. Package includes lifts, lessons, breakfast and lunch each day and other extras.
Value Ladies' Day: Series of three lessons on consecutive December Tuesdays.
Mogul Motion: One-day adult camp on mogul skiing, including video, lunch and other extras.
Tune Up Weeks: Five-day early-season lesson package, including video analysis, fun race and free lift tickets to guests at any on-mountain hotel. Available Monday through Friday.
Ski Improvement Week: Five-day January lesson package, including video analysis, fun race. Free to guests at any on-mountain hotel. Available Monday through Friday.
Mountain Ski Week: Five-day regular season lift-and-lesson package.

Special Program

Ski Partners is a host program providing free guided tours of the mountain daily at 10:00 A.M. and 1:00 P.M.

For Families

Nonskiing Children

Playroom: Newly relocated and expanded day care facility for children from 18 months to nonskiing 8-year-olds. Includes arts and crafts, storytelling and snacks. Available by the hour or full day, with lunch option. Reservations required; **(250) 558-6028.**

Skiing Children

Full Day Ski School: Two two-hour group lessons for ages 4 to 8; parents must arrange for lunch break.
Star Club: Outdoor activity program to supplement ski lessons, above.
Vacation Club: Five-day lift-and-lesson package. Ski or snowboard lessons. Available Monday through Friday, during Christmas and March school holidays.
Much Too Cool for School: Five-day lift-and-lesson package. Ski or snowboard lessons. Available Monday through Friday, non-holiday weeks.

Noteworthy

In addition to children's rates for youngsters ages 6 to 12, Silver Star offers a youth ticket for ages 13 to 17. At some lodgings and on some packages, children to age 16 stay free in parents' room. The resort center is a compact, car-free village where children can feel safe. Youngsters also love night skiing.

You can get children's, youth and family tickets for ice skating, tubing and tobogganing, all just a short walk from the village center near the Silver Queen lift, and all lift tickets include these family-pleasing evening activities as well.

Mountain Stats—
Silver Star

Resort elevation 5,280 feet (1,609 meters)
Top of highest lift 6,280 feet (1,915 meters)
Bottom of lowest lift 3,780 feet (1,155 meters)
Total vertical 2,500 feet (760 meters)
Longest run 5 miles (8 kilometers)
Average annual snowfall 250 inches (635 centimeters)
Ski season mid-November to mid-April
Lifts 2 high-speed detachable quad chairlifts, 1 fixed-grip quad, 2 double chairs, 2 T-bars, 1 handle tow
Capacity 11,800 skiers per hour
Terrain 81 trails, 1,200 acres (20% beginner and novice, 50% intermediate, 30% advanced and expert)
Night skiing 50 acres
Mountain dining Paradise Camp at the Putnam Express mid-station
Snow reports (250) 542-1745 in Vernon, **(250) 860-7817** in Kelowna

NORDIC SKIING

Silver Star, which shares an expansive network with the Sovereign Lake Cross-Country Ski Area, ranks as one of Canada's premier Nordic meccas. Most of the 25 kilometers of trails are groomed for diagonal or skating, but a few are left natural. In addition, 80 kilometers in adjacent Silver Star Provincial Park are marked but not groomed. Experienced skiers can ski into the Sovereign Lake system directly from Silver Star's Summit Lift, but most people drive to the commodious new day lodge at the Sovereign Lake portion of the trail system, where trail tickets are sold. Seventeen trails from an easy half-kilometer teaching track to several advanced trails up to 4.8 kilometers long comprise the entire network, which is regularly the site of serious training camps and cross-country races. World-class racers train at Silver Star because of the trail facilities and the National Altitude Training Centre, which offers comprehensive fitness testing, weight training and on-skis training. The Silver Star Ski School offers beginner packages, advanced packages, ski weeks and tune-up programs for Nordic skiers that are similar to the Alpine program. Seven kilometers of trails accessible from Silver Star are lit for night skiing. Sovereign Lake facilities are maintained by the North Okanagan Cross Country Ski Club; the snow reports number is **(250) 494-0321.**

WHERE TO STAY

Reservations are available through **Silver Star Mountain Ski Holidays, P.O. Box 2, Silver Star Mountain, BC V0E 1G0; (800) 663-4431, (250) 542-0224.**

Silver Star

Mid-Priced Accommodations

Putnam Station
Railroad theme in centrally located hotel with 32 standard hotel rooms, kitchenette units and two-bedroom suites. Some units with fireplaces. Hotel also handles some home rentals. Restaurant, lounge, outdoor hot tub. Daily housekeeping. **P.O. Box 4, Silver Star, BC V0E 1G0; (800) 489-0599, (250) 542-2459.**

Silver Star's compact village and slopeside lodging make it popular with families.

Photo by Don Weixl/Silver Star

Swiss Hotel Silver Lode Inn
Western outside, but Swiss inside. Continental charm and ambiance. Twenty-room hotel, six with kitchenettes. Optional meal plan. Pets permitted. Dining room, lounge, hot tub, recreation room. Daily housekeeping. **P.O. Box 5, Silver Star, BC V0E 1G0; (250) 549-5105.**

Vance Creek Hotel
With 84 rooms in two buildings, resort's largest hotel. Regular hotel rooms, kitchenette units and one-bedroom units with full kitchen. Simple but charming decor. Lobby, corridors and other public spaces filled with antiques and memorabilia. Restaurant, lounge, hot tub. Daily housekeeping. **P.O. Box 3, Silver Star, BC V0E 1G0; (800) 663-4431, (250) 549-5191.**

Economy Accommodations

Kickwillie Inn
Convenient slopeside inn with one- and two-bedroom family units, most with lofts. Some with fireplace. Units each sleep six to eight and have full kitchens. Hot tub. **9883 Pinnacles Rd., P.O. Box 7, Silver Star, BC V0E 1G0; (250) 542-4548.**

The Pinnacles
Silver Star's original base lodge, now a budget inn for families and groups. Two- to four-bedroom suites with full kitchens, many with lofts, fireplaces and/or sundecks. Smallest unit sleeps eight, largest 16. Pets permitted. Rooftop hot tub. **9889 Pinnacles Rd., P.O. Box 8, Silver Star, BC V0E 1G0; (250) 542-4548.**

Condominiums and Homes

Grandview
Thirty-three luxurious two-bedroom, two-bath units with full kitchens. Ski-out to Vance Creek Express and ski-in from Silver Queen chair. Outdoor hot tub. **(250) 542-0224.**

Lord Aberdeen Apartment Hotel
Sixteen one- and new two-bedroom apartments, each with private entrance directly from the village. Largest unit accommodates up to six. Site of resort's deli, cappuccino bar, general store and liquor store. Sauna. **P.O. Box 1, Silver Star, BC V0E 1G0; (800) 553-5885, (250) 542-1992.**

Monashee Vacation Homes

Homes of various sizes. Non-smoking properties. **15850 Whiskey Cove Rd., Winfield, BC V4V 1C4; (250) 766-9947.**

RV Parking

Parking lot near village for recreational vehicles and trailers with electrical plug-ins for engines. Guests may use showers and laundry at Doc Simmons Soak and Swim. Call resort reservations number for details.

On and Near Silver Star Road

Luxury Accommodations

Castle on the Mountain

Chateau-style inn with grandiose valley views. Five rooms, honeymoon suite and family apartment. Private and shared baths. Art gallery and studio on premises. Non-smoking inn. Outdoor hot tub, living room with fireplace. Daily housekeeping, full breakfast. **8227 Silver Star Rd., Vernon, BC V1T 6L6; (250) 542-4593.**

Mid-Priced Accommodations

Maria Rose

Quaint and cozy B&B. Quiet hillside location. Very European, like your "Tante Maria's" place. Four rooms, two with private and two with shared bath, in carriage house adjacent to main house. Non-smoking inn. Daily housekeeping, full breakfast. Sauna, ski racks in barn. **8083 Aspen Rd., Vernon, BC V1T 6L6; (250) 549-4773.**

Silver Star Bed & Breakfast

Spacious new inn, traditionally styled like an "executive home." Four rooms with private baths and private entrances; family suite with crib. Sun and sitting rooms, library, hot tub, grand piano. Non-smoking inn. Daily housekeeping, full breakfast. Ten-minute drive from resort. **8538 Silver Star Rd., Vernon, BC V1T 6L6; (250) 558-1688.**

Economy Accommodations

Wildwood Bed and Breakfast

Sparkling-clean B&B in down-valley ranch house with shared- and private-bath rooms; one suite with fireplace, private bath and kitchen. Non-smoking inn. Virtually a private bird sanctuary, with bird feeders on property that draw many species in winter. Fireplace guest lounge, outdoor hot tub. Full breakfast with vegetarian specialties and home-baked breads. **7454 Wildwood Rd., Vernon, BC V1T 6L6; (800) 545-1558, (250) 545-2747.**

Vernon

A variety of motels and B&B inns are located in Vernon. Some offer ski packages. For lodging information and reservations, call **(800) 665-0795.** For more information on the town or to request the **Vernon Visitors Guide,** call **(250) 542-1415.**

DINING OUT

Clementine's

Hotel restaurant, done in a comforting country style. Buffet and à la carte breakfasts. Also, lunch and dinner. Steak and other beef entrées a specialty. Full bar and wine list. Dinner reservations accepted. **Vance Creek Hotel, Silver Star; (250) 549-5191.**

Craigellachi Dining Room

Hotel restaurant with terrific ambiance. Model train and other railroad memorabilia set the tone for a casual fun dinner. Beef, chicken and other popular dishes. Full bar. Children's menu. **Putnam Station Hotel, Silver Star; (250) 542-2459.**

Lucciano's Trattoria

Stylish restaurant serving pasta, pizza and other Italian favorites. Sleek decor. Reservations accepted. **Vance Creek Hotel, Silver Star; (250) 549-5191.**

Paradise Camp Snowmobile Dinners

Diners board snowmobiles for a roaring good time procession to Paradise Camp on-mountain restaurant. Barbecued steak and side dishes, with entertainment too. Reservations required. **Silver Star Snowmobile Guided Tours, Silver Star; (250) 553-5575.**

Even the smallest detail harmonizes with Silver Star's old western theme.

Photo by Don Weixl/Silver Star

Silver Lode Inn

Top restaurant in resort. Looks and feels like a corner of Switzerland. Known for outstanding and authentic Swiss and other continental dishes, including *Emince de Veau* Zurichoise, Wiener Schnitzel and fondue. Excellent service. Fine wine list. Terrific pastries. Thursday buffet features prime rib, chicken, fish, salads and home-baked bread and pastries. Reservations recommended. **Silver Lode Inn, Silver Star; (250) 549-5105.**

430

NIGHTLIFE

There's enough to do in the evening to ward off boredom but not so much that you'll feel as if you're missing the action if you just feel like returning to your hotel or condo and gazing at the a fire or the television. Clementine's at the Vance Creek Hotel has a popular lounge, and in spring, a deck overlooking "main street" gets some lively spillover. Putnam Station Hotel's Craigellachie Restaurant incorporates a casual bar, while the downstairs lounge resembles a wine cellar and offers nectar from keg and barrel. Don't miss an evening at the Silver Lode. Its Swiss lounge serves commendable local and imported wines, and on Wednesdays, you can sample a wonderful cheese specialty called raclette and a suitable wine. You can also be continental by stopping in for an après-ski pastry and coffee at the Silver Lode, the New Silver Star Bakery in the Vance Creek Hotel or a quick espresso at the neighboring Lord Aberdeen.

For more information, contact **Silver Star Mountain Resort, P.O. Box 2, Silver Star, BV V0E 1G0; (800) 663-4431, (250) 542-0224,** fax **(250) 542-1236.**

BIG WHITE

BACKDROP

Big White is one of those western Canadian secrets, popular with enthusiastic locals, known by
British Columbians and skiers from the Pacific
Northwest, but virtually unheard of by skiers
from elsewhere. With increased air service to
Kelowna, a good little airport just down the road
in the Okanagan Valley, and an ambitious expansion plan, it becomes a worthwhile and economical vacation spot for people from farther afield.
This huge ski area boasts vast uncrowded acreage and consistent, if not ultra-abundant, snow.
The landscape is beguiling, with old-growth pine
forests on the lower mountain, balsam and
spruce higher up and sparse balsams at the timberline. The top of the mountain is at 7,600 feet,
tundra at Big White's latitude, which Canadians
refer to as "the Alpine." The summit elevation
surpasses those of Whistler and Blackcomb, and
with a mid-province location, Big White gets reliable drops of dry western snow instead of the
damp dumps that you often find in the Coast
Mountains where those British Columbia superstar areas are located.

Big White long lingered in limbo between a
local area for day skiers and a resort. The scope
and variety of the terrain and rudimentary overnight accommodations long said "resort," while
the limitations of those same accommodations,
low prices and accessibility to a good-sized city
bespoke "day-skiing area." The recent infusion
of capital is tilting the balance toward real resort status. Millions of dollars have gone into
speedy new lifts, additional terrain and a village in the making. An ambitious development
plan is finally shifting into high gear. A village
core was built in 1996 as a focus for the
rather random base accommodations, and a
second and better-planned development
called Snow Pines Estates is underway. Big
White is definitely an up-and-coming resort
worth a long, hard look.

Inside Big White

THE LAY OF THE LAND

Big White sits squarely in the central British Columbian mountain range known as the Okanagan Highlands of the Monashees. The area burst onto the scene in 1979, with lift service practically to the summit. Subsequent development has involved adding lifts and terrain, relocating liftlines and lowering the base elevation to achieve a greater vertical. This growth pattern has spawned a layered arrangement, with "base areas" and day lodges at three levels. The original day lodge is now a central mid-mountain facility called the Alpine Centre, the next generation is a day lodge just below the main village development and the newest and latest base area is at the bottom of Westridge, a new second-home development begun in 1996. As you drive up to Big White, you first reach Westridge and the new Gem Lake Express chair, then pass one day lodge and finally end up at the resort center. With the expansion of the village in 1996, a new 24-hour central check-in and resort-wide front desk was established. Day skiers can cut up to 20 minutes off their ride by hopping aboard the new chairlift, and vacationers have less competition in the newly expanded resort village.

GETTING THERE

Big White is 55 kilometers (about 35 miles) east of Kelowna, whose airport has flights from Vancouver, Calgary, Edmonton and Toronto. The drive is straightforward, via Route 33 up the canyon to the Big White access road. Rental cars are available at the airport, and shuttle service is available if you book through Big White Central Reservations. There is currently no bus service at the resort, but the village is really compact and self-contained. With the development of Westridge, intraresort shuttle service will probably be introduced as need materializes. The resort is a five-hour drive from Vancouver or Spokane and seven hours from Seattle. Kelowna is also served by **Greyhound Lines of Canada, (800) 661-8747, (604) 662-3222.**

Big White ranks as one of central British Columbia's big snow resorts.

PROFILE

Most of Big White's lifts run due north, meaning that the majority of the ski runs face south and snare the sun's rays all day long, not inconsequential in western Canada. The area's lift and trail system sprawls across three major ridges and five big drainages, yet the layout is so sensible and there's so much wide-open terrain and big vistas that orientation is surprisingly easy. If you are staying at or near the village center which most people still do, you'll find the beginner hill below and most of the novice and intermediate terrain directly above and easily accessible. Better skiers and snowboarders have to earn their turns by skimming past the easy terrain to high-intermediate to high-expert turf on both corners of the ski area. Skiing from one lift to the other is straightforward: stay high and traverse.

Big White presents new and sometime skiers with a great deal of moderate terrain, but it is never boring. There are few boulevards, but rather a lot of dips and curves, drop-offs and rolls, so that even the easiest runs are distinctive and interesting. The great array of green-circle and blue-square runs which make it so perfect for casual cruising skiers are accessed by a trio of high-speed quad chairlifts—Ridge Rocket Express, Bullet Express and Black Forest Express—from three points on the bottom of the mountain, climbing three ridges. Literally dozens of groomed runs from quite mild to decently pitched with lots of cross-overs and connectors make for oodles of options without much risk of getting stuck on unexpected steeps. Unless you're a rank beginner, you can't go wrong on this lacework of gentle and medium trails. Occasional mogul fields, an opportunity to slip into the trees for some glade skiing, and the combination of uncrowded slopes and one of western Canada's highest elevations create the challenge on much of the mountain. The lower stretches of the Black Forest Express are cut through especially tranquil and beautiful stands of big, old pines. This section is understandably popular in flat light.

From the top of the Ridge Rocket or Bullet Express chairs, you can ski down to a T-bar which climbs to Big White's highest point. At- and above-timberline snowfields, sparsely populated by rime-covered trees that bend into snow ghosts, make this a hauntingly beautiful parcel of ski terrain. With wide open slopes on top funneling quickly into light glades and all with a moderate pitch, there's a rare opportunity for intermediate-level glade and bowl skiing. There's nothing moderate about the huge cirque carved out of the side of the mountaintop as if by a voracious giant. Control gates access perpendicular walls, and from a distance, skiers and riders resemble spiders clinging to the mountainside.

The remainder of Big White's black diamonds are liberally sprinkled on the far side of the mountain. The Powder triple chairlift accesses some steep (and some not so steep) runs that snake through the trees, as well as some of British Columbia's all-around best tree skiing. Flagpole Glades, Powder Glades and Corkscrew Glades, all roughly at mid-mountain and Dragon Glades lower down are long and steep. The Falcon double chair tucked off in a high corner of Big White serves another steep-walled cirque called Whitefoot Bowl. Chutes, trees, double-diamond pitches and a real high-Alpine flavor characterize this prize part of the mountain. With the construction of the new Gem Lake Express in

1996 to ferry skiers up from the Westridge area to a knoll between the Falcon and Powder chairs, this heretofore underskied part of the mountain will become more mainstream. The lift falls into the gee-whiz category. At 8,000 feet long and with a 2,330-foot vertical rise, the Gem Lake Express is one of Canada's longest and has the greatest vertical of any high-speed detachable quad in the country. Yet with a ride time of just seven minutes, this lift is more than just a transport lift. Many skiers will take to the new trails cut along with the installation of the new lift. More glades and additional trails, mostly on the moderate to upper-intermediate side, represent a continuation of the Big White's strong emphasis on a combination of recreational skiing and real challenge, all with the resort's new commitment to easy and fast lift access.

SNOWBOARDING

With so many little cut-offs, drop-away steeps and fabulous tree terrain, Big White is a free rider's paradise. There's a dynamite snowboard park on Speculation, off the Ridge Rocket chair, complete with a buried school bus, good half-pipe and other features. A terrain garden on the Sundance trail, accessible via the Bullet and Black Forest Express lifts, boasts a sound system for special events.

SKI SCHOOL PROGRAMS

Introductory Programs

Learn to Ski: Beginner lift ticket and lesson, with equipment rental option, for adults and juniors.
Learn to Snowboard: Introductory package with lift/lesson, lesson/rental and lift/lesson/rental options.

Advanced and Specialty Programs

Ski Improvement Sessions: 1¹/₂-hour lessons for intermediate and advanced skiers.
Snowboarding Sessions: 1¹/₂-hour lessons for intermediate and advanced riders.

British Columbia

Ladies' Day: Lift-and-lesson package, offered Wednesdays from January through March, including lunch and après-ski party.

50 Plus Program: Lift-and-lesson package, offered Thursdays from January through March, including lunch and après-ski party; drop-ins welcome.

Greg Athans Ski Camps: Recreational racing camps and clinics hosted by former Canadian National Team member and Olympian; available in corporate versions for groups.

Special Programs

Snowhosts: Complimentary mountain tours at 10:00 A.M. daily.

Noteworthy

Big White lends helmets to skiing children, compliments of Wendy's restaurants. They are available at the ski school desk. Kettle Valley Park, the sizable children's terrain garden, is served by the Plaza quad chairlift. Older children appreciate night skiing, and the resort also schedules such after-ski activities as children's movie night, casino and bingo night, fun races, Kids' Night Out and other favorites.

For Families

Nonskiing Children

Daycare: For non-skiers from 6 months to 6 years. Indoor and outdoor activities, depending on age and weather conditions. Hourly and daily rates available. Large new children's facility built in 1996, with increased capacity and vibrant indoor play area. Reservations recommended.

Skiing Children

Lessons only or full-day program including lessons and lunch for ages 3 to 5. Program can also be combined with hourly Daycare.

Kids' Klub: Two-hour lessons or all-day option with lessons, lunch and supervision. Lifts additional or available on special packages. Clever booklet, with space for new ski buddies' names and specific skills to be checked off, serves as progress report.

Mountain Stats— Big White

Resort elevation 1,768 meters (5,450 feet)
Top of highest lift 2,319 meters (7,606 feet)
Bottom of lowest lift 1,523 meters (4,950 feet)
Total vertical 850 meters (2,550 feet)
Longest run 7.2 kilometers (4½ miles)
Average annual snowfall 600 centimeters (236 inches)
Ski season mid-November to mid-April
Lifts 4 high-speed detachable quad chairlifts, 1 fixed-grip quad, 1 triple, 1 double, 1 T-bar
Capacity 18,000 skiers per hour
Terrain 105 trails and glade areas plus bowls; 2,300 acres (15% beginner and novice, 50% intermediate, 35% advanced and expert)
Night skiing nightly except Sunday and Monday, on the beginner hill and off the Ridge Rocket Express
Snow reports (250) 765-SNOW

NORDIC SKIING

Big White's 25 kilometers (15 miles) of cross-country trails are accessible from the village and free.

WHERE TO STAY

Big White Central Reservations, P.O. Box 2039, Stn. R, Big White, BC V1X 4K5; (800) 663-2772, (250) 765-8888; fax (250) 765-1822.

Mid-Priced Accommodations

White Crystal Inn

Big White's most luxurious lodging. Comfortable and affordable. Chalet-style 14-room inn in village and close to the lifts. Children 5 and under free. B&B plan, plus discount for guests on other meals. Restaurant, lounge. Daily housekeeping, room service, valet service. **P.O. Box 2365, Stn.**

R, Big White, BC V1X 4K5; (800) 663-2772, (250) 765-4611.

Whitefoot Lodge

Large complex with center-village location. Units range from sparsely furnished budget hotel rooms to multibedroom condominium apartments. Most units with kitchens, some with fireplaces. No in-room phones. All individually furnished. Sauna, hot tub, cold plunge pool, ski lockers, guest laundry, grocery store. Daily housekeeping (towels and trash). **P.O. Box 2039, Stn. R, Big White, BC V1X 4K5; (800) 663-2772, (250) 765-8888.**

RV Lots

Forty RV lots with 30-amp electrical, water, sewer and television hookups. Washroom and shower facilities; outdoor hot tub, ski-in/ski-out sites. Short walk to village. Nightly and weekly rates. Book through Central Reservations.

Noteworthy

Big White offers exceptionally well-priced packages including lessons during non-peak seasons. Ask about Super Saver, January Getaway and Midwinter Magic packages when calling the resort's central reservations number.

Condominiums

The Eagles Resort

Slopeside location at top of beginner area. Comfortable to luxurious units. Sleep up to 10 and range from two bedrooms with den to three bedrooms with loft, all with fireplace, two bathrooms and full kitchen. All non-smoking. Indoor/outdoor pool, spa, sauna, game room. **P.O. Box 22060, Kelowna, BC V1Y 9N9; (800) 563-EAGLES, (604) 765-4883.**

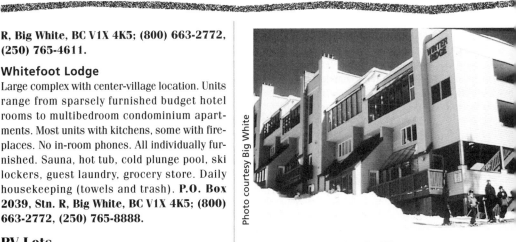

Photo courtesy Big White

Slopeside lodging abounds at Big White.

Plaza and Chateau on the Ridge

Fine slopeside location. One- to four-bedroom condominiums. Two buildings, Chateau on the Ridge and Plaza on the Ridge. Gas fireplaces and washer and dryer in some units. Ski lockers, three hot tubs. **657 Westside Rd., Kelowna, BC V1Y 8B2; (800) 661-7708, (250) 769-3155.**

435

The resort has additional condominium complexes and some vacation homes of various styles and vintages. All are ski-in/ski-out or a very short walk to the slopes and can be booked through the resort's central reservations number. There are no phones in individual rooms or units; daily housekeeping is restricted to towel and trash services. Most have covered parking, and some are elevator buildings. Individual properties and their features include

Das Hofbräuhaus (atrium design with swimming pool in courtyard plus hot tub, saunas, racquetball court, video arcade, restaurant and lounge)

Graystoke Inn (outdoor hot tub, sauna, guest laundry, ski storage)

Monashee Inn (one of older complexes, full kitchens, many fireplace units, ski storage)

The Moguls (studios to three-bedroom units with fireplaces, hot tub, sauna, guest laundry, ski storage)

The Ponderosa (good-sized units, hot tub, sauna)

Ptarmigan Inn (sauna, hot tub, cold plunge area, ski storage, guest laundry)

Tamarack Inn (among Big White's most deluxe, with fireplace and some sauna units)

Kelowna offers abundant accommodations within an easy commute of Big White. They range from budget motels to elaborate resorts, built for golf and offering excellent off-season rates. Many properties have budget ski packages. Information is available from the **Kelowna Visitor Information Centre, 544 Harvey Ave., Kelowna, BC V1Y 6C9; (250) 861-1515,** fax **(250) 861-3624.**

DINING OUT

436 Dom's

Breezy and casual restaurant. American or continental breakfast, including buffet option. Light lunches such as sandwiches and pizza. Dinner is largely Italian, with lots of pasta. Innovative specialties such as Dom's Creation, which is chicken breast with a light cranberry chutney. Aged

The White Crystal Inn combines chalet charm and convenience.

Photo courtesy Big White

steaks. Earlybird children's specials (half-price until 7:00 P.M.). Also, dinner buffet with baron of beef, ham and turkey, with ample accompaniments. Children 6 and under free at dinner buffet. **Whitefoot Lodge, Big White.**

Loose Moose

Après-ski segues into dinner at this lively slopeside spot. Casual and pub food, merriment, and entertainment. Nightly specials. **Alpine Centre, Big White.**

Raakel's

Lounge and restaurant with casual almost coffee-shop decor. Soups, sandwiches, salads, burgers and pizza. Very good munchies, including garlic pork buttons, poutine and Middle Eastern favorites like hummus. Also such specials as two-for-one pizza on Tuesdays, wings on Wednesdays and prime rib on Saturdays. **Das Hofbräuhaus, Big White.**

Snowshoe Sam's

Downstairs is lively lounge; upstairs is fine dining with views of the slopes. Rustic ambiance, with big windows, wooden floors, beamed ceilings and roaring fire. Interesting combinations, including Hot and Sour Prawn Soup, Camembert Chicken Kiev, and Italian and Thai specialties with a twist. Daily specials. Children's menu. Knockout desserts, included Baked Alaska flamed with lit Grand Marnier poured down a gunbarrel. Lunch and dinner. Located next to **Whitefoot Lodge, Big White.**

White Crystal

Hotel restaurant serving breakfast, lunch and dinner. Good soups, salads and sandwiches dominate lunch menu. Dinner features Italian specialties, steaks, seafood, and poultry well prepared and served in a pleasant, traditional atmosphere. Restaurant decorated with wonderful photos of old Big White. **White Crystal Inn, Big White.**

NIGHTLIFE

Early après-ski centers at the Loose Moose Tap and Grille in the Alpine Centre and at Raakel's in the Hofbräuhaus near the bottom of the Ridge Rocket Express. At either, you're likely to find live entertainment. Raakel's has pool, darts and other games and is the best bet for dancing till 1:00 A.M. with a deejay or band. The Loose Moose and Dom's generally have live entertainment on Friday, Saturday and Sunday evenings. If you're in the mood for a somewhat quieter evening, the Grizzly Bear Lounge in the White Crystal Inn is a good choice, and if you're feeling like a really quiet evening, a private hot tub rental at the Alpine Health Centre in the Alpine Centre lodge is just the ticket. But *the* place to be for nightlife is Snowshoe Sam's, a big barn of a place that gets going early and keeps on rocking. The big downstairs bar boasts, "Party Every Night," and that's no idle claim. A congenial atmosphere, pool,

darts and Foozball, and a live band on weekends and holidays set the tone. The music might be blues, rock or something more exotic like a seven-piece horn band. The Bear Trap Lounge upstairs is quieter, with mellow music and a relaxed atmosphere. As Big White's village mushrooms, so—no doubt—will the après-ski options. Big White also puts on a Monday welcome reception for vacationers and features kids' movies or other diversions several evenings.

For more information, contact **Big White, P.O. Box 2039, Stn. R, Big White, BC V1X 4K5; (800) 663-2772, (250) 765-8888,** fax **(250) 765-1822; Kelowna Visitor Information Centre, 544 Harvey Ave., Kelowna, BC V1Y 6C9; (250) 861-1515,** fax **(250) 861-3624.**

SUN PEAKS

BACKDROP

If you ever wished you'd skied Vail in the 1960s or Whistler in the 1970s, before these resorts became what they now are, you can capture the experience at Sun Peaks. This nascent resort is the contemporary reincarnation of Tod Mountain, a rugged and steep "ski hill" founded, funded and skied largely by locals from Kamloops. The resort buildings are being developed in the substantial rustic design that has become the signature style of mountain resorts in the waning years of the 20th century—natural woods, natural stone, patterns derived from folk crafts—whether the "folk" are Scandinavian, Alpine or indigenous North Americans.

438   Sun Peaks is in a growth spurt. The barest nucleus of village and the first two up-to-date ski lifts were in place for the 1995–96 ski season. Development is proceeding at such breakneck speed that the descriptions here will quickly be outdated as more growth occurs in the resort and on the mountain. Meanwhile, as it is in the process of "becoming," Sun Peaks offers mind-bending terrain, an absence of crowds and moderate prices that many people think are missing from the contemporary skiing scene.

THE LAY OF THE LAND

The mountains of British Columbia's central interior are hulking humps whose gentle profile masks a variety of pitch and configuration. Sun Peaks lies at the head of a long, rural valley cut through the high country by Heffley Creek. Deep woods and pastureland line the long access road, while the ski area projects a top-of-the-world that belies a relatively modest 6,882-foot summit elevation.

As you approach the Sun Peaks Resort, you first pass the original Tod Mountain base area.

Minimal accommodations surround the old Burfield Day Lodge, which has gotten a facelift, but this part of the resort is nowhere near the toney and tasteful standards of the new development—and perhaps it never will be too fancy. Homesites and condominiums are sprinkled throughout the lower valley, culminating the village area. The plan includes a core pedestrian zone surrounded by shops, restaurants and lodgings, with the ski lifts just a few steps away.

GETTING THERE

Sun Peaks is about a 45-minute drive from Kamloops. Follow Route 5 north to the Heffley Creek turn-off. Several Canadian airlines fly between Kamloops and Vancouver, Calgary and Edmonton. Rental cars are available. At this writing, there was still no demand for regular shuttle service between the airport and the resort, but this could change as Sun Peaks' business grows. Vancouver is approximately a 3½-hour drive, Seattle 5 hours and Calgary 7½.

PROFILE

Sun Peaks has artfully merged seemingly conflicting components into one, interesting whole that it has won awards for ski-trail layout and area design. The original ski area was known for relentlessly steep skiing. A handful of steep trails were cut on the bottom of the mountain, while the upper area was a wonderland of equally steep open slopes, glades, chutes and bowls. Tod Mountain skiers were known to be good skiers, capable of handling incredibly challenging terrain even in awful conditions, with slopes overgrown and minimally groomed. Some of the old runs have been reconfigured, and other new ones have been added to tame the mountain and make it suitable for less-skilled skiers too. In addition, snowboarders have a field day on a mountain with so much radical terrain. Although the snowfall figure totals are not as impressive as at many other areas (you only ski on the top few inches), and in British Columbia's interior, those inches comprise snow that is often light and dry.

For vacationers, the Sunburst Express, a high-speed quad chairlift, is unquestionably the most logical and best way to get into the heart of Sun Peaks' sprawling terrain, more than a quarter of which is high Alpine-style bowls. This bubble lift takes just eight minutes to speed skiers nearly 2,000 vertical feet from the sparkling Village Day Lodge to a knubby plateau on which the mid-mountain Sunburst Lodge is located. All the skiing below is on tree-lined trails and slopes, while much of that above is headwalls, chutes through the timber and grandiose open bowls. It gives Sun Peaks a convenient two-dimensional quality: when it's stormy and visibility is low, you can ski the lower mountain, and when the sky clears and the sun comes out to create see-for-ever conditions, the upper slopes beckon.

If you get off the Sunburst Express to the right, you'll have your choice of five ridge-side, black-diamond runs that range from Cariboo which has length, width and pitch to Fifth Avenue which is shorter, narrower and also steep. These are bracketed by Boardwalk, which offers the benefit or drawback of being largely visible from the lift, and Coquihalla, which has the ski-down-the-side quality but only wears a blue circle. All of these runs feed into lower 5 Mile, a green-circle boulevard. If you turn left off the express lift, the selection is among half a dozen mid-level cruisers, including skiing the ridgetop which leads to the old Burfield base area.

When you see the expansive white world at the top, it is not surprising that some of the local ranchers called it Mt. Baldy, and for many skiers, the splendor and uniqueness of Sun Peaks are concentrated at the top. The two chairlifts that reach the summit unload on high points of a pair of ridges, the Burfield chair at the top of Juniper Ridge and the Crystal chair high on Crystal Ridge. The broad expanse of Crystal Bowl is scooped between them, and steep runs cascade down into the trough from both. By contemporary standards, riding the old Burfield chair, an antiquated double, is an exercise in patience, but it nevertheless commands the loyalty of some Kamloops regulars. The lift painstakingly rises from 3,969 feet, the lowest part of the ski mountain, to the top at 6,814 feet. The upper reaches are an experts' paradise of chutes, drop-offs and rifle-shot steeps from down ridge walls. Single and double diamonds abound. The signature run on the Burfield sector is a double-diamond called

Photo courtesy Sun Peaks Resort

Inside Sun Peaks

British Columbia

Challenger, a long bump run that drops down a consistent fall-line pitch and narrows into a near slot at the bottom. At the top, good skiers groove on the Chief slots off the side of Juniper Ridge, while even better ones ski a near-freefall called Kukamungas. The West Bowl T-bar serves a passle of blue-square slopes down the far end of the bowl.

While Kamloops regulars will probably continue to ride the Burfield chair (just as they will long insist on calling the place Tod Mountain), the Crystal chair, which is reached by a road from the top of the Sunburst Express, is a better option for vacationers. This conventional-speed triple also serves the upper mountain. The Headwall offers a feast of double-black routes through stands of trees. Intermediates can ski the Crystal Run down the center of the bowl between the Burfield and Crystal chairs, and nearly anyone can navigate 5 Mile, a broad, gentle parkway around the perimeter of the terrain.

440   The Sundance Express rises more than 1,500 vertical feet from the resort base to the top of Sundance Ridge. While the ridges on the main mountain are sharp-walled steeps, Sundance is a milder ridge, which provides exceptional, uncrowded learning and practice terrain for new skiers. On snow days, when experts are carving up the powder on high, you can lay first tracks on Sundance's trails run after run—unless the snowcat beats you and packs it down first. Before long, another lift will probably climb from the gully between Sundance Ridge and lower 5 Mile to the top of The Gills, which is currently a hike-

Riding above the clouds.

Photo courtesy Sun Peaks Resort

Mountain Stats—
Sun Peaks

Resort elevation 4,117 feet (1,255 meters)
Top of highest lift 6,814 feet (2,077 meters)
Bottom of lowest lift 3,969 feet (1,121 meters)
Total vertical 2,844 feet (867 meters)
Longest run 5 miles (8 kilometers)
Average annual snowfall 177 inches (449 centimeters)
Ski season mid-November to mid-April
Lifts 2 high-speed quad chairlifts, 1 triple, 1 double, 1 T-bar, 1 platterpull
Capacity 6,371 skiers per hour
Terrain 63 trails, 1,000 acres (24% beginner and novice, 54% intermediate, 22% advanced and expert)
Snowmaking 120 acres
Mountain dining Sunburst Lodge at the top of the Sunburst chair
Snow reports (250) 578-7232 in Kamloops, **(604) 290-0754** in Vancouver

to area of out-of-bounds powder fields. A long-range dream involves yet another lift and more runs on Mt. Morrisey, which would give Sun Peaks skiing on three interconnected mountains on three sides of the resort village.

SNOWBOARDING

Sun Peaks hangs out the welcome sign to snowboarders. High-level free riders love the upper mountain's awesome stands of trees, rocket-sided chutes and airworthy drop-offs, while young riders in the wannabe stage love to play in an impromptu natural half-pipe next to 5 Mile. A 3,000-foot-long, exceptionally well sculpted snowboard park on the lower Sunrise run, off the Sundance chairlift, features two half-pipes, one for experienced riders and one for novices, plus handrails, cars, fun box, hips, quarter-pipes, transfers and fat gaps. Since Sun Peaks sells a cheaper novice ticket for this lift, budget-conscious snowboarders can use a high-speed chair and ride in a knock-out terrain park.

SKI SCHOOL PROGRAMS

For details on ski and snowboarding instruction, call **(250) 578-7232.**

Introductory Programs

First Turns: Four-day intro program, with two-hour daily lesson, four-day lift pass and learn-to-ski guarantee.

Discovery to Skiing: All-day program with three-hour lesson, lunch and beginner lift ticket, with equipment rental option.

Discovery to Snowboard Programs: All-day program with three-hour lesson, lunch and Sundance Express lift ticket, with equipment rental option. Geared for adult beginners.

Advanced and Specialty Programs

Perfectly Parallel: Multiday program for high-novice and intermediate skiers.

Mountain Adventures: Two-hour class lesson for all levels, with rental equipment option.

Peak Perfection Clinics: Two-hour lessons on consecutive weeks (Fridays through Mondays) for high-intermediate and advanced skiers seeking to master ice, bumps, powder and steeps.

Mountain Adventures: Daily ski or snowboard lessons, with rental equipment option, for all levels.

Instructor Training: Course for upper-level skiers and snowboarders interested in teaching. Leads to Level 1 certification respectively from the Canadian Ski Instructors' Alliance or Canadian Association of Snowboard Instructors.

Nancy Greene Ski Clinics: Two-day workshops monthly during the season with coaching by the Olympic champion and her coaching staff. Some one-day clinics are geared for women only.

Graham Swann's Mountain Masters: Learn-to-ski-better clinics several times during the season with a local ex-racer.

Special Program

Ski With Nancy: Complimentary skiing with Nancy Greene. Usually Mondays, Thursdays and Saturdays, but schedule is posted at guest service desk and in hotels.

For Families
Nonskiing Children

Sundance Playschool: Indoor play and activities for 18 months to 5 years. Full-and half-day options, with or without lunch and with early drop-off or late pick-up available at an extra fee. Reservations required.

Skiing Children

Sun Tots: Two two-hour lessons each day, with rental equipment option for ages 3 to 6 (lift ticket required for 6-year-olds).

Sun Kids: Series of five lessons available on consecutive weekends for local youngsters (charter bus on weekends and holidays from Kamloops optional) or on consecutive days during vacations. Classes at all levels for ages 5 to 14.

Teens

Team Teen Weekday Adventure: Holiday instruction for all levels of skiing and snowboarding for ages 13 to 18, with rental equipment option.

441

Noteworthy

Sun Peaks is developing as a compact, family-friendly, walk-around village. Lift ticket pricing is equally congenial, with varying reductions from the adult price for seniors 65 and over, youths from 13 to 18, children from 9 to 12, and young children from 6 to 8 and free skiing for tots 5 and under. In addition, beginners and novices in all age groups may buy reduced-rate tickets for the Sundance Express only, including free skiing for children 8 and younger.

The resort has developed a full program of organized evening activities for vacationing youngsters, starting with an orientation, face painting and games on Monday night through such outdoor adventures as supervised snowshoeing, tobogganing, broomball and snowplay on Thursday. In between, there's games night, family casino night and kids' movie night.

Photo courtesy Sun Peaks Resort

Popular Nancy Greene, Olympic medalist and still a Canadian sports star, is Sun Peaks' director of skiing.

NORDIC SKIING

442

Twenty-five miles (40 kilometers) of Nordic trails adjoin the resort. Five kilometers are groomed for skating, and four are trackset. The remainder are marked but ungroomed. Some are interwoven with snowmobile trails, but the aim is to separate these two activities as much as possible. Logan Lake, west of Kamloops, offers 23 miles (36 kilometers) of cross-country trails, groomed by volunteers from the Highland Valley Outdoor Association. Several shelters and privies are available along the network. Two kilometers are lit for night skiing. There is no trail fee, but donation boxes are located at the trailhead. For information, call **(250) 523-6225.**

WHERE TO STAY

The limited accommodations at this writing will most certainly expand annually, including an announced involvement by Vancouver-based IntraWest, which has developed base villages at Whistler and Panorama, B.C.; Tremblant, P.Q.; Stratton, VT, and Keystone, CO. The Sun Peaks Resort Association has current information on lodging, as well as other programs and facilities. They can be contacted at **P.O. Box 869,**

Kamloops, BC V2C 5M8; (250) 578-7842, fax (250) 578-7843. The **Central Reservations** number is **(800) 807-3257.**

Mid-Priced Accommodations
Father's Country Inn
Warm B&B, 5 miles (8 kilometers) from Sun Peaks. Ranch house with some first floor and some basement rooms, with private or shared baths. Inn's name honors owner's father, who "discovered" and photographed Norma Jean Baker before she became Marilyn Monroe. Dinner available on advance request. Huge solarium room with large pool and indoor hot tub. Daily housekeeping. **McGillivary Creek Rd., P.O. Box 152, Heffley Creek, BC V0E 1Z0; (800) 578-7322, (250) 578-7308.**

Nancy Greene's Cahilty Lodge
Well-appointed slopeside lodge with efficiency studios, studio lofts, one-bedroom units and suites, plus hotel rooms. On-site restaurant, convenience store, hot tub, ski room. Daily housekeeping for hotel rooms and deluxe suites; for kitchenette units, daily towel change and trash removal, plus cleaning every third day. **P.O. Box 728, Kamloops, BC V2C 5M4; (800) 244-8424, (800) 578-7322, (250) 578-7454.**

Stumböck Club, Sun Peaks Lodge
Authentic European hotel, designed and operated by a leading German tour company. Forty-four attractive rooms, all with mini-bar and some with balconies. Rooms and public spaces decorated in modern Alpine style. Short walk to lifts. Lobby bar, restaurant, cafe, on-site rental and convenience shops, fitness center, hot tub, wax room. Daily housekeeping. **P.O. Box 1187, Kamloops, BC V1C 6H3; (800) 333-9112, (250) 578-7878.**

Vacation Homes and Condominiums
The **Burfield Chalets** are a handful of budget cottages at the base of the Burfield chair. Various more comfortable condominiums and luxurious townhouse and rental homes are also available, and more developments are in the planning stages. For reservations, phone **(800) 807-3257.**

Staying in Kamloops and commuting to Sun Peaks is an economical option throughout the winter and may be the only alternative during busy holiday periods. A number of the town's numerous motels and hotels offer packages that include Sun Peaks lift tickets. For details, contact the **Kamloops Tourist Information Centre, 1290 West TransCanada Hwy., Kamloops, BC V2C 623; (800) 662-1994, (250) 374-3377.**

DINING OUT

All restaurants are at Sun Peaks.

Lachmann's
Tasteful lunch and dinner spot. Predictably features German specialties in a pleasant continental setting. **Stumböck Club; (250) 578-7260.**

Macker's
Spacious restaurant beside Nancy Greene's Cahilty Lodge, specializing the unique cuisine of Canada's West Coast, plus pasta specials. **(250) 578-7454.**

Masa's
Informal spot for breakfast, lunch and dinner at the base of the lifts. Casual dining with eclectic offerings. **Village Day Lodge; (250) 578-5484.**

Sunburst Lodge
Mid-mountain day lodge serves typical skiers' breakfasts and lunches, but also does fondue dinner every Thursday evening, including a chairlift ride up the mountain and a torchlight ski-down to the village. Reservations required. **(250) 578-7222.**

Tequilleria
Casual Mexican restaurant in refurbished original day lodge. Serves lunch daily and dinner Wednesday through Sunday. **Burfield Lodge; (250) 578-7222.**

NIGHTLIFE

Most of the crowd heads to the fireplace bar area of Masa's after the lifts close. Rounds of beer and plates of nachos are prime. On weekends, there's live entertainment and even dancing. Teens too young to drink hang out at the video games in the lower level of the Village Day Lodge. Locals like Tequilleria, the new Mexican hangout in the old Burfield Day Lodge. Later, the action, such as it is, shifts to Batida's Bar & Lounge in the Sun Peaks Lodge. Macker's also has après-ski specials. Vacationers can also tap into scheduled evening activities. A wine and cheese social and resort orientation is scheduled every Sunday evening. It is followed, in order, by Monday Night Football and comedy night at Masa's bar, casino night on Tuesday, line dancing on Wednesday and moonlight fondue dinner at the Sunburst Lodge on Thursday.

It's also possible to head to Kamloops for a change-of-pace evening. For those who can't get **443** enough sliding, a small local area called **Harper Mountain** turns on the lights for night skiing, **(250) 828-0336** for information. Kamloops is a lively college town with an abundance of places to dine and party. Hockey is big, so getting tickets for a Blazers home game at **Riverside Coliseum** is quite a coup, **(250) 828-3339.** To sample the popular Canadian pastime of curling, call the **Kamloops Curling Club, (250) 372-5432,** or the **North Kamloops Curling Club, (250) 554-1911** to see what's up and how you can tap in. **Kamloops' Lake City Casino** offers blackjack, roulette and other games, with proceeds earmarked for local charities, **(250) 372-3333** for details.

For more information, contact **Sun Peaks Resort, P.O. Box 869, Kamloops, BC V2C 5M8; (250) 578-7222,** fax **(250) 578-7843.**

Touching Other Bases

In addition to established destination resorts of all sizes, the Rocky Mountains have a number of worthy local ski areas with 1,000 vertical feet or more which merit a visit if you are in the region. Most have no (or very limited) slopeside lodging or other resort amenities, but the size and the price are right. Here's the scoop on some you might want to consider if you want to discover a place your friends haven't heard of, let alone skied. You might find yourself ahead of the curve. For instance, if you'd explored Tod Mountain, B.C., a few years ago, you would have spent very little to ski a big, tough mountain—way before real estate development, high-speed quads or ski stars like Nancy Greene came on the scene and the area was renamed Sun Peaks.

COLORADO

Powderhorn

Mid-size ski area 35 miles from Grand Junction and 8 miles from the Grand Mesa in the western part of the state. Some on-site condos. Of the 240 skiable acres and 20 miles of trails on 1,640 vertical feet, two-thirds are intermediate terrain. **(970) 242-5637.**

IDAHO

Pebble Creek

Surprising ski area with 2,000 feet of vertical in southeastern Idaho. Bargain lift tickets. Day and night skiing. Nearest lodging 15 miles away in Pocatello. Lava Hot Springs pool 20 miles away. **(208) 775-4451.**

Pomerelle

Day- and night-skiing area with 17 trails on 1,000 vertical feet and budget-priced lift tickets. Nearest lodging in Albion (25 miles away) or Burley (28 miles away). **(208) 638-5599.**

Soldier Mountain

South-central Idaho's top area, 100 miles southeast of Boise, 70 miles northwest of Twin Falls and 10 miles from Fairfield. Offers 36 trails on 1,400 vertical feet. Low-cost lift tickets and two nearby motels. Bought by Bruce Willis in late 1996 and slated for an upgrade. **(208) 764-2300.**

MONTANA

Discovery Basin

A nearly even split between novice, intermediate and advanced terrain on 1,300 vertical feet. This ski area in west-central Montana recently added 120 skiable acres for a total of 280. Three lodges within 5 miles and Hot Springs Resort 20 miles away. Low-cost lift tickets. **(406) 563-2184.**

Great Divide

Located 22 miles northwest of Helena, this is where the Montana's "state capital-ists" ski.

Low-priced day and night tickets buy skiing on 1,330 vertical feet. **(406) 449-3746.**

Lost Trail

Located 90 miles south of Missoula. Mostly open bowl skiing on 1,100 vertical feet and 20 miles of cross-country trails. Several lodges are located nearby, and the lift ticket prices are low. **(406) 821-3211.**

Marshall Mountain

A 1,500-vertical-foot ski area with 17 slopes and trails would be a giant in the Middle Atlantic or southern New England states, but in Montana, it's a minor player. Rock-bottom rates and unsurpassed proximity to Missoula make it a local favorite for day and night skiing. For more information, call **(406) 258-6000.**

446 Maverick Mountain

Just nine "major runs" and two lifts (one chair) on 1,920 vertical feet, but lots of tree skiing and small side trails. The nearest accommodations to this ski area in southwestern Montana are in Dillon, 38 miles away. Nearby are natural hot springs pools and cross-country skiing trails beginning at the summit. **(406) 834-3454.**

Showdown

With 50 runs and 600 acres of skiable terrain (65 percent for intermediate and advanced skiers) on a 1,400-foot vertical, Showdown is one of Montana's biggest mid-size ski areas. Open Wednesday through Sunday, plus holidays. Lodging in White Sulphur Springs, 8 miles away. **(406) 771-1300.**

Turner Mountain

Weekend area with just one T-bar and one rope tow (and tickets priced accordingly) but a whopping 2,165-foot vertical. Located 22 miles from Libby in Montana's northwest corner. **(406) 293-4317.**

NEW MEXICO

Pajarito

Known as a tough little 1,141-vertical-foot ski area. Open Wednesdays, weekends and federal holidays. Skied mostly by Los Alamos scientists and their families. Low-cost lift tickets and lodging at four motels in town. **(505) 662-5722.**

Sandia Peak

Albuquerque's home hill. Access by road or scenic tram from the city's outskirts. Vertical of 1,700 feet and 85 percent of the terrain for novices and intermediates. Ample accommodations in the city. **(505) 242-9133.**

Snow Canyon

The small village of Cloudcroft is 45 miles southwest of Ruidoso, and if you ski there at Snow Canyon, you'll rack up bragging rights for skiing at the country's southernmost area. Located on high terrain above the Tularosa Basin, it is an intimate, family-oriented resort. One double chairlift and two beginner tows serve a complex of mild trails on a 700-foot vertical. When conditions permit, there's cross-country skiing on the local golf course. **(800) 333-7542.**

UTAH

Beaver Mountain

Tucked into the Utah panhandle's northeast corner near Logan. Sixteen groomed runs (three-quarters for intermediate and advanced skiers) plus powder glades. Snowfall averages 350 inches a year. Motels and condos within 15 miles. **(801) 753-0921.**

Brian Head Ski Resort

Utah's southernmost ski area, and not really in the Rockies, but with 1,400 vertical feet of skiing topping out at 11,000 feet. Snow averaging 400 inches a year falls on 48 trails served by seven chairlifts. Accommodations at area. Located 30 miles from Cedar City, but drive market stretches to Las Vegas (three hours) and even Los Angeles (eight hours). **(801) 943-8309.**

Elk Meadows

Commendable intermediate area with 30 runs and ample off-piste skiing on 1,200 vertical feet. Located in south-central Utah, not in the Rockies. Gets up to 400 inches of snow annually. Limited lodging at ski area; more at Beaver, 17 miles away. Roughly equidistant to Las Vegas and Salt Lake City; 500 miles from Los Angeles. **(801) 438-5433.**

WYOMING

Antelope Butte

Wyoming's northernmost ski area. Two lifts on a 1,000-foot vertical. Open weekends. Very inexpensive. Lodging in several not-too-far-away (for northern Wyoming) towns. **(307) 655-9530.**

Pine Creek

Quaint 13-run, 1,150-vertical-foot ski area near Utah border. Three lifts (two tows and a single chair!). Weekend skiing only. Lodging in Cokeville. **(307) 279-3201.**

ALBERTA

Canada Olympic Park

Doesn't approach the arbitrary 1,000-foot vertical of the other areas here, but interesting for other reasons. Site of the bobsled and luge run and the ski jumps for the 1988 Winter Olympics, it still operates these facilities for training and competition. Also, a day and night skiing area for beginners just west of Calgary, directly off the TransCanada Highway. Decidedly worth visiting

en route to or from the Banff/Lake Louise area of Kananaskis Valley. **(403) 247-5452.**

Westcastle Park

Alberta's most southwesterly ski area. A low-key local treasure near the town of Pincher Creek with three T-bars on a 1,650-foot vertical. Combine skiing and sightseeing in one trip. Not far from Head-Smashed-In Buffalo Jump, one of the oldest, best-preserved buffalo jump sites, used as an Indian hunting practice, in the Plains and a UNESCO World Heritage Site. **(403) 627-5101, (403) 627-2605.**

BRITISH COLUMBIA

Apex Resort

With Big White and Silver Star, one of the wonderful ski areas in the mountains just east of the Okanagan Valley, near Penticton. Four lifts, including a high-speed quad, on a 2,000-foot vertical—and even some slopeside lodging, cross-country trails and ice skating. However, troubled in recent years by disputes regarding Native land claims, including some harassment of skiers. When this is mitigated, it will be right up there. **(250) 492-2880.**

Fairmont Hot Springs

Major hot springs resort with Canada's largest complex of spring-fed mineral pools and the added benefit of skiing on a 1,000-vertical-foot mountain nearby. Ski area known for long, wide, gentle runs, ideal for beginners and novices. Accommodations are very good. **(250) 345-6311.**

Fernie Snow Valley

Excellent family area with 2,400 vertical feet of varied terrain, from cut runs through the woods to high open bowls. Seventy percent for intermediate to expert skiers. Good snowfall record and excellent reputation for powder. Limited

447

slopeside lodging; other accommodations a short drive. **(250) 423-4655.**

Kimberley

Congenial resort near the namesake town of Kimberley—and its airport. Big broad mountain with half-a-dozen lifts on a 2,400-foot vertical and many ultrawide runs and abundant cross-country trails. Top night-skiing operation. Bavarian-style village at the base. **(250) 427-4881.**

Red Mountain

Tough behemoth just outside the gritty former mining town of Rossland. Big 2,800-foot vertical—but just three chairlifts (and only one to the top) and one T-bar. Known for tremendous tree

skiing, great powder and virtual absence of crowds. **(250) 362-7384.**

Whitetooth

The town of Golden is known as one of Canada's early heli-skiing centers, but it's also got a ski area. This one measures 1,740 vertical feet and is open Fridays through Mondays, plus holiday weeks. One double chair and one T-bar provide the uphill. **(250) 344-6114.**

Whitewater

This one's not in Arkansas. Brassy ski area with three chairlifts on 1,300 vertical feet of challenging trails, glades and open bowls—and a mind-blowing, Utah-size average annual snowfall of 500 inches. Located 12 miles from Nelson. **(250) 354-4944.**

Information Sources

SKI AND TOURISM INFORMATION

Colorado

Bed & Breakfast Innkeepers of Colorado, **1102 W. Pikes Peak Ave., Colorado Springs, CO 80904; (800) 83-BOOKS.**

Colorado Avalanche Information Center, **(303) 371-1080.**

Colorado/Ski Country USA, **1560 Broadway, Ste. 1440, Denver, CO 80202; (303) 831-SNOW** for statewide ski conditions reports, **(303) 837-0793** for general information.

Colorado Cross-Country Ski Association, **P.O. Box 1292, Kremmling, CO 80459; (800) 869-4560.**

Colorado Guest and Dude Ranch Association, **P.O. Box 300, Tabernash, CO 80478; (970) 887-3128.**

Colorado Travel & Tourism Authority, **P.O. Box 3524, Englewood, CO 80155; (800) COLORADO, or 707 Seventh St., Ste. 3500, Denver, CO 80202; (303) 296-3384.**

Distinctive Inns of Colorado, **205 Park Lane, P.O. Box 1061, Estes Park, CO 80527; (800) 866-0621.**

Idaho

Idaho Travel Council, **700 W. State St., Boise, ID 83720; (800) 635-7820, (208) 334-2470.**

Montana

Montana Avalanche Information, **(800) 281-1030, (406) 549-4488.**

For a free Montana Winter Recreation Guide, call or write *Travel Montana,* **1424 Ninth Ave., P.O. Box 200533, Helena, MT 59620; (800) VISIT-MT** out of state, **(406) 444-2654.**

New Mexico

New Mexico Department of Tourism, **491 Old Santa Fe Trail, Santa Fe, NM 87503; (800) 545-2040** out of state, **(505) 827-7400.**

Ski New Mexico, **P.O. Box 1104, Santa Fe, NM 87594; (505) 984-0606** for statewide ski conditions reports, **(505) 982-5300** for general information.

Utah

Utah Travel Council, **Council Hall, Capitol Hill, Salt Lake City, UT 84114; (801) 538-1030.**

Ski Utah (Utah Ski Association), **150 W. 500 South, Salt Lake City, UT 84101; (801) 521-8102** for statewide ski conditions report, **(801) 534-1779** for general information.

Appendix 2

Wyoming

Wyoming Travel Commission, **I-25 at College Dr., Cheyenne, WY 82002; (800) 225-5996, (307) 777-7777.** The Travel Commission phone number also issues statewide ski conditions reports.

Alberta

Alberta Tourism Partnership, **10155 102nd Street, Commerce Place, 3rd Floor, Edmonton, AB T5J 4L6; (800) 661-8888, (407) 427-4321.**

Northern Alberta Hostelling Association, **(403) 432-7798** for information, **(403) 439-3089** for reservations.

Southern Alberta Hostelling Association, **(403) 762-4122.**

British Columbia

450

Rocky Mountain Visitors Assn. of British Columbia, **P.O. Box 10, Kimberley, BC V1A 2YS; (250) 427-4838.**

Tourism British Columbia, **802, 865 Hornby St., Vancouver, BC V6Z 2G3; (800) 663-6000, (604) 663-6000.**

Miscellaneous

Dude Ranchers Association, **P.O. Box 471, Laporte, CO 80535; (970) 223-8440.**

Ski Tour Operators Association, **P.O. Box 19181, Sacramento, CA 95819.**

SKI WEBSITES

Ski areas, local tourism-infomation sources and other information providers have launched into cyberspace. Addresses change with cyberspeed, but among the Web addresses available as this book was being prepared are the following.

Author's website, http//www.netone.com/cmwalter
Consummate Skiing List, http://ski.websmith.ca/ski/
iski, http://www.iski.com/

The Mountain Zone, http://www.iski.com/
National Ski Patrol, http://www.skipatrol.org/
Ski America (magazine), http://www.skiamerica.com
Ski Central, http://www.skicentral.com/
SkiFest (annual nationwide Nordic day),
http://www.xcski.org/
SkiNet (*Skiing* and *Ski* magazines on-line),
http://skinet.com/
Ski Tour Operators Association, http://skitops.com
Snow Country (magazine), http://www.skicentral.com/
Snow Net, http://www.snownet.com/
Snow Web, http://www.snoweb.com/
University of Maryland Ski Map Server,
http://www.cs.umd.edu/~regli/ski.html
Usenet newsgroups, rec.skiing.alpine,
rec.skiing.nordic, and
rec.skiing.snowboard

Colorado

Colorado Ski Country USA,
http://www.skicolorado.org/
Colorado Travel & Tourism Authority,
http://www.colorado.com/
Arapahoe Basin, http://www.csn.net/resorts/abasin.html
Aspen Skiing Co., http://skiaspen.com/
Aspen (community), http://www.aspenonline.com/aspenonline/
Breckenridge (ski area), http://www.csn.net/resorts/breck.html
Breckenridge Resort Chamber,
http://www.gobreck.com/
Copper Mountain, http://www.ski-copper.com/
Crested Butte, http://www.csn.net/cbws/skiing/
Keystone, http://www.csn.net/resorts/keyst.html
Monarch, http://www.rmi.net/monarch/
Purgatory, http://www.ski-purg.com/
Steamboat (ski area and resort),
http://www.steamboat-ski.com/
Steamboat Springs (town), http://www.steamboat-chamber.com/
Telluride, http://www.telluridegateway.com/
Vail, http://www.vail.net/
Winter Park, http://www.skiwinterpark.com/wpmj/
TravelBank Systems, http://www.travelbank.com/tbs/
Also operates a non-Web bulletin board with computer-accessed ski information and snow reports, mainly on Colorado but also on other

states, **(303) 671-7669** modem, **(303) 320-8550** voice
YMCA of the Rockies: http://www.ymcarockies.org

Idaho

Sandpoint (resort town near Schweitzer), http://www.keokee.com/sptonlin.html
Schweitzer Mountain Resort, http://www.keokee.com/schweitzer/schhome.htm
Sun Valley, http://www.sunvalley.com/

Montana

Big Sky, http://www.bigskyresort.com/
Lone Mountain Ranch (at Big Sky), http://www.gomontana.com/lmrhome.html
Montana Bed and Breakfast Assn., http://www.wtp.net/go/montana/

New Mexico

Santa Fe Convention and Visitors Bureau, http://nets.com/santafe/
Ski New Mexico, http://www.skinewmexico.com/
Taos Ski Valley, http://taoswebb.com/nmusa/skitaos/

Utah

Deer Valley Resort, http://www.deervalley.com/
Homestead X-Country Area, http://www.homestead-ut.com/
Park City Ski Area, http://www.pcski.com/
Snowbird Ski Resort, http://www.snowbird.com/
Solitude Ski Resort, http://www.skisolitude.com/

Wyoming

Grand Targhee, http://idahonews.com/targhee/powder.htm
Jackson Hole (town), http://www.info@jacksonhole.com/
Jackson Hole (ski area), http://www.jacksonhole.com/ski/

Alberta

Banff and Lake Louise, http://www.skibanfflakelouise.com/
Jasper and Mountain Park Lodges, http://www.mtn-park-lodges.com/
Lake Louise, http://skilouise.softnc.com/louise.html

ALTITUDE CONSIDERATIONS

If you live at or near sea level, you may be uncomfortable at the altitudes of many Rocky Mountain ski resorts. To combat the effects of the high altitude, spend a night or two at about 5,000 feet (Denver, Salt Lake City, Calgary, etc.) if possible, take it slow and easy your first couple of days on the slopes, cut down on consumption of alcohol, caffeine and salty foods and drink plenty of other liquids. Also remember that the sun is stronger in the thinner air of altitude, so be sure to use a high-SPF sunscreen. "Altitude Awareness" is a useful little brochure available from the **Colorado Altitude Research Institute, P.O. Box 38, Keystone, CO 80435; (970) 262-1114.**

SENIOR PERKS

Over the Hill Gang: **6355 S. Dayton St., #220, Englewood, CO 80011; (303) 790-2720.**
70 Plus Ski Club: **104 East Side Dr., Ballston Lake, NY 12109; no phone.**

In addition to the two organizations above, which offer day and vacation trips for their members, many ski areas—successfully lobbied by these organizations—offer discounted or free skiing for seniors. Typically, though not always, skiers somewhere in the 60 to 70 bracket (often 60 to 65 or 65 to 70) ski at junior or other reduced rates while those over 70 (and sometimes over 65) ski free.

INDEX

453

Index

454

Index

Index

Index

Index

459

Index

461

Index

463

Index

465

Index